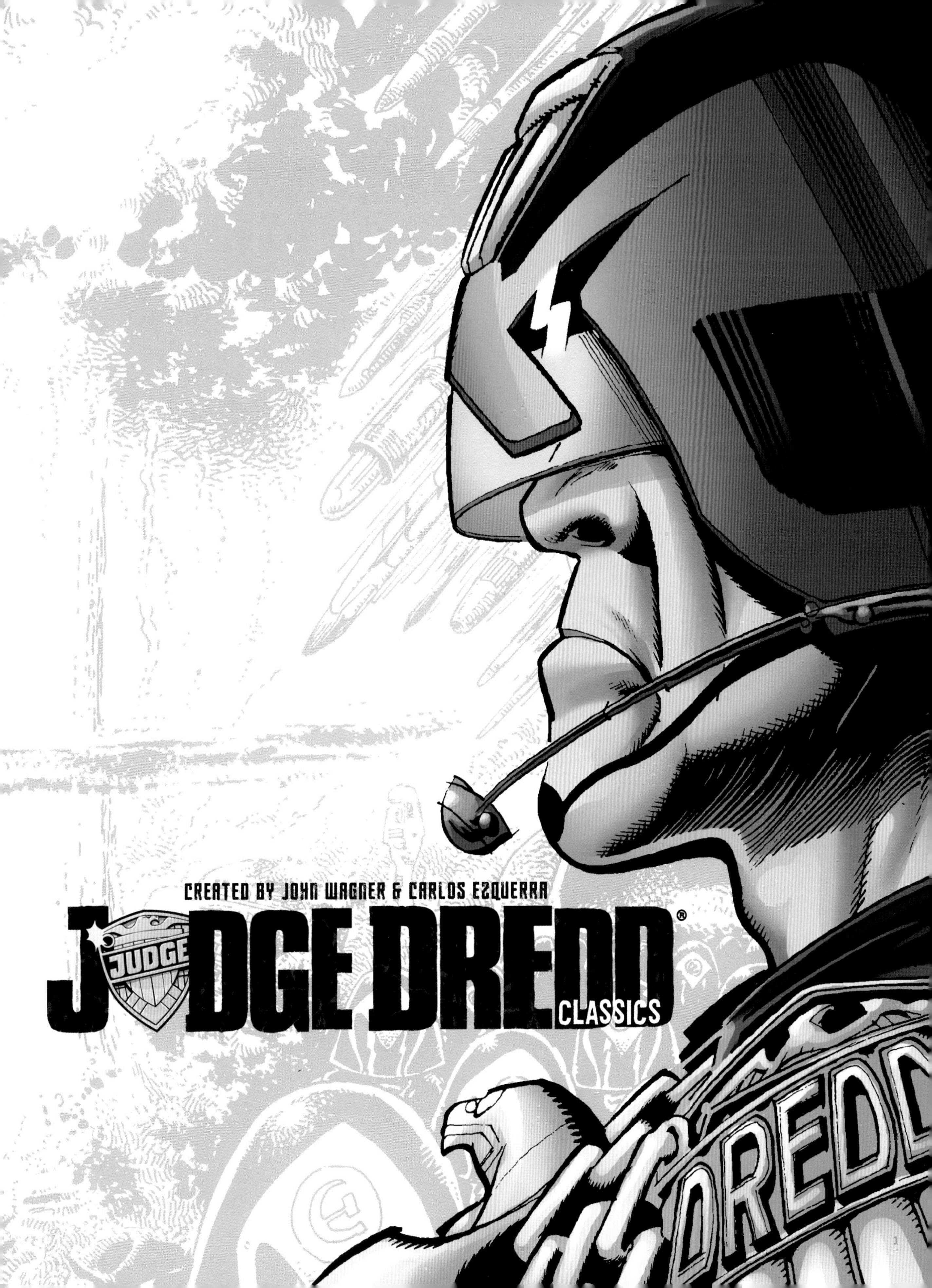
DREDD

CREATED BY JOHN WAGNER & CARLOS EZQUERRA

JUDGE DREDD® CLASSICS

CREATED BY JOHN WAGNER & CARLOS EZQUERRA

JUDGE DREDD® CLASSICS

WRITTEN BY **JOHN WAGNER** & **ALAN GRANT** CREDITED AS T. B. GROVER

"BLOCK MANIA"

ART BY **MIKE McMAHON** PARTS 1 & 2 • **RON SMITH** PARTS 3 - 6
STEVE DILLON PARTS 7 & 8 • **BRIAN BOLLAND** PART 9
COLORS BY **CHARLIE KIRCHOFF** • LETTERS BY **TOM FRAME**

"THE APOCALYPSE WAR"

ART BY **CARLOS EZQUERRA** • COLORS BY **TOM MULLIN**
LETTERS BY **STEVE POTTER** PARTS 1 - 12 • **TOM FRAME** PARTS 13 - 25

IDW Series Edits by **CHRIS RYALL** & **CHRIS SCHRAFF**
Cover by **JIM FERN**
Cover Colors by **CHARLIE KIRCHOFF**
Collection Edits by **JUSTIN EISINGER** & **ALONZO SIMON**
Collection Design by **TOM B. LONG**

Special thanks to Ben Smith and Matt Smith for their invaluable assistance.

ISBN: 978-1-61377-935-4

17 16 15 14   1 2 3 4

Ted Adams, CEO & Publisher
Greg Goldstein, President & COO
Robbie Robbins, EVP/Sr. Graphic Artist
Chris Ryall, Chief Creative Officer/Editor-in-Chief
Matthew Ruzicka, CPA, Chief Financial Officer
Alan Payne, VP of Sales
Dirk Wood, VP of Marketing
Lorelei Bunjes, VP of Digital Services
Jeff Webber, VP of Digital Publishing & Business Development

IDW 2000 AD
www.IDWPUBLISHING.com
IDW founded by Ted Adams, Alex Garner, Kris Oprisko, and Robbie Robbins

Facebook: **facebook.com/idwpublishing**
Twitter: **@idwpublishing**
YouTube: **youtube.com/idwpublishing**
Instagram: **instagram.com/idwpublishing**
deviantART: **idwpublishing.deviantart.com**
Pinterest: **pinterest.com/idwpublishing/idw-staff-faves**

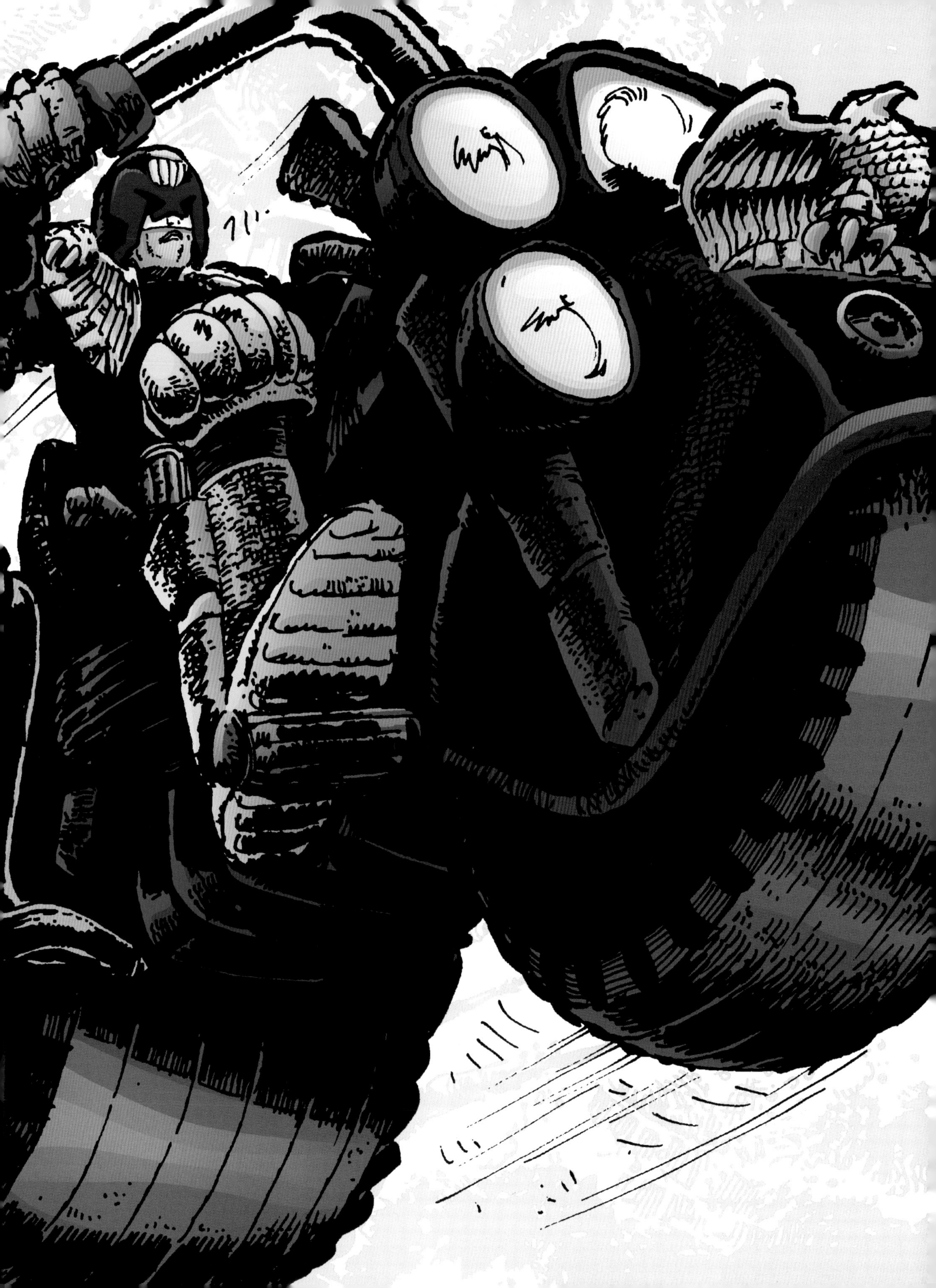

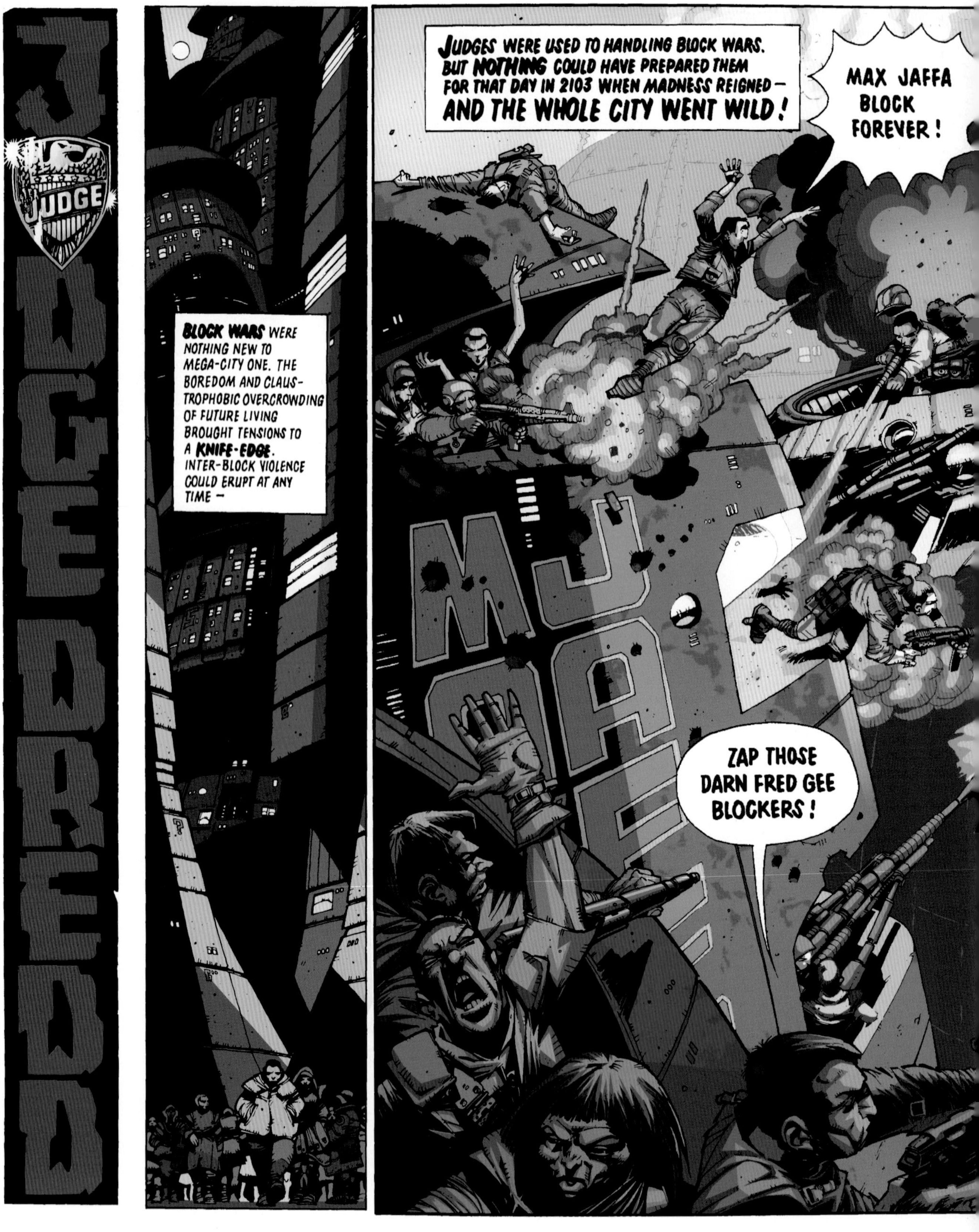
JUDGE DREDD
BLOCK WARS WERE NOTHING NEW TO MEGA-CITY ONE. THE BOREDOM AND CLAUSTROPHOBIC OVERCROWDING OF FUTURE LIVING BROUGHT TENSIONS TO A KNIFE-EDGE. INTER-BLOCK VIOLENCE COULD ERUPT AT ANY TIME —
JUDGES WERE USED TO HANDLING BLOCK WARS. BUT NOTHING COULD HAVE PREPARED THEM FOR THAT DAY IN 2103 WHEN MADNESS REIGNED — AND THE WHOLE CITY WENT WILD!
MAX JAFFA BLOCK FOREVER!
ZAP THOSE DARN FRED GEE BLOCKERS!

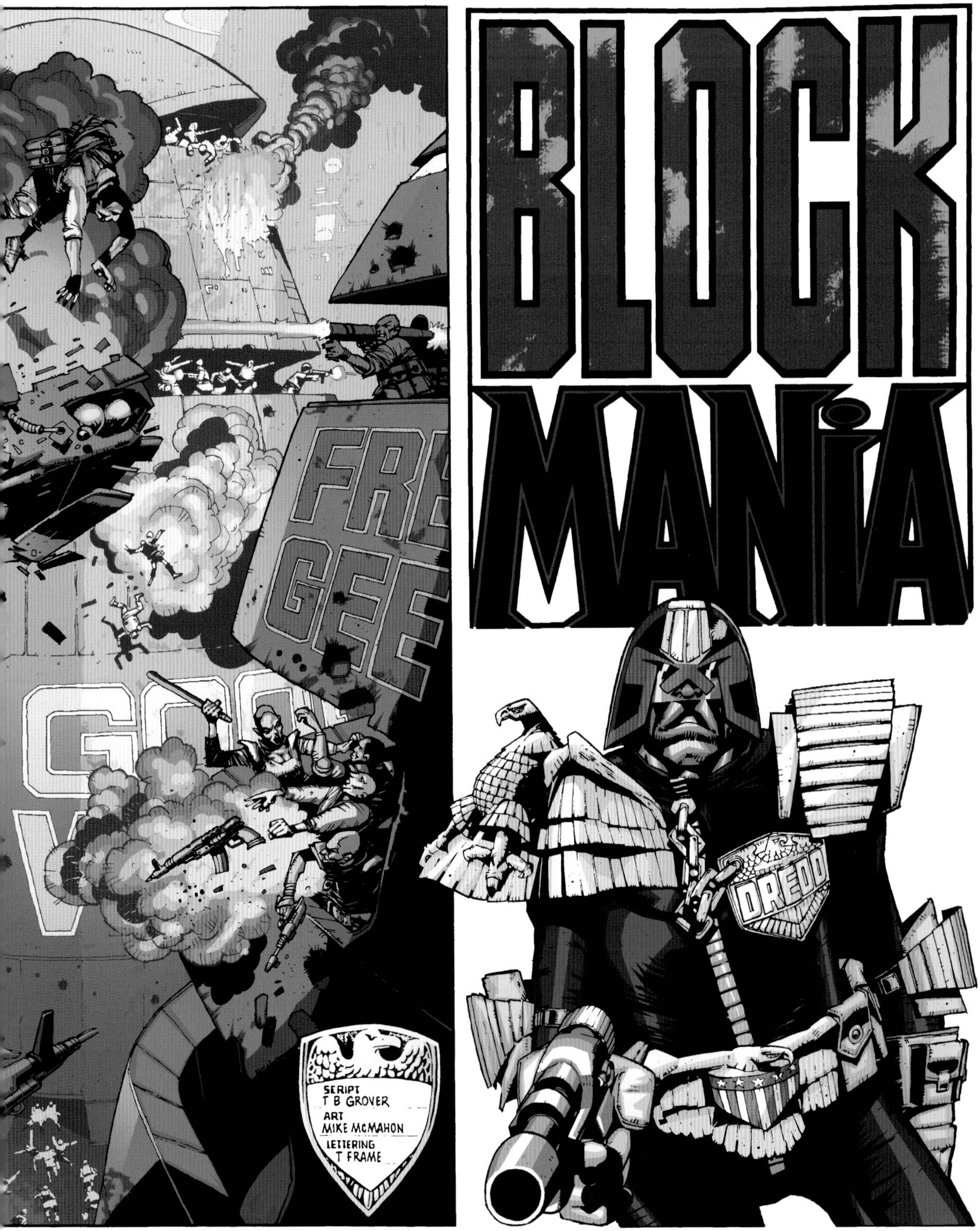
BLOCK MANIA
DREDD
SCRIPT T B GROVER
ART MIKE MCMAHON
LETTERING T FRAME

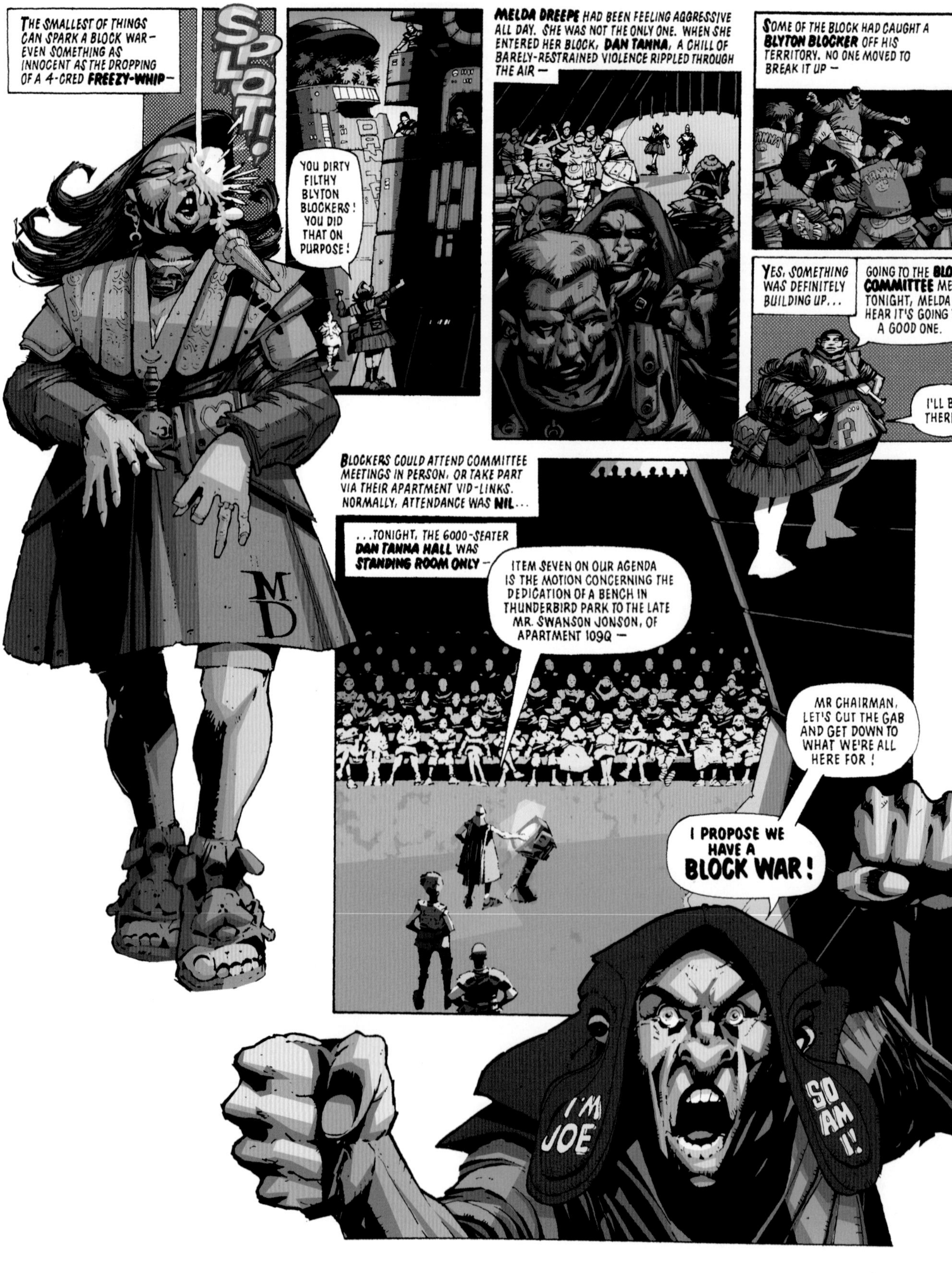

THE SMALLEST OF THINGS CAN SPARK A BLOCK WAR – EVEN SOMETHING AS INNOCENT AS THE DROPPING OF A 4-CRED FREEZY-WHIP –
SPLOT!
YOU DIRTY FILTHY BLYTON BLOCKERS! YOU DID THAT ON PURPOSE!
MELDA DREEPE HAD BEEN FEELING AGGRESSIVE ALL DAY. SHE WAS NOT THE ONLY ONE. WHEN SHE ENTERED HER BLOCK, DAN TANNA, A CHILL OF BARELY-RESTRAINED VIOLENCE RIPPLED THROUGH THE AIR –
SOME OF THE BLOCK HAD CAUGHT A BLYTON BLOCKER OFF HIS TERRITORY. NO ONE MOVED TO BREAK IT UP –
YES, SOMETHING WAS DEFINITELY BUILDING UP...
GOING TO THE BLOCK COMMITTEE MEETING TONIGHT, MELDA? I HEAR IT'S GOING TO BE A GOOD ONE.
I'LL BE THERE!
BLOCKERS COULD ATTEND COMMITTEE MEETINGS IN PERSON, OR TAKE PART VIA THEIR APARTMENT VID-LINKS. NORMALLY, ATTENDANCE WAS NIL...
...TONIGHT, THE 6000-SEATER DAN TANNA HALL WAS STANDING ROOM ONLY –
ITEM SEVEN ON OUR AGENDA IS THE MOTION CONCERNING THE DEDICATION OF A BENCH IN THUNDERBIRD PARK TO THE LATE MR. SWANSON JONSON, OF APARTMENT 109Q –
MR CHAIRMAN, LET'S CUT THE GAB AND GET DOWN TO WHAT WE'RE ALL HERE FOR!
I PROPOSE WE HAVE A BLOCK WAR!
I'M JOE
SO AM I!

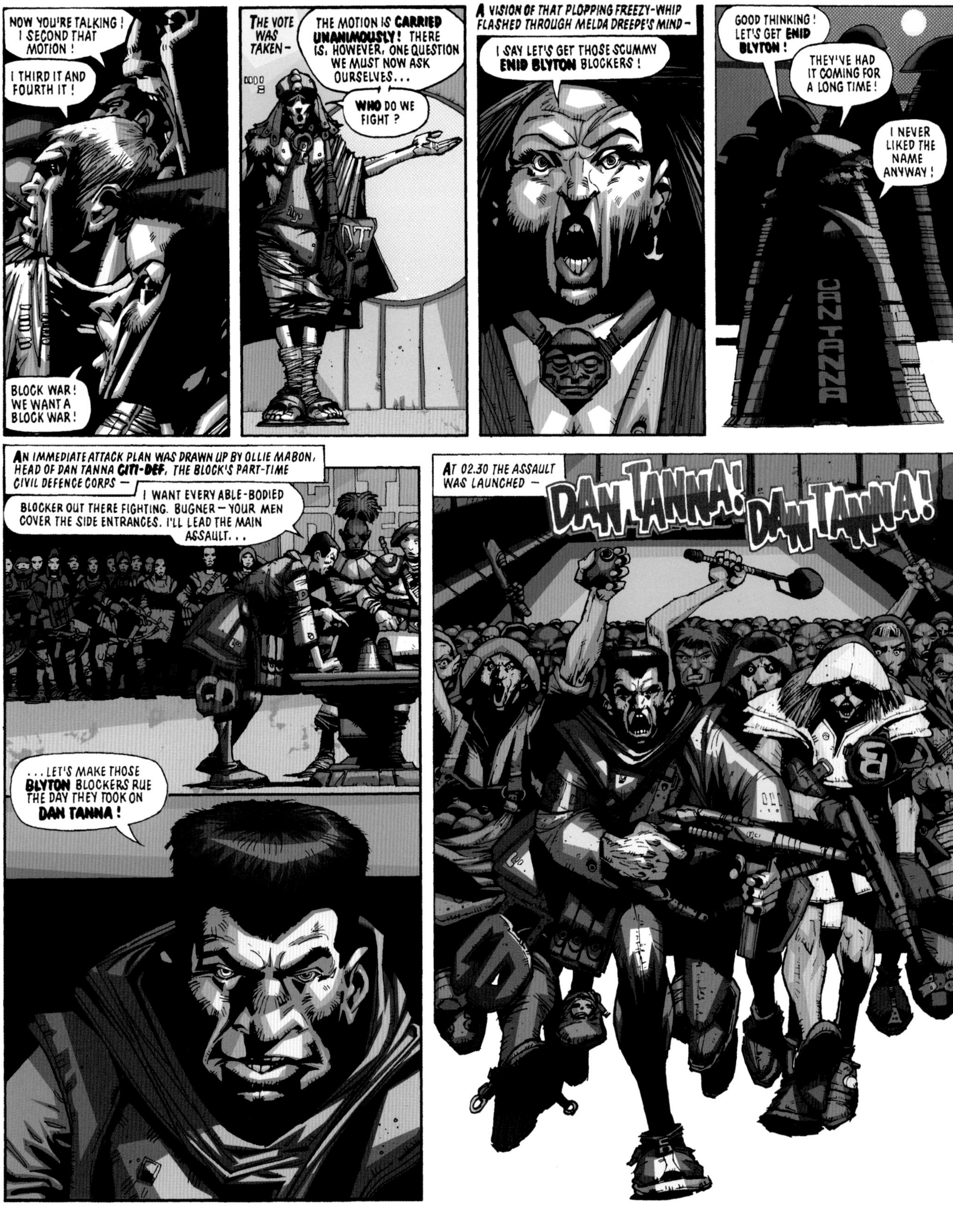
NOW YOU'RE TALKING! I SECOND THAT MOTION!
I THIRD IT AND FOURTH IT!
BLOCK WAR! WE WANT A BLOCK WAR!
THE VOTE WAS TAKEN –
THE MOTION IS CARRIED UNANIMOUSLY! THERE IS, HOWEVER, ONE QUESTION WE MUST NOW ASK OURSELVES...
WHO DO WE FIGHT?
A VISION OF THAT PLOPPING FREEZY-WHIP FLASHED THROUGH MELDA DREEPE'S MIND –
I SAY LET'S GET THOSE SCUMMY ENID BLYTON BLOCKERS!
GOOD THINKING! LET'S GET ENID BLYTON!
THEY'VE HAD IT COMING FOR A LONG TIME!
I NEVER LIKED THE NAME ANYWAY!
DAN TANNA
AN IMMEDIATE ATTACK PLAN WAS DRAWN UP BY OLLIE MABON, HEAD OF DAN TANNA CITI-DEF, THE BLOCK'S PART-TIME CIVIL DEFENCE CORPS –
I WANT EVERY ABLE-BODIED BLOCKER OUT THERE FIGHTING. BUGNER – YOUR MEN COVER THE SIDE ENTRANCES. I'LL LEAD THE MAIN ASSAULT...
...LET'S MAKE THOSE BLYTON BLOCKERS RUE THE DAY THEY TOOK ON DAN TANNA!
AT 02.30 THE ASSAULT WAS LAUNCHED –
DAN TANNA! DAN TANNA!

THE ENID BLYTON BLOCKERS WERE WAITING. THEY TOO HAD FELT THE TENSION OF THE DAY. SOON IT WOULD FIND *RELEASE* —

THOSE DUMB TANNAS! WALKIN' RIGHT INTO OUR EVER-LOVIN' ARMS —

LET 'EM HAVE IT!

AIEEE!

AAAAH!

THEY GOT OLLIE MABON!

HE DIED LIKE A REAL TANNA! LET'S PAY 'EM BACK!

SMOKE BOMB!

FROM THE NEARBY **RIKKI FULTON BLOCK**, THE BATTLE WAS WATCHED WITH KEEN INTEREST —

THEY'RE GOING AT IT LIKE LARRY! SOME TANNAS MAKING A BREAKTHROUGH INTO THE PLAZA —

A BLOCK WAR'S JUST WHAT WE NEED! IT'S TIME WE GOT INVOLVED!

RIKKI FULTON BLOCK HAD BEEN IN A FIGHTING MOOD ALL DAY —

WE'RE READY TO MOVE IMMEDIATELY!

JUST TELL ME WHOSE **SIDE** WE'RE ON!

UH, I'VE GOT A SLIGHT FANCY FOR BLYTON!

BLYTON IT IS, THEN!

A VID-CALL CAME THROUGH FROM NEIGHBOURING **HENRY KISSINGER** —

WE'RE FIGHTIN' FOR BLYTON!

US TOO! WATCH OUT FOR THE **BETTY CROCKER** BLOCKERS — THEY'RE SIDING WITH **TANNA**!

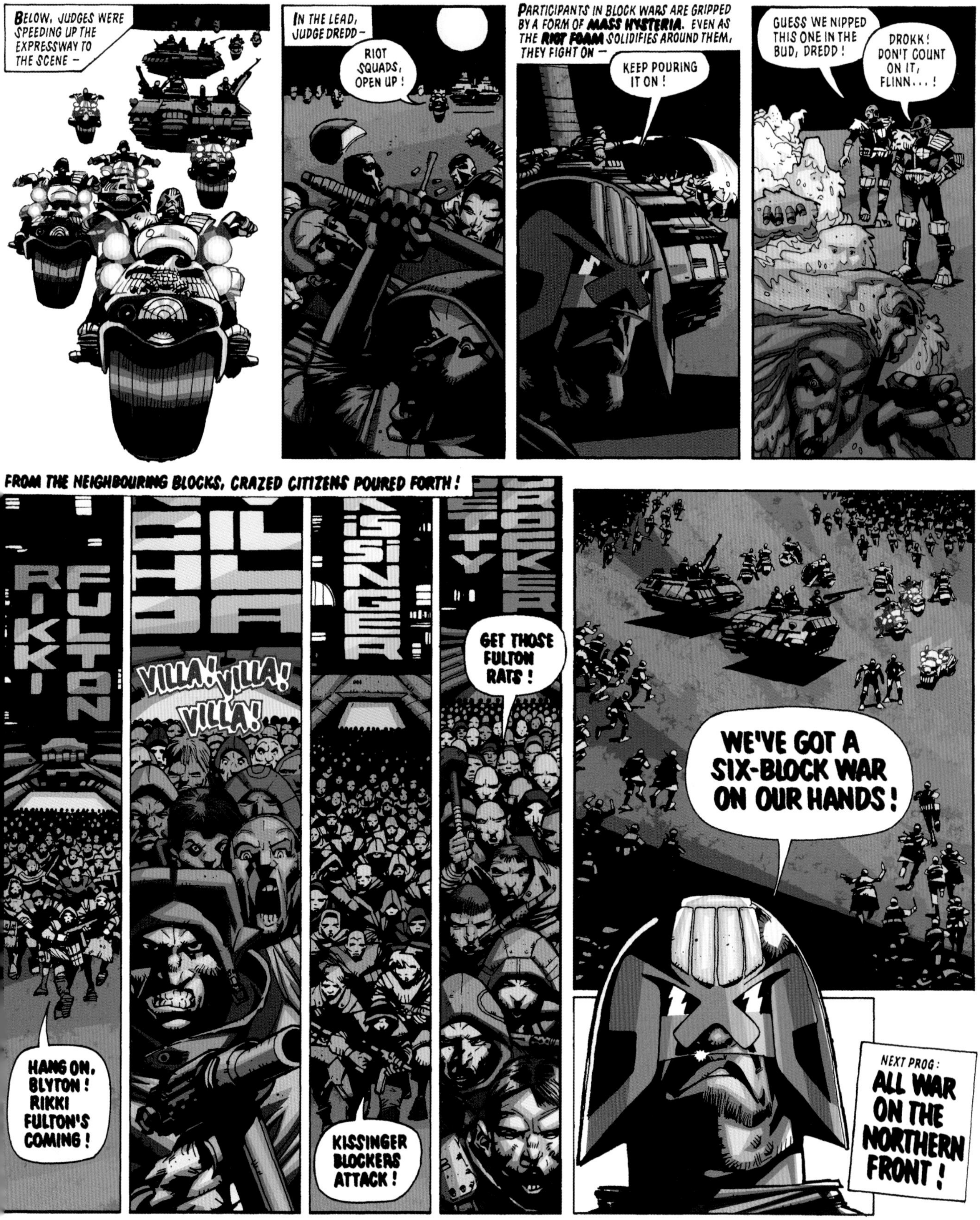
BELOW, JUDGES WERE SPEEDING UP THE EXPRESSWAY TO THE SCENE –
IN THE LEAD, JUDGE DREDD –
RIOT SQUADS, OPEN UP!
PARTICIPANTS IN BLOCK WARS ARE GRIPPED BY A FORM OF MASS HYSTERIA. EVEN AS THE RIOT FOAM SOLIDIFIES AROUND THEM, THEY FIGHT ON –
KEEP POURING IT ON!
GUESS WE NIPPED THIS ONE IN THE BUD, DREDD!
DROKK! DON'T COUNT ON IT, FLINN...!
FROM THE NEIGHBOURING BLOCKS, CRAZED CITIZENS POURED FORTH!
RIKKI FULTON
HANG ON, BLYTON! RIKKI FULTON'S COMING!
VILLA! VILLA! VILLA!
KISSINGER
KISSINGER BLOCKERS ATTACK!
GET THOSE FULTON RATS!
WE'VE GOT A SIX-BLOCK WAR ON OUR HANDS!
NEXT PROG: ALL WAR ON THE NORTHERN FRONT!

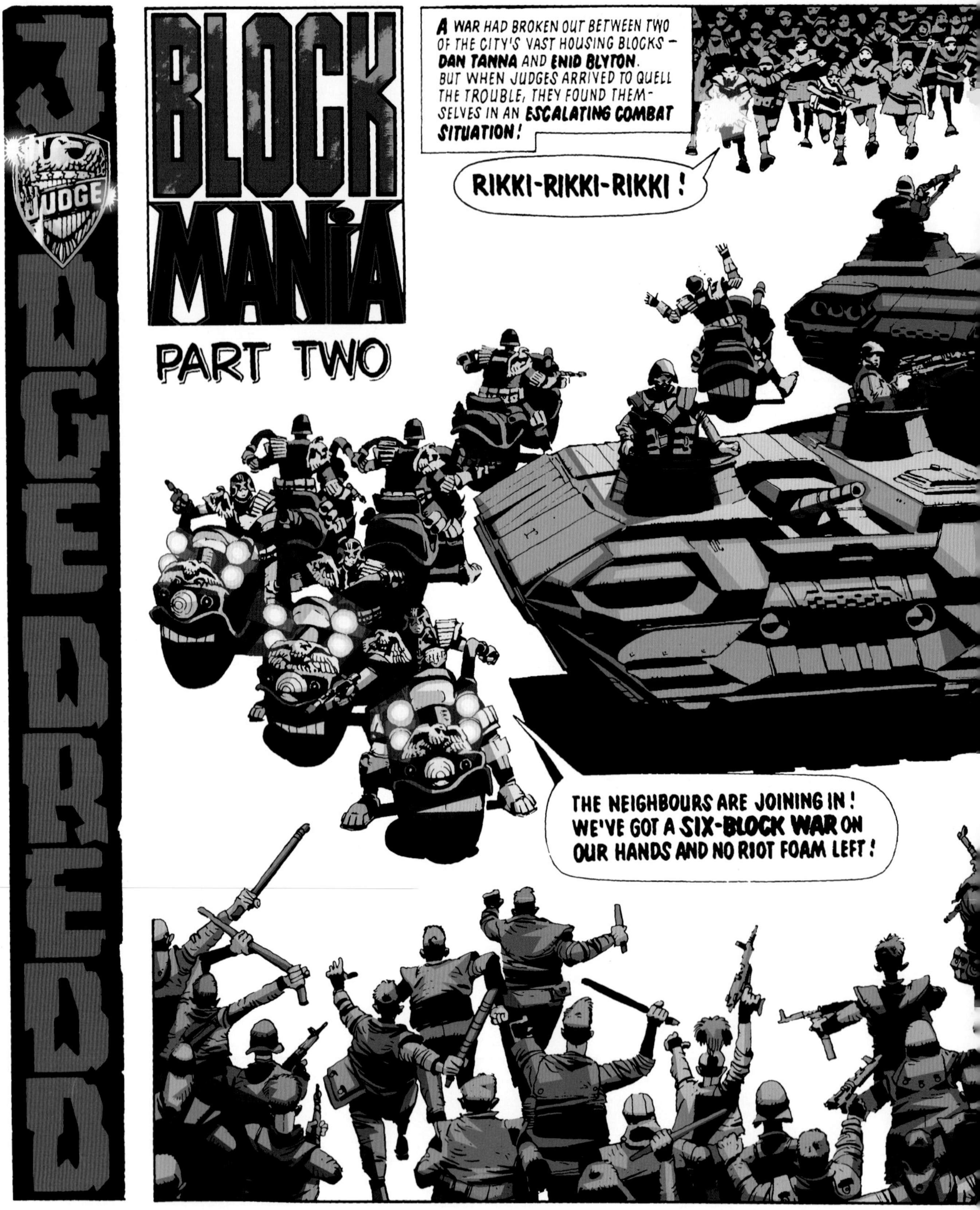
JUDGE DREDD
BLOCK MANIA
PART TWO
A WAR HAD BROKEN OUT BETWEEN TWO OF THE CITY'S VAST HOUSING BLOCKS — DAN TANNA AND ENID BLYTON. BUT WHEN JUDGES ARRIVED TO QUELL THE TROUBLE, THEY FOUND THEMSELVES IN AN ESCALATING COMBAT SITUATION!
RIKKI-RIKKI-RIKKI!
THE NEIGHBOURS ARE JOINING IN! WE'VE GOT A SIX-BLOCK WAR ON OUR HANDS AND NO RIOT FOAM LEFT!

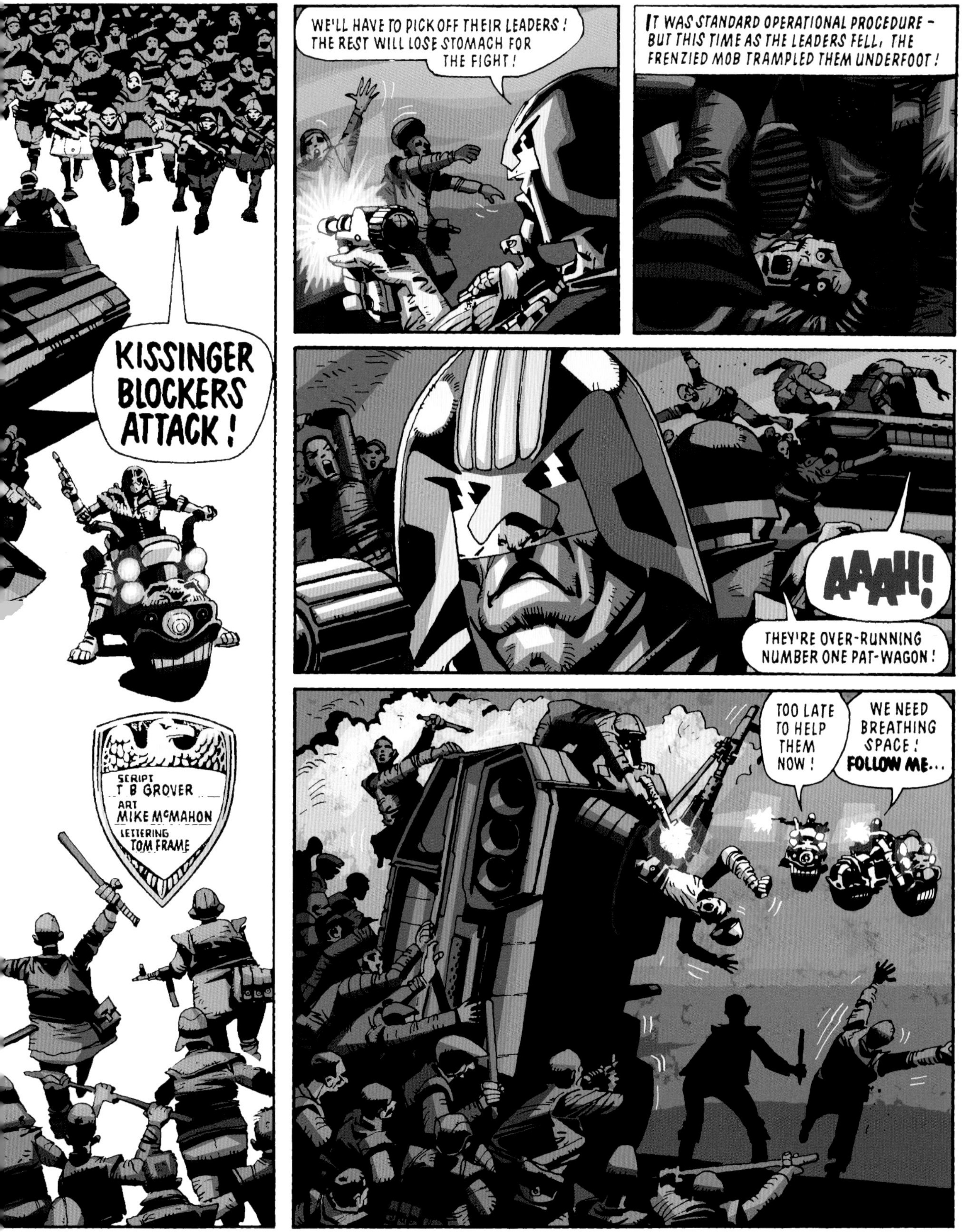
KISSINGER BLOCKERS ATTACK!
SCRIPT T B GROVER
ART MIKE McMAHON
LETTERING TOM FRAME
WE'LL HAVE TO PICK OFF THEIR LEADERS! THE REST WILL LOSE STOMACH FOR THE FIGHT!
IT WAS STANDARD OPERATIONAL PROCEDURE - BUT THIS TIME AS THE LEADERS FELL, THE FRENZIED MOB TRAMPLED THEM UNDERFOOT!
AAAH!
THEY'RE OVER-RUNNING NUMBER ONE PAT-WAGON!
TOO LATE TO HELP THEM NOW!
WE NEED BREATHING SPACE! FOLLOW ME...

WE'RE **BLASTING** OUR WAY OUT!

THE SEETHING MASS OF BLOCKERS **PARTED** BEFORE THE JUDGES' AWESOME FIREPOWER —

AIEEE!

WE'RE CLEAR!

I WANT **REINFORCEMENTS** DOWN HERE — **PRIORITY ONE!**

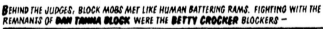

BEHIND THE JUDGES, BLOCK MOBS MET LIKE HUMAN BATTERING RAMS. FIGHTING WITH THE REMNANTS OF **DAN TANNA BLOCK** WERE THE **BETTY CROCKER** BLOCKERS —

RIKKI-RIKKI-RIKKI!

CROCKER 'EM!

AGAINST THEM, THE CONCERTED MIGHT OF **HENRY KISSINGER**, **RIKKI FULTON** AND **ENID BLYTON**!

ALL THE WAY WITH HENRY K — **AAAGH!**

A SIXTH BLOCK HAD JOINED THE WAR. **PANCHO VILLA**. THEY WERE FIGHTING EVERYONE —

PANCHO VILLA BLOCK WILL SETTLE FOR NOTHING LESS THAN **TOTAL DOMINATION!**

ZAP THEM ALL!

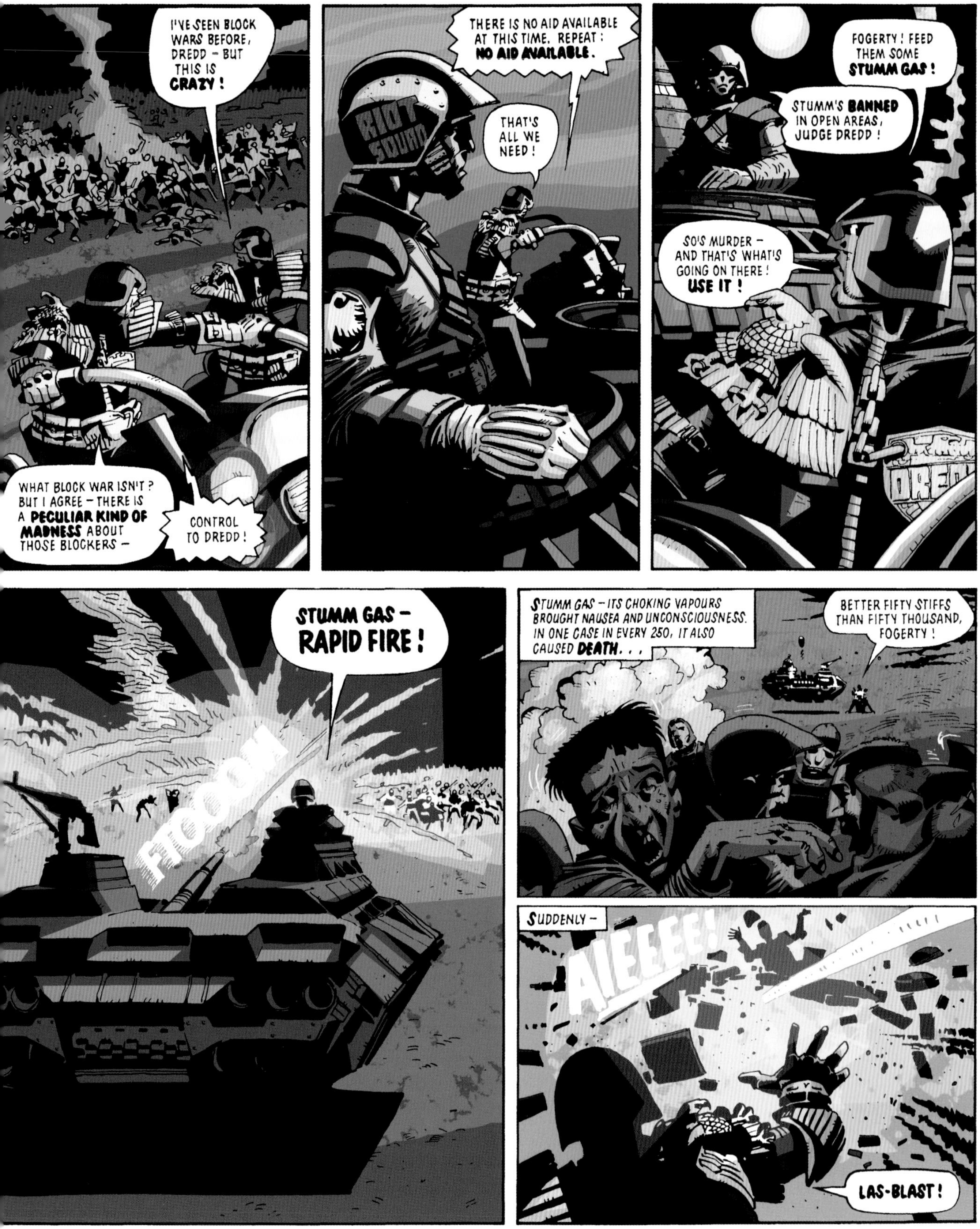
I'VE SEEN BLOCK WARS BEFORE, DREDD – BUT THIS IS **CRAZY**!
WHAT BLOCK WAR ISN'T? BUT I AGREE – THERE IS A **PECULIAR KIND OF MADNESS** ABOUT THOSE BLOCKERS –
CONTROL TO DREDD!
THERE IS NO AID AVAILABLE AT THIS TIME. REPEAT: **NO AID AVAILABLE**.
RIOT SQUAD
THAT'S ALL WE NEED!
FOGERTY! FEED THEM SOME **STUMM GAS**!
STUMM'S **BANNED** IN OPEN AREAS, JUDGE DREDD!
SO'S MURDER – AND THAT'S WHAT'S GOING ON THERE! **USE IT**!
STUMM GAS – **RAPID FIRE!**
STUMM GAS – ITS CHOKING VAPOURS BROUGHT NAUSEA AND UNCONSCIOUSNESS. IN ONE CASE IN EVERY 250, IT ALSO CAUSED **DEATH**. . .
BETTER FIFTY STIFFS THAN FIFTY THOUSAND, FOGERTY!
SUDDENLY –
AIEEEE!
LAS-BLAST!

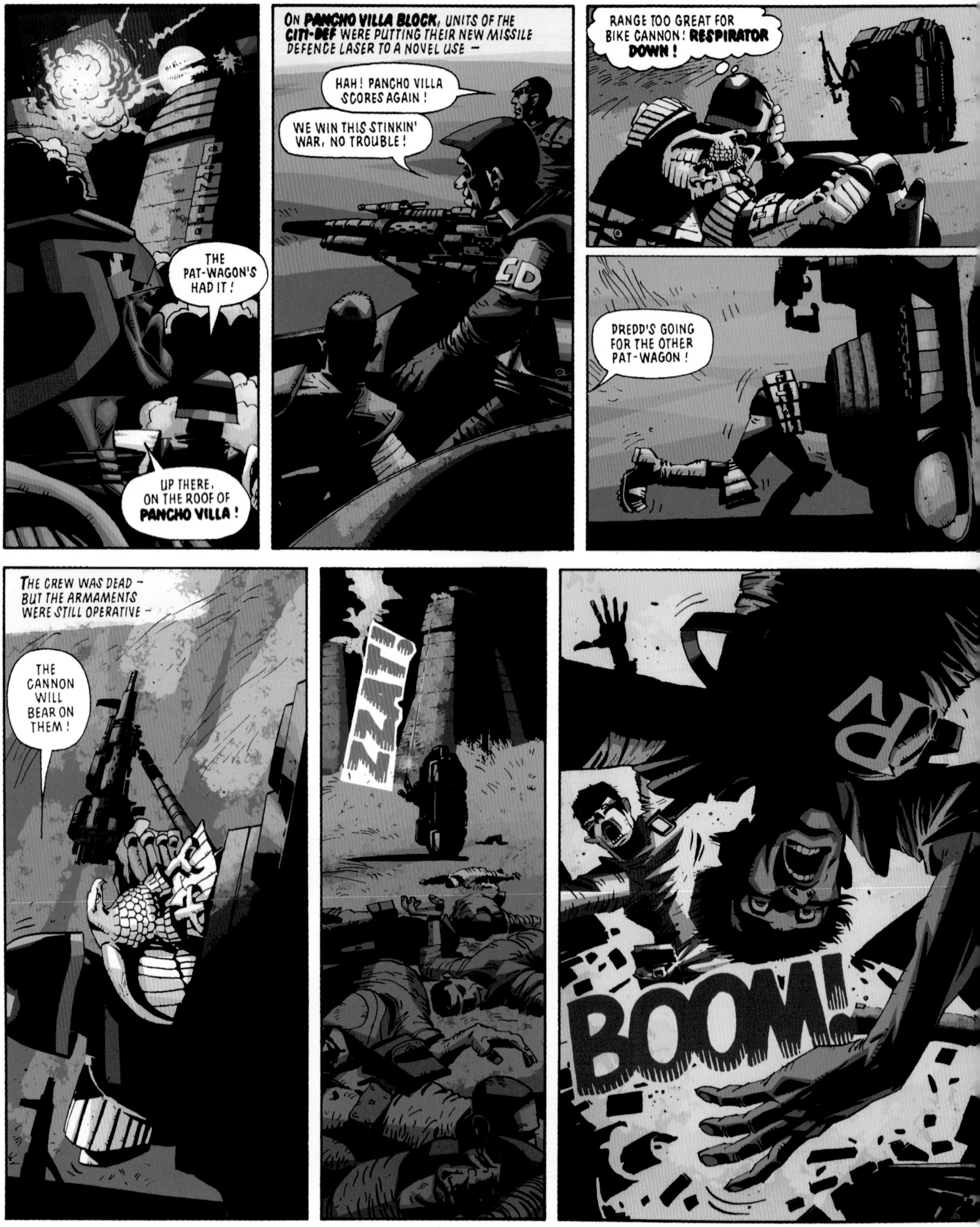
THE PAT-WAGON'S HAD IT!
UP THERE, ON THE ROOF OF PANCHO VILLA!
ON PANCHO VILLA BLOCK, UNITS OF THE CITI-DEF WERE PUTTING THEIR NEW MISSILE DEFENCE LASER TO A NOVEL USE –
HAH! PANCHO VILLA SCORES AGAIN!
WE WIN THIS STINKIN' WAR, NO TROUBLE!
CD
RANGE TOO GREAT FOR BIKE CANNON: RESPIRATOR DOWN!
DREDD'S GOING FOR THE OTHER PAT-WAGON!
THE CREW WAS DEAD – BUT THE ARMAMENTS WERE STILL OPERATIVE –
THE CANNON WILL BEAR ON THEM!
ZZAT!
BOOM!

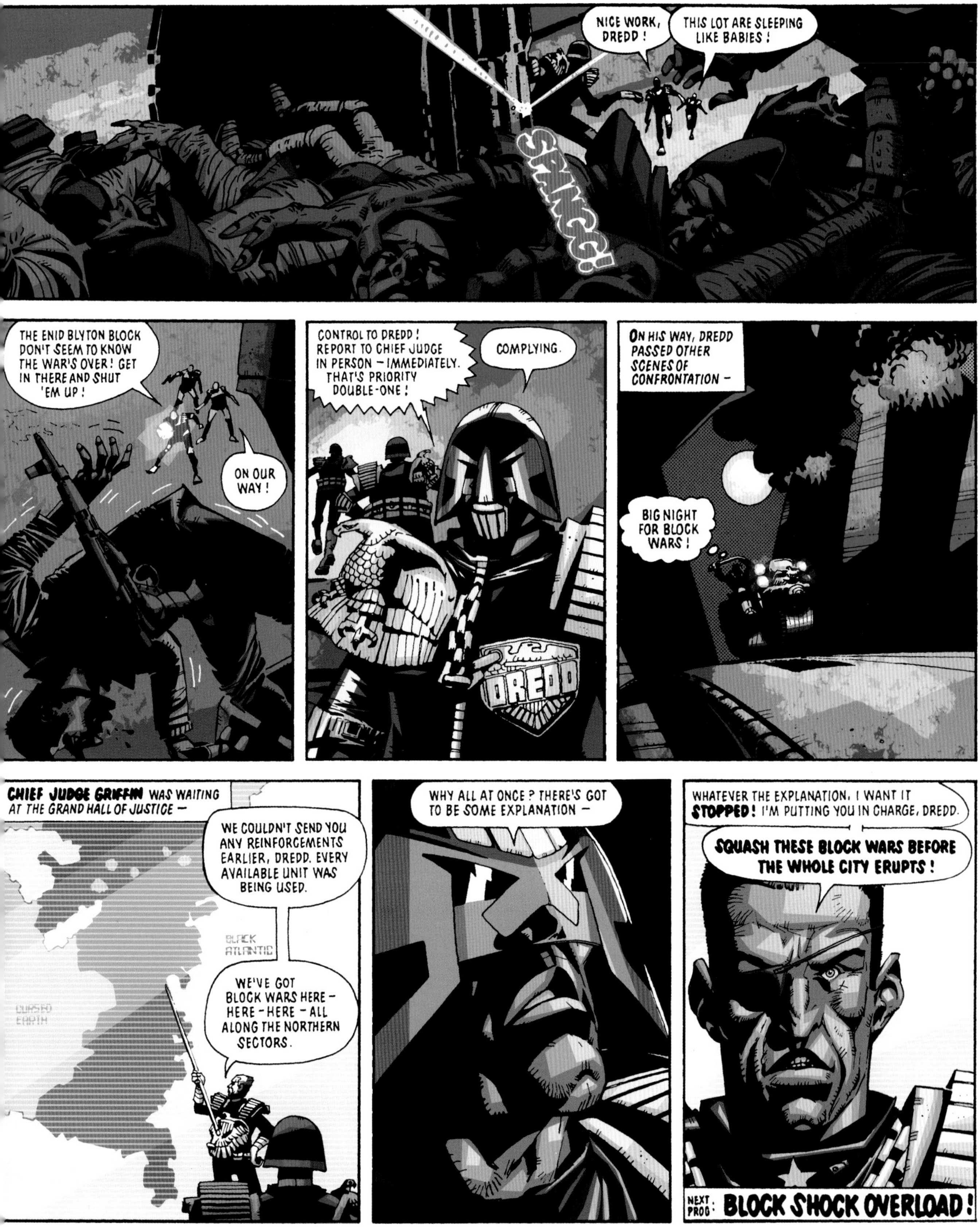
NICE WORK, DREDD!
THIS LOT ARE SLEEPING LIKE BABIES!
SPANGG!
THE ENID BLYTON BLOCK DON'T SEEM TO KNOW THE WAR'S OVER! GET IN THERE AND SHUT 'EM UP!
ON OUR WAY!
CONTROL TO DREDD! REPORT TO CHIEF JUDGE IN PERSON – IMMEDIATELY. THAT'S PRIORITY DOUBLE-ONE!
COMPLYING.
DREDD
ON HIS WAY, DREDD PASSED OTHER SCENES OF CONFRONTATION –
BIG NIGHT FOR BLOCK WARS!
CHIEF JUDGE GRIFFIN WAS WAITING AT THE GRAND HALL OF JUSTICE –
WE COULDN'T SEND YOU ANY REINFORCEMENTS EARLIER, DREDD. EVERY AVAILABLE UNIT WAS BEING USED.
BLACK ATLANTIC
CURSED EARTH
WE'VE GOT BLOCK WARS HERE – HERE – HERE – ALL ALONG THE NORTHERN SECTORS.
WHY ALL AT ONCE? THERE'S GOT TO BE SOME EXPLANATION –
WHATEVER THE EXPLANATION, I WANT IT STOPPED! I'M PUTTING YOU IN CHARGE, DREDD.
SQUASH THESE BLOCK WARS BEFORE THE WHOLE CITY ERUPTS!
NEXT PROG: BLOCK SHOCK OVERLOAD!

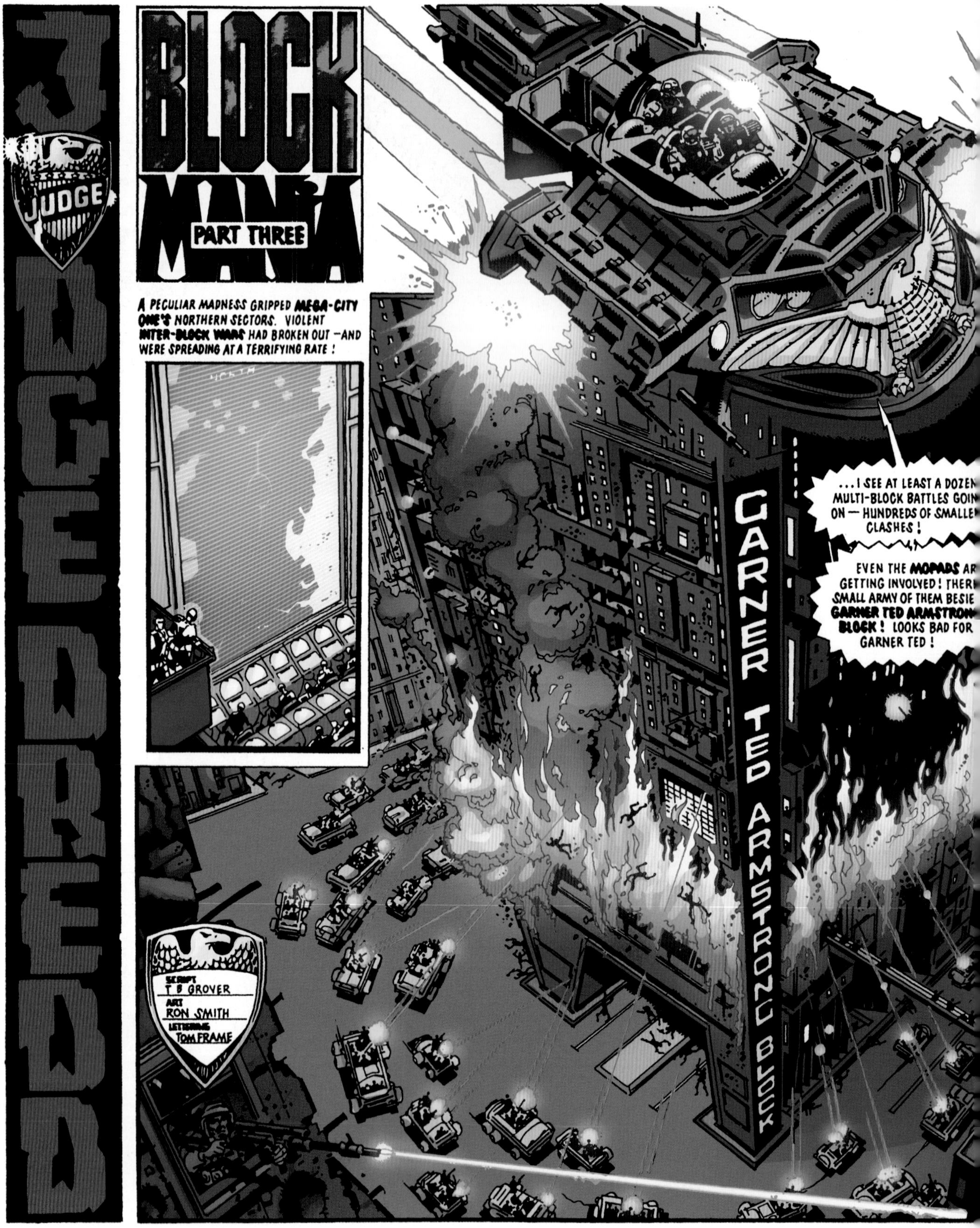
JUDGE DREDD
BLOCK MANIA
PART THREE
A PECULIAR MADNESS GRIPPED MEGA-CITY ONE'S NORTHERN SECTORS. VIOLENT INTER-BLOCK WARS HAD BROKEN OUT —AND WERE SPREADING AT A TERRIFYING RATE !
...I SEE AT LEAST A DOZEN MULTI-BLOCK BATTLES GOIN ON — HUNDREDS OF SMALLE CLASHES !
EVEN THE MOPADS AR GETTING INVOLVED ! THER SMALL ARMY OF THEM BESIE GARNER TED ARMSTRONG BLOCK ! LOOKS BAD FOR GARNER TED !
GARNER TED ARMSTRONG BLOCK
SCRIPT T B GROVER
ART RON SMITH
LETTERING TOM FRAME

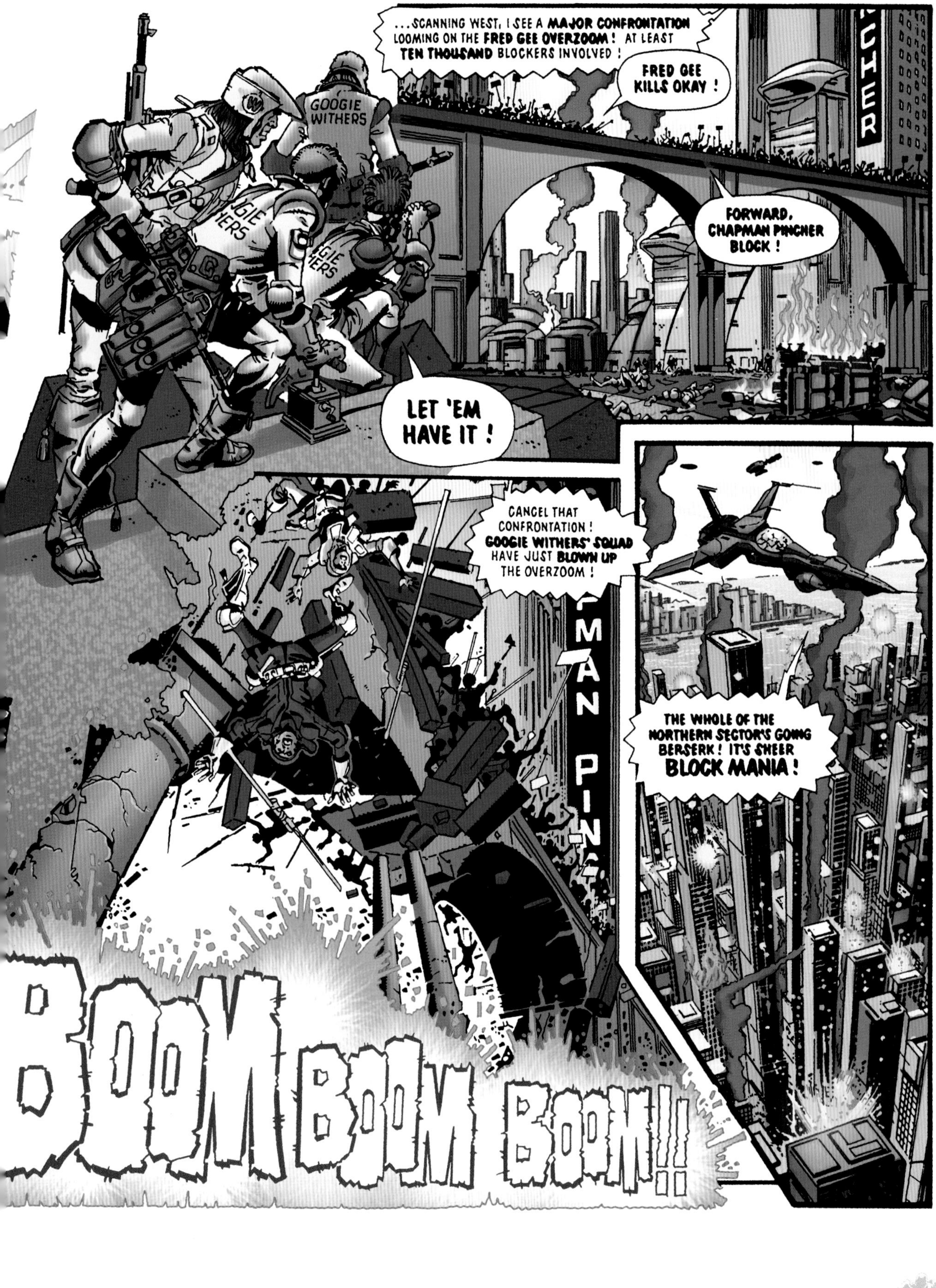
...SCANNING WEST, I SEE A MAJOR CONFRONTATION LOOMING ON THE FRED GEE OVERZOOM! AT LEAST TEN THOUSAND BLOCKERS INVOLVED!
FRED GEE KILLS OKAY!
FORWARD, CHAPMAN PINCHER BLOCK!
LET 'EM HAVE IT!
CANCEL THAT CONFRONTATION! GOOGIE WITHERS' SQUAD HAVE JUST BLOWN UP THE OVERZOOM!
THE WHOLE OF THE NORTHERN SECTOR'S GOING BERSERK! IT'S SHEER BLOCK MANIA!
BOOM BOOM BOOM!!

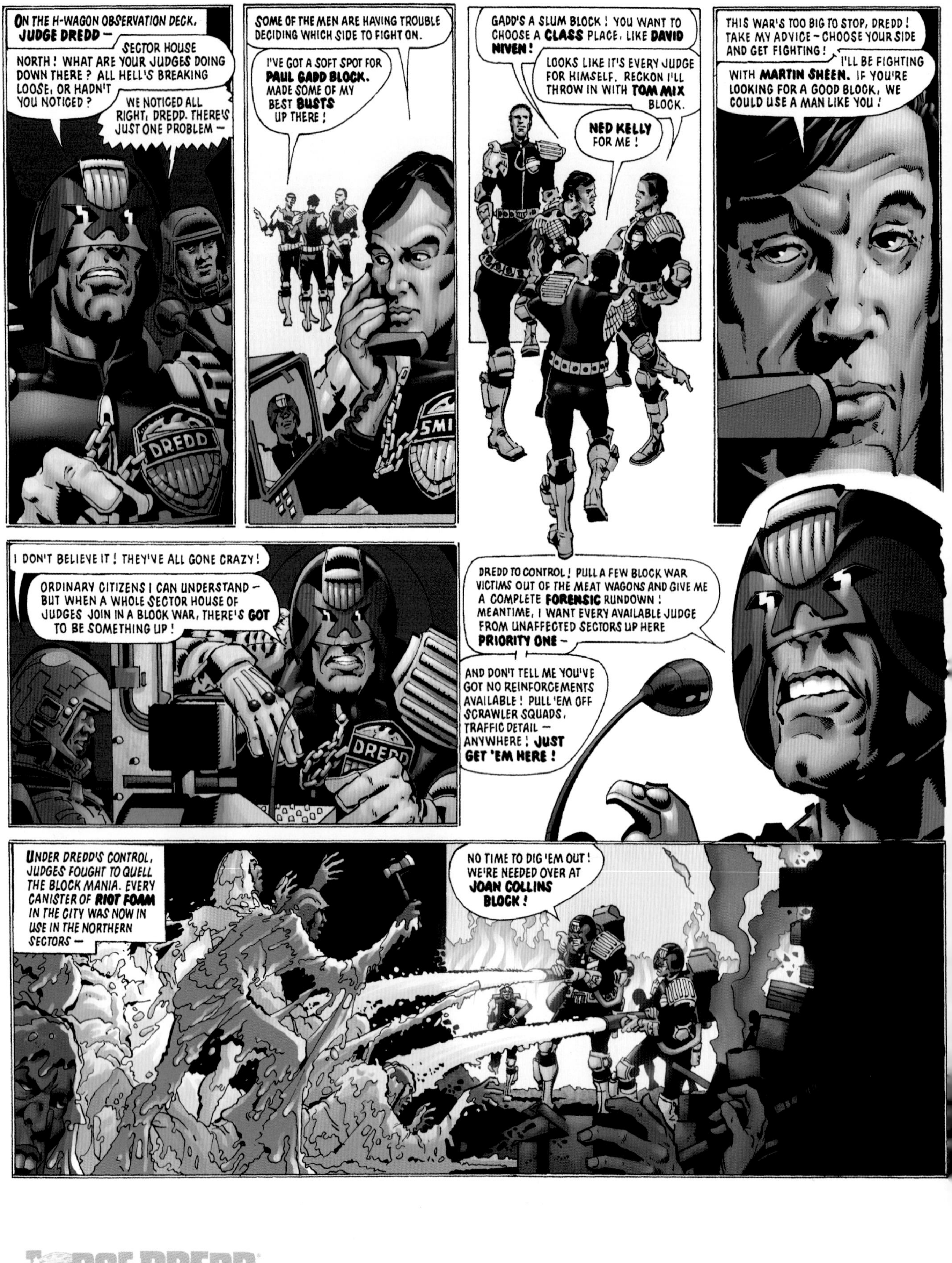

ON THE H-WAGON OBSERVATION DECK, JUDGE DREDD —
SECTOR HOUSE NORTH ! WHAT ARE YOUR JUDGES DOING DOWN THERE ? ALL HELL'S BREAKING LOOSE, OR HADN'T YOU NOTICED ?
WE NOTICED ALL RIGHT, DREDD. THERE'S JUST ONE PROBLEM —
DREDD
SOME OF THE MEN ARE HAVING TROUBLE DECIDING WHICH SIDE TO FIGHT ON.
I'VE GOT A SOFT SPOT FOR PAUL GADD BLOCK. MADE SOME OF MY BEST BUSTS UP THERE !
SMI
GADD'S A SLUM BLOCK ! YOU WANT TO CHOOSE A CLASS PLACE, LIKE DAVID NIVEN !
LOOKS LIKE IT'S EVERY JUDGE FOR HIMSELF. RECKON I'LL THROW IN WITH TOM MIX BLOCK.
NED KELLY FOR ME !
THIS WAR'S TOO BIG TO STOP, DREDD ! TAKE MY ADVICE — CHOOSE YOUR SIDE AND GET FIGHTING !
I'LL BE FIGHTING WITH MARTIN SHEEN. IF YOU'RE LOOKING FOR A GOOD BLOCK, WE COULD USE A MAN LIKE YOU !
I DON'T BELIEVE IT ! THEY'VE ALL GONE CRAZY !
ORDINARY CITIZENS I CAN UNDERSTAND — BUT WHEN A WHOLE SECTOR HOUSE OF JUDGES JOIN IN A BLOCK WAR, THERE'S GOT TO BE SOMETHING UP !
DREDD
DREDD TO CONTROL ! PULL A FEW BLOCK WAR VICTIMS OUT OF THE MEAT WAGONS AND GIVE ME A COMPLETE FORENSIC RUNDOWN ! MEANTIME, I WANT EVERY AVAILABLE JUDGE FROM UNAFFECTED SECTORS UP HERE PRIORITY ONE —
AND DON'T TELL ME YOU'VE GOT NO REINFORCEMENTS AVAILABLE ! PULL 'EM OFF SCRAWLER SQUADS, TRAFFIC DETAIL — ANYWHERE ! JUST GET 'EM HERE !
UNDER DREDD'S CONTROL, JUDGES FOUGHT TO QUELL THE BLOCK MANIA. EVERY CANISTER OF RIOT FOAM IN THE CITY WAS NOW IN USE IN THE NORTHERN SECTORS —
NO TIME TO DIG 'EM OUT ! WE'RE NEEDED OVER AT JOAN COLLINS BLOCK !

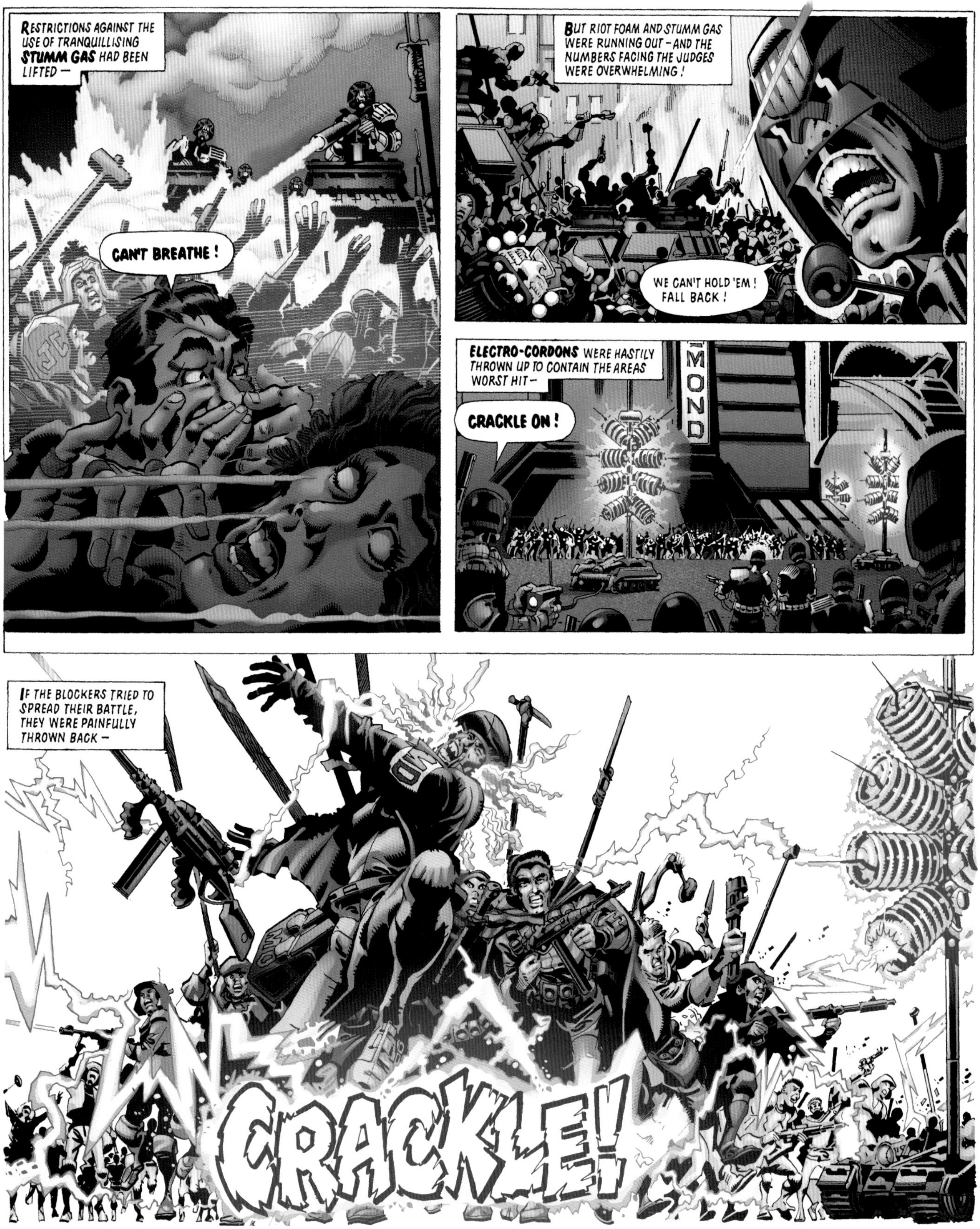
RESTRICTIONS AGAINST THE USE OF TRANQUILLISING STUMM GAS HAD BEEN LIFTED –
CAN'T BREATHE !
BUT RIOT FOAM AND STUMM GAS WERE RUNNING OUT – AND THE NUMBERS FACING THE JUDGES WERE OVERWHELMING !
WE CAN'T HOLD 'EM ! FALL BACK !
ELECTRO-CORDONS WERE HASTILY THROWN UP TO CONTAIN THE AREAS WORST HIT –
CRACKLE ON !
IF THE BLOCKERS TRIED TO SPREAD THEIR BATTLE, THEY WERE PAINFULLY THROWN BACK –
CRACKLE!

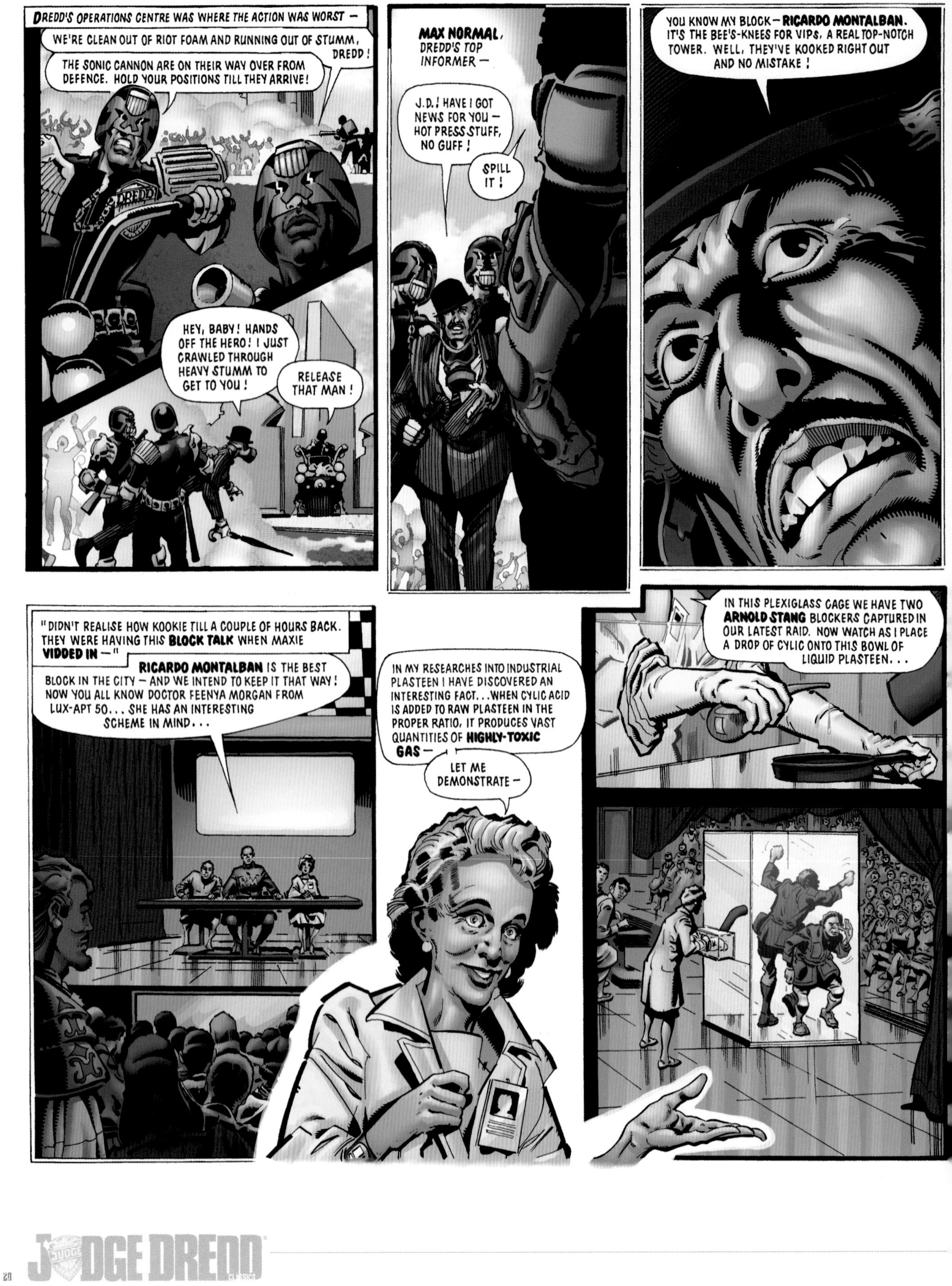

DREDD'S OPERATIONS CENTRE WAS WHERE THE ACTION WAS WORST –
WE'RE CLEAN OUT OF RIOT FOAM AND RUNNING OUT OF STUMM, DREDD!
THE SONIC CANNON ARE ON THEIR WAY OVER FROM DEFENCE. HOLD YOUR POSITIONS TILL THEY ARRIVE!
HEY, BABY! HANDS OFF THE HERO! I JUST CRAWLED THROUGH HEAVY STUMM TO GET TO YOU!
RELEASE THAT MAN!
MAX NORMAL, DREDD'S TOP INFORMER –
J.D.! HAVE I GOT NEWS FOR YOU – HOT PRESS STUFF, NO GUFF!
SPILL IT!
YOU KNOW MY BLOCK – RICARDO MONTALBAN. IT'S THE BEE'S-KNEES FOR VIPS, A REAL TOP-NOTCH TOWER. WELL, THEY'VE KOOKED RIGHT OUT AND NO MISTAKE!
"DIDN'T REALISE HOW KOOKIE TILL A COUPLE OF HOURS BACK. THEY WERE HAVING THIS BLOCK TALK WHEN MAXIE VIDDED IN –"
RICARDO MONTALBAN IS THE BEST BLOCK IN THE CITY – AND WE INTEND TO KEEP IT THAT WAY! NOW YOU ALL KNOW DOCTOR FEENYA MORGAN FROM LUX-APT 50... SHE HAS AN INTERESTING SCHEME IN MIND...
IN MY RESEARCHES INTO INDUSTRIAL PLASTEEN I HAVE DISCOVERED AN INTERESTING FACT... WHEN CYLIC ACID IS ADDED TO RAW PLASTEEN IN THE PROPER RATIO, IT PRODUCES VAST QUANTITIES OF HIGHLY-TOXIC GAS –
LET ME DEMONSTRATE –
IN THIS PLEXIGLASS CAGE WE HAVE TWO ARNOLD STANG BLOCKERS CAPTURED IN OUR LATEST RAID. NOW WATCH AS I PLACE A DROP OF CYLIC ONTO THIS BOWL OF LIQUID PLASTEEN...

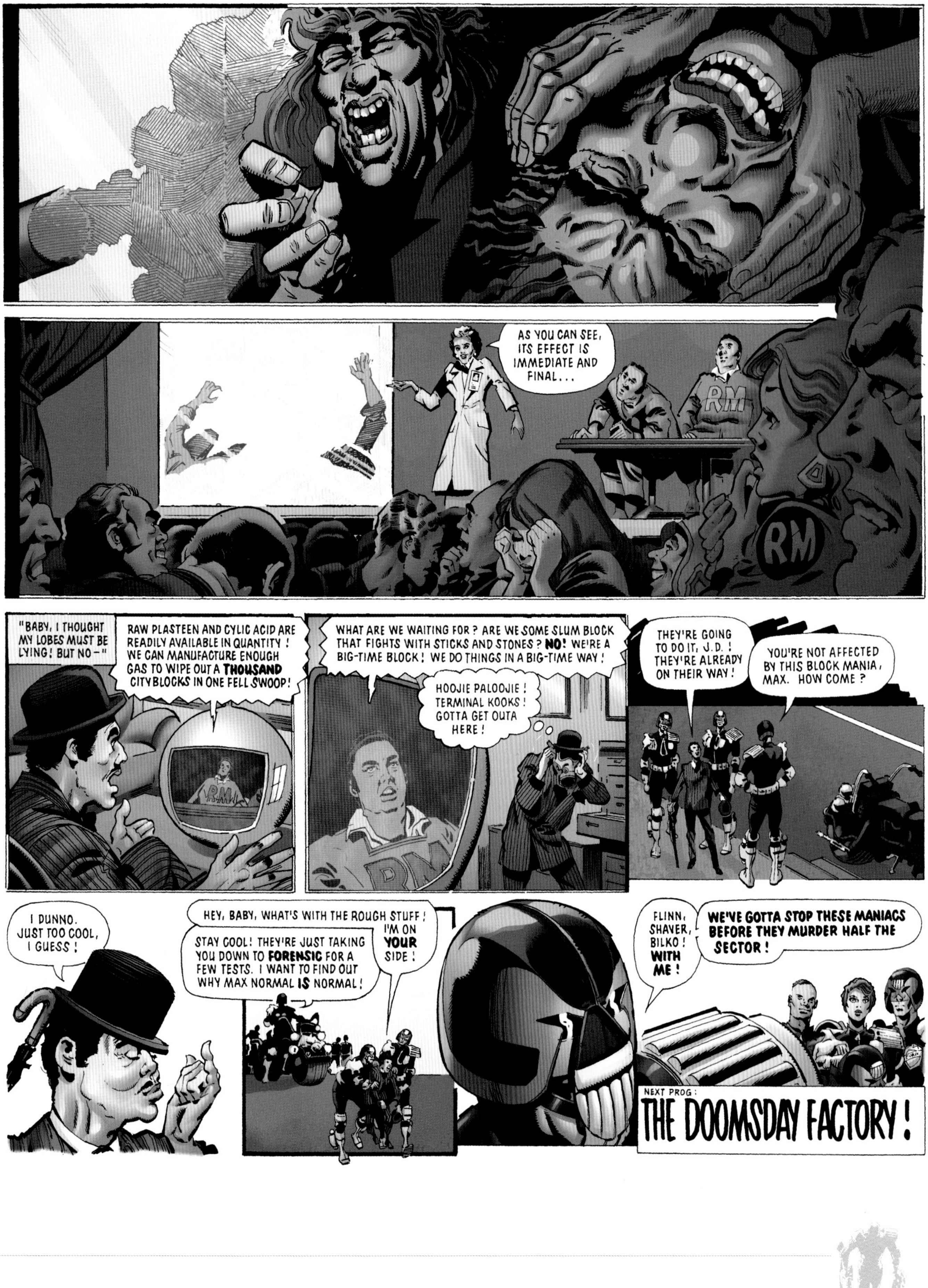

AS YOU CAN SEE, ITS EFFECT IS IMMEDIATE AND FINAL...
"BABY, I THOUGHT MY LOBES MUST BE LYING! BUT NO–"
RAW PLASTEEN AND CYLIC ACID ARE READILY AVAILABLE IN QUANTITY! WE CAN MANUFACTURE ENOUGH GAS TO WIPE OUT A THOUSAND CITY BLOCKS IN ONE FELL SWOOP!
WHAT ARE WE WAITING FOR? ARE WE SOME SLUM BLOCK THAT FIGHTS WITH STICKS AND STONES? NO! WE'RE A BIG-TIME BLOCK! WE DO THINGS IN A BIG-TIME WAY!
HOOJIE PALOOJIE! TERMINAL KOOKS! GOTTA GET OUTA HERE!
THEY'RE GOING TO DO IT, J.D.! THEY'RE ALREADY ON THEIR WAY!
YOU'RE NOT AFFECTED BY THIS BLOCK MANIA, MAX. HOW COME?
I DUNNO. JUST TOO COOL, I GUESS!
HEY, BABY, WHAT'S WITH THE ROUGH STUFF! I'M ON YOUR SIDE!
STAY COOL! THEY'RE JUST TAKING YOU DOWN TO FORENSIC FOR A FEW TESTS. I WANT TO FIND OUT WHY MAX NORMAL IS NORMAL!
FLINN, SHAVER, BILKO! WITH ME!
WE'VE GOTTA STOP THESE MANIACS BEFORE THEY MURDER HALF THE SECTOR!
NEXT PROG:
THE DOOMSDAY FACTORY!

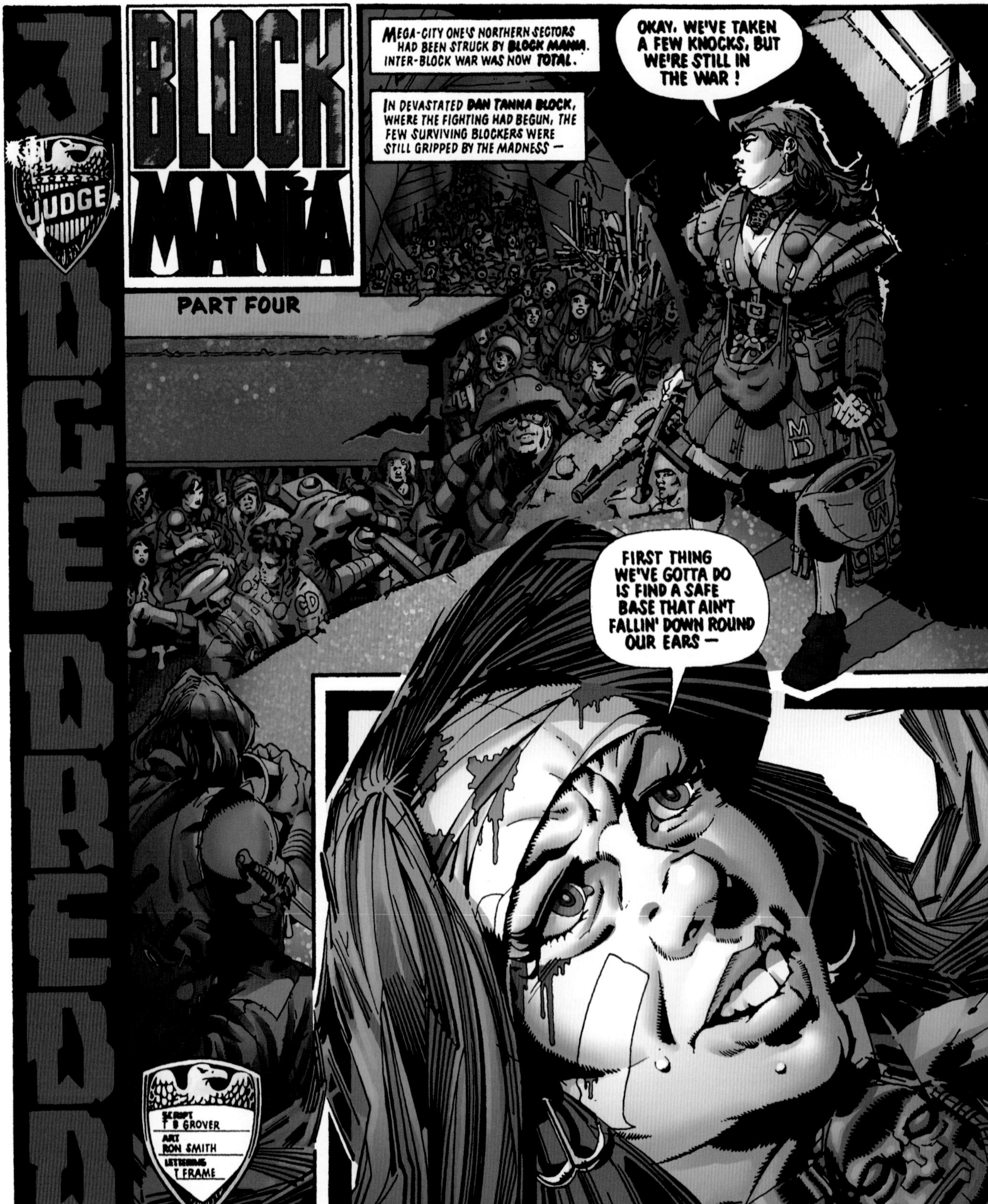
JUDGE DREDD
JUDGE
BLOCK MANIA
PART FOUR
MEGA-CITY ONE'S NORTHERN SECTORS HAD BEEN STRUCK BY BLOCK MANIA. INTER-BLOCK WAR WAS NOW TOTAL.
IN DEVASTATED DAN TANNA BLOCK, WHERE THE FIGHTING HAD BEGUN, THE FEW SURVIVING BLOCKERS WERE STILL GRIPPED BY THE MADNESS —
OKAY, WE'VE TAKEN A FEW KNOCKS, BUT WE'RE STILL IN THE WAR !
FIRST THING WE'VE GOTTA DO IS FIND A SAFE BASE THAT AIN'T FALLIN' DOWN ROUND OUR EARS —
SCRIPT T B GROVER
ART RON SMITH
LETTERING T FRAME

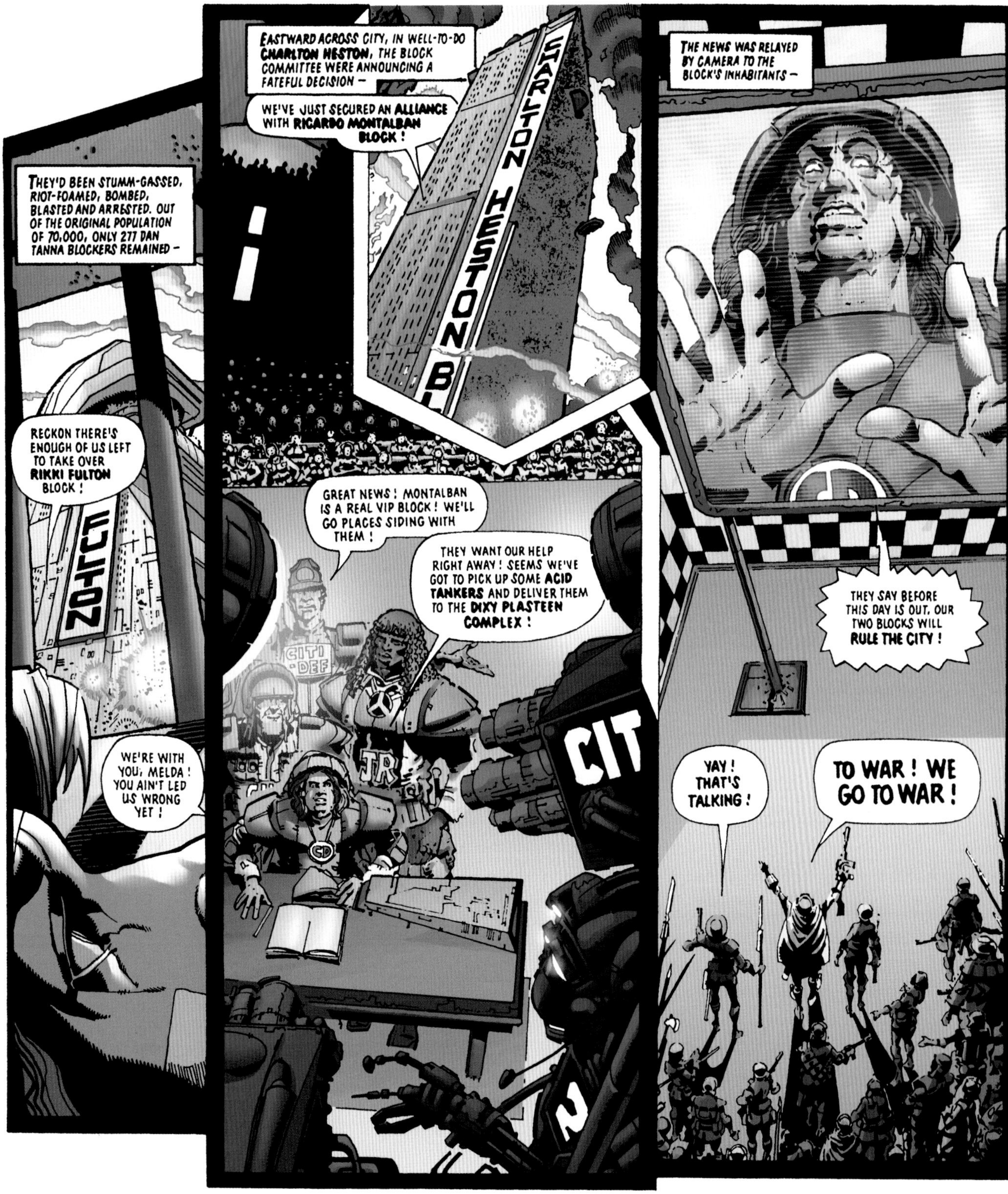

THEY'D BEEN STUMM-GASSED, RIOT-FOAMED, BOMBED, BLASTED AND ARRESTED. OUT OF THE ORIGINAL POPULATION OF 70,000, ONLY 277 DAN TANNA BLOCKERS REMAINED –
RECKON THERE'S ENOUGH OF US LEFT TO TAKE OVER RIKKI FULTON BLOCK !
FULTON
WE'RE WITH YOU, MELDA ! YOU AIN'T LED US WRONG YET !
EASTWARD ACROSS CITY, IN WELL-TO-DO CHARLTON HESTON, THE BLOCK COMMITTEE WERE ANNOUNCING A FATEFUL DECISION –
WE'VE JUST SECURED AN ALLIANCE WITH RICARDO MONTALBAN BLOCK !
CHARLTON HESTON BL
GREAT NEWS ! MONTALBAN IS A REAL VIP BLOCK ! WE'LL GO PLACES SIDING WITH THEM !
THEY WANT OUR HELP RIGHT AWAY ! SEEMS WE'VE GOT TO PICK UP SOME ACID TANKERS AND DELIVER THEM TO THE DIXY PLASTEEN COMPLEX !
CITI DEF
CIT
THE NEWS WAS RELAYED BY CAMERA TO THE BLOCK'S INHABITANTS –
THEY SAY BEFORE THIS DAY IS OUT, OUR TWO BLOCKS WILL RULE THE CITY !
YAY ! THAT'S TALKING !
TO WAR ! WE GO TO WAR !

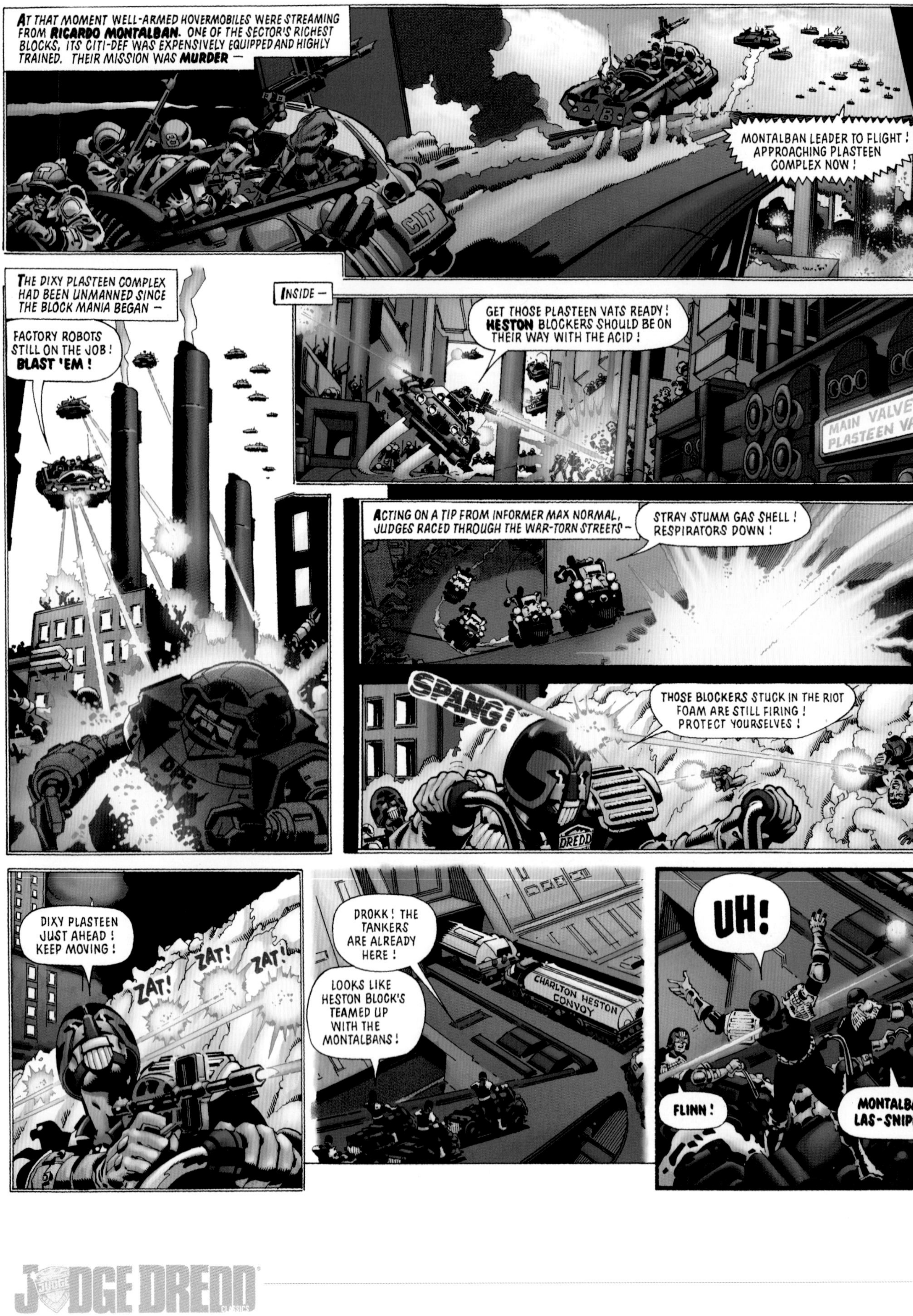
AT THAT MOMENT WELL-ARMED HOVERMOBILES WERE STREAMING FROM RICARDO MONTALBAN. ONE OF THE SECTOR'S RICHEST BLOCKS, ITS CITI-DEF WAS EXPENSIVELY EQUIPPED AND HIGHLY TRAINED. THEIR MISSION WAS MURDER –
MONTALBAN LEADER TO FLIGHT! APPROACHING PLASTEEN COMPLEX NOW!
THE DIXY PLASTEEN COMPLEX HAD BEEN UNMANNED SINCE THE BLOCK MANIA BEGAN –
FACTORY ROBOTS STILL ON THE JOB! BLAST 'EM!
INSIDE –
GET THOSE PLASTEEN VATS READY! HESTON BLOCKERS SHOULD BE ON THEIR WAY WITH THE ACID!
MAIN VALVES PLASTEEN VATS
ACTING ON A TIP FROM INFORMER MAX NORMAL, JUDGES RACED THROUGH THE WAR-TORN STREETS –
STRAY STUMM GAS SHELL! RESPIRATORS DOWN!
SPANG!
THOSE BLOCKERS STUCK IN THE RIOT FOAM ARE STILL FIRING! PROTECT YOURSELVES!
DREDD
DIXY PLASTEEN JUST AHEAD! KEEP MOVING!
ZAT! ZAT! ZAT!
DROKK! THE TANKERS ARE ALREADY HERE!
LOOKS LIKE HESTON BLOCK'S TEAMED UP WITH THE MONTALBANS!
CHARLTON HESTON CONVOY
UH!
FLINN!
MONTALBAN LAS-SNIPERS!

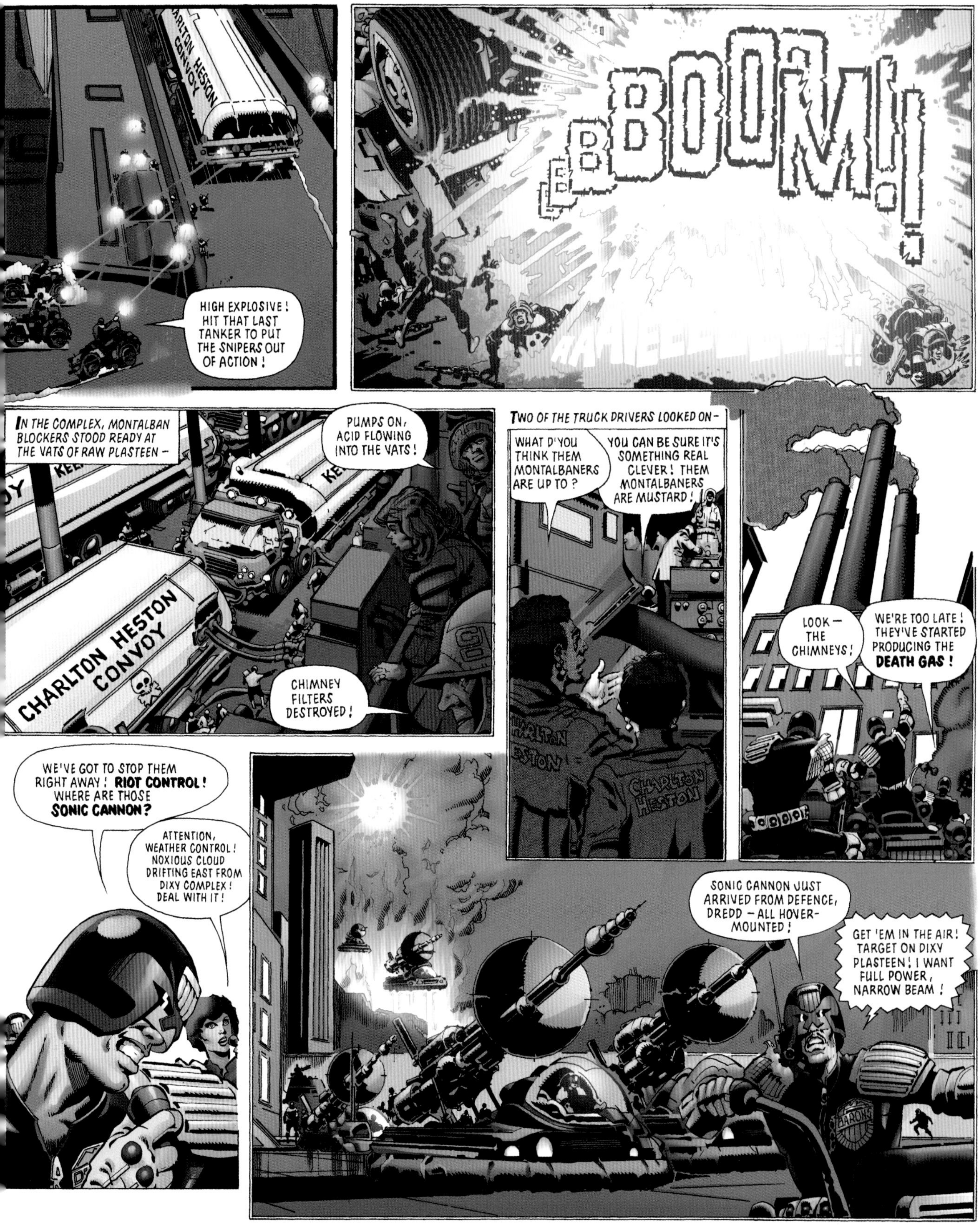
CHARLTON HESTON CONVOY
HIGH EXPLOSIVE! HIT THAT LAST TANKER TO PUT THE SNIPERS OUT OF ACTION!
BBBOOOM!!
IN THE COMPLEX, MONTALBAN BLOCKERS STOOD READY AT THE VATS OF RAW PLASTEEN –
PUMPS ON, ACID FLOWING INTO THE VATS!
CHARLTON HESTON CONVOY
CHIMNEY FILTERS DESTROYED!
TWO OF THE TRUCK DRIVERS LOOKED ON –
WHAT D'YOU THINK THEM MONTALBANERS ARE UP TO?
YOU CAN BE SURE IT'S SOMETHING REAL CLEVER! THEM MONTALBANERS ARE MUSTARD!
CHARLTON HESTON
LOOK – THE CHIMNEYS!
WE'RE TOO LATE! THEY'VE STARTED PRODUCING THE DEATH GAS!
WE'VE GOT TO STOP THEM RIGHT AWAY! RIOT CONTROL! WHERE ARE THOSE SONIC CANNON?
ATTENTION, WEATHER CONTROL! NOXIOUS CLOUD DRIFTING EAST FROM DIXY COMPLEX! DEAL WITH IT!
SONIC CANNON JUST ARRIVED FROM DEFENCE, DREDD – ALL HOVER-MOUNTED!
GET 'EM IN THE AIR! TARGET ON DIXY PLASTEEN! I WANT FULL POWER, NARROW BEAM!

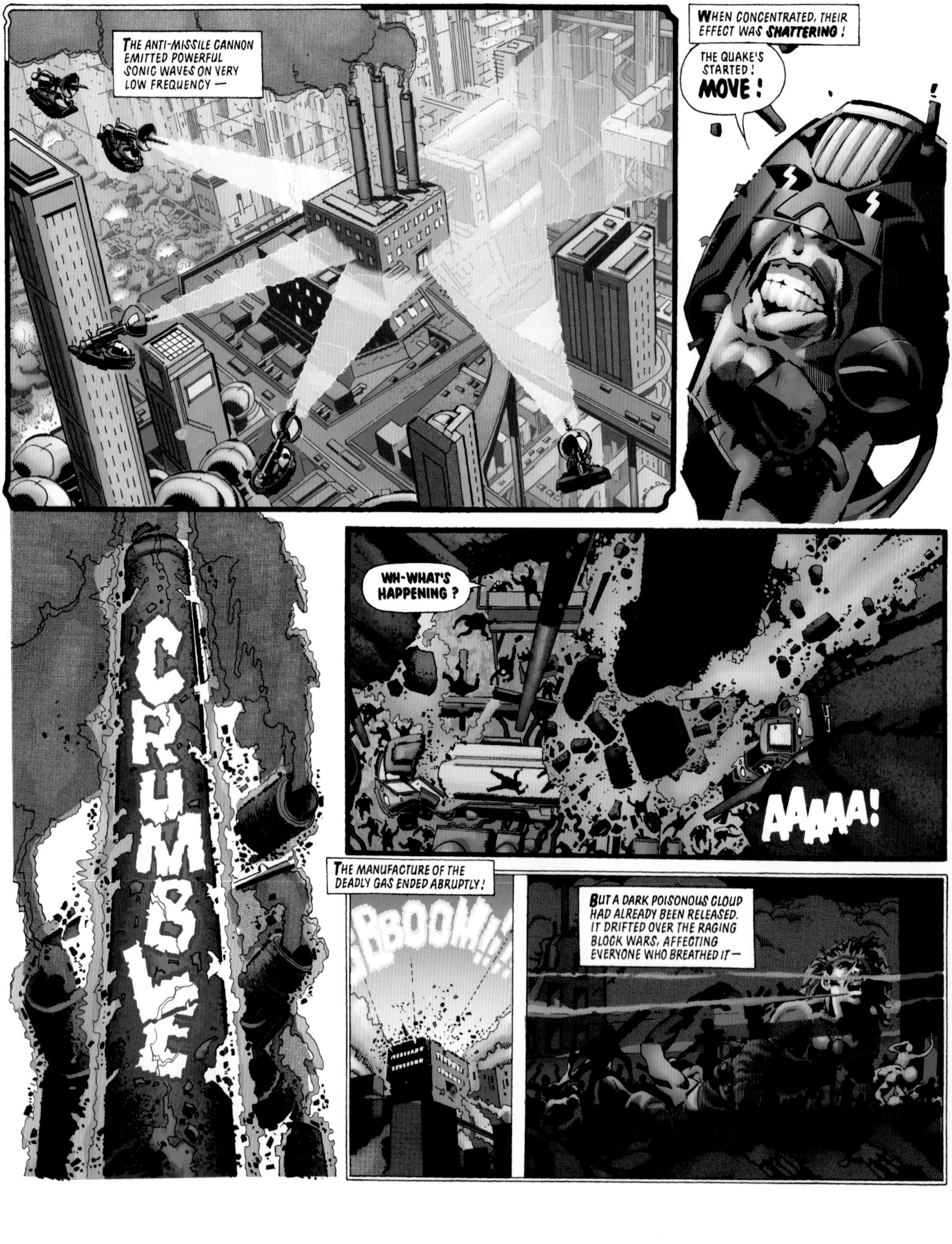
THE ANTI-MISSILE CANNON EMITTED POWERFUL SONIC WAVES ON VERY LOW FREQUENCY —
WHEN CONCENTRATED, THEIR EFFECT WAS SHATTERING!
THE QUAKE'S STARTED! MOVE!
CRUMBLE
WH-WHAT'S HAPPENING?
AAAAA!
THE MANUFACTURE OF THE DEADLY GAS ENDED ABRUPTLY!
BBOOM!!!
BUT A DARK POISONOUS CLOUD HAD ALREADY BEEN RELEASED. IT DRIFTED OVER THE RAGING BLOCK WARS, AFFECTING EVERYONE WHO BREATHED IT —

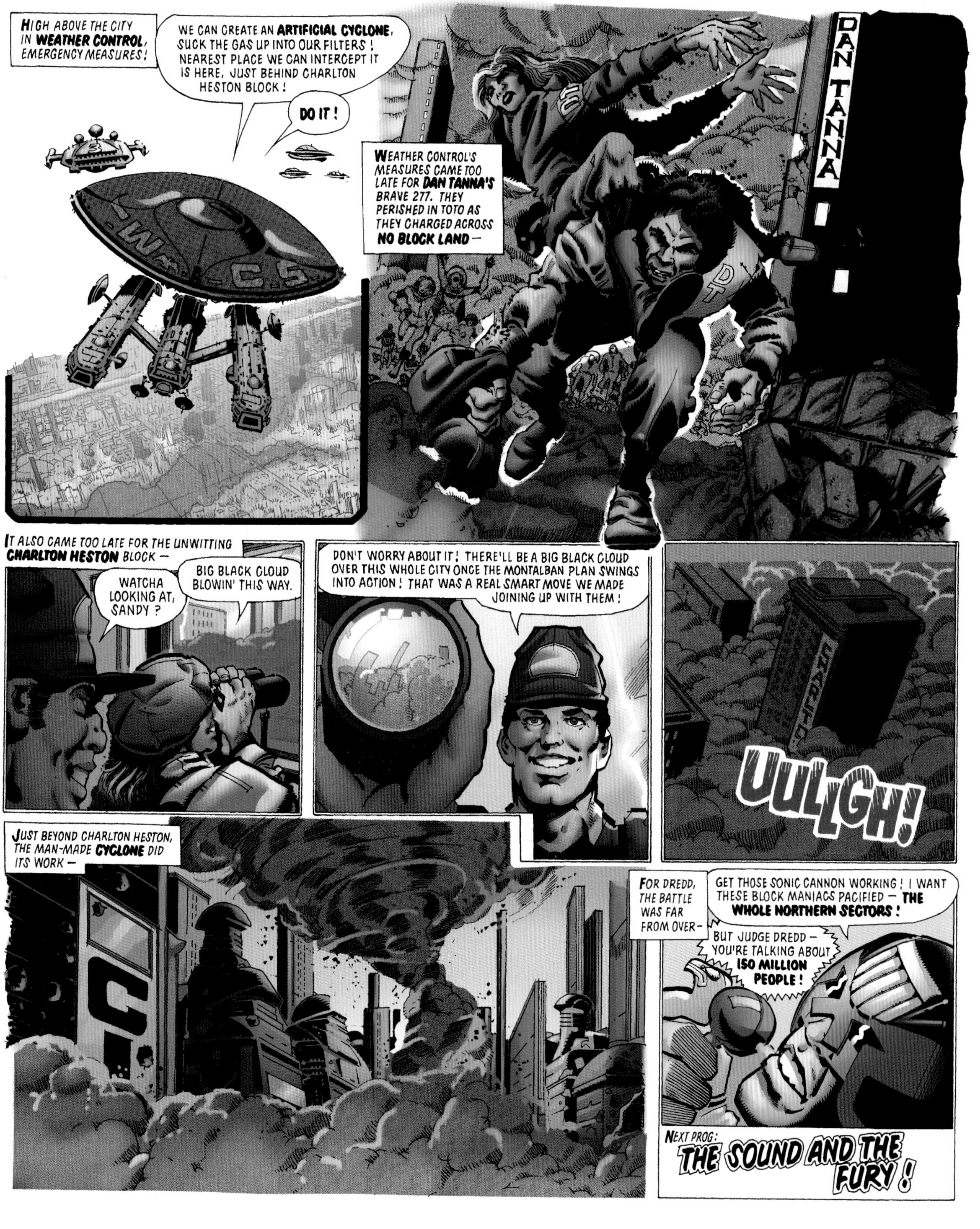
HIGH ABOVE THE CITY IN WEATHER CONTROL, EMERGENCY MEASURES!
WE CAN CREATE AN ARTIFICIAL CYCLONE, SUCK THE GAS UP INTO OUR FILTERS! NEAREST PLACE WE CAN INTERCEPT IT IS HERE, JUST BEHIND CHARLTON HESTON BLOCK!
DO IT!
W.C.S.
WEATHER CONTROL'S MEASURES CAME TOO LATE FOR DAN TANNA'S BRAVE 277. THEY PERISHED IN TOTO AS THEY CHARGED ACROSS NO BLOCK LAND —
DAN TANNA
IT ALSO CAME TOO LATE FOR THE UNWITTING CHARLTON HESTON BLOCK —
WATCHA LOOKING AT, SANDY?
BIG BLACK CLOUD BLOWIN' THIS WAY.
DON'T WORRY ABOUT IT! THERE'LL BE A BIG BLACK CLOUD OVER THIS WHOLE CITY ONCE THE MONTALBAN PLAN SWINGS INTO ACTION! THAT WAS A REAL SMART MOVE WE MADE JOINING UP WITH THEM!
UULLGH!
JUST BEYOND CHARLTON HESTON, THE MAN-MADE CYCLONE DID ITS WORK —
FOR DREDD, THE BATTLE WAS FAR FROM OVER—
GET THOSE SONIC CANNON WORKING! I WANT THESE BLOCK MANIACS PACIFIED — THE WHOLE NORTHERN SECTORS!
BUT JUDGE DREDD — YOU'RE TALKING ABOUT 150 MILLION PEOPLE!
NEXT PROG:
THE SOUND AND THE FURY!

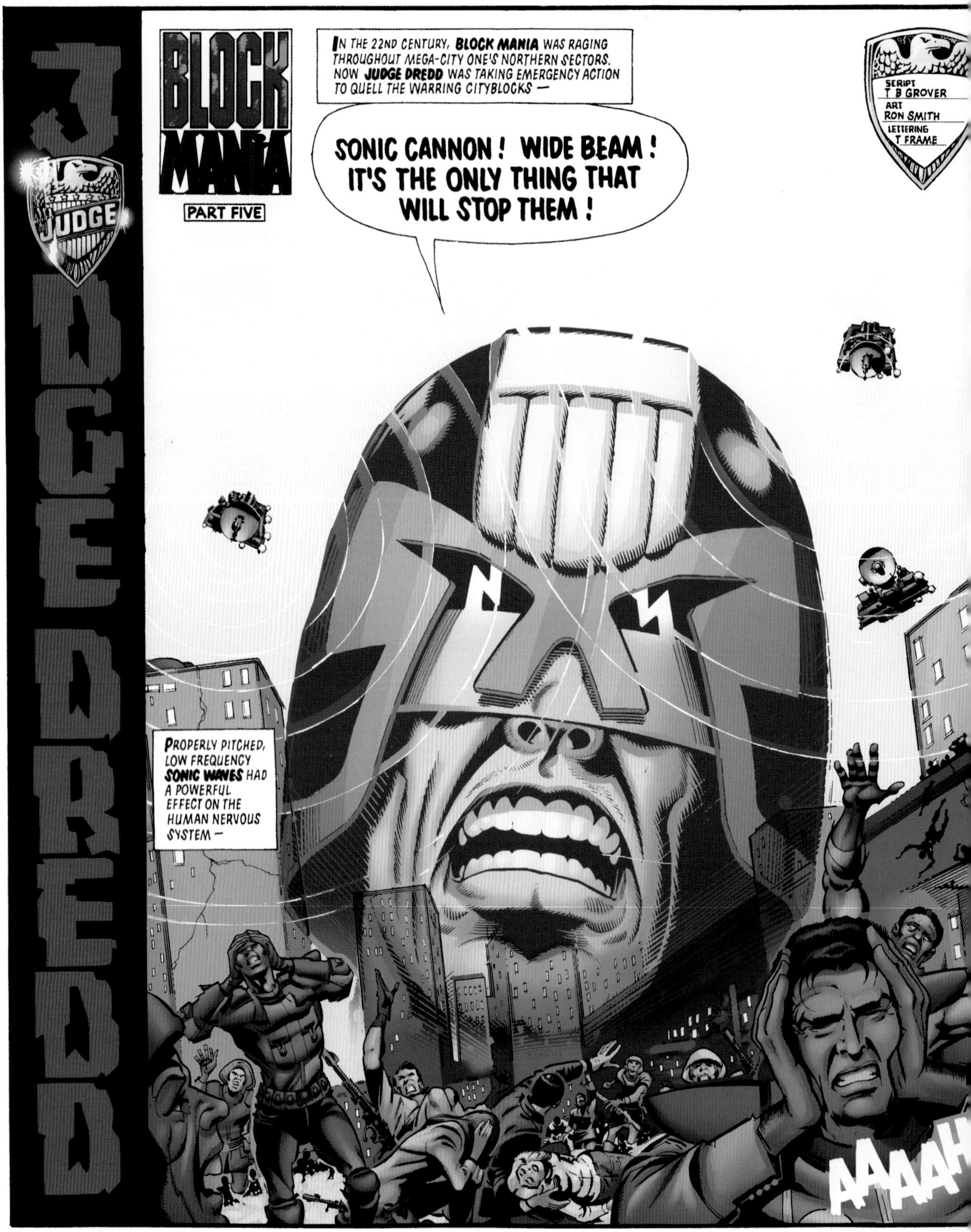
JUDGE DREDD
BLOCK MANIA
PART FIVE
IN THE 22ND CENTURY, BLOCK MANIA WAS RAGING THROUGHOUT MEGA-CITY ONE'S NORTHERN SECTORS. NOW JUDGE DREDD WAS TAKING EMERGENCY ACTION TO QUELL THE WARRING CITYBLOCKS —
SONIC CANNON! WIDE BEAM! IT'S THE ONLY THING THAT WILL STOP THEM!
SCRIPT T B GROVER
ART RON SMITH
LETTERING T FRAME
PROPERLY PITCHED, LOW FREQUENCY SONIC WAVES HAD A POWERFUL EFFECT ON THE HUMAN NERVOUS SYSTEM —
AAAAH

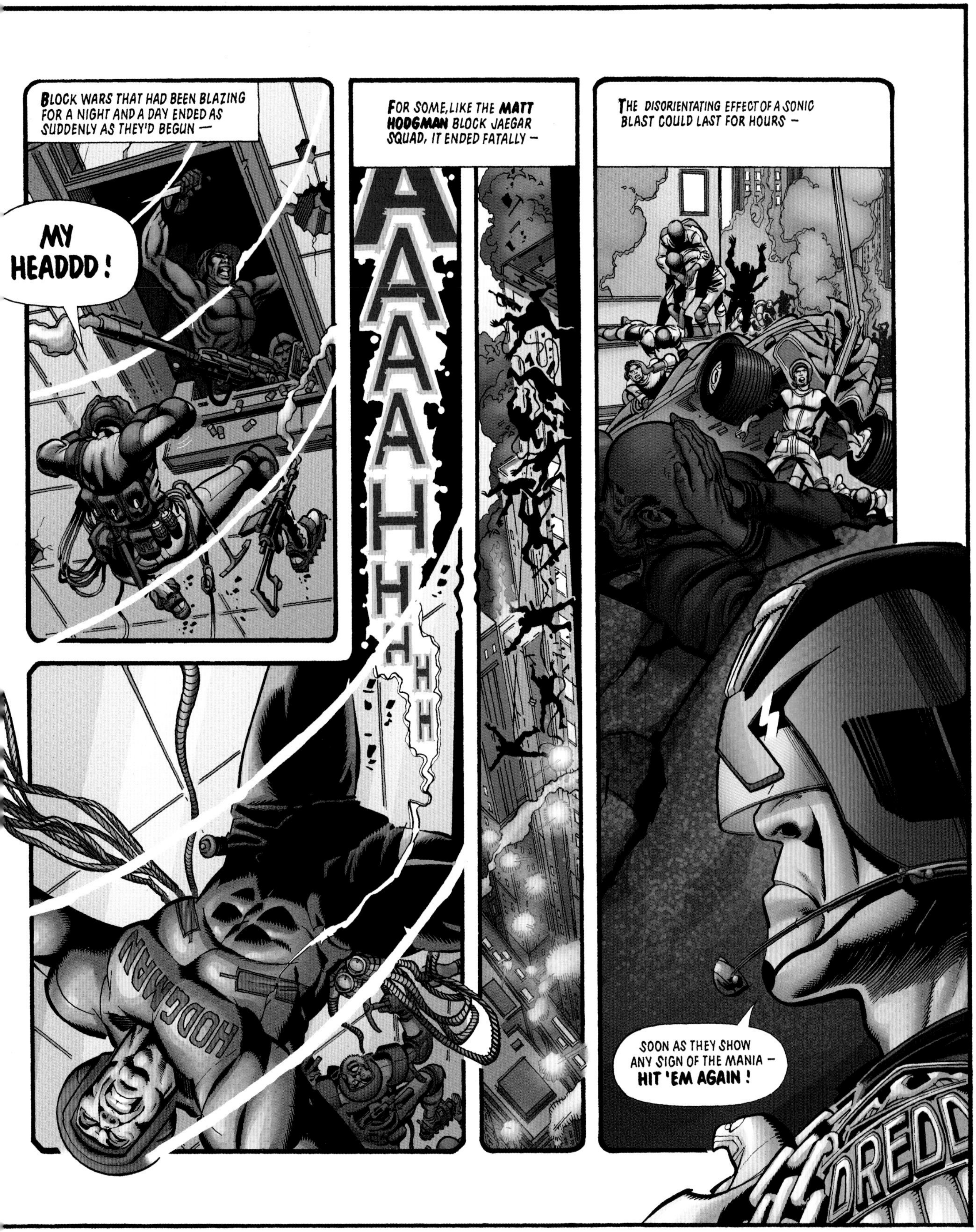
BLOCK WARS THAT HAD BEEN BLAZING FOR A NIGHT AND A DAY ENDED AS SUDDENLY AS THEY'D BEGUN —
MY HEADDD!
FOR SOME, LIKE THE MATT HODGMAN BLOCK JAEGAR SQUAD, IT ENDED FATALLY —
AAAAAHHHHHH
HODGMAN
THE DISORIENTATING EFFECT OF A SONIC BLAST COULD LAST FOR HOURS —
SOON AS THEY SHOW ANY SIGN OF THE MANIA — HIT 'EM AGAIN!
DREDD

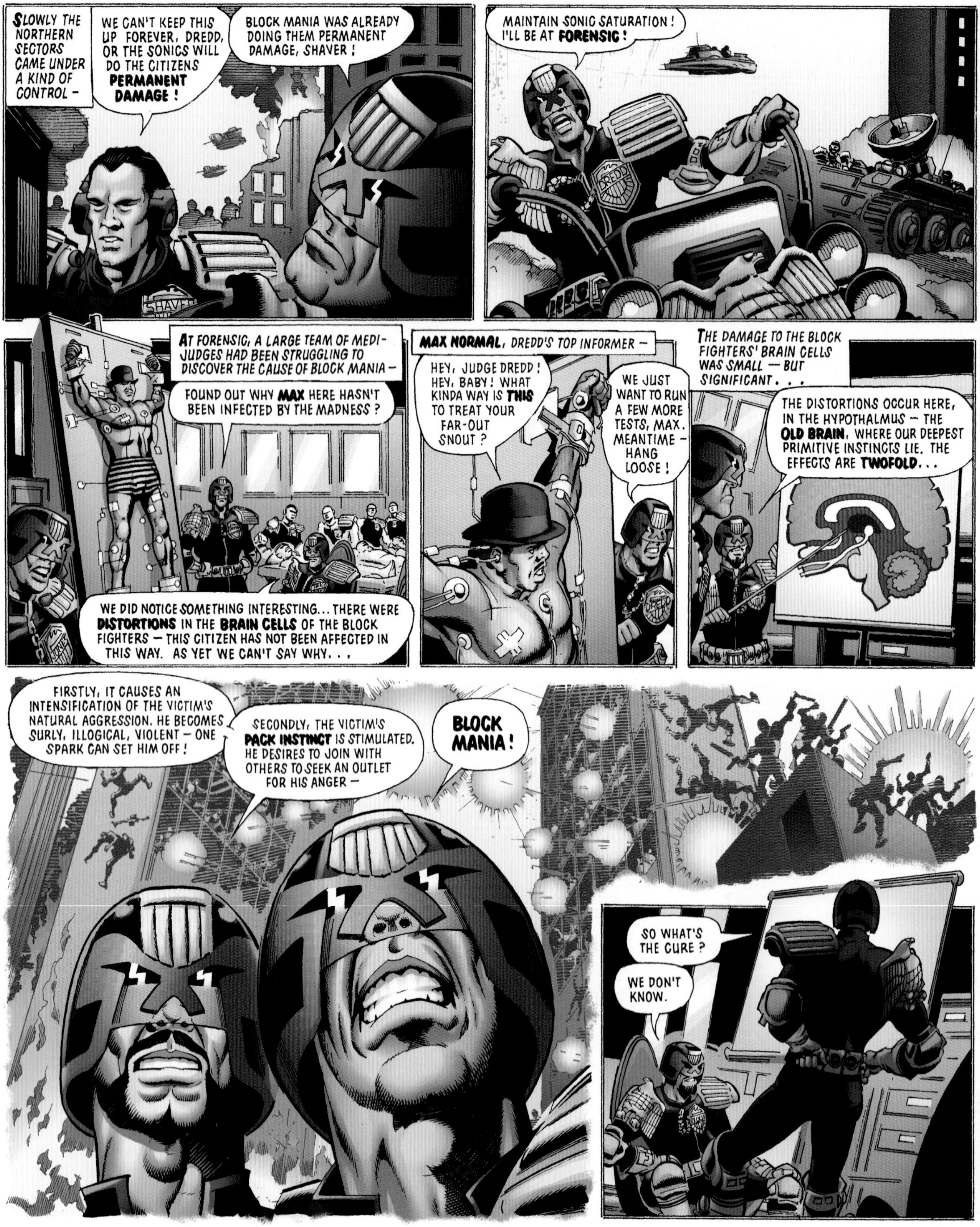
SLOWLY THE NORTHERN SECTORS CAME UNDER A KIND OF CONTROL -
WE CAN'T KEEP THIS UP FOREVER, DREDD, OR THE SONICS WILL DO THE CITIZENS PERMANENT DAMAGE!
BLOCK MANIA WAS ALREADY DOING THEM PERMANENT DAMAGE, SHAVER!
MAINTAIN SONIC SATURATION! I'LL BE AT FORENSIC!
AT FORENSIC, A LARGE TEAM OF MEDI-JUDGES HAD BEEN STRUGGLING TO DISCOVER THE CAUSE OF BLOCK MANIA -
FOUND OUT WHY MAX HERE HASN'T BEEN INFECTED BY THE MADNESS?
WE DID NOTICE SOMETHING INTERESTING... THERE WERE DISTORTIONS IN THE BRAIN CELLS OF THE BLOCK FIGHTERS - THIS CITIZEN HAS NOT BEEN AFFECTED IN THIS WAY. AS YET WE CAN'T SAY WHY...
MAX NORMAL, DREDD'S TOP INFORMER -
HEY, JUDGE DREDD! HEY, BABY! WHAT KINDA WAY IS THIS TO TREAT YOUR FAR-OUT SNOUT?
WE JUST WANT TO RUN A FEW MORE TESTS, MAX. MEANTIME - HANG LOOSE!
THE DAMAGE TO THE BLOCK FIGHTERS' BRAIN CELLS WAS SMALL — BUT SIGNIFICANT...
THE DISTORTIONS OCCUR HERE, IN THE HYPOTHALMUS — THE OLD BRAIN, WHERE OUR DEEPEST PRIMITIVE INSTINCTS LIE. THE EFFECTS ARE TWOFOLD...
FIRSTLY, IT CAUSES AN INTENSIFICATION OF THE VICTIM'S NATURAL AGGRESSION. HE BECOMES SURLY, ILLOGICAL, VIOLENT — ONE SPARK CAN SET HIM OFF!
SECONDLY, THE VICTIM'S PACK INSTINCT IS STIMULATED. HE DESIRES TO JOIN WITH OTHERS TO SEEK AN OUTLET FOR HIS ANGER —
BLOCK MANIA!
SO WHAT'S THE CURE?
WE DON'T KNOW.

AND WE **WON'T** KNOW UNTIL WE FIND OUT WHAT'S **CAUSING** IT. THERE'S NO TRACE OF ANY FOREIGN SUBSTANCE IN VICTIMS' BODIES. EVERY POSSIBLE SOURCE OF CONTAMINATION HAS BEEN CHECKED — WATER, AIR, SANITATION . . . ALL CLEAN.

PSI-DIVISION HAVE BEEN MONITORING FOR FOR PSYCHIC INTERFERENCE — **NOTHING!**

WE'RE STUMPED, DREDD! ALL I CAN SAY IS, THANK GOD YOU'VE MANAGED TO CONTAIN IT TO THE NORTHERN SECTORS!

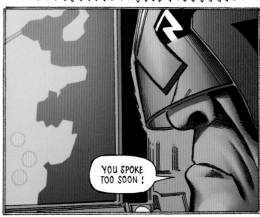

ATTENTION, JUDGE DREDD! WE HAVE **MULTI-BLOCK FLARE-UP** IN **SOUTH SECTOR 7.** STATUS: **WAR AND ESCALATING!**

YOU SPOKE TOO SOON!

THE WAR IN THE CITY'S VAST SOUTH SECTOR WAS LAUNCHED BY **FATS DOMINO BLOCK** —

PRESENT FOR YOU, RUDI!

BOOM! BOOM! BOOM!

IT WAS THE SPARK THAT IGNITED THE SOUTH —

YOU HEARD THAT, VALLI BLOCKERS! THE WAR'S ON!

IT'S EVERY BLOCK FOR ITSELF!

EVERY SPARE JUDGE HAD BEEN PULLED OUT TO FIGHT IN THE NORTH. WITH MINIMAL LAW ENFORCEMENT, **BLOCK MANIA** *SPREAD LIKE WILDFIRE —*

THE BRONTE CONURB'S GOING! STRIKE TWO TO FATS DOMINO!

LOOK OUT! VIC HUGO HOVER-STRIKE!

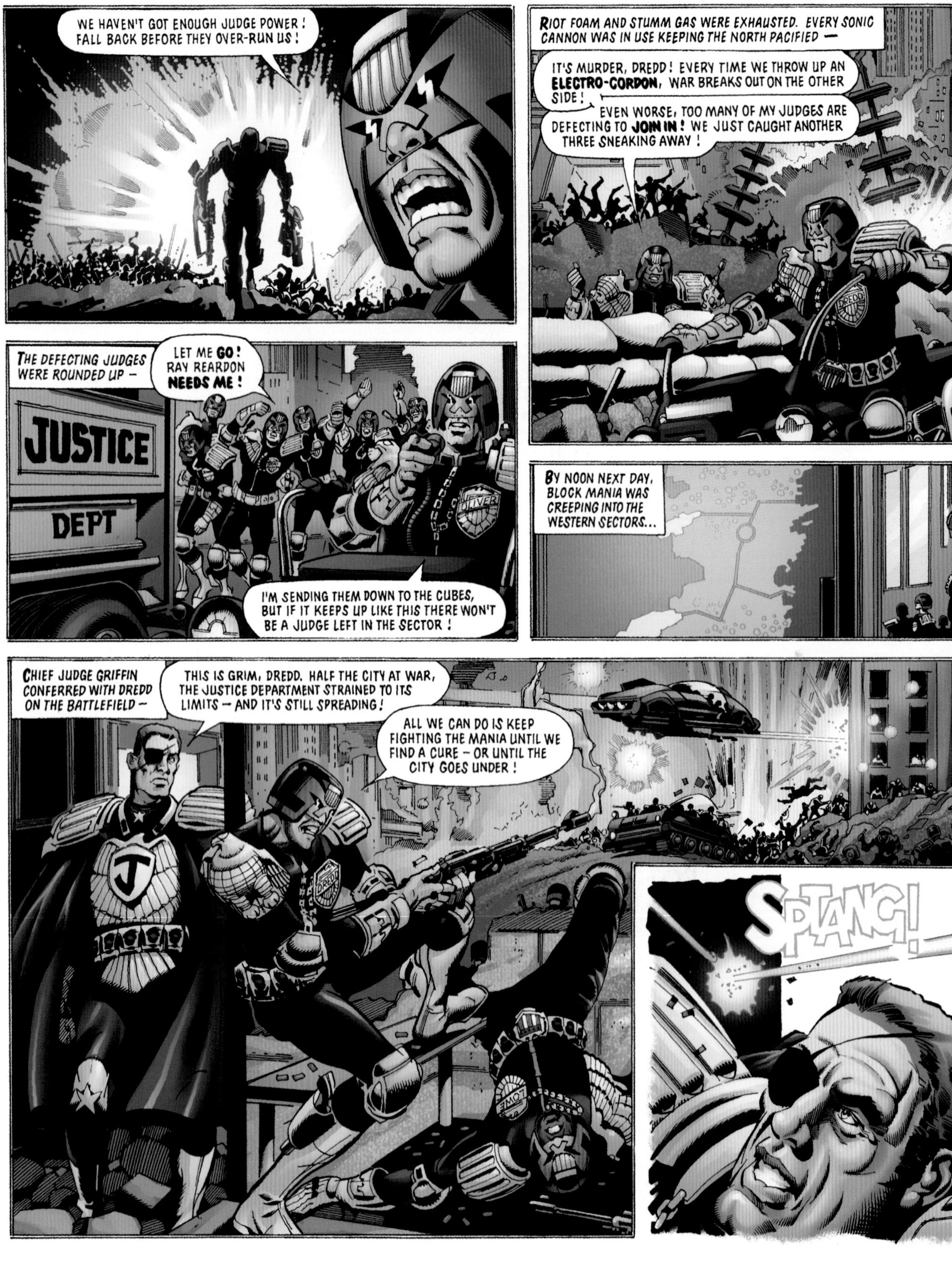
WE HAVEN'T GOT ENOUGH JUDGE POWER! FALL BACK BEFORE THEY OVER-RUN US!
RIOT FOAM AND STUMM GAS WERE EXHAUSTED. EVERY SONIC CANNON WAS IN USE KEEPING THE NORTH PACIFIED —
IT'S MURDER, DREDD! EVERY TIME WE THROW UP AN ELECTRO-CORDON, WAR BREAKS OUT ON THE OTHER SIDE!
EVEN WORSE, TOO MANY OF MY JUDGES ARE DEFECTING TO JOIN IN! WE JUST CAUGHT ANOTHER THREE SNEAKING AWAY!
THE DEFECTING JUDGES WERE ROUNDED UP —
LET ME GO! RAY REARDON NEEDS ME!
JUSTICE
DEPT
I'M SENDING THEM DOWN TO THE CUBES, BUT IF IT KEEPS UP LIKE THIS THERE WON'T BE A JUDGE LEFT IN THE SECTOR!
BY NOON NEXT DAY, BLOCK MANIA WAS CREEPING INTO THE WESTERN SECTORS...
CHIEF JUDGE GRIFFIN CONFERRED WITH DREDD ON THE BATTLEFIELD —
THIS IS GRIM, DREDD. HALF THE CITY AT WAR, THE JUSTICE DEPARTMENT STRAINED TO ITS LIMITS — AND IT'S STILL SPREADING!
ALL WE CAN DO IS KEEP FIGHTING THE MANIA UNTIL WE FIND A CURE — OR UNTIL THE CITY GOES UNDER!
SPTANG!

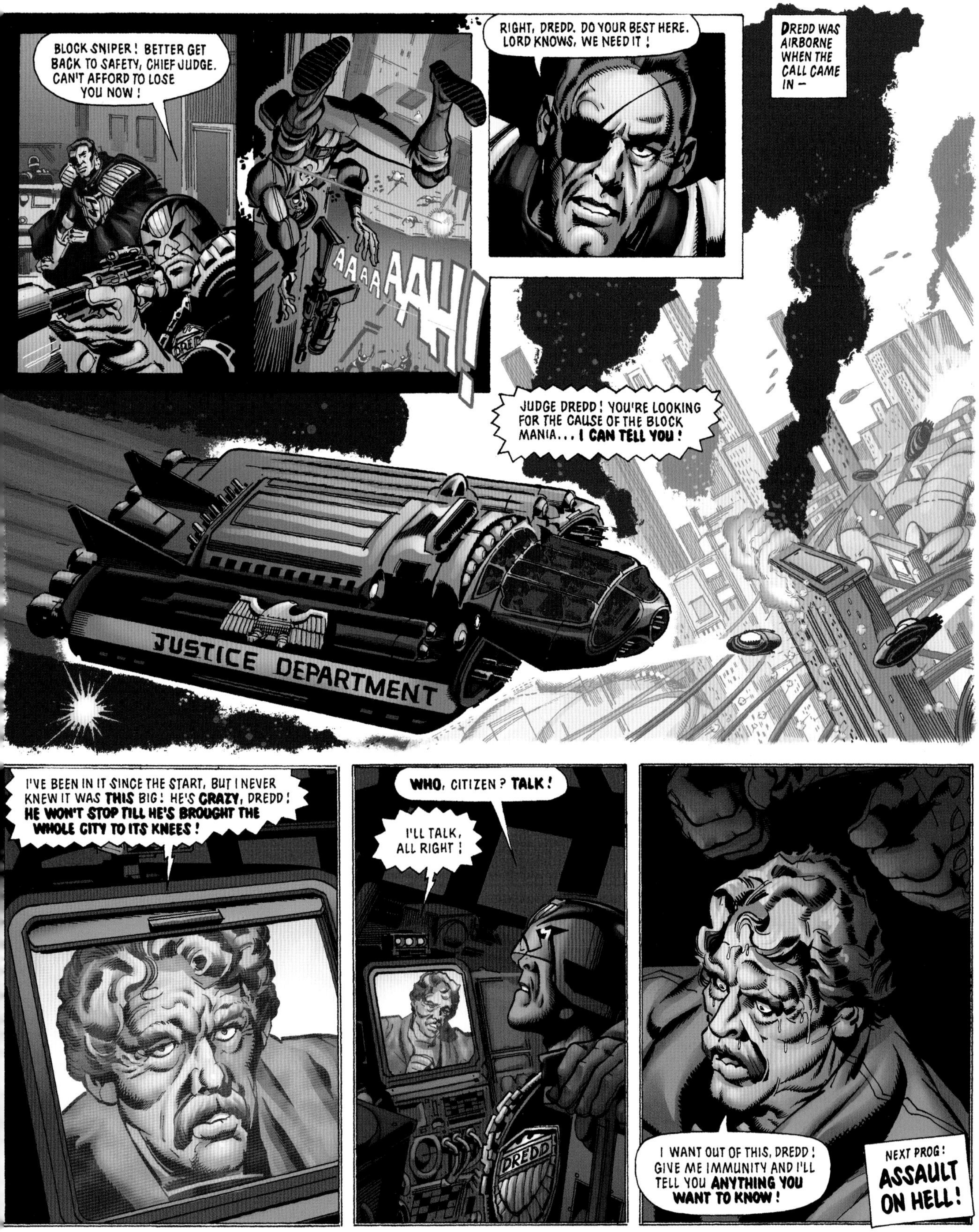
BLOCK SNIPER! BETTER GET BACK TO SAFETY, CHIEF JUDGE. CAN'T AFFORD TO LOSE YOU NOW!
AAAAAAAH!
RIGHT, DREDD. DO YOUR BEST HERE. LORD KNOWS, WE NEED IT!
DREDD WAS AIRBORNE WHEN THE CALL CAME IN –
JUDGE DREDD! YOU'RE LOOKING FOR THE CAUSE OF THE BLOCK MANIA... I CAN TELL YOU!
JUSTICE DEPARTMENT
I'VE BEEN IN IT SINCE THE START, BUT I NEVER KNEW IT WAS THIS BIG! HE'S CRAZY, DREDD! HE WON'T STOP TILL HE'S BROUGHT THE WHOLE CITY TO ITS KNEES!
WHO, CITIZEN? TALK!
I'LL TALK, ALL RIGHT!
DREDD
I WANT OUT OF THIS, DREDD! GIVE ME IMMUNITY AND I'LL TELL YOU ANYTHING YOU WANT TO KNOW!
NEXT PROG: ASSAULT ON HELL!

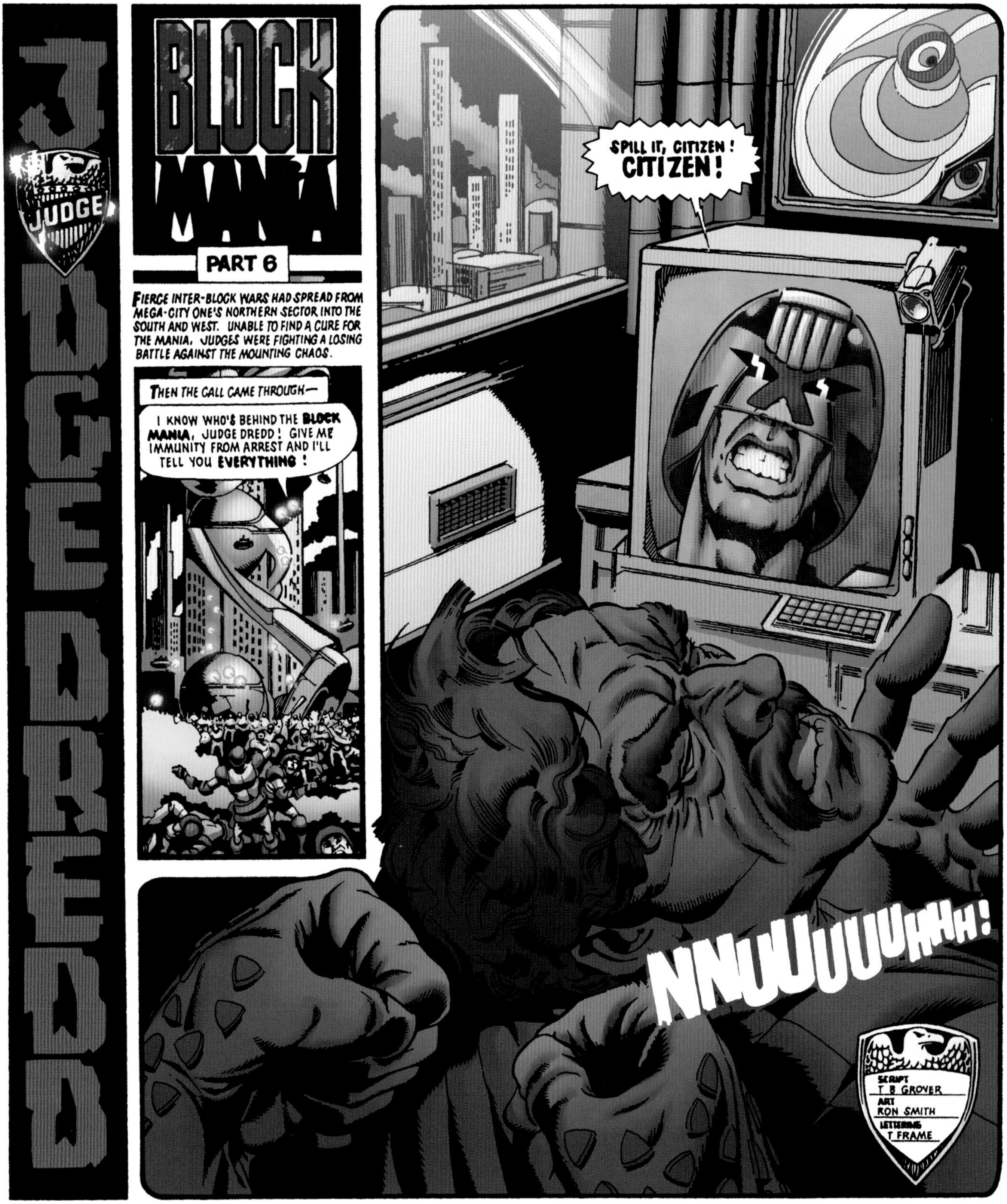
JUDGE DREDD
JUDGE
BLOCK MANIA
PART 6
FIERCE INTER-BLOCK WARS HAD SPREAD FROM MEGA-CITY ONE'S NORTHERN SECTOR INTO THE SOUTH AND WEST. UNABLE TO FIND A CURE FOR THE MANIA, JUDGES WERE FIGHTING A LOSING BATTLE AGAINST THE MOUNTING CHAOS.
THEN THE CALL CAME THROUGH—
I KNOW WHO'S BEHIND THE BLOCK MANIA, JUDGE DREDD! GIVE ME IMMUNITY FROM ARREST AND I'LL TELL YOU EVERYTHING!
SPILL IT, CITIZEN! CITIZEN!
NNUUUUUUHHH!
SCRIPT T B GROVER
ART RON SMITH
LETTERING T FRAME

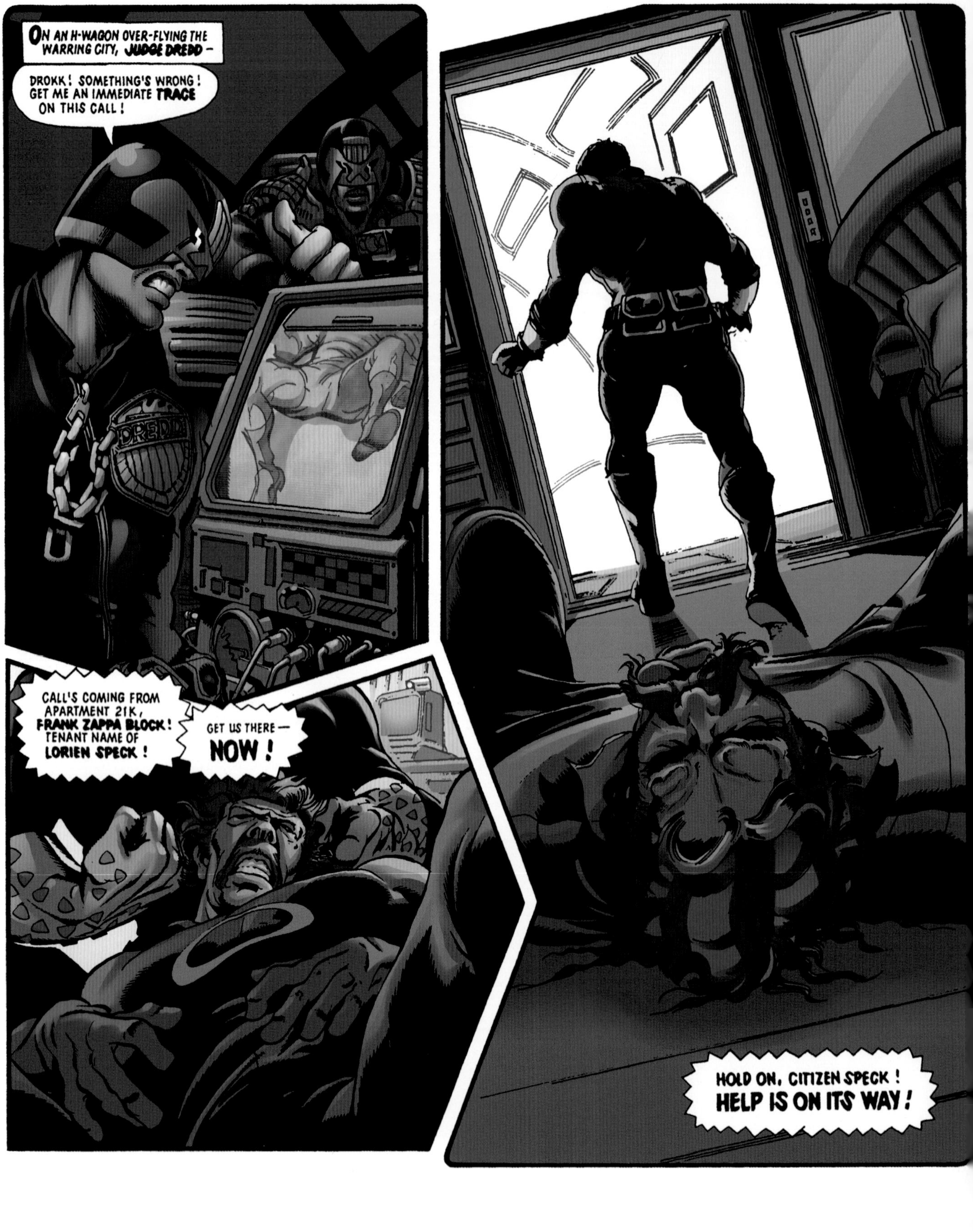

ON AN H-WAGON OVER-FLYING THE WARRING CITY, JUDGE DREDD –
DROKK! SOMETHING'S WRONG! GET ME AN IMMEDIATE TRACE ON THIS CALL!
CALL'S COMING FROM APARTMENT 21K, FRANK ZAPPA BLOCK! TENANT NAME OF LORIEN SPECK!
GET US THERE — NOW!
HOLD ON, CITIZEN SPECK! HELP IS ON ITS WAY!

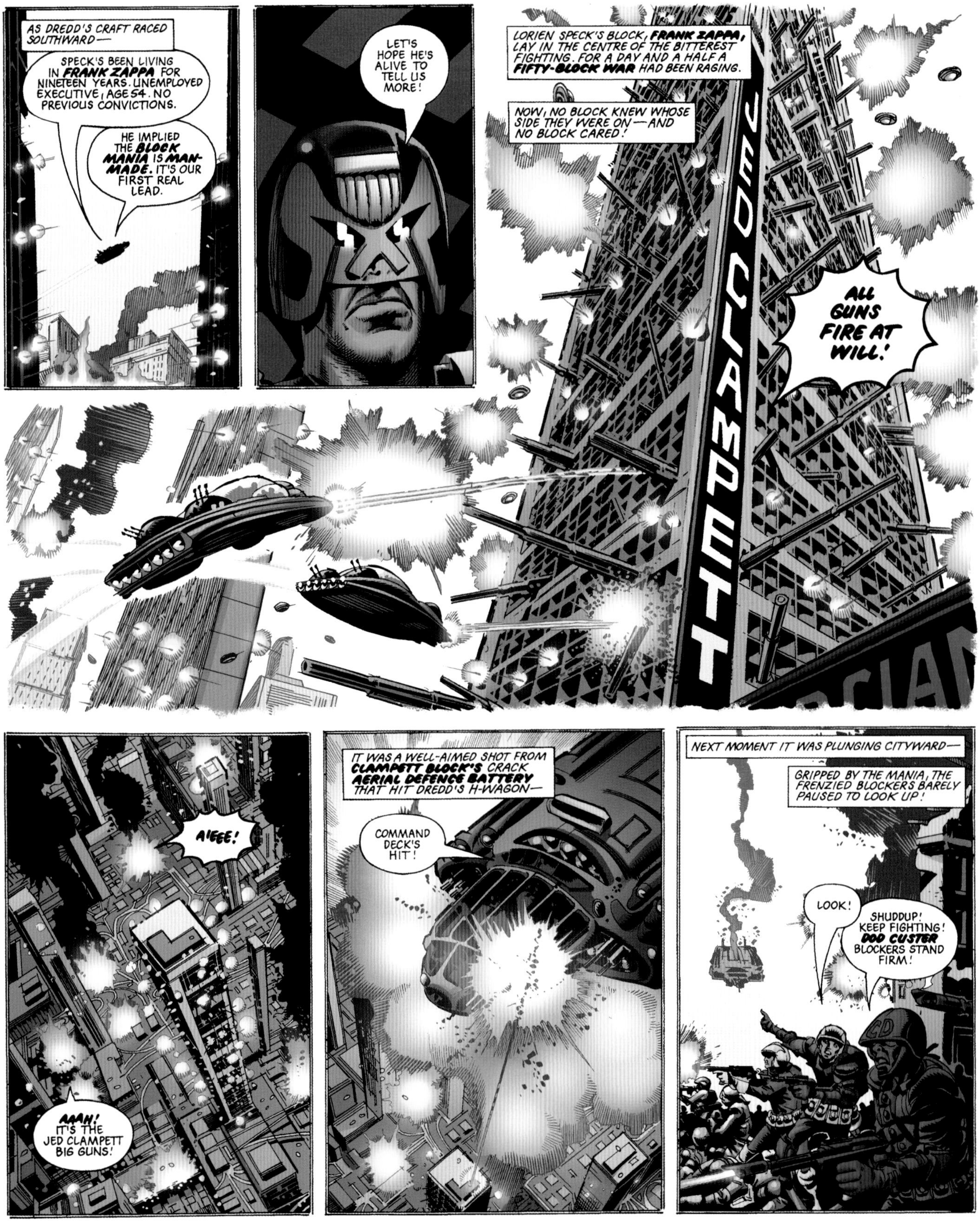
AS DREDD'S CRAFT RACED SOUTHWARD—
SPECK'S BEEN LIVING IN FRANK ZAPPA FOR NINETEEN YEARS. UNEMPLOYED EXECUTIVE, AGE 54. NO PREVIOUS CONVICTIONS.
HE IMPLIED THE BLOCK MANIA IS MAN-MADE. IT'S OUR FIRST REAL LEAD.
LET'S HOPE HE'S ALIVE TO TELL US MORE!
LORIEN SPECK'S BLOCK, FRANK ZAPPA, LAY IN THE CENTRE OF THE BITTEREST FIGHTING. FOR A DAY AND A HALF A FIFTY-BLOCK WAR HAD BEEN RAGING.
NOW, NO BLOCK KNEW WHOSE SIDE THEY WERE ON—AND NO BLOCK CARED!
JED CLAMPETT
ALL GUNS FIRE AT WILL!
AIEEE!
AAAH! IT'S THE JED CLAMPETT BIG GUNS!
IT WAS A WELL-AIMED SHOT FROM CLAMPETT BLOCK'S CRACK AERIAL DEFENCE BATTERY THAT HIT DREDD'S H-WAGON—
COMMAND DECK'S HIT!
NEXT MOMENT IT WAS PLUNGING CITYWARD—
GRIPPED BY THE MANIA, THE FRENZIED BLOCKERS BARELY PAUSED TO LOOK UP!
LOOK!
SHUDDUP! KEEP FIGHTING! DOD CUSTER BLOCKERS STAND FIRM!

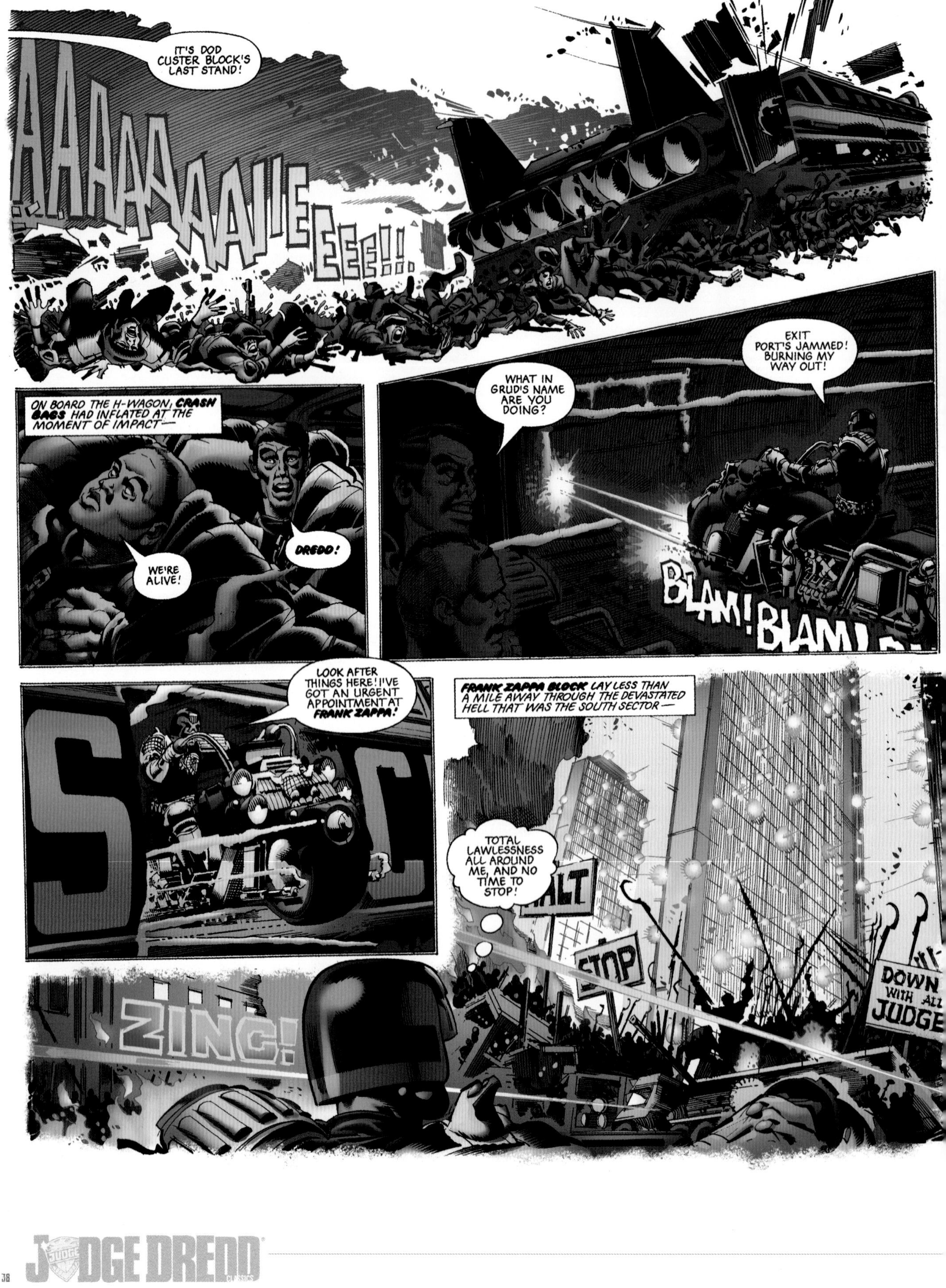
IT'S DOD CUSTER BLOCK'S LAST STAND!
AAAAAAAIIEEEE!!
ON BOARD THE H-WAGON, CRASH BAGS HAD INFLATED AT THE MOMENT OF IMPACT—
WE'RE ALIVE!
DREDD!
WHAT IN GRUD'S NAME ARE YOU DOING?
EXIT PORT'S JAMMED! BURNING MY WAY OUT!
BLAM! BLAM!
LOOK AFTER THINGS HERE! I'VE GOT AN URGENT APPOINTMENT AT FRANK ZAPPA!
FRANK ZAPPA BLOCK LAY LESS THAN A MILE AWAY THROUGH THE DEVASTATED HELL THAT WAS THE SOUTH SECTOR—
TOTAL LAWLESSNESS ALL AROUND ME, AND NO TIME TO STOP!
HALT
STOP
DOWN WITH ALL JUDGE
ZING!

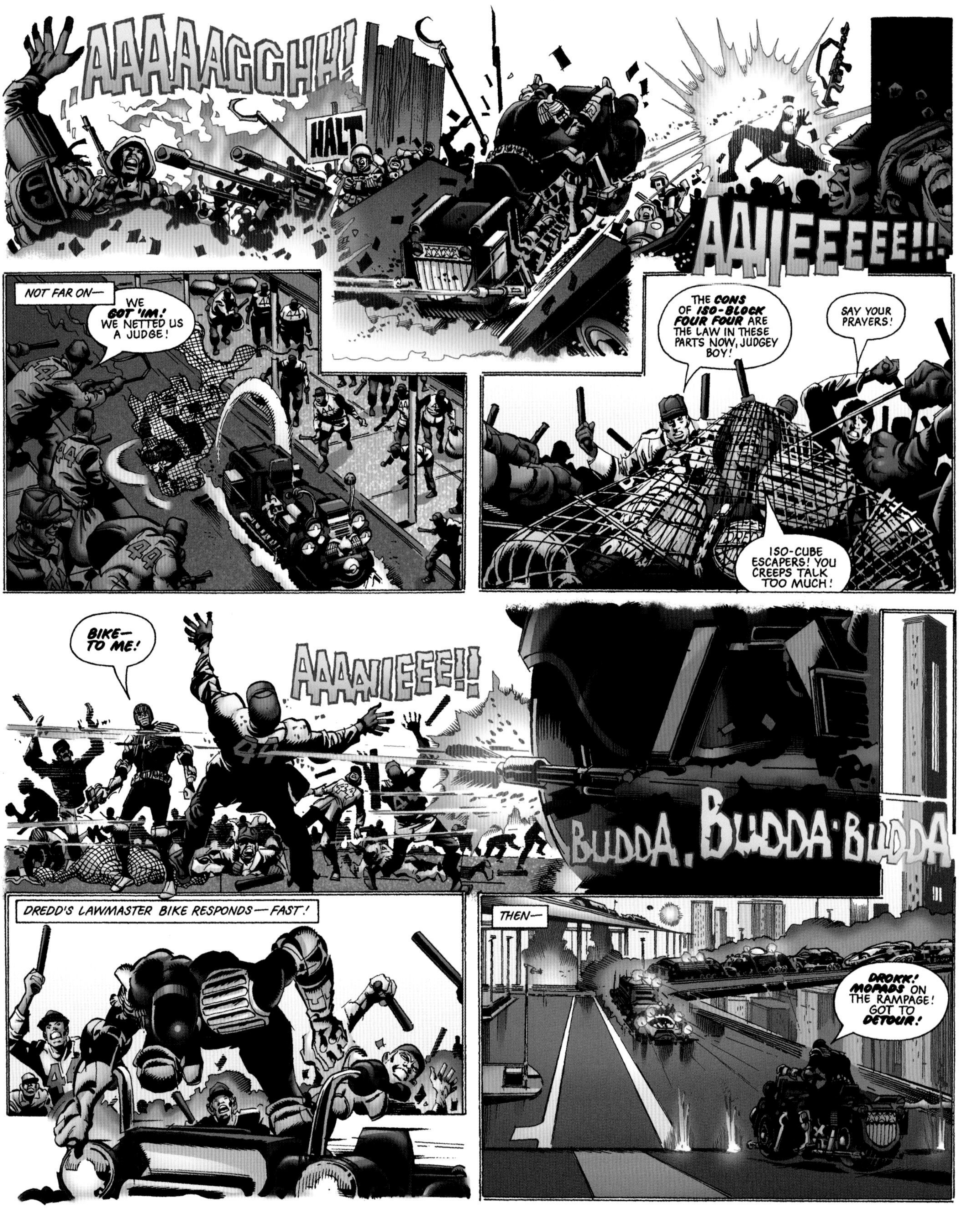

AAAAACGHH!
HALT
AAIEEEEE!!
NOT FAR ON—
WE GOT 'IM! WE NETTED US A JUDGE!
THE CONS OF ISO-BLOCK FOUR FOUR ARE THE LAW IN THESE PARTS NOW, JUDGEY BOY!
SAY YOUR PRAYERS!
ISO-CUBE ESCAPERS! YOU CREEPS TALK TOO MUCH!
BIKE— TO ME!
AAAAIEEE!!
BUDDA. BUDDA·BUDDA
DREDD'S LAWMASTER BIKE RESPONDS — FAST!
THEN—
DROKK! MOPADS ON THE RAMPAGE! GOT TO DETOUR!

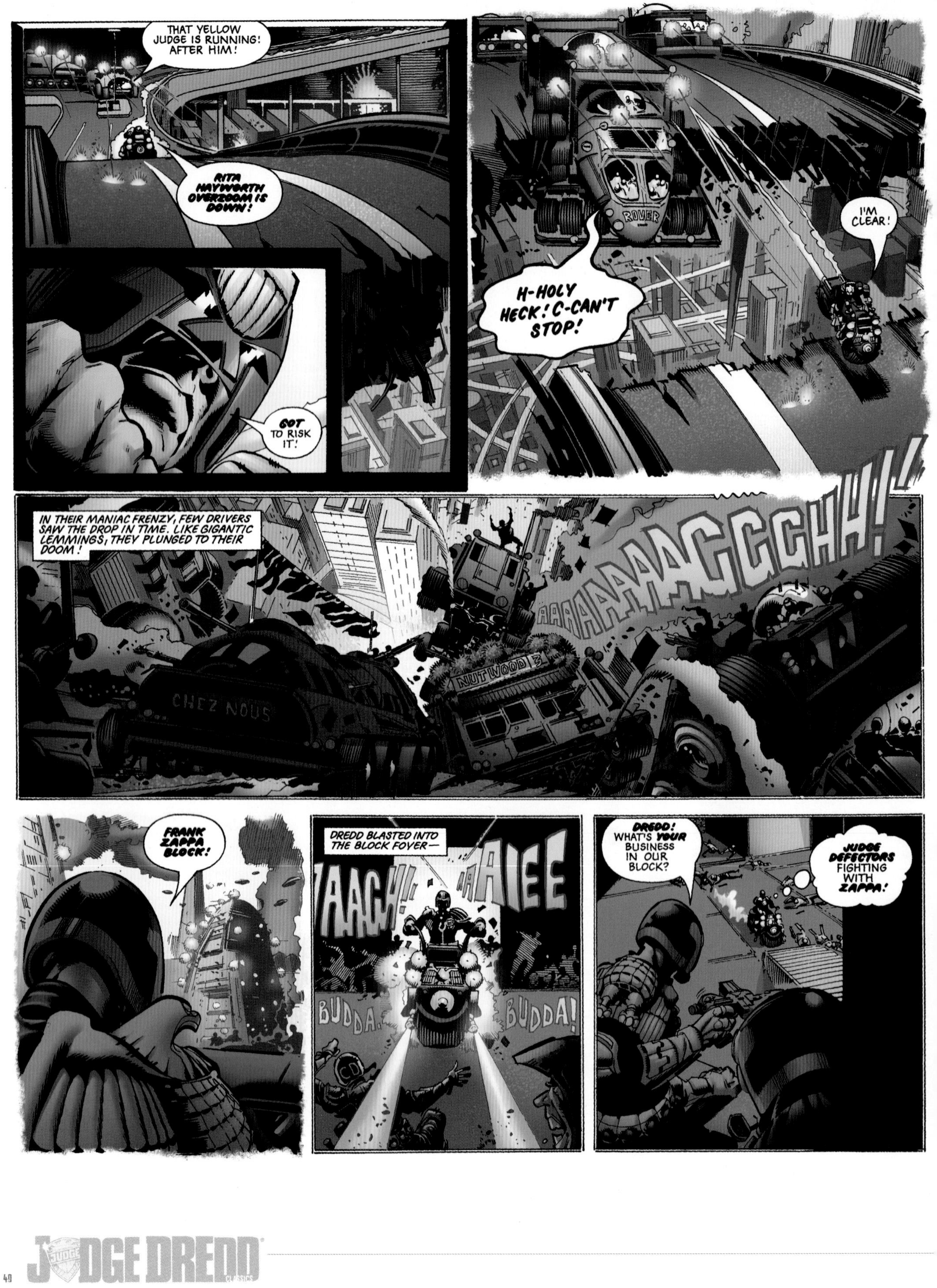
THAT YELLOW JUDGE IS RUNNING! AFTER HIM!
RITA HAYWORTH OVERZOOM IS DOWN!
GOT TO RISK IT!
H-HOLY HECK! C-CAN'T STOP!
ROVER
I'M CLEAR!
IN THEIR MANIAC FRENZY, FEW DRIVERS SAW THE DROP IN TIME. LIKE GIGANTIC LEMMINGS, THEY PLUNGED TO THEIR DOOM!
AAAAAAAAGCCHH!
CHEZ NOUS
NUTWOOD 3
FRANK ZAPPA BLOCK!
DREDD BLASTED INTO THE BLOCK FOYER—
AACH!
AIEE
BUDDA.
BUDDA!
DREDD! WHAT'S YOUR BUSINESS IN OUR BLOCK?
JUDGE DEFECTORS FIGHTING WITH ZAPPA!

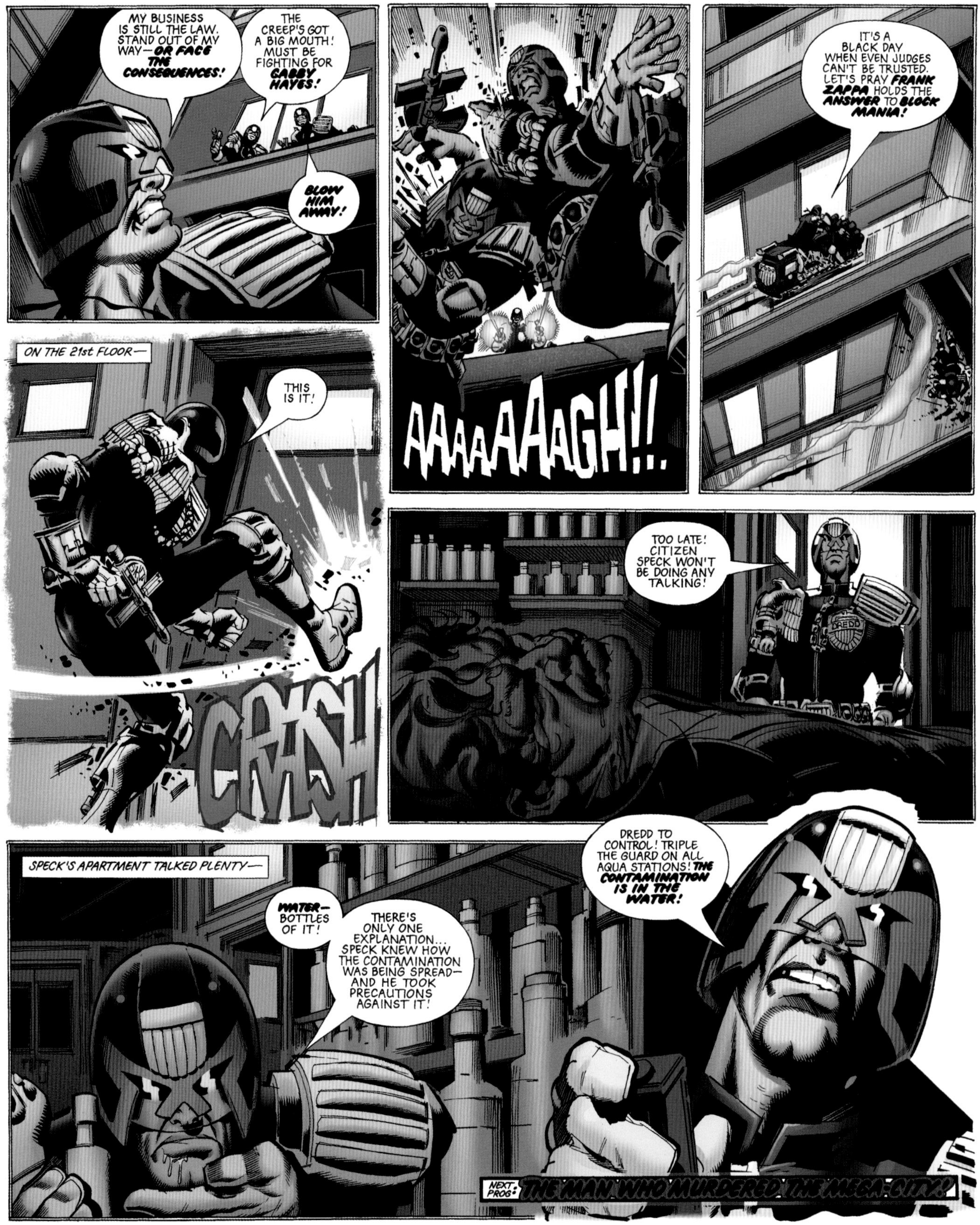

MY BUSINESS IS STILL THE LAW. STAND OUT OF MY WAY—OR FACE THE CONSEQUENCES!
THE CREEP'S GOT A BIG MOUTH! MUST BE FIGHTING FOR GABBY HAYES!
BLOW HIM AWAY!
AAAAAAAGH!!!
IT'S A BLACK DAY WHEN EVEN JUDGES CAN'T BE TRUSTED. LET'S PRAY FRANK ZAPPA HOLDS THE ANSWER TO BLOCK MANIA!
ON THE 21st FLOOR—
THIS IS IT!
CRASH
TOO LATE! CITIZEN SPECK WON'T BE DOING ANY TALKING!
DREDD
SPECK'S APARTMENT TALKED PLENTY—
WATER—BOTTLES OF IT!
THERE'S ONLY ONE EXPLANATION... SPECK KNEW HOW THE CONTAMINATION WAS BEING SPREAD—AND HE TOOK PRECAUTIONS AGAINST IT!
DREDD TO CONTROL! TRIPLE THE GUARD ON ALL AQUA STATIONS! THE CONTAMINATION IS IN THE WATER!
NEXT PROG: THE MAN WHO MURDERED THE MEGA-CITY!

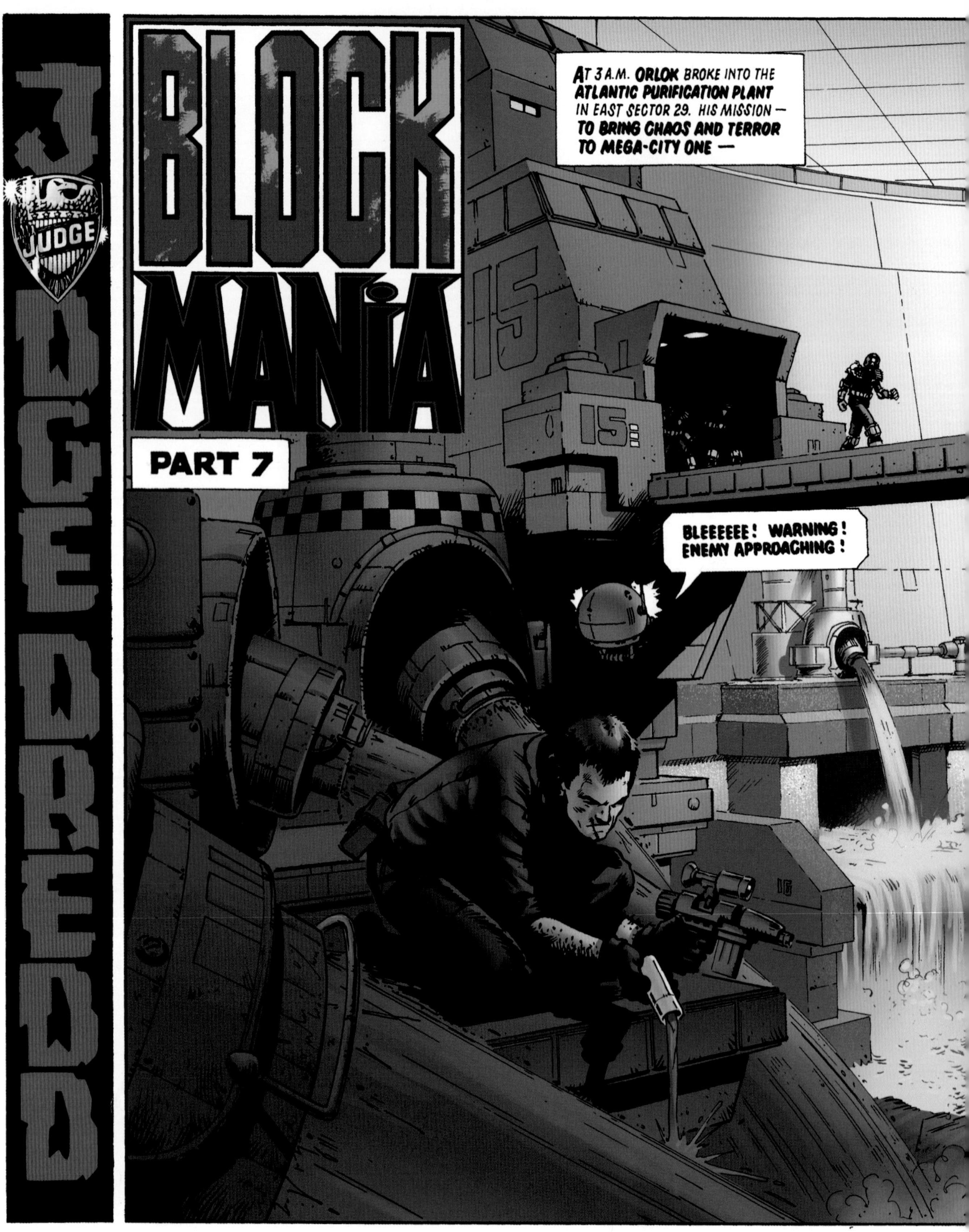
JUDGE DREDD
BLOCK MANIA
PART 7
AT 3 A.M. ORLOK BROKE INTO THE ATLANTIC PURIFICATION PLANT IN EAST SECTOR 29. HIS MISSION — TO BRING CHAOS AND TERROR TO MEGA-CITY ONE —
BLEEEEEE! WARNING! ENEMY APPROACHING!

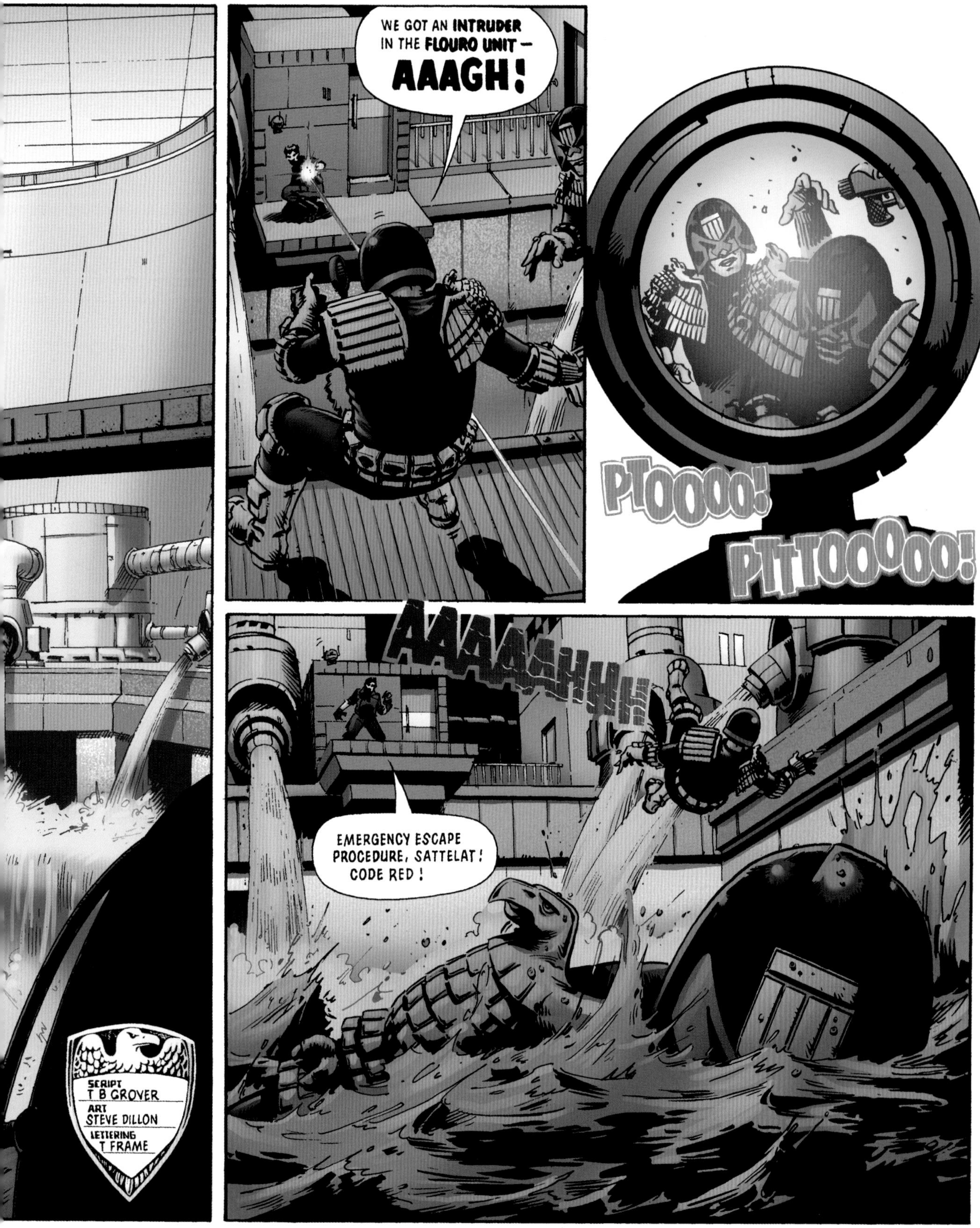

WE GOT AN INTRUDER IN THE FLOURO UNIT — AAAGH!
PTOOOO!
PTTTOOOOOO!
AAAAAHHHH!
EMERGENCY ESCAPE PROCEDURE, SATTELAT! CODE RED!
SCRIPT T B GROVER
ART STEVE DILLON
LETTERING T FRAME

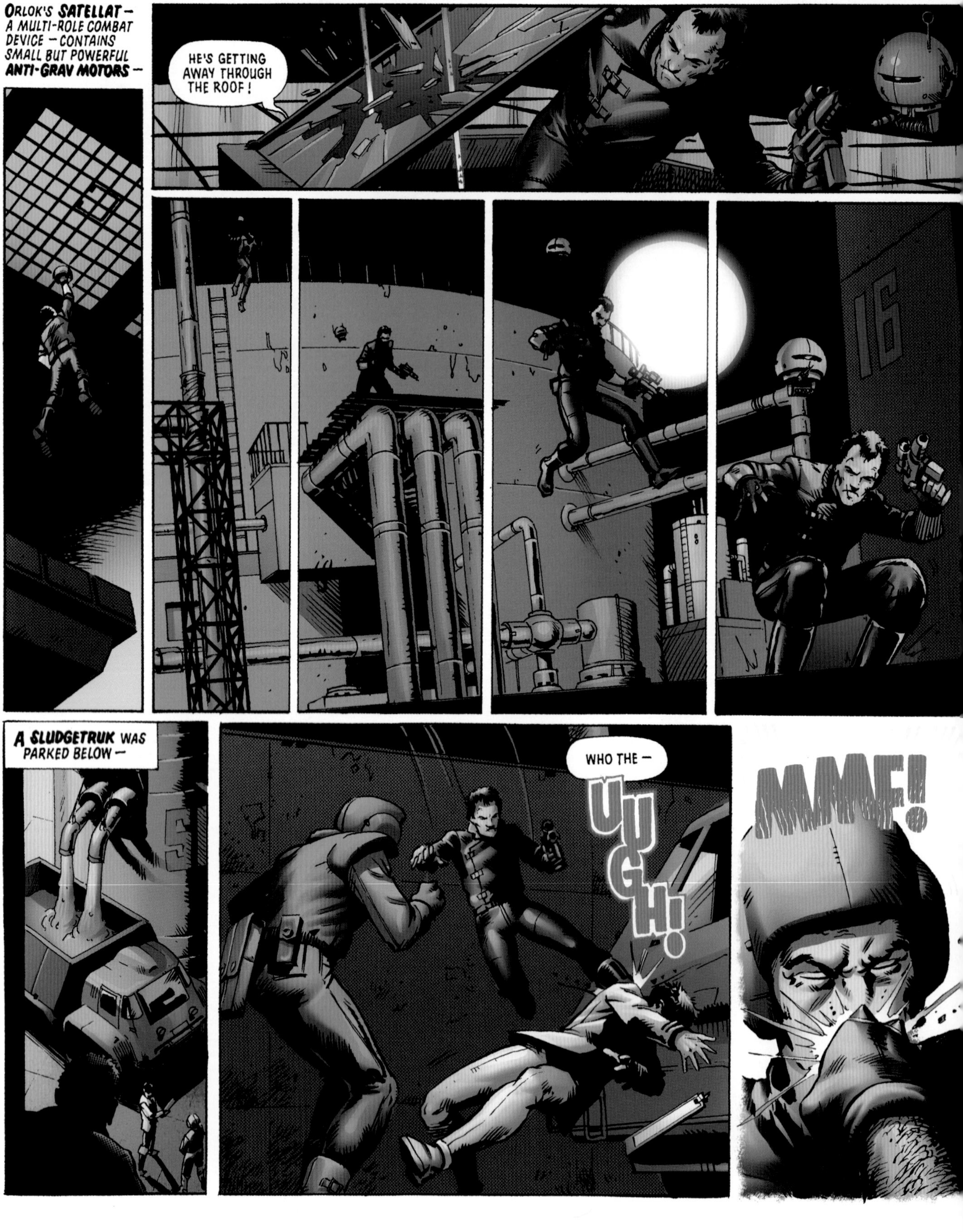

ORLOK'S SATELLAT – A MULTI-ROLE COMBAT DEVICE – CONTAINS SMALL BUT POWERFUL ANTI-GRAV MOTORS –
HE'S GETTING AWAY THROUGH THE ROOF !
16
A SLUDGETRUK WAS PARKED BELOW –
WHO THE –
UUGH!
MMMF!!

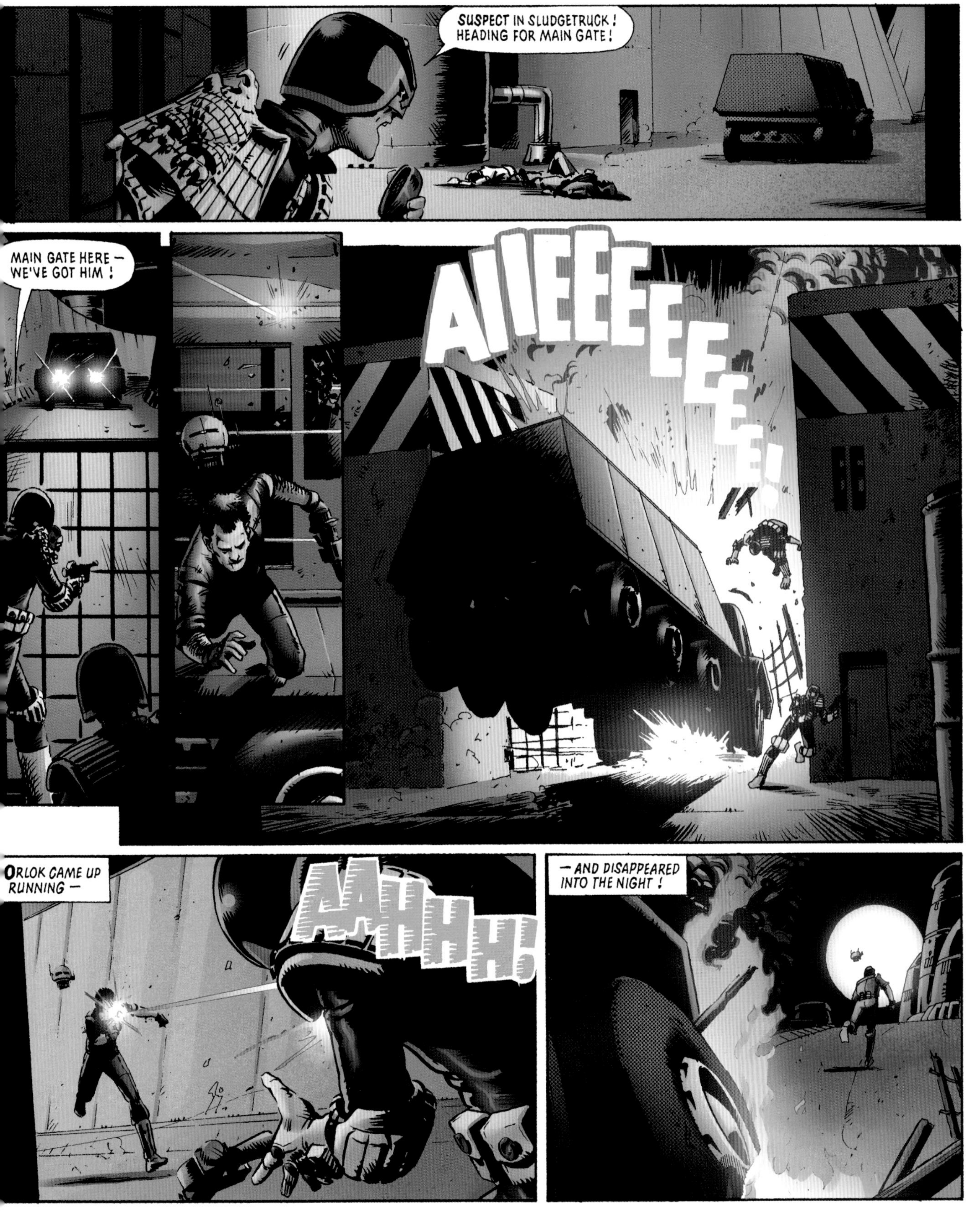
SUSPECT IN SLUDGETRUCK! HEADING FOR MAIN GATE!
MAIN GATE HERE — WE'VE GOT HIM!
AIIEEEEEEEE!
ORLOK CAME UP RUNNING —
AAHHHH!
— AND DISAPPEARED INTO THE NIGHT!

IN HIS OPERATIONS CENTRE IN THE GRAND HALL OF JUSTICE, *JUDGE DREDD* WAS LEADING THE FIGHT AGAINST *BLOCK MANIA*—

INTER-BLOCK WAR IS NOW *TOTAL* IN SECTORS *NORTH*, *SOUTH* AND *WEST*!

THERE'S NOTHING WE CAN DO UNTIL WE FIND A CURE. PULL EVERY UNAFFECTED JUDGE BACK TO *EAST* AND *CENTRAL*!

IF THE MANIA IS BEING SPREAD VIA THE *WATER SUPPLY*, WHY HAVE SO MANY *JUDGES* ESCAPED IT? AND WHAT ABOUT YOUR *INFORMER*— HE *LIVED* IN AN AFFECTED BLOCK!

JUDGES ON PATROL DRAW THEIR WATER FROM THEIR *BIKES'* SUPPLY. THAT'S *STATIC*, CHIEF JUDGE. AS FOR MY INFORMER—

MAX NORMAL IS ONE OF A KIND! NEVER *TOUCHES* WATER—RECKONS IT'S BAD FOR THE HEALTH. HE'S STRICTLY A *SHAMPAGNE* AND *CLEAN-O-SPRAY* MAN.

I SHOULD'VE TWIGGED—I FORGOT HOW NUTS MAX IS!

BUT FORENSIC HAVE CHECKED THE WATER! THERE'S NOTHING THERE, DREDD! *NOTHING!*

IT'S THERE, ALL RIGHT. WE JUST HAVEN'T FOUND IT YET!

THIS IS THE *ATLANTIC PLANT!* WE FOUND AN *INTRUDER* IN THE FLUORO UNIT! I'VE SHUT OFF THE WATER SUPPLY AND ORDERED AN IMMEDIATE SCANALYSIS!

AND THE INTRUDER— YOU *GOT* HIM?

GOT HIM, NOTHING! I'VE GOT SIX DEAD JUDGES AND ONE ON THE CRITICAL LIST!

THIS IS NO *MONKEY* WE'RE DEALING WITH, DREDD! THIS GUY'S A *PRO*— I'D STAKE MY LIFE ON IT!

DREDD PUT OUT ORLOK'S DESCRIPTION TO ALL UNITS—

I DON'T CARE WHAT YOU'RE DOING—DROP IT! CHECK EVERY HIDING PLACE— EVERY SUSPICIOUS CHARACTER! I WANT THIS CREEP *ALIVE*—AND I WANT HIM *NOW!*

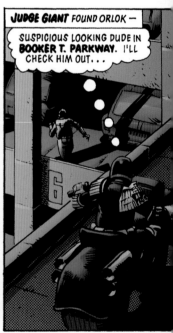

JUDGE GIANT FOUND ORLOK—

SUSPICIOUS LOOKING DUDE IN *BOOKER T. PARKWAY*. I'LL CHECK HIM OUT...

JUDGE DREDD

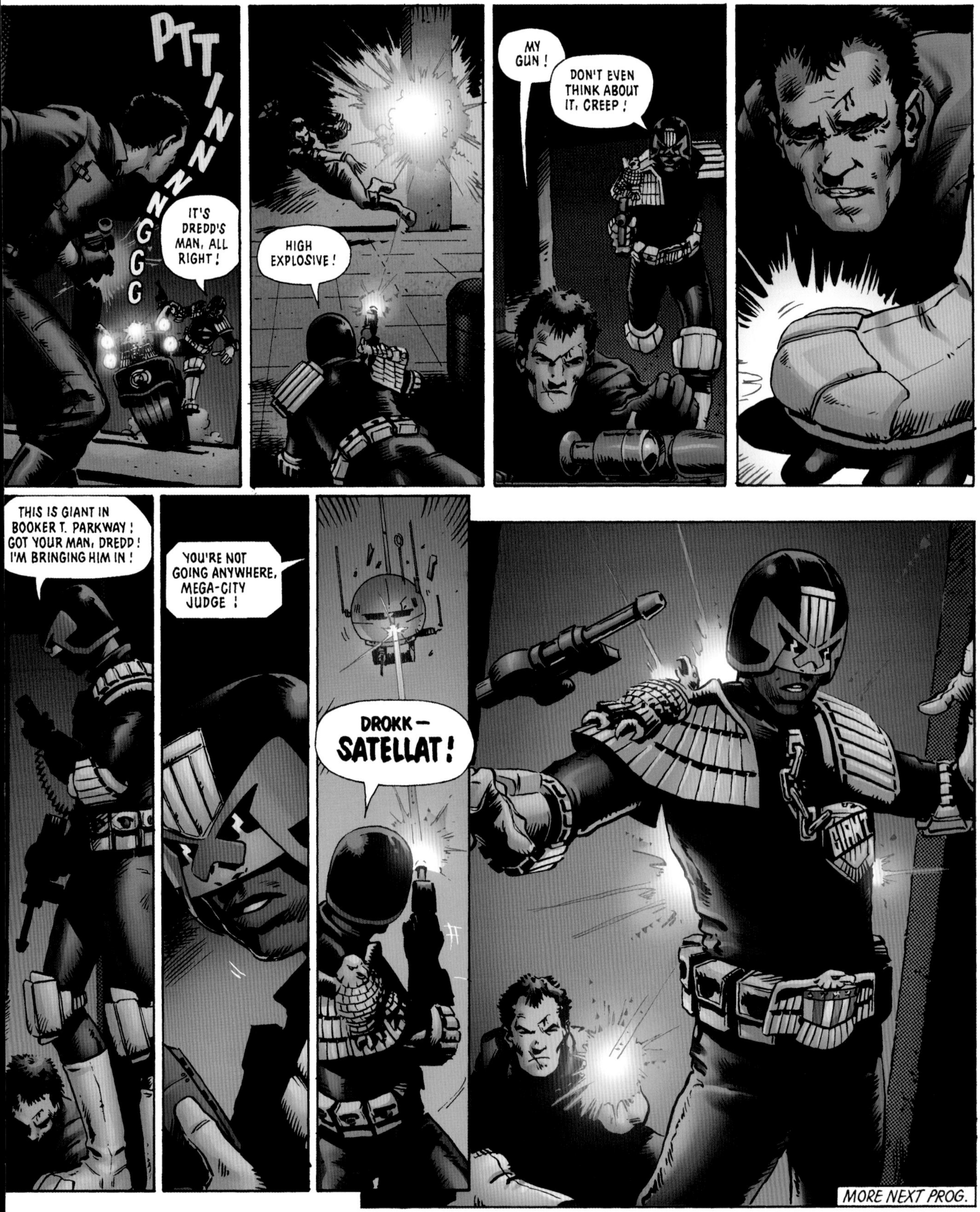
PTTINNNNGGG
IT'S DREDD'S MAN, ALL RIGHT!
HIGH EXPLOSIVE!
MY GUN!
DON'T EVEN THINK ABOUT IT, CREEP!
THIS IS GIANT IN BOOKER T. PARKWAY! GOT YOUR MAN, DREDD! I'M BRINGING HIM IN!
YOU'RE NOT GOING ANYWHERE, MEGA-CITY JUDGE!
DROKK — SATELLAT!
MORE NEXT PROG.

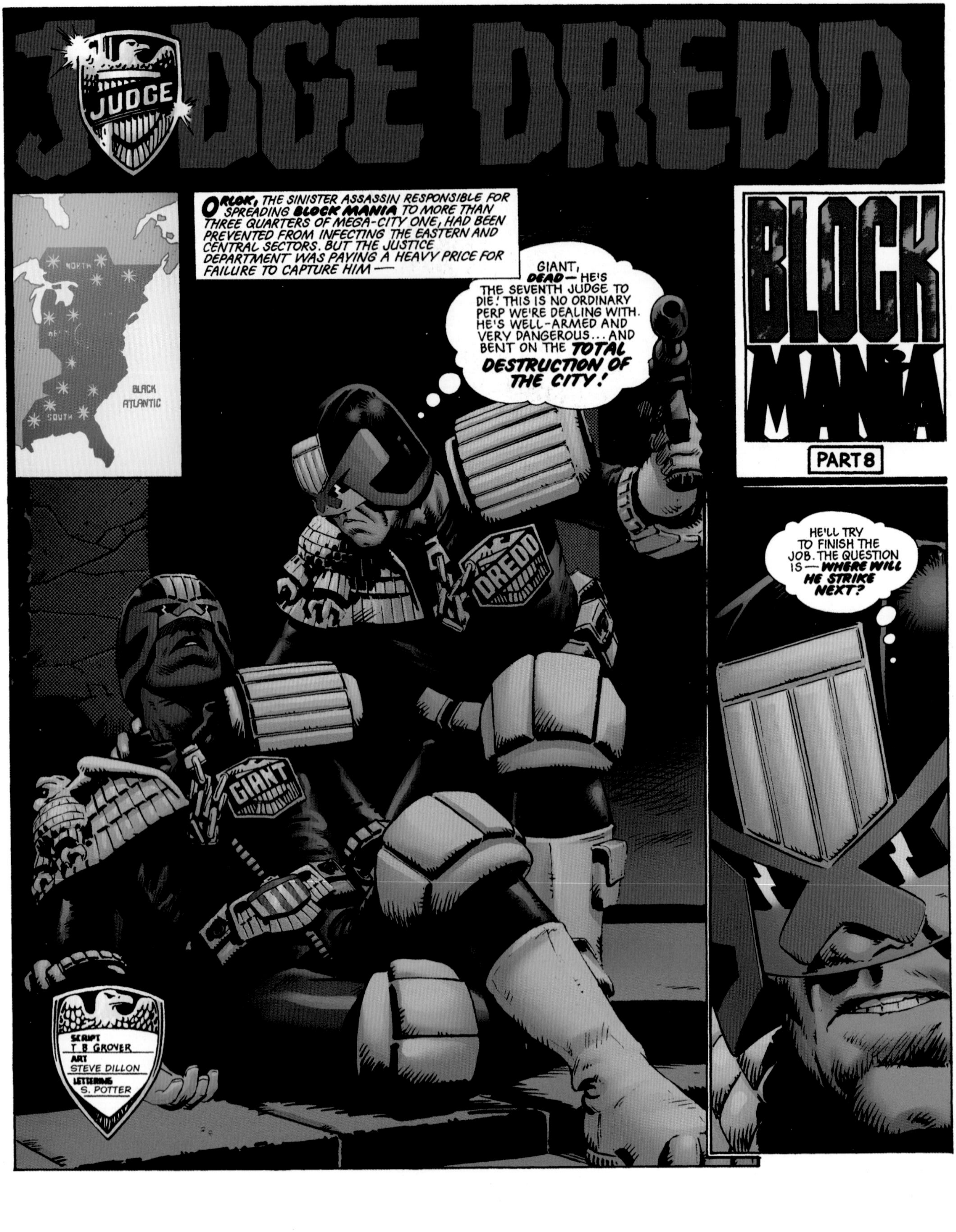

JUDGE DREDD
JUDGE
NORTH
WEST
SOUTH
BLACK ATLANTIC
ORLOK, THE SINISTER ASSASSIN RESPONSIBLE FOR SPREADING BLOCK MANIA TO MORE THAN THREE QUARTERS OF MEGA-CITY ONE, HAD BEEN PREVENTED FROM INFECTING THE EASTERN AND CENTRAL SECTORS. BUT THE JUSTICE DEPARTMENT WAS PAYING A HEAVY PRICE FOR FAILURE TO CAPTURE HIM—
GIANT, DEAD— HE'S THE SEVENTH JUDGE TO DIE! THIS IS NO ORDINARY PERP WE'RE DEALING WITH. HE'S WELL-ARMED AND VERY DANGEROUS... AND BENT ON THE TOTAL DESTRUCTION OF THE CITY!
BLOCK MANIA
PART 8
DREDD
GIANT
HE'LL TRY TO FINISH THE JOB. THE QUESTION IS— WHERE WILL HE STRIKE NEXT?
SCRIPT T B GROVER
ART STEVE DILLON
LETTERING S. POTTER

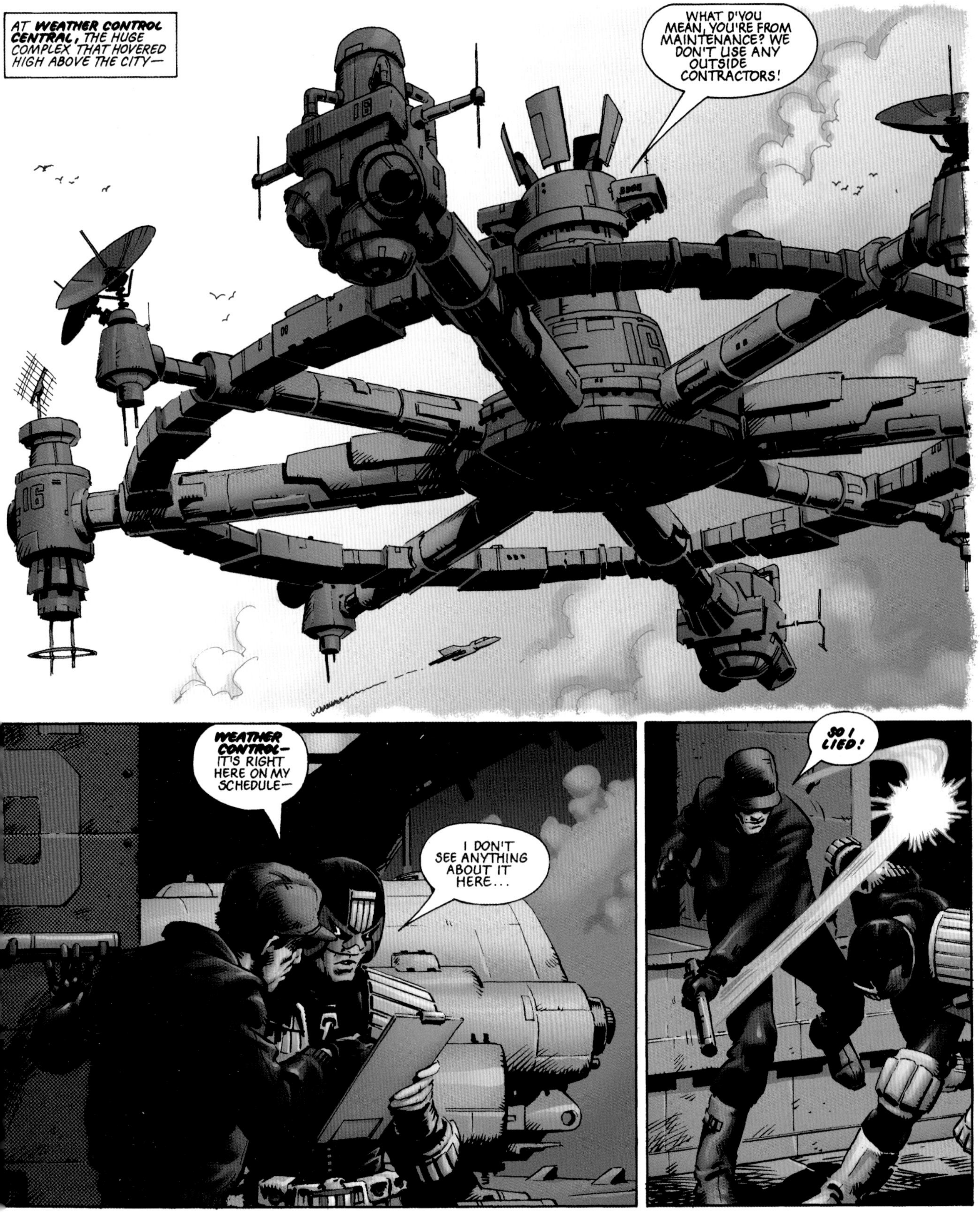
AT WEATHER CONTROL CENTRAL, THE HUGE COMPLEX THAT HOVERED HIGH ABOVE THE CITY—
WHAT D'YOU MEAN, YOU'RE FROM MAINTENANCE? WE DON'T USE ANY OUTSIDE CONTRACTORS!
WEATHER CONTROL— IT'S RIGHT HERE ON MY SCHEDULE—
I DON'T SEE ANYTHING ABOUT IT HERE...
SO I LIED!

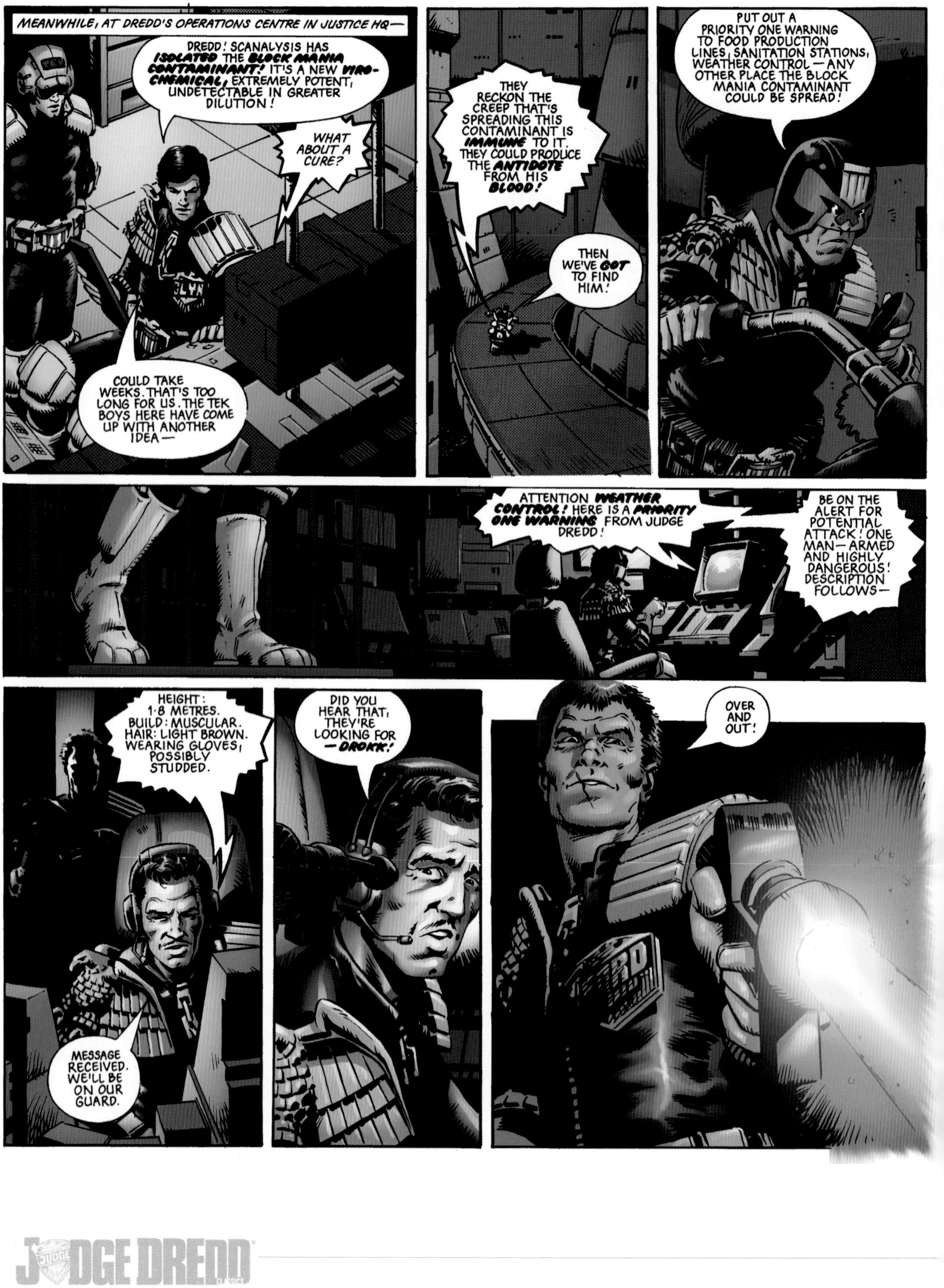
MEANWHILE, AT DREDD'S OPERATIONS CENTRE IN JUSTICE HQ—
DREDD! SCANALYSIS HAS ISOLATED THE BLOCK MANIA CONTAMINANT! IT'S A NEW VIRO-CHEMICAL, EXTREMELY POTENT, UNDETECTABLE IN GREATER DILUTION!
WHAT ABOUT A CURE?
COULD TAKE WEEKS. THAT'S TOO LONG FOR US. THE TEK BOYS HERE HAVE COME UP WITH ANOTHER IDEA—
THEY RECKON THE CREEP THAT'S SPREADING THIS CONTAMINANT IS IMMUNE TO IT. THEY COULD PRODUCE THE ANTIDOTE FROM HIS BLOOD!
THEN WE'VE GOT TO FIND HIM!
PUT OUT A PRIORITY ONE WARNING TO FOOD PRODUCTION LINES, SANITATION STATIONS, WEATHER CONTROL—ANY OTHER PLACE THE BLOCK MANIA CONTAMINANT COULD BE SPREAD!
ATTENTION WEATHER CONTROL! HERE IS A PRIORITY ONE WARNING FROM JUDGE DREDD!
BE ON THE ALERT FOR POTENTIAL ATTACK! ONE MAN—ARMED AND HIGHLY DANGEROUS! DESCRIPTION FOLLOWS—
HEIGHT: 1·8 METRES. BUILD: MUSCULAR. HAIR: LIGHT BROWN. WEARING GLOVES, POSSIBLY STUDDED.
MESSAGE RECEIVED. WE'LL BE ON OUR GUARD.
DID YOU HEAR THAT, THEY'RE LOOKING FOR —DROKK!
OVER AND OUT!

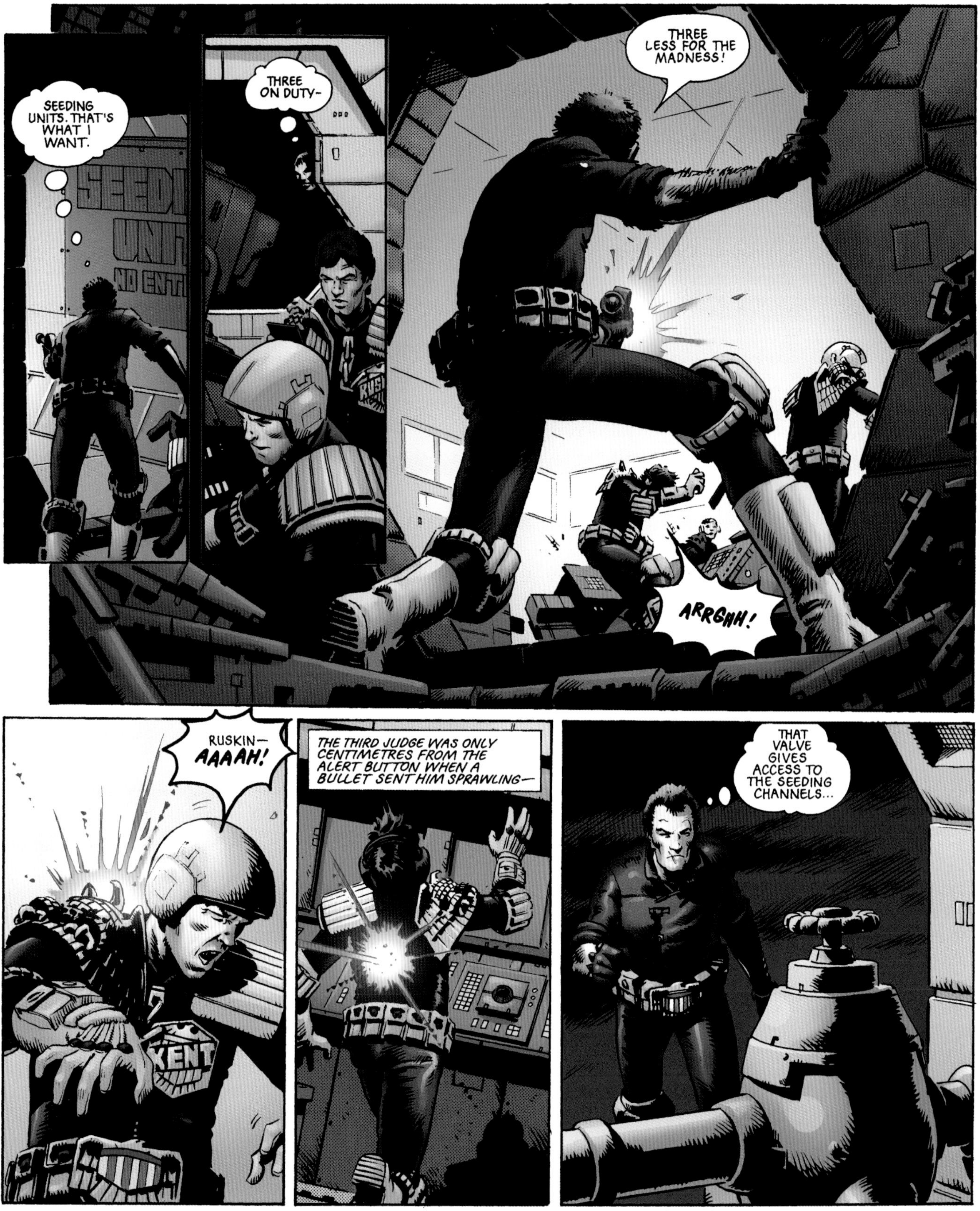

SEEDING UNITS. THAT'S WHAT I WANT.
SEEDING UNITS NO ENTRY
THREE ON DUTY-
THREE LESS FOR THE MADNESS!
ARRGHH!
RUSKIN— AAAAH!
THE THIRD JUDGE WAS ONLY CENTIMETRES FROM THE ALERT BUTTON WHEN A BULLET SENT HIM SPRAWLING—
KENT
THAT VALVE GIVES ACCESS TO THE SEEDING CHANNELS...

THE CONTENTS OF THESE PHIALS WILL BRING THE REST OF THIS CURSED CITY TO ITS KNEES!

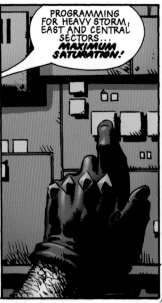

PROGRAMMING FOR HEAVY STORM, EAST AND CENTRAL SECTORS... *MAXIMUM SATURATION!*

MINUTE *SEEDING CRYSTALS* HISSED FROM CENTRAL *WEATHER CONTROL'S* VAST NETWORK OF *ATMOSPHERIC MODULATORS*—

AS THEY FELL THE CRYSTALS DREW TO THEM THE WATER VAPOUR IN THE SURROUNDING AIR... *RAIN!*

A *DELUGE* OF RAIN— *CONTAMINATED* WITH THE SEEDS OF *MADNESS* AND *DESTRUCTION!*

DROKK! IT'S HIM— GOT TO BE!

DREDD TO WEATHER CONTROL! *STOP THAT RAIN!*

WE CAN'T! WHOLE CONTROL UNIT IS *FUSED!* IT'S MAYHEM IN HERE, DREDD!

ATTENTION! MAINTENANCE POD LEAVING HUB BAY! SUSPECT MAY BE ON BOARD!

AN H-WAGON SPED TO INTERCEPT—

THIS IS DREDD! MAINTAIN SURVEILLANCE! ON NO ACCOUNTS SHOOT IT DOWN! WE WANT THIS CREEP *ALIVE!*

WILCO! POD HEADING FOR LANDING— REGION *BUDDY EBSEN SPIRAL!*

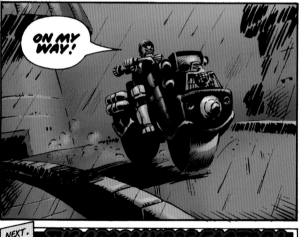

ON MY WAY!

NEXT PROG: *THE APOCALYPSE FACTOR!*

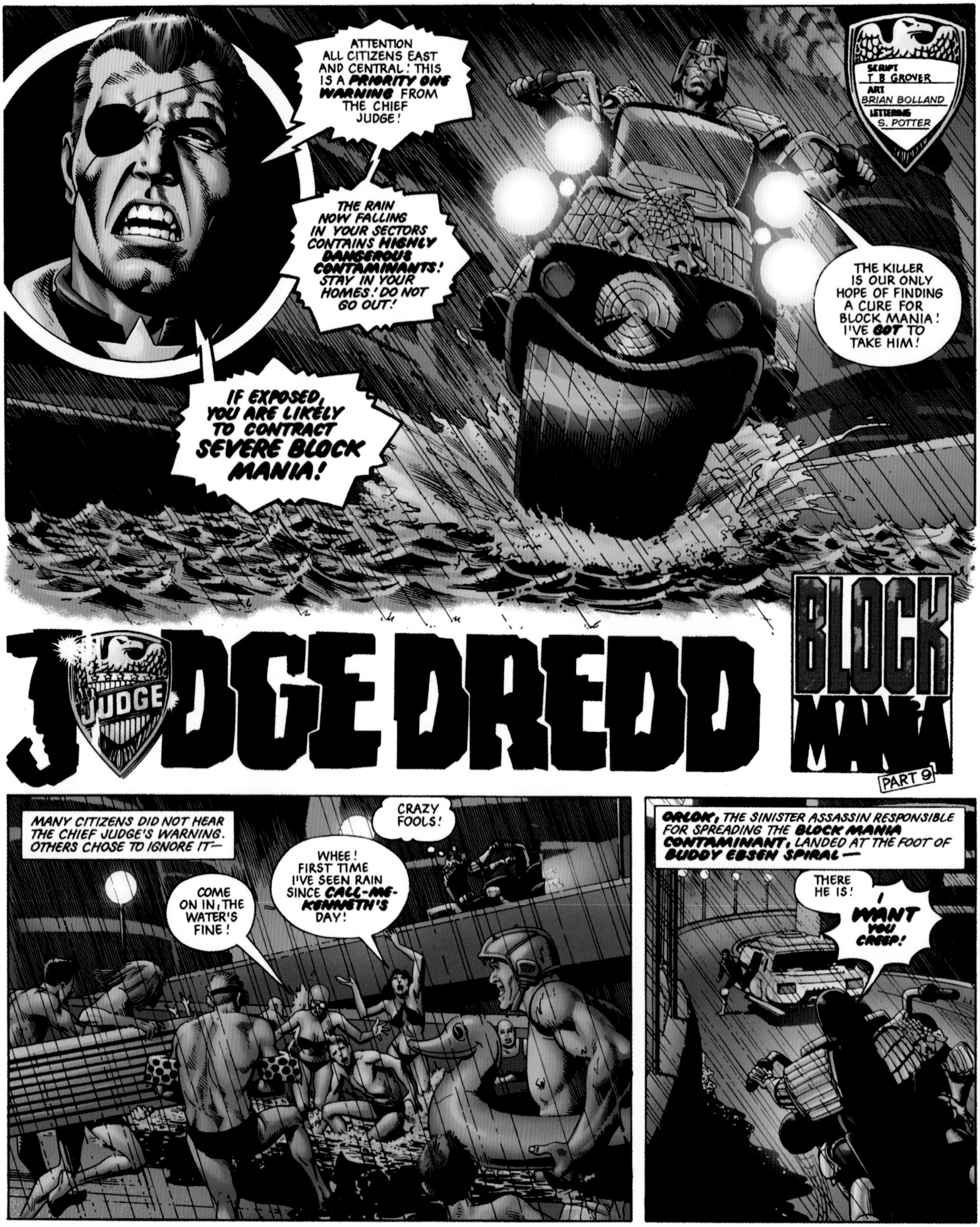
ATTENTION ALL CITIZENS EAST AND CENTRAL! THIS IS A PRIORITY ONE WARNING FROM THE CHIEF JUDGE!
THE RAIN NOW FALLING IN YOUR SECTORS CONTAINS HIGHLY DANGEROUS CONTAMINANTS! STAY IN YOUR HOMES! DO NOT GO OUT!
IF EXPOSED, YOU ARE LIKELY TO CONTRACT SEVERE BLOCK MANIA!
SCRIPT T B GROVER
ART BRIAN BOLLAND
LETTERING S. POTTER
THE KILLER IS OUR ONLY HOPE OF FINDING A CURE FOR BLOCK MANIA! I'VE GOT TO TAKE HIM!
JUDGE
JUDGE DREDD
BLOCK MANIA
PART 9
MANY CITIZENS DID NOT HEAR THE CHIEF JUDGE'S WARNING. OTHERS CHOSE TO IGNORE IT—
COME ON IN, THE WATER'S FINE!
WHEE! FIRST TIME I'VE SEEN RAIN SINCE CALL-ME-KENNETH'S DAY!
CRAZY FOOLS!
ORLOK, THE SINISTER ASSASSIN RESPONSIBLE FOR SPREADING THE BLOCK MANIA CONTAMINANT, LANDED AT THE FOOT OF BUDDY EBSEN SPIRAL—
THERE HE IS!
I WANT YOU CREEP!

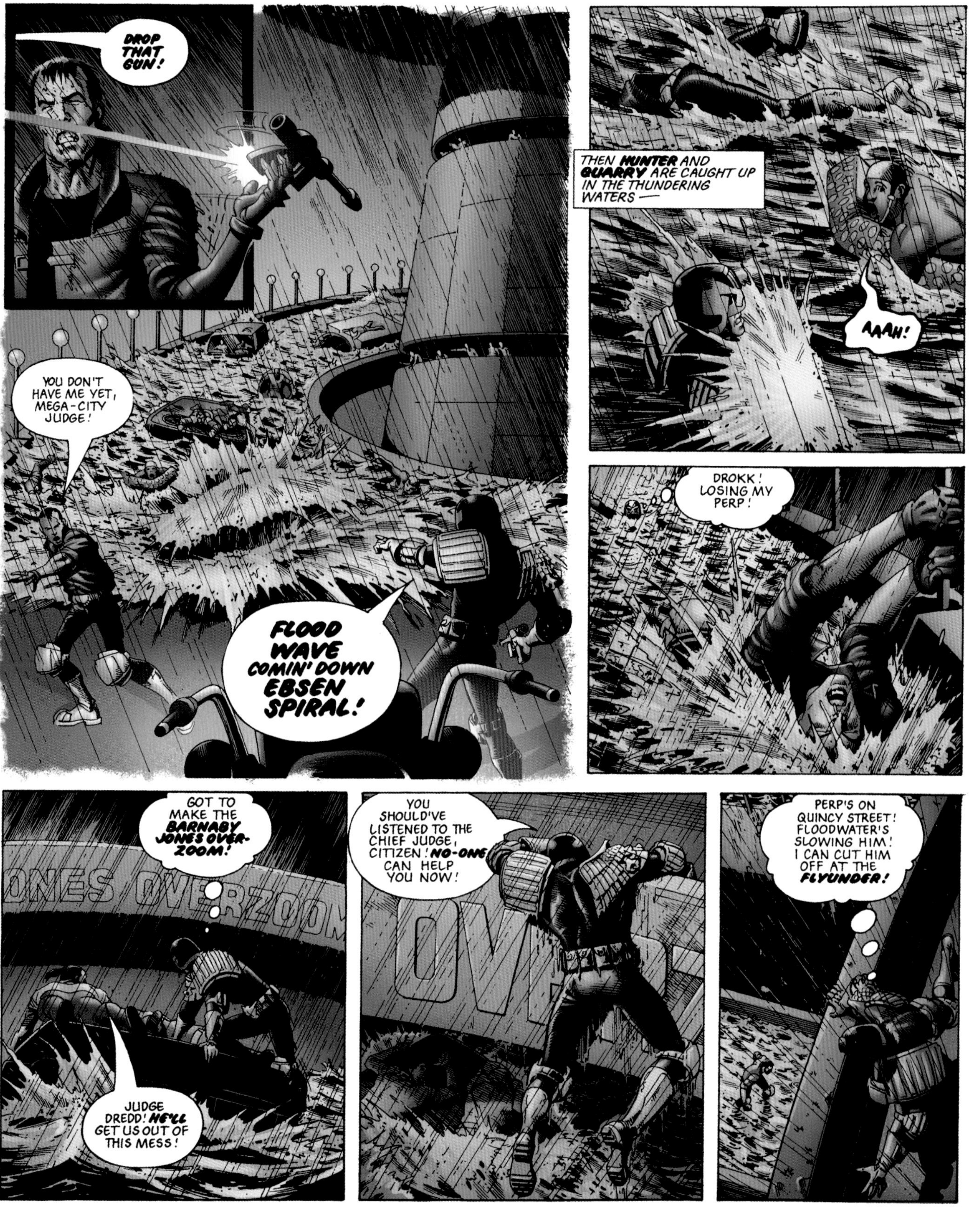

DROP THAT GUN!
YOU DON'T HAVE ME YET, MEGA-CITY JUDGE!
FLOOD WAVE COMIN' DOWN EBSEN SPIRAL!
THEN HUNTER AND QUARRY ARE CAUGHT UP IN THE THUNDERING WATERS —
AAAH!
DROKK! LOSING MY PERP!
GOT TO MAKE THE BARNABY JONES OVER-ZOOM!
ONES OVERZOOM
JUDGE DREDD! HE'LL GET US OUT OF THIS MESS!
YOU SHOULD'VE LISTENED TO THE CHIEF JUDGE, CITIZEN! NO-ONE CAN HELP YOU NOW!
PERP'S ON QUINCY STREET! FLOODWATER'S SLOWING HIM! I CAN CUT HIM OFF AT THE FLYUNDER!

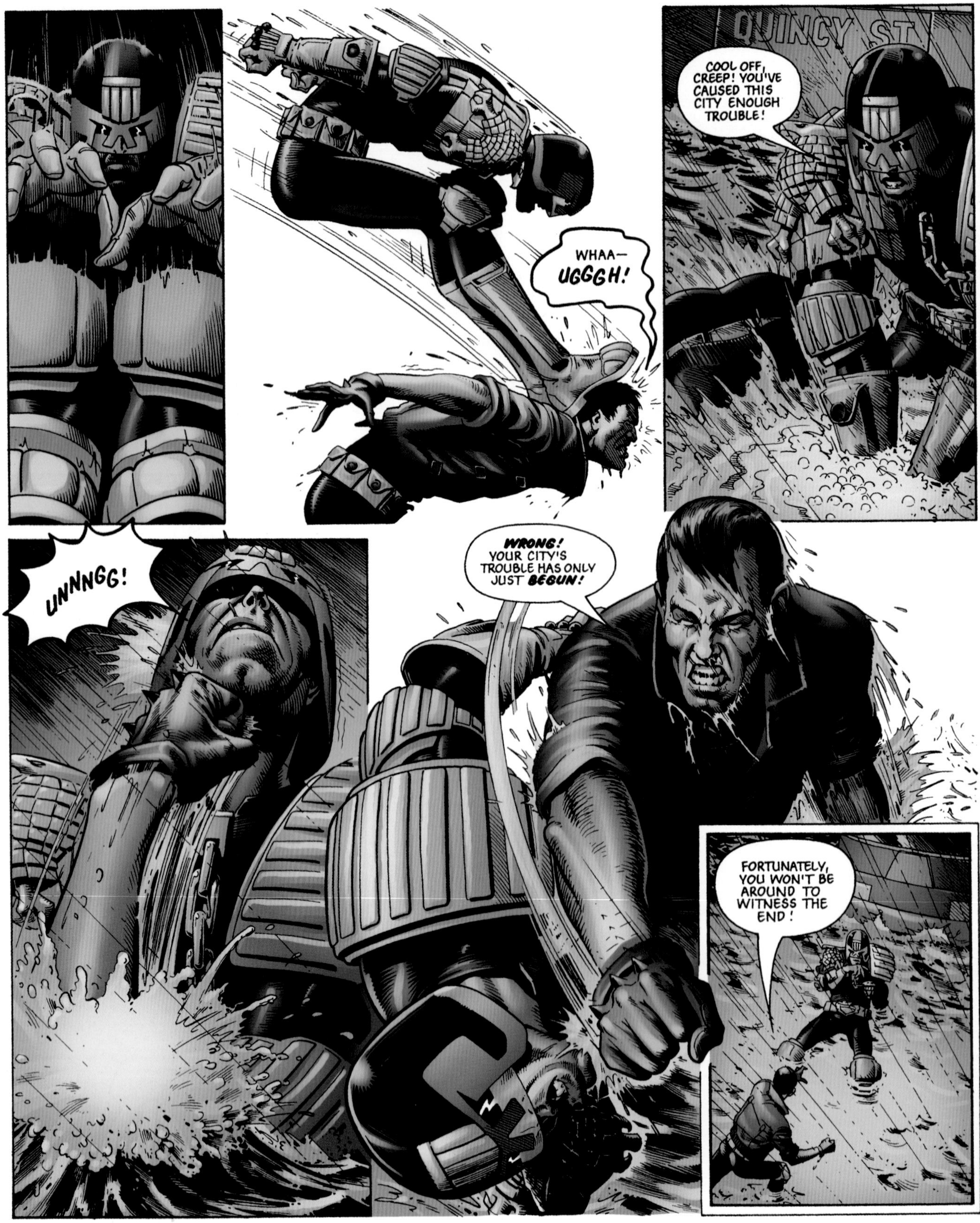
WHAA—
UGGGH!
QUINCY ST
COOL OFF, CREEP! YOU'VE CAUSED THIS CITY ENOUGH TROUBLE!
UNNNGG!
WRONG! YOUR CITY'S TROUBLE HAS ONLY JUST BEGUN!
FORTUNATELY, YOU WON'T BE AROUND TO WITNESS THE END!

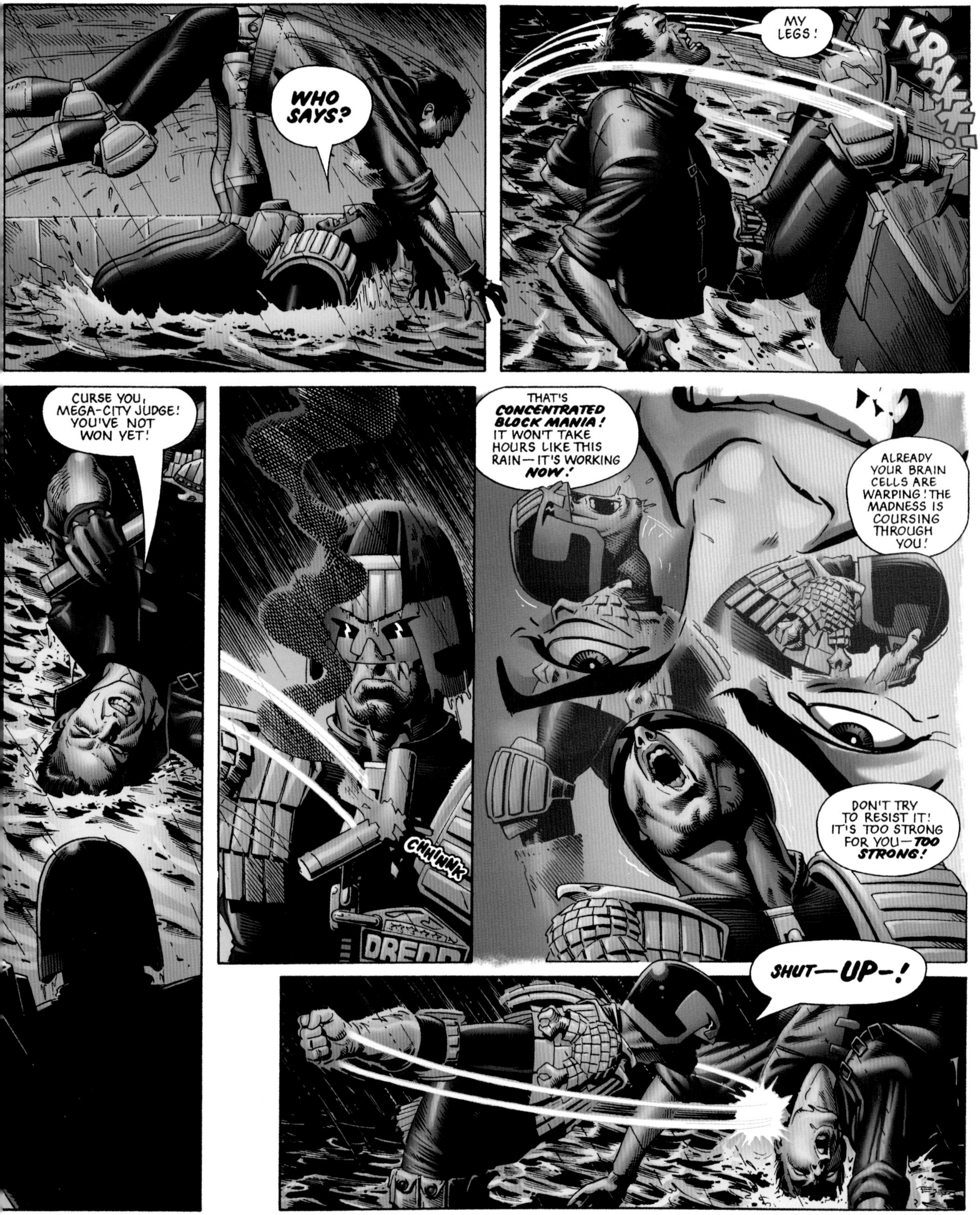

WHO SAYS?
MY LEGS!
KRAKK!
CURSE YOU, MEGA-CITY JUDGE! YOU'VE NOT WON YET!
CHHNNK
DREDD
THAT'S CONCENTRATED BLOCK MANIA! IT WON'T TAKE HOURS LIKE THIS RAIN—IT'S WORKING NOW!
ALREADY YOUR BRAIN CELLS ARE WARPING! THE MADNESS IS COURSING THROUGH YOU!
DON'T TRY TO RESIST IT! IT'S TOO STRONG FOR YOU—TOO STRONG!
SHUT—UP-!

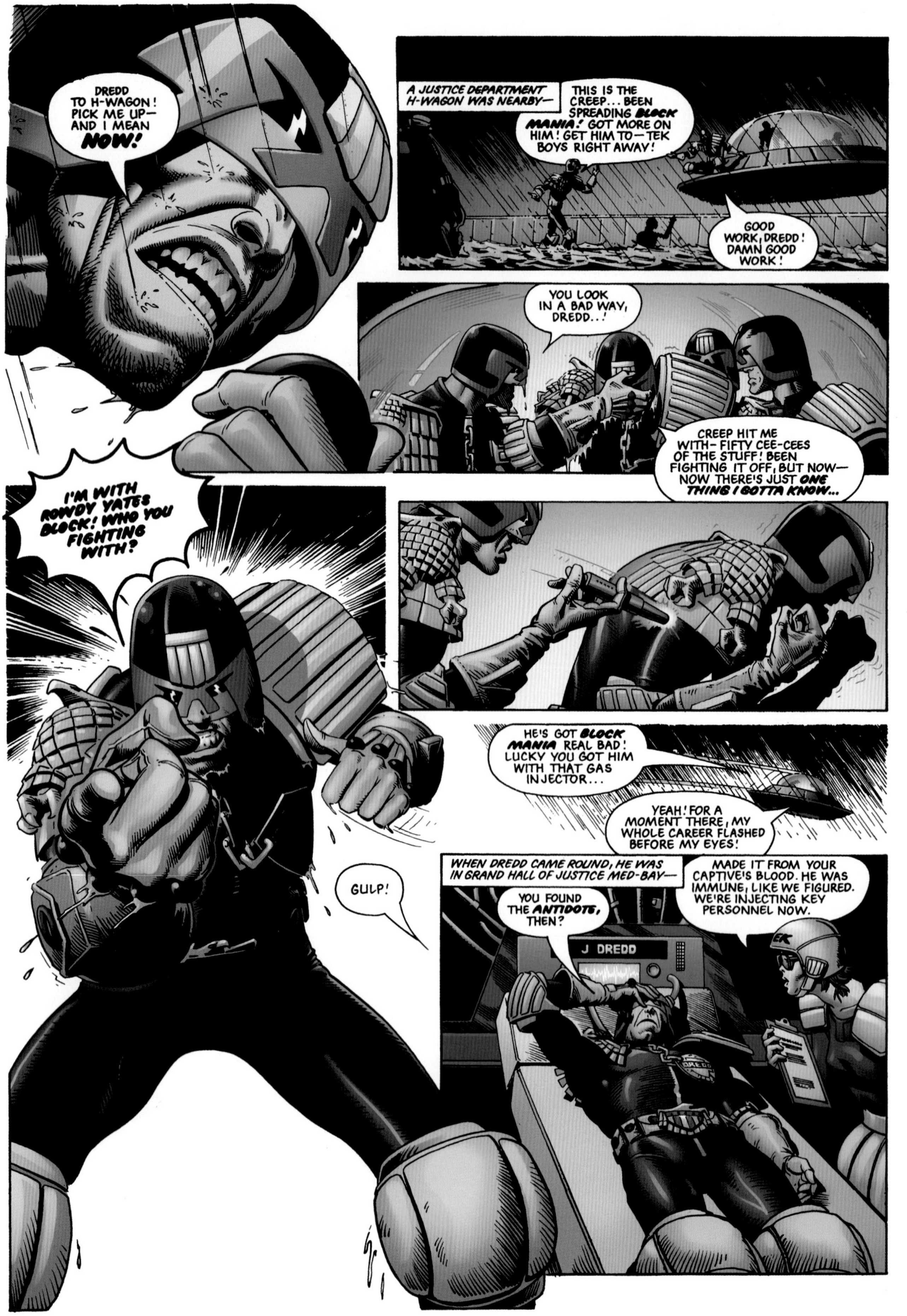
DREDD TO H-WAGON! PICK ME UP— AND I MEAN NOW!
A JUSTICE DEPARTMENT H-WAGON WAS NEARBY—
THIS IS THE CREEP... BEEN SPREADING BLOCK MANIA! GOT MORE ON HIM! GET HIM TO—TEK BOYS RIGHT AWAY!
GOOD WORK, DREDD! DAMN GOOD WORK!
YOU LOOK IN A BAD WAY, DREDD..!
CREEP HIT ME WITH—FIFTY CEE-CEES OF THE STUFF! BEEN FIGHTING IT OFF, BUT NOW— NOW THERE'S JUST ONE THING I GOTTA KNOW...
I'M WITH ROWDY YATES BLOCK! WHO YOU FIGHTING WITH?
GULP!
HE'S GOT BLOCK MANIA REAL BAD! LUCKY YOU GOT HIM WITH THAT GAS INJECTOR...
YEAH! FOR A MOMENT THERE, MY WHOLE CAREER FLASHED BEFORE MY EYES!
WHEN DREDD CAME ROUND, HE WAS IN GRAND HALL OF JUSTICE MED-BAY—
YOU FOUND THE ANTIDOTE, THEN?
MADE IT FROM YOUR CAPTIVE'S BLOOD. HE WAS IMMUNE, LIKE WE FIGURED. WE'RE INJECTING KEY PERSONNEL NOW.
J DREDD

OUTSIDE, CHAOS HAD ERUPTED IN THE EAST AND CENTRAL SECTORS—

WEATHER CONTROL GOT THE RAIN STOPPED, BUT IT WAS TOO LATE! BLOCK MANIA IS NOW CITY-WIDE!

WE'VE GOT YOUR CAPTIVE UNDER INTERROGATION NOW, DREDD. CHIEF JUDGE WANTS YOU THERE.

ORLOK HAD BEEN SUBJECTED TO A BATTERY OF TRUTH SERUMS. HE HAD INEVITABLY CRACKED—

THE NEWS IS BAD, DREDD— THE WORST! HIS NAME IS ORLOK... JUDGE OF EAST-MEG ONE.

BLOCK MANIA WAS A SOV PLOT!

A PLOT OF MONSTROUS PROPORTION!

MY MISSION HAS...SUCCEEDED! MADNESS REIGNS IN YOUR...STREETS— YOUR JUDGE FORCE IS CRIPPLED— YOU...ARE DEFENCELESS!

EAST-MEG WEAPONS ARE AIMED AND READY! THE WAR TO END ALL WARS IS EVEN NOW BEGINNING!

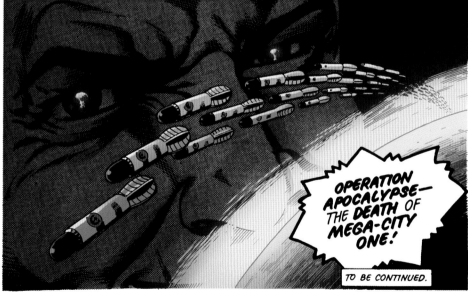

OPERATION APOCALYPSE— THE DEATH OF MEGA-CITY ONE!

TO BE CONTINUED.

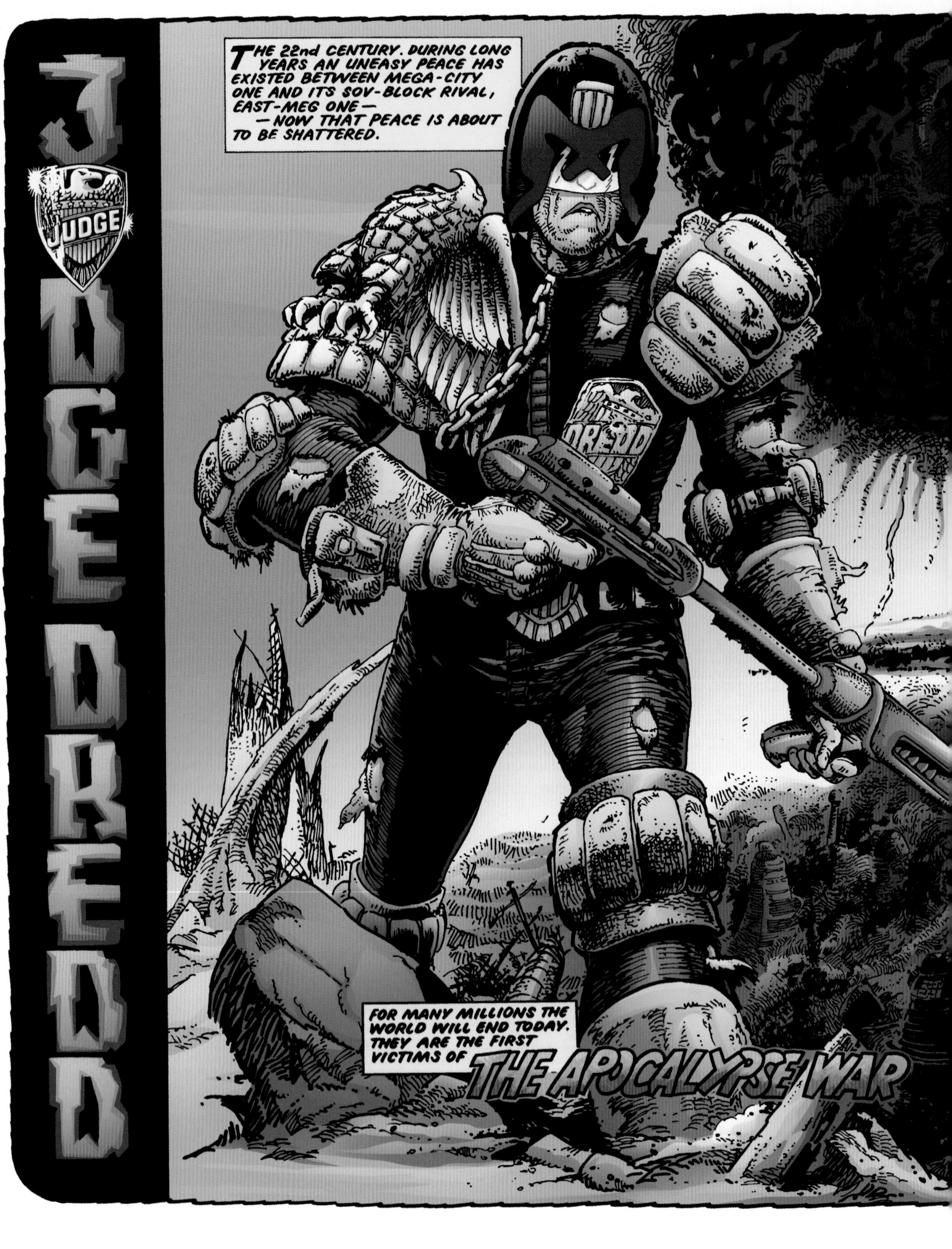
JUDGE DREDD
JUDGE
THE 22nd CENTURY. DURING LONG YEARS AN UNEASY PEACE HAS EXISTED BETWEEN MEGA-CITY ONE AND ITS SOV-BLOCK RIVAL, EAST-MEG ONE— —NOW THAT PEACE IS ABOUT TO BE SHATTERED.
DREDD
FOR MANY MILLIONS THE WORLD WILL END TODAY. THEY ARE THE FIRST VICTIMS OF
THE APOCALYPSE WAR

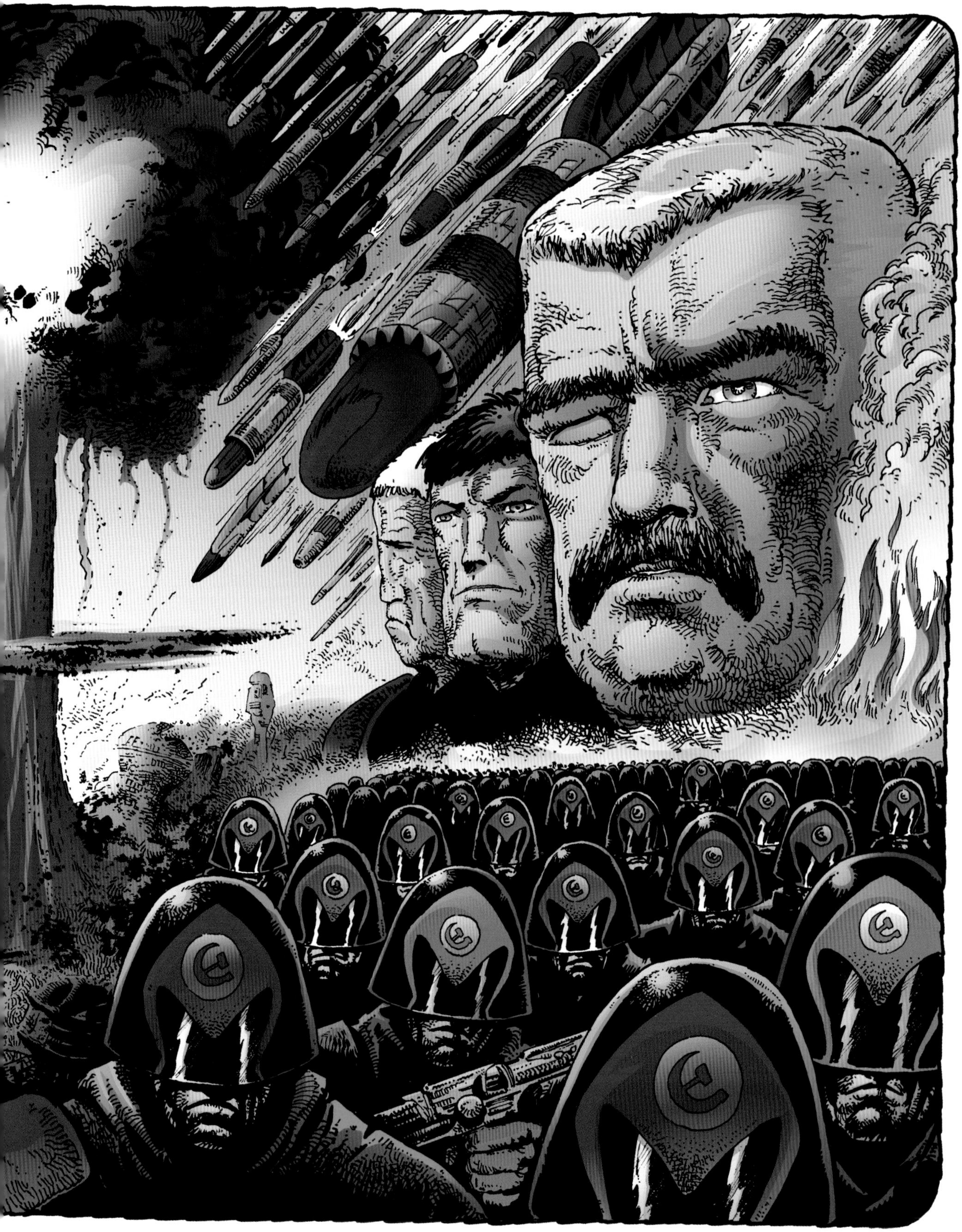

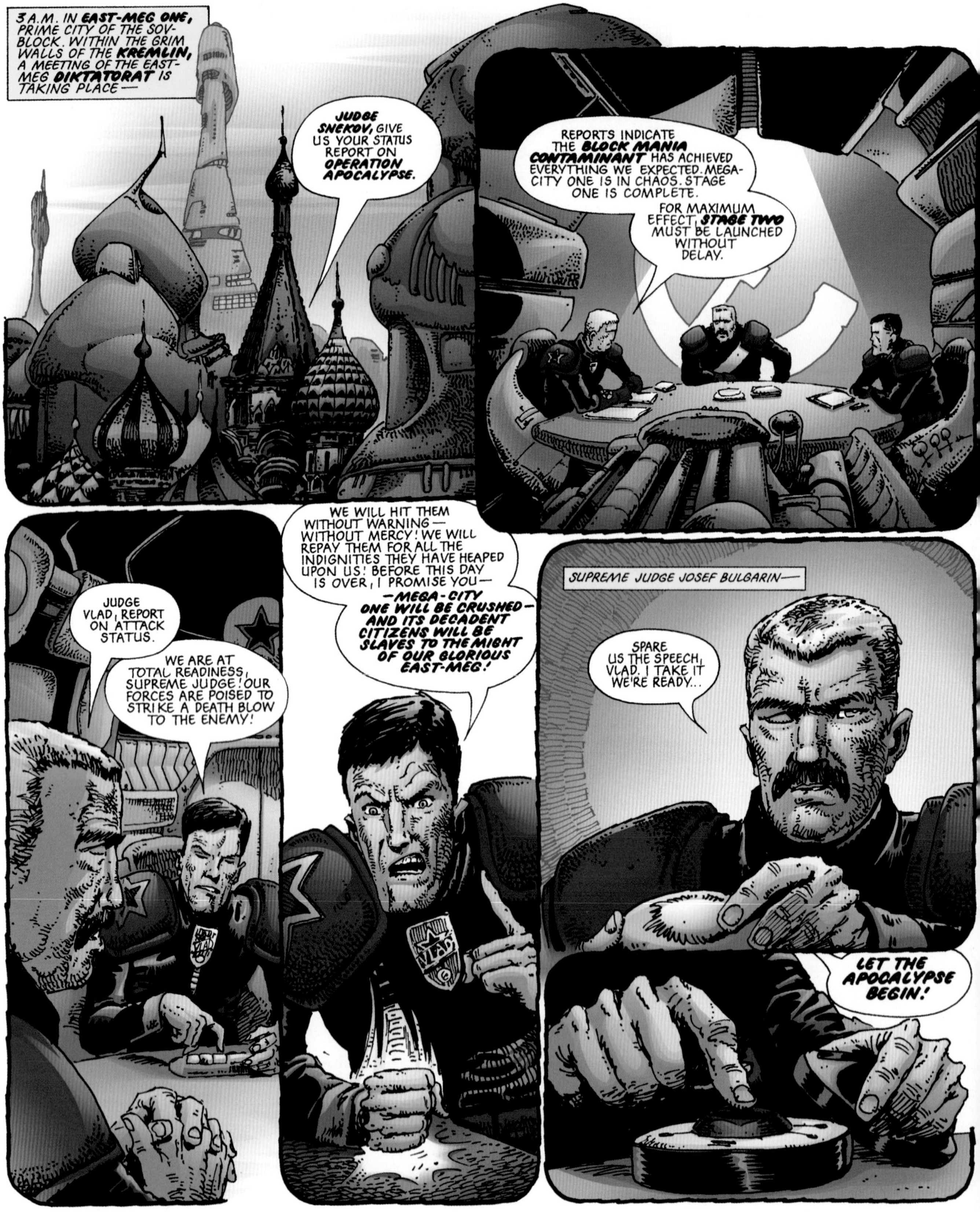

3 A.M. IN EAST-MEG ONE, PRIME CITY OF THE SOV-BLOCK. WITHIN THE GRIM WALLS OF THE KREMLIN, A MEETING OF THE EAST-MEG DIKTATORAT IS TAKING PLACE—
JUDGE SNEKOV, GIVE US YOUR STATUS REPORT ON OPERATION APOCALYPSE.
REPORTS INDICATE THE BLOCK MANIA CONTAMINANT HAS ACHIEVED EVERYTHING WE EXPECTED. MEGA-CITY ONE IS IN CHAOS. STAGE ONE IS COMPLETE.
FOR MAXIMUM EFFECT, STAGE TWO MUST BE LAUNCHED WITHOUT DELAY.
JUDGE VLAD, REPORT ON ATTACK STATUS.
WE ARE AT TOTAL READINESS, SUPREME JUDGE! OUR FORCES ARE POISED TO STRIKE A DEATH BLOW TO THE ENEMY!
WE WILL HIT THEM WITHOUT WARNING— WITHOUT MERCY! WE WILL REPAY THEM FOR ALL THE INDIGNITIES THEY HAVE HEAPED UPON US! BEFORE THIS DAY IS OVER, I PROMISE YOU—
—MEGA-CITY ONE WILL BE CRUSHED— AND ITS DECADENT CITIZENS WILL BE SLAVES TO THE MIGHT OF OUR GLORIOUS EAST-MEG!
SUPREME JUDGE JOSEF BULGARIN—
SPARE US THE SPEECH, VLAD. I TAKE IT WE'RE READY...
LET THE APOCALYPSE BEGIN!

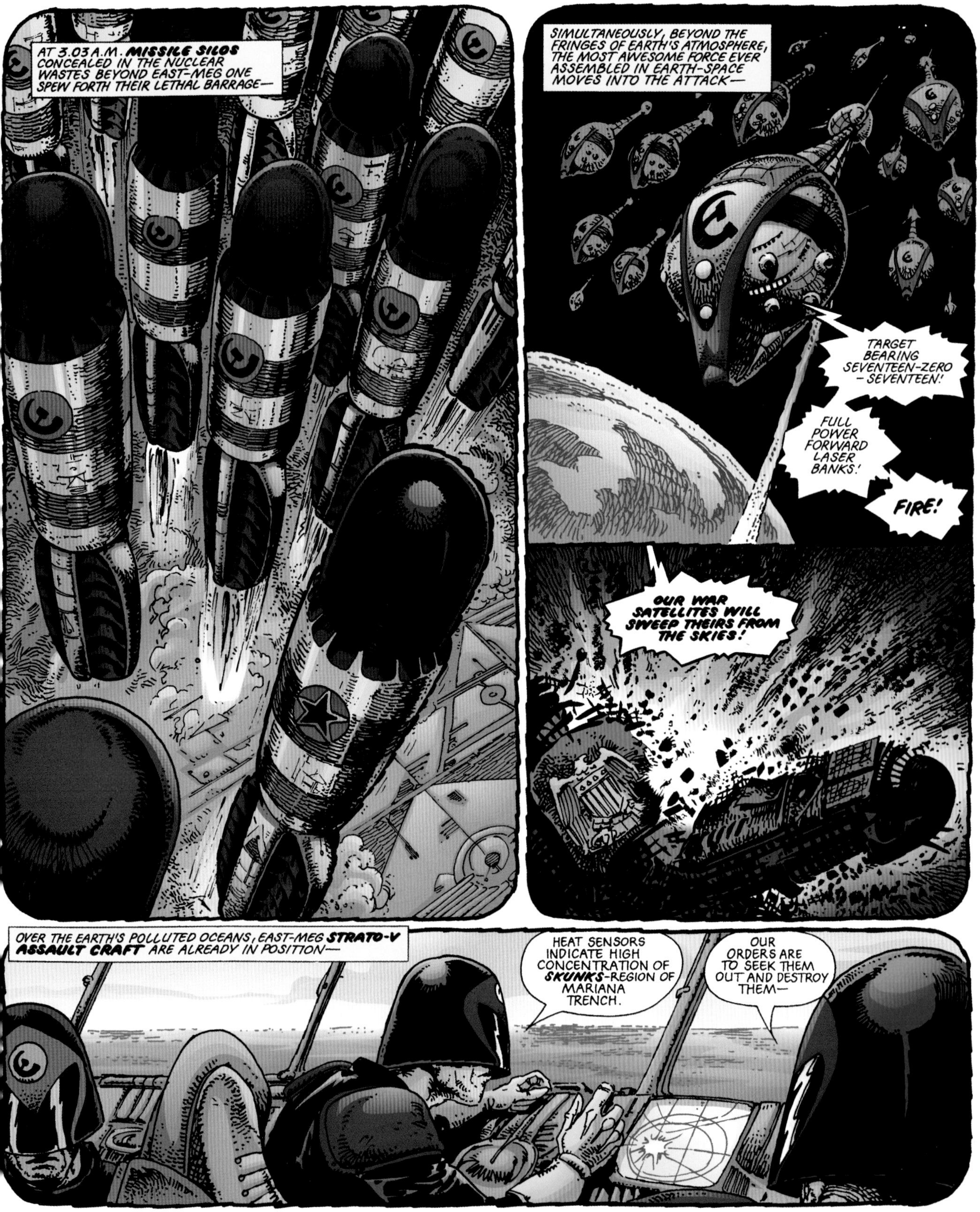
AT 3.03 A.M. MISSILE SILOS CONCEALED IN THE NUCLEAR WASTES BEYOND EAST-MEG ONE SPEW FORTH THEIR LETHAL BARRAGE—
SIMULTANEOUSLY, BEYOND THE FRINGES OF EARTH'S ATMOSPHERE, THE MOST AWESOME FORCE EVER ASSEMBLED IN EARTH-SPACE MOVES INTO THE ATTACK—
TARGET BEARING SEVENTEEN-ZERO - SEVENTEEN!
FULL POWER FORWARD LASER BANKS!
FIRE!
OUR WAR SATELLITES WILL SWEEP THEIRS FROM THE SKIES!
OVER THE EARTH'S POLLUTED OCEANS, EAST-MEG STRATO-V ASSAULT CRAFT ARE ALREADY IN POSITION—
HEAT SENSORS INDICATE HIGH CONCENTRATION OF SKUNKS-REGION OF MARIANA TRENCH.
OUR ORDERS ARE TO SEEK THEM OUT AND DESTROY THEM—

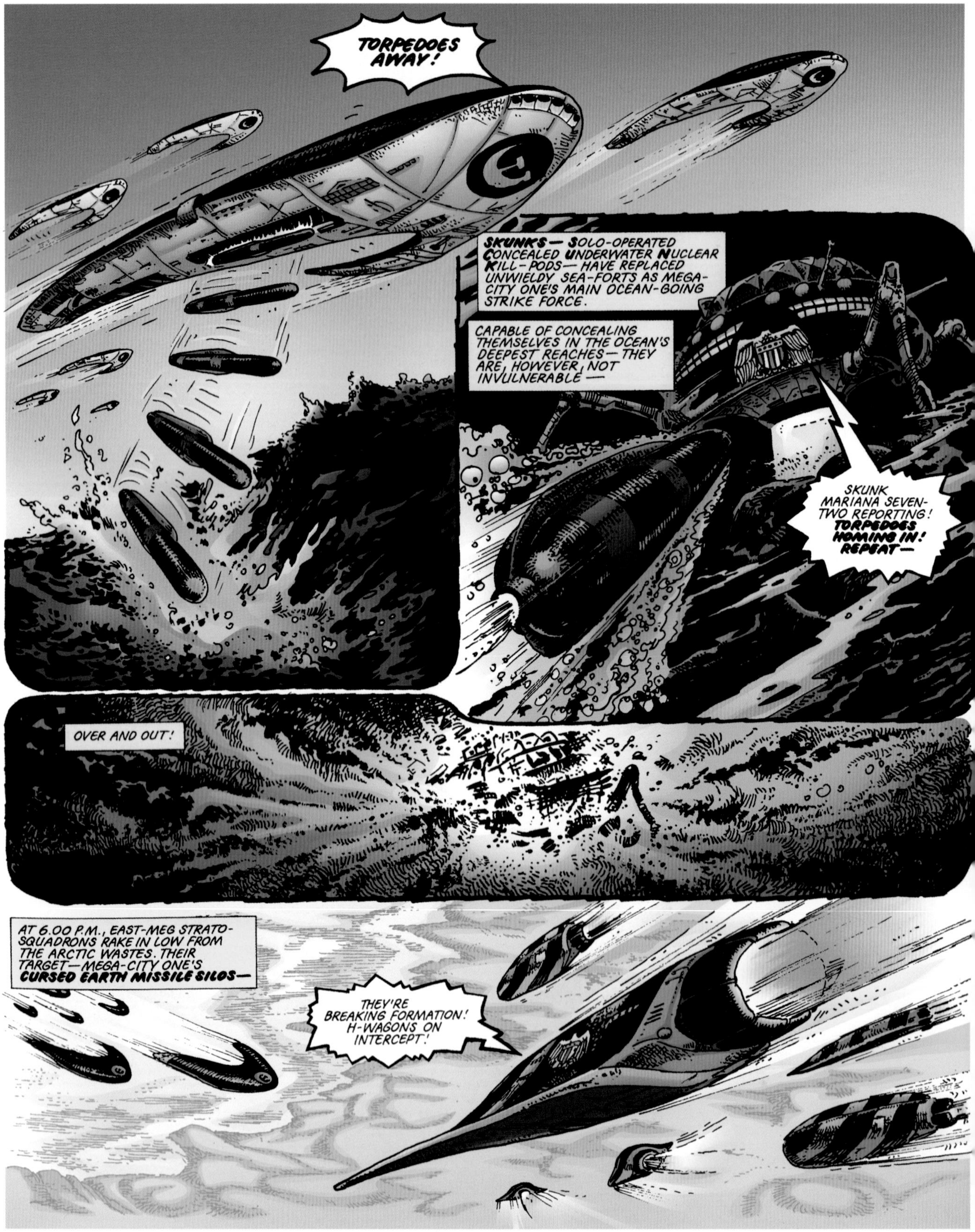
TORPEDOES AWAY!
SKUNKS— SOLO-OPERATED CONCEALED UNDERWATER NUCLEAR KILL-PODS— HAVE REPLACED UNWIELDY SEA-FORTS AS MEGA-CITY ONE'S MAIN OCEAN-GOING STRIKE FORCE.
CAPABLE OF CONCEALING THEMSELVES IN THE OCEAN'S DEEPEST REACHES— THEY ARE, HOWEVER, NOT INVULNERABLE—
SKUNK MARIANA SEVEN-TWO REPORTING! TORPEDOES HOMING IN! REPEAT—
OVER AND OUT!
AT 6.00 P.M., EAST-MEG STRATO-SQUADRONS RAKE IN LOW FROM THE ARCTIC WASTES. THEIR TARGET—MEGA-CITY ONE'S CURSED EARTH MISSILE SILOS—
THEY'RE BREAKING FORMATION! H-WAGONS ON INTERCEPT!

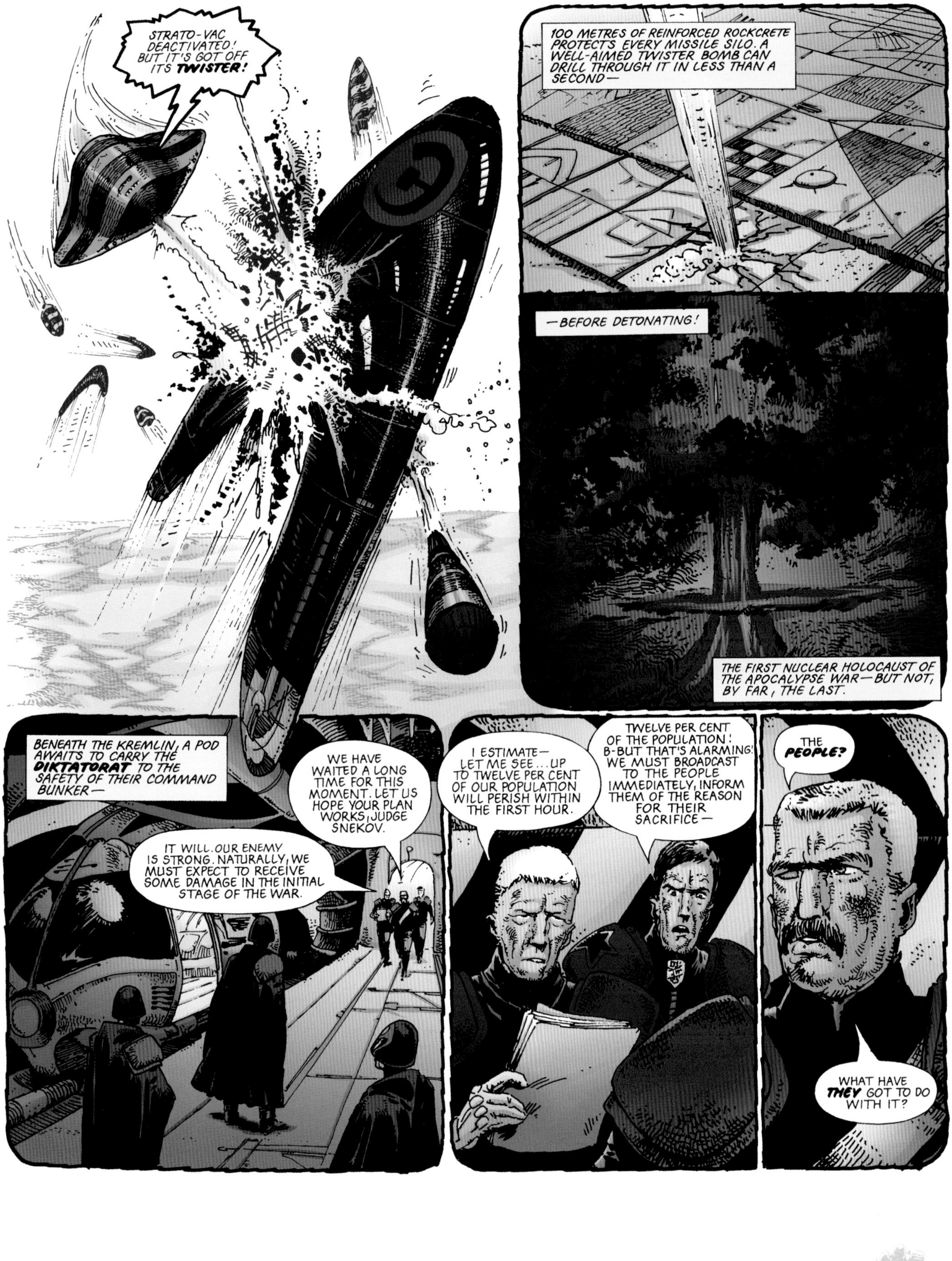
STRATO-VAC DEACTIVATED! BUT IT'S GOT OFF ITS TWISTER!
100 METRES OF REINFORCED ROCKCRETE PROTECTS EVERY MISSILE SILO. A WELL-AIMED TWISTER BOMB CAN DRILL THROUGH IT IN LESS THAN A SECOND—
—BEFORE DETONATING!
THE FIRST NUCLEAR HOLOCAUST OF THE APOCALYPSE WAR—BUT NOT, BY FAR, THE LAST.
BENEATH THE KREMLIN, A POD AWAITS TO CARRY THE DIKTATORAT TO THE SAFETY OF THEIR COMMAND BUNKER—
WE HAVE WAITED A LONG TIME FOR THIS MOMENT. LET US HOPE YOUR PLAN WORKS, JUDGE SNEKOV.
IT WILL. OUR ENEMY IS STRONG. NATURALLY, WE MUST EXPECT TO RECEIVE SOME DAMAGE IN THE INITIAL STAGE OF THE WAR.
I ESTIMATE— LET ME SEE... UP TO TWELVE PER CENT OF OUR POPULATION WILL PERISH WITHIN THE FIRST HOUR.
TWELVE PER CENT OF THE POPULATION! B-BUT THAT'S ALARMING! WE MUST BROADCAST TO THE PEOPLE IMMEDIATELY, INFORM THEM OF THE REASON FOR THEIR SACRIFICE—
THE PEOPLE?
WHAT HAVE THEY GOT TO DO WITH IT?

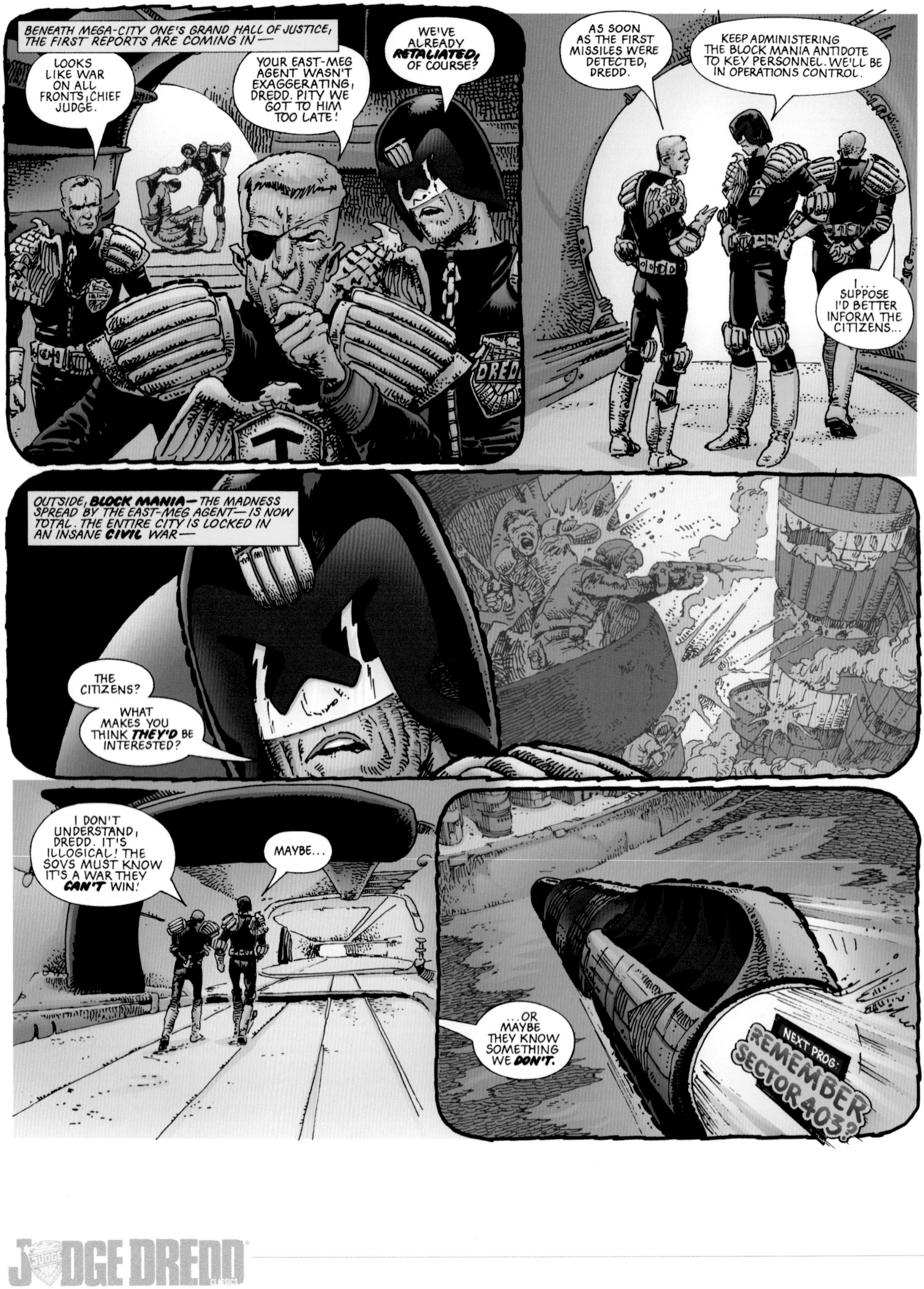

BENEATH MEGA-CITY ONE'S GRAND HALL OF JUSTICE, THE FIRST REPORTS ARE COMING IN—
LOOKS LIKE WAR ON ALL FRONTS, CHIEF JUDGE.
YOUR EAST-MEG AGENT WASN'T EXAGGERATING, DREDD. PITY WE GOT TO HIM TOO LATE!
WE'VE ALREADY **RETALIATED,** OF COURSE?
AS SOON AS THE FIRST MISSILES WERE DETECTED, DREDD.
KEEP ADMINISTERING THE BLOCK MANIA ANTIDOTE TO KEY PERSONNEL. WE'LL BE IN OPERATIONS CONTROL.
I... SUPPOSE I'D BETTER INFORM THE CITIZENS...
OUTSIDE, **BLOCK MANIA**— THE MADNESS SPREAD BY THE EAST-MEG AGENT— IS NOW TOTAL. THE ENTIRE CITY IS LOCKED IN AN INSANE **CIVIL** WAR—
THE CITIZENS?
WHAT MAKES YOU THINK **THEY'D** BE INTERESTED?
I DON'T UNDERSTAND, DREDD. IT'S ILLOGICAL! THE SOVS MUST KNOW IT'S A WAR THEY **CAN'T** WIN!
MAYBE...
...OR MAYBE THEY KNOW SOMETHING WE **DON'T.**
NEXT PROG:
REMEMBER SECTOR 403?

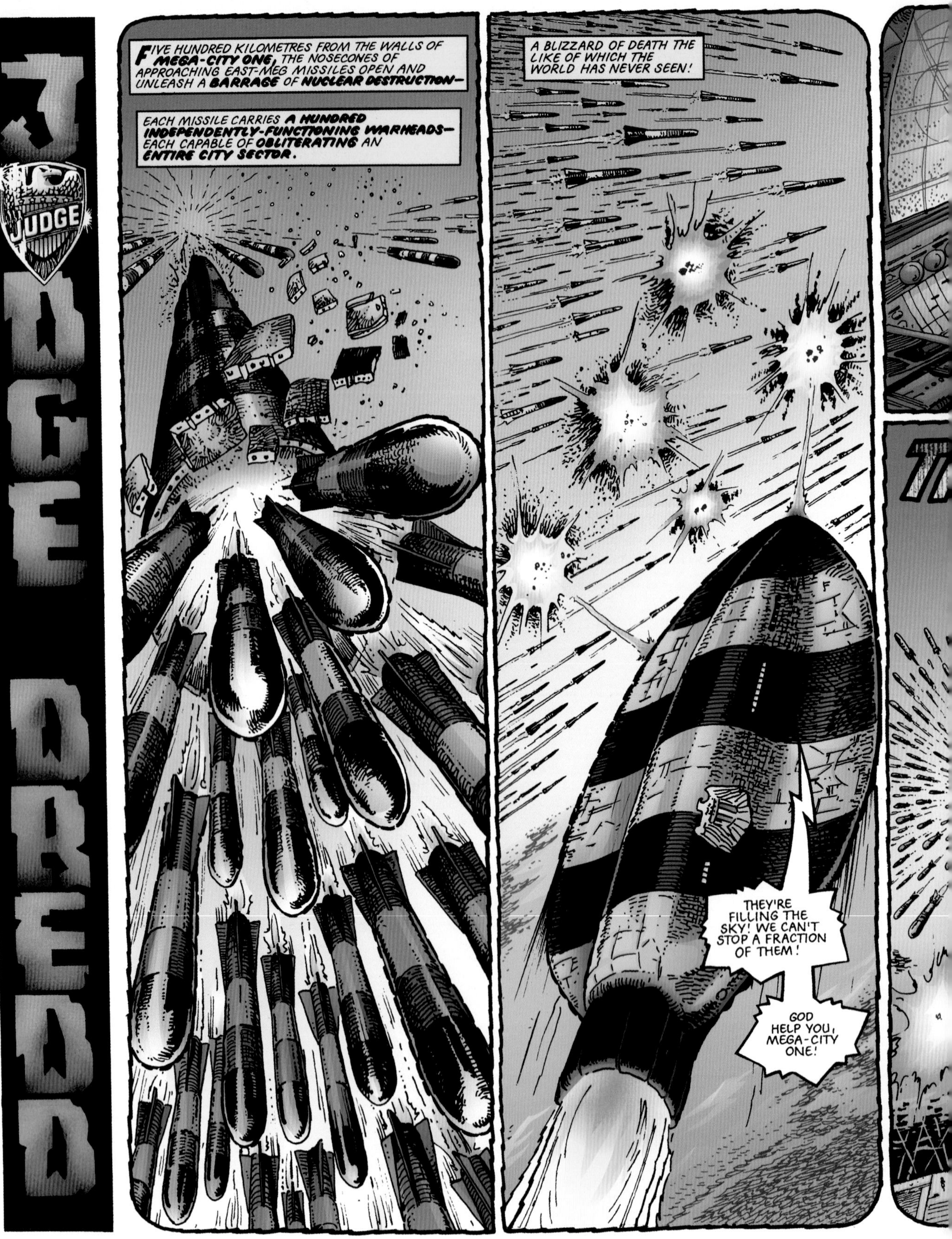
JUDGE DREDD
JUDGE
FIVE HUNDRED KILOMETRES FROM THE WALLS OF MEGA-CITY ONE, THE NOSECONES OF APPROACHING EAST-MEG MISSILES OPEN AND UNLEASH A BARRAGE OF NUCLEAR DESTRUCTION—
EACH MISSILE CARRIES A HUNDRED INDEPENDENTLY-FUNCTIONING WARHEADS— EACH CAPABLE OF OBLITERATING AN ENTIRE CITY SECTOR.
A BLIZZARD OF DEATH THE LIKE OF WHICH THE WORLD HAS NEVER SEEN!
THEY'RE FILLING THE SKY! WE CAN'T STOP A FRACTION OF THEM!
GOD HELP YOU, MEGA-CITY ONE!

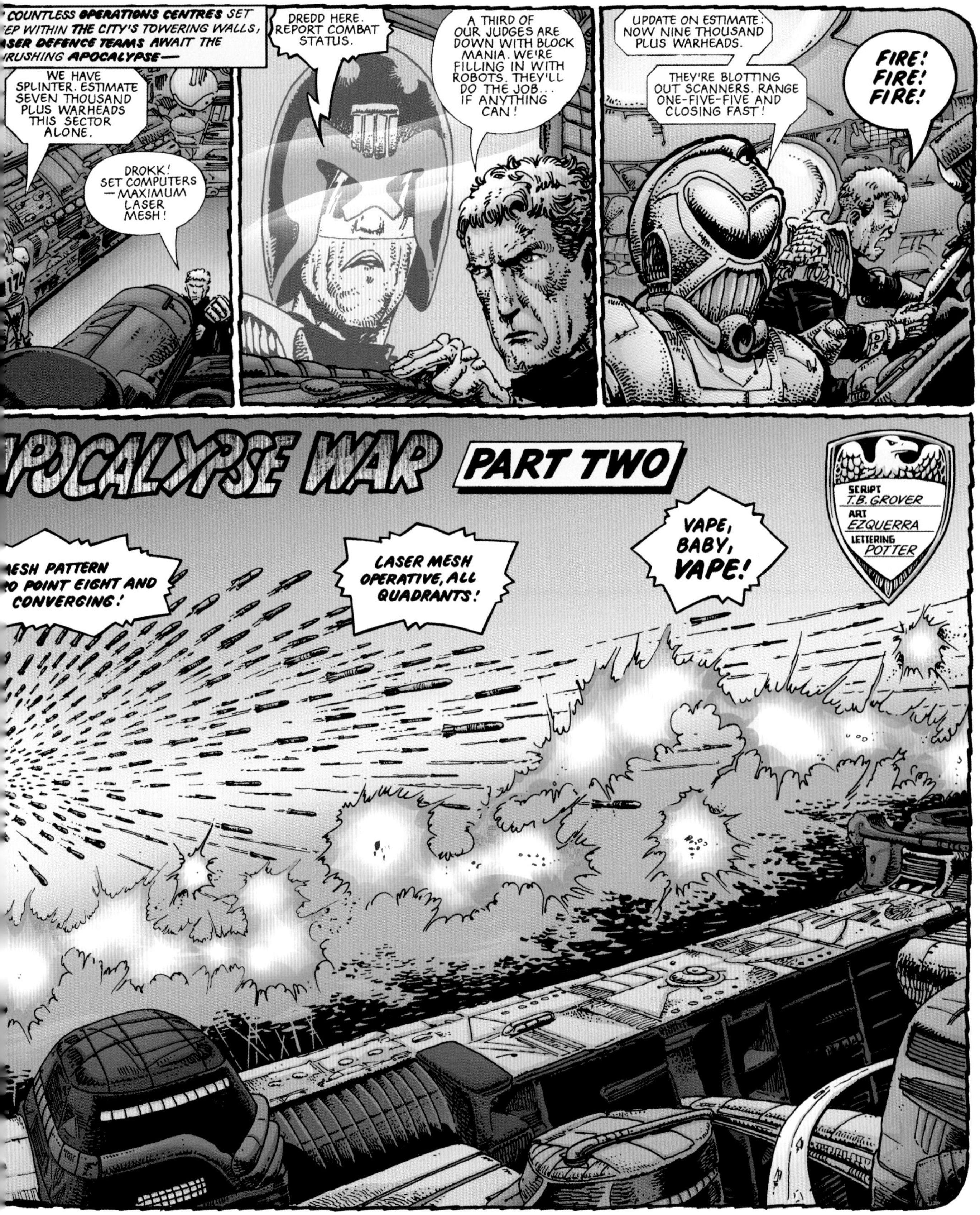

COUNTLESS OPERATIONS CENTRES SET
EP WITHIN THE CITY'S TOWERING WALLS,
ASER DEFENCE TEAMS AWAIT THE
RUSHING APOCALYPSE—
WE HAVE SPLINTER. ESTIMATE SEVEN THOUSAND PLUS WARHEADS THIS SECTOR ALONE.
DROKK! SET COMPUTERS —MAXIMUM LASER MESH!
DREDD HERE. REPORT COMBAT STATUS.
A THIRD OF OUR JUDGES ARE DOWN WITH BLOCK MANIA. WE'RE FILLING IN WITH ROBOTS. THEY'LL DO THE JOB... IF ANYTHING CAN!
UPDATE ON ESTIMATE: NOW NINE THOUSAND PLUS WARHEADS.
THEY'RE BLOTTING OUT SCANNERS. RANGE ONE-FIVE-FIVE AND CLOSING FAST!
FIRE! FIRE! FIRE!
POCALYPSE WAR
PART TWO
SCRIPT T.B. GROVER
ART EZQUERRA
LETTERING POTTER
ESH PATTERN
O POINT EIGHT AND
CONVERGING!
LASER MESH OPERATIVE, ALL QUADRANTS!
VAPE, BABY, VAPE!

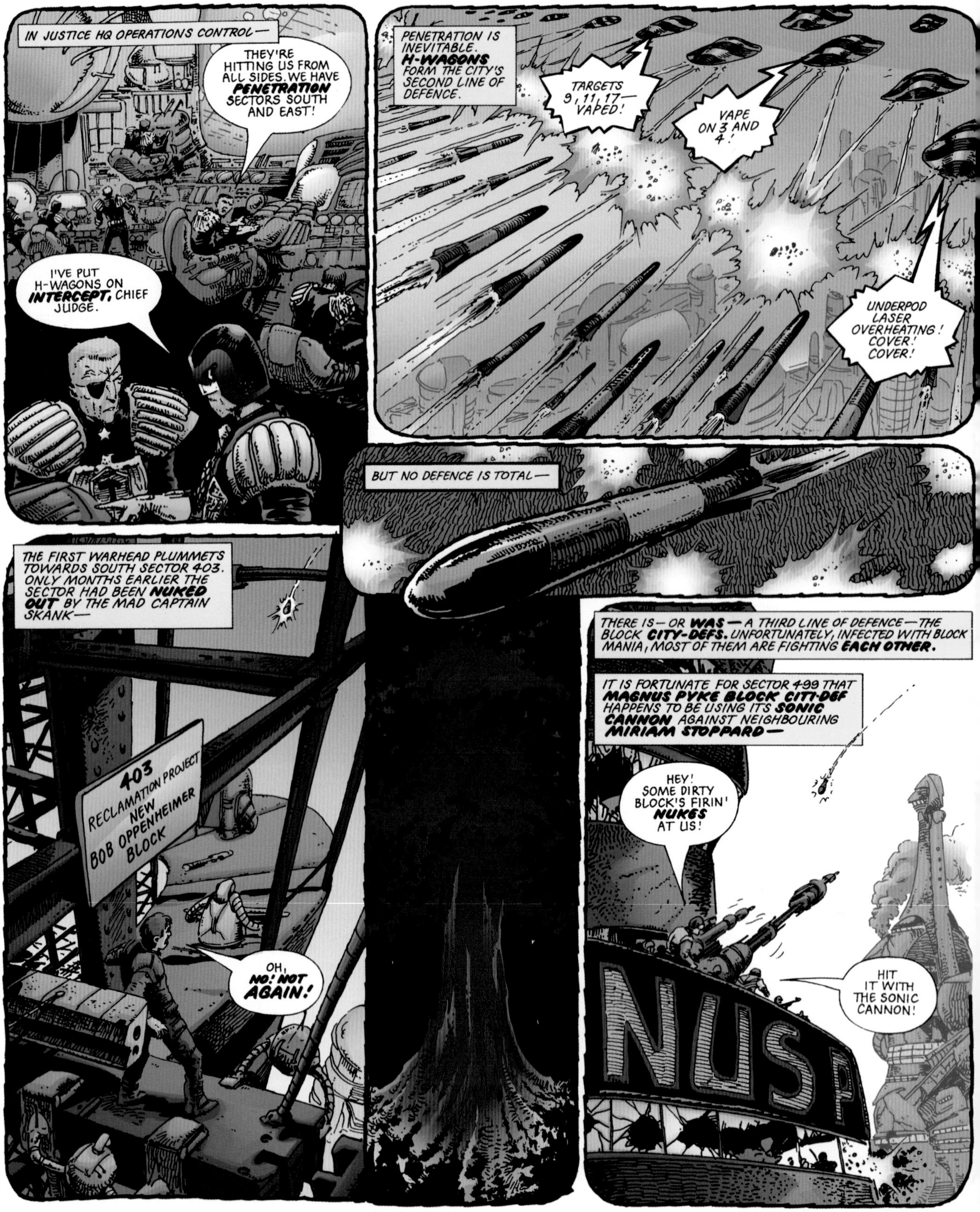
IN JUSTICE HQ OPERATIONS CONTROL—
THEY'RE HITTING US FROM ALL SIDES. WE HAVE PENETRATION SECTORS SOUTH AND EAST!
I'VE PUT H-WAGONS ON INTERCEPT, CHIEF JUDGE.
PENETRATION IS INEVITABLE. H-WAGONS FORM THE CITY'S SECOND LINE OF DEFENCE.
TARGETS 9, 11, 17— VAPED!
VAPE ON 3 AND 4!
UNDERPOD LASER OVERHEATING! COVER! COVER!
BUT NO DEFENCE IS TOTAL—
THE FIRST WARHEAD PLUMMETS TOWARDS SOUTH SECTOR 403. ONLY MONTHS EARLIER THE SECTOR HAD BEEN NUKED OUT BY THE MAD CAPTAIN SKANK—
403 RECLAMATION PROJECT NEW BOB OPPENHEIMER BLOCK
OH, NO! NOT AGAIN!
THERE IS— OR WAS — A THIRD LINE OF DEFENCE—THE BLOCK CITY-DEFS. UNFORTUNATELY, INFECTED WITH BLOCK MANIA, MOST OF THEM ARE FIGHTING EACH OTHER.
IT IS FORTUNATE FOR SECTOR 499 THAT MAGNUS PYKE BLOCK CITI-DEF HAPPENS TO BE USING ITS SONIC CANNON AGAINST NEIGHBOURING MIRIAM STOPPARD—
HEY! SOME DIRTY BLOCK'S FIRIN' NUKES AT US!
HIT IT WITH THE SONIC CANNON!
NUS P

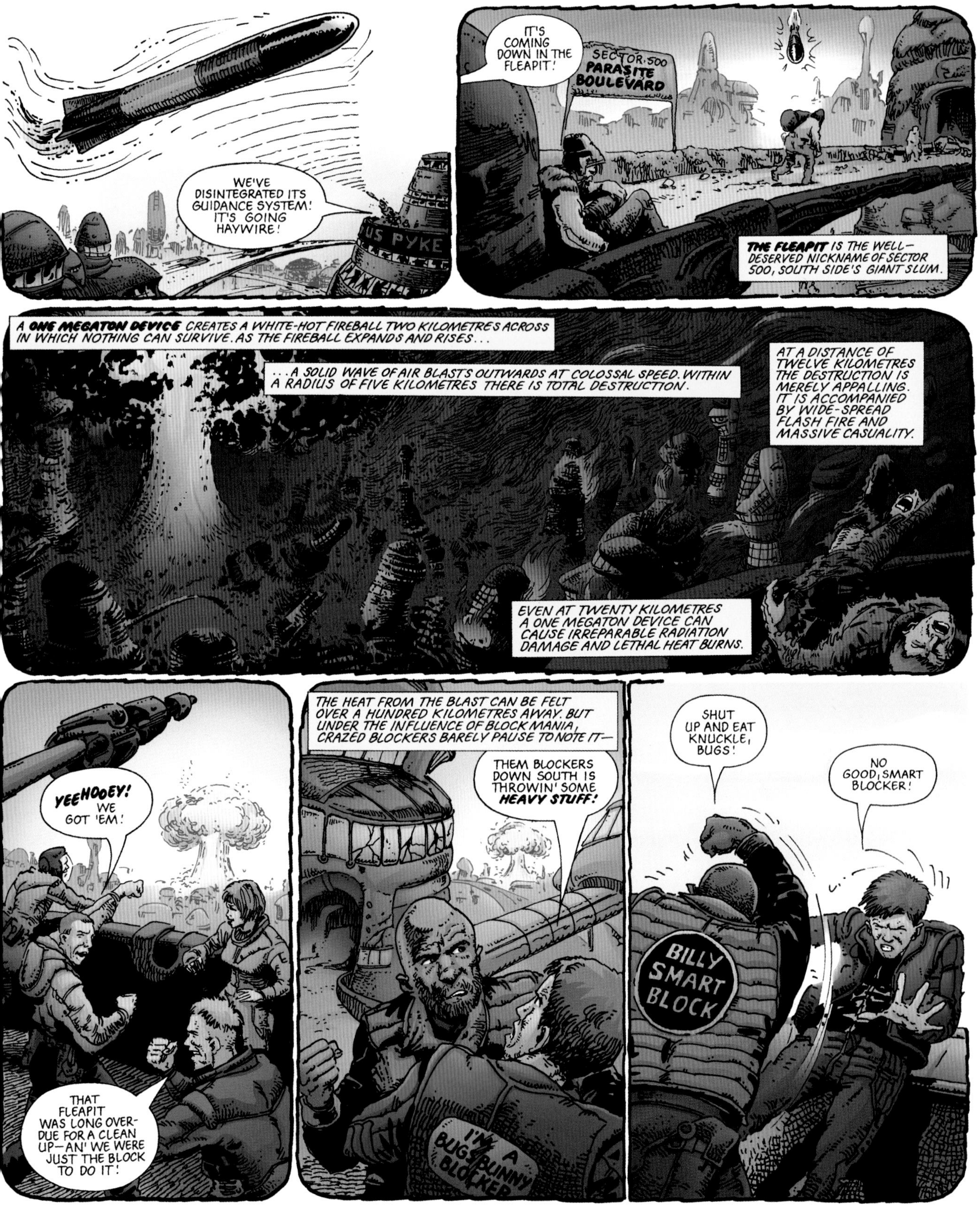
WE'VE DISINTEGRATED ITS GUIDANCE SYSTEM! IT'S GOING HAYWIRE!
US PYKE
IT'S COMING DOWN IN THE FLEAPIT!
SECTOR 500
PARASITE BOULEVARD
THE FLEAPIT IS THE WELL-DESERVED NICKNAME OF SECTOR 500, SOUTH SIDE'S GIANT SLUM.
A ONE MEGATON DEVICE CREATES A WHITE-HOT FIREBALL TWO KILOMETRES ACROSS IN WHICH NOTHING CAN SURVIVE. AS THE FIREBALL EXPANDS AND RISES...
...A SOLID WAVE OF AIR BLASTS OUTWARDS AT COLOSSAL SPEED. WITHIN A RADIUS OF FIVE KILOMETRES THERE IS TOTAL DESTRUCTION.
AT A DISTANCE OF TWELVE KILOMETRES THE DESTRUCTION IS MERELY APPALLING. IT IS ACCOMPANIED BY WIDE-SPREAD FLASH FIRE AND MASSIVE CASUALITY.
EVEN AT TWENTY KILOMETRES A ONE MEGATON DEVICE CAN CAUSE IRREPARABLE RADIATION DAMAGE AND LETHAL HEAT BURNS.
YEEHOOEY! WE GOT 'EM!
THAT FLEAPIT WAS LONG OVERDUE FOR A CLEAN UP—AN' WE WERE JUST THE BLOCK TO DO IT!
THE HEAT FROM THE BLAST CAN BE FELT OVER A HUNDRED KILOMETRES AWAY. BUT UNDER THE INFLUENCE OF BLOCK MANIA, CRAZED BLOCKERS BARELY PAUSE TO NOTE IT—
THEM BLOCKERS DOWN SOUTH IS THROWIN' SOME HEAVY STUFF!
I'M A BUGS BUNNY BLOCKER
SHUT UP AND EAT KNUCKLE, BUGS!
NO GOOD, SMART BLOCKER!
BILLY SMART BLOCK

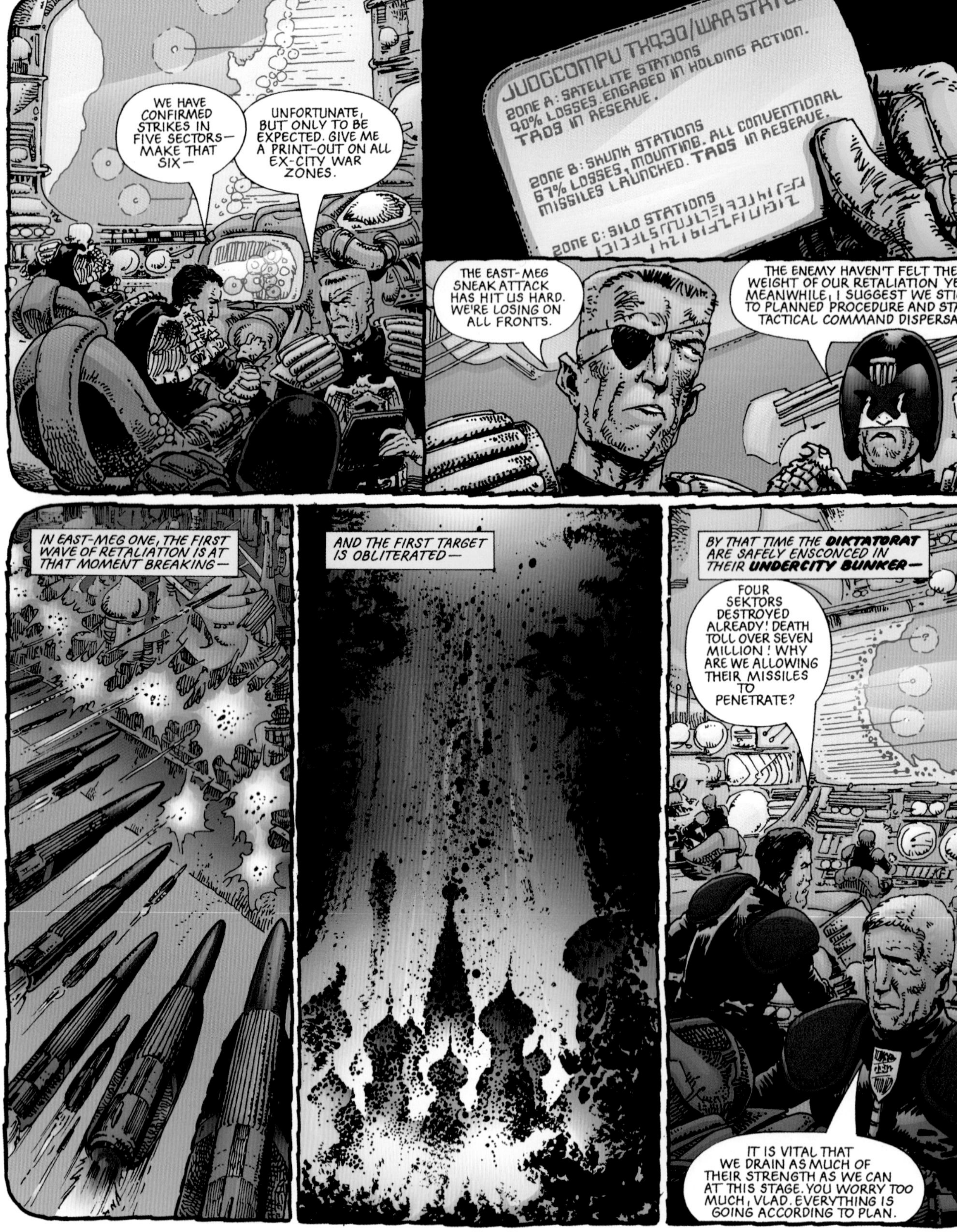
WE HAVE CONFIRMED STRIKES IN FIVE SECTORS— MAKE THAT SIX—
UNFORTUNATE, BUT ONLY TO BE EXPECTED. GIVE ME A PRINT-OUT ON ALL EX-CITY WAR ZONES.
JUDGCOMPU TX430/WAR STATUS
ZONE A: SATELLITE STATIONS
40% LOSSES. ENGAGED IN HOLDING ACTION.
TADS IN RESERVE.
ZONE B: SKUNK STATIONS
67% LOSSES, MOUNTING. ALL CONVENTIONAL
MISSILES LAUNCHED. TADS IN RESERVE.
ZONE C: SILO STATIONS
THE EAST-MEG SNEAK ATTACK HAS HIT US HARD. WE'RE LOSING ON ALL FRONTS.
THE ENEMY HAVEN'T FELT THE WEIGHT OF OUR RETALIATION YET. MEANWHILE, I SUGGEST WE STICK TO PLANNED PROCEDURE AND START TACTICAL COMMAND DISPERSAL.
IN EAST-MEG ONE, THE FIRST WAVE OF RETALIATION IS AT THAT MOMENT BREAKING—
AND THE FIRST TARGET IS OBLITERATED—
BY THAT TIME THE DIKTATORAT ARE SAFELY ENSCONCED IN THEIR UNDERCITY BUNKER—
FOUR SEKTORS DESTROYED ALREADY! DEATH TOLL OVER SEVEN MILLION! WHY ARE WE ALLOWING THEIR MISSILES TO PENETRATE?
IT IS VITAL THAT WE DRAIN AS MUCH OF THEIR STRENGTH AS WE CAN AT THIS STAGE. YOU WORRY TOO MUCH, VLAD. EVERYTHING IS GOING ACCORDING TO PLAN.

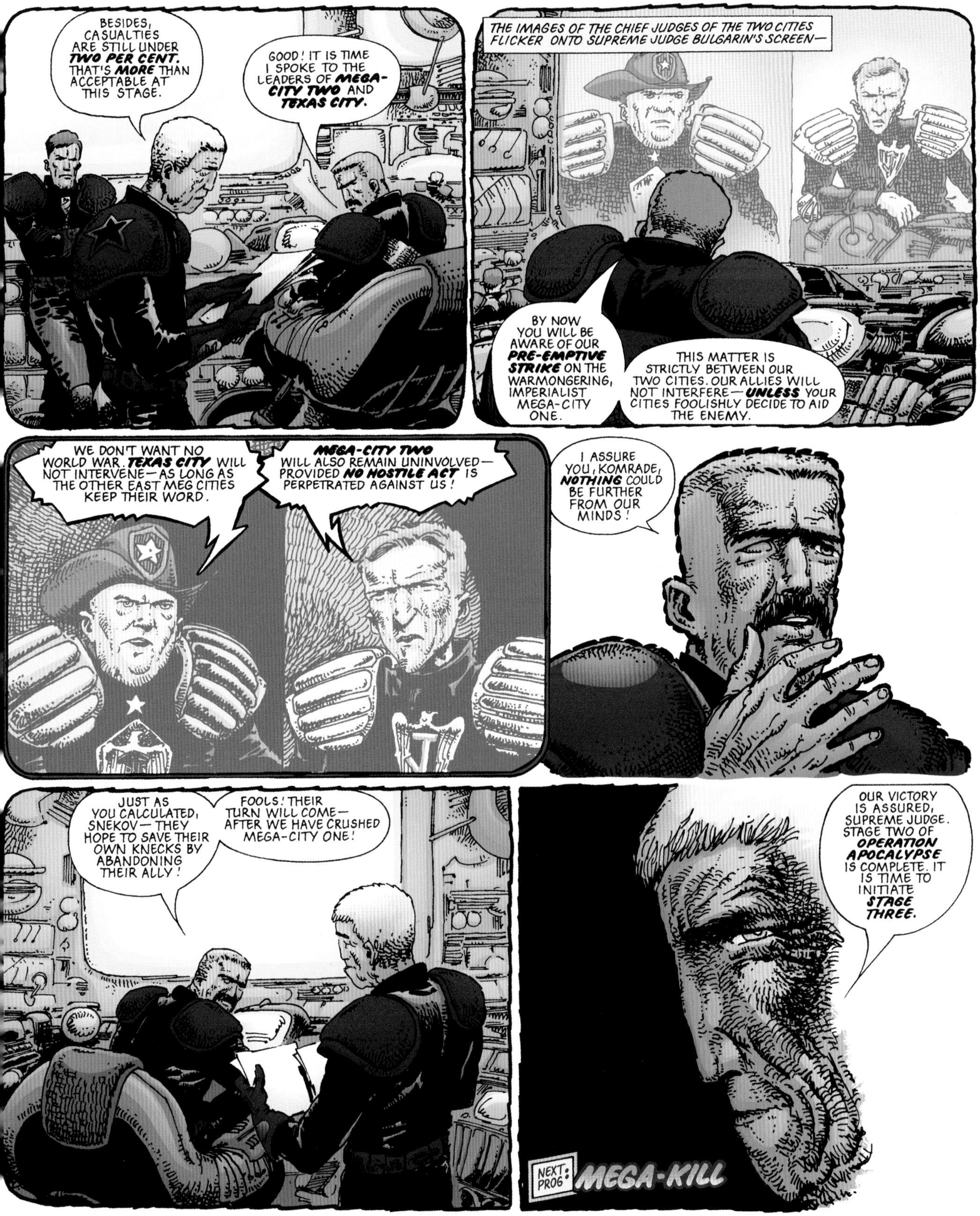
BESIDES, CASUALTIES ARE STILL UNDER **TWO PER CENT.** THAT'S **MORE** THAN ACCEPTABLE AT THIS STAGE.
GOOD! IT IS TIME I SPOKE TO THE LEADERS OF **MEGA-CITY TWO** AND **TEXAS CITY.**
THE IMAGES OF THE CHIEF JUDGES OF THE TWO CITIES FLICKER ONTO SUPREME JUDGE BULGARIN'S SCREEN—
BY NOW YOU WILL BE AWARE OF OUR **PRE-EMPTIVE STRIKE** ON THE WARMONGERING, IMPERIALIST MEGA-CITY ONE.
THIS MATTER IS STRICTLY BETWEEN OUR TWO CITIES. OUR ALLIES WILL NOT INTERFERE— **UNLESS** YOUR CITIES FOOLISHLY DECIDE TO AID THE ENEMY.
WE DON'T WANT NO WORLD WAR. **TEXAS CITY** WILL NOT INTERVENE— AS LONG AS THE OTHER EAST MEG CITIES KEEP THEIR WORD.
MEGA-CITY TWO WILL ALSO REMAIN UNINVOLVED— PROVIDED **NO HOSTILE ACT** IS PERPETRATED AGAINST US!
I ASSURE YOU, KOMRADE, **NOTHING** COULD BE FURTHER FROM OUR MINDS!
JUST AS YOU CALCULATED, SNEKOV— THEY HOPE TO SAVE THEIR OWN KNECKS BY ABANDONING THEIR ALLY!
FOOLS! THEIR TURN WILL COME— AFTER WE HAVE CRUSHED MEGA-CITY ONE!
OUR VICTORY IS ASSURED, SUPREME JUDGE. STAGE TWO OF **OPERATION APOCALYPSE** IS COMPLETE. IT IS TIME TO INITIATE **STAGE THREE.**
NEXT PROG: MEGA-KILL

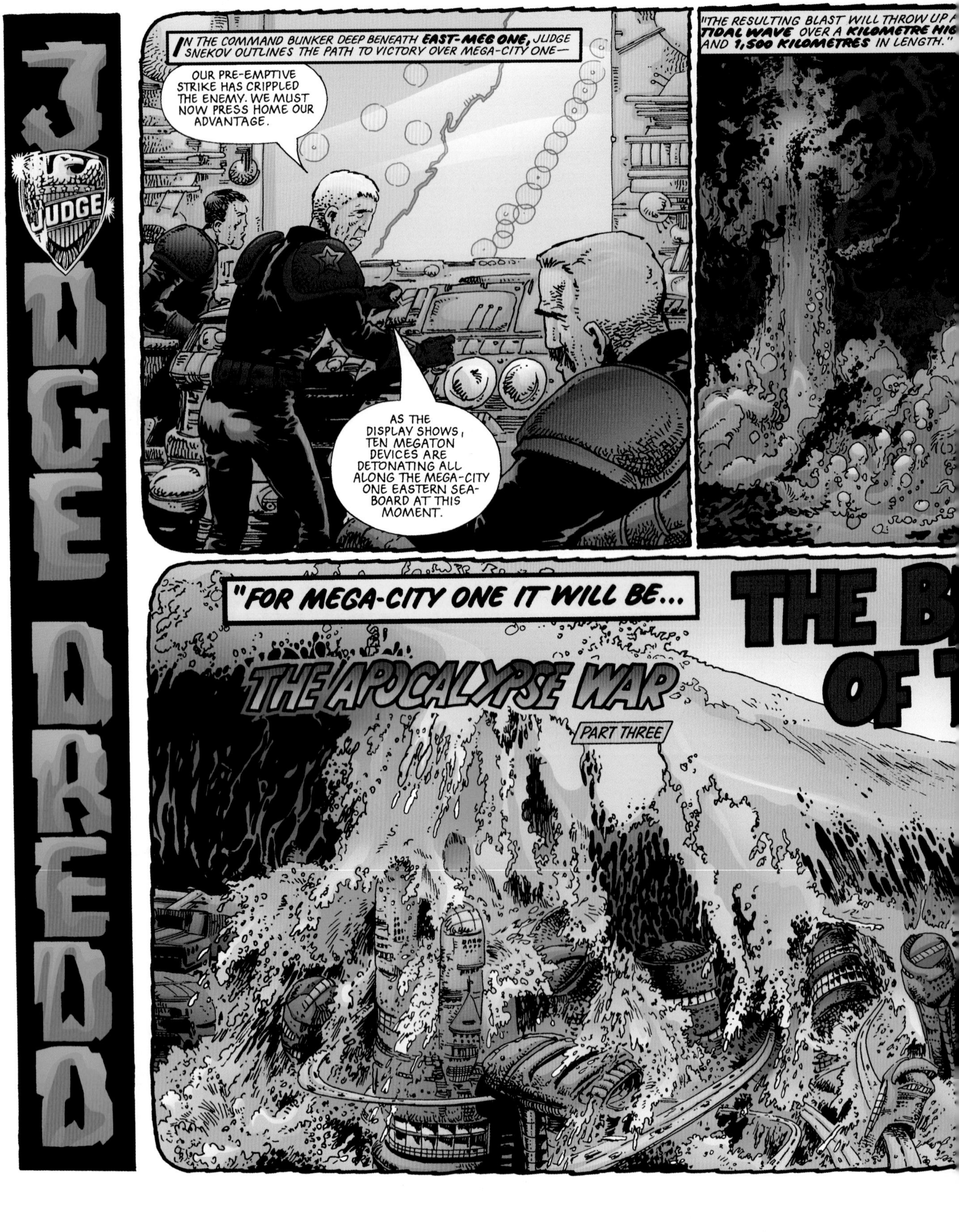
JUDGE DREDD
IN THE COMMAND BUNKER DEEP BENEATH EAST-MEG ONE, JUDGE SNEKOV OUTLINES THE PATH TO VICTORY OVER MEGA-CITY ONE—
OUR PRE-EMPTIVE STRIKE HAS CRIPPLED THE ENEMY. WE MUST NOW PRESS HOME OUR ADVANTAGE.
AS THE DISPLAY SHOWS, TEN MEGATON DEVICES ARE DETONATING ALL ALONG THE MEGA-CITY ONE EASTERN SEA-BOARD AT THIS MOMENT.
"THE RESULTING BLAST WILL THROW UP A TIDAL WAVE OVER A KILOMETRE HIG AND 1,500 KILOMETRES IN LENGTH."
"FOR MEGA-CITY ONE IT WILL BE...
THE APOCALYPSE WAR
PART THREE

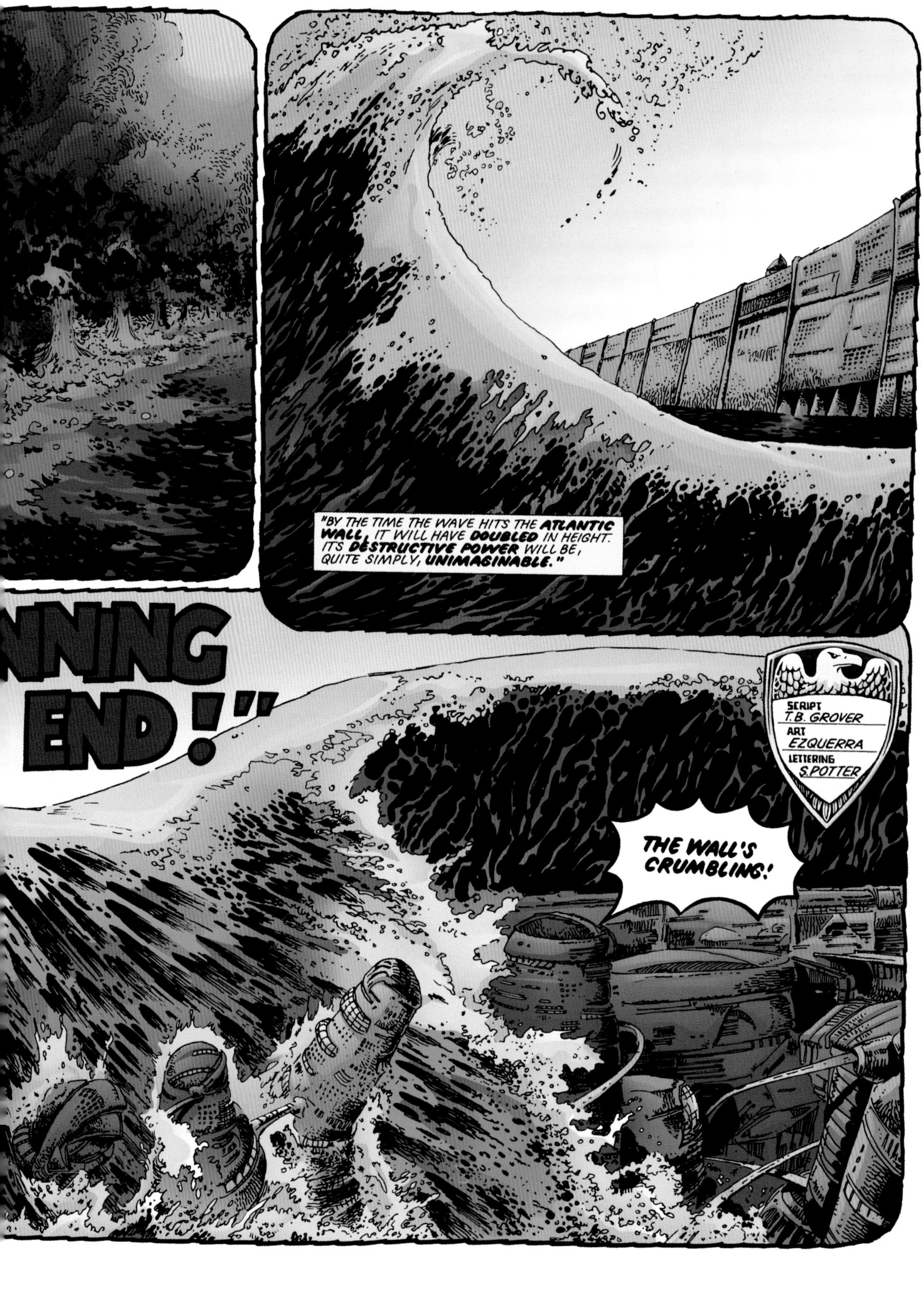

"BY THE TIME THE WAVE HITS THE ATLANTIC WALL, IT WILL HAVE DOUBLED IN HEIGHT. ITS DESTRUCTIVE POWER WILL BE, QUITE SIMPLY, UNIMAGINABLE."
NNING
END!"
SCRIPT
T.B. GROVER
ART
EZQUERRA
LETTERING
S.POTTER
THE WALL'S CRUMBLING!

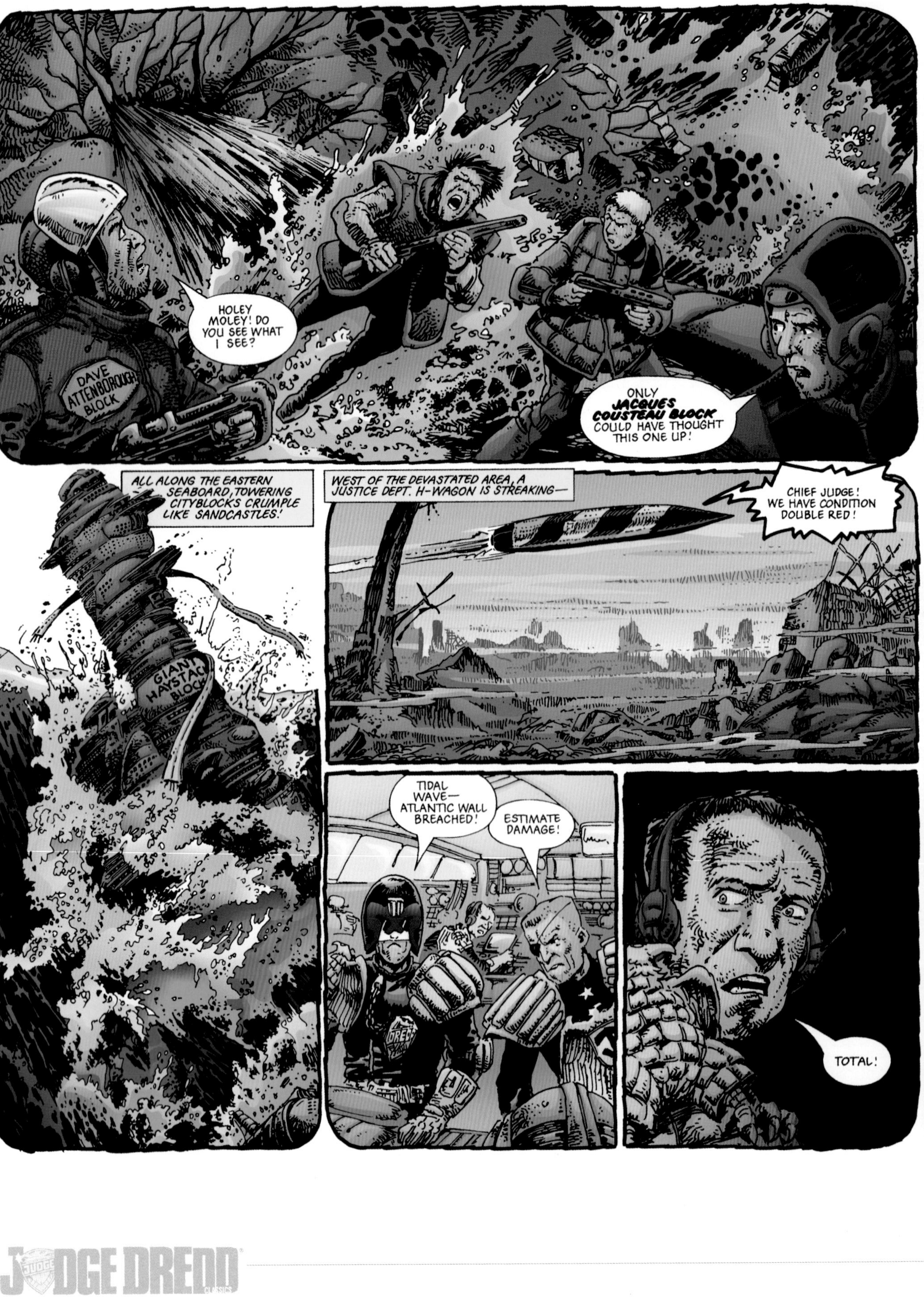
HOLEY MOLEY! DO YOU SEE WHAT I SEE?
DAVE ATTENBOROUGH BLOCK
ONLY JACQUES COUSTEAU BLOCK COULD HAVE THOUGHT THIS ONE UP!
ALL ALONG THE EASTERN SEABOARD, TOWERING CITYBLOCKS CRUMPLE LIKE SANDCASTLES!
GIANT HAYSTACK BLOCK
WEST OF THE DEVASTATED AREA, A JUSTICE DEPT. H-WAGON IS STREAKING—
CHIEF JUDGE! WE HAVE CONDITION DOUBLE RED!
TIDAL WAVE— ATLANTIC WALL BREACHED!
ESTIMATE DAMAGE!
TOTAL!

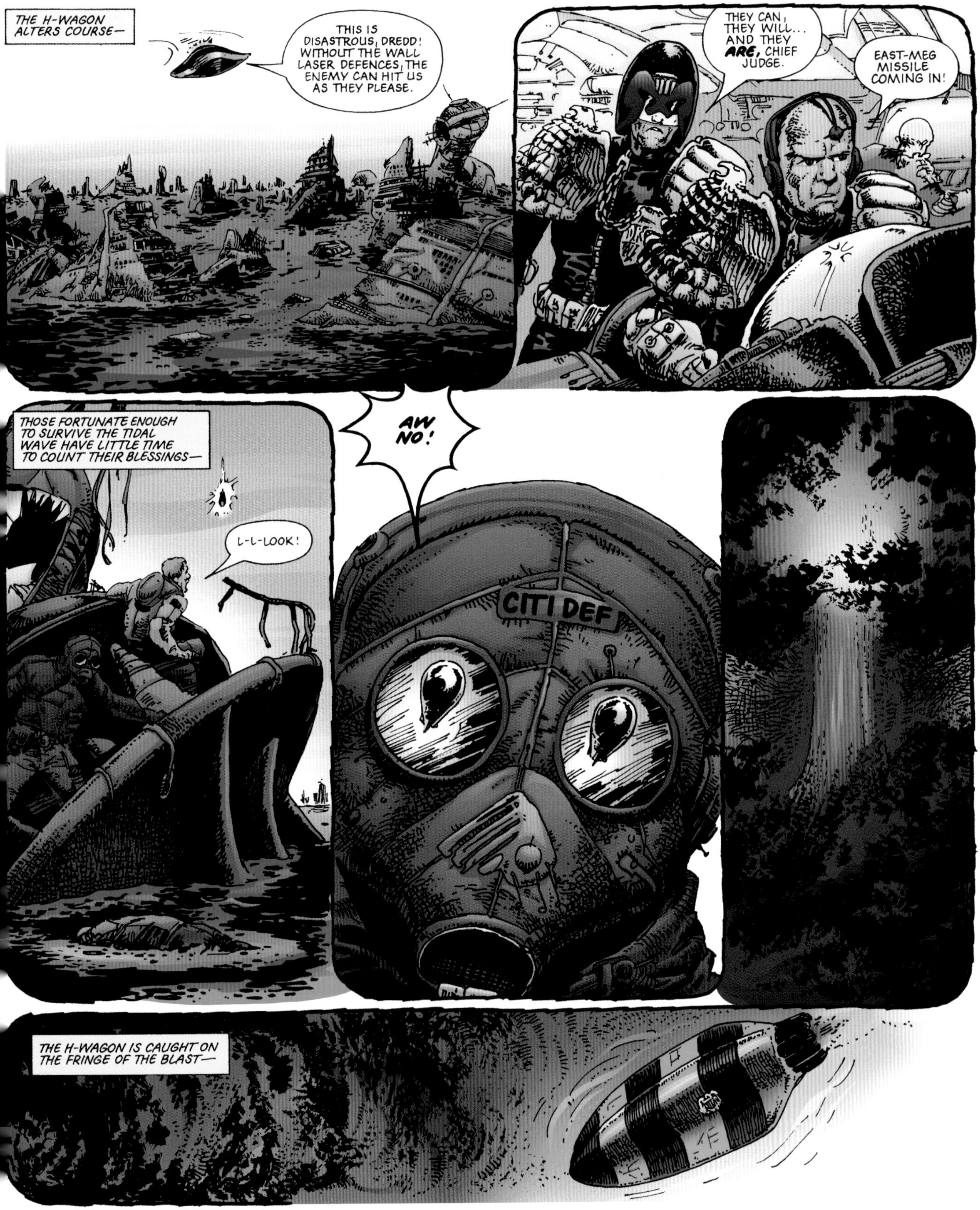

THE H-WAGON ALTERS COURSE—
THIS IS DISASTROUS, DREDD! WITHOUT THE WALL LASER DEFENCES, THE ENEMY CAN HIT US AS THEY PLEASE.
THEY CAN, THEY WILL... AND THEY ARE, CHIEF JUDGE.
EAST-MEG MISSILE COMING IN!
THOSE FORTUNATE ENOUGH TO SURVIVE THE TIDAL WAVE HAVE LITTLE TIME TO COUNT THEIR BLESSINGS—
L-L-LOOK!
AW NO!
CITI DEF
THE H-WAGON IS CAUGHT ON THE FRINGE OF THE BLAST—

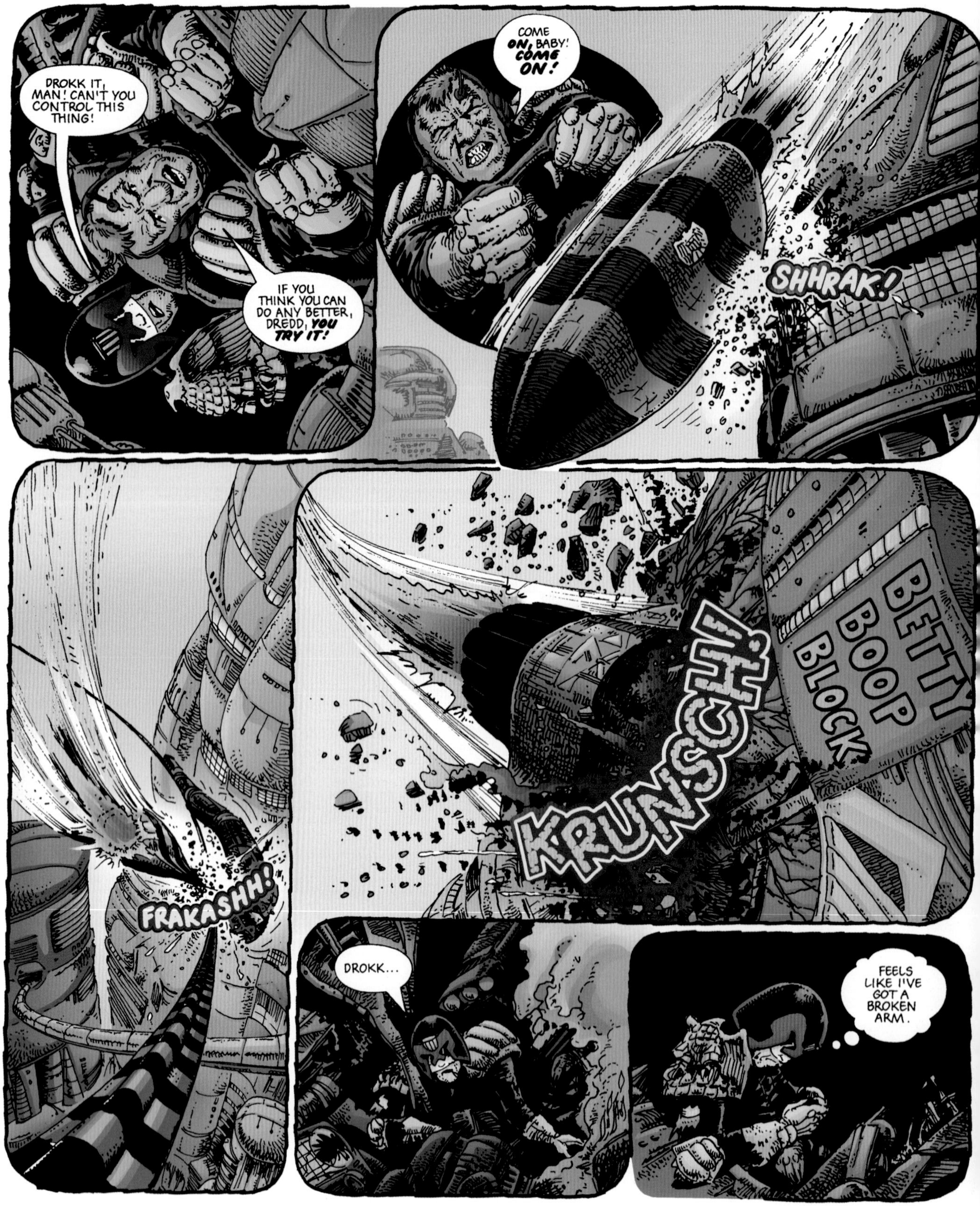
DROKK IT, MAN! CAN'T YOU CONTROL THIS THING!
IF YOU THINK YOU CAN DO ANY BETTER, DREDD, YOU TRY IT!
COME ON, BABY! COME ON!
SHHRAK!
FRAKASHH!
BETTY BOOP BLOCK
KRUNSCH!
DROKK...
FEELS LIKE I'VE GOT A BROKEN ARM.

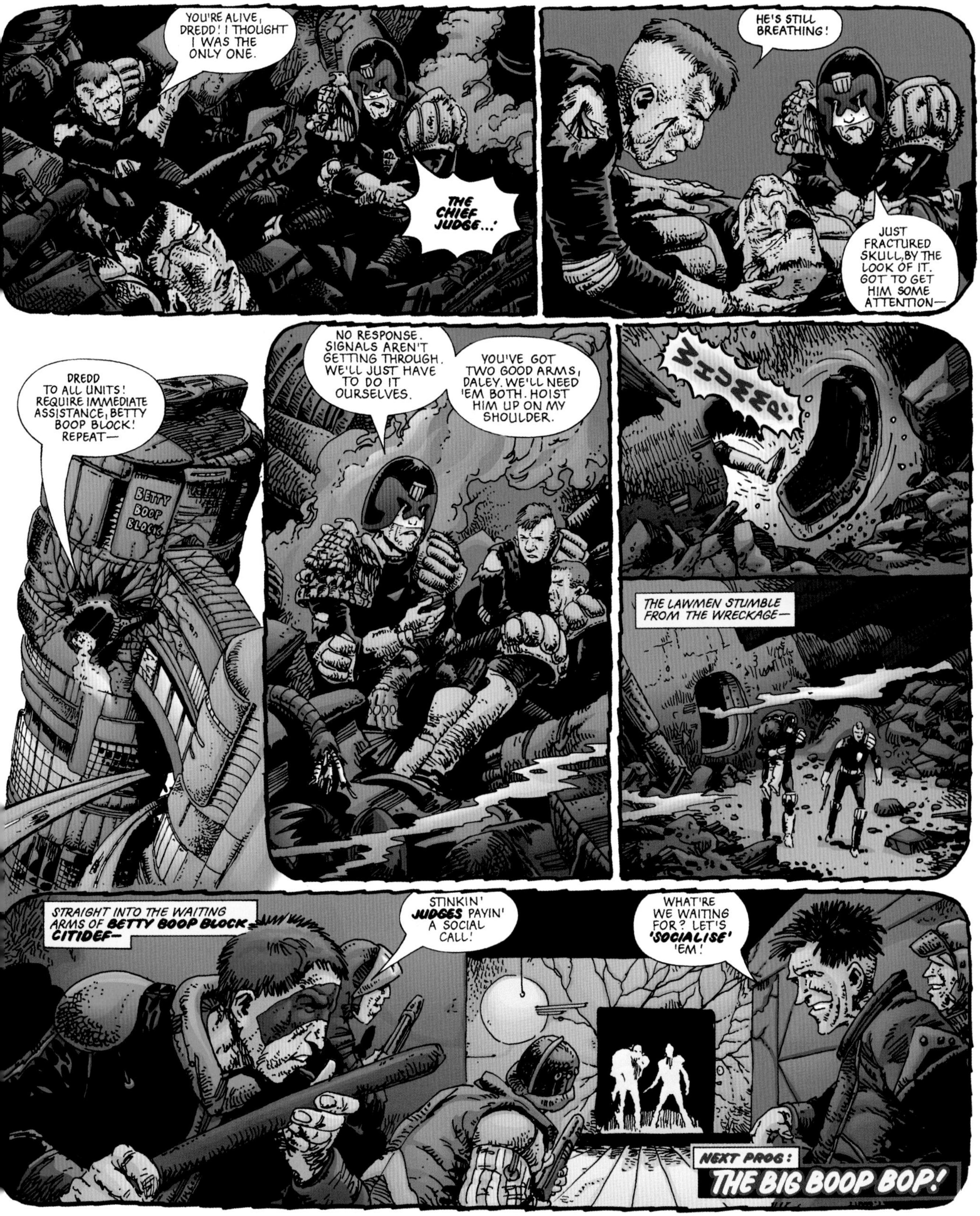
YOU'RE ALIVE, DREDD! I THOUGHT I WAS THE ONLY ONE.
'THE CHIEF JUDGE...'
HE'S STILL BREATHING!
JUST FRACTURED SKULL, BY THE LOOK OF IT. GOT TO GET HIM SOME ATTENTION—
DREDD TO ALL UNITS! REQUIRE IMMEDIATE ASSISTANCE, BETTY BOOP BLOCK! REPEAT—
BETTY BOOP BLOCK
NO RESPONSE. SIGNALS AREN'T GETTING THROUGH. WE'LL JUST HAVE TO DO IT OURSELVES.
YOU'VE GOT TWO GOOD ARMS, DALEY. WE'LL NEED 'EM BOTH. HOIST HIM UP ON MY SHOULDER.
WHUMMP!
THE LAWMEN STUMBLE FROM THE WRECKAGE—
STRAIGHT INTO THE WAITING ARMS OF BETTY BOOP BLOCK CITIDEF—
STINKIN' JUDGES PAYIN' A SOCIAL CALL!
WHAT'RE WE WAITING FOR? LET'S 'SOCIALISE' 'EM!
NEXT PROG:
THE BIG BOOP BOP!

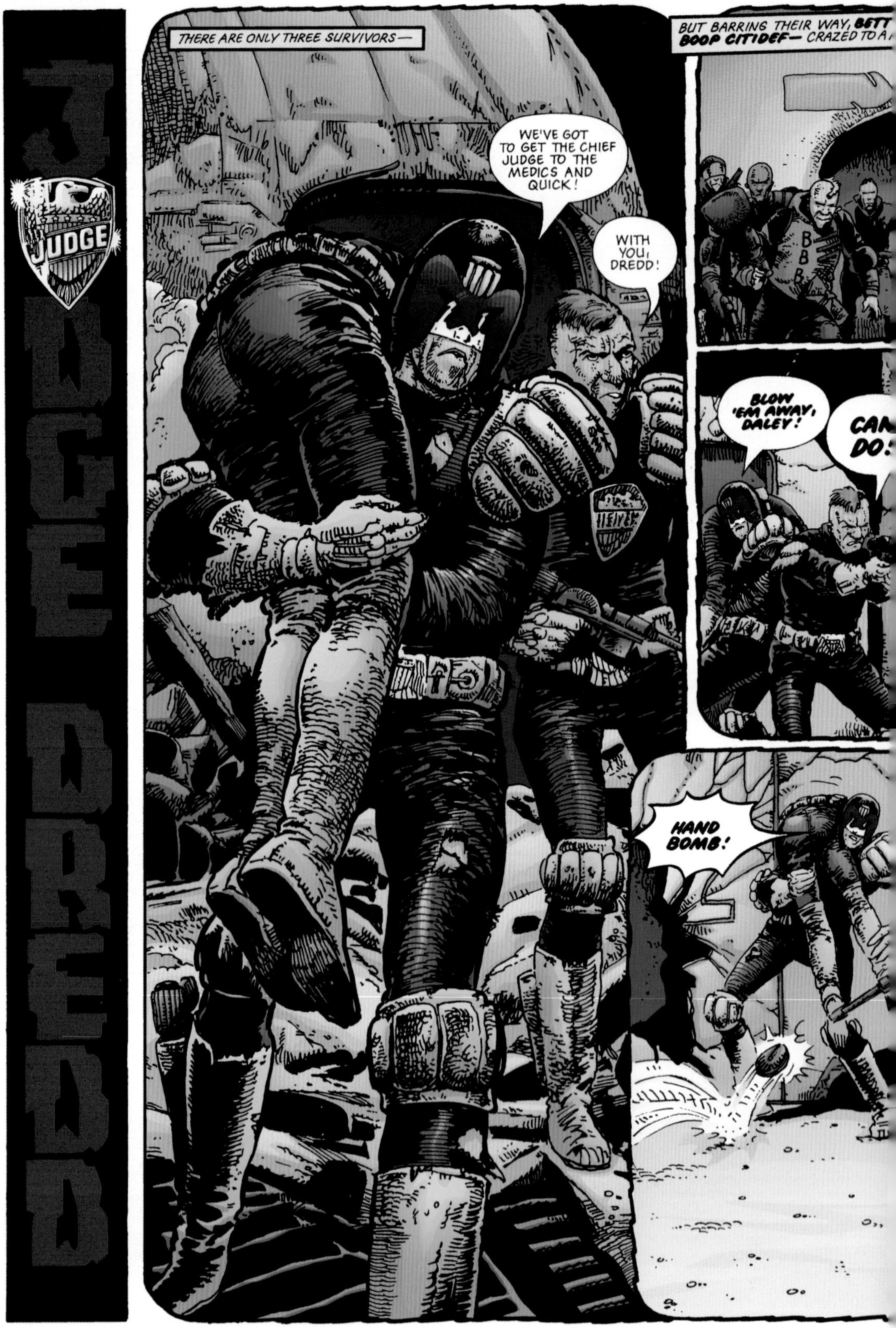
JUDGE DREDD
THERE ARE ONLY THREE SURVIVORS—
WE'VE GOT TO GET THE CHIEF JUDGE TO THE MEDICS AND QUICK!
WITH YOU, DREDD!
BUT BARRING THEIR WAY, BETT
BOOP CITIDEF— CRAZED TO A
BLOW 'EM AWAY, DALEY!
HAND BOMB!

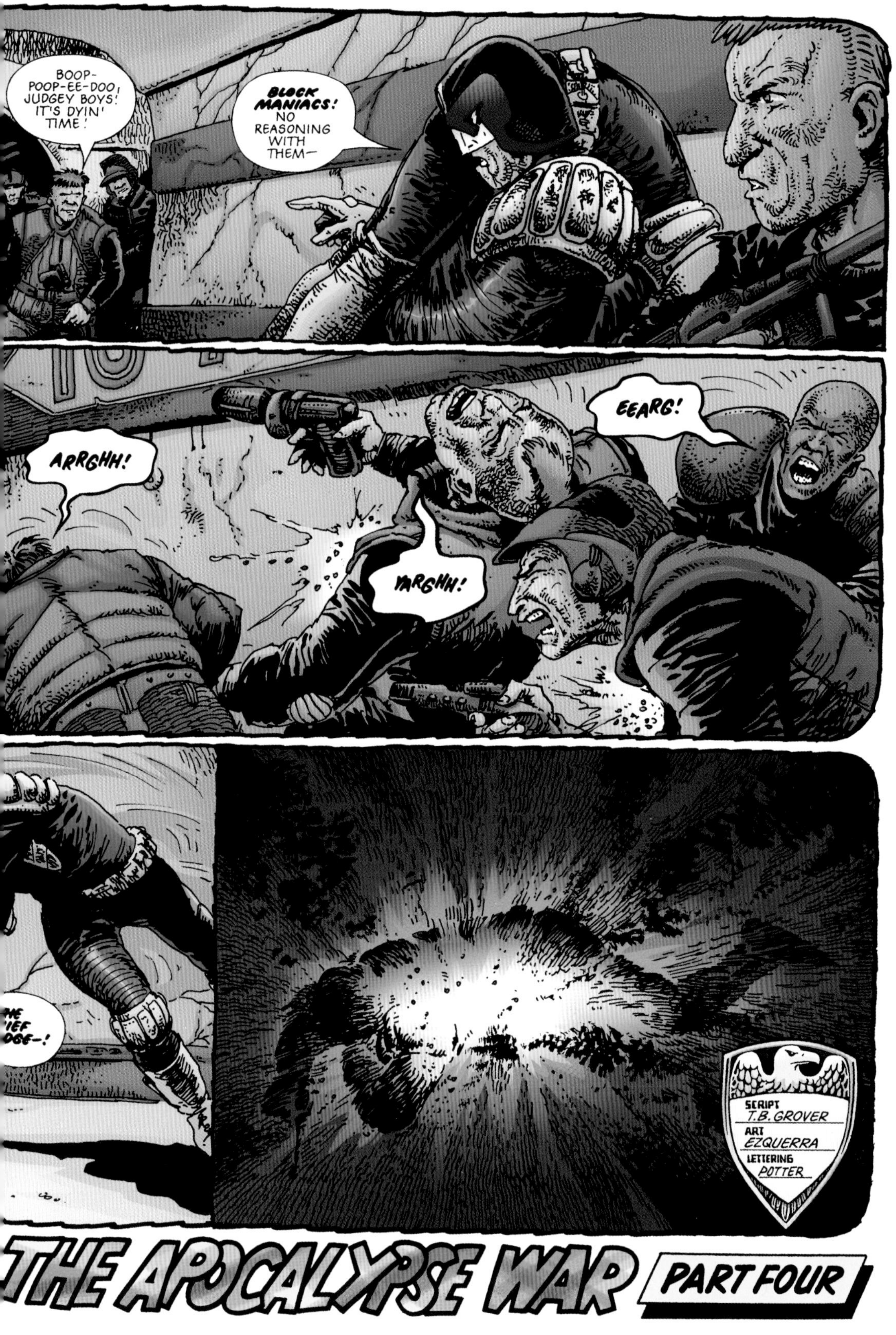
BOOP-POOP-EE-DOO, JUDGEY BOYS! IT'S DYIN' TIME!
BLOCK MANIACS! NO REASONING WITH THEM—
ARRGHH!
EEARG!
YARGHH!
SCRIPT T.B. GROVER
ART EZQUERRA
LETTERING POTTER
THE APOCALYPSE WAR
PART FOUR

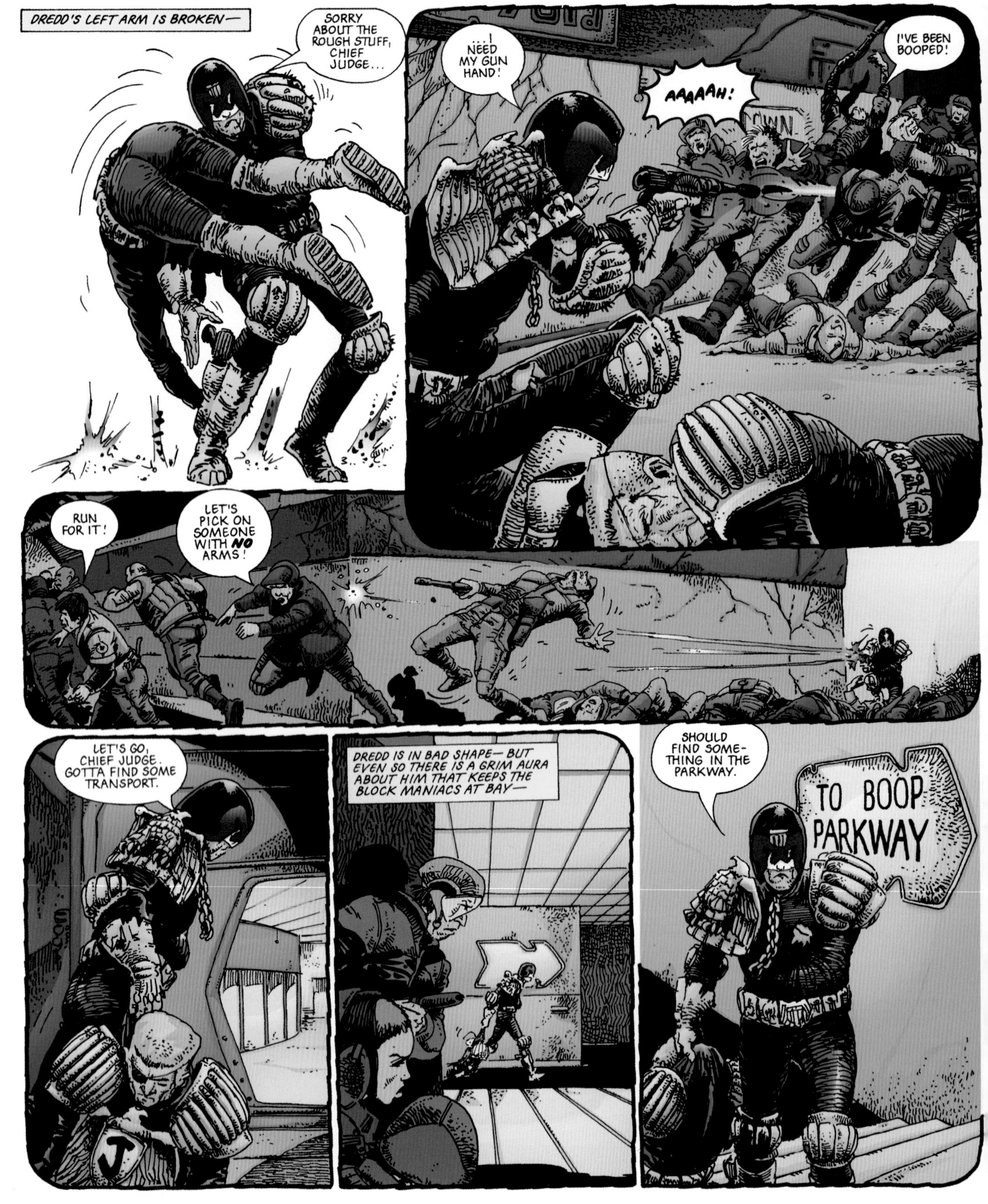
DREDD'S LEFT ARM IS BROKEN—
SORRY ABOUT THE ROUGH STUFF, CHIEF JUDGE...
...I NEED MY GUN HAND!
AAAAAH!
I'VE BEEN BOOPED!
RUN FOR IT!
LET'S PICK ON SOMEONE WITH NO ARMS!
LET'S GO, CHIEF JUDGE. GOTTA FIND SOME TRANSPORT.
DREDD IS IN BAD SHAPE— BUT EVEN SO THERE IS A GRIM AURA ABOUT HIM THAT KEEPS THE BLOCK MANIACS AT BAY—
SHOULD FIND SOMETHING IN THE PARKWAY.
TO BOOP PARKWAY

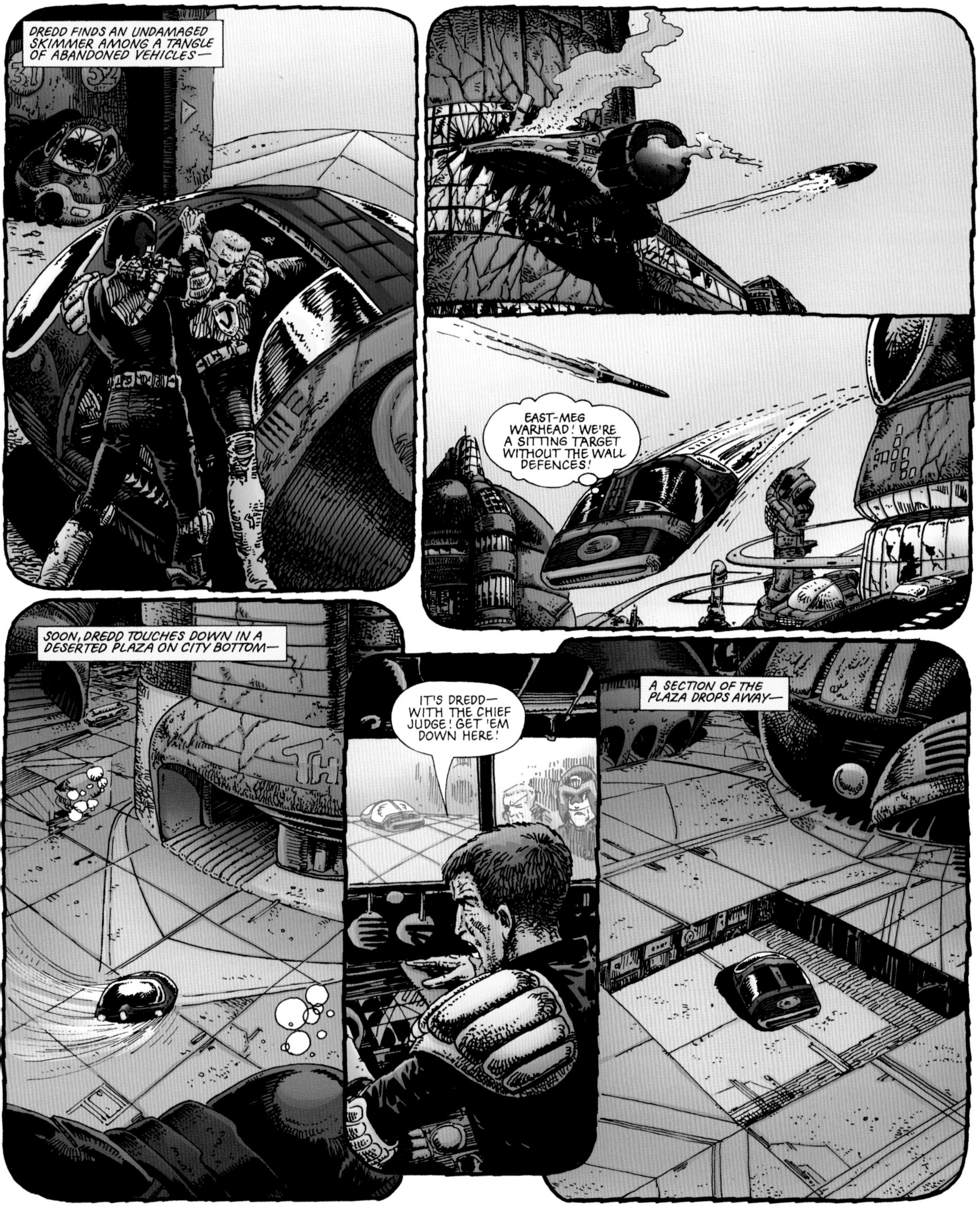
DREDD FINDS AN UNDAMAGED SKIMMER AMONG A TANGLE OF ABANDONED VEHICLES—
EAST-MEG WARHEAD! WE'RE A SITTING TARGET WITHOUT THE WALL DEFENCES!
SOON, DREDD TOUCHES DOWN IN A DESERTED PLAZA ON CITY BOTTOM—
IT'S DREDD— WITH THE CHIEF JUDGE! GET 'EM DOWN HERE!
A SECTION OF THE PLAZA DROPS AWAY—

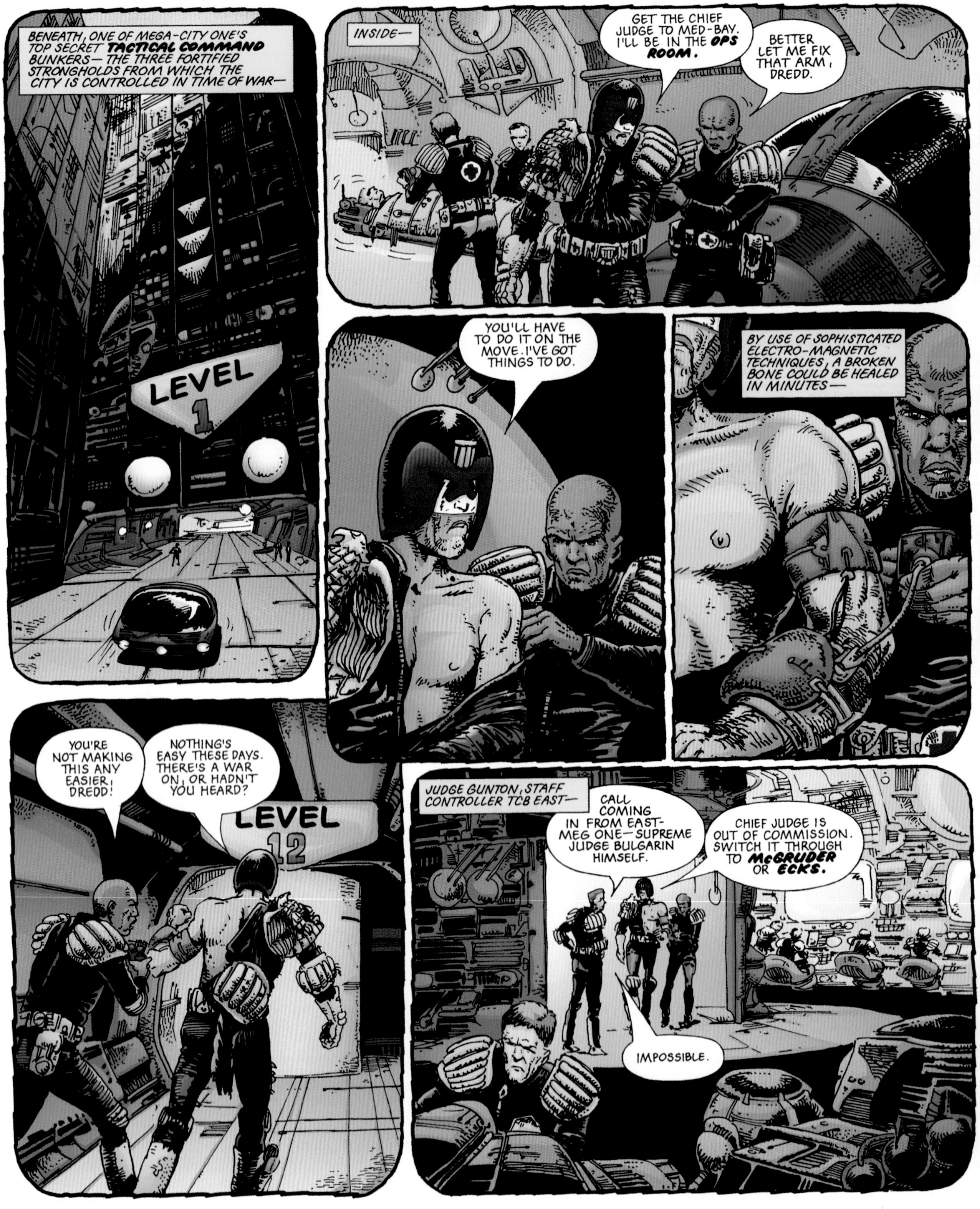
BENEATH, ONE OF MEGA-CITY ONE'S TOP SECRET TACTICAL COMMAND BUNKERS— THE THREE FORTIFIED STRONGHOLDS FROM WHICH THE CITY IS CONTROLLED IN TIME OF WAR—
LEVEL 1
INSIDE—
GET THE CHIEF JUDGE TO MED-BAY. I'LL BE IN THE OPS ROOM.
BETTER LET ME FIX THAT ARM, DREDD.
YOU'LL HAVE TO DO IT ON THE MOVE. I'VE GOT THINGS TO DO.
BY USE OF SOPHISTICATED ELECTRO-MAGNETIC TECHNIQUES, A BROKEN BONE COULD BE HEALED IN MINUTES—
YOU'RE NOT MAKING THIS ANY EASIER, DREDD!
NOTHING'S EASY THESE DAYS. THERE'S A WAR ON, OR HADN'T YOU HEARD?
LEVEL 12
JUDGE GUNTON, STAFF CONTROLLER TCB EAST—
CALL COMING IN FROM EAST-MEG ONE— SUPREME JUDGE BULGARIN HIMSELF.
CHIEF JUDGE IS OUT OF COMMISSION. SWITCH IT THROUGH TO McGRUDER OR ECKS.
IMPOSSIBLE.

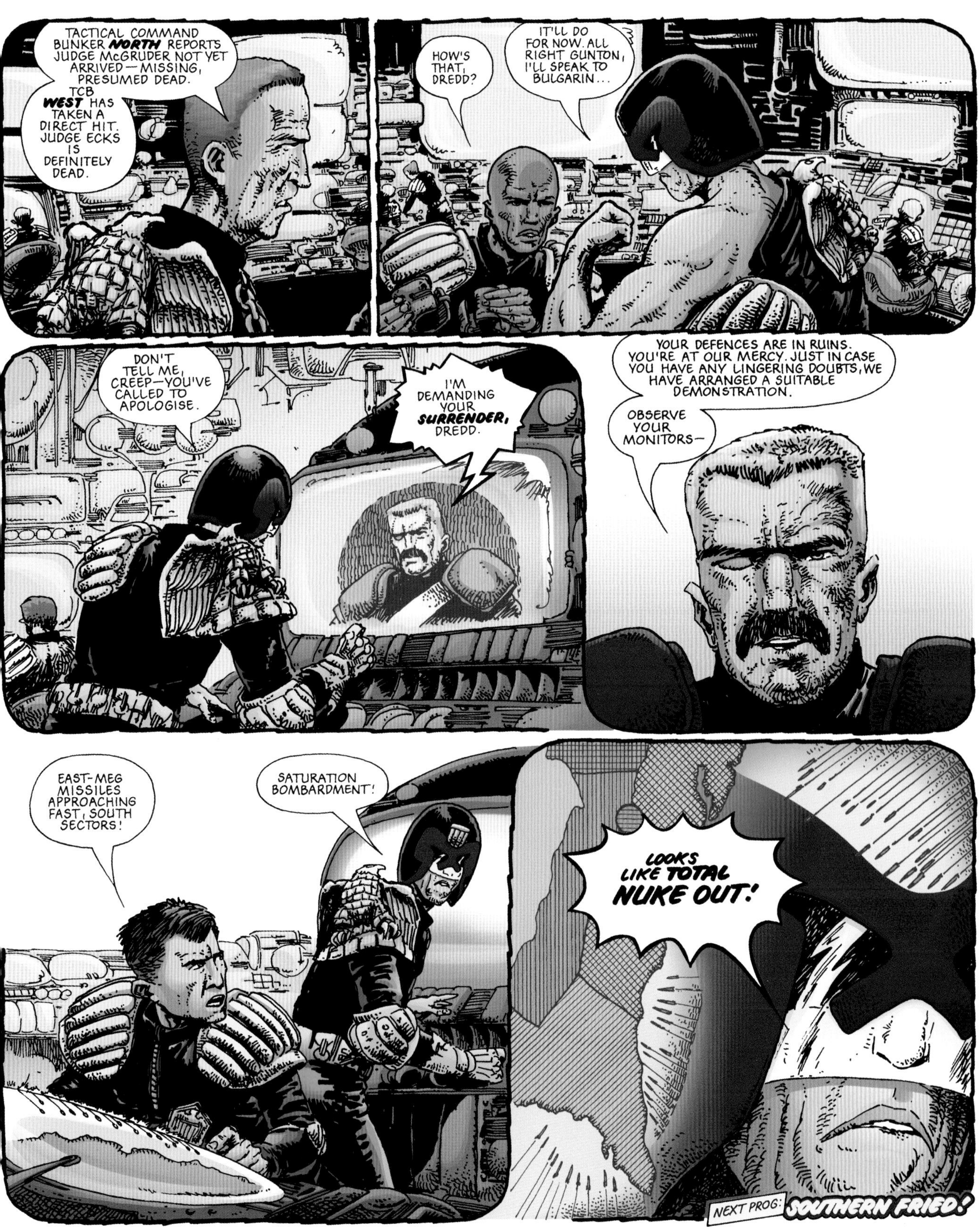

TACTICAL COMMAND BUNKER NORTH REPORTS JUDGE McGRUDER NOT YET ARRIVED—MISSING, PRESUMED DEAD.
TCB WEST HAS TAKEN A DIRECT HIT. JUDGE ECKS IS DEFINITELY DEAD.
HOW'S THAT, DREDD?
IT'LL DO FOR NOW. ALL RIGHT GUNTON, I'LL SPEAK TO BULGARIN...
DON'T TELL ME, CREEP—YOU'VE CALLED TO APOLOGISE.
I'M DEMANDING YOUR SURRENDER, DREDD.
YOUR DEFENCES ARE IN RUINS. YOU'RE AT OUR MERCY. JUST IN CASE YOU HAVE ANY LINGERING DOUBTS, WE HAVE ARRANGED A SUITABLE DEMONSTRATION.
OBSERVE YOUR MONITORS—
EAST-MEG MISSILES APPROACHING FAST, SOUTH SECTORS!
SATURATION BOMBARDMENT!
LOOKS LIKE TOTAL NUKE OUT!
NEXT PROG: SOUTHERN FRIED!

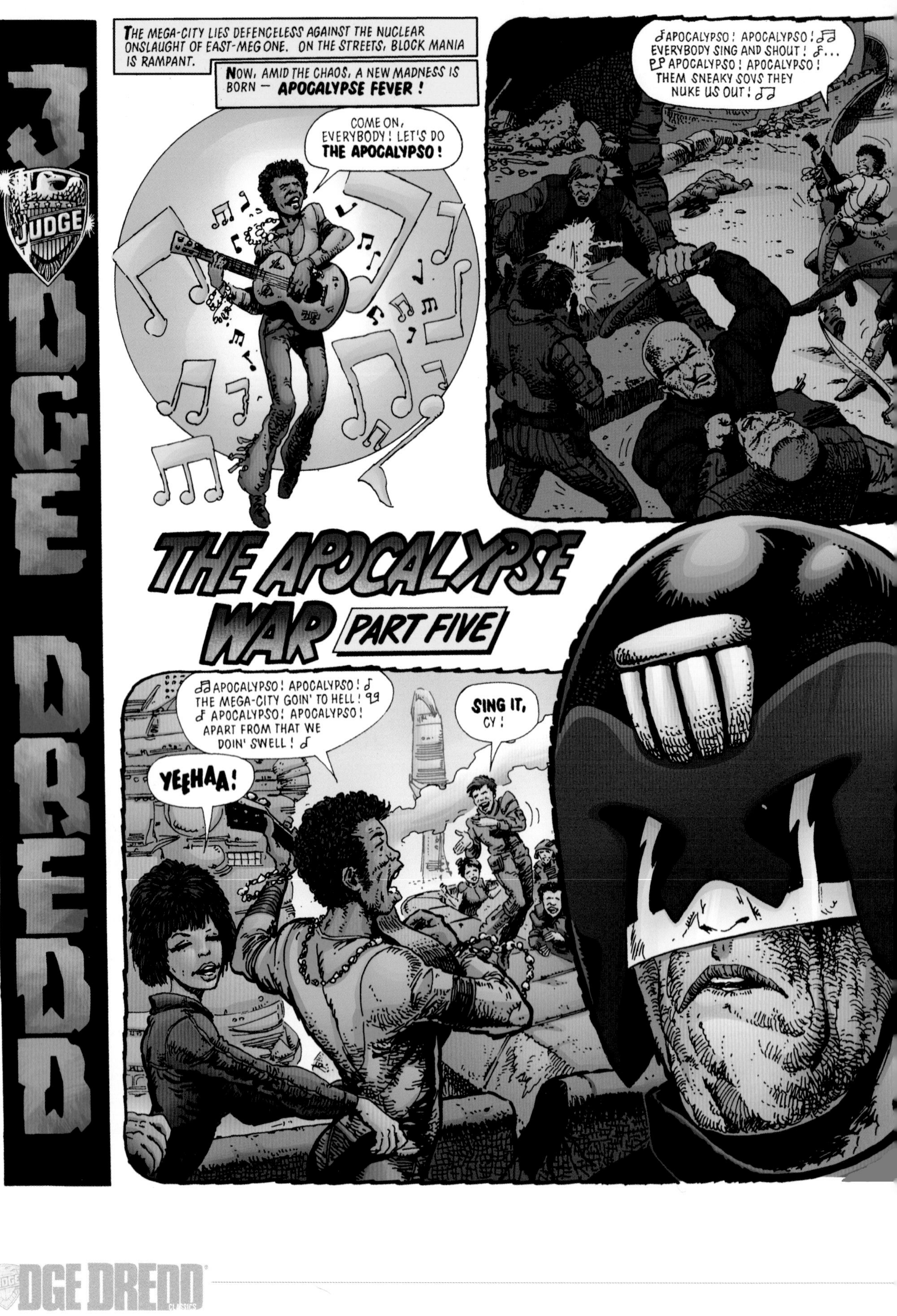
JUDGE DREDD
THE MEGA-CITY LIES DEFENCELESS AGAINST THE NUCLEAR ONSLAUGHT OF EAST-MEG ONE. ON THE STREETS, BLOCK MANIA IS RAMPANT.
NOW, AMID THE CHAOS, A NEW MADNESS IS BORN — APOCALYPSE FEVER!
COME ON, EVERYBODY! LET'S DO THE APOCALYPSO!
APOCALYPSO! APOCALYPSO! EVERYBODY SING AND SHOUT! ... APOCALYPSO! APOCALYPSO! THEM SNEAKY SOVS THEY NUKE US OUT!
THE APOCALYPSE WAR PART FIVE
APOCALYPSO! APOCALYPSO! THE MEGA-CITY GOIN' TO HELL! APOCALYPSO! APOCALYPSO! APART FROM THAT WE DOIN' SWELL!
YEEHAA!
SING IT, CY!

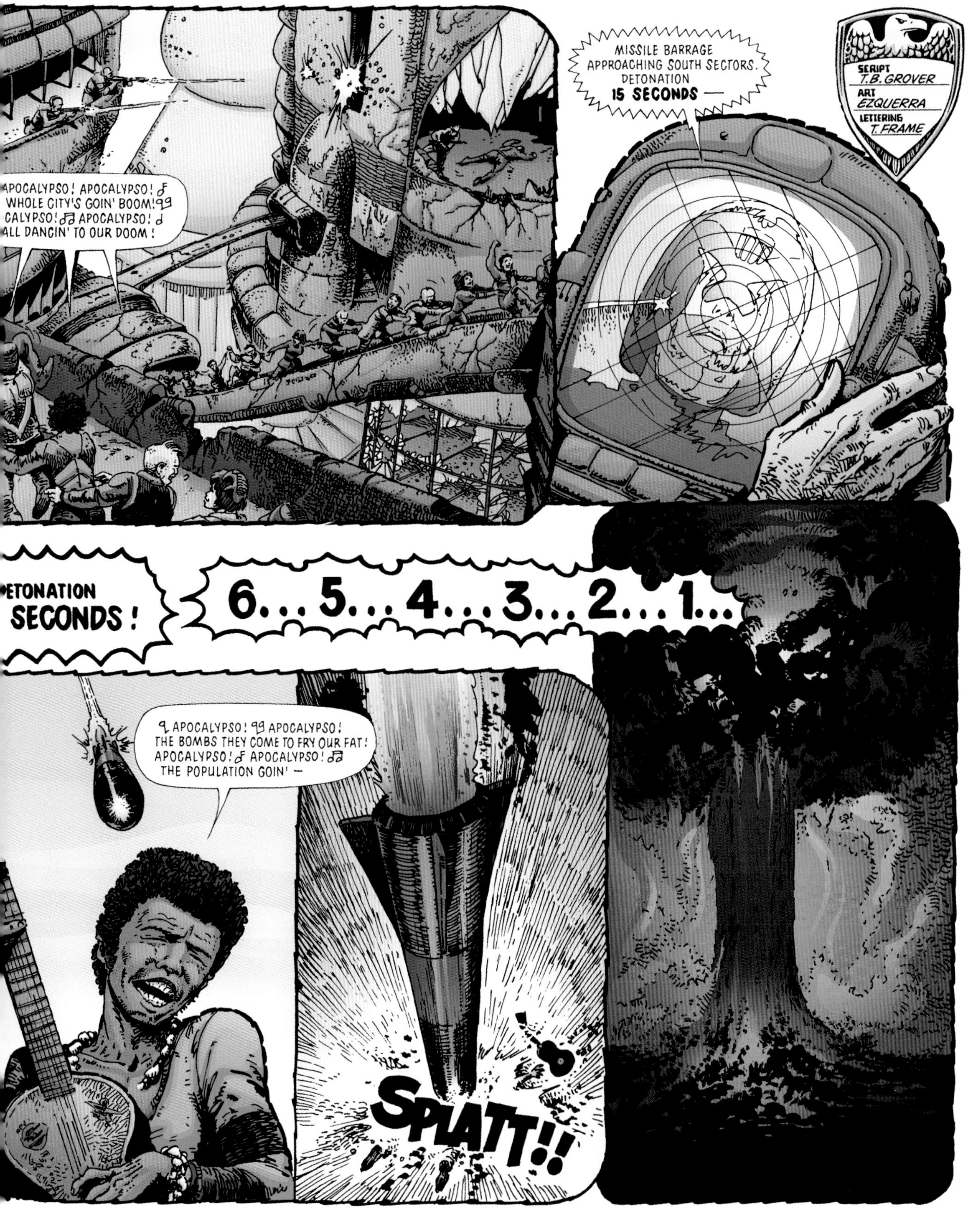

SCRIPT T.B. GROVER
ART EZQUERRA
LETTERING T. FRAME
APOCALYPSO! APOCALYPSO! WHOLE CITY'S GOIN' BOOM! CALYPSO! APOCALYPSO! ALL DANCIN' TO OUR DOOM!
MISSILE BARRAGE APPROACHING SOUTH SECTORS. DETONATION 15 SECONDS —
ETONATION SECONDS!
6... 5... 4... 3... 2... 1...
APOCALYPSO! APOCALYPSO! THE BOMBS THEY COME TO FRY OUR FAT! APOCALYPSO! APOCALYPSO! THE POPULATION GOIN' —
SPLATT!!

IN A TACTICAL COMMAND BUNKER DEEP BENEATH THE CITY —

THOSE MURDERING EAST-MEGGERS! EVERY SECTOR SOUTH OF THE 35TH PARALLEL — **NUKED OUT!**

GET A GRIP ON YOURSELF, HACKETT!

DON'T YOU UNDERSTAND, DREDD! WE'RE TALKING ABOUT 150 MILLION PEOPLE! WIPED OUT — JUST LIKE THAT!

IT-IT'S MONSTROUS! I CAN'T BELIEVE IT — I WON'T!

PRONE TO HYSTERIA. SOMEBODY AT THE ACADEMY SHOULD HAVE SPOTTED IT.

SOMEWHAT UNDERSTANDABLE UNDER THE CIRCUMSTANCES.

GET HIM TO MED-BAY.

ON SCREEN FROM EAST-MEG ONE, **SUPREME JUDGE JOSEF BULGARIN** —

YOU'RE BEATEN, DREDD. ADMIT IT! WE HAVE THE CAPABILITY TO DESTROY **EVERY SECTOR** IN YOUR CITY.

YOU'RE OUT OF YOUR TINY MIND, BULGARIN! YOU MUST REALISE **NO-ONE** CAN WIN THIS WAR!

THERE IS NO MORE TO BE SAID. YOU HAVE OUR TERMS: **UNCONDITIONAL SURRENDER — OR THE APOCALYPSE!**

SURRENDER? AND CONDEMN MY CITY TO SOV-BLOCK SLAVERY? **NEVER!**

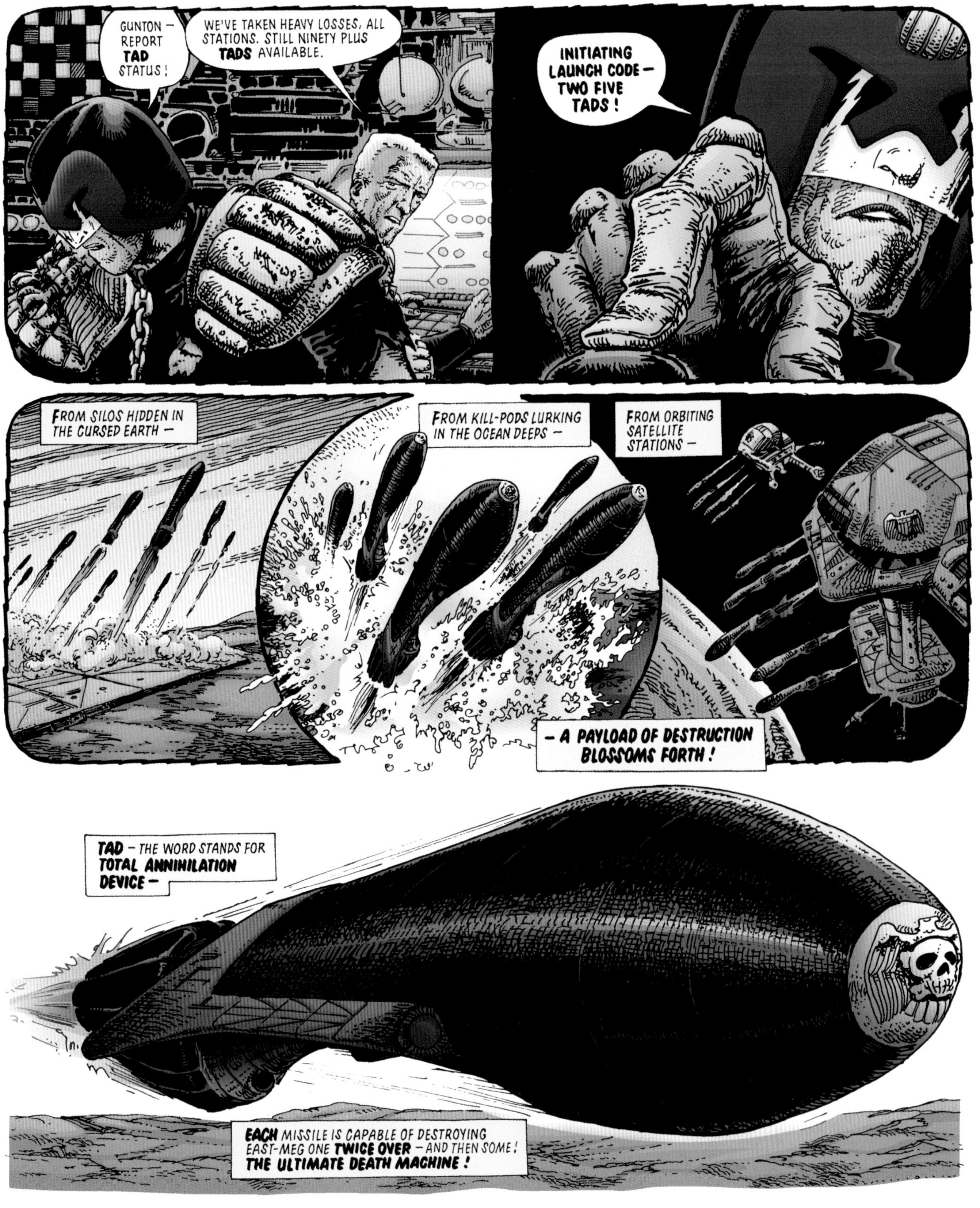
GUNTON — REPORT TAD STATUS!
WE'VE TAKEN HEAVY LOSSES, ALL STATIONS. STILL NINETY PLUS TADS AVAILABLE.
INITIATING LAUNCH CODE — TWO FIVE TADS!
FROM SILOS HIDDEN IN THE CURSED EARTH —
FROM KILL-PODS LURKING IN THE OCEAN DEEPS —
FROM ORBITING SATELLITE STATIONS —
— A PAYLOAD OF DESTRUCTION BLOSSOMS FORTH!
TAD — THE WORD STANDS FOR TOTAL ANNIHILATION DEVICE —
EACH MISSILE IS CAPABLE OF DESTROYING EAST-MEG ONE TWICE OVER — AND THEN SOME! THE ULTIMATE DEATH MACHINE!

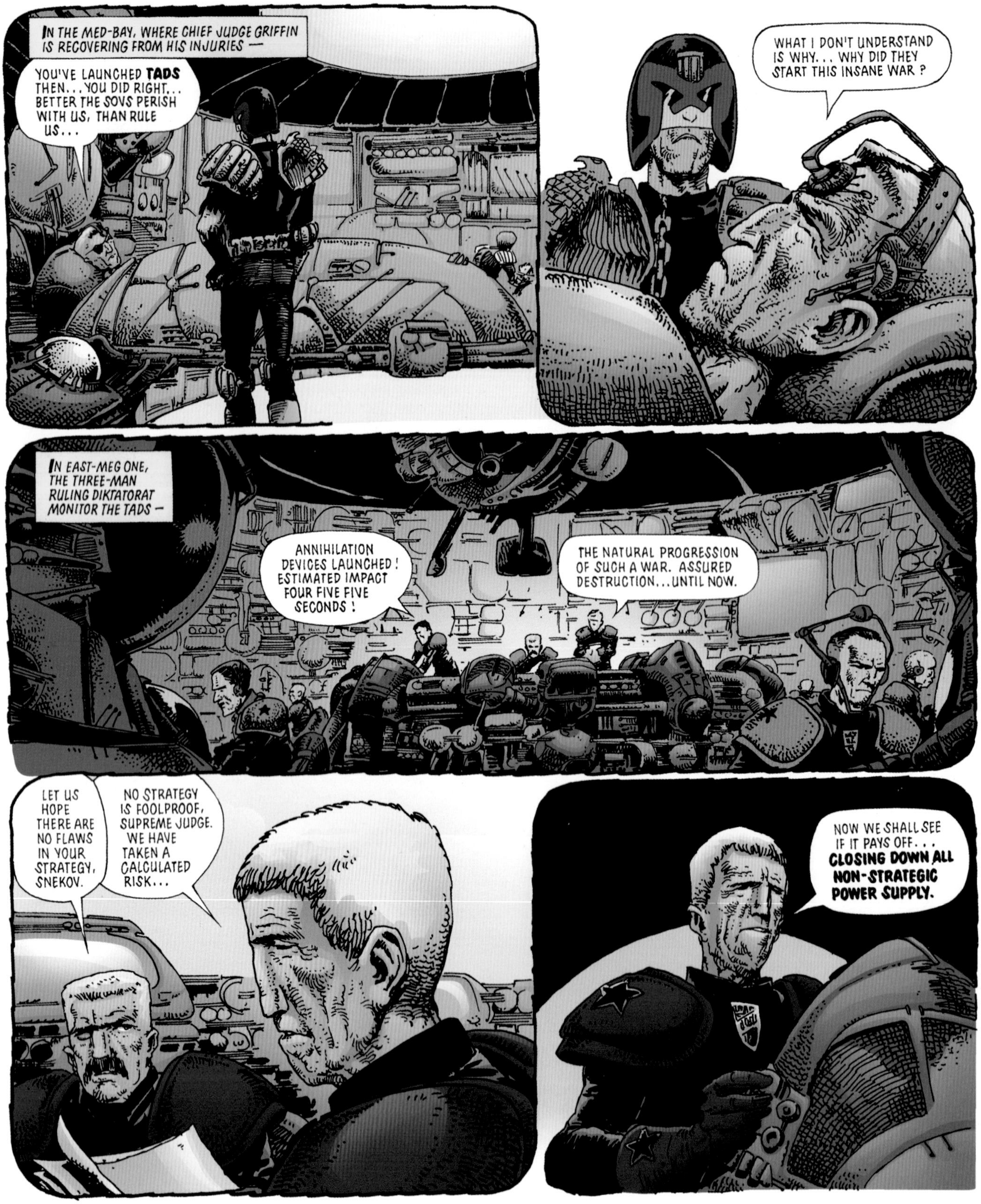
IN THE MED-BAY, WHERE CHIEF JUDGE GRIFFIN IS RECOVERING FROM HIS INJURIES —
YOU'VE LAUNCHED TADS THEN... YOU DID RIGHT... BETTER THE SOVS PERISH WITH US, THAN RULE US...
WHAT I DON'T UNDERSTAND IS WHY... WHY DID THEY START THIS INSANE WAR ?
IN EAST-MEG ONE, THE THREE-MAN RULING DIKTATORAT MONITOR THE TADS —
ANNIHILATION DEVICES LAUNCHED ! ESTIMATED IMPACT FOUR FIVE FIVE SECONDS !
THE NATURAL PROGRESSION OF SUCH A WAR. ASSURED DESTRUCTION... UNTIL NOW.
LET US HOPE THERE ARE NO FLAWS IN YOUR STRATEGY, SNEKOV.
NO STRATEGY IS FOOLPROOF, SUPREME JUDGE. WE HAVE TAKEN A CALCULATED RISK...
NOW WE SHALL SEE IF IT PAYS OFF... CLOSING DOWN ALL NON-STRATEGIC POWER SUPPLY.

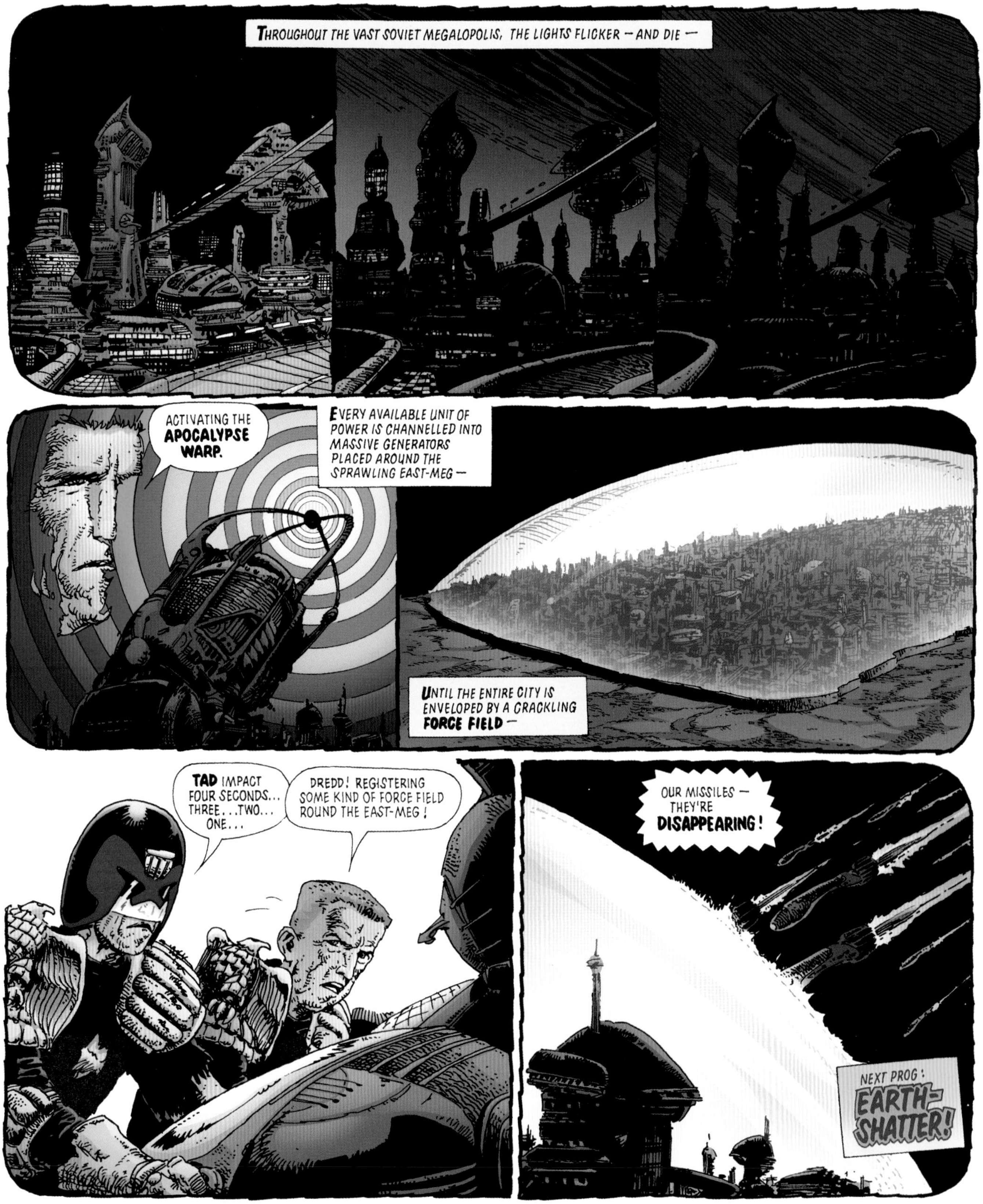
THROUGHOUT THE VAST SOVIET MEGALOPOLIS, THE LIGHTS FLICKER — AND DIE —
ACTIVATING THE APOCALYPSE WARP.
EVERY AVAILABLE UNIT OF POWER IS CHANNELLED INTO MASSIVE GENERATORS PLACED AROUND THE SPRAWLING EAST-MEG —
UNTIL THE ENTIRE CITY IS ENVELOPED BY A CRACKLING FORCE FIELD —
TAD IMPACT FOUR SECONDS... THREE...TWO... ONE...
DREDD! REGISTERING SOME KIND OF FORCE FIELD ROUND THE EAST-MEG!
OUR MISSILES — THEY'RE DISAPPEARING!
NEXT PROG: EARTH-SHATTER!

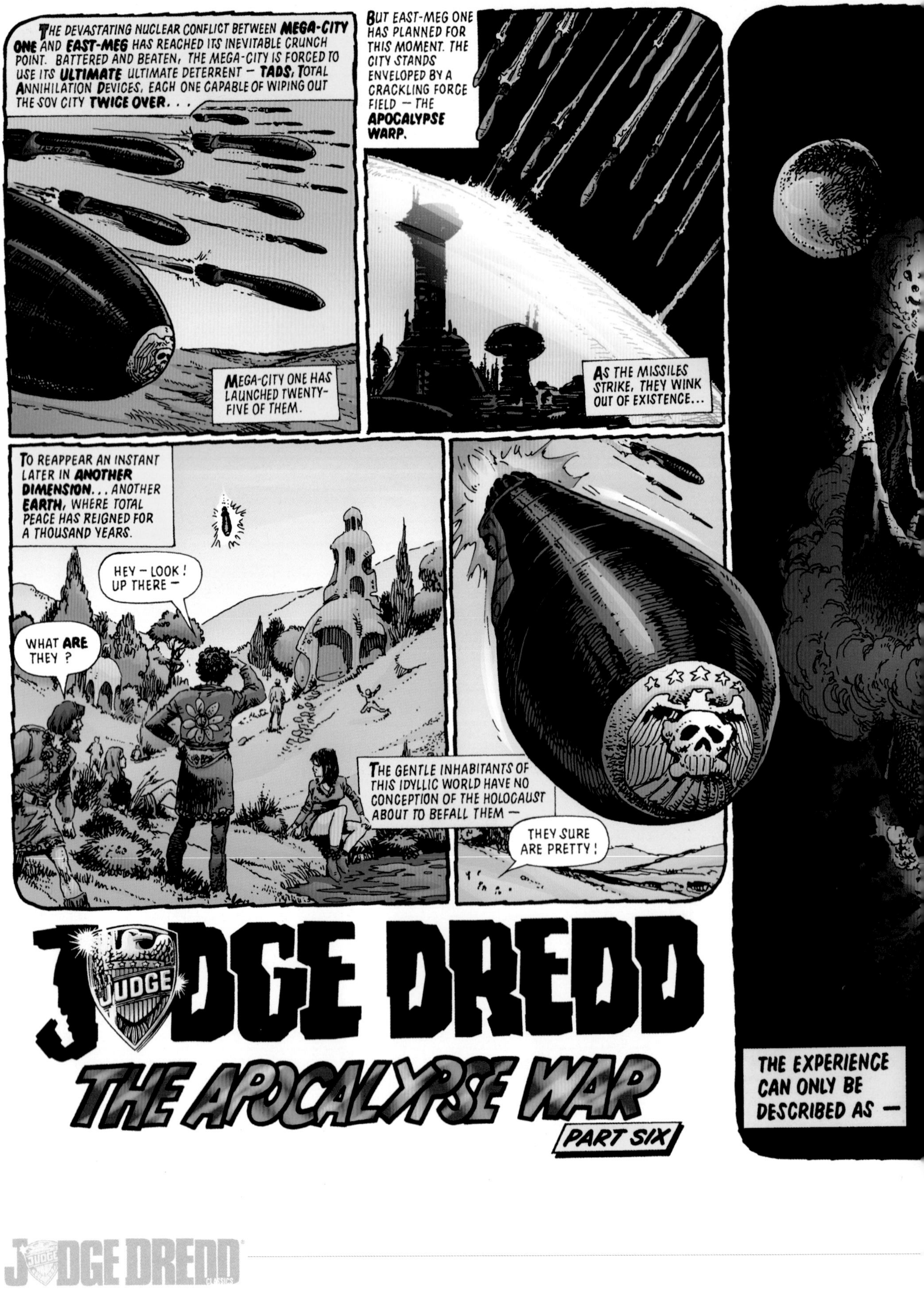
THE DEVASTATING NUCLEAR CONFLICT BETWEEN MEGA-CITY ONE AND EAST-MEG HAS REACHED ITS INEVITABLE CRUNCH POINT. BATTERED AND BEATEN, THE MEGA-CITY IS FORCED TO USE ITS ULTIMATE ULTIMATE DETERRENT — TADS, TOTAL ANNIHILATION DEVICES, EACH ONE CAPABLE OF WIPING OUT THE SOV CITY TWICE OVER. . .
MEGA-CITY ONE HAS LAUNCHED TWENTY-FIVE OF THEM.
BUT EAST-MEG ONE HAS PLANNED FOR THIS MOMENT. THE CITY STANDS ENVELOPED BY A CRACKLING FORCE FIELD — THE APOCALYPSE WARP.
AS THE MISSILES STRIKE, THEY WINK OUT OF EXISTENCE...
TO REAPPEAR AN INSTANT LATER IN ANOTHER DIMENSION. . . ANOTHER EARTH, WHERE TOTAL PEACE HAS REIGNED FOR A THOUSAND YEARS.
HEY — LOOK! UP THERE —
WHAT ARE THEY ?
THE GENTLE INHABITANTS OF THIS IDYLLIC WORLD HAVE NO CONCEPTION OF THE HOLOCAUST ABOUT TO BEFALL THEM —
THEY SURE ARE PRETTY!
JUDGE DREDD
THE APOCALYPSE WAR
PART SIX
THE EXPERIENCE CAN ONLY BE DESCRIBED AS —

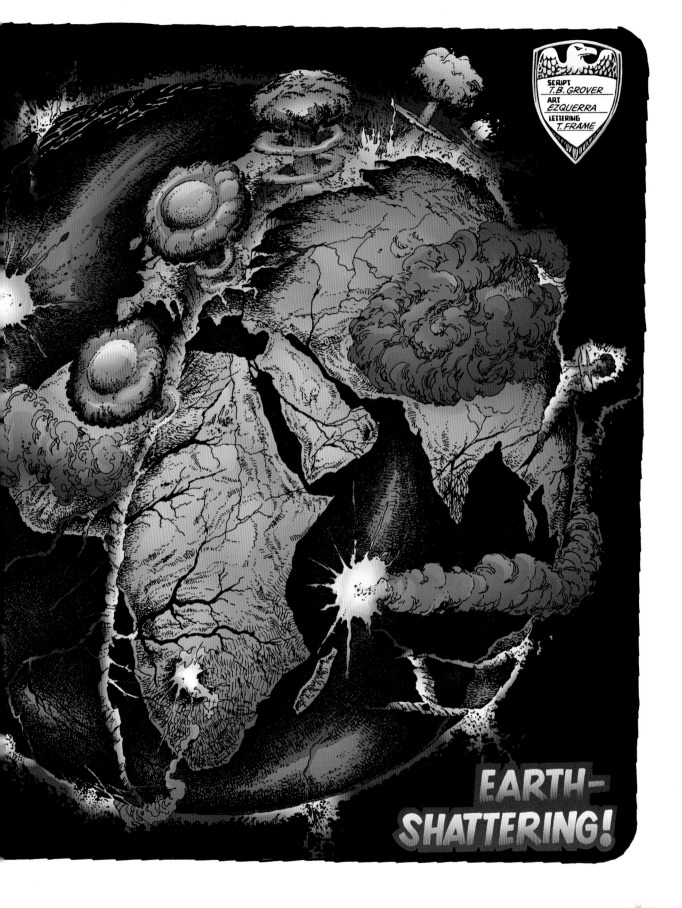

SCRIPT
T.B. GROVER
ART
EZQUERRA
LETTERING
T. FRAME

EARTH-
SHATTERING!

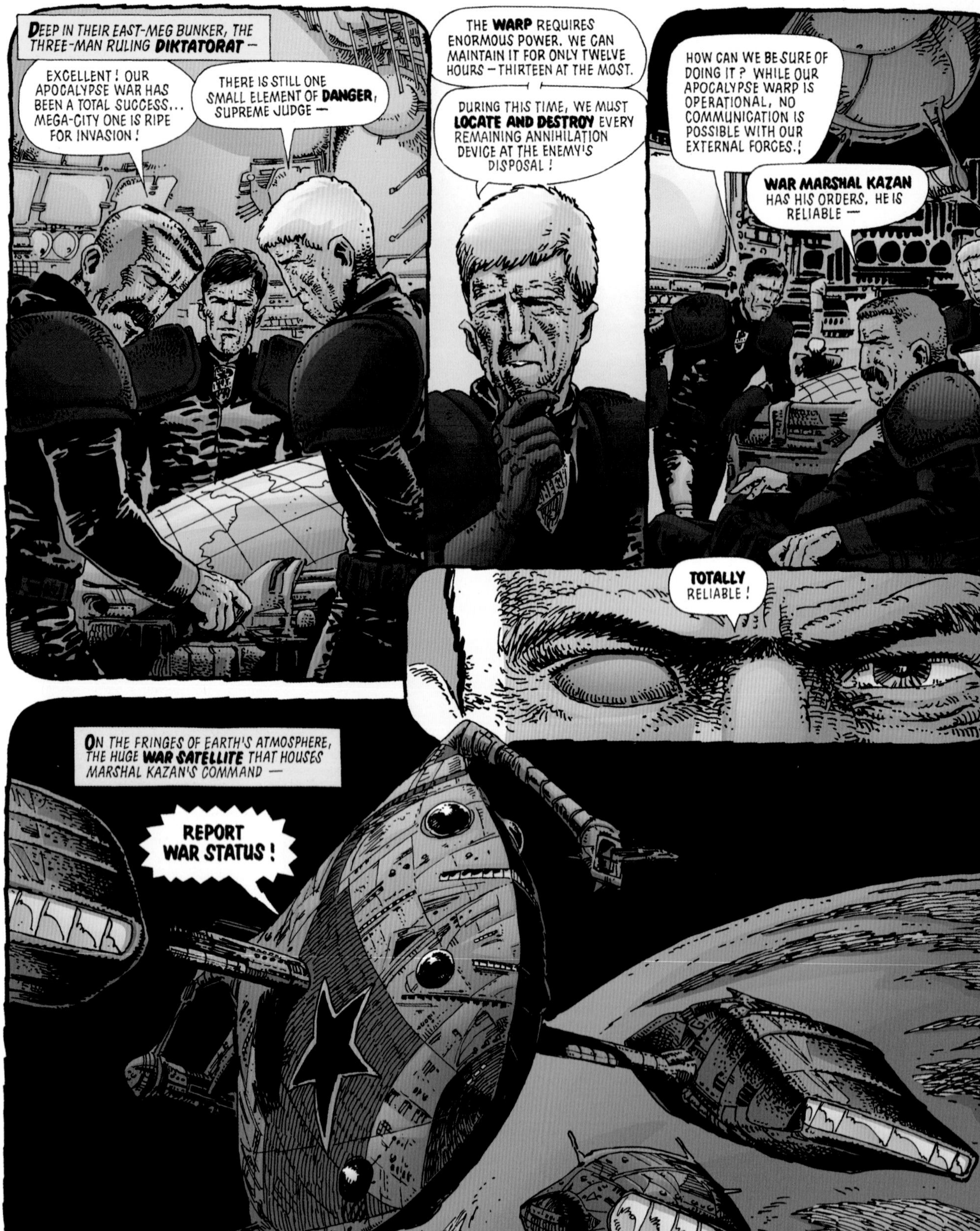
DEEP IN THEIR EAST-MEG BUNKER, THE THREE-MAN RULING DIKTATORAT —
EXCELLENT! OUR APOCALYPSE WAR HAS BEEN A TOTAL SUCCESS... MEGA-CITY ONE IS RIPE FOR INVASION!
THERE IS STILL ONE SMALL ELEMENT OF DANGER, SUPREME JUDGE —
THE WARP REQUIRES ENORMOUS POWER. WE CAN MAINTAIN IT FOR ONLY TWELVE HOURS — THIRTEEN AT THE MOST.
DURING THIS TIME, WE MUST LOCATE AND DESTROY EVERY REMAINING ANNIHILATION DEVICE AT THE ENEMY'S DISPOSAL!
HOW CAN WE BE SURE OF DOING IT? WHILE OUR APOCALYPSE WARP IS OPERATIONAL, NO COMMUNICATION IS POSSIBLE WITH OUR EXTERNAL FORCES.!
WAR MARSHAL KAZAN HAS HIS ORDERS. HE IS RELIABLE —
TOTALLY RELIABLE!
ON THE FRINGES OF EARTH'S ATMOSPHERE, THE HUGE WAR SATELLITE THAT HOUSES MARSHAL KAZAN'S COMMAND —
REPORT WAR STATUS!

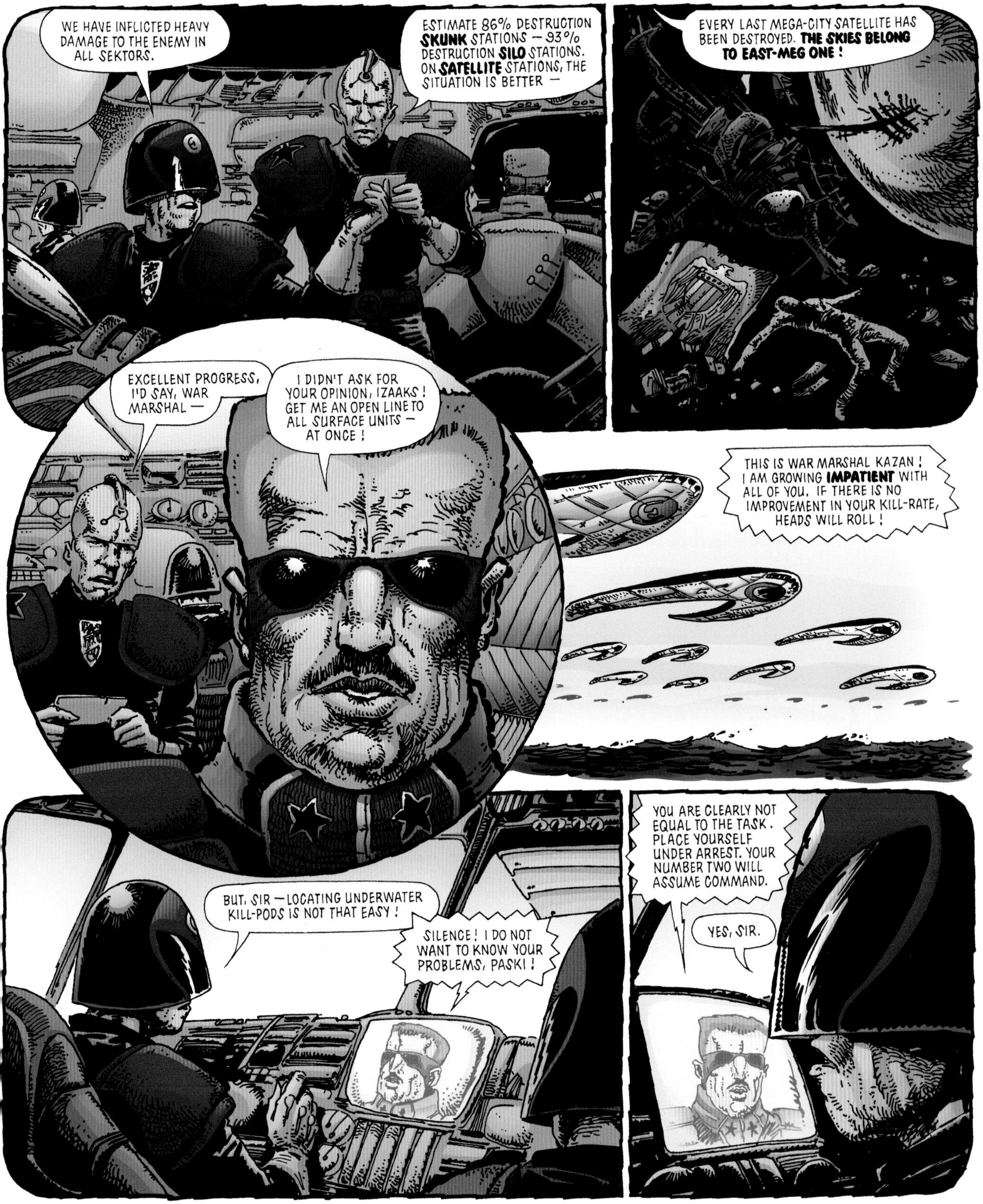
WE HAVE INFLICTED HEAVY DAMAGE TO THE ENEMY IN ALL SEKTORS.
ESTIMATE 86% DESTRUCTION SKUNK STATIONS — 93% DESTRUCTION SILO STATIONS. ON SATELLITE STATIONS, THE SITUATION IS BETTER —
EVERY LAST MEGA-CITY SATELLITE HAS BEEN DESTROYED. THE SKIES BELONG TO EAST-MEG ONE!
EXCELLENT PROGRESS, I'D SAY, WAR MARSHAL —
I DIDN'T ASK FOR YOUR OPINION, IZAAKS! GET ME AN OPEN LINE TO ALL SURFACE UNITS — AT ONCE!
THIS IS WAR MARSHAL KAZAN! I AM GROWING IMPATIENT WITH ALL OF YOU. IF THERE IS NO IMPROVEMENT IN YOUR KILL-RATE, HEADS WILL ROLL!
BUT, SIR — LOCATING UNDERWATER KILL-PODS IS NOT THAT EASY!
SILENCE! I DO NOT WANT TO KNOW YOUR PROBLEMS, PASKI!
YOU ARE CLEARLY NOT EQUAL TO THE TASK. PLACE YOURSELF UNDER ARREST. YOUR NUMBER TWO WILL ASSUME COMMAND.
YES, SIR.

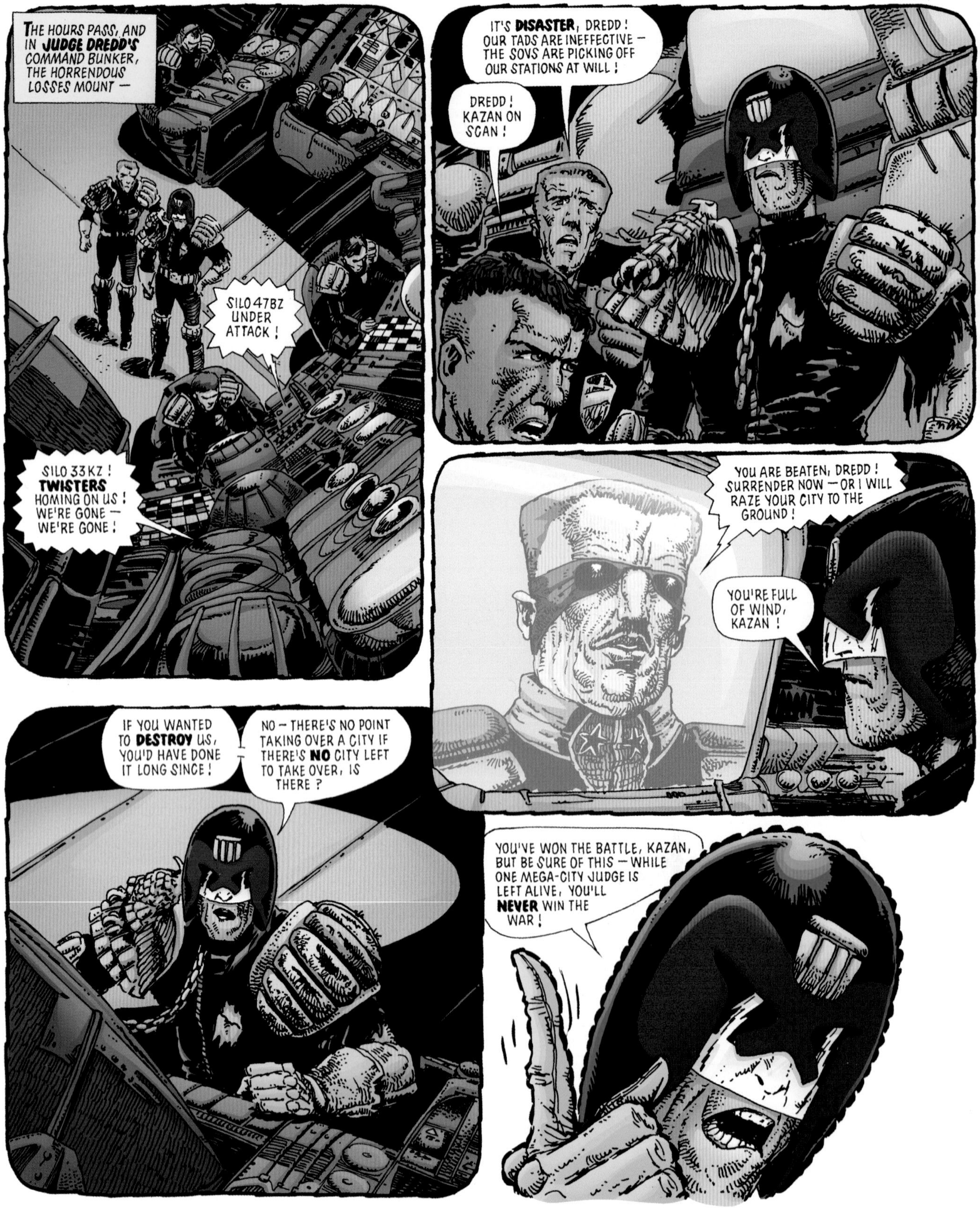
THE HOURS PASS, AND IN JUDGE DREDD'S COMMAND BUNKER, THE HORRENDOUS LOSSES MOUNT —
SILO 47BZ UNDER ATTACK!
SILO 33KZ! TWISTERS HOMING ON US! WE'RE GONE — WE'RE GONE!
IT'S DISASTER, DREDD! OUR TADS ARE INEFFECTIVE — THE SOVS ARE PICKING OFF OUR STATIONS AT WILL!
DREDD! KAZAN ON SCAN!
YOU ARE BEATEN, DREDD! SURRENDER NOW — OR I WILL RAZE YOUR CITY TO THE GROUND!
YOU'RE FULL OF WIND, KAZAN!
IF YOU WANTED TO DESTROY US, YOU'D HAVE DONE IT LONG SINCE!
NO — THERE'S NO POINT TAKING OVER A CITY IF THERE'S NO CITY LEFT TO TAKE OVER, IS THERE?
YOU'VE WON THE BATTLE, KAZAN, BUT BE SURE OF THIS — WHILE ONE MEGA-CITY JUDGE IS LEFT ALIVE, YOU'LL NEVER WIN THE WAR!

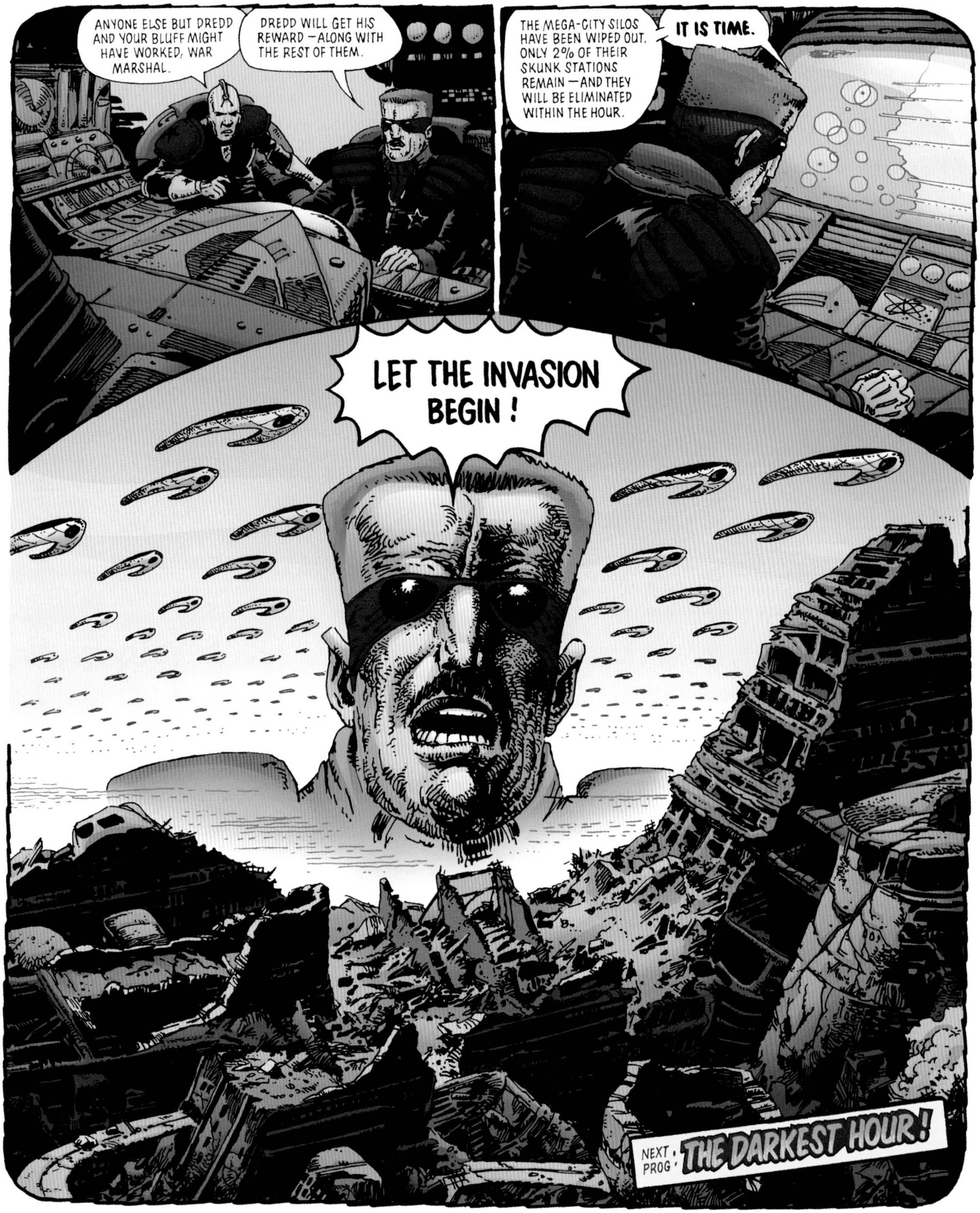
ANYONE ELSE BUT DREDD AND YOUR BLUFF MIGHT HAVE WORKED, WAR MARSHAL.
DREDD WILL GET HIS REWARD — ALONG WITH THE REST OF THEM.
THE MEGA-CITY SILOS HAVE BEEN WIPED OUT. ONLY 2% OF THEIR SKUNK STATIONS REMAIN — AND THEY WILL BE ELIMINATED WITHIN THE HOUR.
IT IS TIME.
LET THE INVASION BEGIN!
NEXT PROG: THE DARKEST HOUR!

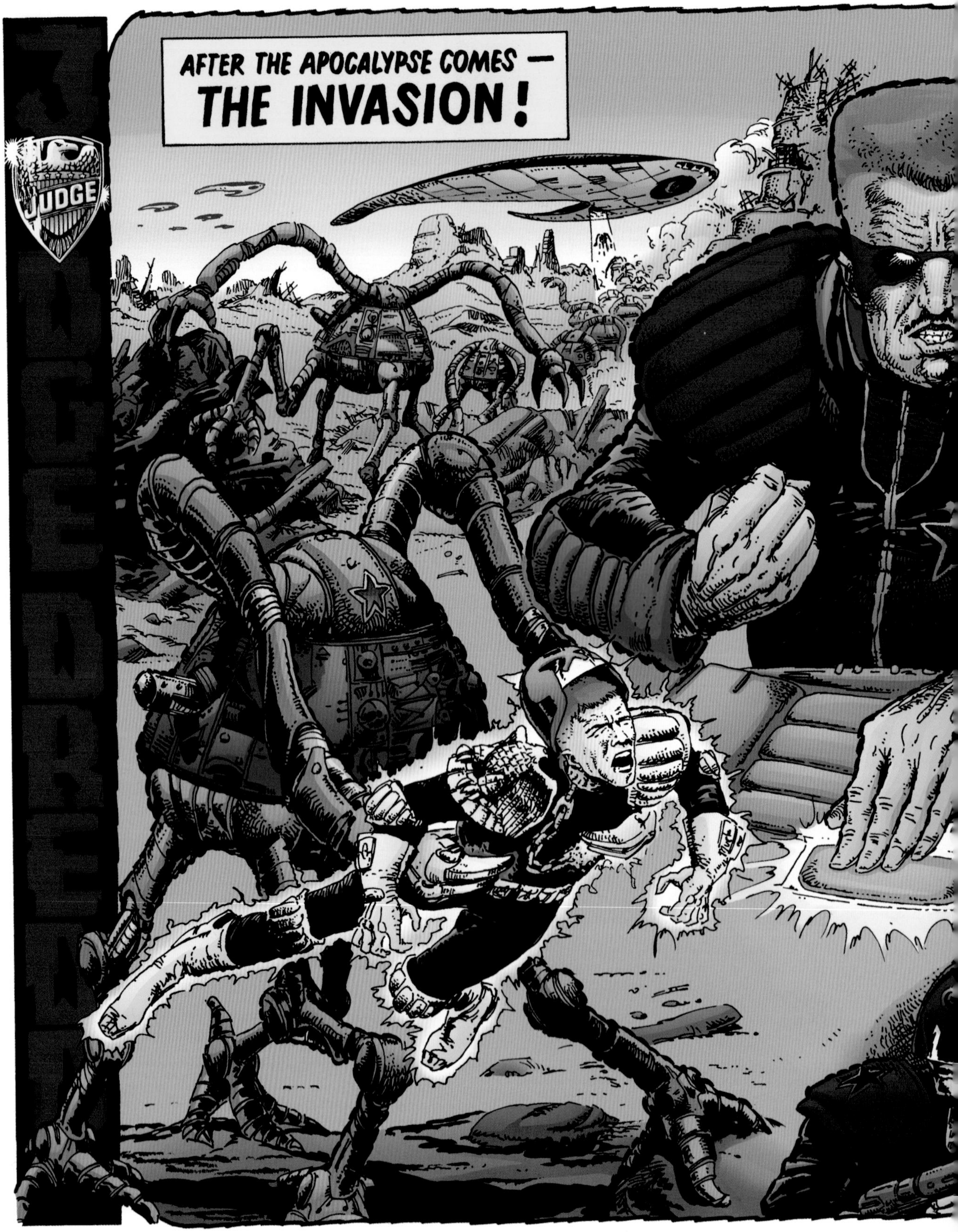
AFTER THE APOCALYPSE COMES —
THE INVASION!

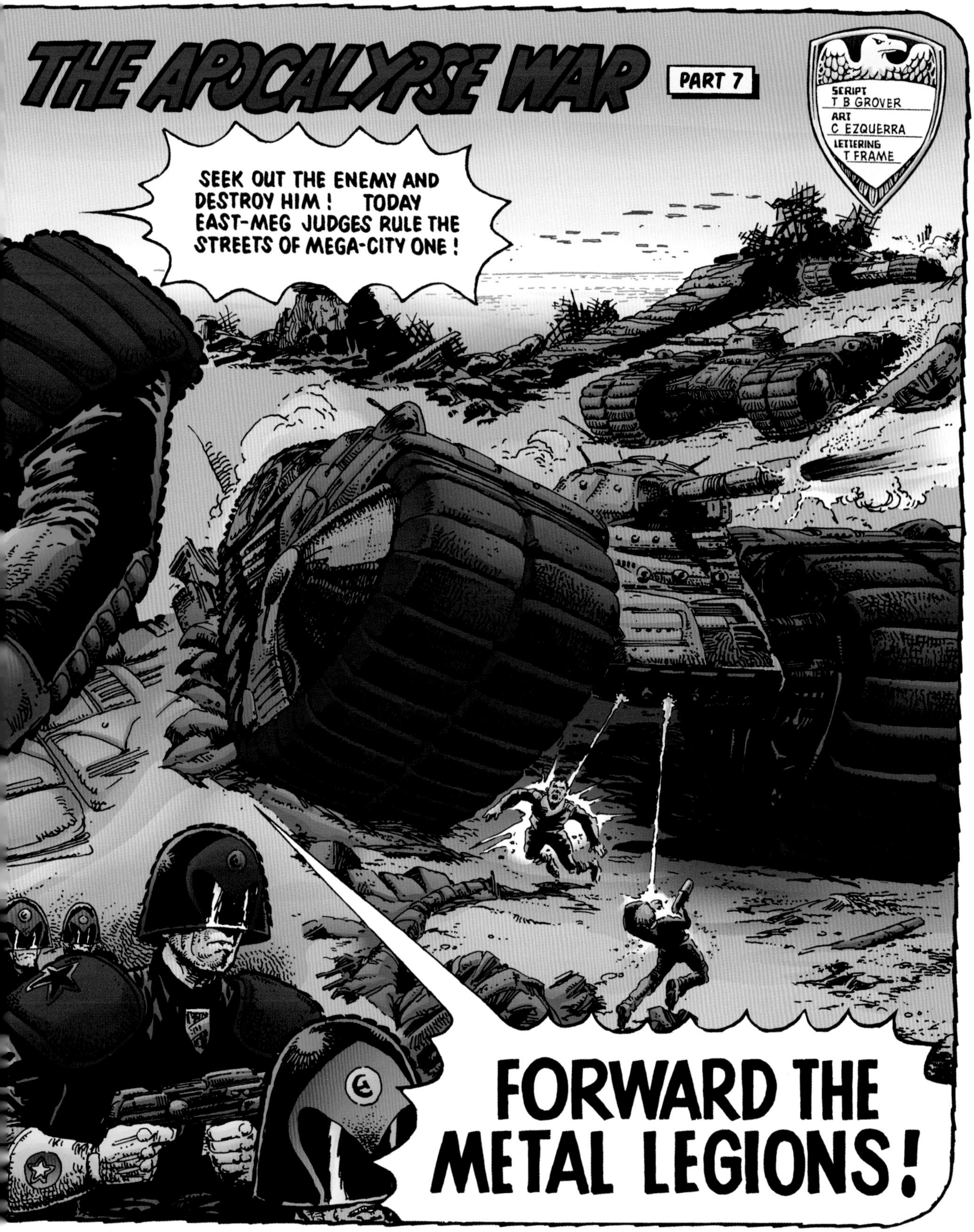
THE APOCALYPSE WAR
PART 7
SCRIPT T B GROVER
ART C EZQUERRA
LETTERING T FRAME
SEEK OUT THE ENEMY AND DESTROY HIM! TODAY EAST-MEG JUDGES RULE THE STREETS OF MEGA-CITY ONE!
FORWARD THE METAL LEGIONS!

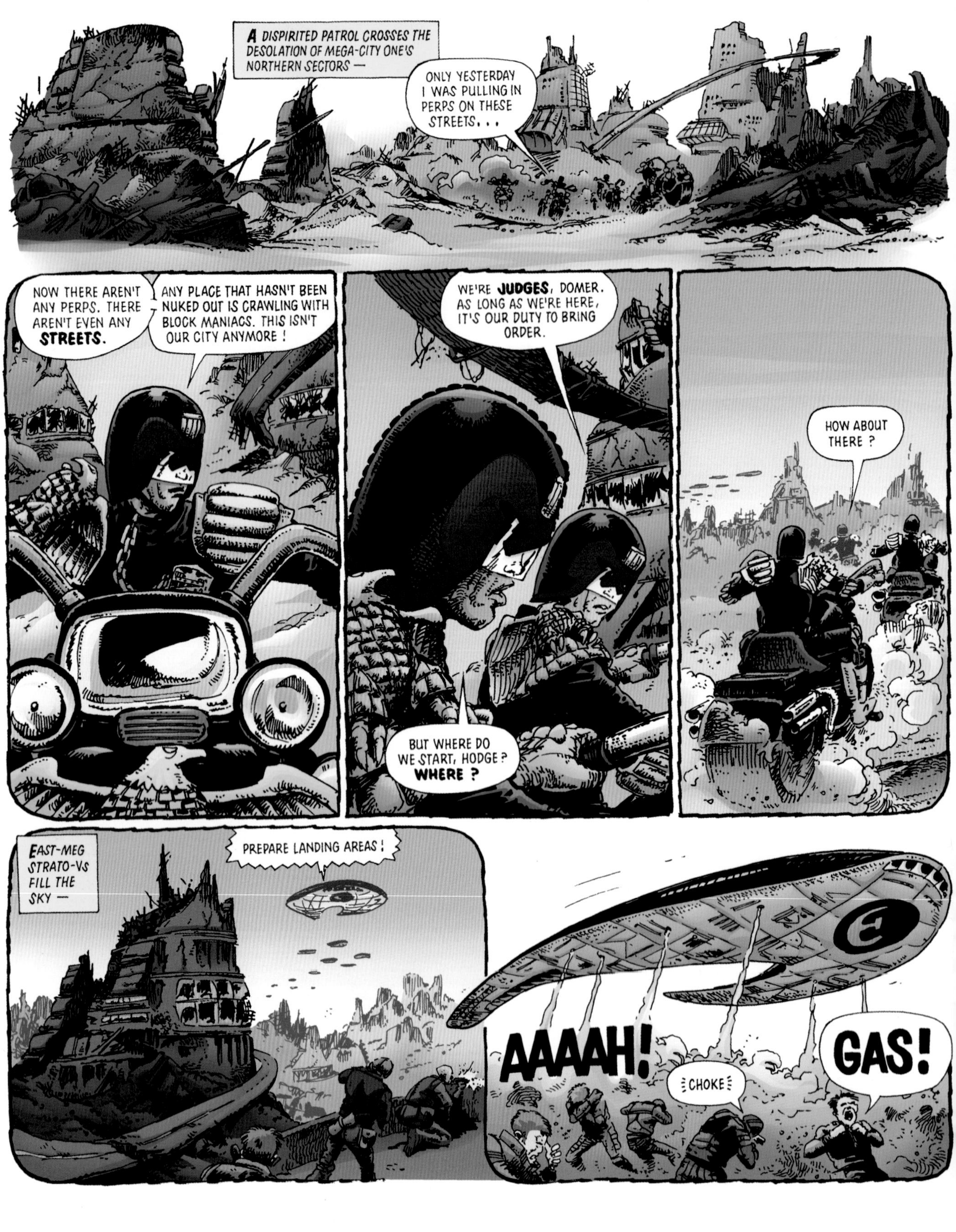
A DISPIRITED PATROL CROSSES THE DESOLATION OF MEGA-CITY ONE'S NORTHERN SECTORS —
ONLY YESTERDAY I WAS PULLING IN PERPS ON THESE STREETS...
NOW THERE AREN'T ANY PERPS. THERE AREN'T EVEN ANY STREETS.
ANY PLACE THAT HASN'T BEEN NUKED OUT IS CRAWLING WITH BLOCK MANIACS. THIS ISN'T OUR CITY ANYMORE !
WE'RE JUDGES, DOMER. AS LONG AS WE'RE HERE, IT'S OUR DUTY TO BRING ORDER.
BUT WHERE DO WE START, HODGE ? WHERE ?
HOW ABOUT THERE ?
EAST-MEG STRATO-VS FILL THE SKY —
PREPARE LANDING AREAS !
AAAAH!
CHOKE
GAS!

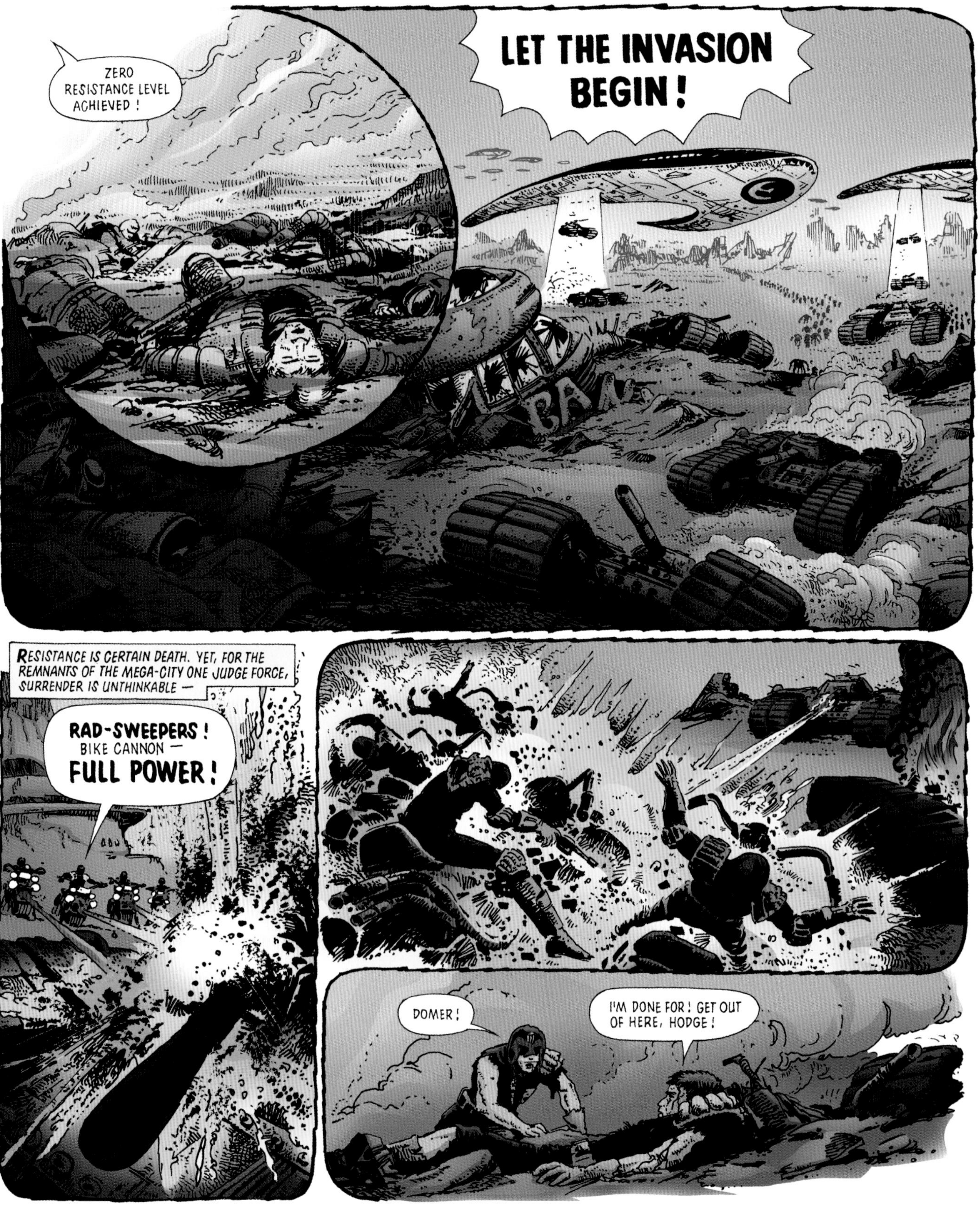
ZERO RESISTANCE LEVEL ACHIEVED !
LET THE INVASION BEGIN !
RESISTANCE IS CERTAIN DEATH. YET, FOR THE REMNANTS OF THE MEGA-CITY ONE JUDGE FORCE, SURRENDER IS UNTHINKABLE —
RAD-SWEEPERS ! BIKE CANNON — FULL POWER !
DOMER !
I'M DONE FOR ! GET OUT OF HERE, HODGE !

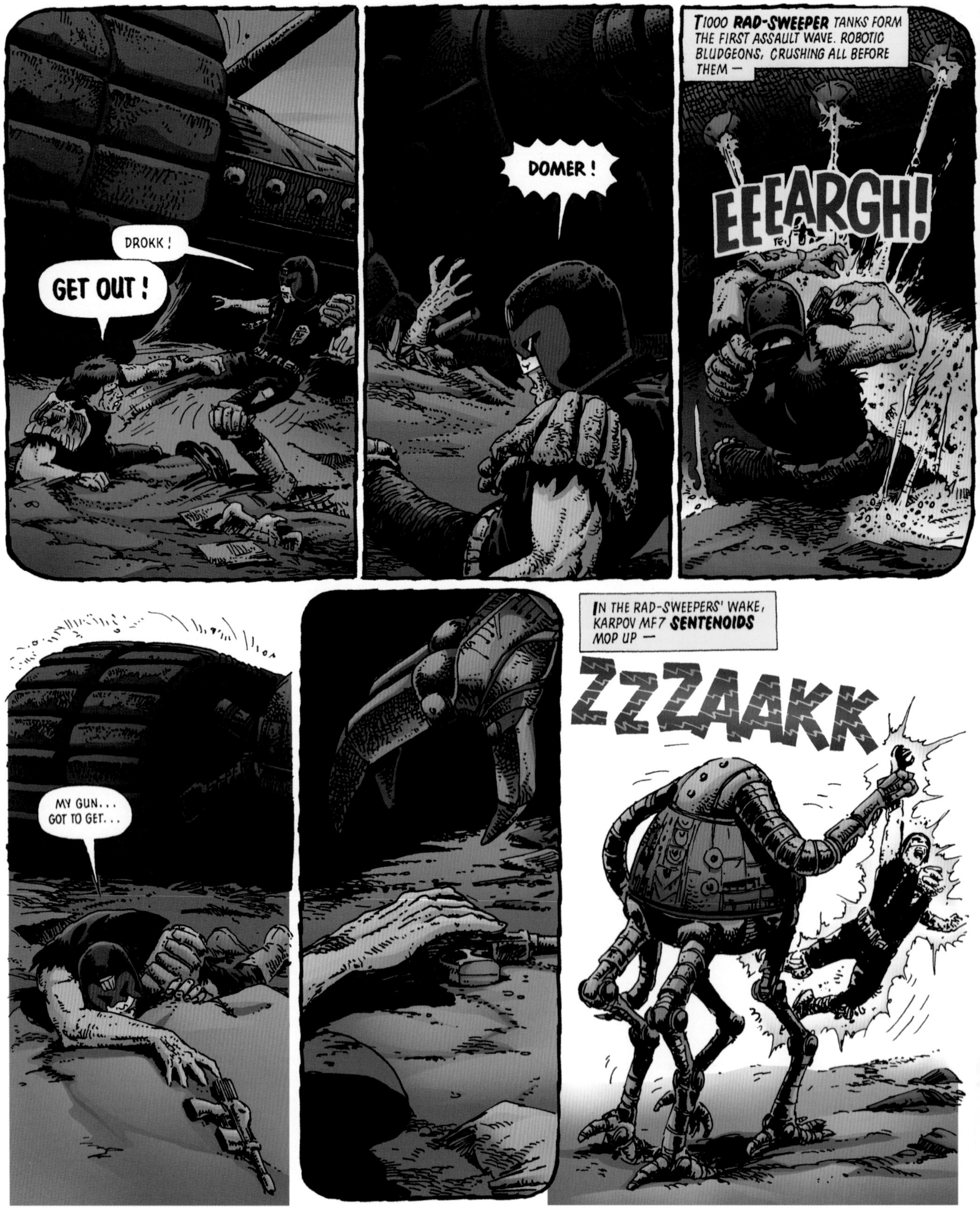
DROKK!
GET OUT!
DOMER!
T1000 RAD-SWEEPER TANKS FORM THE FIRST ASSAULT WAVE. ROBOTIC BLUDGEONS, CRUSHING ALL BEFORE THEM —
EEEARGH!
MY GUN... GOT TO GET...
IN THE RAD-SWEEPERS' WAKE, KARPOV MF7 SENTENOIDS MOP UP —
ZZZAAKK

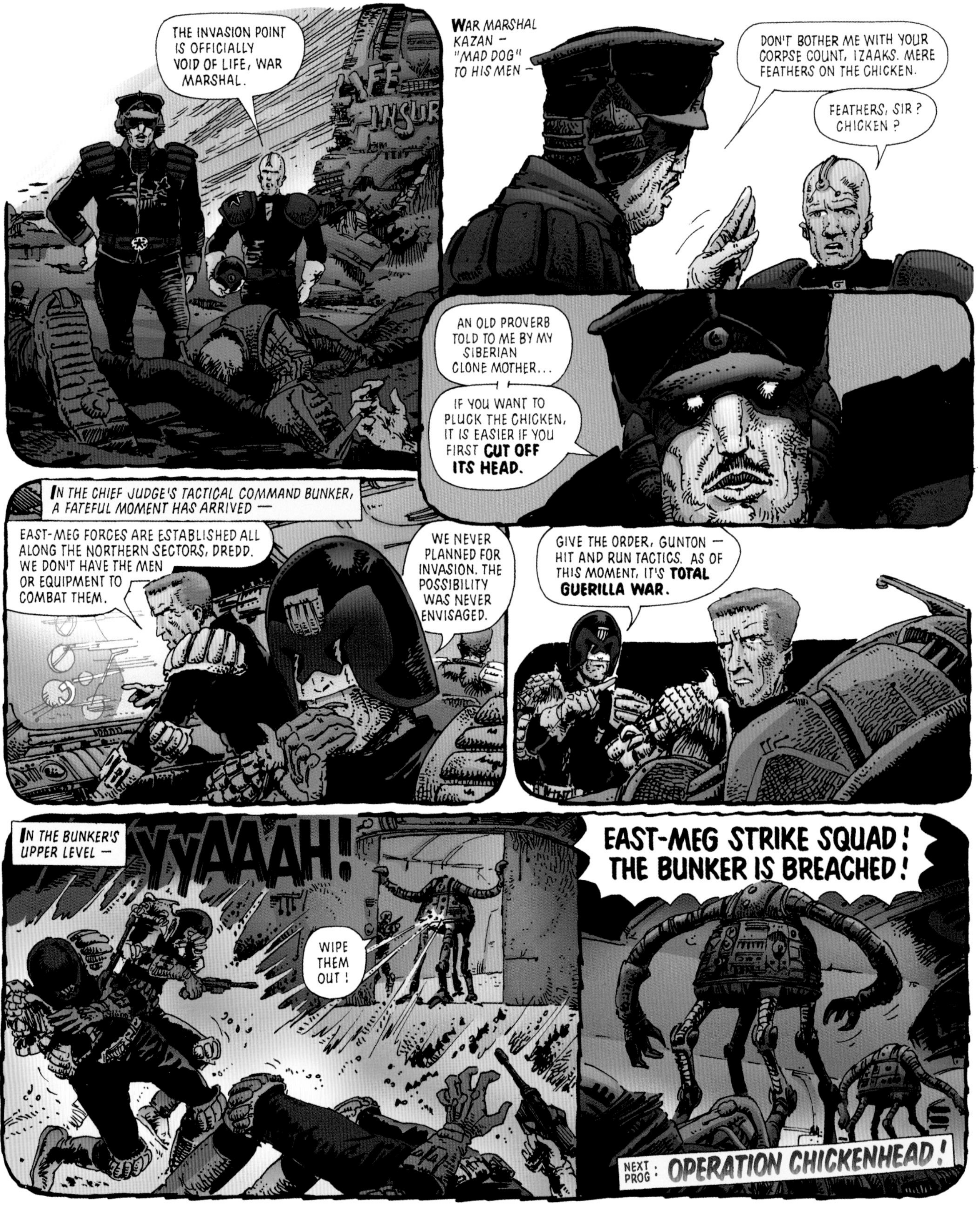

THE INVASION POINT IS OFFICIALLY VOID OF LIFE, WAR MARSHAL.
LIFE INSUR
WAR MARSHAL KAZAN — "MAD DOG" TO HIS MEN —
DON'T BOTHER ME WITH YOUR CORPSE COUNT, IZAAKS. MERE FEATHERS ON THE CHICKEN.
FEATHERS, SIR? CHICKEN?
AN OLD PROVERB TOLD TO ME BY MY SIBERIAN CLONE MOTHER...
IF YOU WANT TO PLUCK THE CHICKEN, IT IS EASIER IF YOU FIRST CUT OFF ITS HEAD.
IN THE CHIEF JUDGE'S TACTICAL COMMAND BUNKER, A FATEFUL MOMENT HAS ARRIVED —
EAST-MEG FORCES ARE ESTABLISHED ALL ALONG THE NORTHERN SECTORS, DREDD. WE DON'T HAVE THE MEN OR EQUIPMENT TO COMBAT THEM.
WE NEVER PLANNED FOR INVASION. THE POSSIBILITY WAS NEVER ENVISAGED.
GIVE THE ORDER, GUNTON — HIT AND RUN TACTICS. AS OF THIS MOMENT, IT'S TOTAL GUERILLA WAR.
IN THE BUNKER'S UPPER LEVEL —
YYAAAH!
WIPE THEM OUT!
EAST-MEG STRIKE SQUAD! THE BUNKER IS BREACHED!
NEXT PROG: OPERATION CHICKENHEAD!

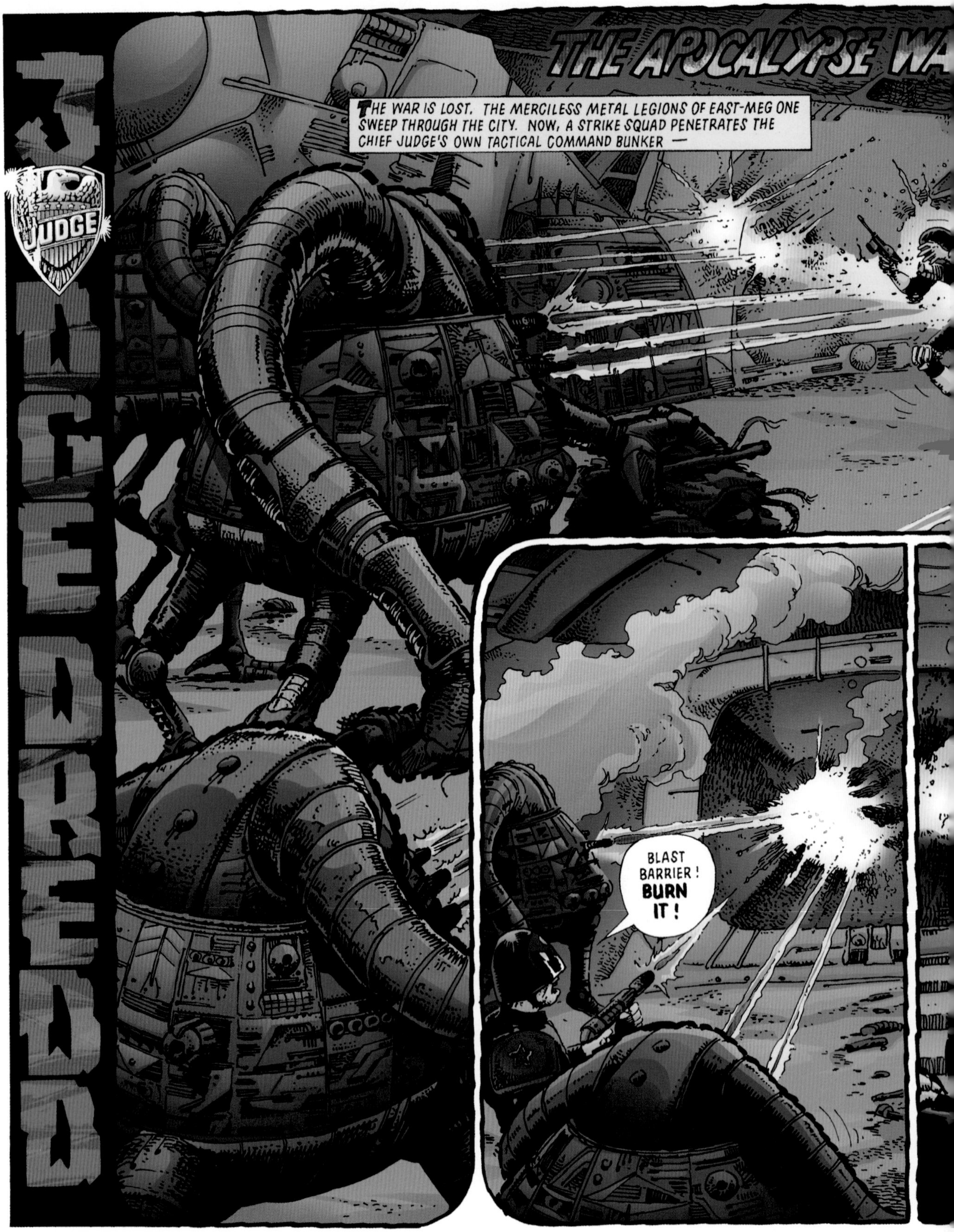
JUDGE DREDD
THE APOCALYPSE WA
THE WAR IS LOST. THE MERCILESS METAL LEGIONS OF EAST-MEG ONE SWEEP THROUGH THE CITY. NOW, A STRIKE SQUAD PENETRATES THE CHIEF JUDGE'S OWN TACTICAL COMMAND BUNKER —
BLAST BARRIER! **BURN IT!**

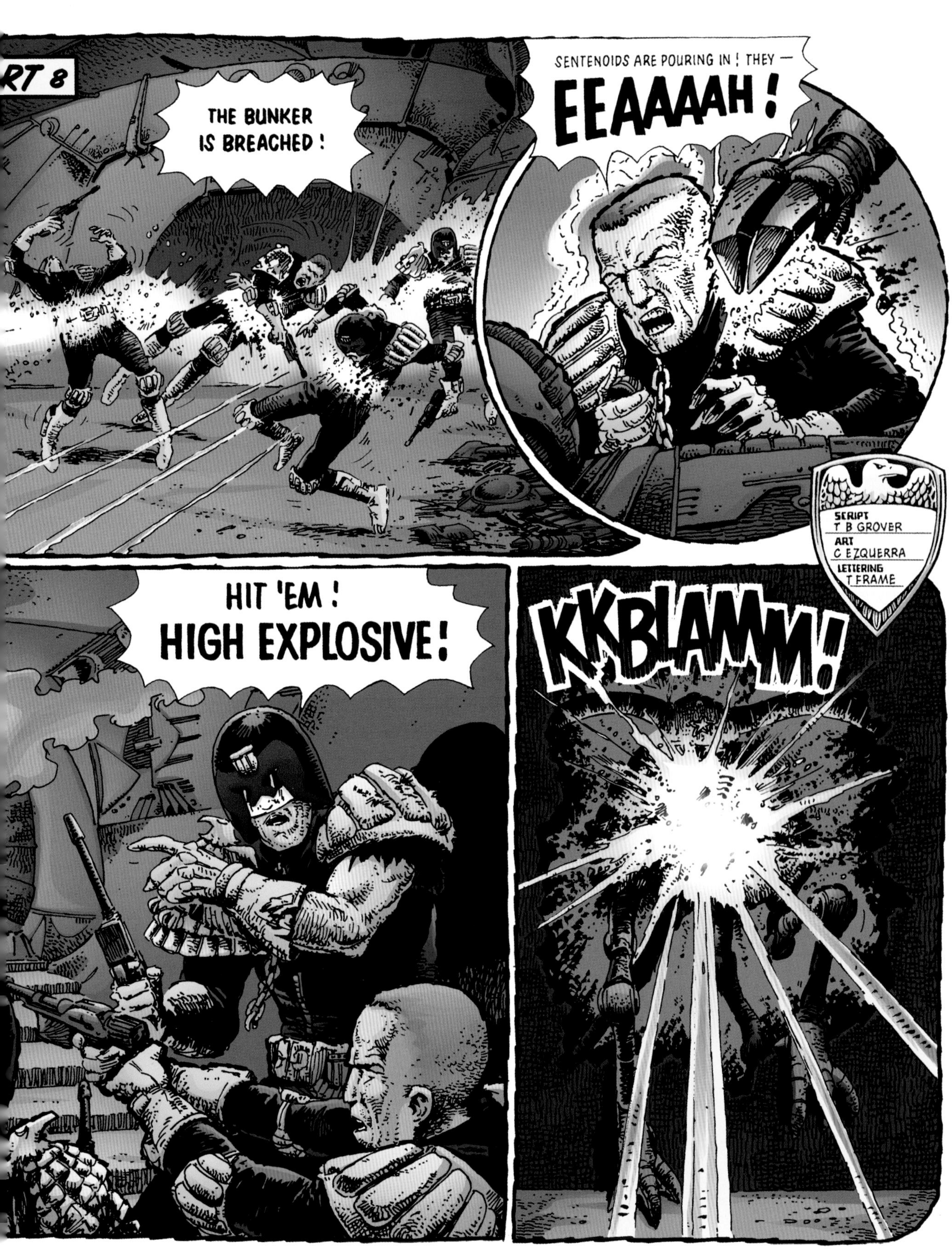
RT 8
THE BUNKER IS BREACHED!
SENTENOIDS ARE POURING IN! THEY —
EEAAAAH!
SCRIPT
T B GROVER
ART
C EZQUERRA
LETTERING
T FRAME
HIT 'EM! HIGH EXPLOSIVE!
KKBLAMMM!

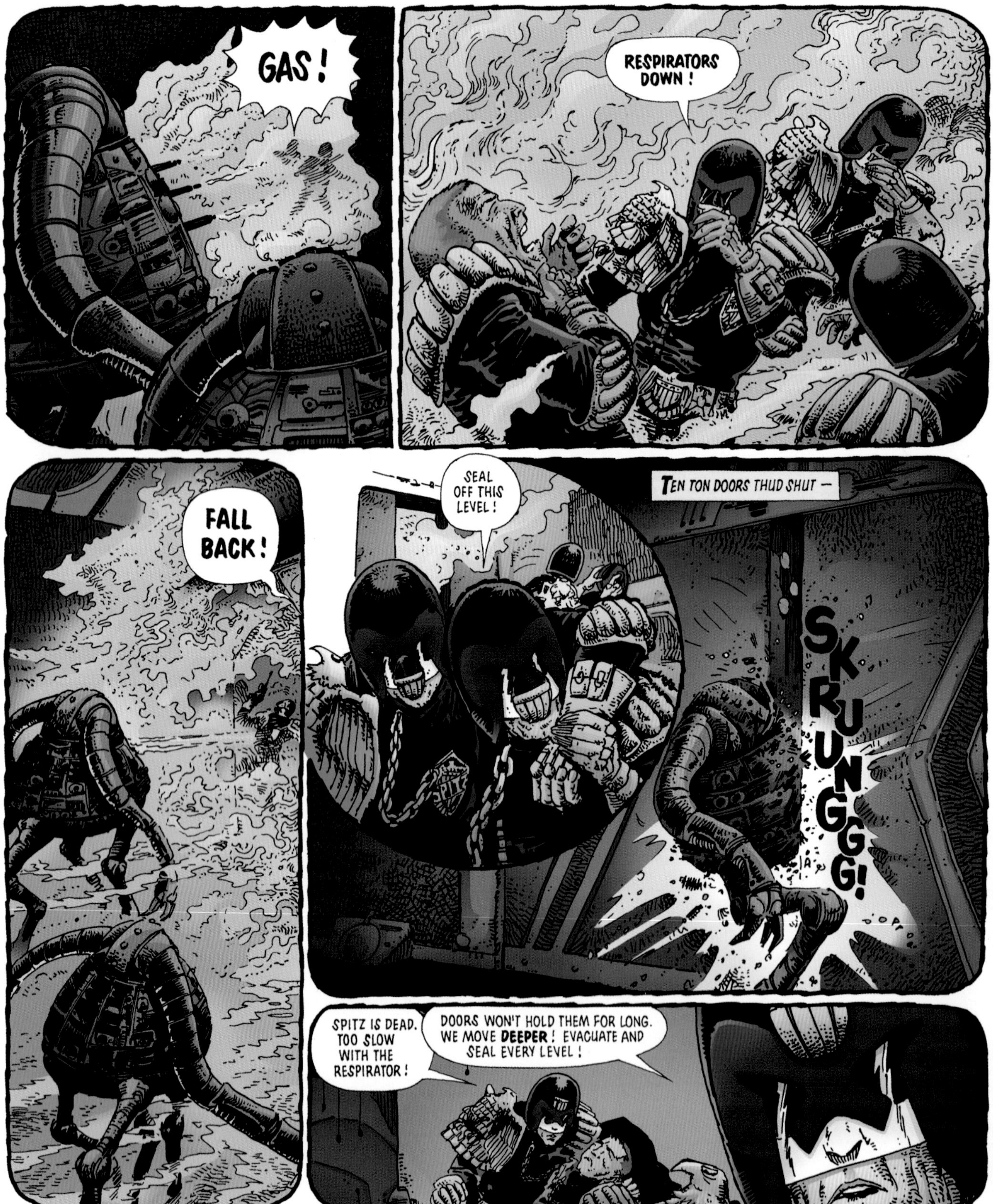
GAS!
RESPIRATORS DOWN!
FALL BACK!
SEAL OFF THIS LEVEL!
TEN TON DOORS THUD SHUT —
SKRUNGGG!
SPITZ IS DEAD. TOO SLOW WITH THE RESPIRATOR!
DOORS WON'T HOLD THEM FOR LONG. WE MOVE DEEPER! EVACUATE AND SEAL EVERY LEVEL!

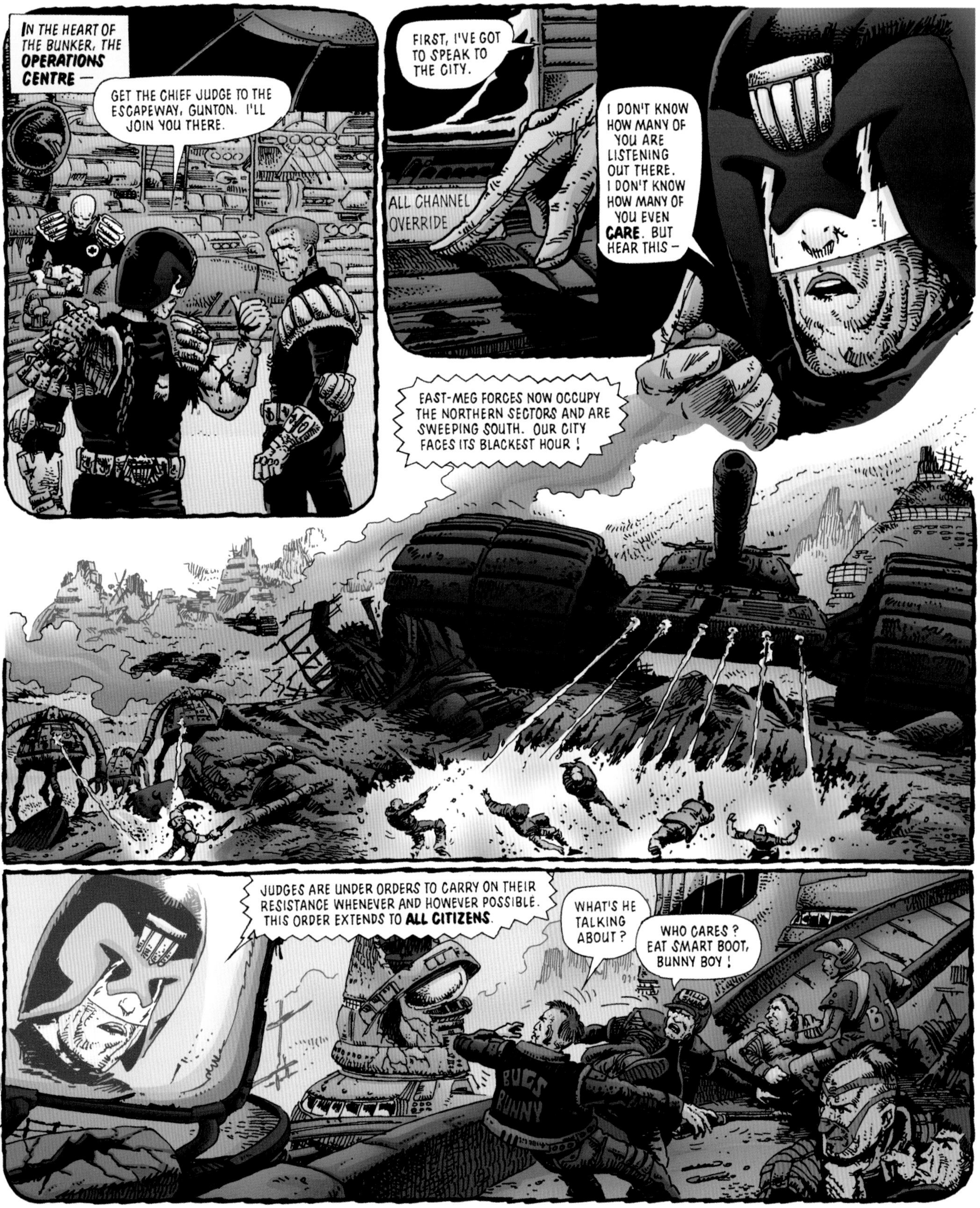

IN THE HEART OF THE BUNKER, THE OPERATIONS CENTRE —
GET THE CHIEF JUDGE TO THE ESCAPEWAY, GUNTON. I'LL JOIN YOU THERE.
FIRST, I'VE GOT TO SPEAK TO THE CITY.
ALL CHANNEL OVERRIDE
I DON'T KNOW HOW MANY OF YOU ARE LISTENING OUT THERE. I DON'T KNOW HOW MANY OF YOU EVEN CARE. BUT HEAR THIS —
EAST-MEG FORCES NOW OCCUPY THE NORTHERN SECTORS AND ARE SWEEPING SOUTH. OUR CITY FACES ITS BLACKEST HOUR!
JUDGES ARE UNDER ORDERS TO CARRY ON THEIR RESISTANCE WHENEVER AND HOWEVER POSSIBLE. THIS ORDER EXTENDS TO ALL CITIZENS.
WHAT'S HE TALKING ABOUT?
WHO CARES? EAT SMART BOOT, BUNNY BOY!
BUGS BUNNY

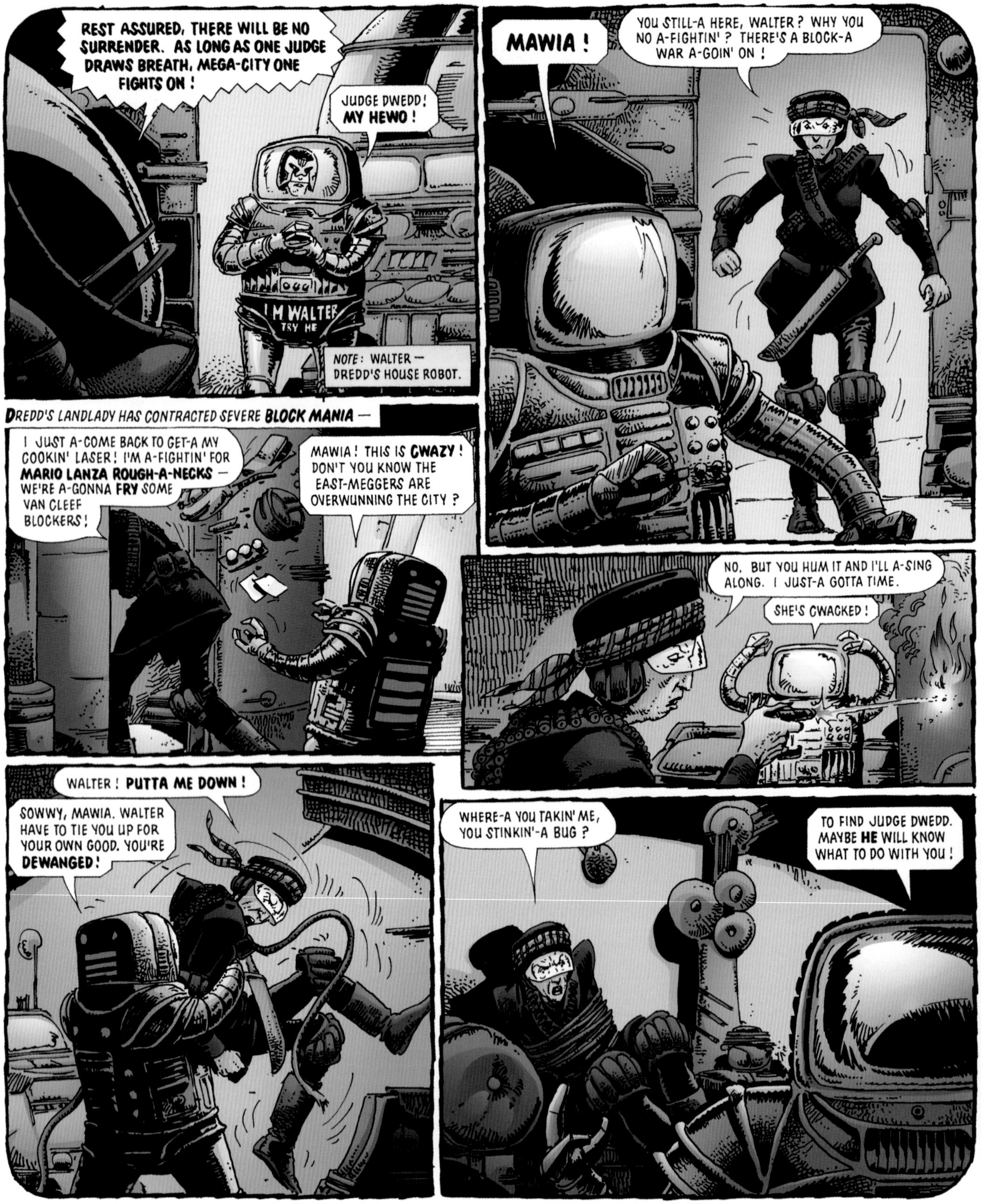

REST ASSURED, THERE WILL BE NO SURRENDER. AS LONG AS ONE JUDGE DRAWS BREATH, MEGA-CITY ONE FIGHTS ON!
JUDGE DWEDD! MY HEWO!
I M WALTER TRY ME
NOTE: WALTER — DREDD'S HOUSE ROBOT.
MAWIA!
YOU STILL-A HERE, WALTER? WHY YOU NO A-FIGHTIN'? THERE'S A BLOCK-A WAR A-GOIN' ON!
DREDD'S LANDLADY HAS CONTRACTED SEVERE BLOCK MANIA —
I JUST A-COME BACK TO GET-A MY COOKIN' LASER! I'M A-FIGHTIN' FOR MARIO LANZA ROUGH-A-NECKS — WE'RE A-GONNA FRY SOME VAN CLEEF BLOCKERS!
MAWIA! THIS IS CWAZY! DON'T YOU KNOW THE EAST-MEGGERS ARE OVERWUNNING THE CITY?
NO. BUT YOU HUM IT AND I'LL A-SING ALONG. I JUST-A GOTTA TIME.
SHE'S CWACKED!
WALTER! PUTTA ME DOWN!
SOWWY, MAWIA. WALTER HAVE TO TIE YOU UP FOR YOUR OWN GOOD. YOU'RE DEWANGED!
WHERE-A YOU TAKIN' ME, YOU STINKIN'-A BUG?
TO FIND JUDGE DWEDD. MAYBE HE WILL KNOW WHAT TO DO WITH YOU!

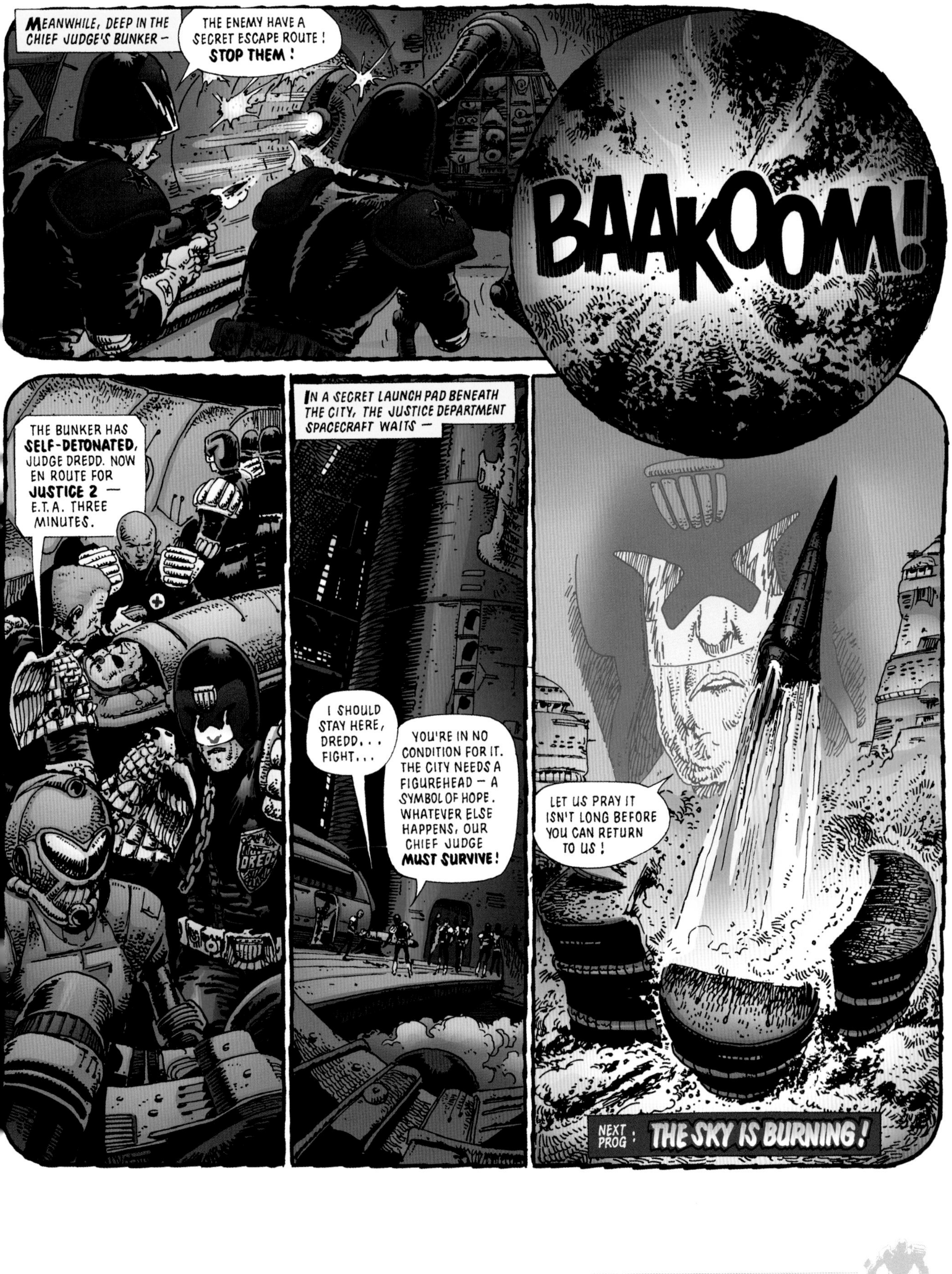
MEANWHILE, DEEP IN THE CHIEF JUDGE'S BUNKER —
THE ENEMY HAVE A SECRET ESCAPE ROUTE ! STOP THEM !
BAAKOOM!
THE BUNKER HAS SELF-DETONATED, JUDGE DREDD. NOW EN ROUTE FOR JUSTICE 2 — E.T.A. THREE MINUTES.
IN A SECRET LAUNCH PAD BENEATH THE CITY, THE JUSTICE DEPARTMENT SPACECRAFT WAITS —
I SHOULD STAY HERE, DREDD. . . FIGHT. . .
YOU'RE IN NO CONDITION FOR IT. THE CITY NEEDS A FIGUREHEAD — A SYMBOL OF HOPE. WHATEVER ELSE HAPPENS, OUR CHIEF JUDGE MUST SURVIVE !
LET US PRAY IT ISN'T LONG BEFORE YOU CAN RETURN TO US !
NEXT PROG : THE SKY IS BURNING !

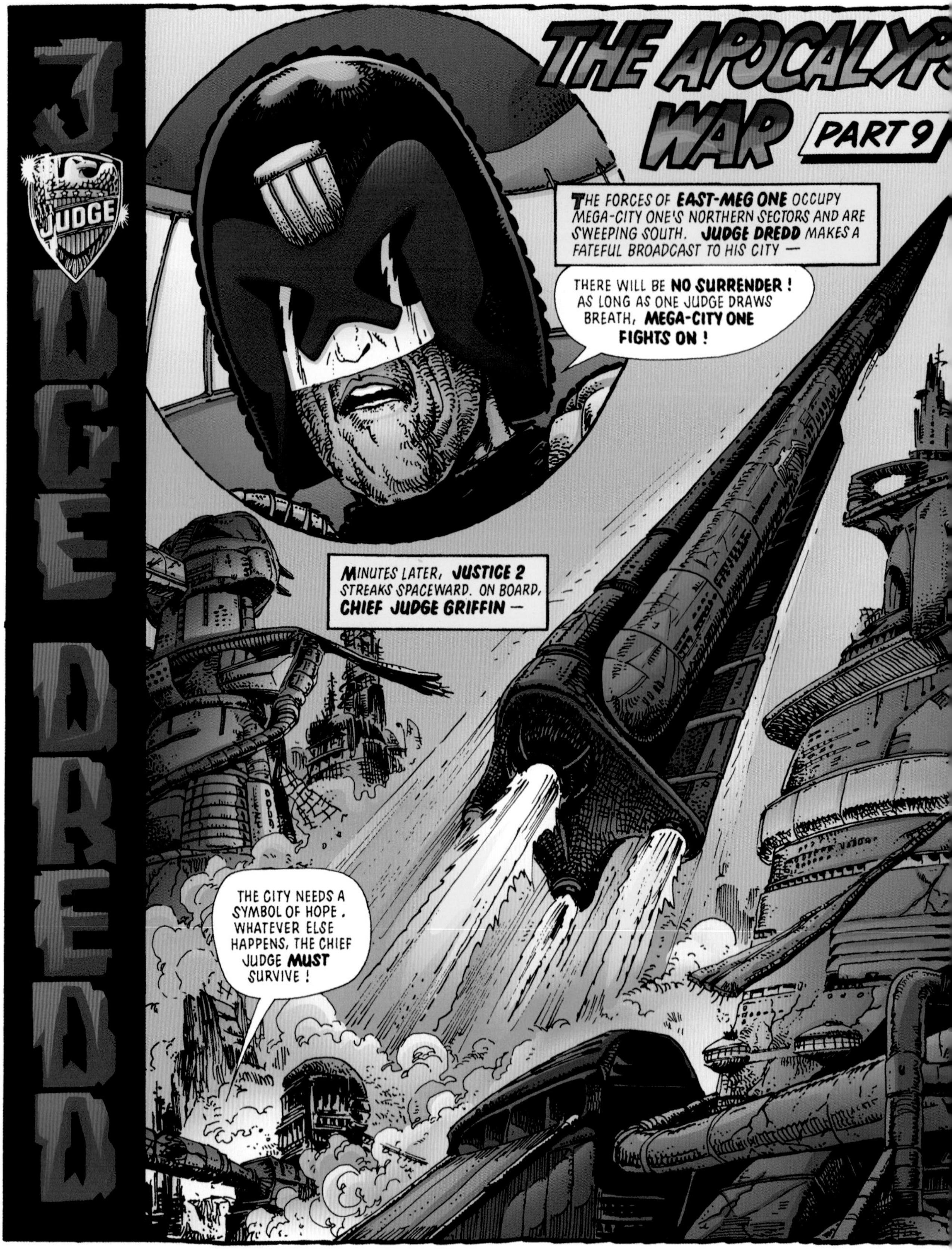
JUDGE DREDD
THE APOCALYPSE WAR
PART 9
THE FORCES OF EAST-MEG ONE OCCUPY MEGA-CITY ONE'S NORTHERN SECTORS AND ARE SWEEPING SOUTH. JUDGE DREDD MAKES A FATEFUL BROADCAST TO HIS CITY —
THERE WILL BE NO SURRENDER ! AS LONG AS ONE JUDGE DRAWS BREATH, MEGA-CITY ONE FIGHTS ON !
MINUTES LATER, JUSTICE 2 STREAKS SPACEWARD. ON BOARD, CHIEF JUDGE GRIFFIN —
THE CITY NEEDS A SYMBOL OF HOPE . WHATEVER ELSE HAPPENS, THE CHIEF JUDGE MUST SURVIVE !

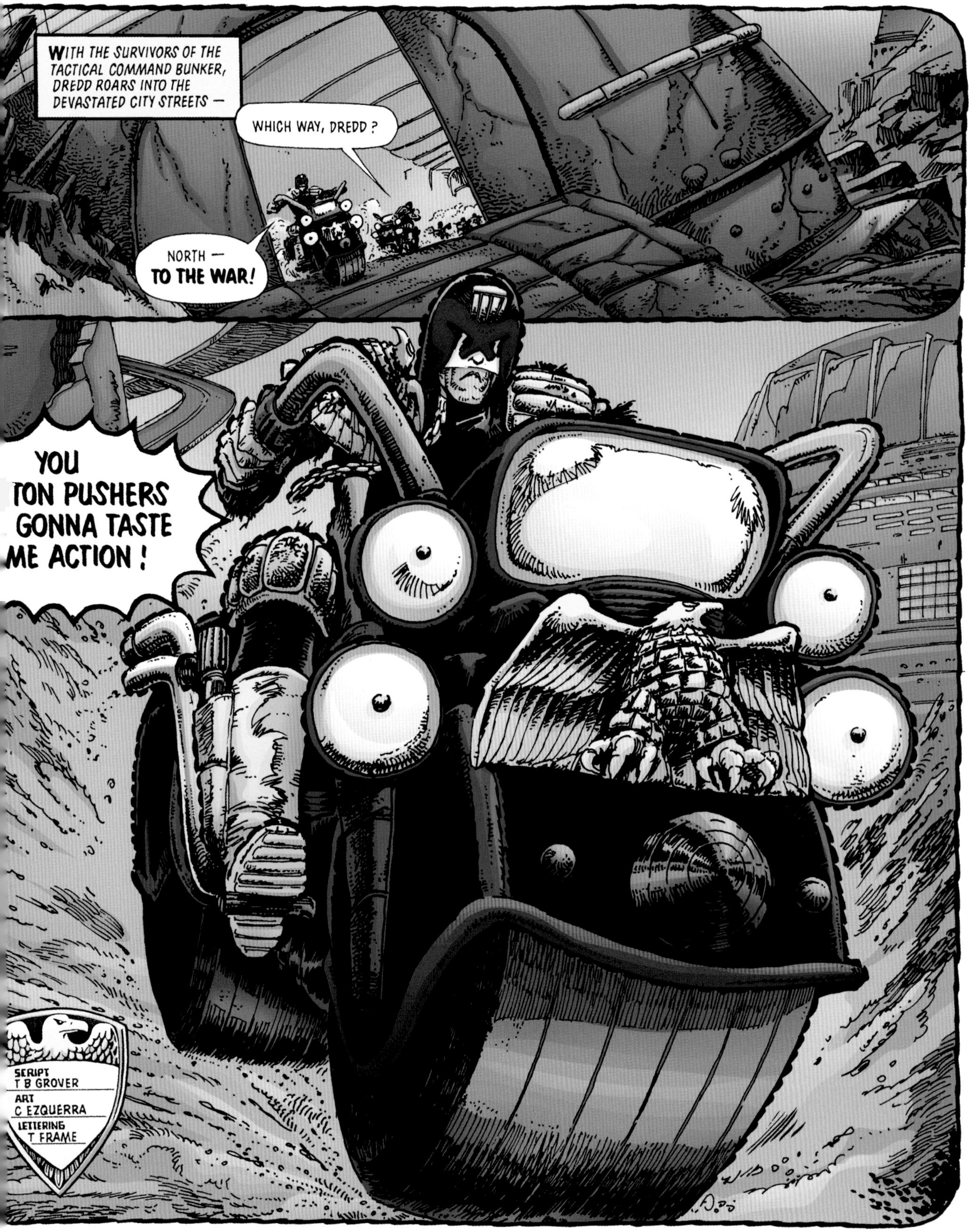
WITH THE SURVIVORS OF THE TACTICAL COMMAND BUNKER, DREDD ROARS INTO THE DEVASTATED CITY STREETS —
WHICH WAY, DREDD ?
NORTH — TO THE WAR!
YOU TON PUSHERS GONNA TASTE ME ACTION !
SCRIPT T B GROVER
ART C EZQUERRA
LETTERING T FRAME

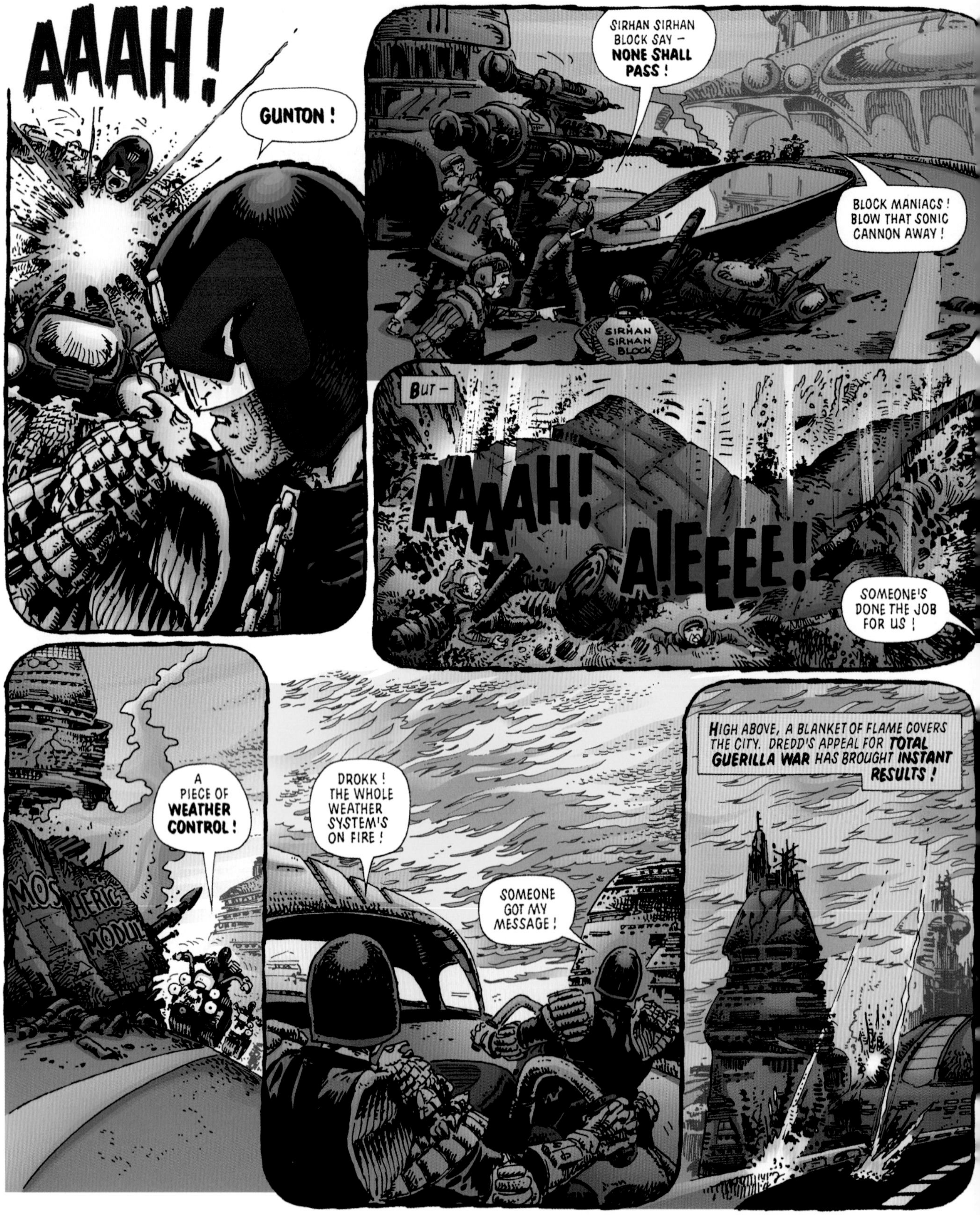
AAAH!
GUNTON!
SIRHAN SIRHAN BLOCK SAY — NONE SHALL PASS!
BLOCK MANIACS! BLOW THAT SONIC CANNON AWAY!
SIRHAN SIRHAN BLOCK
BUT —
AAAAH!
AIEEEE!
SOMEONE'S DONE THE JOB FOR US!
A PIECE OF WEATHER CONTROL!
DROKK! THE WHOLE WEATHER SYSTEM'S ON FIRE!
SOMEONE GOT MY MESSAGE!
HIGH ABOVE, A BLANKET OF FLAME COVERS THE CITY. DREDD'S APPEAL FOR TOTAL GUERILLA WAR HAS BROUGHT INSTANT RESULTS!

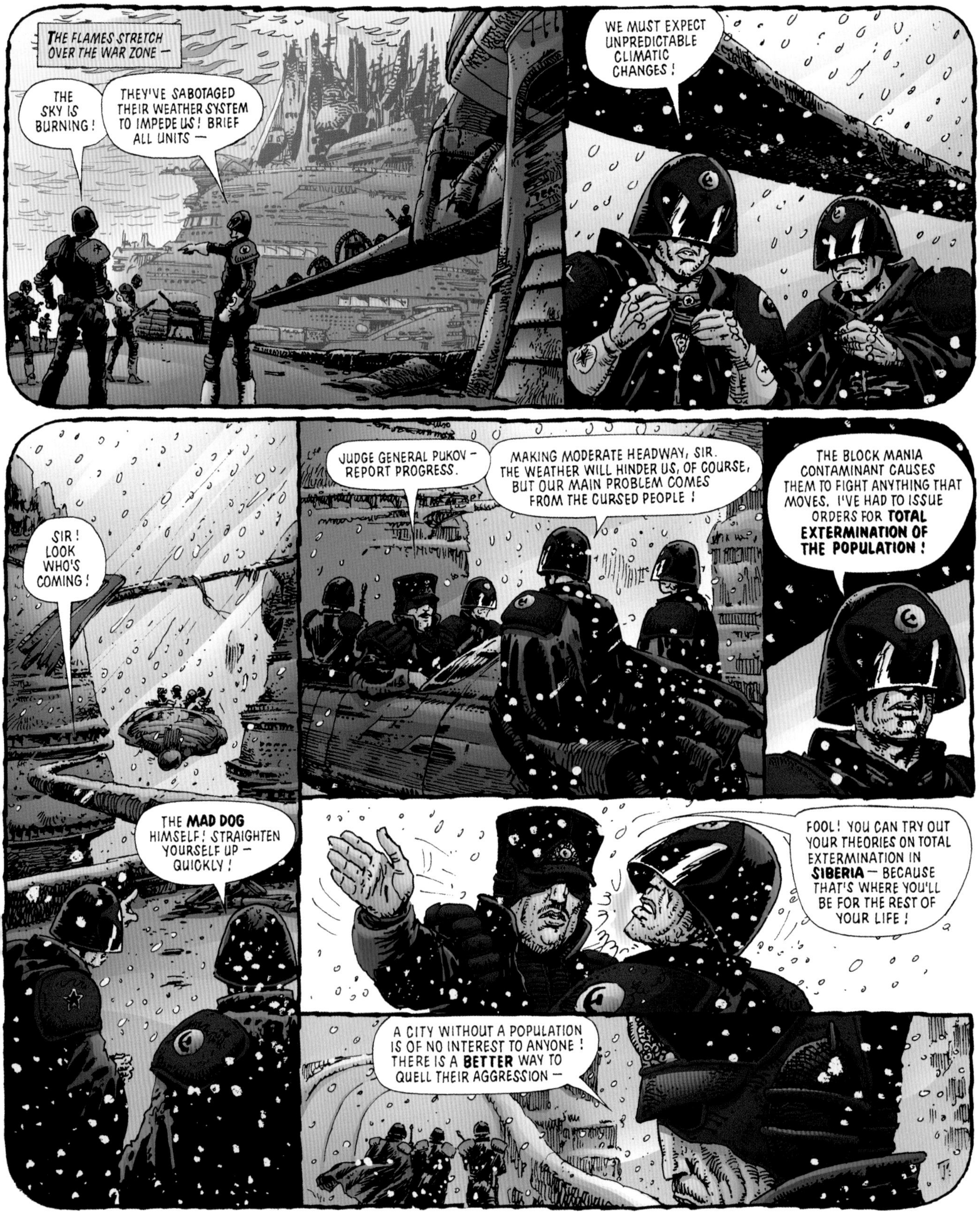
THE FLAMES STRETCH OVER THE WAR ZONE —
THE SKY IS BURNING!
THEY'VE SABOTAGED THEIR WEATHER SYSTEM TO IMPEDE US! BRIEF ALL UNITS —
WE MUST EXPECT UNPREDICTABLE CLIMATIC CHANGES!
SIR! LOOK WHO'S COMING!
JUDGE GENERAL PUKOV — REPORT PROGRESS.
MAKING MODERATE HEADWAY, SIR. THE WEATHER WILL HINDER US, OF COURSE, BUT OUR MAIN PROBLEM COMES FROM THE CURSED PEOPLE!
THE BLOCK MANIA CONTAMINANT CAUSES THEM TO FIGHT ANYTHING THAT MOVES. I'VE HAD TO ISSUE ORDERS FOR TOTAL EXTERMINATION OF THE POPULATION!
THE MAD DOG HIMSELF! STRAIGHTEN YOURSELF UP — QUICKLY!
FOOL! YOU CAN TRY OUT YOUR THEORIES ON TOTAL EXTERMINATION IN SIBERIA — BECAUSE THAT'S WHERE YOU'LL BE FOR THE REST OF YOUR LIFE!
A CITY WITHOUT A POPULATION IS OF NO INTEREST TO ANYONE! THERE IS A BETTER WAY TO QUELL THEIR AGGRESSION —

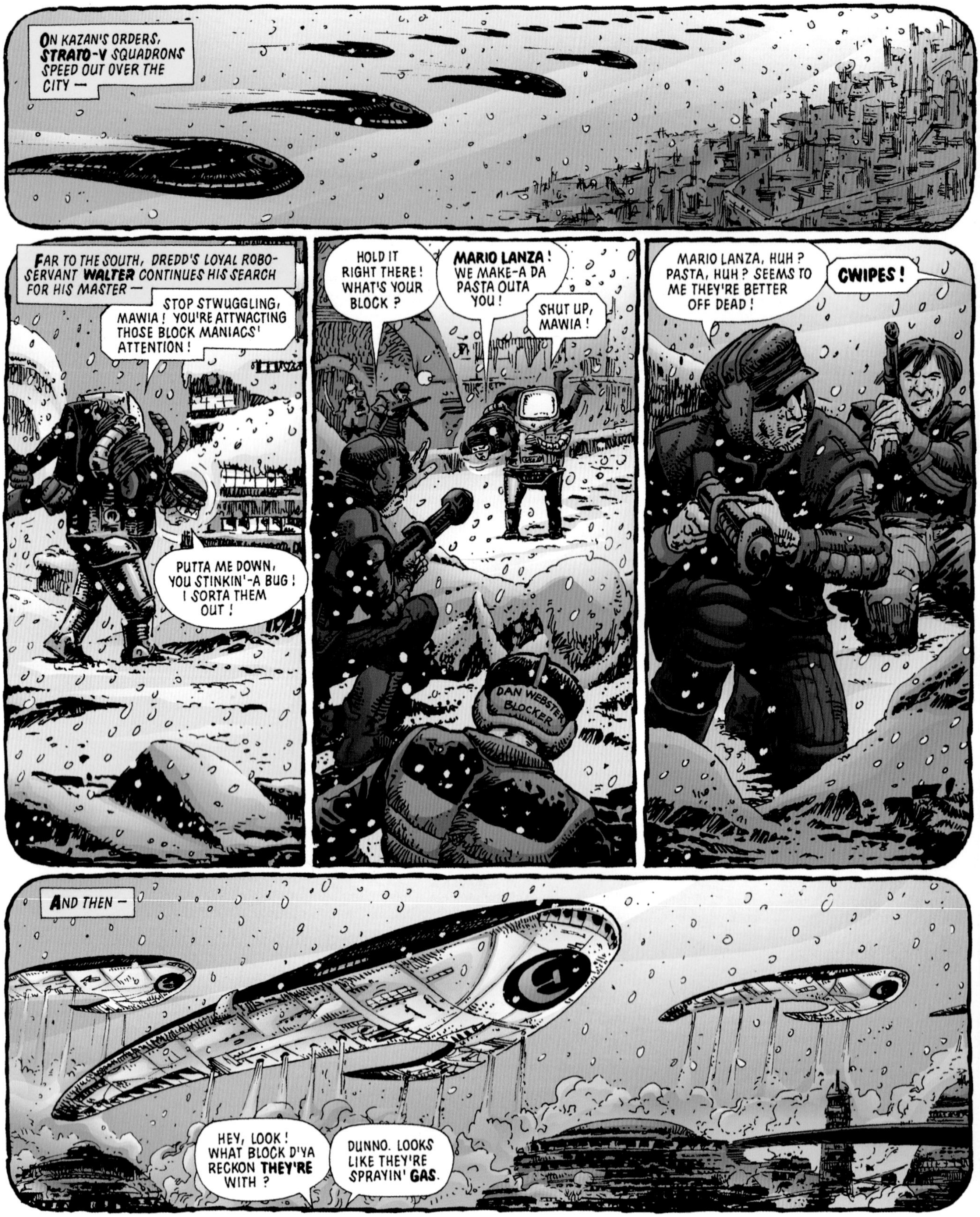

ON KAZAN'S ORDERS, STRATO-V SQUADRONS SPEED OUT OVER THE CITY —
FAR TO THE SOUTH, DREDD'S LOYAL ROBO-SERVANT WALTER CONTINUES HIS SEARCH FOR HIS MASTER —
STOP STWUGGLING, MAWIA! YOU'RE ATTWACTING THOSE BLOCK MANIACS' ATTENTION!
PUTTA ME DOWN, YOU STINKIN'-A BUG! I SORTA THEM OUT!
HOLD IT RIGHT THERE! WHAT'S YOUR BLOCK?
MARIO LANZA! WE MAKE-A DA PASTA OUTA YOU!
SHUT UP, MAWIA!
DAN WEBSTER BLOCKER
MARIO LANZA, HUH? PASTA, HUH? SEEMS TO ME THEY'RE BETTER OFF DEAD!
CWIPES!
AND THEN —
HEY, LOOK! WHAT BLOCK D'YA RECKON THEY'RE WITH?
DUNNO. LOOKS LIKE THEY'RE SPRAYIN' GAS.

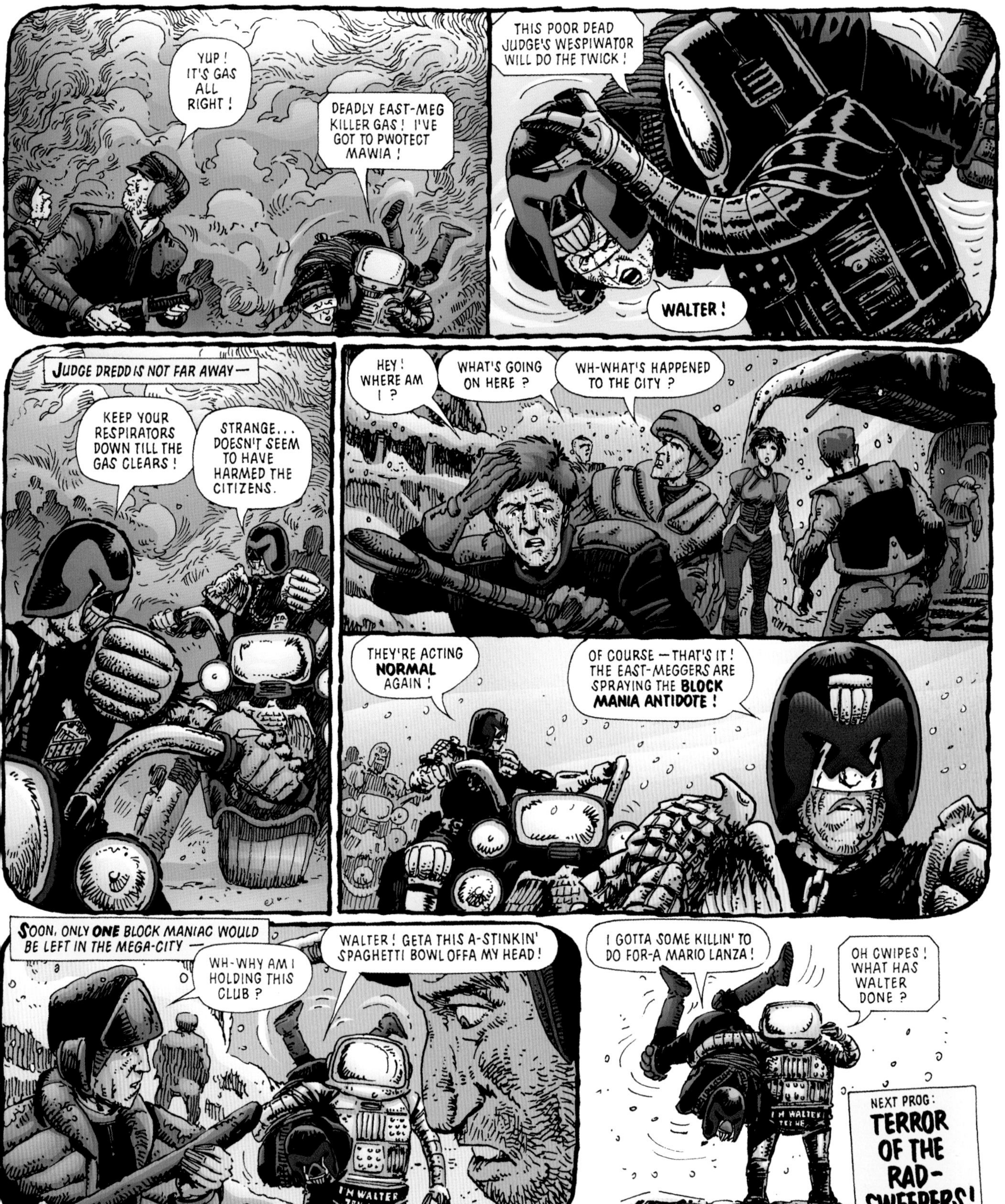
YUP! IT'S GAS ALL RIGHT!
DEADLY EAST-MEG KILLER GAS! I'VE GOT TO PWOTECT MAWIA!
THIS POOR DEAD JUDGE'S WESPIWATOR WILL DO THE TWICK!
WALTER!
JUDGE DREDD IS NOT FAR AWAY—
KEEP YOUR RESPIRATORS DOWN TILL THE GAS CLEARS!
STRANGE... DOESN'T SEEM TO HAVE HARMED THE CITIZENS.
HEY! WHERE AM I?
WHAT'S GOING ON HERE?
WH-WHAT'S HAPPENED TO THE CITY?
THEY'RE ACTING NORMAL AGAIN!
OF COURSE — THAT'S IT! THE EAST-MEGGERS ARE SPRAYING THE BLOCK MANIA ANTIDOTE!
SOON, ONLY ONE BLOCK MANIAC WOULD BE LEFT IN THE MEGA-CITY —
WH-WHY AM I HOLDING THIS CLUB?
WALTER! GETA THIS A-STINKIN' SPAGHETTI BOWL OFFA MY HEAD!
I'M WALTER TRY ME
I GOTTA SOME KILLIN' TO DO FOR-A MARIO LANZA!
OH CWIPES! WHAT HAS WALTER DONE?
NEXT PROG: TERROR OF THE RAD-SWEEPERS!

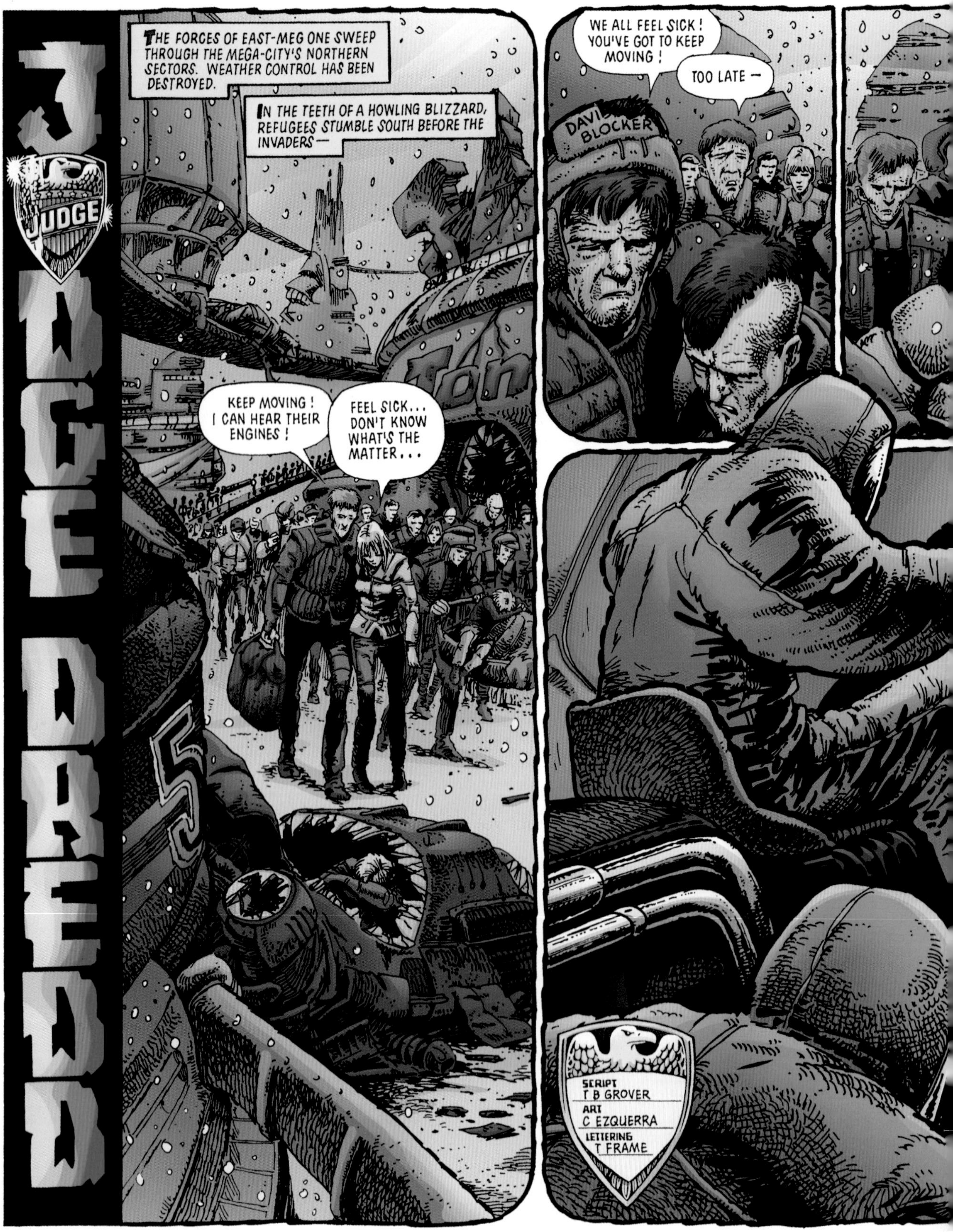
JUDGE DREDD
JUDGE
THE FORCES OF EAST-MEG ONE SWEEP THROUGH THE MEGA-CITY'S NORTHERN SECTORS. WEATHER CONTROL HAS BEEN DESTROYED.
IN THE TEETH OF A HOWLING BLIZZARD, REFUGEES STUMBLE SOUTH BEFORE THE INVADERS—
KEEP MOVING ! I CAN HEAR THEIR ENGINES !
FEEL SICK... DON'T KNOW WHAT'S THE MATTER...
WE ALL FEEL SICK ! YOU'VE GOT TO KEEP MOVING !
TOO LATE—
BLOCKER
SCRIPT
T B GROVER
ART
C EZQUERRA
LETTERING
T FRAME

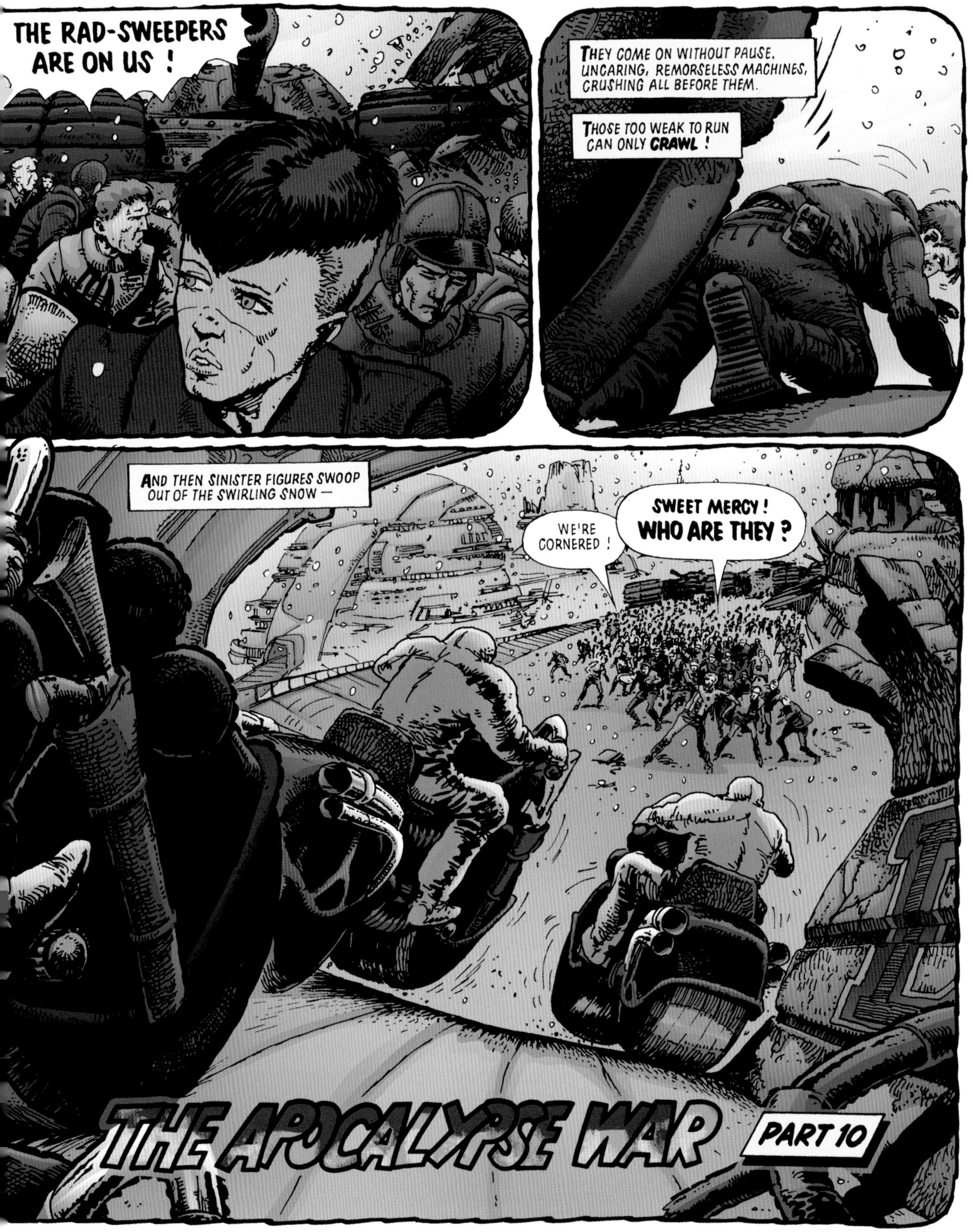
THE RAD-SWEEPERS ARE ON US !
THEY COME ON WITHOUT PAUSE. UNCARING, REMORSELESS MACHINES, CRUSHING ALL BEFORE THEM.
THOSE TOO WEAK TO RUN CAN ONLY CRAWL !
AND THEN SINISTER FIGURES SWOOP OUT OF THE SWIRLING SNOW —
WE'RE CORNERED !
SWEET MERCY ! WHO ARE THEY ?
THE APOCALYPSE WAR
PART 10

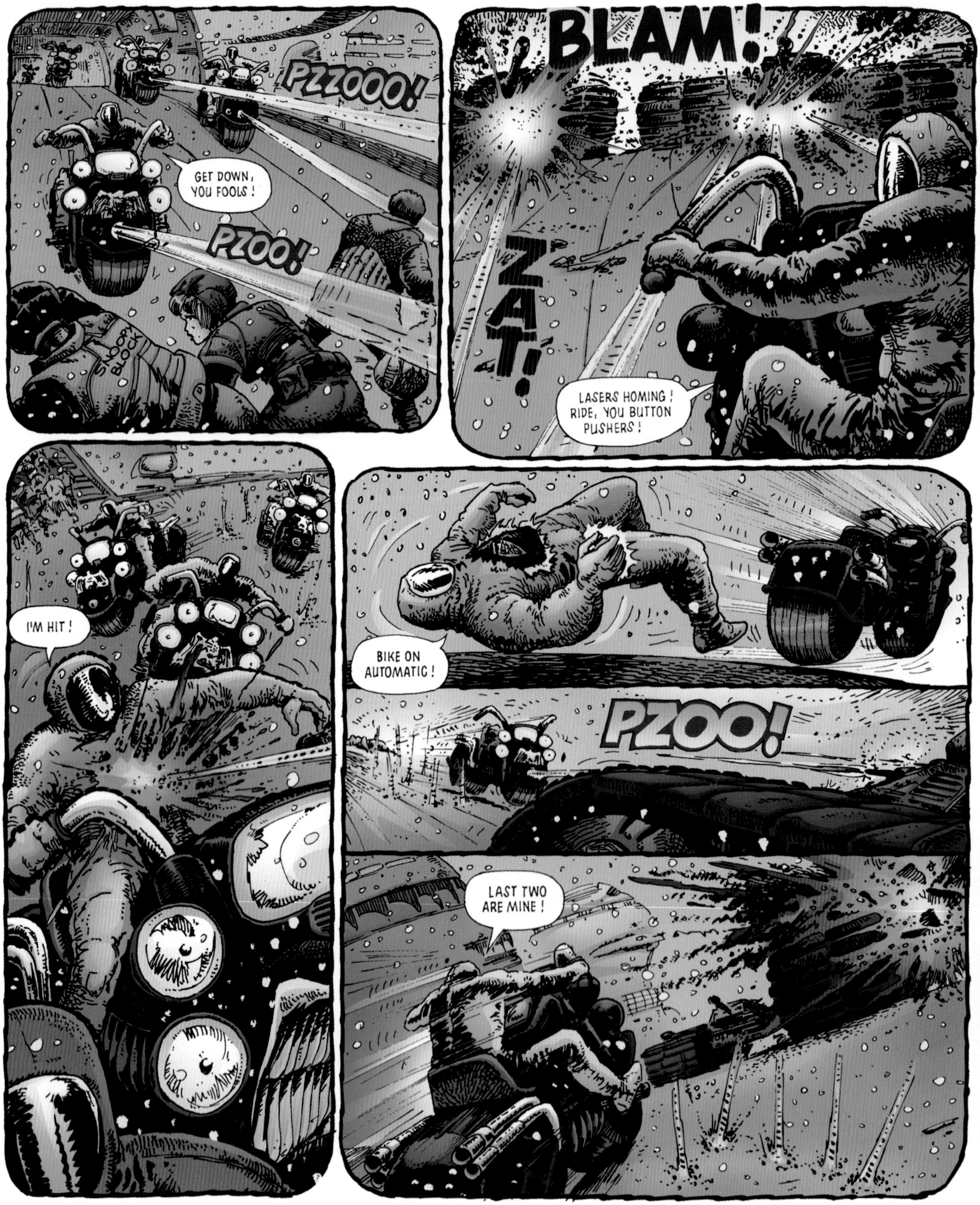
PZZOOO!
GET DOWN, YOU FOOLS!
PZOO!
BLAM!
ZAT!
LASERS HOMING! RIDE, YOU BUTTON PUSHERS!
I'M HIT!
BIKE ON AUTOMATIC!
PZOO!
LAST TWO ARE MINE!

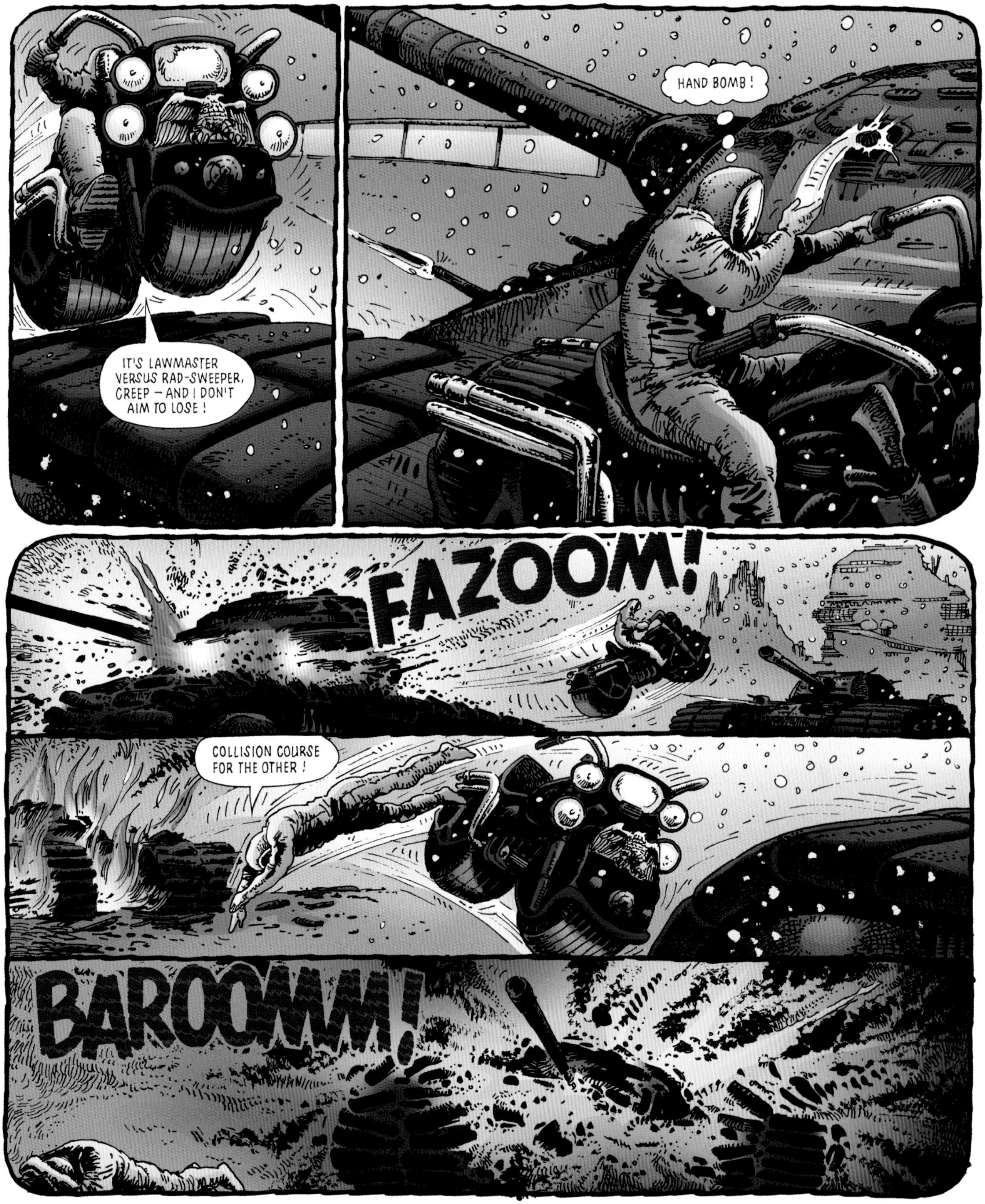
IT'S LAWMASTER VERSUS RAD-SWEEPER, CREEP – AND I DON'T AIM TO LOSE !
HAND BOMB !
FAZOOM!
COLLISION COURSE FOR THE OTHER !
BAROOMM!

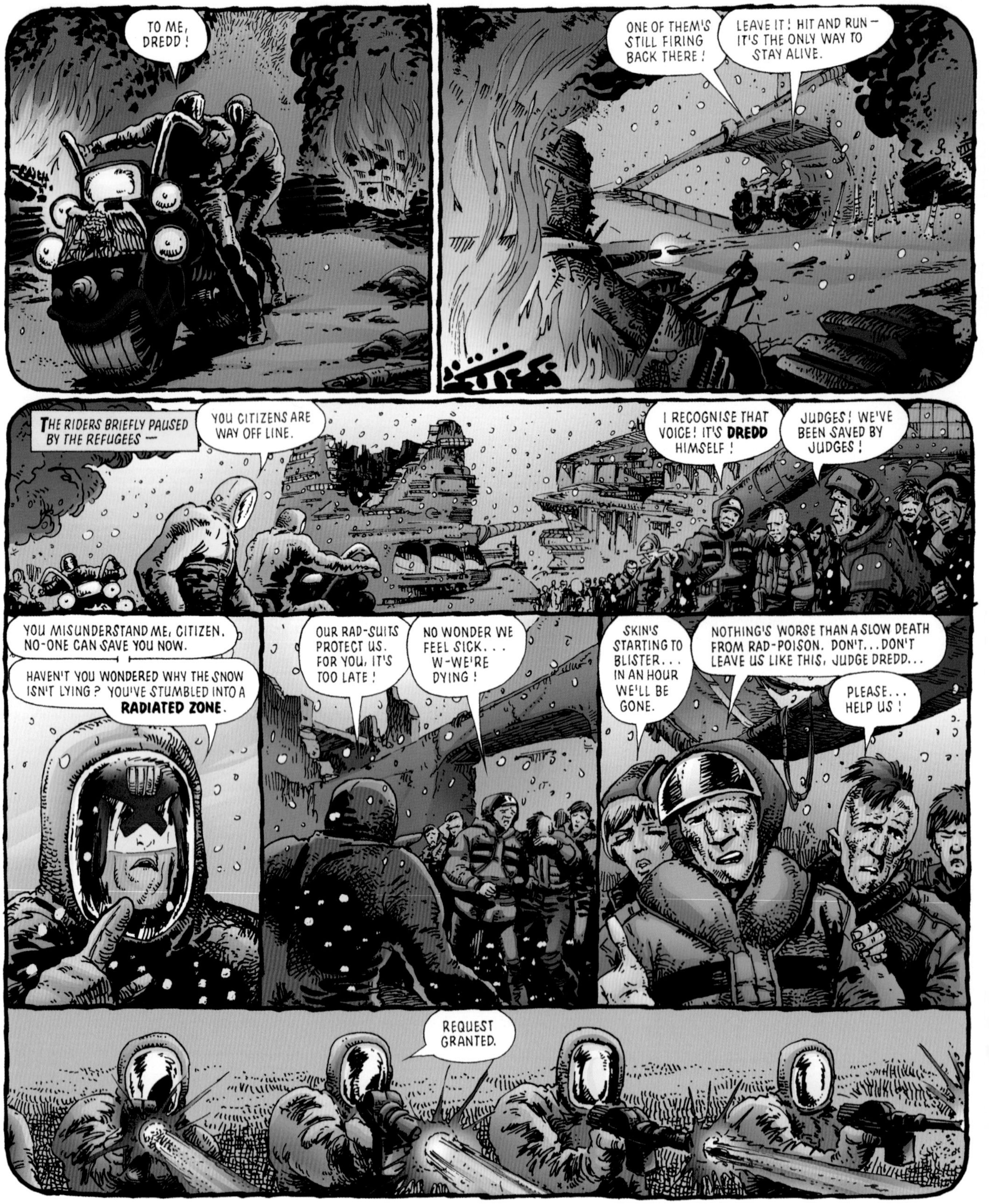
TO ME, DREDD!
ONE OF THEM'S STILL FIRING BACK THERE!
LEAVE IT! HIT AND RUN — IT'S THE ONLY WAY TO STAY ALIVE.
THE RIDERS BRIEFLY PAUSED BY THE REFUGEES —
YOU CITIZENS ARE WAY OFF LINE.
I RECOGNISE THAT VOICE! IT'S DREDD HIMSELF!
JUDGES! WE'VE BEEN SAVED BY JUDGES!
YOU MISUNDERSTAND ME, CITIZEN. NO-ONE CAN SAVE YOU NOW.
HAVEN'T YOU WONDERED WHY THE SNOW ISN'T LYING? YOU'VE STUMBLED INTO A RADIATED ZONE.
OUR RAD-SUITS PROTECT US. FOR YOU, IT'S TOO LATE!
NO WONDER WE FEEL SICK... W-WE'RE DYING!
SKIN'S STARTING TO BLISTER... IN AN HOUR WE'LL BE GONE.
NOTHING'S WORSE THAN A SLOW DEATH FROM RAD-POISON. DON'T... DON'T LEAVE US LIKE THIS, JUDGE DREDD...
PLEASE... HELP US!
REQUEST GRANTED.

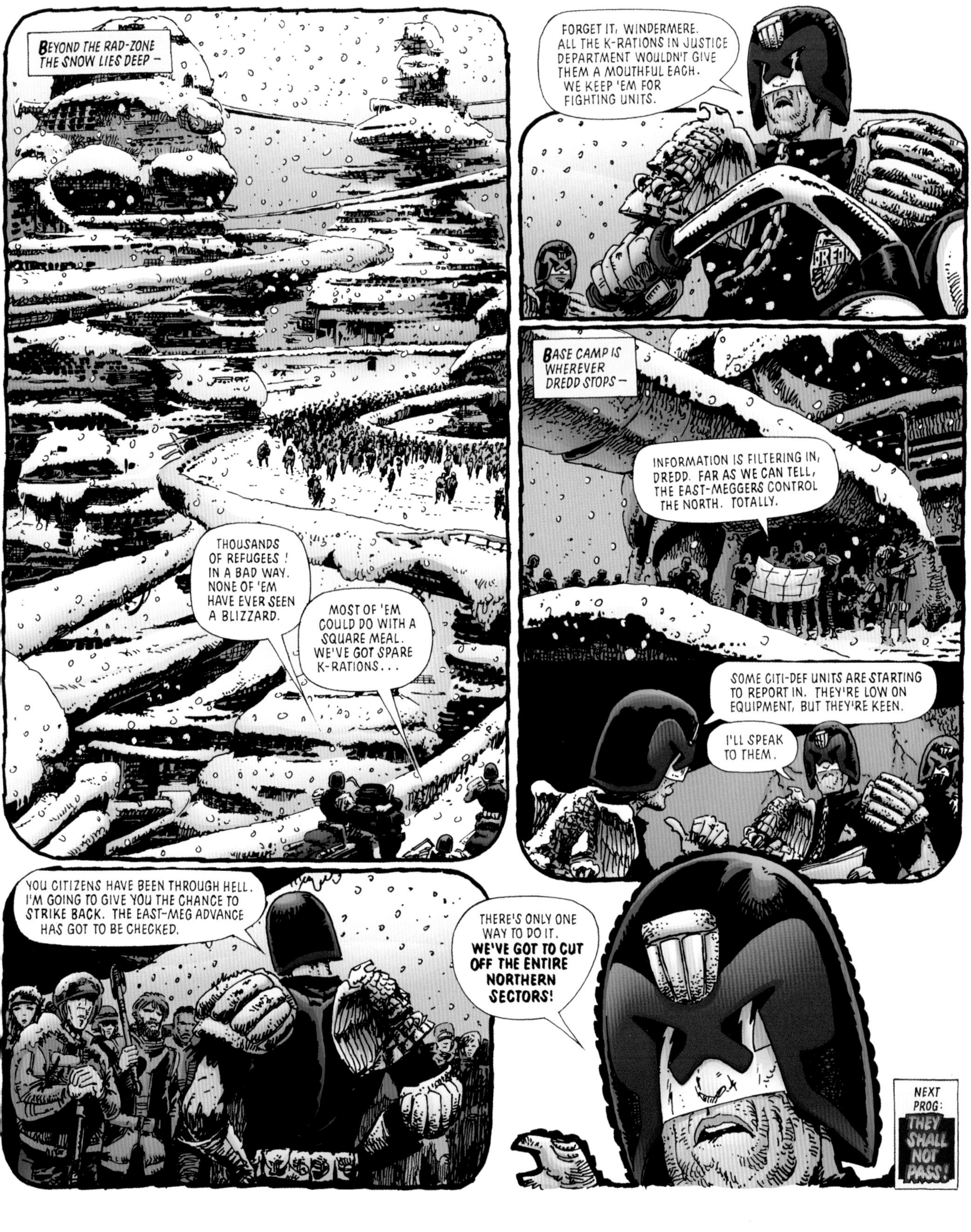

BEYOND THE RAD-ZONE THE SNOW LIES DEEP –
THOUSANDS OF REFUGEES ! IN A BAD WAY. NONE OF 'EM HAVE EVER SEEN A BLIZZARD.
MOST OF 'EM COULD DO WITH A SQUARE MEAL. WE'VE GOT SPARE K-RATIONS...
FORGET IT, WINDERMERE. ALL THE K-RATIONS IN JUSTICE DEPARTMENT WOULDN'T GIVE THEM A MOUTHFUL EACH. WE KEEP 'EM FOR FIGHTING UNITS.
BASE CAMP IS WHEREVER DREDD STOPS –
INFORMATION IS FILTERING IN, DREDD. FAR AS WE CAN TELL, THE EAST-MEGGERS CONTROL THE NORTH. TOTALLY.
SOME CITI-DEF UNITS ARE STARTING TO REPORT IN. THEY'RE LOW ON EQUIPMENT, BUT THEY'RE KEEN.
I'LL SPEAK TO THEM.
YOU CITIZENS HAVE BEEN THROUGH HELL. I'M GOING TO GIVE YOU THE CHANCE TO STRIKE BACK. THE EAST-MEG ADVANCE HAS GOT TO BE CHECKED.
THERE'S ONLY ONE WAY TO DO IT. WE'VE GOT TO CUT OFF THE ENTIRE NORTHERN SECTORS!
NEXT PROG: THEY SHALL NOT PASS!

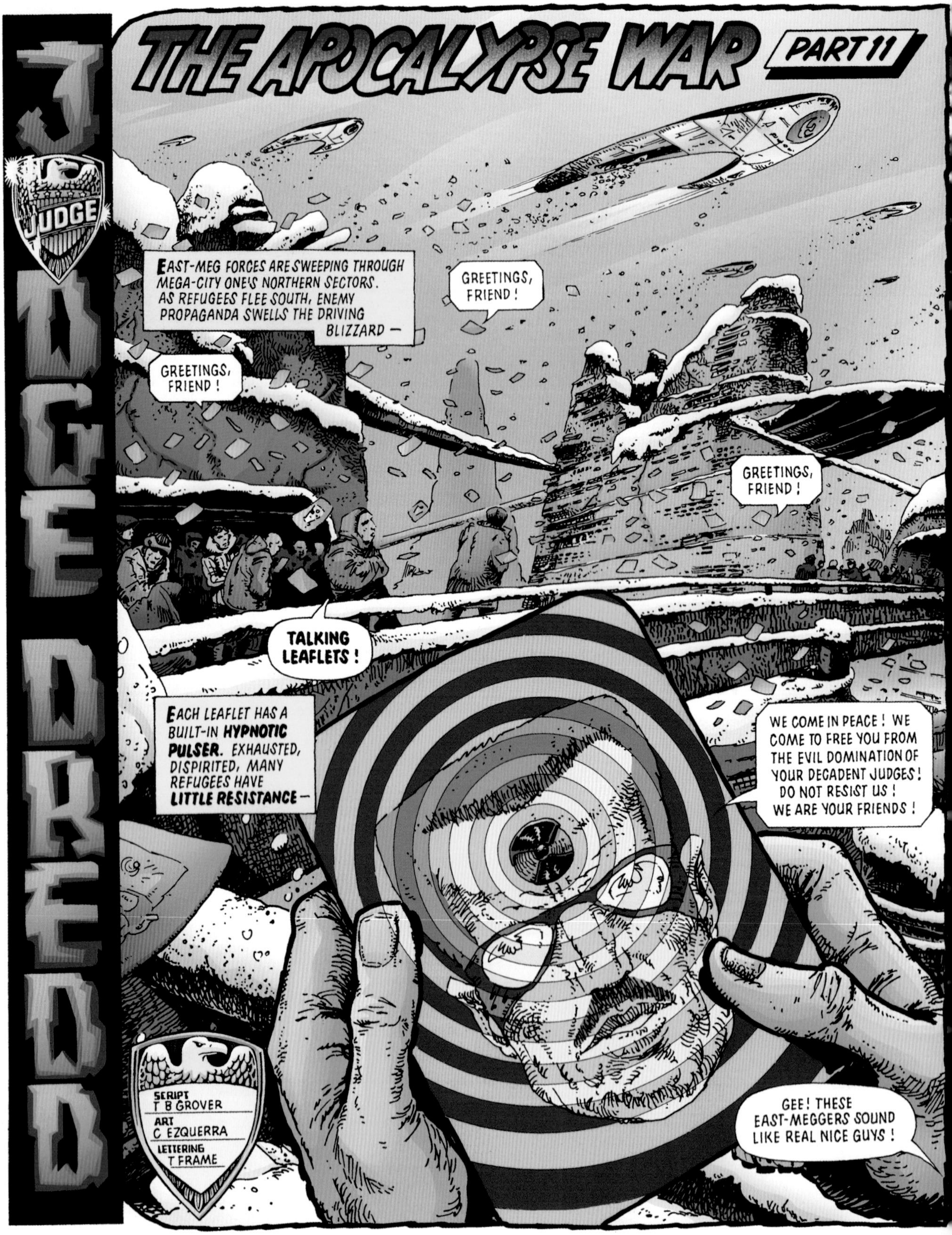
JUDGE DREDD
THE APOCALYPSE WAR PART 11
EAST-MEG FORCES ARE SWEEPING THROUGH MEGA-CITY ONE'S NORTHERN SECTORS. AS REFUGEES FLEE SOUTH, ENEMY PROPAGANDA SWELLS THE DRIVING BLIZZARD —
GREETINGS, FRIEND!
GREETINGS, FRIEND!
GREETINGS, FRIEND!
TALKING LEAFLETS!
EACH LEAFLET HAS A BUILT-IN HYPNOTIC PULSER. EXHAUSTED, DISPIRITED, MANY REFUGEES HAVE LITTLE RESISTANCE —
WE COME IN PEACE! WE COME TO FREE YOU FROM THE EVIL DOMINATION OF YOUR DECADENT JUDGES! DO NOT RESIST US! WE ARE YOUR FRIENDS!
GEE! THESE EAST-MEGGERS SOUND LIKE REAL NICE GUYS!
SCRIPT T B GROVER
ART C EZQUERRA
LETTERING T FRAME

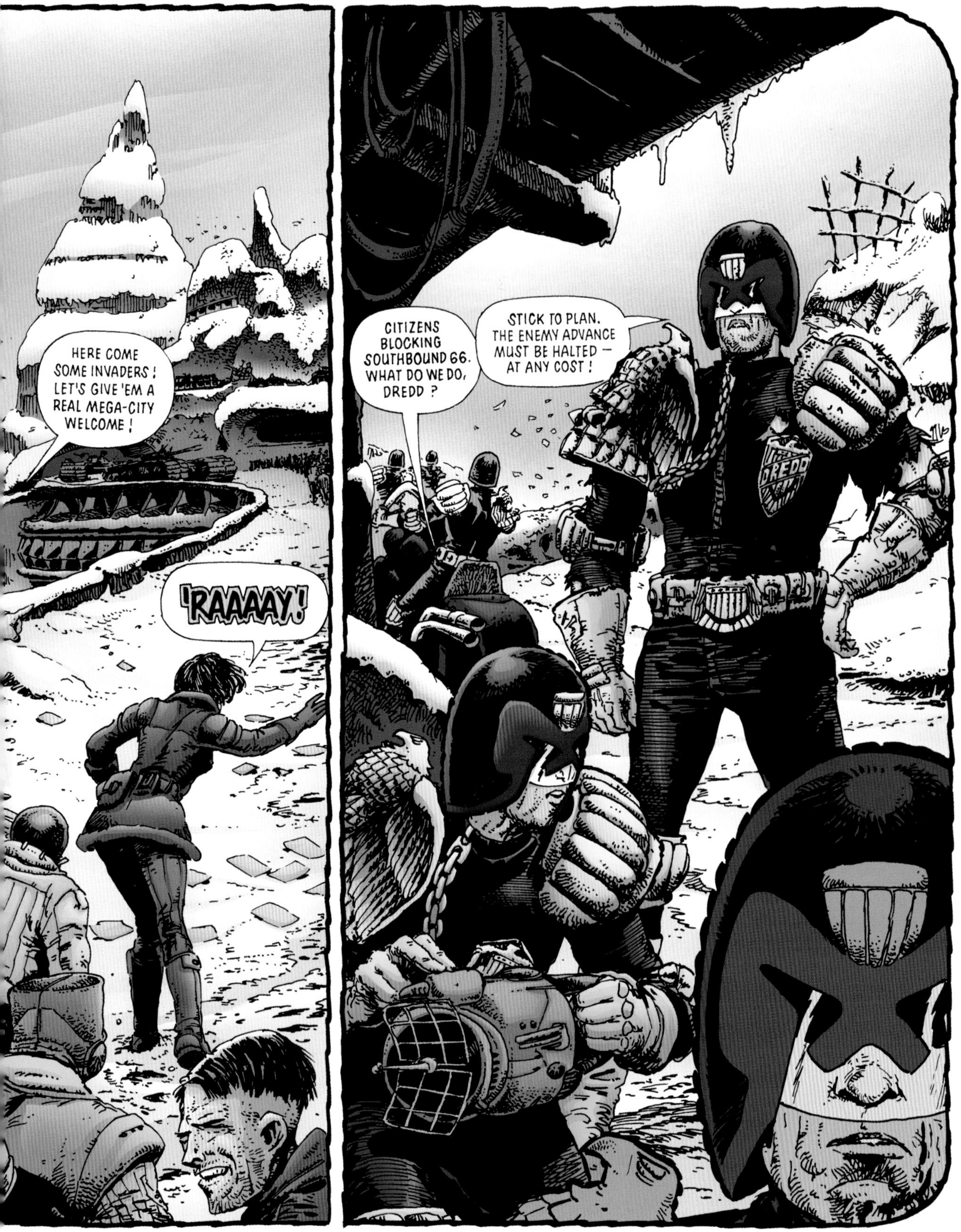

HERE COME SOME INVADERS! LET'S GIVE 'EM A REAL MEGA-CITY WELCOME!
'RAAAAY!
CITIZENS BLOCKING SOUTHBOUND 66. WHAT DO WE DO, DREDD?
STICK TO PLAN. THE ENEMY ADVANCE MUST BE HALTED — AT ANY COST!
DREDD

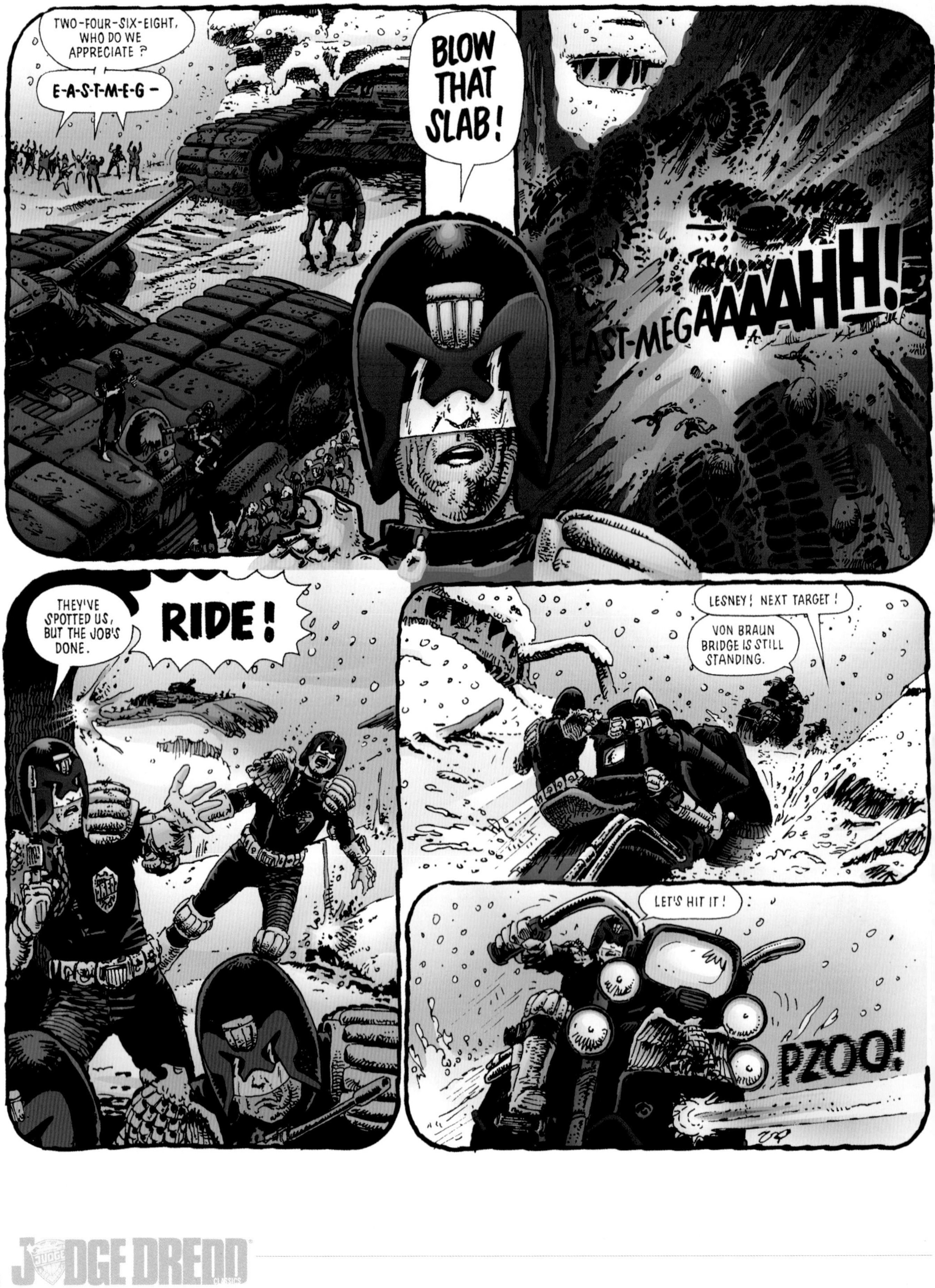
TWO-FOUR-SIX-EIGHT, WHO DO WE APPRECIATE ?
E-A-S-T-M-E-G -
BLOW THAT SLAB !
EAST-MEGAAAAAHH!
THEY'VE SPOTTED US, BUT THE JOB'S DONE.
RIDE !
LESNEY ! NEXT TARGET !
VON BRAUN BRIDGE IS STILL STANDING.
LET'S HIT IT !
PZOO!

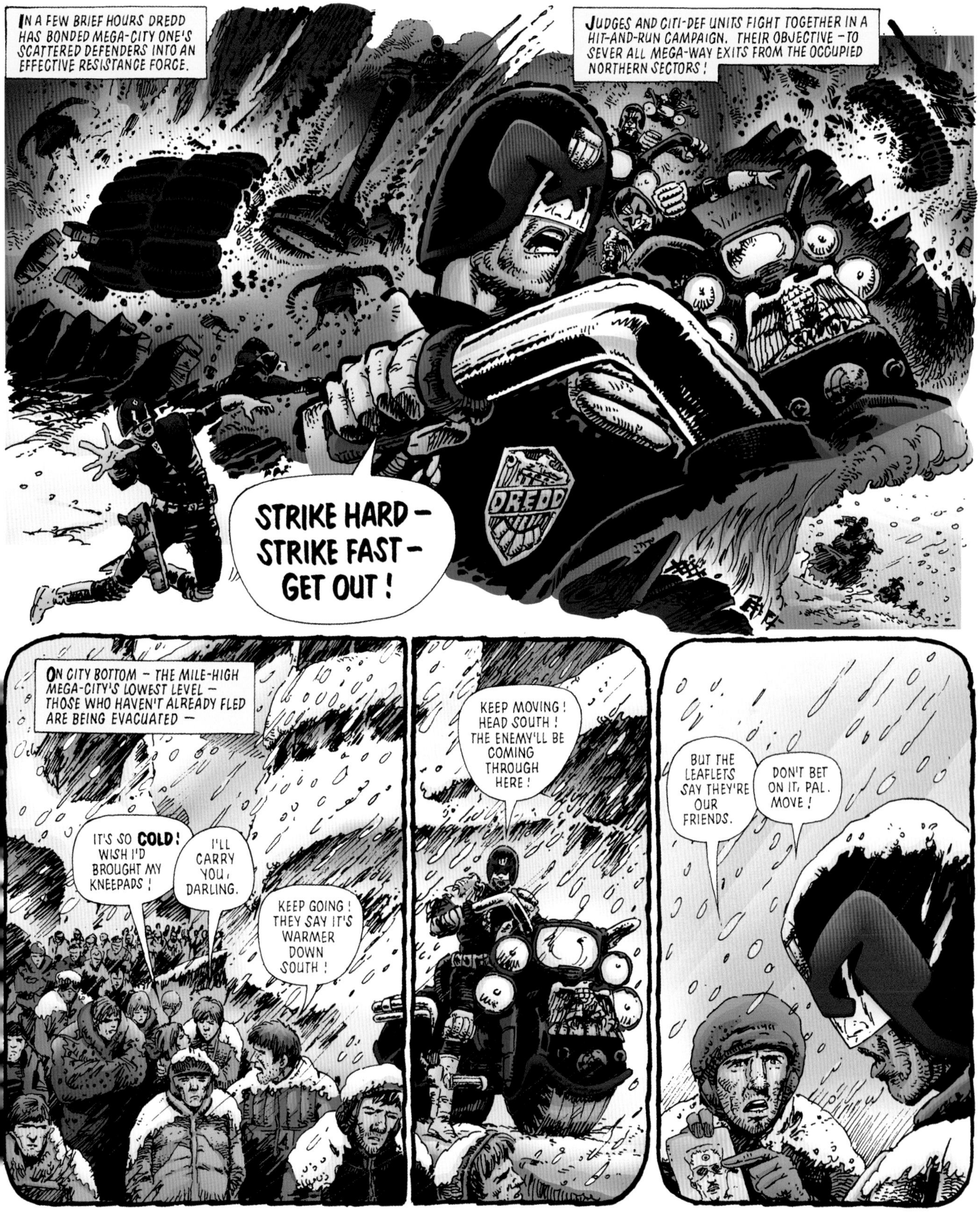
IN A FEW BRIEF HOURS DREDD HAS BONDED MEGA-CITY ONE'S SCATTERED DEFENDERS INTO AN EFFECTIVE RESISTANCE FORCE.
JUDGES AND CITI-DEF UNITS FIGHT TOGETHER IN A HIT-AND-RUN CAMPAIGN. THEIR OBJECTIVE – TO SEVER ALL MEGA-WAY EXITS FROM THE OCCUPIED NORTHERN SECTORS!
STRIKE HARD – STRIKE FAST – GET OUT!
DREDD
ON CITY BOTTOM – THE MILE-HIGH MEGA-CITY'S LOWEST LEVEL – THOSE WHO HAVEN'T ALREADY FLED ARE BEING EVACUATED –
IT'S SO **COLD**! WISH I'D BROUGHT MY KNEEPADS!
I'LL CARRY YOU, DARLING.
KEEP GOING! THEY SAY IT'S WARMER DOWN SOUTH!
KEEP MOVING! HEAD SOUTH! THE ENEMY'LL BE COMING THROUGH HERE!
BUT THE LEAFLETS SAY THEY'RE OUR FRIENDS.
DON'T BET ON IT, PAL. MOVE!

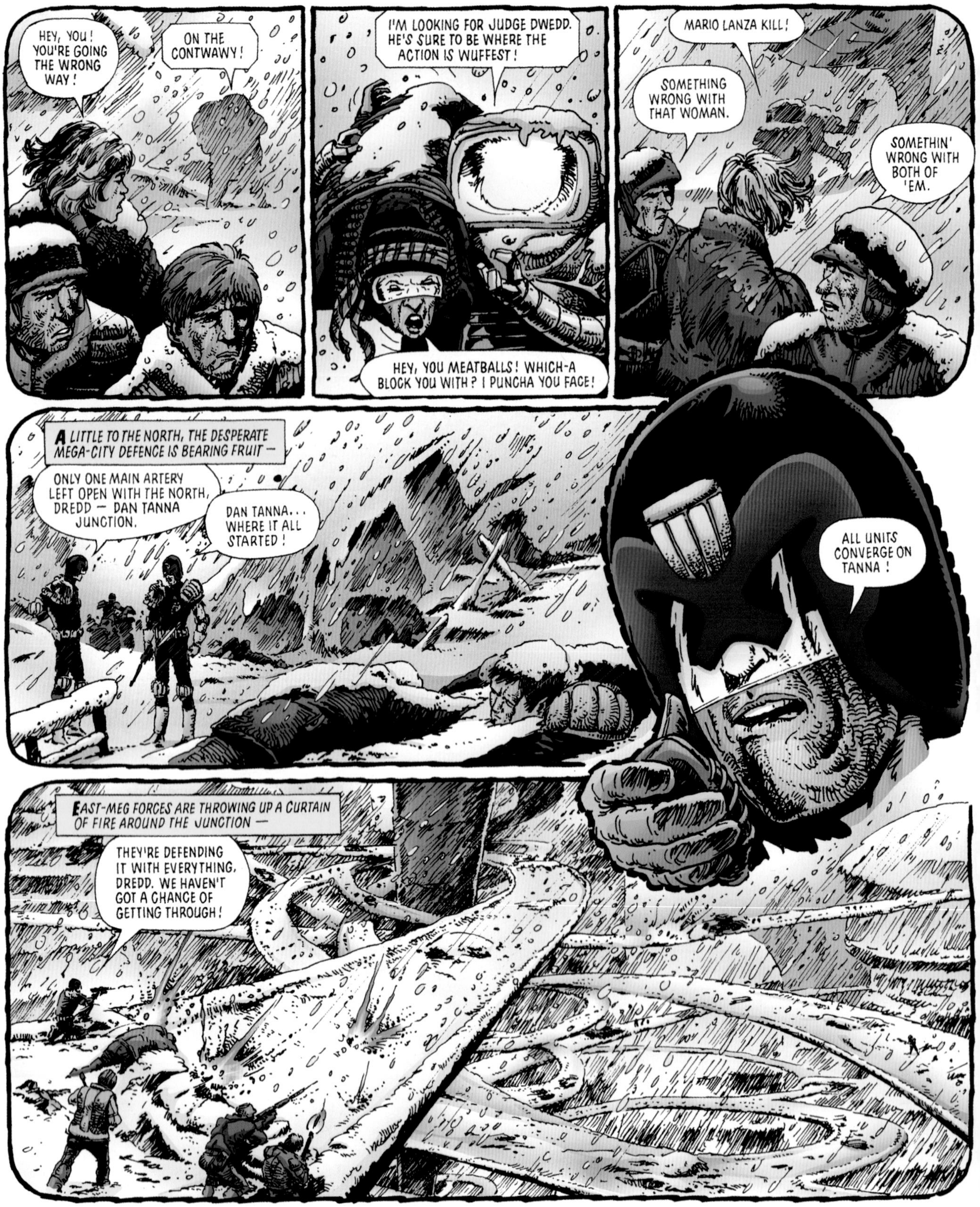
HEY, YOU! YOU'RE GOING THE WRONG WAY!
ON THE CONTWAWY!
I'M LOOKING FOR JUDGE DWEDD. HE'S SURE TO BE WHERE THE ACTION IS WUFFEST!
HEY, YOU MEATBALLS! WHICH-A BLOCK YOU WITH? I PUNCHA YOU FACE!
MARIO LANZA KILL!
SOMETHING WRONG WITH THAT WOMAN.
SOMETHIN' WRONG WITH BOTH OF 'EM.
A LITTLE TO THE NORTH, THE DESPERATE MEGA-CITY DEFENCE IS BEARING FRUIT —
ONLY ONE MAIN ARTERY LEFT OPEN WITH THE NORTH, DREDD — DAN TANNA JUNCTION.
DAN TANNA... WHERE IT ALL STARTED!
ALL UNITS CONVERGE ON TANNA!
EAST-MEG FORCES ARE THROWING UP A CURTAIN OF FIRE AROUND THE JUNCTION —
THEY'RE DEFENDING IT WITH EVERYTHING, DREDD. WE HAVEN'T GOT A CHANCE OF GETTING THROUGH!

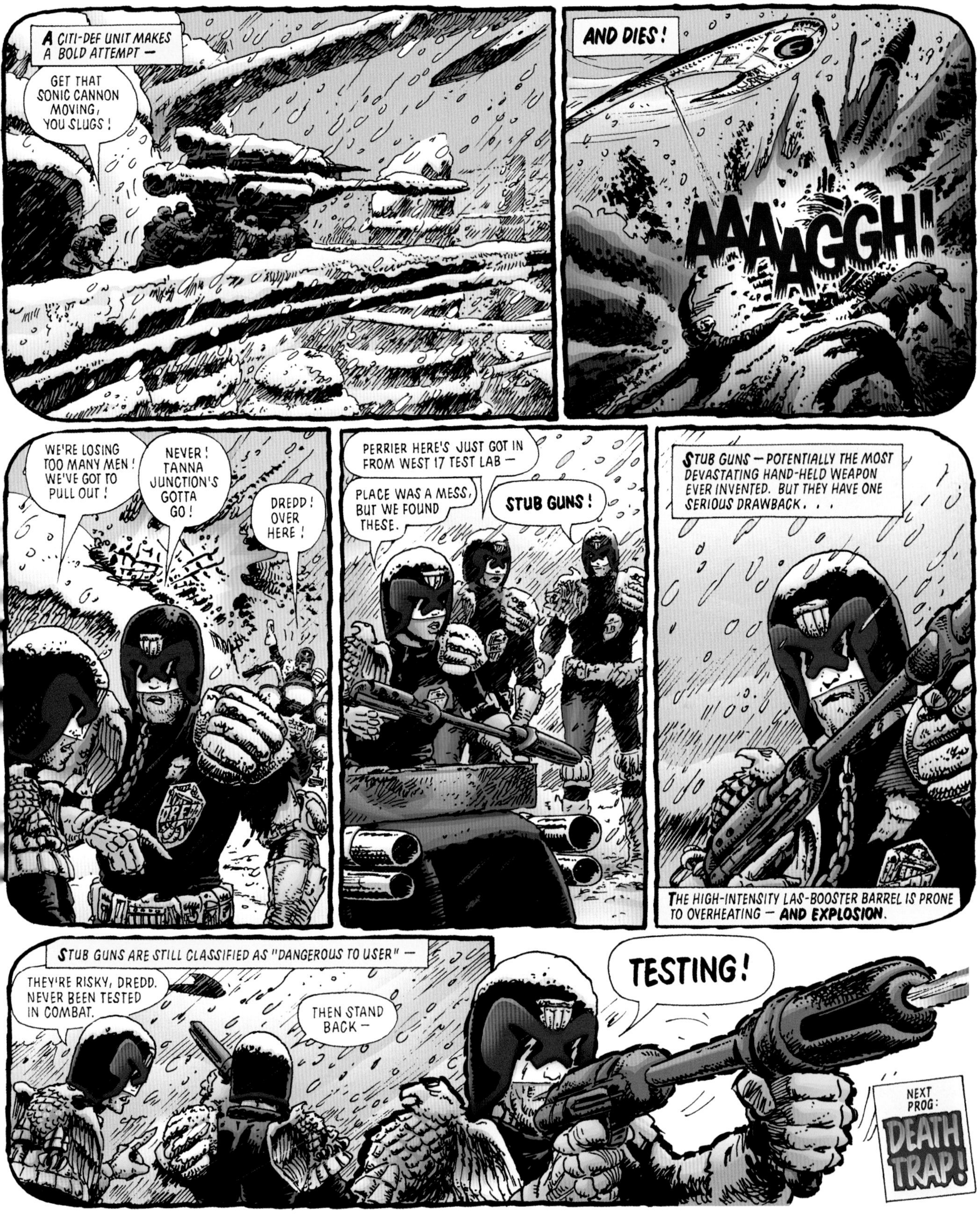
A CITI-DEF UNIT MAKES A BOLD ATTEMPT —
GET THAT SONIC CANNON MOVING, YOU SLUGS!
AND DIES!
AAAAGGH!
WE'RE LOSING TOO MANY MEN! WE'VE GOT TO PULL OUT!
NEVER! TANNA JUNCTION'S GOTTA GO!
DREDD! OVER HERE!
PERRIER HERE'S JUST GOT IN FROM WEST 17 TEST LAB —
PLACE WAS A MESS, BUT WE FOUND THESE.
STUB GUNS!
STUB GUNS — POTENTIALLY THE MOST DEVASTATING HAND-HELD WEAPON EVER INVENTED. BUT THEY HAVE ONE SERIOUS DRAWBACK. . .
THE HIGH-INTENSITY LAS-BOOSTER BARREL IS PRONE TO OVERHEATING — AND EXPLOSION.
STUB GUNS ARE STILL CLASSIFIED AS "DANGEROUS TO USER" —
THEY'RE RISKY, DREDD. NEVER BEEN TESTED IN COMBAT.
THEN STAND BACK —
TESTING!
NEXT PROG:
DEATH TRAP!

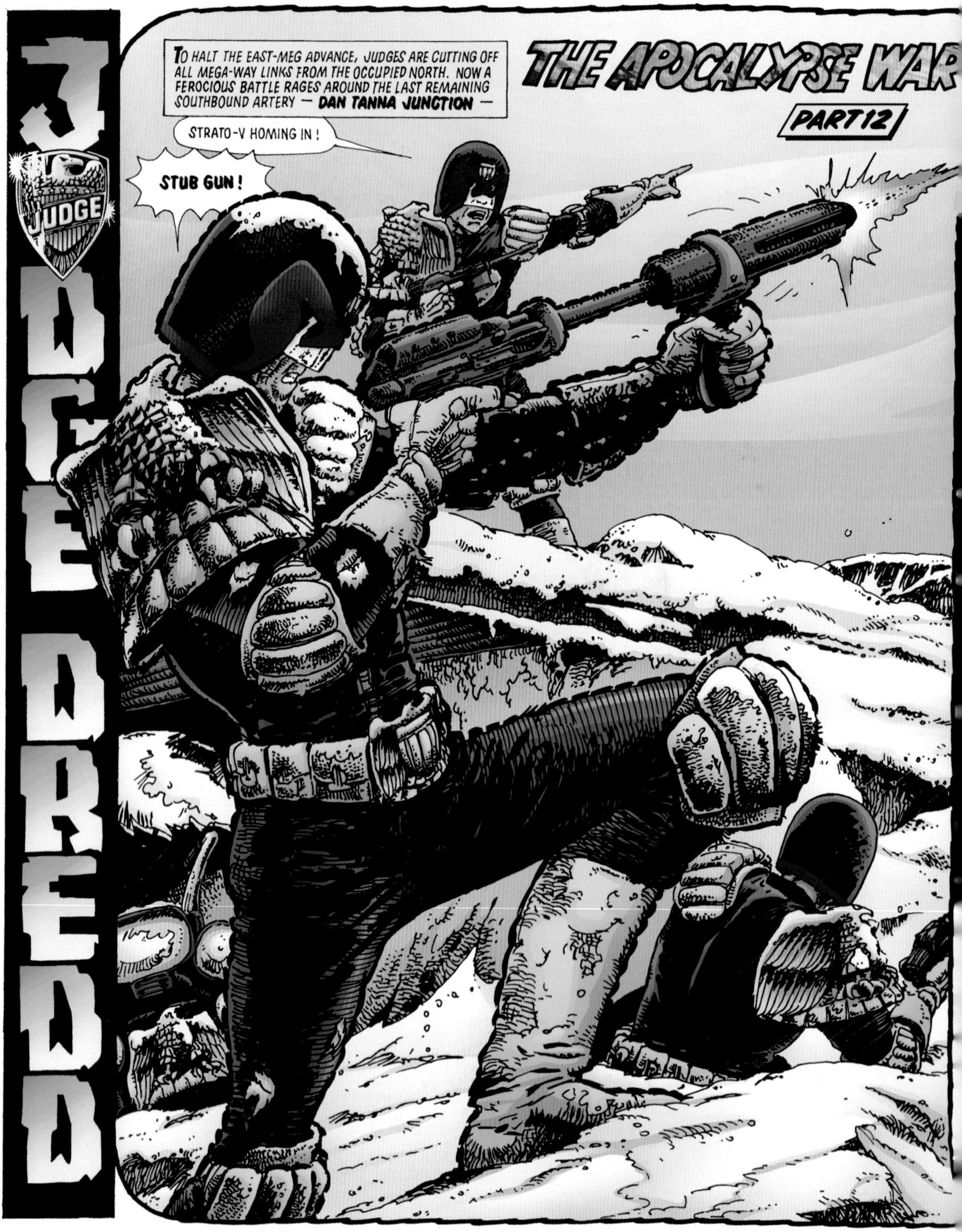
JUDGE DREDD
THE APOCALYPSE WAR
PART 12
TO HALT THE EAST-MEG ADVANCE, JUDGES ARE CUTTING OFF ALL MEGA-WAY LINKS FROM THE OCCUPIED NORTH. NOW A FEROCIOUS BATTLE RAGES AROUND THE LAST REMAINING SOUTHBOUND ARTERY — DAN TANNA JUNCTION —
STRATO-V HOMING IN!
STUB GUN!

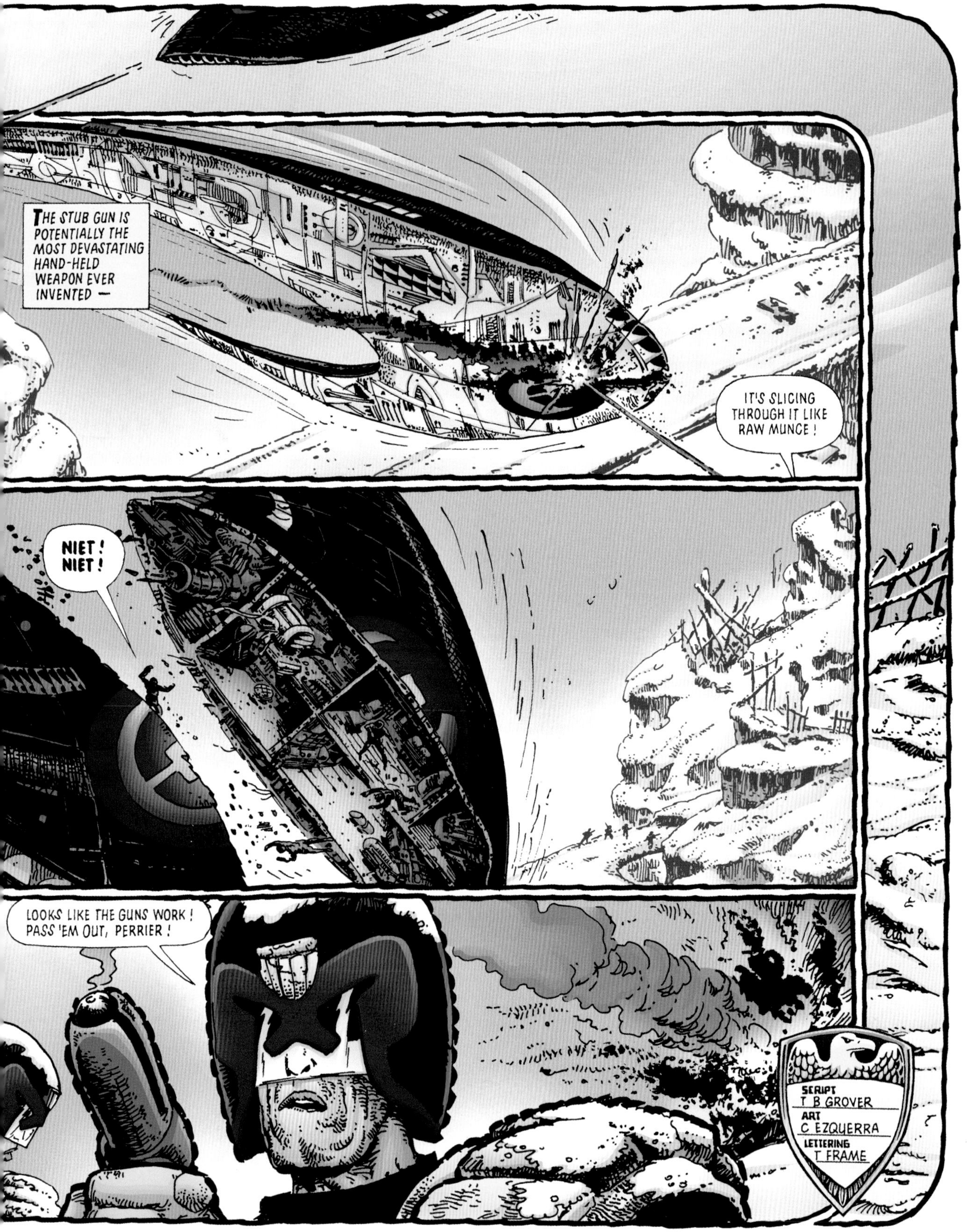
THE STUB GUN IS POTENTIALLY THE MOST DEVASTATING HAND-HELD WEAPON EVER INVENTED —
IT'S SLICING THROUGH IT LIKE RAW MUNCE !
NIET ! NIET !
LOOKS LIKE THE GUNS WORK ! PASS 'EM OUT, PERRIER !
SCRIPT T B GROVER
ART C EZQUERRA
LETTERING T FRAME

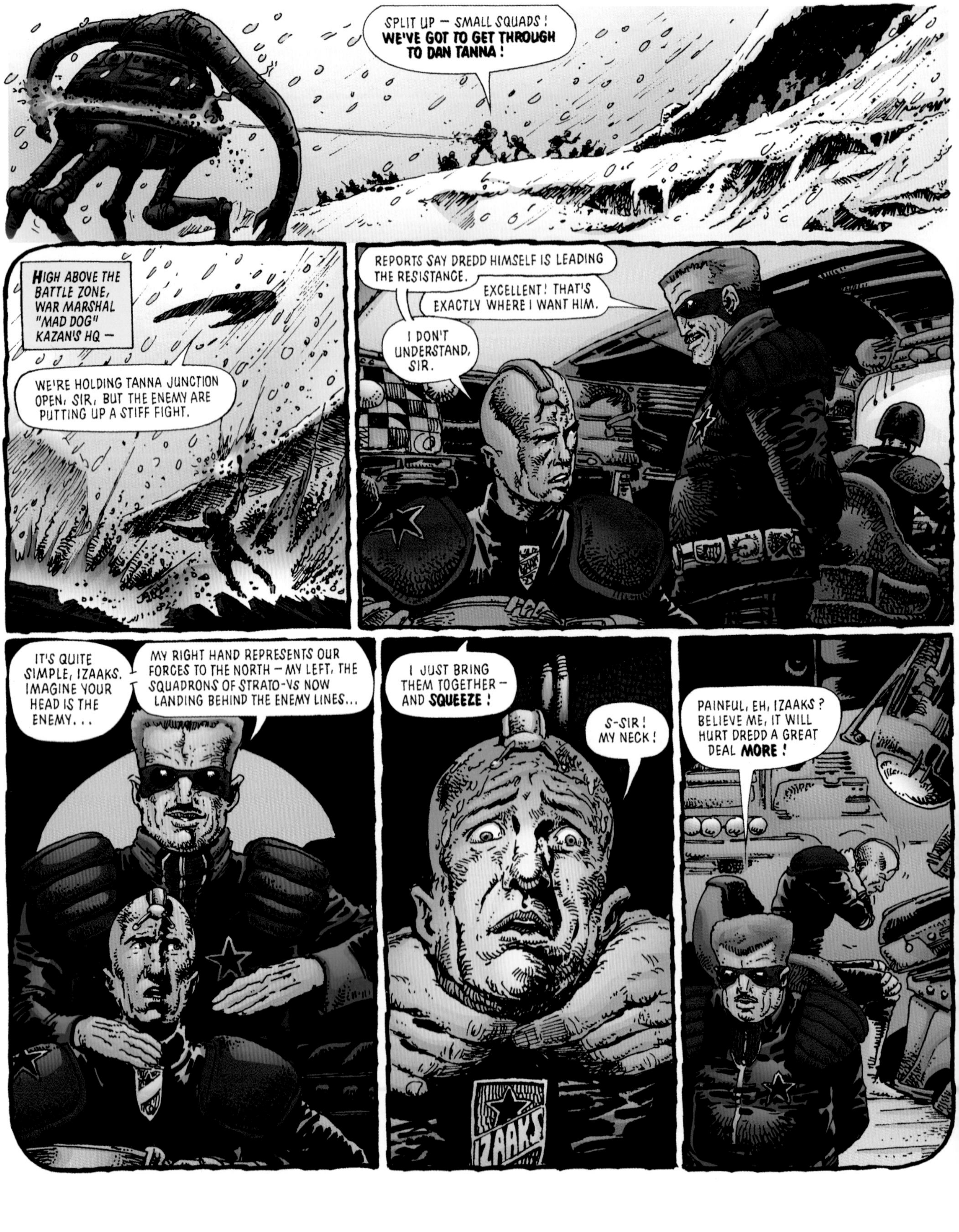

SPLIT UP — SMALL SQUADS! **WE'VE GOT TO GET THROUGH TO DAN TANNA!**
HIGH ABOVE THE BATTLE ZONE, WAR MARSHAL "MAD DOG" KAZAN'S HQ —
WE'RE HOLDING TANNA JUNCTION OPEN, SIR, BUT THE ENEMY ARE PUTTING UP A STIFF FIGHT.
REPORTS SAY DREDD HIMSELF IS LEADING THE RESISTANCE.
EXCELLENT! THAT'S EXACTLY WHERE I WANT HIM.
I DON'T UNDERSTAND, SIR.
IT'S QUITE SIMPLE, IZAAKS. IMAGINE YOUR HEAD IS THE ENEMY...
MY RIGHT HAND REPRESENTS OUR FORCES TO THE NORTH — MY LEFT, THE SQUADRONS OF STRATO-VS NOW LANDING BEHIND THE ENEMY LINES...
I JUST BRING THEM TOGETHER — AND **SQUEEZE!**
S-SIR! MY NECK!
IZAAKS
PAINFUL, EH, IZAAKS? BELIEVE ME, IT WILL HURT DREDD A GREAT DEAL **MORE!**

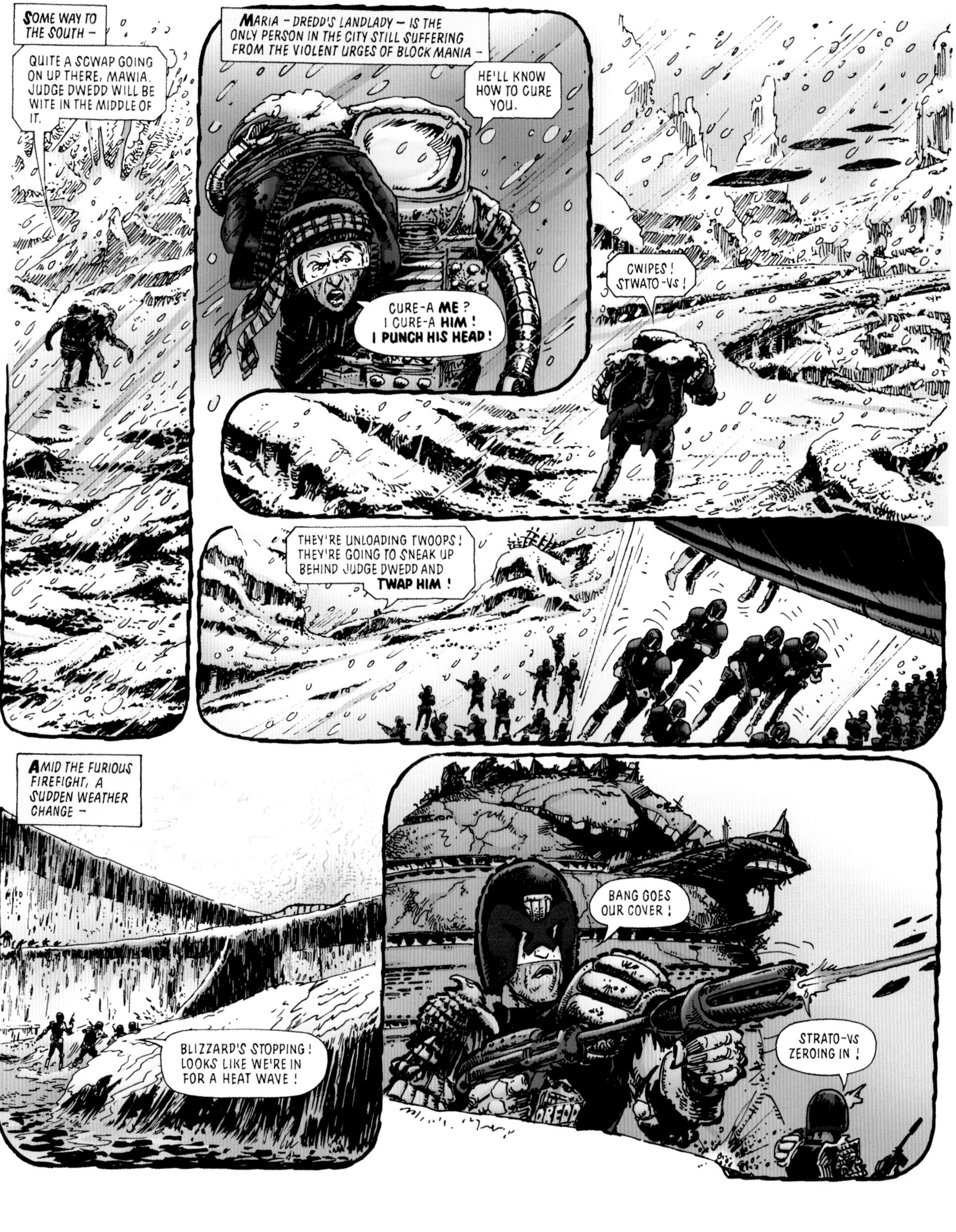
SOME WAY TO THE SOUTH –
QUITE A SCWAP GOING ON UP THERE, MAWIA. JUDGE DWEDD WILL BE WITE IN THE MIDDLE OF IT.
MARIA – DREDD'S LANDLADY – IS THE ONLY PERSON IN THE CITY STILL SUFFERING FROM THE VIOLENT URGES OF BLOCK MANIA –
HE'LL KNOW HOW TO CURE YOU.
CURE-A **ME**? I CURE-A **HIM**! **I PUNCH HIS HEAD!**
CWIPES! STWATO-VS!
THEY'RE UNLOADING TWOOPS! THEY'RE GOING TO SNEAK UP BEHIND JUDGE DWEDD AND **TWAP HIM**!
AMID THE FURIOUS FIREFIGHT, A SUDDEN WEATHER CHANGE –
BLIZZARD'S STOPPING! LOOKS LIKE WE'RE IN FOR A HEAT WAVE!
BANG GOES OUR COVER!
STRATO-VS ZEROING IN!

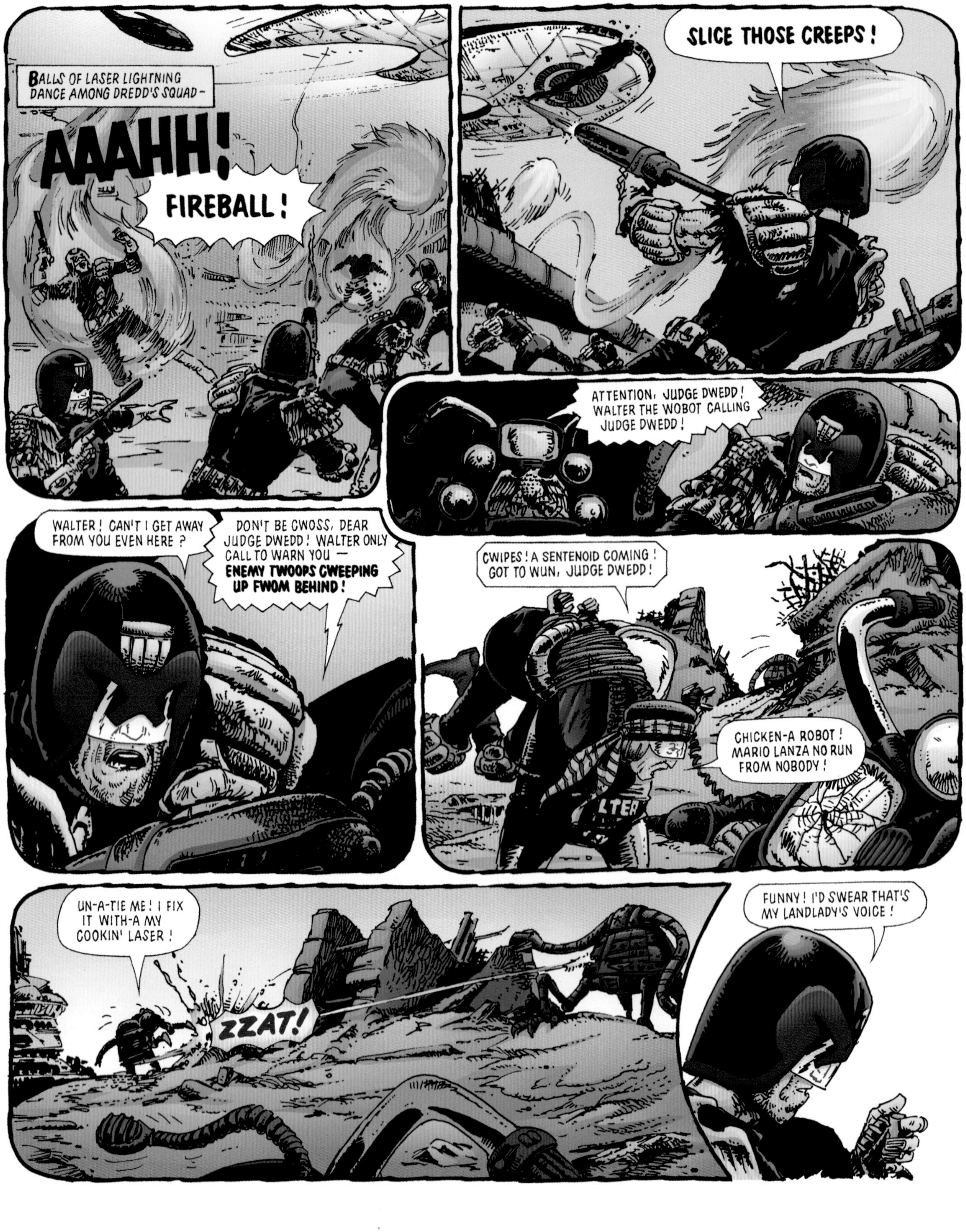
BALLS OF LASER LIGHTNING DANCE AMONG DREDD'S SQUAD –
AAAHH!
FIREBALL!
SLICE THOSE CREEPS!
ATTENTION, JUDGE DWEDD! WALTER THE WOBOT CALLING JUDGE DWEDD!
WALTER! CAN'T I GET AWAY FROM YOU EVEN HERE?
DON'T BE CWOSS, DEAR JUDGE DWEDD! WALTER ONLY CALL TO WARN YOU — ENEMY TWOOPS CWEEPING UP FWOM BEHIND!
CWIPES! A SENTENOID COMING! GOT TO WUN, JUDGE DWEDD!
CHICKEN-A ROBOT! MARIO LANZA NO RUN FROM NOBODY!
UN-A-TIE ME! I FIX IT WITH-A MY COOKIN' LASER!
ZZAT!
FUNNY! I'D SWEAR THAT'S MY LANDLADY'S VOICE!

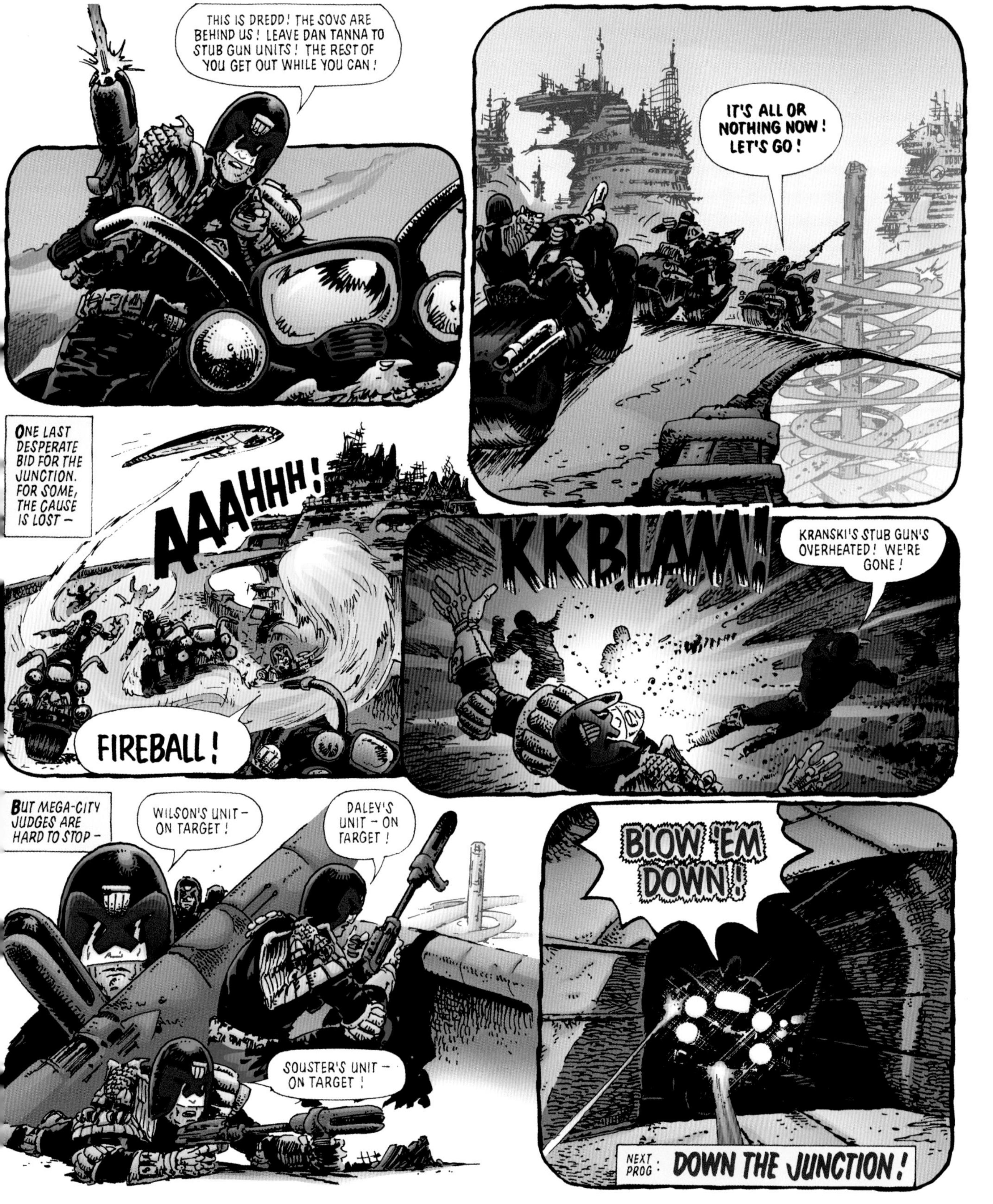
THIS IS DREDD! THE SOVS ARE BEHIND US! LEAVE DAN TANNA TO STUB GUN UNITS! THE REST OF YOU GET OUT WHILE YOU CAN!
IT'S ALL OR NOTHING NOW! LET'S GO!
ONE LAST DESPERATE BID FOR THE JUNCTION. FOR SOME, THE CAUSE IS LOST –
AAAHHH!
FIREBALL!
KKBLAM!
KRANSKI'S STUB GUN'S OVERHEATED! WE'RE GONE!
BUT MEGA-CITY JUDGES ARE HARD TO STOP –
WILSON'S UNIT – ON TARGET!
DALEY'S UNIT – ON TARGET!
SOUSTER'S UNIT – ON TARGET!
BLOW 'EM DOWN!
NEXT PROG: DOWN THE JUNCTION!

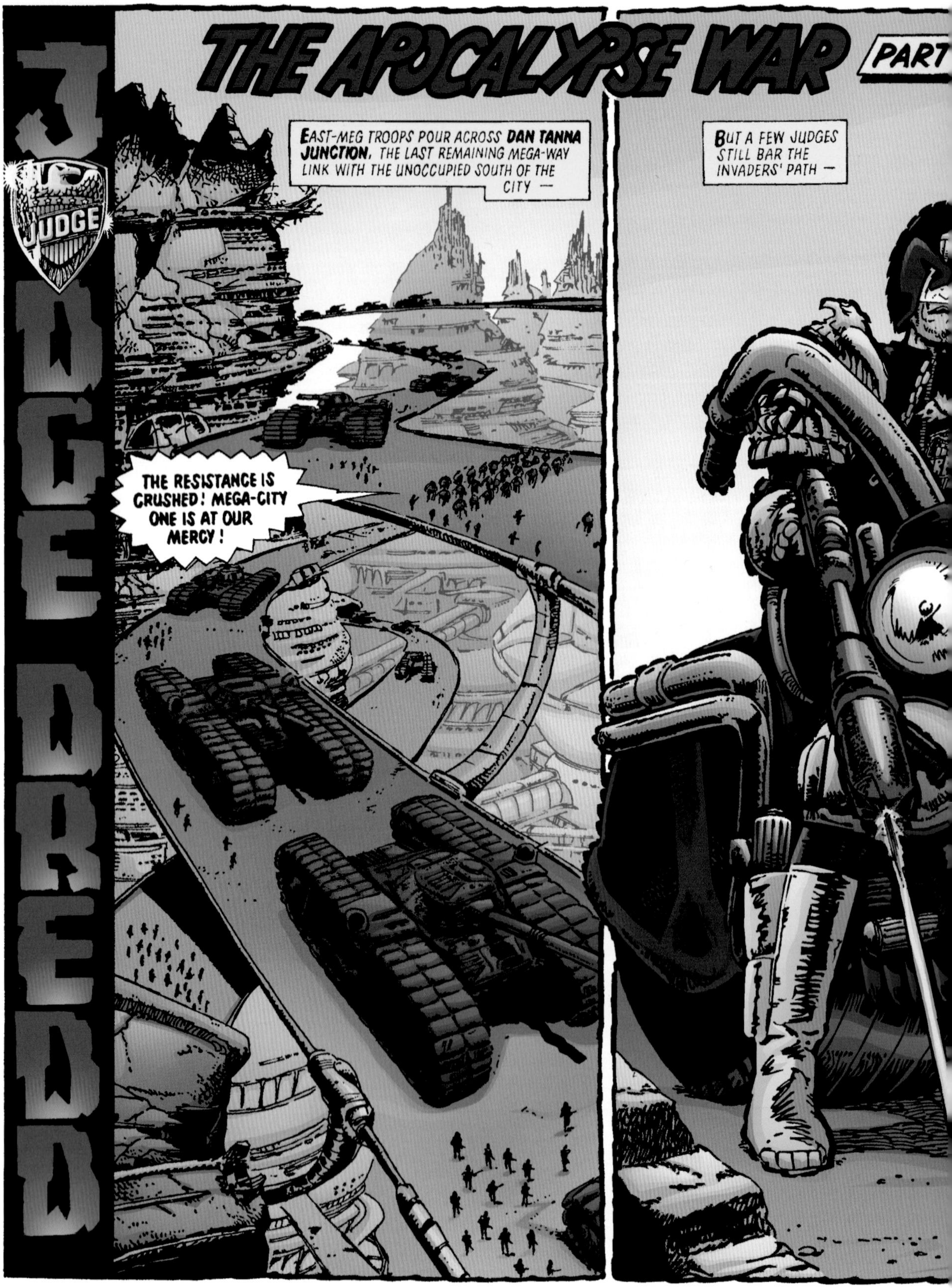
JUDGE DREDD
THE APOCALYPSE WAR PART
EAST-MEG TROOPS POUR ACROSS DAN TANNA JUNCTION, THE LAST REMAINING MEGA-WAY LINK WITH THE UNOCCUPIED SOUTH OF THE CITY —
BUT A FEW JUDGES STILL BAR THE INVADERS' PATH —
THE RESISTANCE IS CRUSHED! MEGA-CITY ONE IS AT OUR MERCY!

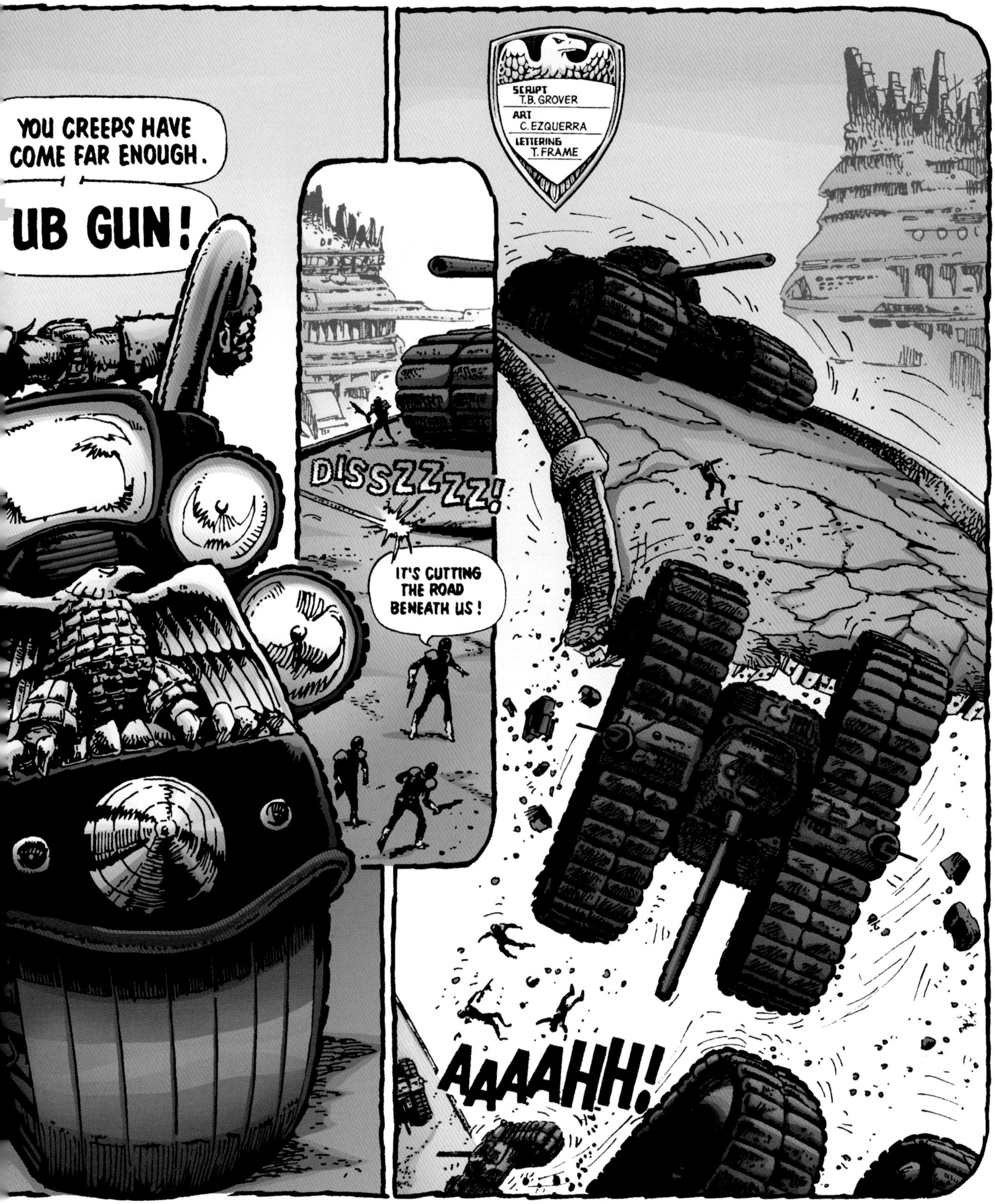
YOU CREEPS HAVE COME FAR ENOUGH.
UB GUN!
SCRIPT T.B. GROVER
ART C. EZQUERRA
LETTERING T. FRAME
DISSZZZZZ!
IT'S CUTTING THE ROAD BENEATH US!
AAAAHH!

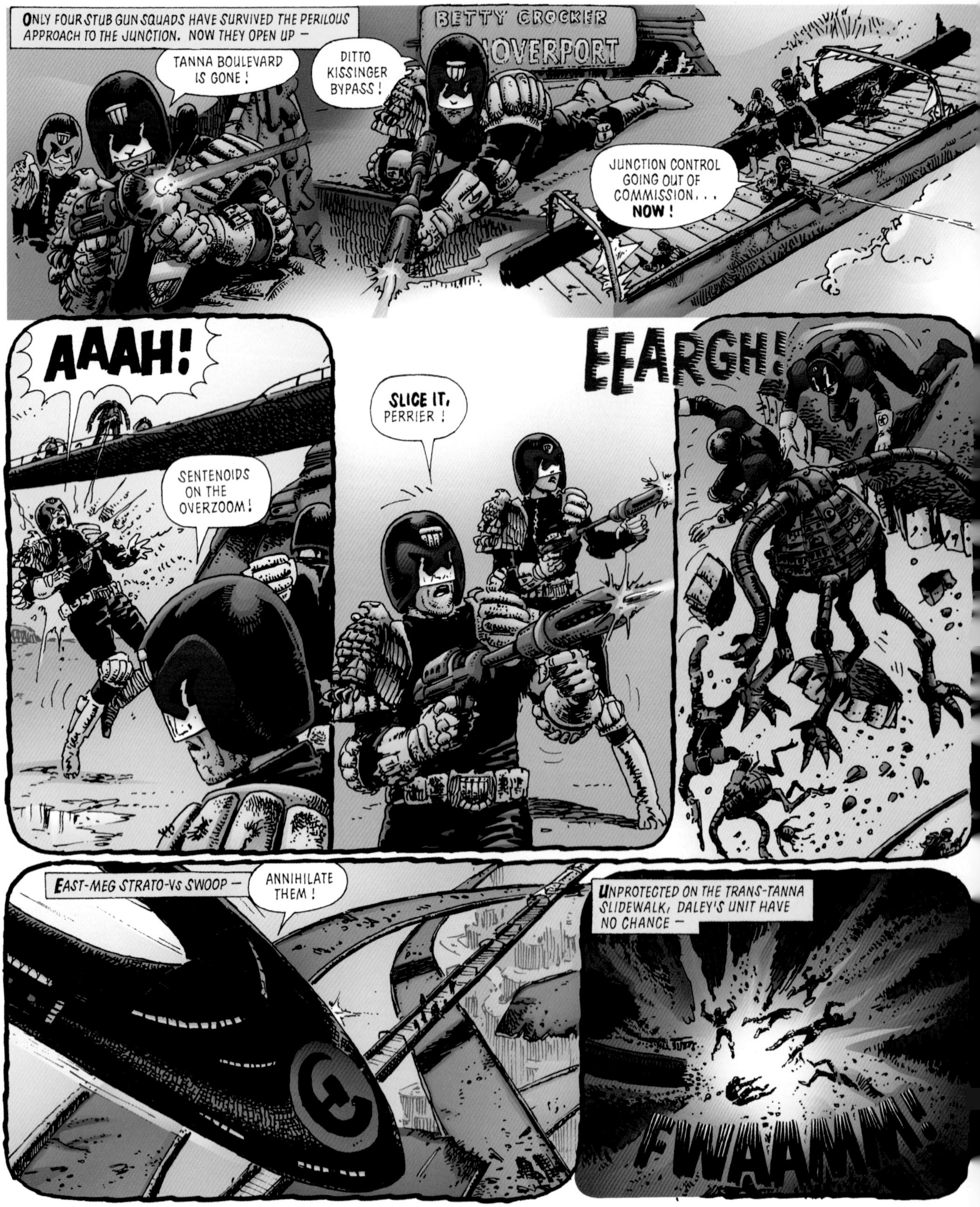
ONLY FOUR STUB GUN SQUADS HAVE SURVIVED THE PERILOUS APPROACH TO THE JUNCTION. NOW THEY OPEN UP –
BETTY CROCKER HOVERPORT
TANNA BOULEVARD IS GONE!
DITTO KISSINGER BYPASS!
JUNCTION CONTROL GOING OUT OF COMMISSION. . . NOW!
AAAH!
SENTENOIDS ON THE OVERZOOM!
SLICE IT, PERRIER!
EEARGH!
EAST-MEG STRATO-VS SWOOP –
ANNIHILATE THEM!
UNPROTECTED ON THE TRANS-TANNA SLIDEWALK, DALEY'S UNIT HAVE NO CHANCE –
FWAAMM!

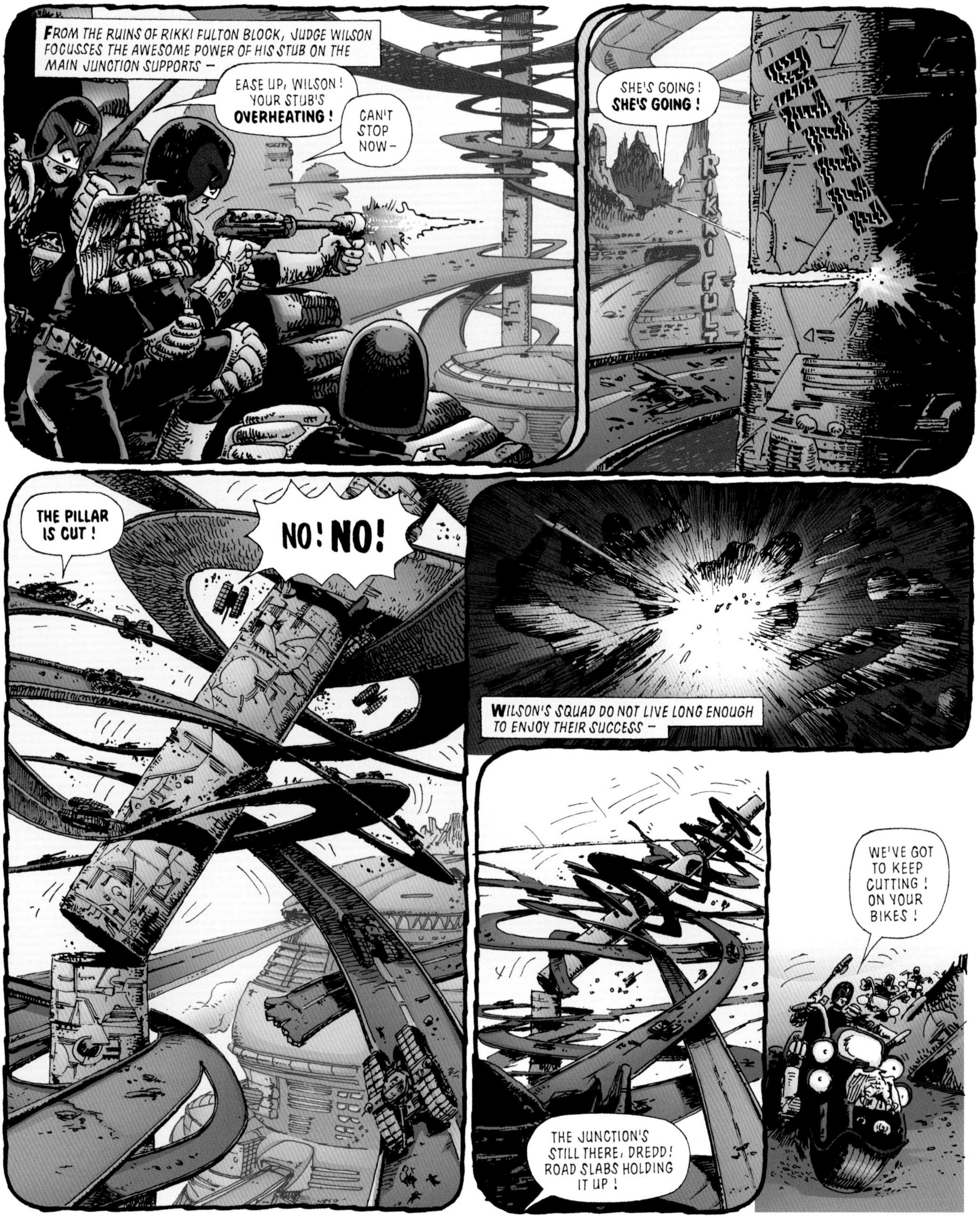
FROM THE RUINS OF RIKKI FULTON BLOCK, JUDGE WILSON FOCUSSES THE AWESOME POWER OF HIS STUB ON THE MAIN JUNCTION SUPPORTS –
EASE UP, WILSON! YOUR STUB'S OVERHEATING!
CAN'T STOP NOW –
SHE'S GOING! SHE'S GOING!
RIKKI FULT
THE PILLAR IS CUT!
NO! NO!
WILSON'S SQUAD DO NOT LIVE LONG ENOUGH TO ENJOY THEIR SUCCESS –
THE JUNCTION'S STILL THERE, DREDD! ROAD SLABS HOLDING IT UP!
WE'VE GOT TO KEEP CUTTING! ON YOUR BIKES!

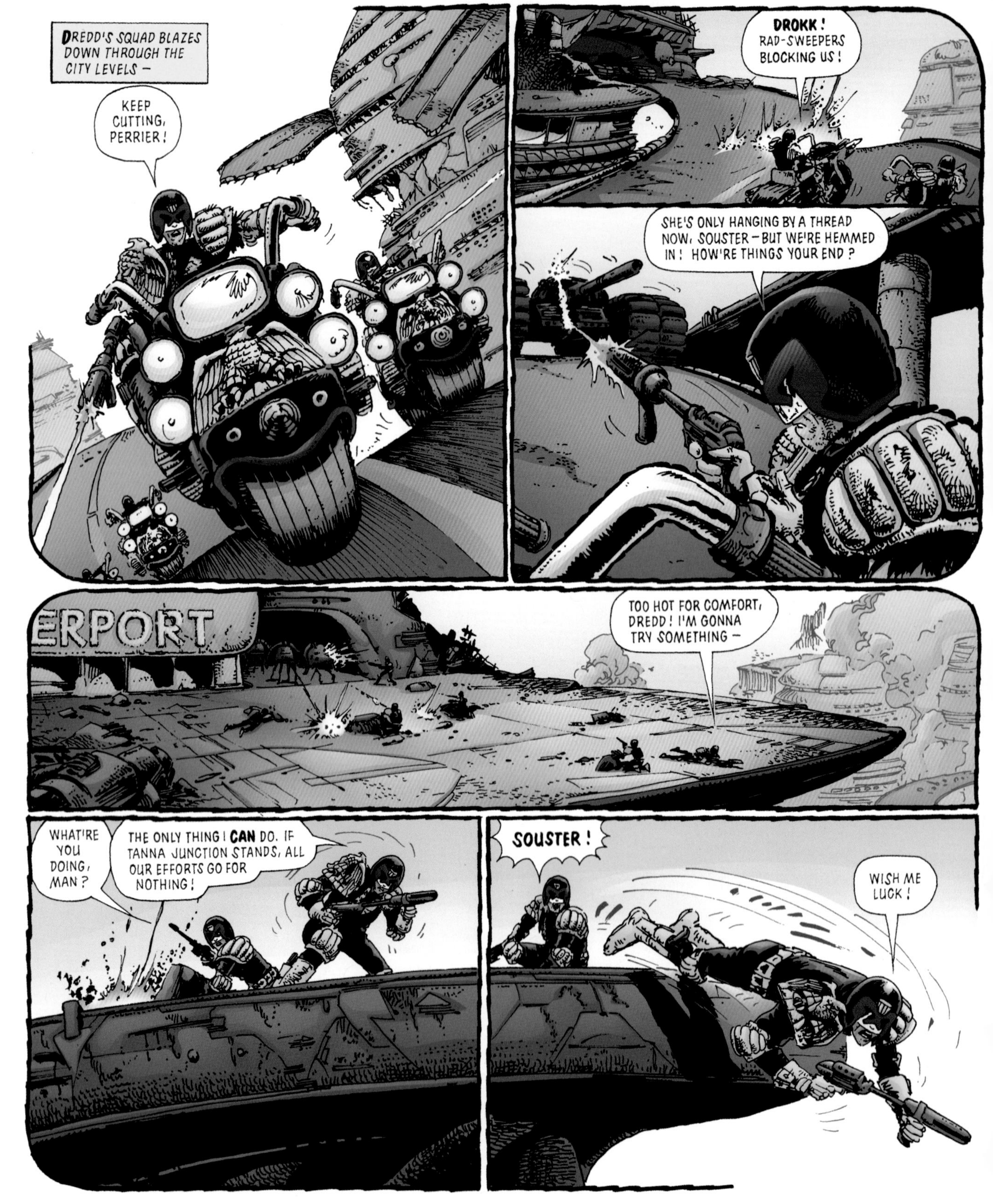
DREDD'S SQUAD BLAZES DOWN THROUGH THE CITY LEVELS –
KEEP CUTTING, PERRIER!
DROKK! RAD-SWEEPERS BLOCKING US!
SHE'S ONLY HANGING BY A THREAD NOW, SOUSTER – BUT WE'RE HEMMED IN! HOW'RE THINGS YOUR END?
ERPORT
TOO HOT FOR COMFORT, DREDD! I'M GONNA TRY SOMETHING –
WHAT'RE YOU DOING, MAN?
THE ONLY THING I **CAN** DO. IF TANNA JUNCTION STANDS, ALL OUR EFFORTS GO FOR NOTHING!
SOUSTER!
WISH ME LUCK!

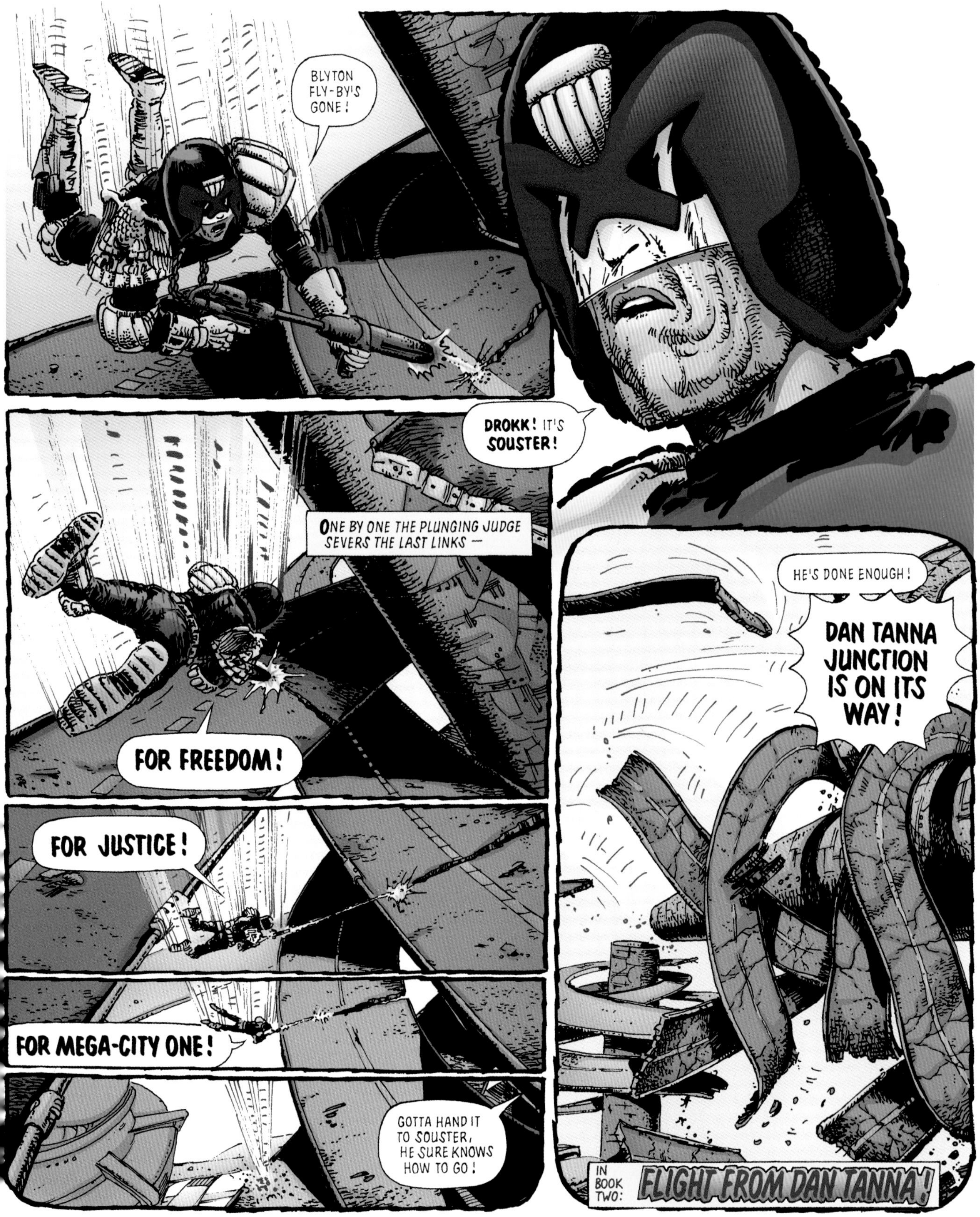
BLYTON FLY-BY'S GONE!
DROKK! IT'S SOUSTER!
ONE BY ONE THE PLUNGING JUDGE SEVERS THE LAST LINKS —
FOR FREEDOM!
FOR JUSTICE!
FOR MEGA-CITY ONE!
GOTTA HAND IT TO SOUSTER, HE SURE KNOWS HOW TO GO!
HE'S DONE ENOUGH!
DAN TANNA JUNCTION IS ON ITS WAY!
IN BOOK TWO:
FLIGHT FROM DAN TANNA!

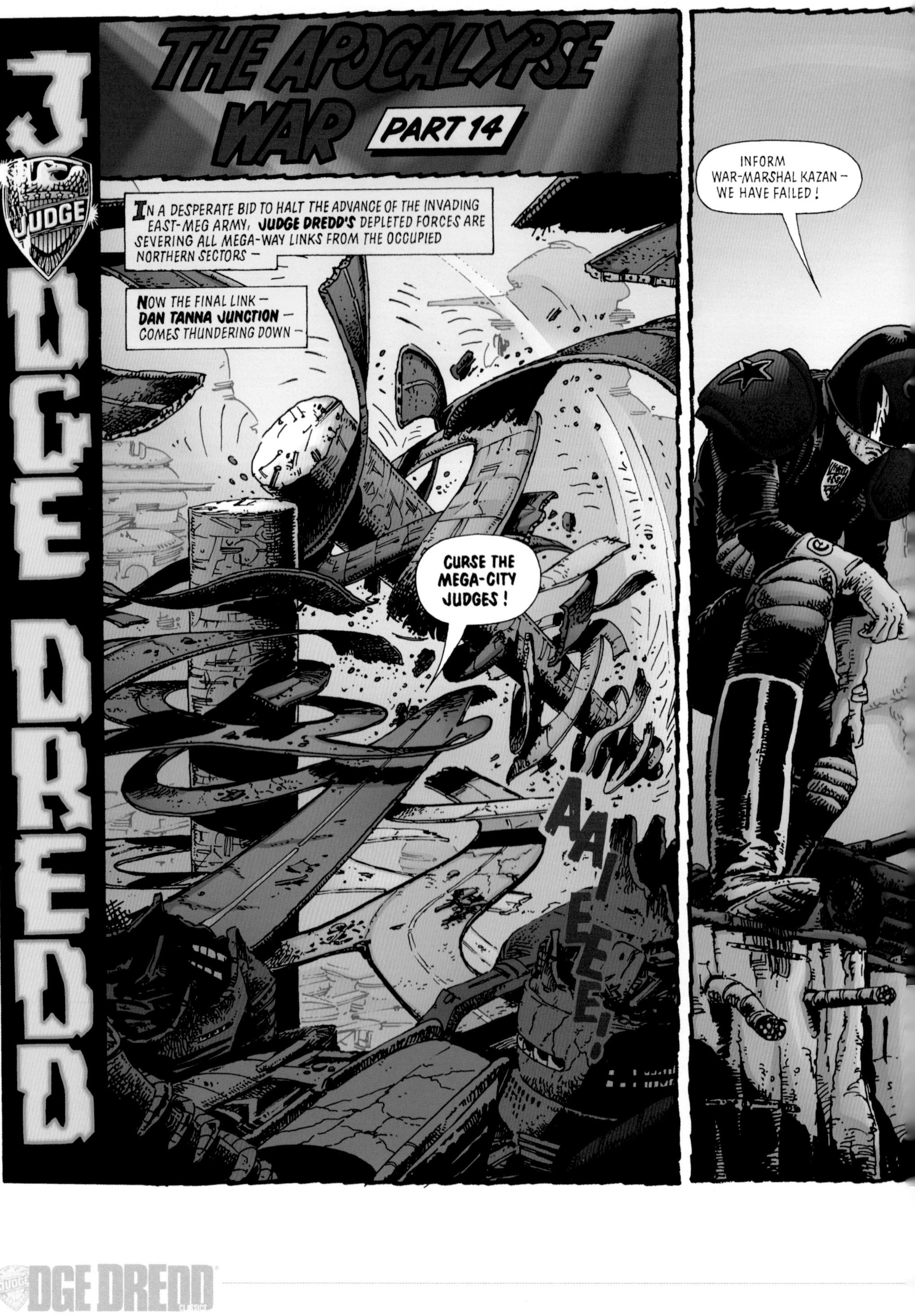
JUDGE DREDD
THE APOCALYPSE WAR
PART 14
IN A DESPERATE BID TO HALT THE ADVANCE OF THE INVADING EAST-MEG ARMY, JUDGE DREDD'S DEPLETED FORCES ARE SEVERING ALL MEGA-WAY LINKS FROM THE OCCUPIED NORTHERN SECTORS –
NOW THE FINAL LINK – DAN TANNA JUNCTION – COMES THUNDERING DOWN –
CURSE THE MEGA-CITY JUDGES !
AAIEEEE!
INFORM WAR-MARSHAL KAZAN – WE HAVE FAILED !

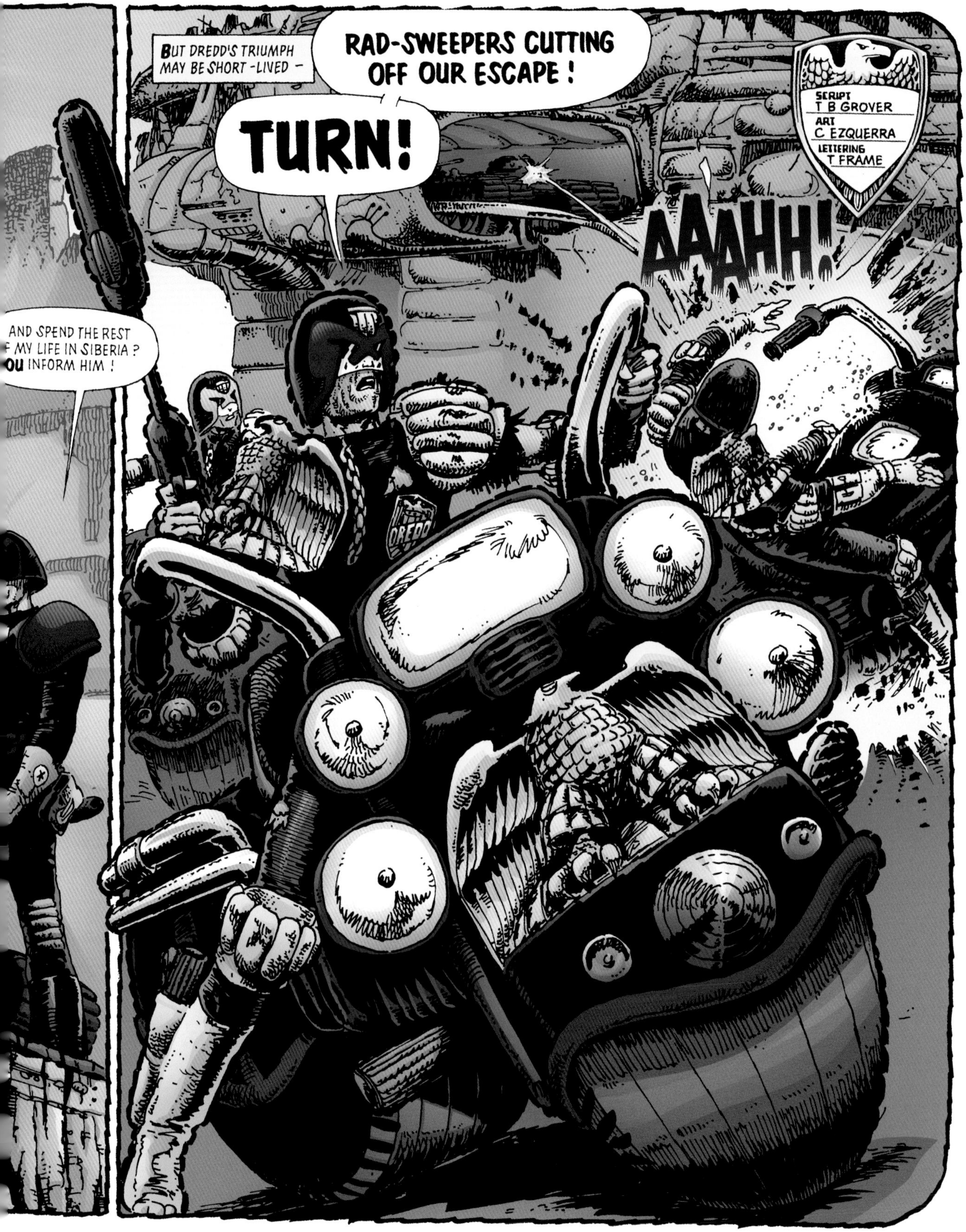
AND SPEND THE REST
F MY LIFE IN SIBERIA ?
OU INFORM HIM !
BUT DREDD'S TRIUMPH MAY BE SHORT-LIVED –
RAD-SWEEPERS CUTTING OFF OUR ESCAPE !
TURN!
SCRIPT T B GROVER
ART C EZQUERRA
LETTERING T FRAME
AAAHH!

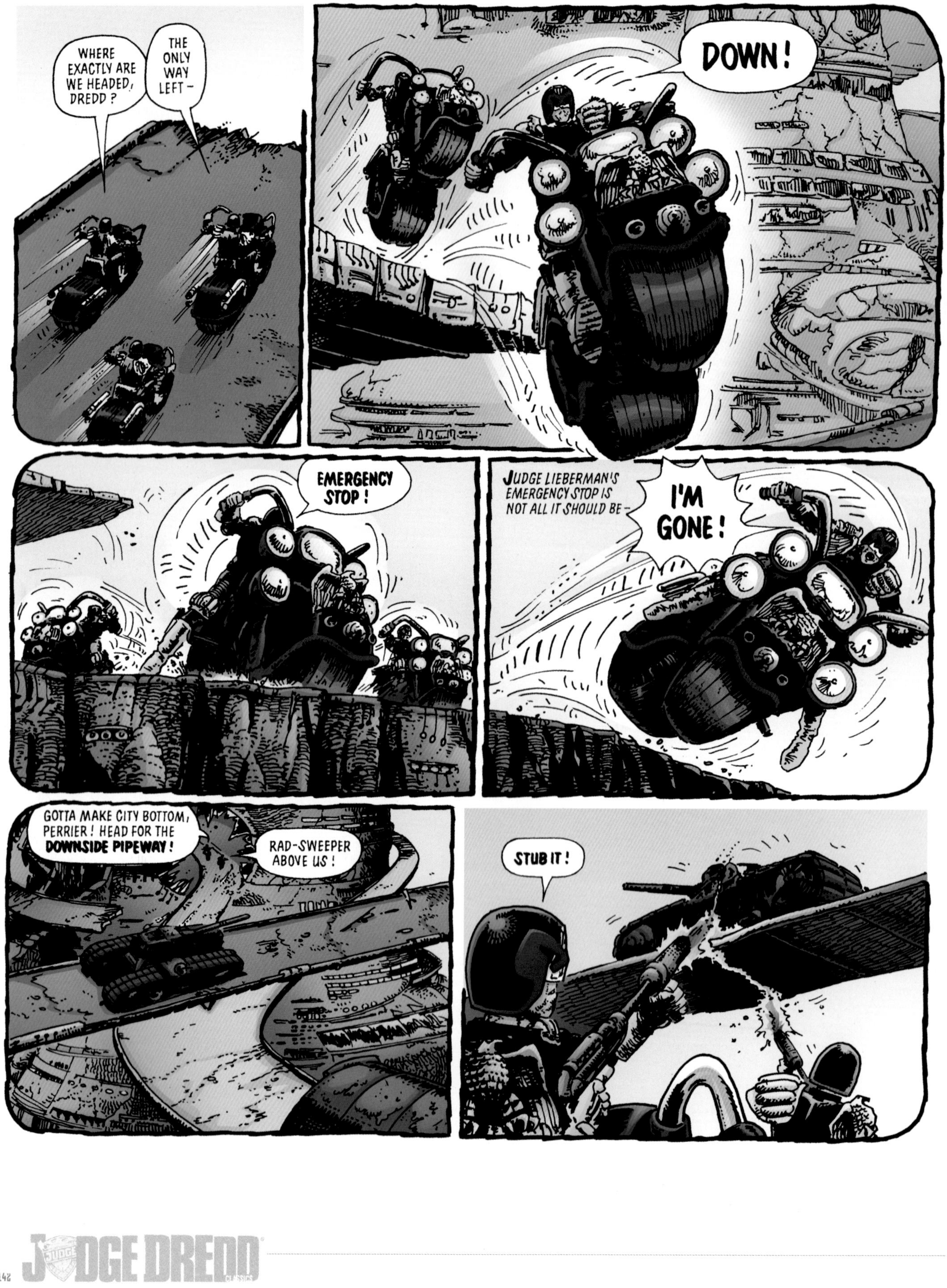
WHERE EXACTLY ARE WE HEADED, DREDD ?
THE ONLY WAY LEFT –
DOWN !
EMERGENCY STOP !
JUDGE LIEBERMAN'S EMERGENCY STOP IS NOT ALL IT SHOULD BE –
I'M GONE !
GOTTA MAKE CITY BOTTOM, PERRIER ! HEAD FOR THE DOWNSIDE PIPEWAY !
RAD-SWEEPER ABOVE US !
STUB IT !

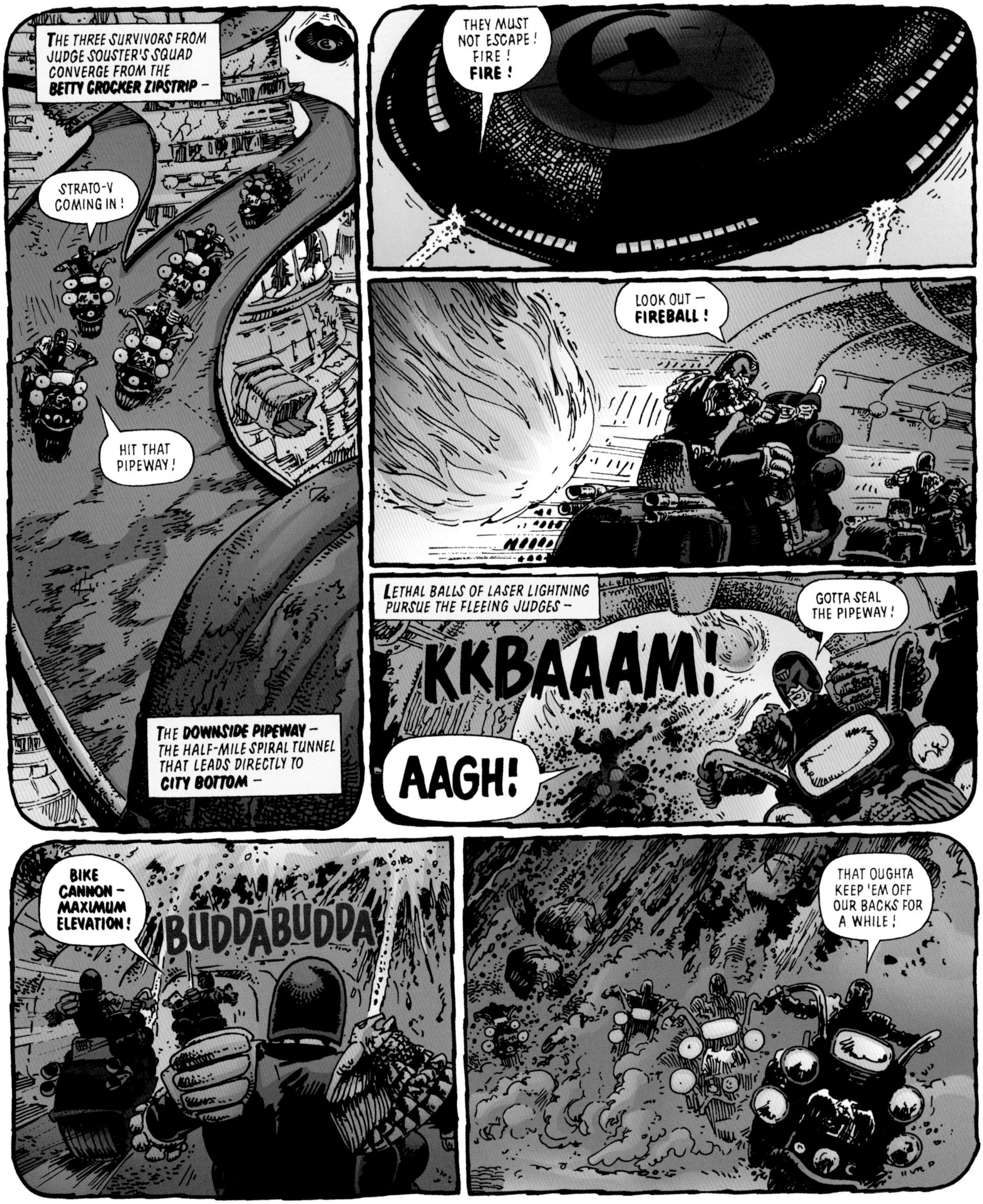
THE THREE SURVIVORS FROM JUDGE SOUSTER'S SQUAD CONVERGE FROM THE BETTY CROCKER ZIPSTRIP –
STRATO-V COMING IN!
HIT THAT PIPEWAY!
THE DOWNSIDE PIPEWAY – THE HALF-MILE SPIRAL TUNNEL THAT LEADS DIRECTLY TO CITY BOTTOM –
THEY MUST NOT ESCAPE! FIRE! FIRE!
LOOK OUT – FIREBALL!
LETHAL BALLS OF LASER LIGHTNING PURSUE THE FLEEING JUDGES –
GOTTA SEAL THE PIPEWAY!
KKBAAAM!
AAGH!
BIKE CANNON – MAXIMUM ELEVATION!
BUDDABUDDA
THAT OUGHTA KEEP 'EM OFF OUR BACKS FOR A WHILE!

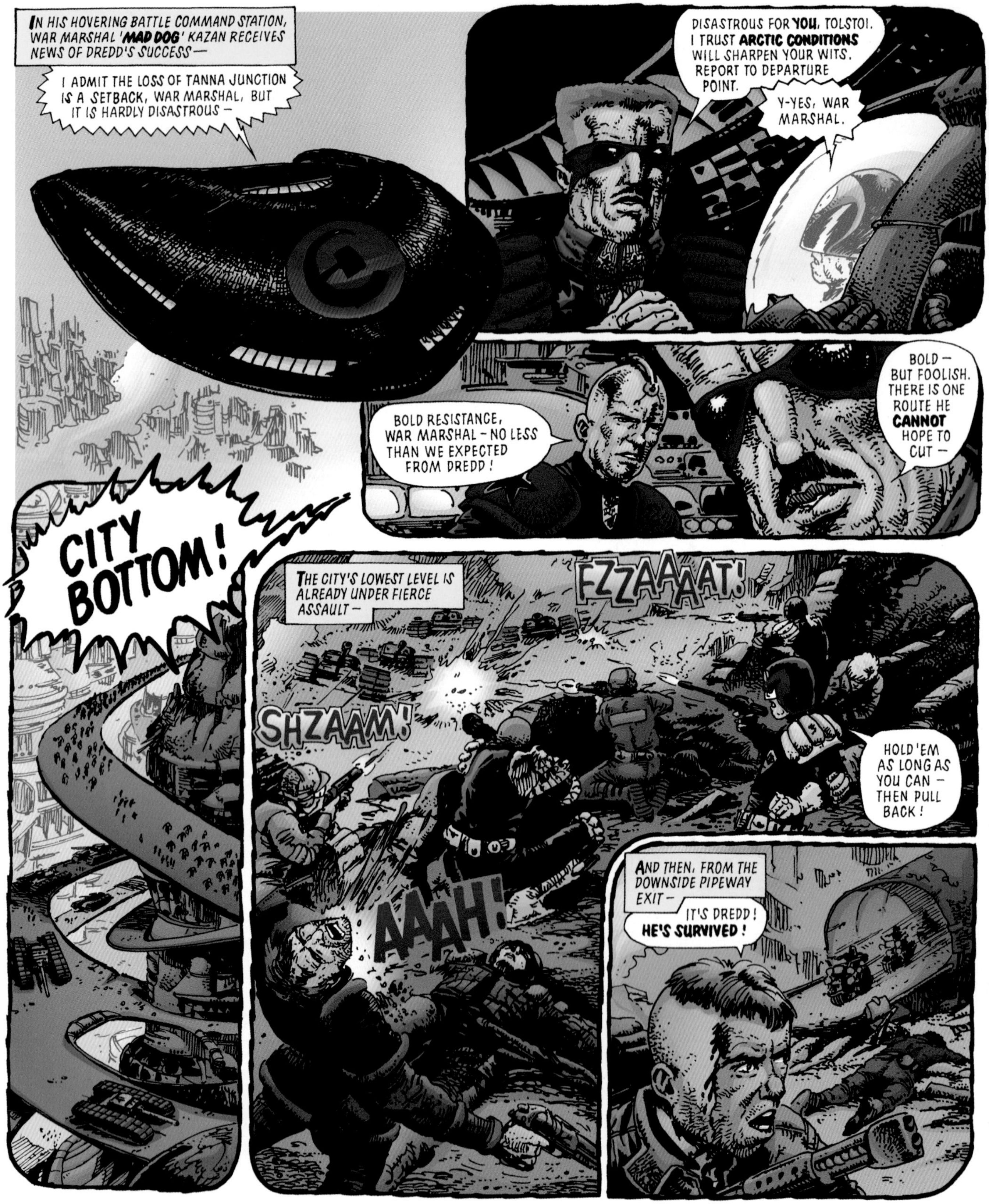
IN HIS HOVERING BATTLE COMMAND STATION, WAR MARSHAL 'MAD DOG' KAZAN RECEIVES NEWS OF DREDD'S SUCCESS —
I ADMIT THE LOSS OF TANNA JUNCTION IS A SETBACK, WAR MARSHAL, BUT IT IS HARDLY DISASTROUS —
DISASTROUS FOR YOU, TOLSTOI. I TRUST ARCTIC CONDITIONS WILL SHARPEN YOUR WITS. REPORT TO DEPARTURE POINT.
Y-YES, WAR MARSHAL.
BOLD RESISTANCE, WAR MARSHAL — NO LESS THAN WE EXPECTED FROM DREDD!
BOLD — BUT FOOLISH. THERE IS ONE ROUTE HE CANNOT HOPE TO CUT —
CITY BOTTOM!
THE CITY'S LOWEST LEVEL IS ALREADY UNDER FIERCE ASSAULT —
FZZAAAAAT!
SHZAAM!
HOLD 'EM AS LONG AS YOU CAN — THEN PULL BACK!
AAAH!
AND THEN, FROM THE DOWNSIDE PIPEWAY EXIT —
IT'S DREDD! HE'S SURVIVED!

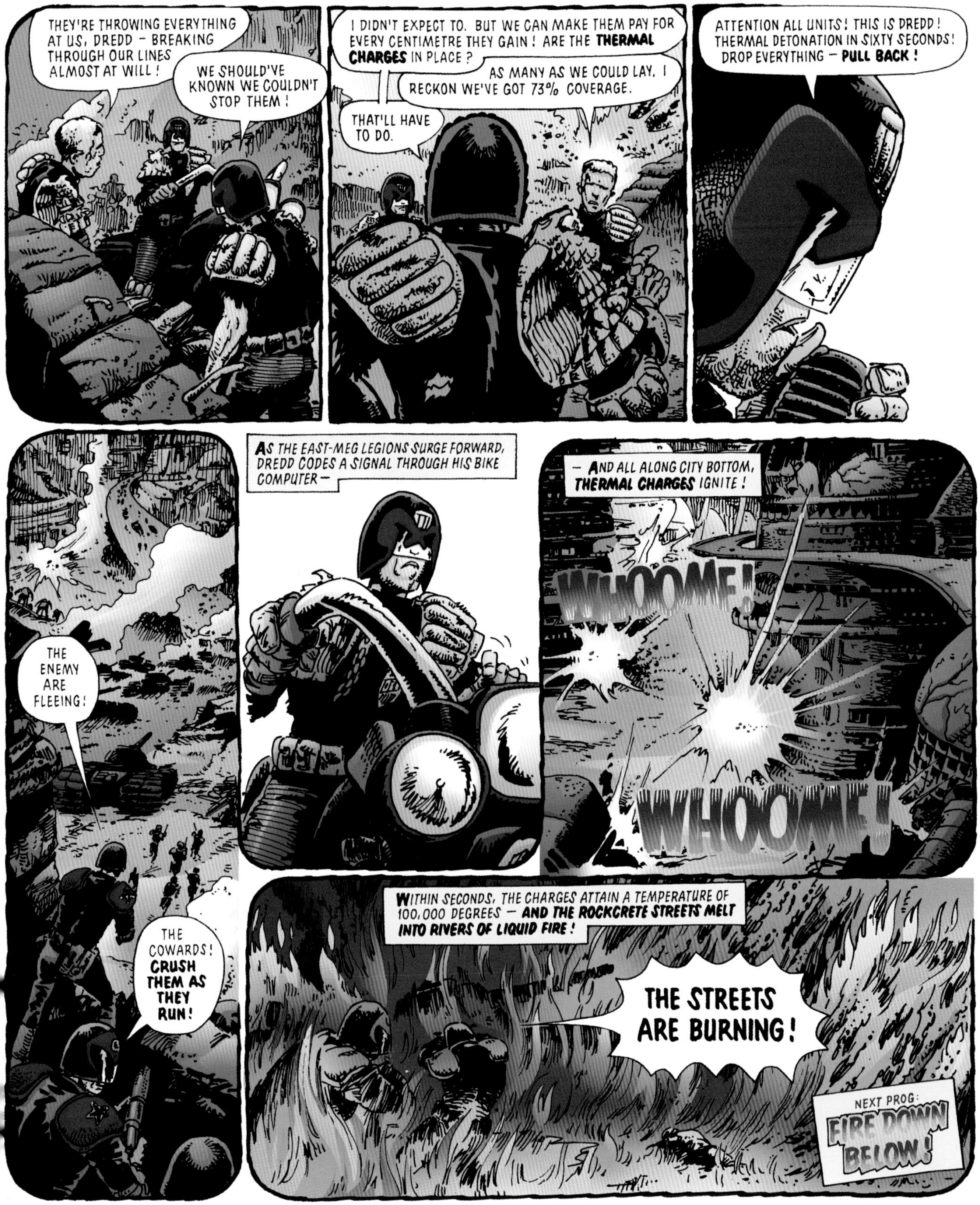

THEY'RE THROWING EVERYTHING AT US, DREDD — BREAKING THROUGH OUR LINES ALMOST AT WILL!
WE SHOULD'VE KNOWN WE COULDN'T STOP THEM!
I DIDN'T EXPECT TO. BUT WE CAN MAKE THEM PAY FOR EVERY CENTIMETRE THEY GAIN! ARE THE THERMAL CHARGES IN PLACE?
AS MANY AS WE COULD LAY, I RECKON WE'VE GOT 73% COVERAGE.
THAT'LL HAVE TO DO.
ATTENTION ALL UNITS! THIS IS DREDD! THERMAL DETONATION IN SIXTY SECONDS! DROP EVERYTHING — PULL BACK!
THE ENEMY ARE FLEEING!
THE COWARDS! CRUSH THEM AS THEY RUN!
AS THE EAST-MEG LEGIONS SURGE FORWARD, DREDD CODES A SIGNAL THROUGH HIS BIKE COMPUTER —
— AND ALL ALONG CITY BOTTOM, THERMAL CHARGES IGNITE!
WHOOMF!
WHOOMF!
WITHIN SECONDS, THE CHARGES ATTAIN A TEMPERATURE OF 100,000 DEGREES — AND THE ROCKCRETE STREETS MELT INTO RIVERS OF LIQUID FIRE!
THE STREETS ARE BURNING!
NEXT PROG:
FIRE DOWN BELOW!

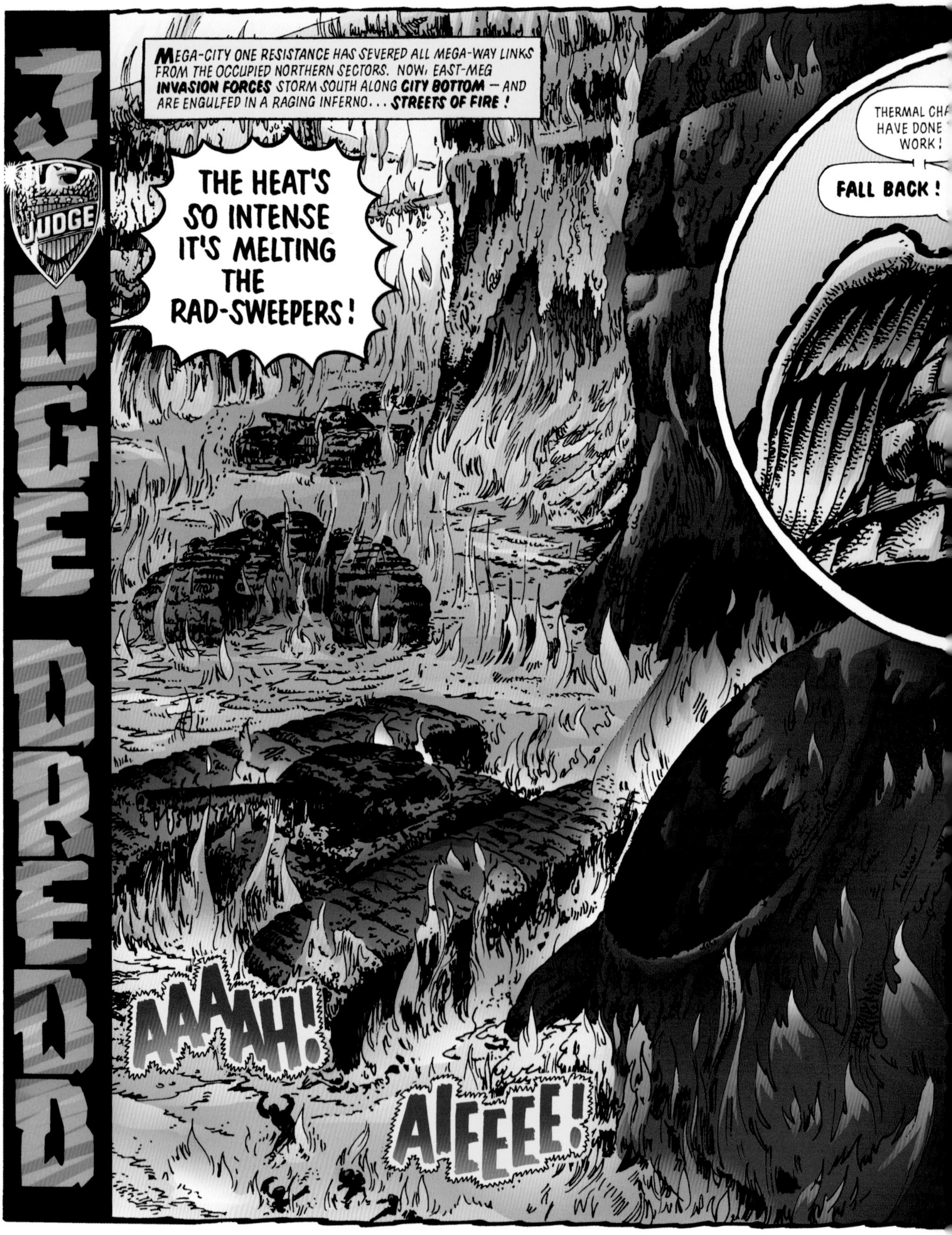
JUDGE DREDD
MEGA-CITY ONE RESISTANCE HAS SEVERED ALL MEGA-WAY LINKS FROM THE OCCUPIED NORTHERN SECTORS. NOW, EAST-MEG **INVASION FORCES** STORM SOUTH ALONG **CITY BOTTOM** — AND ARE ENGULFED IN A RAGING INFERNO... **STREETS OF FIRE!**
THE HEAT'S SO INTENSE IT'S MELTING THE RAD-SWEEPERS!
FALL BACK!
AAAAH!
AIEEEE!

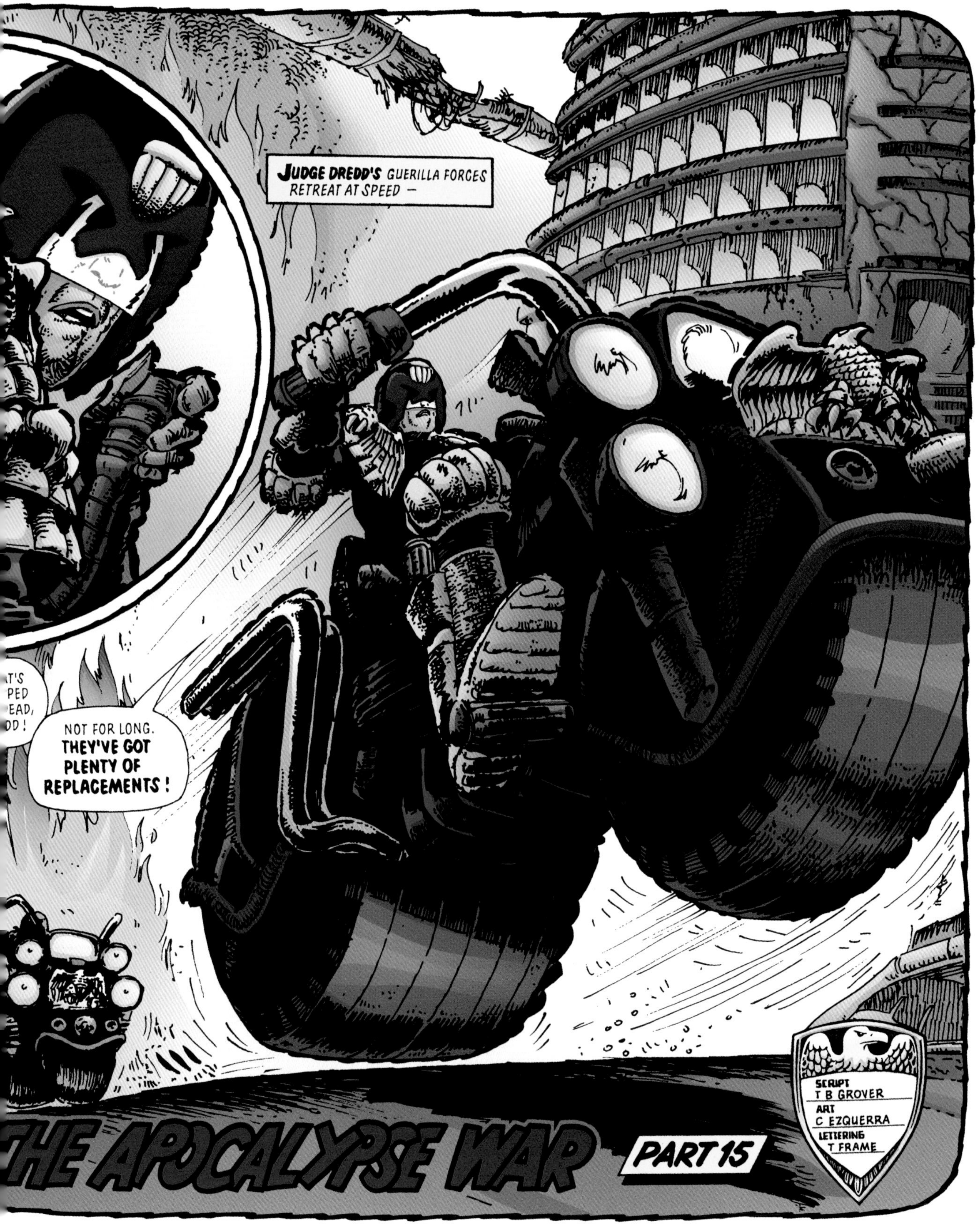
JUDGE DREDD'S GUERILLA FORCES RETREAT AT SPEED —
T'S
PED
EAD,
DD!
NOT FOR LONG. THEY'VE GOT PLENTY OF REPLACEMENTS!
THE APOCALYPSE WAR
PART 15
SCRIPT T B GROVER
ART C EZQUERRA
LETTERING T FRAME

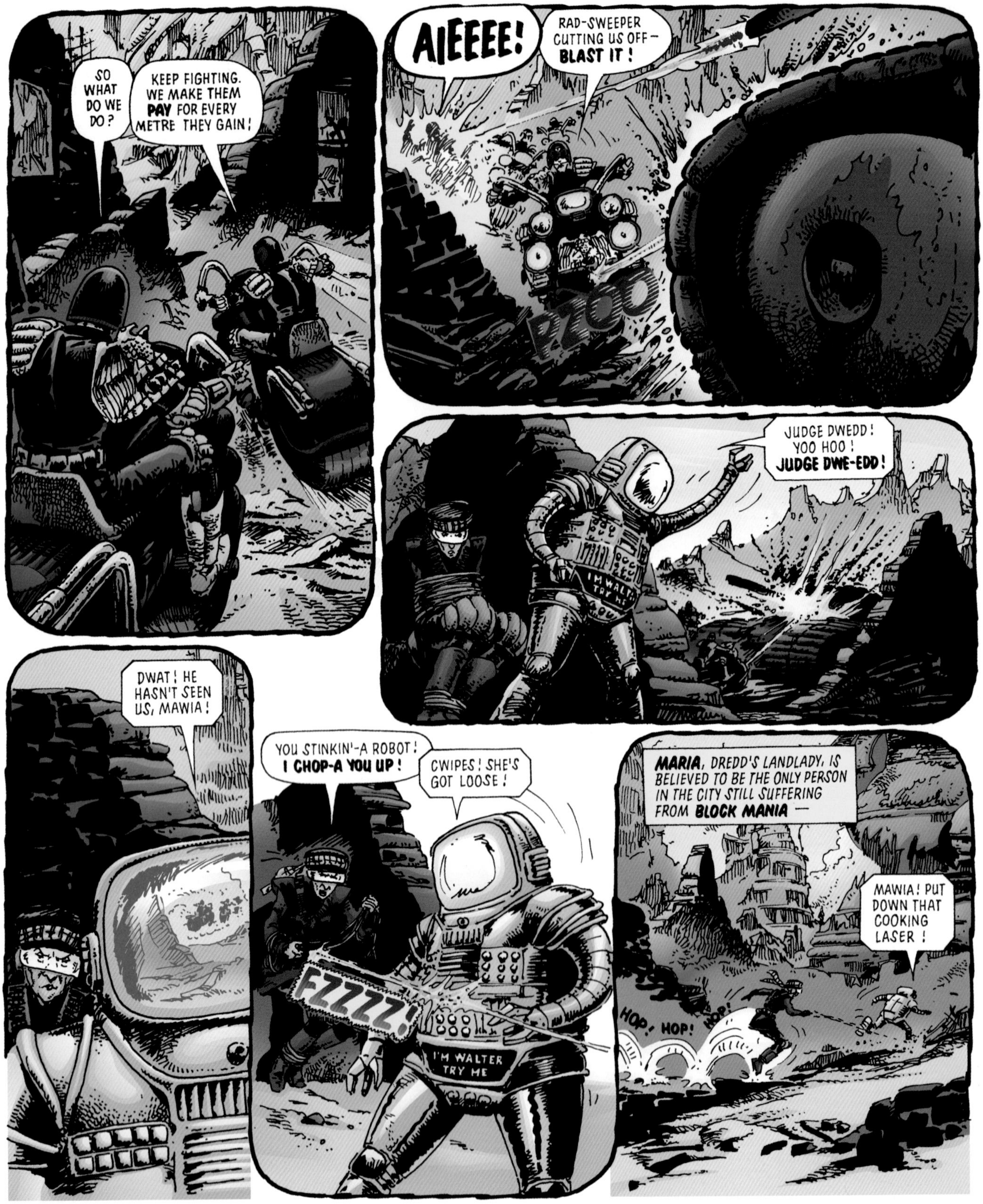
SO WHAT DO WE DO?
KEEP FIGHTING. WE MAKE THEM PAY FOR EVERY METRE THEY GAIN!
AIEEEE!
RAD-SWEEPER CUTTING US OFF — BLAST IT!
PZOO
JUDGE DWEDD! YOO HOO! JUDGE DWE-EDD!
DWAT! HE HASN'T SEEN US, MAWIA!
YOU STINKIN'-A ROBOT! I CHOP-A YOU UP!
CWIPES! SHE'S GOT LOOSE!
FZZZZ!
I'M WALTER TRY ME
MARIA, DREDD'S LANDLADY, IS BELIEVED TO BE THE ONLY PERSON IN THE CITY STILL SUFFERING FROM BLOCK MANIA —
MAWIA! PUT DOWN THAT COOKING LASER!
HOP! HOP! HOP!

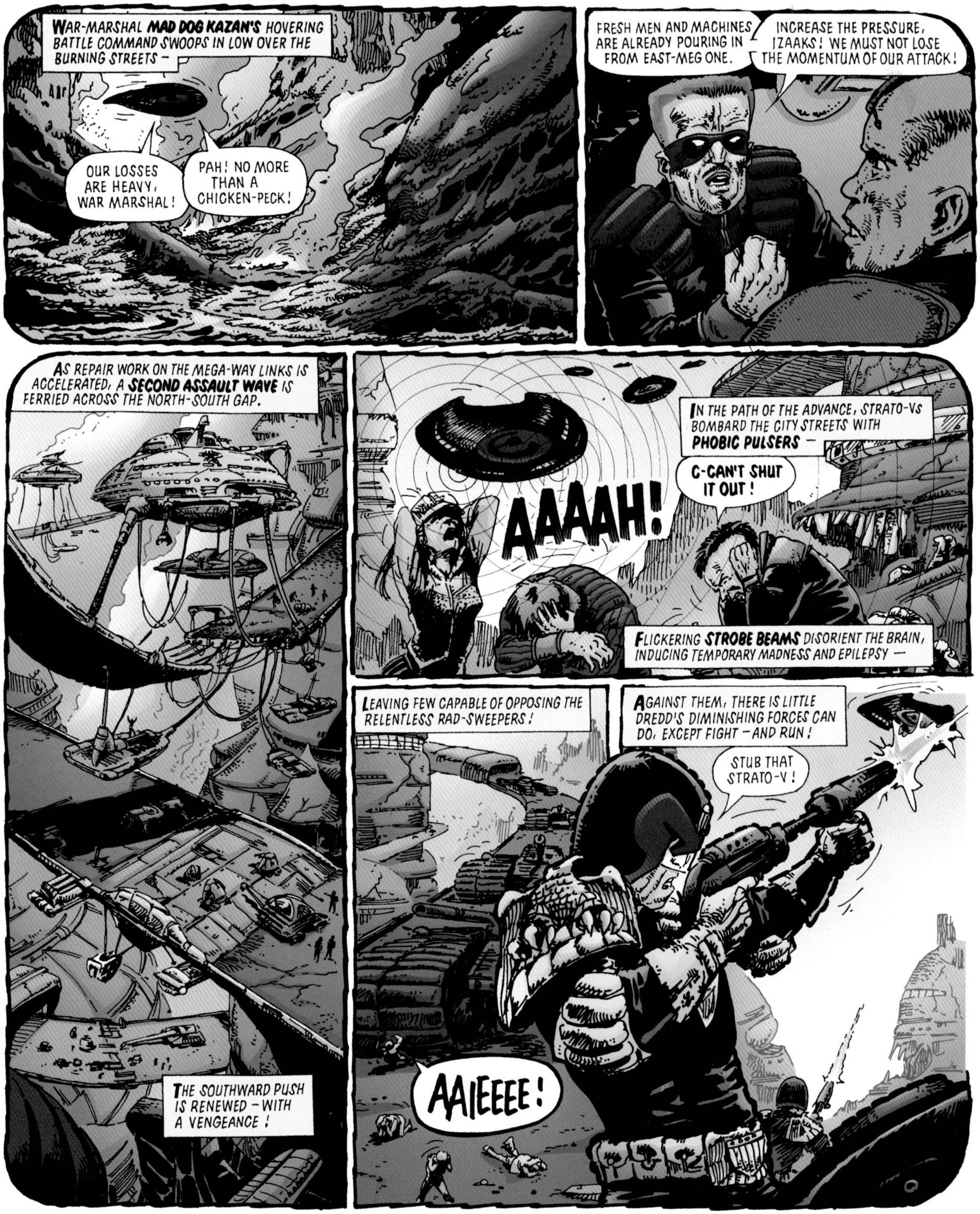
WAR-MARSHAL MAD DOG KAZAN'S HOVERING BATTLE COMMAND SWOOPS IN LOW OVER THE BURNING STREETS –
OUR LOSSES ARE HEAVY, WAR MARSHAL!
PAH! NO MORE THAN A CHICKEN-PECK!
FRESH MEN AND MACHINES ARE ALREADY POURING IN FROM EAST-MEG ONE.
INCREASE THE PRESSURE, IZAAKS! WE MUST NOT LOSE THE MOMENTUM OF OUR ATTACK!
AS REPAIR WORK ON THE MEGA-WAY LINKS IS ACCELERATED, A SECOND ASSAULT WAVE IS FERRIED ACROSS THE NORTH-SOUTH GAP.
THE SOUTHWARD PUSH IS RENEWED – WITH A VENGEANCE!
IN THE PATH OF THE ADVANCE, STRATO-VS BOMBARD THE CITY STREETS WITH PHOBIC PULSERS –
AAAAH!
C-CAN'T SHUT IT OUT!
FLICKERING STROBE BEAMS DISORIENT THE BRAIN, INDUCING TEMPORARY MADNESS AND EPILEPSY –
LEAVING FEW CAPABLE OF OPPOSING THE RELENTLESS RAD-SWEEPERS!
AGAINST THEM, THERE IS LITTLE DREDD'S DIMINISHING FORCES CAN DO, EXCEPT FIGHT – AND RUN!
STUB THAT STRATO-V!
AAIEEEE!

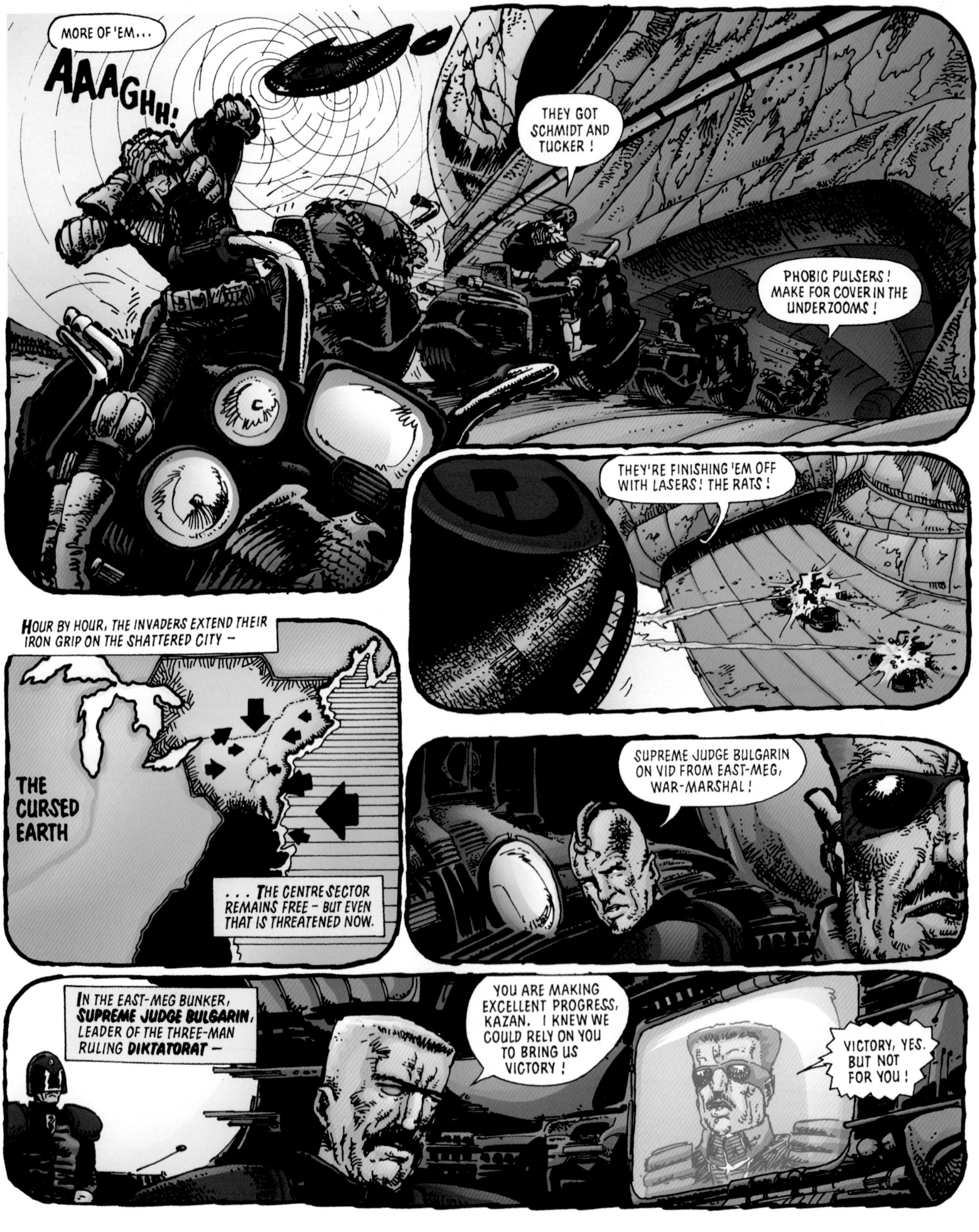
MORE OF 'EM...
AAAGHH!
THEY GOT SCHMIDT AND TUCKER !
PHOBIC PULSERS ! MAKE FOR COVER IN THE UNDERZOOMS !
THEY'RE FINISHING 'EM OFF WITH LASERS ! THE RATS !
HOUR BY HOUR, THE INVADERS EXTEND THEIR IRON GRIP ON THE SHATTERED CITY –
THE CURSED EARTH
. . . THE CENTRE SECTOR REMAINS FREE – BUT EVEN THAT IS THREATENED NOW.
SUPREME JUDGE BULGARIN ON VID FROM EAST-MEG, WAR-MARSHAL !
IN THE EAST-MEG BUNKER, SUPREME JUDGE BULGARIN, LEADER OF THE THREE-MAN RULING DIKTATORAT –
YOU ARE MAKING EXCELLENT PROGRESS, KAZAN. I KNEW WE COULD RELY ON YOU TO BRING US VICTORY !
VICTORY, YES. BUT NOT FOR YOU !

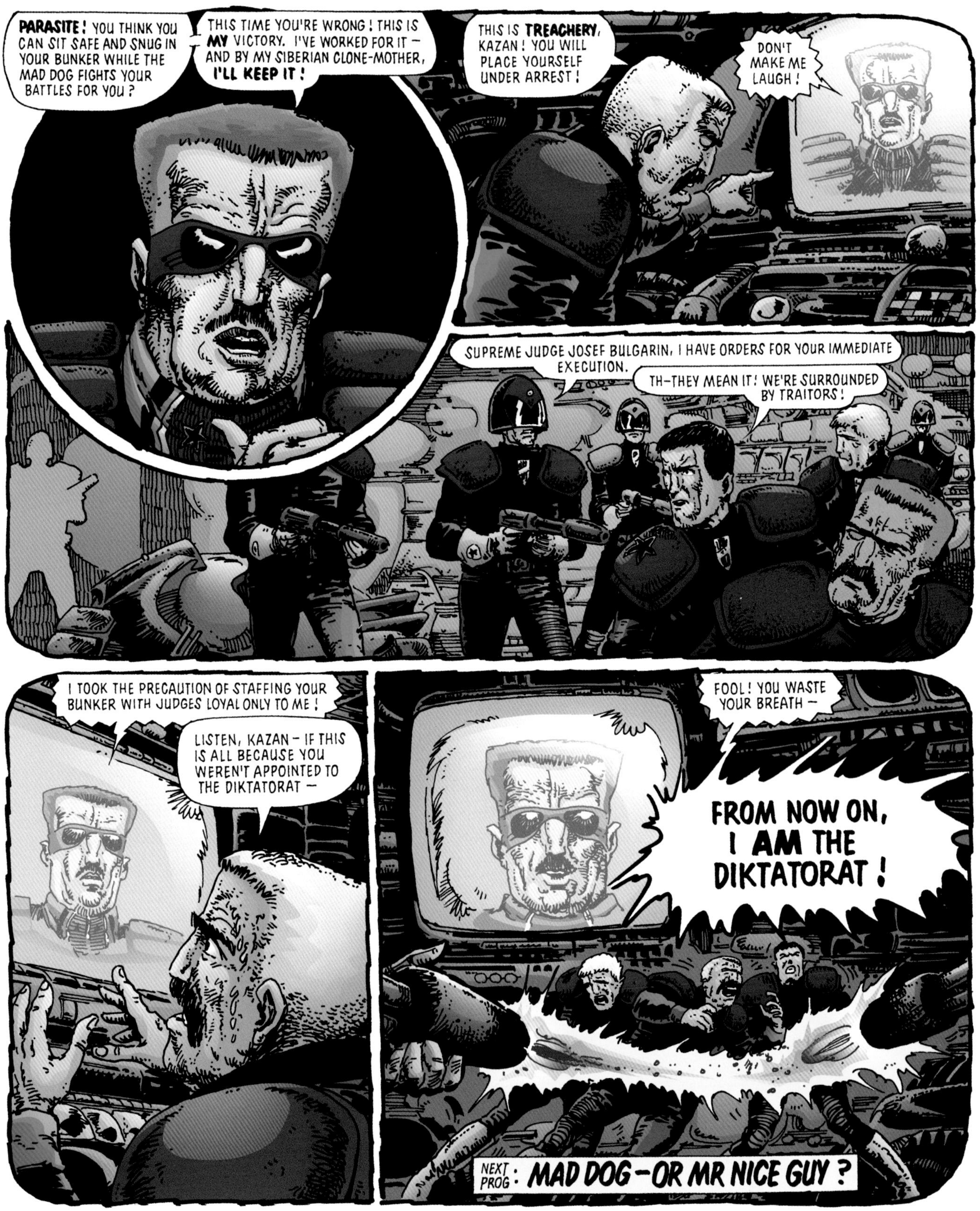
PARASITE! YOU THINK YOU CAN SIT SAFE AND SNUG IN YOUR BUNKER WHILE THE MAD DOG FIGHTS YOUR BATTLES FOR YOU?
THIS TIME YOU'RE WRONG! THIS IS MY VICTORY. I'VE WORKED FOR IT — AND BY MY SIBERIAN CLONE-MOTHER, I'LL KEEP IT!
THIS IS TREACHERY, KAZAN! YOU WILL PLACE YOURSELF UNDER ARREST!
DON'T MAKE ME LAUGH!
SUPREME JUDGE JOSEF BULGARIN, I HAVE ORDERS FOR YOUR IMMEDIATE EXECUTION.
TH-THEY MEAN IT! WE'RE SURROUNDED BY TRAITORS!
I TOOK THE PRECAUTION OF STAFFING YOUR BUNKER WITH JUDGES LOYAL ONLY TO ME!
LISTEN, KAZAN — IF THIS IS ALL BECAUSE YOU WEREN'T APPOINTED TO THE DIKTATORAT —
FOOL! YOU WASTE YOUR BREATH —
FROM NOW ON, I AM THE DIKTATORAT!
NEXT PROG: MAD DOG — OR MR NICE GUY?

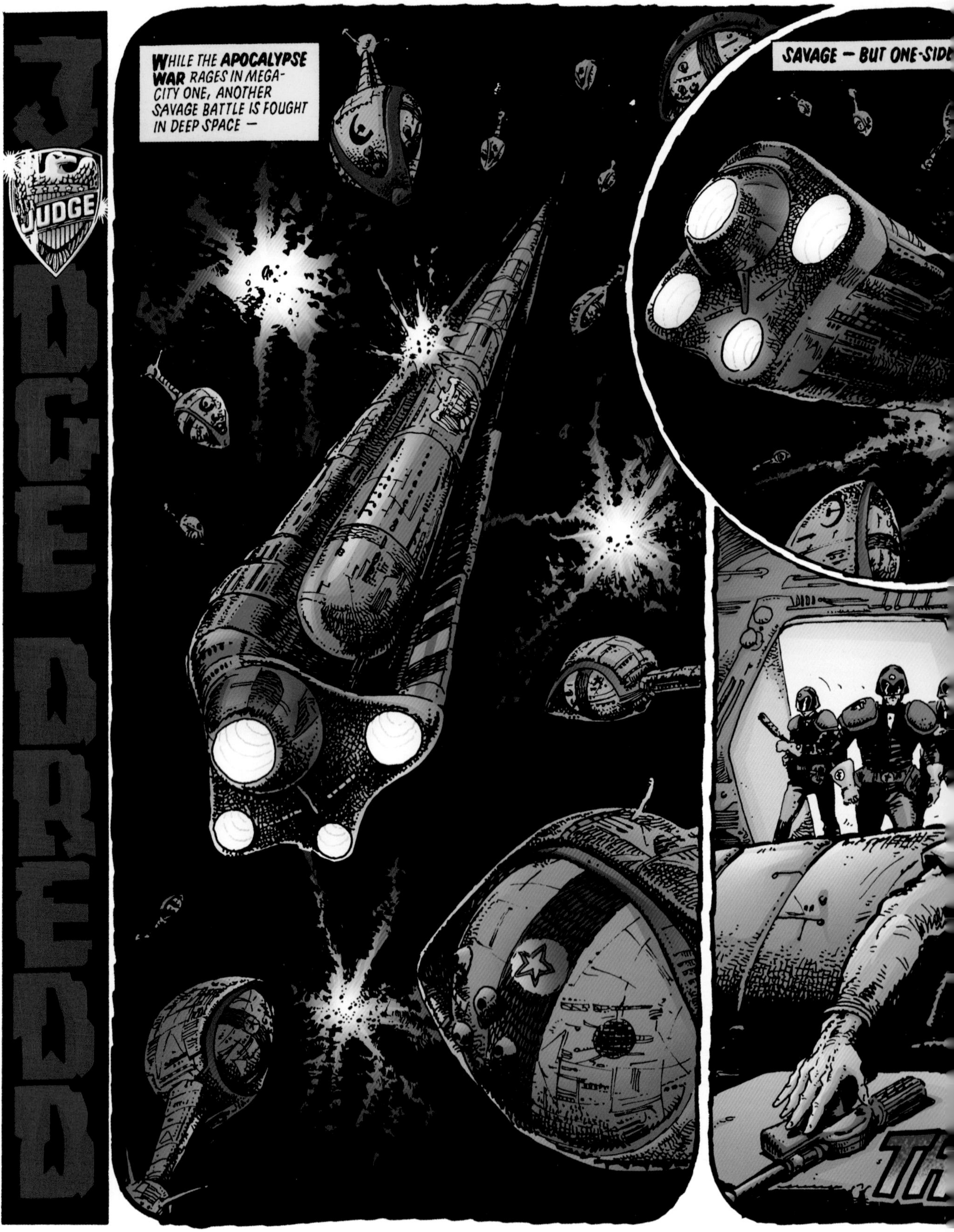
JUDGE DREDD
JUDGE
WHILE THE APOCALYPSE WAR RAGES IN MEGA-CITY ONE, ANOTHER SAVAGE BATTLE IS FOUGHT IN DEEP SPACE —
SAVAGE — BUT ONE-SIDE

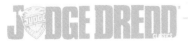

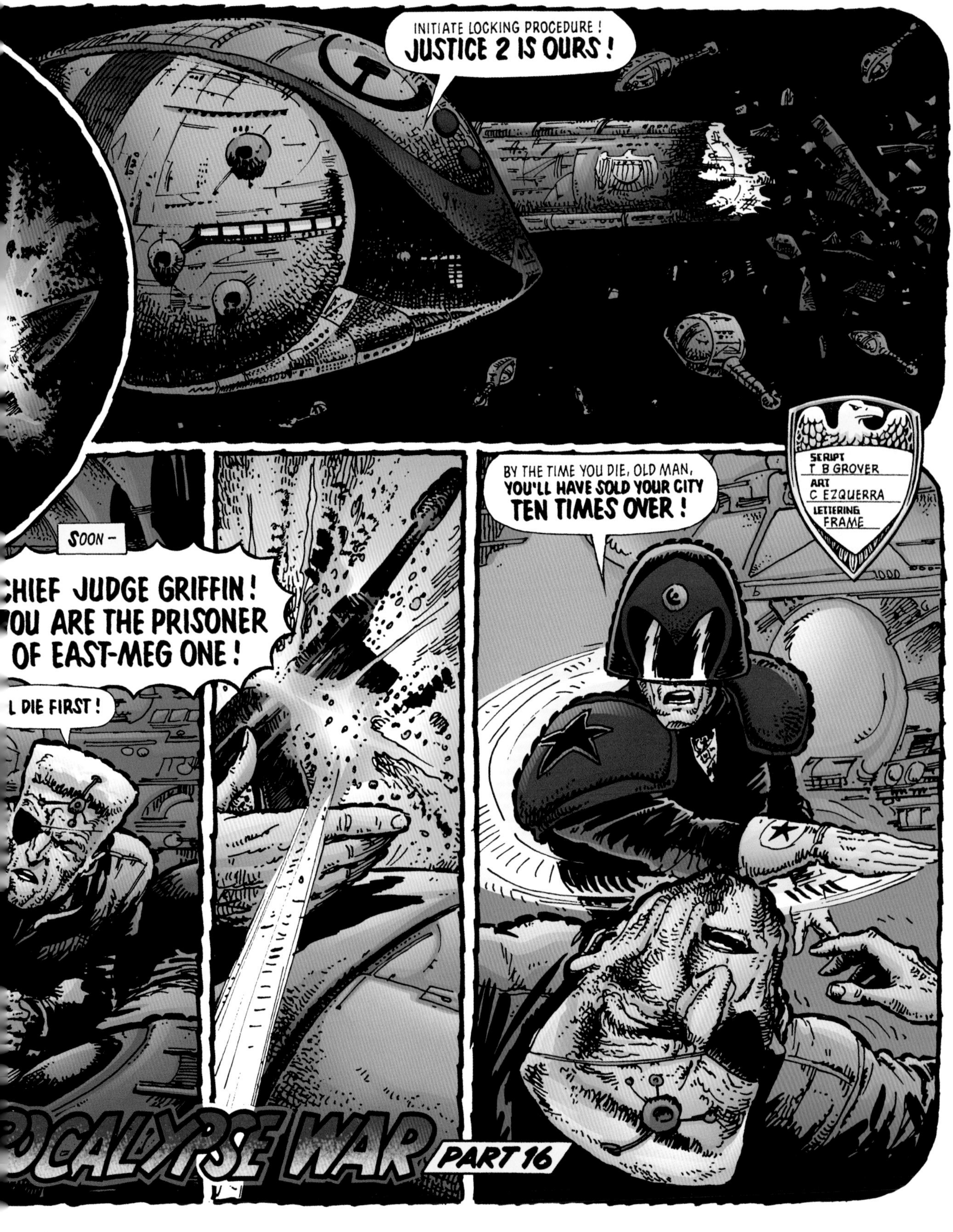

INITIATE LOCKING PROCEDURE ! JUSTICE 2 IS OURS !
SOON -
CHIEF JUDGE GRIFFIN ! YOU ARE THE PRISONER OF EAST-MEG ONE !
L DIE FIRST !
BY THE TIME YOU DIE, OLD MAN, YOU'LL HAVE SOLD YOUR CITY TEN TIMES OVER !
SCRIPT T B GROVER
ART C EZQUERRA
LETTERING FRAME
OCALYPSE WAR
PART 16

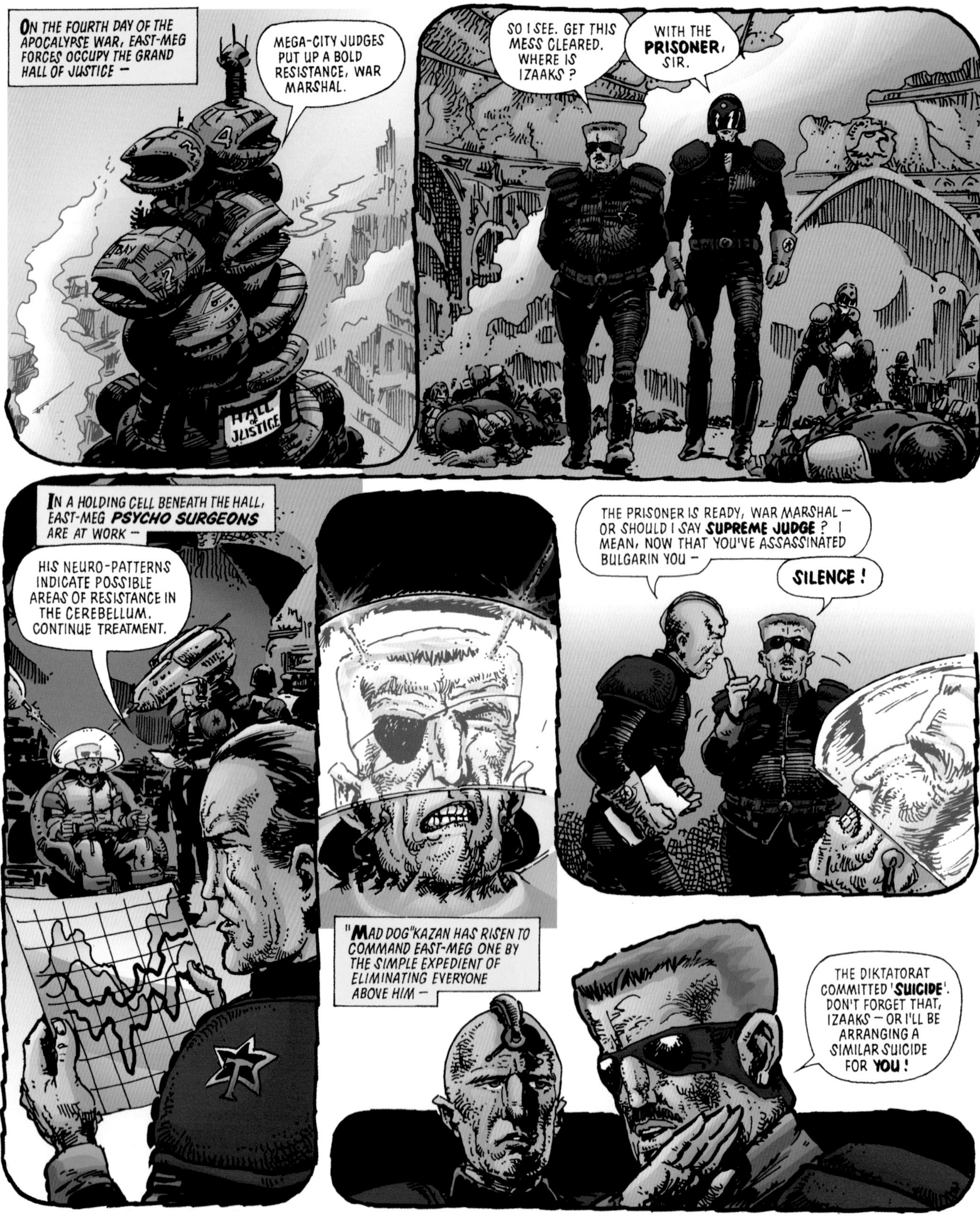

ON THE FOURTH DAY OF THE APOCALYPSE WAR, EAST-MEG FORCES OCCUPY THE GRAND HALL OF JUSTICE –
MEGA-CITY JUDGES PUT UP A BOLD RESISTANCE, WAR MARSHAL.
HALL of JUSTICE
SO I SEE. GET THIS MESS CLEARED. WHERE IS IZAAKS ?
WITH THE **PRISONER**, SIR.
IN A HOLDING CELL BENEATH THE HALL, EAST-MEG **PSYCHO SURGEONS** ARE AT WORK –
HIS NEURO-PATTERNS INDICATE POSSIBLE AREAS OF RESISTANCE IN THE CEREBELLUM. CONTINUE TREATMENT.
THE PRISONER IS READY, WAR MARSHAL – OR SHOULD I SAY **SUPREME JUDGE** ? I MEAN, NOW THAT YOU'VE ASSASSINATED BULGARIN YOU –
SILENCE !
"MAD DOG" KAZAN HAS RISEN TO COMMAND EAST-MEG ONE BY THE SIMPLE EXPEDIENT OF ELIMINATING EVERYONE ABOVE HIM –
THE DIKTATORAT COMMITTED '**SUICIDE**'. DON'T FORGET THAT, IZAAKS – OR I'LL BE ARRANGING A SIMILAR SUICIDE FOR **YOU** !

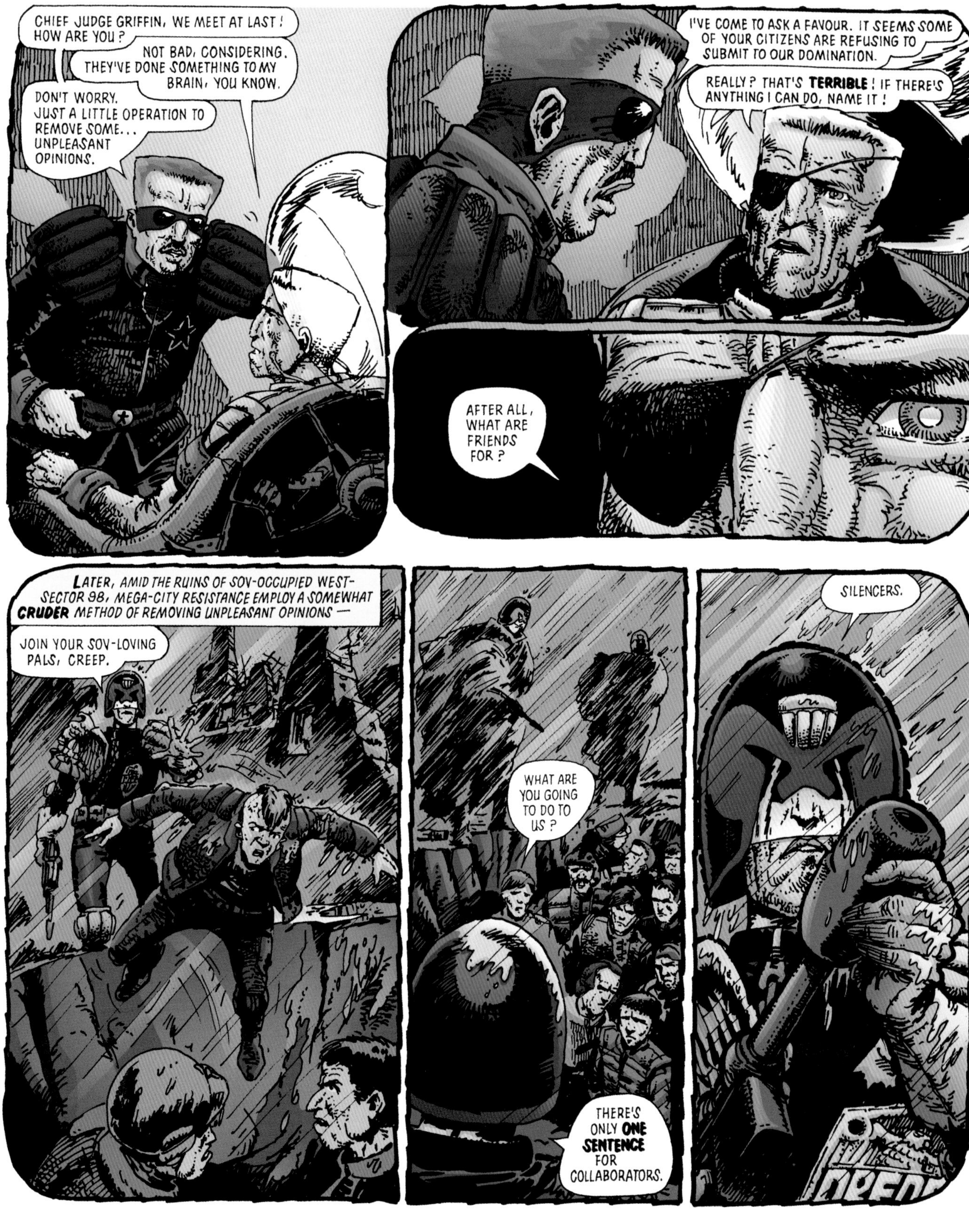

CHIEF JUDGE GRIFFIN, WE MEET AT LAST! HOW ARE YOU?
NOT BAD, CONSIDERING. THEY'VE DONE SOMETHING TO MY BRAIN, YOU KNOW.
DON'T WORRY. JUST A LITTLE OPERATION TO REMOVE SOME... UNPLEASANT OPINIONS.
I'VE COME TO ASK A FAVOUR. IT SEEMS SOME OF YOUR CITIZENS ARE REFUSING TO SUBMIT TO OUR DOMINATION.
REALLY? THAT'S TERRIBLE! IF THERE'S ANYTHING I CAN DO, NAME IT!
AFTER ALL, WHAT ARE FRIENDS FOR?
LATER, AMID THE RUINS OF SOV-OCCUPIED WEST-SECTOR 98, MEGA-CITY RESISTANCE EMPLOY A SOMEWHAT CRUDER METHOD OF REMOVING UNPLEASANT OPINIONS —
JOIN YOUR SOV-LOVING PALS, CREEP.
WHAT ARE YOU GOING TO DO TO US?
THERE'S ONLY ONE SENTENCE FOR COLLABORATORS.
SILENCERS.

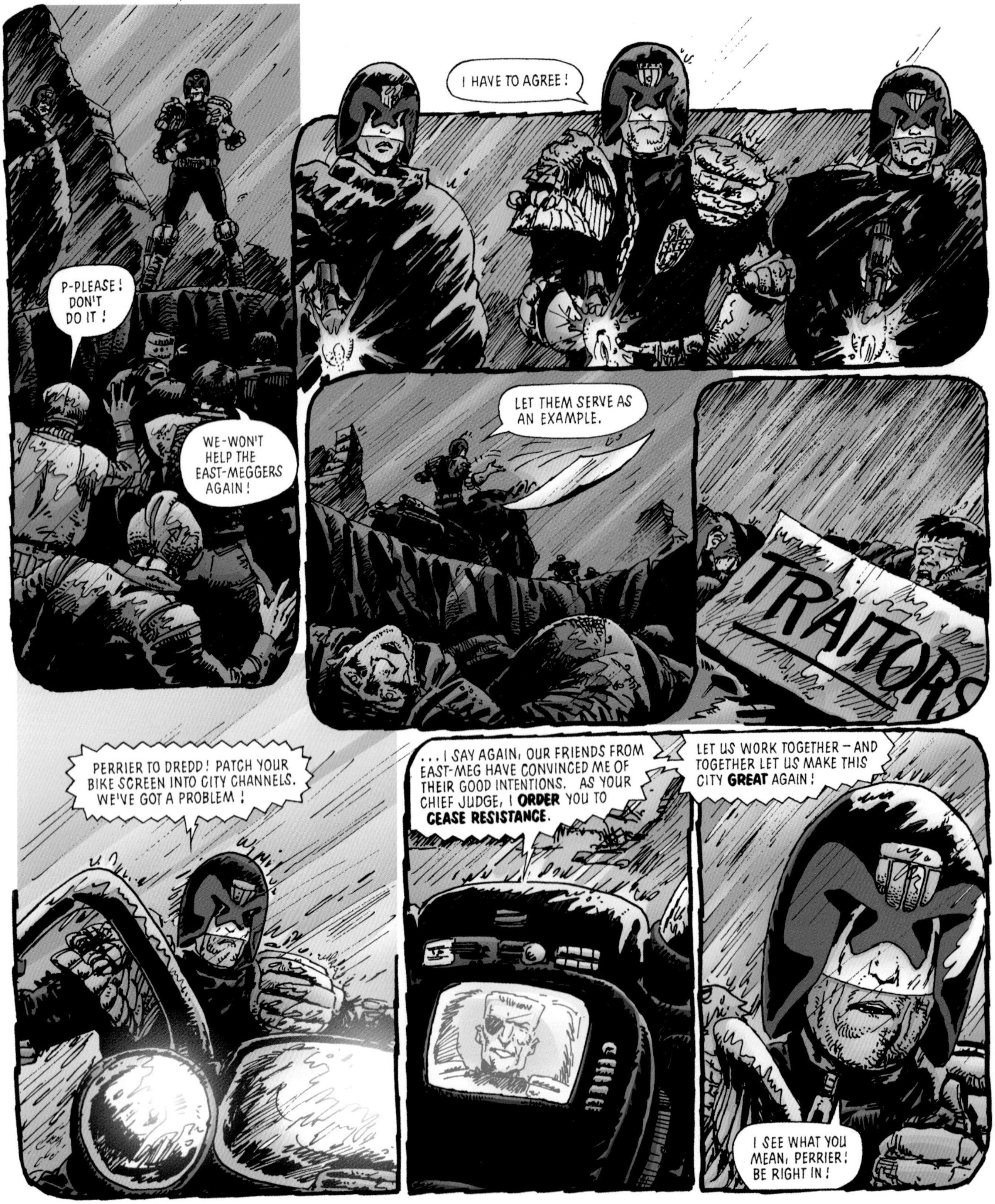
P-PLEASE! DON'T DO IT!
WE-WON'T HELP THE EAST-MEGGERS AGAIN!
I HAVE TO AGREE!
LET THEM SERVE AS AN EXAMPLE.
TRAITORS
PERRIER TO DREDD! PATCH YOUR BIKE SCREEN INTO CITY CHANNELS. WE'VE GOT A PROBLEM!
...I SAY AGAIN, OUR FRIENDS FROM EAST-MEG HAVE CONVINCED ME OF THEIR GOOD INTENTIONS. AS YOUR CHIEF JUDGE, I **ORDER** YOU TO **CEASE RESISTANCE**.
LET US WORK TOGETHER – AND TOGETHER LET US MAKE THIS CITY **GREAT** AGAIN!
I SEE WHAT YOU MEAN, PERRIER! BE RIGHT IN!

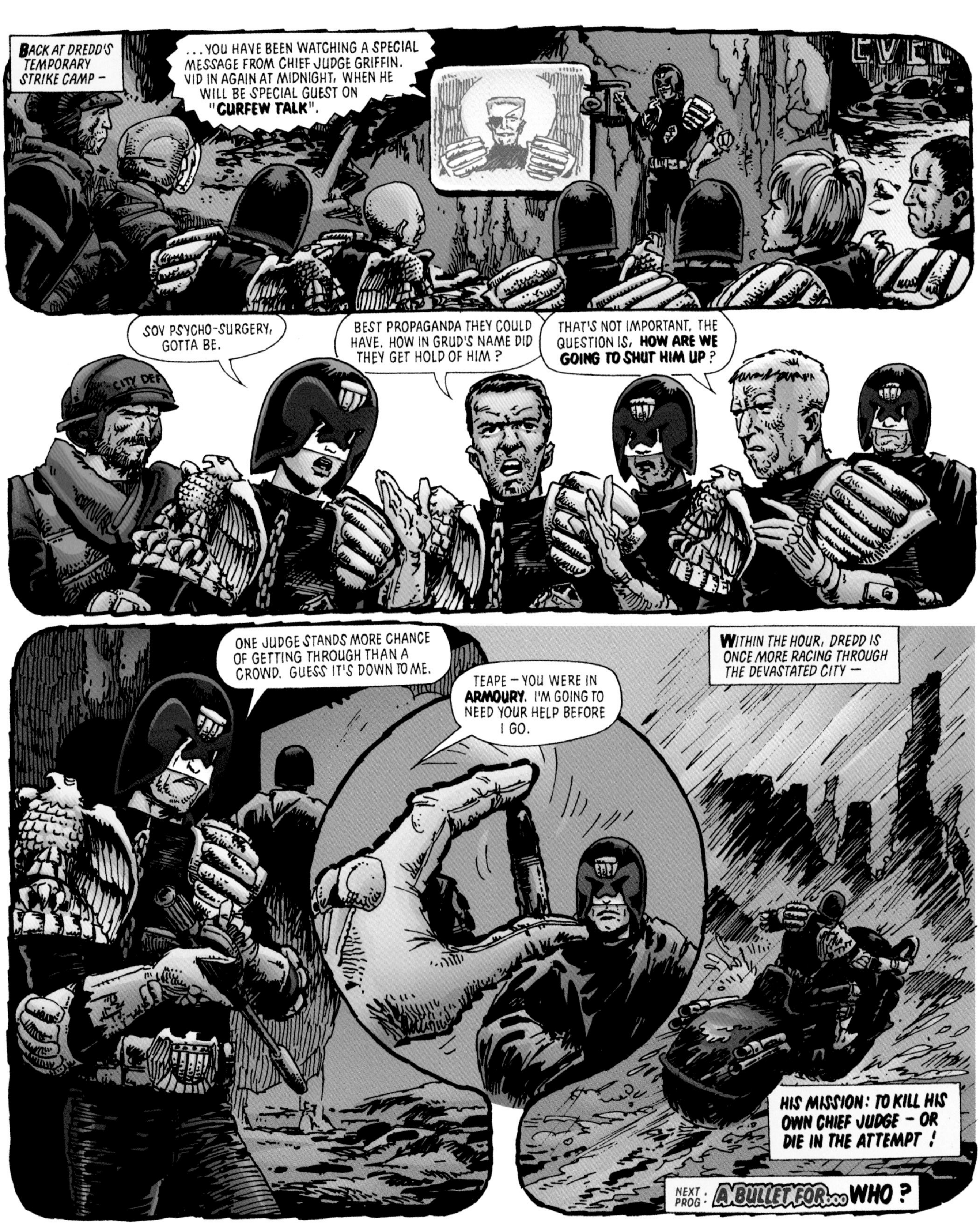
BACK AT DREDD'S TEMPORARY STRIKE CAMP –
...YOU HAVE BEEN WATCHING A SPECIAL MESSAGE FROM CHIEF JUDGE GRIFFIN. VID IN AGAIN AT MIDNIGHT, WHEN HE WILL BE SPECIAL GUEST ON "CURFEW TALK".
SOV PSYCHO-SURGERY, GOTTA BE.
BEST PROPAGANDA THEY COULD HAVE. HOW IN GRUD'S NAME DID THEY GET HOLD OF HIM?
THAT'S NOT IMPORTANT. THE QUESTION IS, HOW ARE WE GOING TO SHUT HIM UP?
ONE JUDGE STANDS MORE CHANCE OF GETTING THROUGH THAN A CROWD. GUESS IT'S DOWN TO ME.
TEAPE – YOU WERE IN ARMOURY. I'M GOING TO NEED YOUR HELP BEFORE I GO.
WITHIN THE HOUR, DREDD IS ONCE MORE RACING THROUGH THE DEVASTATED CITY –
HIS MISSION: TO KILL HIS OWN CHIEF JUDGE – OR DIE IN THE ATTEMPT!
NEXT PROG: A BULLET FOR...WHO?

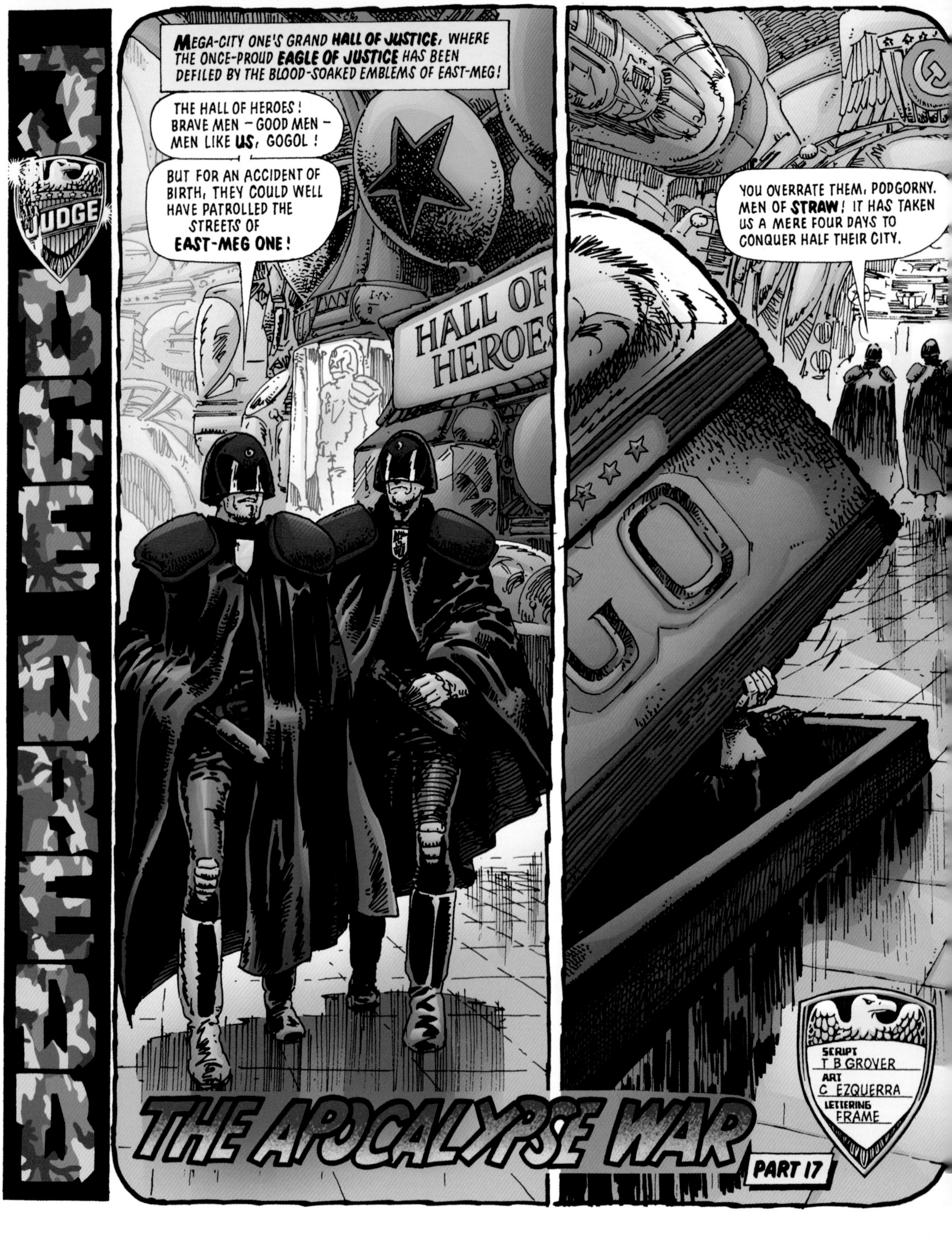
JUDGE DREDD
JUDGE
MEGA-CITY ONE'S GRAND HALL OF JUSTICE, WHERE THE ONCE-PROUD EAGLE OF JUSTICE HAS BEEN DEFILED BY THE BLOOD-SOAKED EMBLEMS OF EAST-MEG!
THE HALL OF HEROES! BRAVE MEN — GOOD MEN — MEN LIKE US, GOGOL!
BUT FOR AN ACCIDENT OF BIRTH, THEY COULD WELL HAVE PATROLLED THE STREETS OF EAST-MEG ONE!
HALL OF HEROES
YOU OVERRATE THEM, PODGORNY. MEN OF STRAW! IT HAS TAKEN US A MERE FOUR DAYS TO CONQUER HALF THEIR CITY.
THE APOCALYPSE WAR
PART 17
SCRIPT T B GROVER
ART C EZQUERRA
LETTERING FRAME

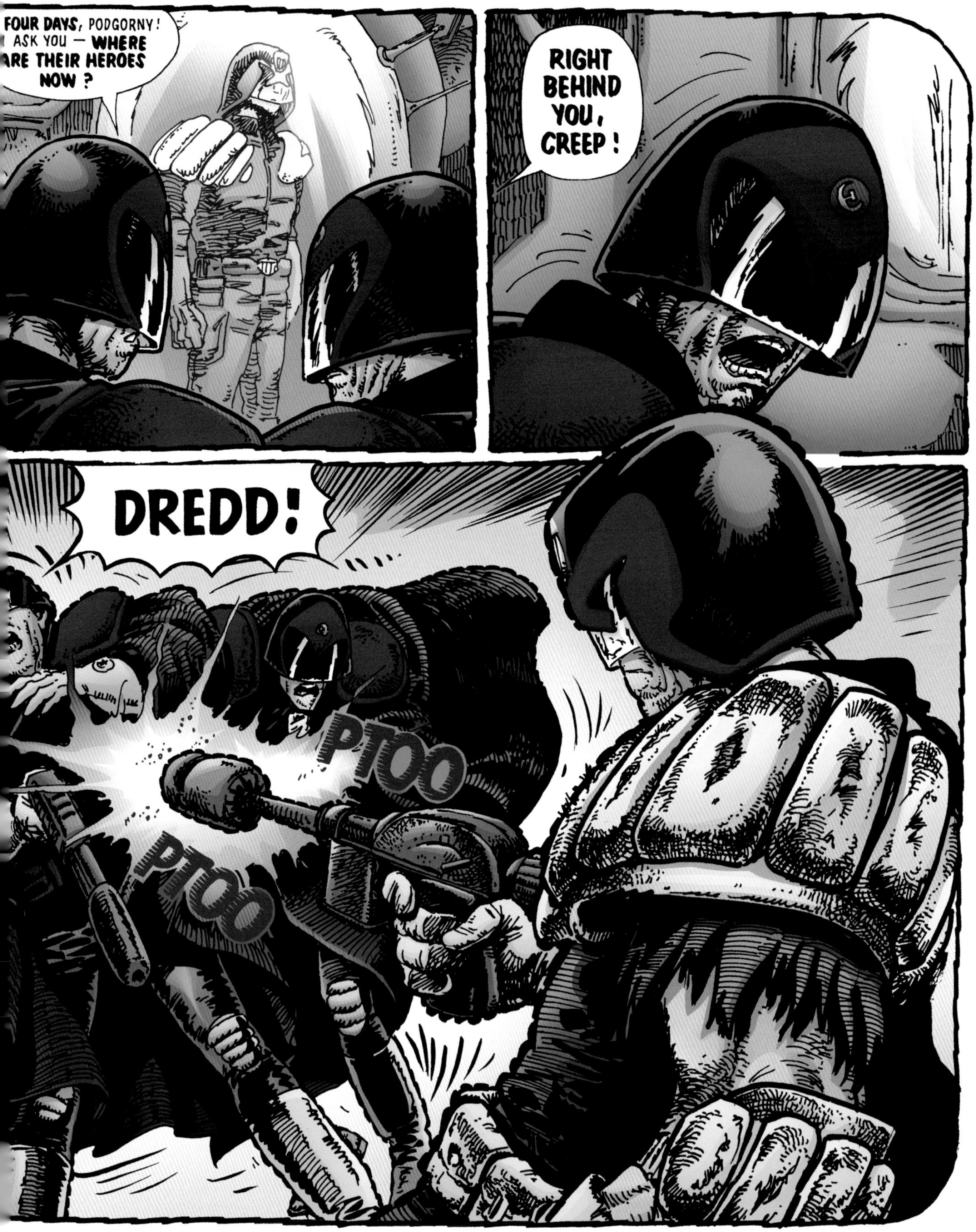
FOUR DAYS, PODGORNY! I ASK YOU — WHERE ARE THEIR HEROES NOW ?
RIGHT BEHIND YOU, CREEP!
DREDD!
PTOO
PTOO

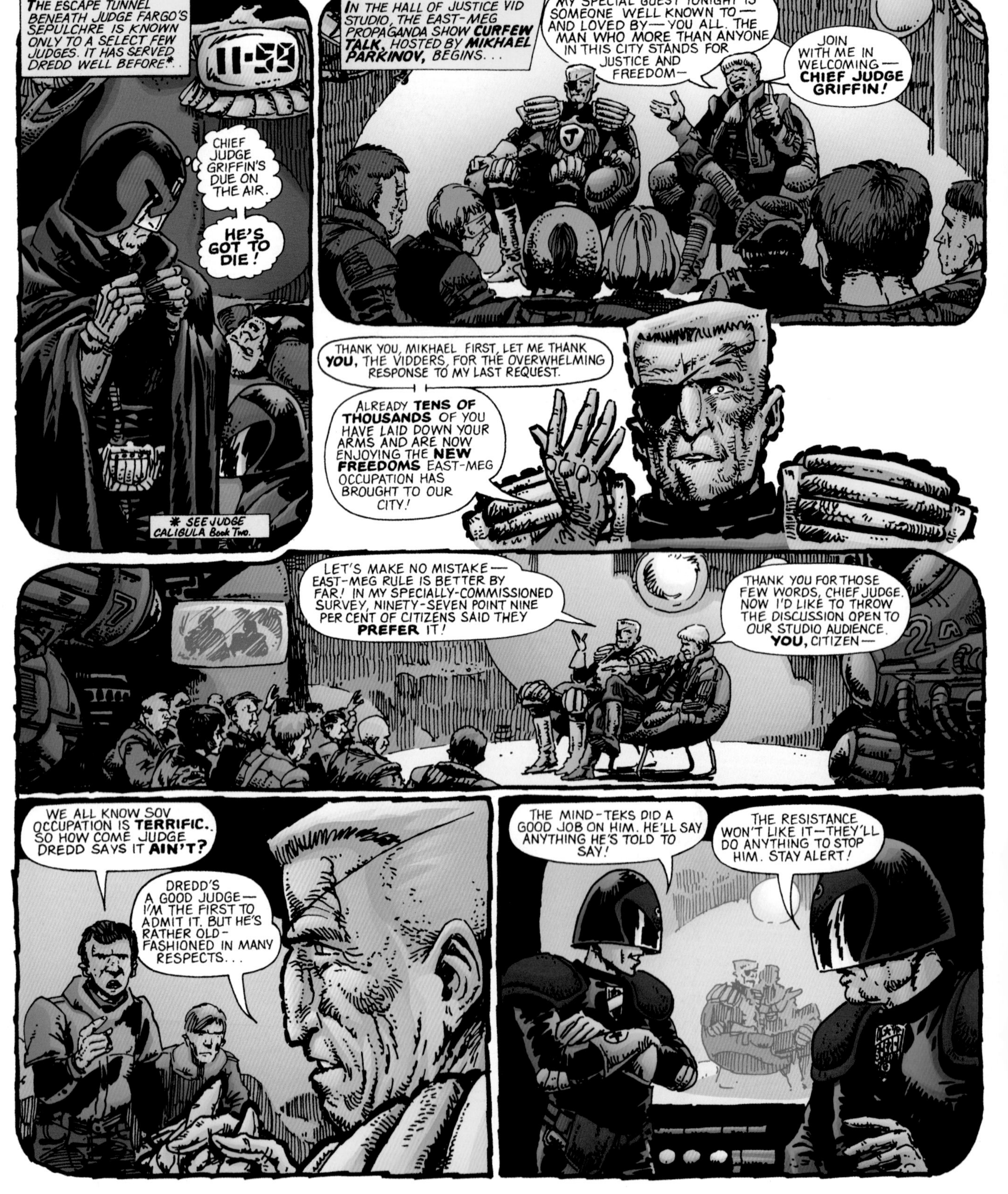
THE ESCAPE TUNNEL BENEATH JUDGE FARGO'S SEPULCHRE IS KNOWN ONLY TO A SELECT FEW JUDGES. IT HAS SERVED DREDD WELL BEFORE*.
11:59
CHIEF JUDGE GRIFFIN'S DUE ON THE AIR.
HE'S GOT TO DIE!
* SEE JUDGE CALIGULA Book Two.
IN THE HALL OF JUSTICE VID STUDIO, THE EAST-MEG PROPAGANDA SHOW CURFEW TALK, HOSTED BY MIKHAEL PARKINOV, BEGINS...
MY SPECIAL GUEST TONIGHT IS SOMEONE WELL KNOWN TO— AND LOVED BY— YOU ALL. THE MAN WHO MORE THAN ANYONE IN THIS CITY STANDS FOR JUSTICE AND FREEDOM—
JOIN WITH ME IN WELCOMING— CHIEF JUDGE GRIFFIN!
THANK YOU, MIKHAEL. FIRST, LET ME THANK YOU, THE VIDDERS, FOR THE OVERWHELMING RESPONSE TO MY LAST REQUEST.
ALREADY TENS OF THOUSANDS OF YOU HAVE LAID DOWN YOUR ARMS AND ARE NOW ENJOYING THE NEW FREEDOMS EAST-MEG OCCUPATION HAS BROUGHT TO OUR CITY!
LET'S MAKE NO MISTAKE— EAST-MEG RULE IS BETTER BY FAR! IN MY SPECIALLY-COMMISSIONED SURVEY, NINETY-SEVEN POINT NINE PER CENT OF CITIZENS SAID THEY PREFER IT!
THANK YOU FOR THOSE FEW WORDS, CHIEF JUDGE. NOW I'D LIKE TO THROW THE DISCUSSION OPEN TO OUR STUDIO AUDIENCE. YOU, CITIZEN—
WE ALL KNOW SOV OCCUPATION IS TERRIFIC. SO HOW COME JUDGE DREDD SAYS IT AIN'T?
DREDD'S A GOOD JUDGE— I'M THE FIRST TO ADMIT IT. BUT HE'S RATHER OLD-FASHIONED IN MANY RESPECTS...
THE MIND-TEKS DID A GOOD JOB ON HIM. HE'LL SAY ANYTHING HE'S TOLD TO SAY!
THE RESISTANCE WON'T LIKE IT—THEY'LL DO ANYTHING TO STOP HIM. STAY ALERT!

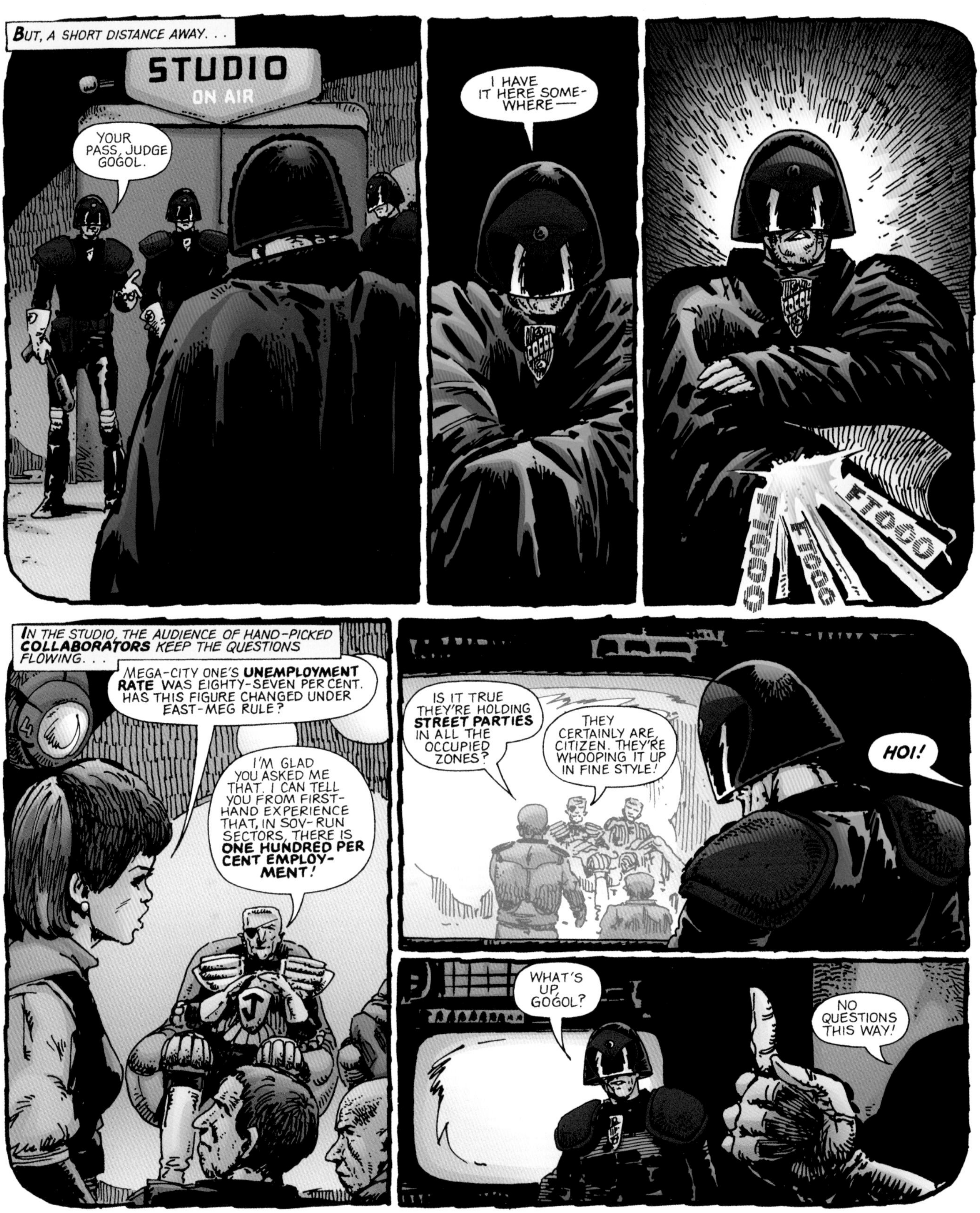
BUT, A SHORT DISTANCE AWAY. . .
STUDIO
ON AIR
YOUR PASS, JUDGE GOGOL.
I HAVE IT HERE SOME-WHERE—
IN THE STUDIO, THE AUDIENCE OF HAND-PICKED COLLABORATORS KEEP THE QUESTIONS FLOWING. . .
MEGA-CITY ONE'S UNEMPLOYMENT RATE WAS EIGHTY-SEVEN PER CENT. HAS THIS FIGURE CHANGED UNDER EAST-MEG RULE?
I'M GLAD YOU ASKED ME THAT. I CAN TELL YOU FROM FIRST-HAND EXPERIENCE THAT, IN SOV-RUN SECTORS, THERE IS ONE HUNDRED PER CENT EMPLOYMENT!
IS IT TRUE THEY'RE HOLDING STREET PARTIES IN ALL THE OCCUPIED ZONES?
THEY CERTAINLY ARE, CITIZEN. THEY'RE WHOOPING IT UP IN FINE STYLE!
HOI!
WHAT'S UP, GOGOL?
NO QUESTIONS THIS WAY!

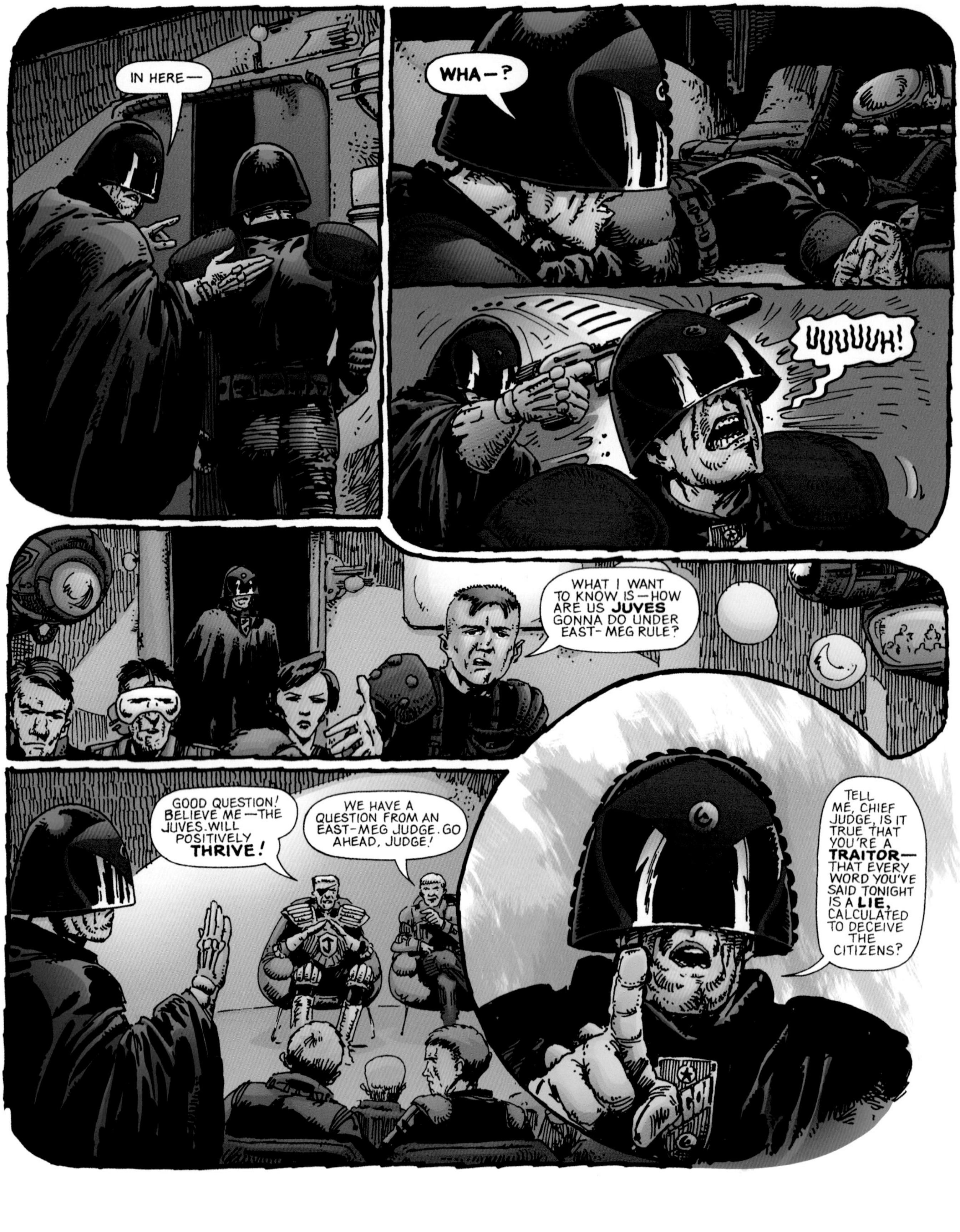

IN HERE—
WHA—?
UUUUUH!
WHAT I WANT TO KNOW IS—HOW ARE US **JUVES** GONNA DO UNDER EAST-MEG RULE?
GOOD QUESTION! BELIEVE ME—THE JUVES WILL POSITIVELY **THRIVE**!
WE HAVE A QUESTION FROM AN EAST-MEG JUDGE. GO AHEAD, JUDGE!
TELL ME, CHIEF JUDGE, IS IT TRUE THAT YOU'RE A **TRAITOR**— THAT EVERY WORD YOU'VE SAID TONIGHT IS A **LIE**, CALCULATED TO DECEIVE THE CITIZENS?

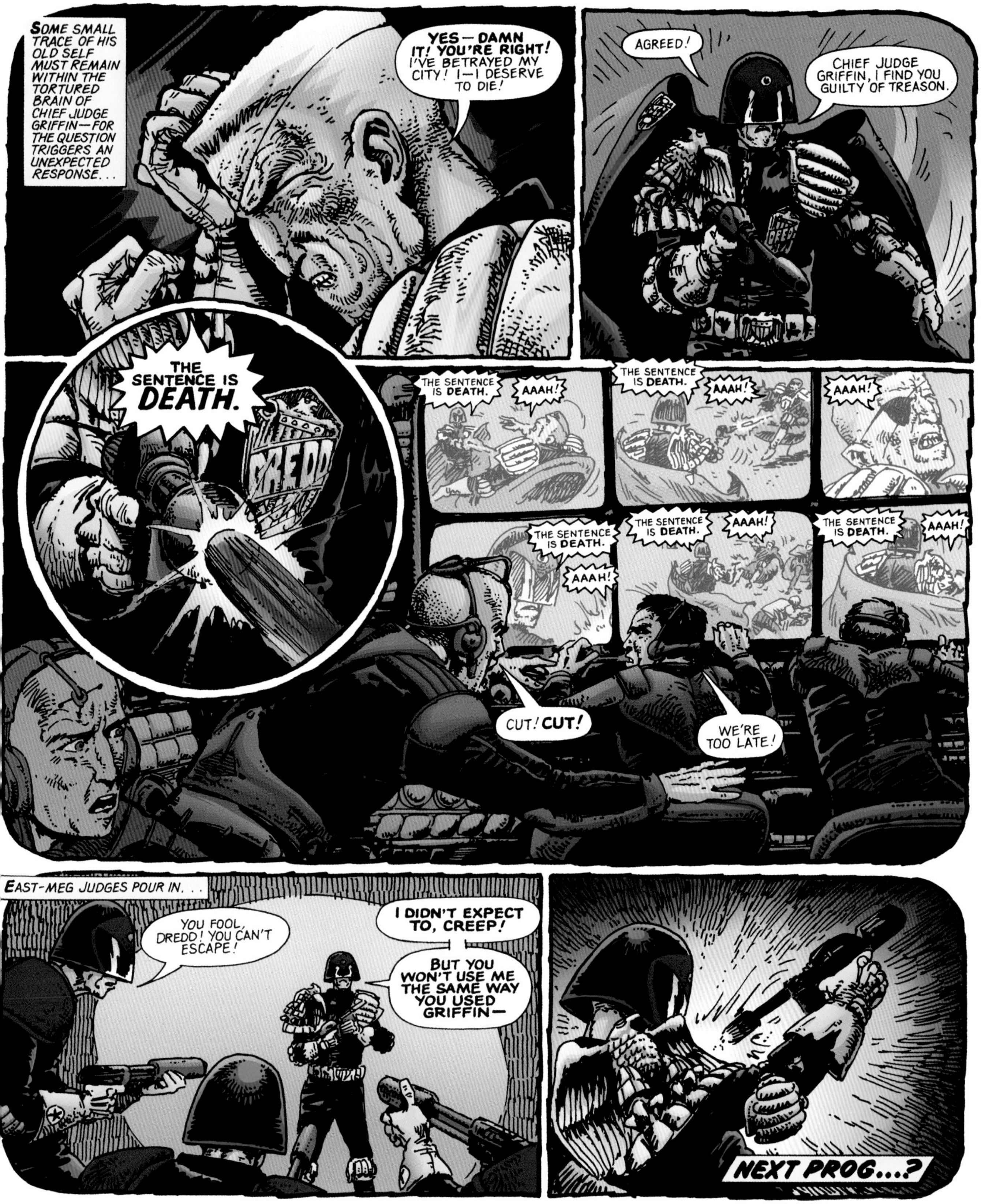

SOME SMALL TRACE OF HIS OLD SELF MUST REMAIN WITHIN THE TORTURED BRAIN OF CHIEF JUDGE GRIFFIN—FOR THE QUESTION TRIGGERS AN UNEXPECTED RESPONSE. . .
YES—DAMN IT! YOU'RE RIGHT! I'VE BETRAYED MY CITY! I—I DESERVE TO DIE!
AGREED!
CHIEF JUDGE GRIFFIN, I FIND YOU GUILTY OF TREASON.
THE SENTENCE IS DEATH.
THE SENTENCE IS DEATH.
AAAH!
THE SENTENCE IS DEATH.
AAAH!
AAAH!
THE SENTENCE IS DEATH.
AAAH!
THE SENTENCE IS DEATH.
AAAH!
THE SENTENCE IS DEATH.
AAAH!
CUT! CUT!
WE'RE TOO LATE!
EAST-MEG JUDGES POUR IN. . .
YOU FOOL, DREDD! YOU CAN'T ESCAPE!
I DIDN'T EXPECT TO, CREEP!
BUT YOU WON'T USE ME THE SAME WAY YOU USED GRIFFIN—
NEXT PROG...?

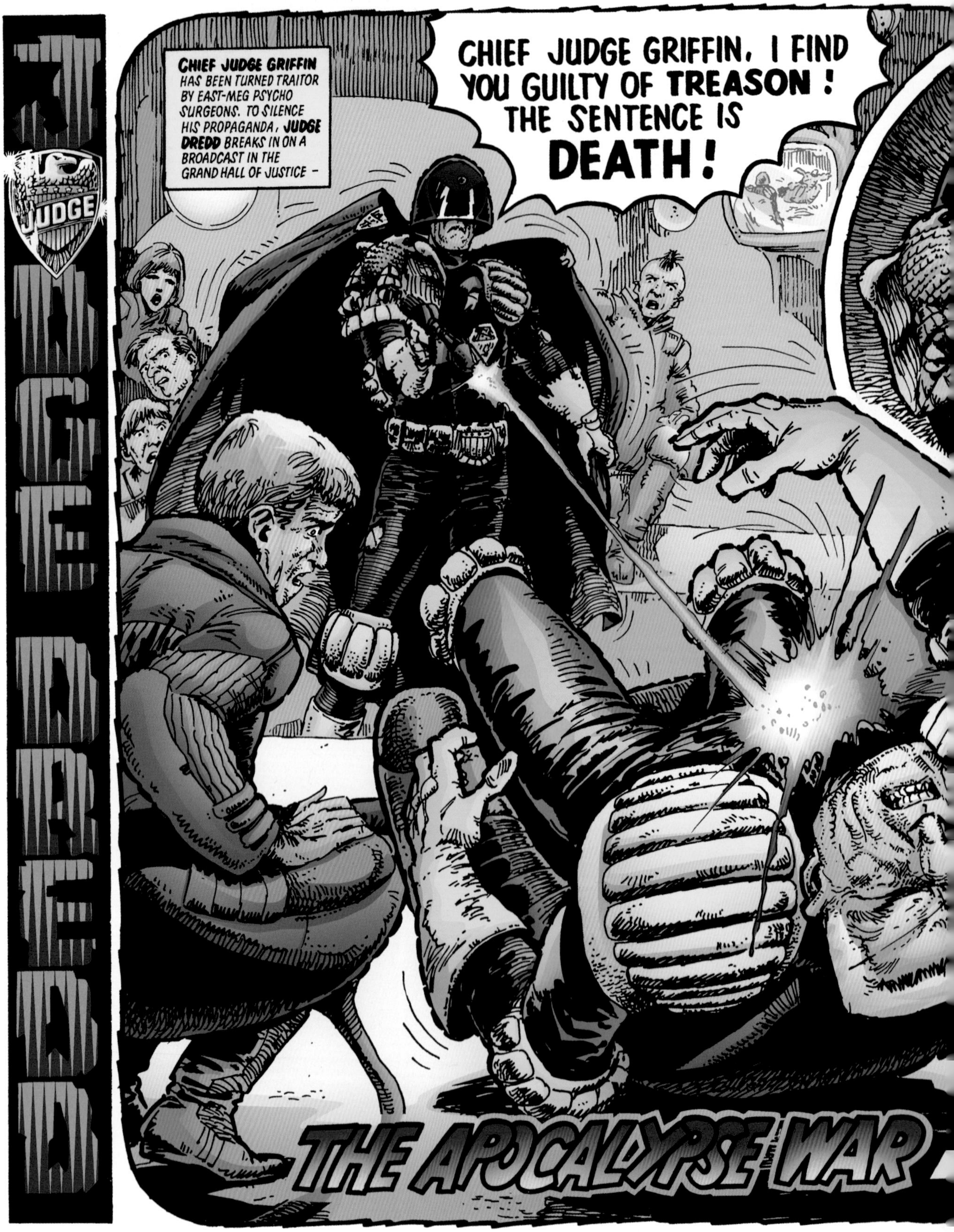
JUDGE DREDD
CHIEF JUDGE GRIFFIN HAS BEEN TURNED TRAITOR BY EAST-MEG PSYCHO SURGEONS. TO SILENCE HIS PROPAGANDA, JUDGE DREDD BREAKS IN ON A BROADCAST IN THE GRAND HALL OF JUSTICE –
CHIEF JUDGE GRIFFIN, I FIND YOU GUILTY OF TREASON! THE SENTENCE IS DEATH!
THE APOCALYPSE WAR

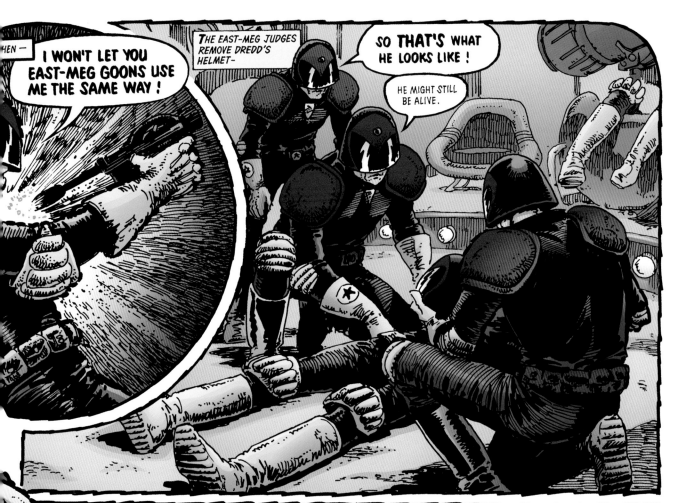

...HEN —

I WON'T LET YOU EAST-MEG GOONS USE ME THE SAME WAY!

THE EAST-MEG JUDGES REMOVE DREDD'S HELMET—

SO **THAT'S** WHAT HE LOOKS LIKE!

HE MIGHT STILL BE ALIVE.

NO CHANCE. **HEART SHOT.**

SCRIPT T B GROVER
ART C EZQUERRA
LETTERING FRAME

MEANWHILE, A SHORT DISTANCE TO THE NORTH, THE TV PICTURES OF DREDD'S DEMISE HAD BEEN SEEN BY HIS LOYAL ROBOT —

JUDGE DWEDD — THE BWAVEST MAN IN ALL THE WORLD — DEAD!

HE MUST BE WEVENGED! YOU'RE GOING TO GET YOUR BLOCK WAR, MAWIA — AGAINST THE BADDEST BLOCK OF ALL — THE SOV BLOCK!

NOW YOU A-TALKIN', WALTER!

MEANWHILE — THE MED-TEKS WILL WANT TO LOOK HIM OVER. TAKE HIM TO THE LABS!

OUT OF SIGHT — THIS IS A DAY WE'LL NEVER FORGET. I'VE GOT A SOUVENIR... HIS LAWGIVER!

I'M GOING TO GET ONE TOO!

BULGARIN'S BONES! HE'S —

NNN GG GG!

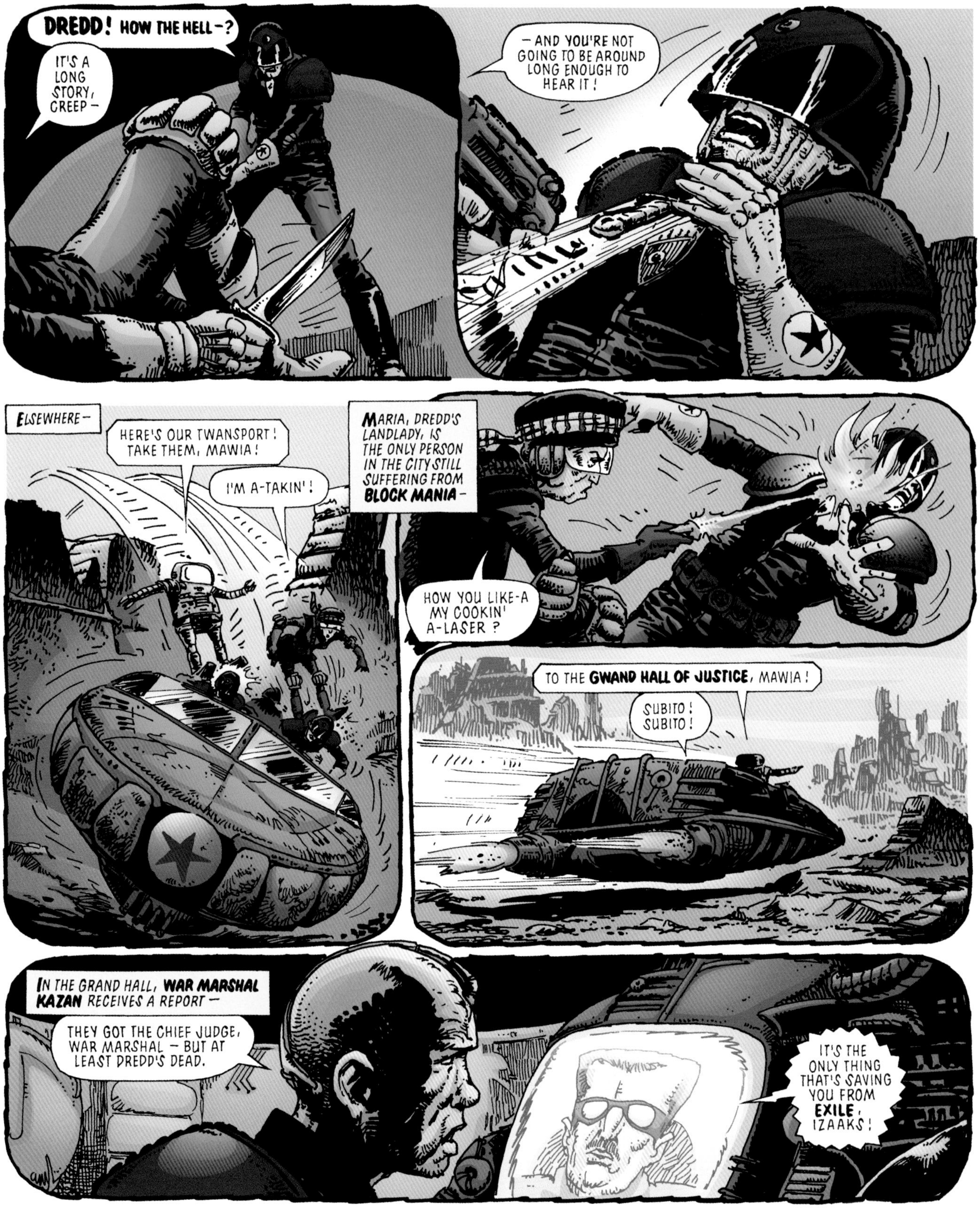
DREDD! HOW THE HELL–?
IT'S A LONG STORY, CREEP–
–AND YOU'RE NOT GOING TO BE AROUND LONG ENOUGH TO HEAR IT!
ELSEWHERE–
HERE'S OUR TWANSPORT! TAKE THEM, MAWIA!
I'M A-TAKIN'!
MARIA, DREDD'S LANDLADY, IS THE ONLY PERSON IN THE CITY STILL SUFFERING FROM BLOCK MANIA–
HOW YOU LIKE-A MY COOKIN' A-LASER?
TO THE GWAND HALL OF JUSTICE, MAWIA!
SUBITO! SUBITO!
IN THE GRAND HALL, WAR MARSHAL KAZAN RECEIVES A REPORT–
THEY GOT THE CHIEF JUDGE, WAR MARSHAL – BUT AT LEAST DREDD'S DEAD.
IT'S THE ONLY THING THAT'S SAVING YOU FROM EXILE, IZAAKS!

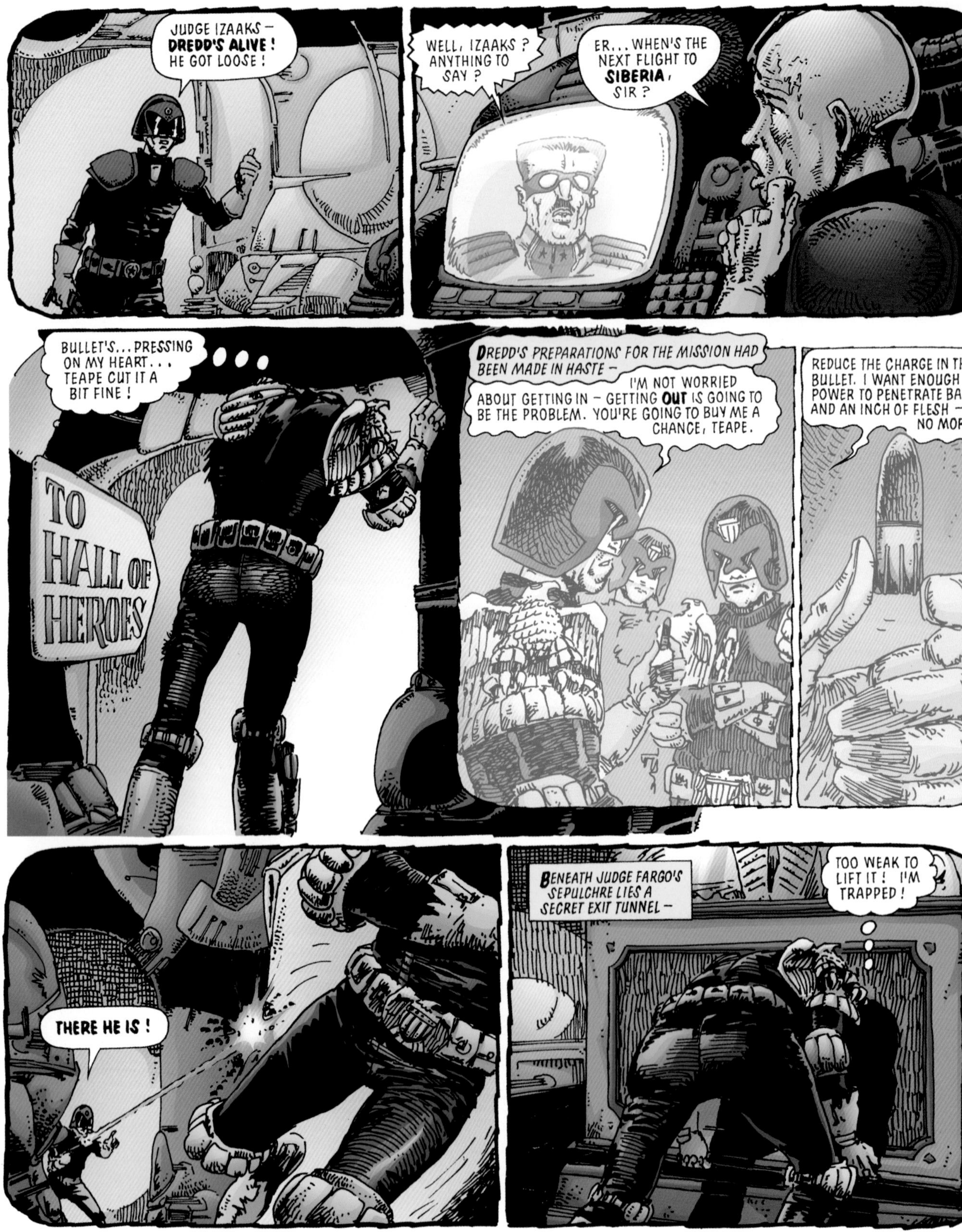
JUDGE IZAAKS — DREDD'S ALIVE! HE GOT LOOSE!
WELL, IZAAKS? ANYTHING TO SAY?
ER... WHEN'S THE NEXT FLIGHT TO SIBERIA, SIR?
BULLET'S... PRESSING ON MY HEART... TEAPE CUT IT A BIT FINE!
TO HALL OF HEROES
DREDD'S PREPARATIONS FOR THE MISSION HAD BEEN MADE IN HASTE —
I'M NOT WORRIED ABOUT GETTING IN — GETTING OUT IS GOING TO BE THE PROBLEM. YOU'RE GOING TO BUY ME A CHANCE, TEAPE.
REDUCE THE CHARGE IN THIS BULLET. I WANT ENOUGH POWER TO PENETRATE BADGE AND AN INCH OF FLESH — NO MORE.
THERE HE IS!
BENEATH JUDGE FARGO'S SEPULCHRE LIES A SECRET EXIT TUNNEL —
TOO WEAK TO LIFT IT! I'M TRAPPED!

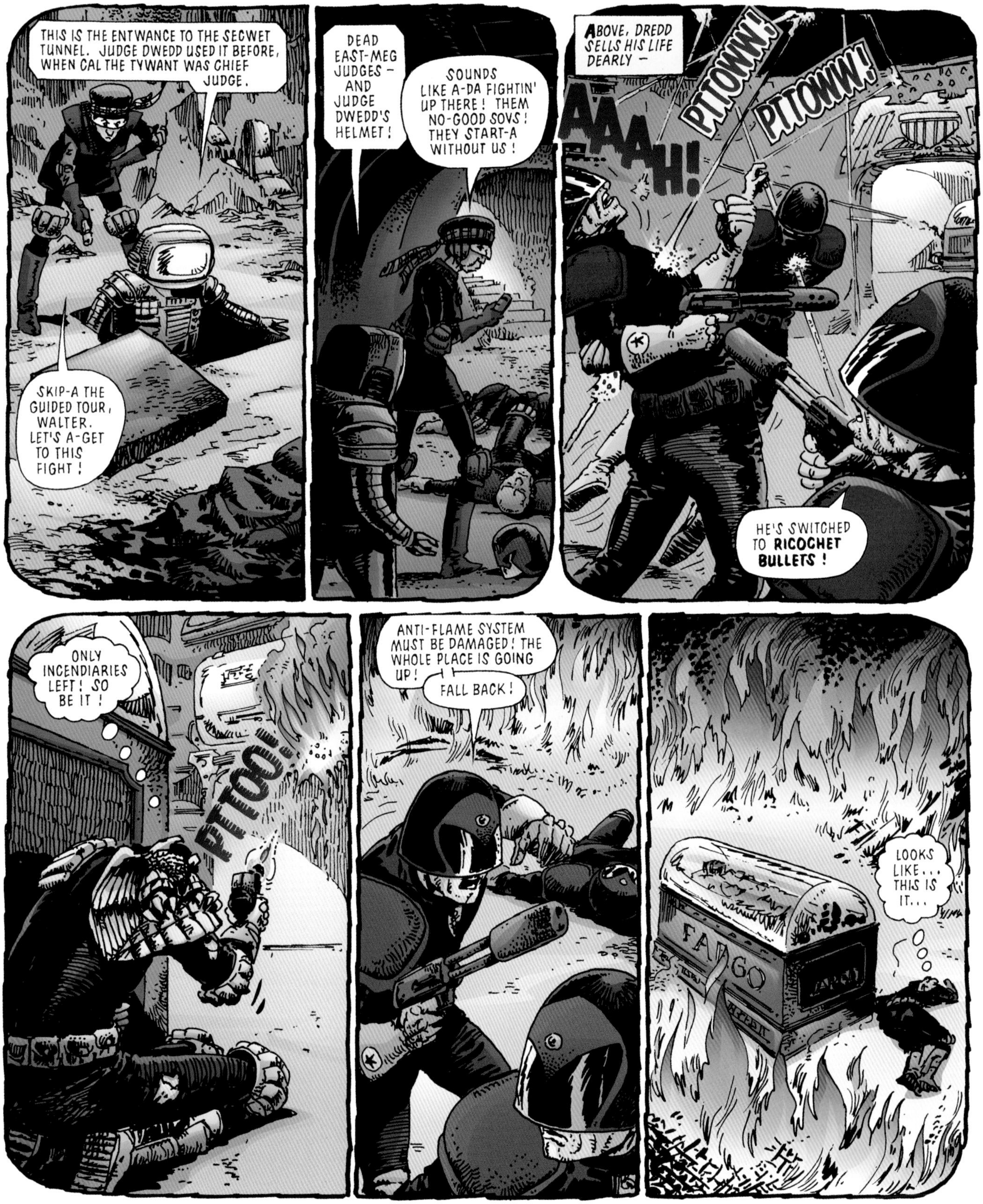
THIS IS THE ENTWANCE TO THE SECWET TUNNEL. JUDGE DWEDD USED IT BEFORE, WHEN CAL THE TYWANT WAS CHIEF JUDGE.
SKIP-A THE GUIDED TOUR, WALTER. LET'S A-GET TO THIS FIGHT!
DEAD EAST-MEG JUDGES — AND JUDGE DWEDD'S HELMET!
SOUNDS LIKE A-DA FIGHTIN' UP THERE! THEM NO-GOOD SOVS! THEY START-A WITHOUT US!
ABOVE, DREDD SELLS HIS LIFE DEARLY —
AAAAH!
PTTOWW!
PTTOWW!
HE'S SWITCHED TO RICOCHET BULLETS!
ONLY INCENDIARIES LEFT! SO BE IT!
PTTOO!
ANTI-FLAME SYSTEM MUST BE DAMAGED! THE WHOLE PLACE IS GOING UP!
FALL BACK!
LOOKS LIKE... THIS IS IT...

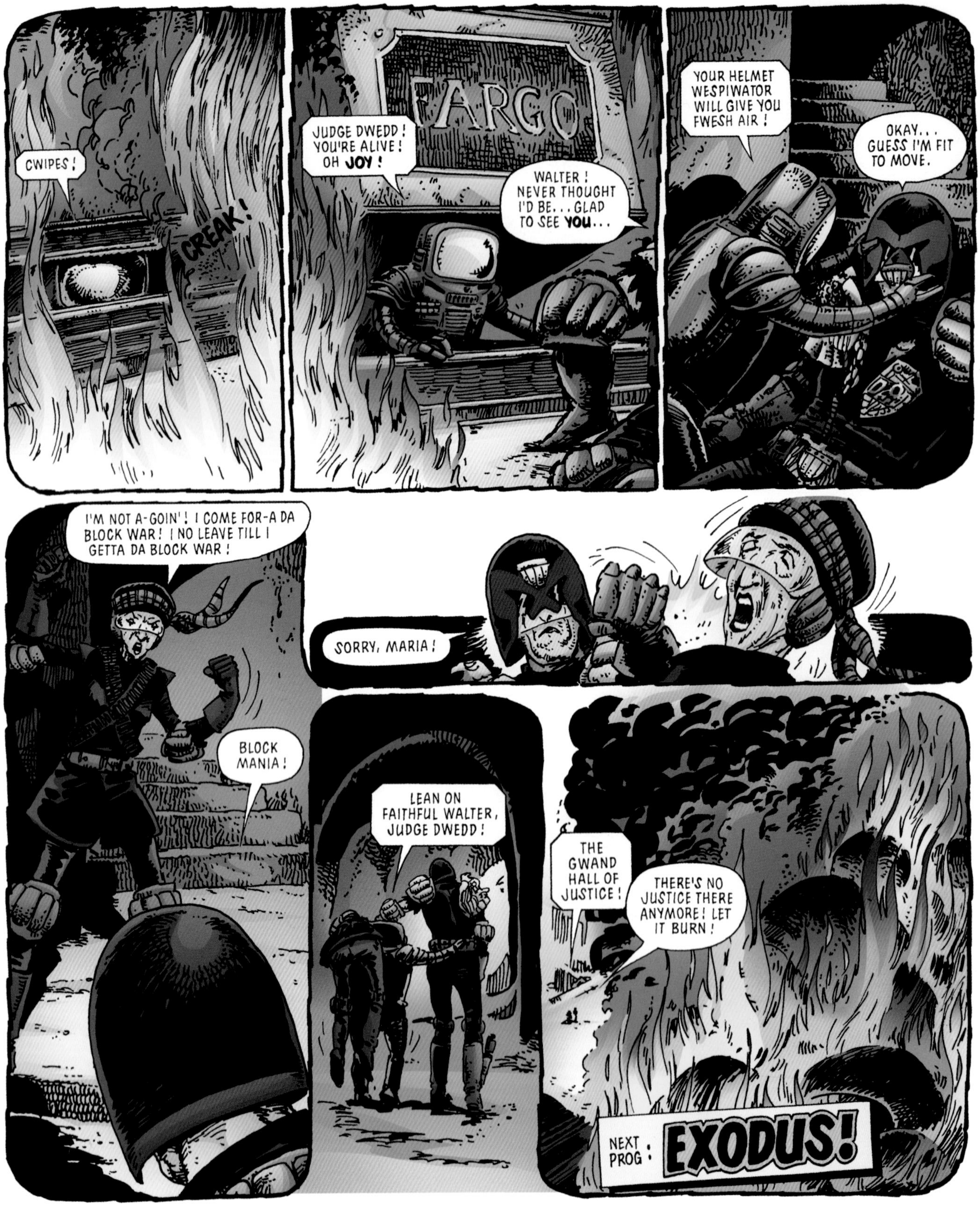
CWIPES!
CREAK!
FARGO
JUDGE DWEDD! YOU'RE ALIVE! OH JOY!
WALTER! NEVER THOUGHT I'D BE... GLAD TO SEE YOU...
YOUR HELMET WESPIWATOR WILL GIVE YOU FWESH AIR!
OKAY... GUESS I'M FIT TO MOVE.
I'M NOT A-GOIN'! I COME FOR-A DA BLOCK WAR! I NO LEAVE TILL I GETTA DA BLOCK WAR!
BLOCK MANIA!
SORRY, MARIA!
LEAN ON FAITHFUL WALTER, JUDGE DWEDD!
THE GWAND HALL OF JUSTICE!
THERE'S NO JUSTICE THERE ANYMORE! LET IT BURN!
NEXT PROG: EXODUS!

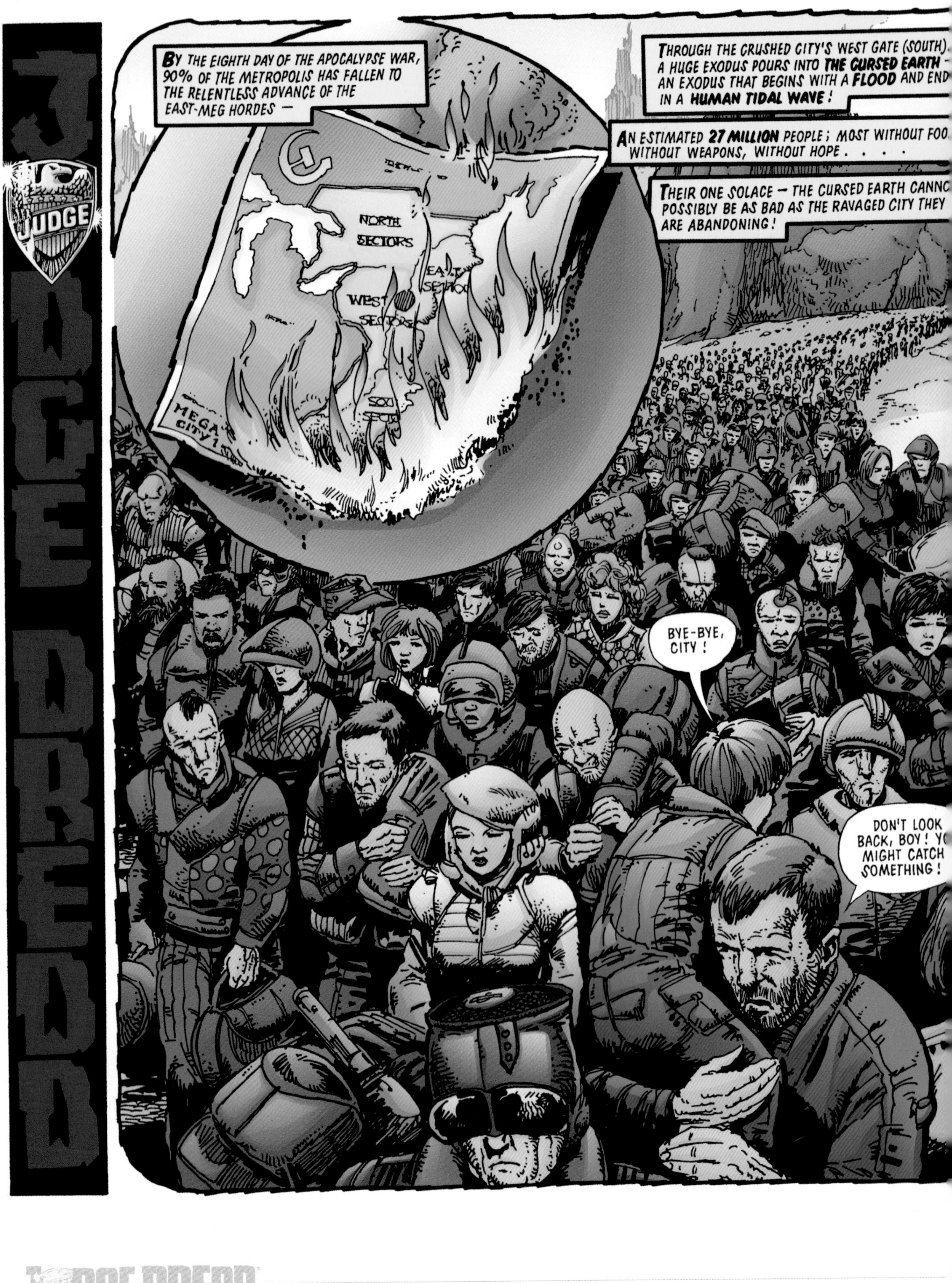
JUDGE DREDD
BY THE EIGHTH DAY OF THE APOCALYPSE WAR, 90% OF THE METROPOLIS HAS FALLEN TO THE RELENTLESS ADVANCE OF THE EAST-MEG HORDES —
THROUGH THE CRUSHED CITY'S WEST GATE (SOUTH) A HUGE EXODUS POURS INTO THE CURSED EARTH — AN EXODUS THAT BEGINS WITH A FLOOD AND ENDS IN A HUMAN TIDAL WAVE!
AN ESTIMATED 27 MILLION PEOPLE; MOST WITHOUT FOO WITHOUT WEAPONS, WITHOUT HOPE . . . .
THEIR ONE SOLACE — THE CURSED EARTH CANNO POSSIBLY BE AS BAD AS THE RAVAGED CITY THEY ARE ABANDONING!
NORTH SECTORS
WEST SECTORS
MEGA CITY 1
BYE-BYE, CITY!
DON'T LOOK BACK, BOY! Y MIGHT CATCH SOMETHING!

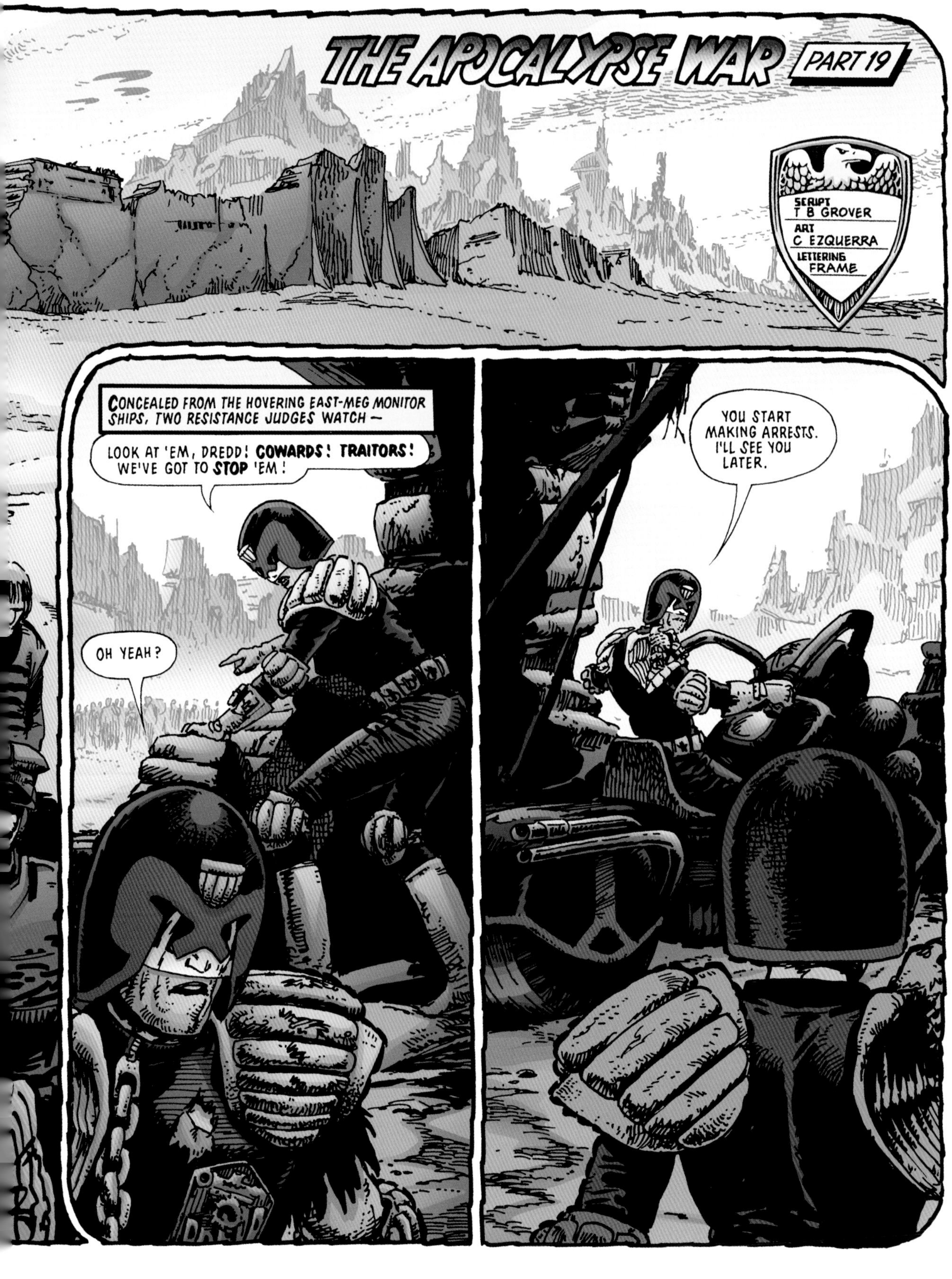
THE APOCALYPSE WAR
PART 19
SCRIPT T B GROVER
ART C EZQUERRA
LETTERING FRAME
CONCEALED FROM THE HOVERING EAST-MEG MONITOR SHIPS, TWO RESISTANCE JUDGES WATCH —
LOOK AT 'EM, DREDD! COWARDS! TRAITORS! WE'VE GOT TO STOP 'EM!
OH YEAH?
YOU START MAKING ARRESTS. I'LL SEE YOU LATER.

AFTER HIS ESCAPE FROM THE BLAZING **HALL OF JUSTICE,*** JUDGE DREDD HAD RETURNED TO HIS STRIKE CAMP FOR URGENT MEDICAL TREATMENT—

TEAPE GOT THE CHARGE WRONG, DREDD. BULLET'S PRESSING ON YOUR **HEART**. LUCKY YOU MADE IT THIS FAR!

NOT LUCK. GWIT! **TWUE GWIT!**

*SEE LAST PROG.

IT'S GONNA HURT SOME WHEN THE LOCAL WEARS OFF!

I'LL LIVE.

DREDD'S LANDLADY, **MARIA**, HAD BEEN GIVEN THE ANTIDOTE TO BLOCK MANIA—

WHEN SHE COMES ROUND, SHE'LL BE NORMAL AGAIN.

SHE'D PROBABLY HAVE BEEN MORE USE TO US AS SHE WAS!

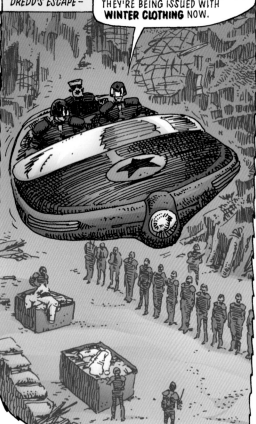

MAD DOG KAZAN HAD BEEN LESS THAN HAPPY ABOUT DREDD'S ESCAPE—

ALL THOSE PRESENT IN THE HALL OF JUSTICE HAVE BEEN ROUNDED UP, AS PER YOUR ORDERS, WAR-MARSHAL. THEY'RE BEING ISSUED WITH **WINTER CLOTHING** NOW.

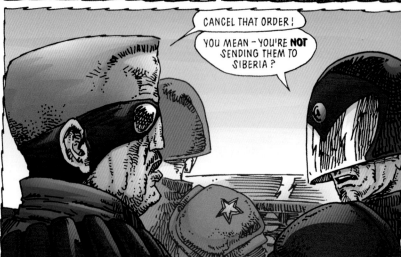

CANCEL THAT ORDER!

YOU MEAN — YOU'RE **NOT** SENDING THEM TO SIBERIA?

NO. I MEAN THEY'RE NOT GETTING ANY WINTER CLOTHING!

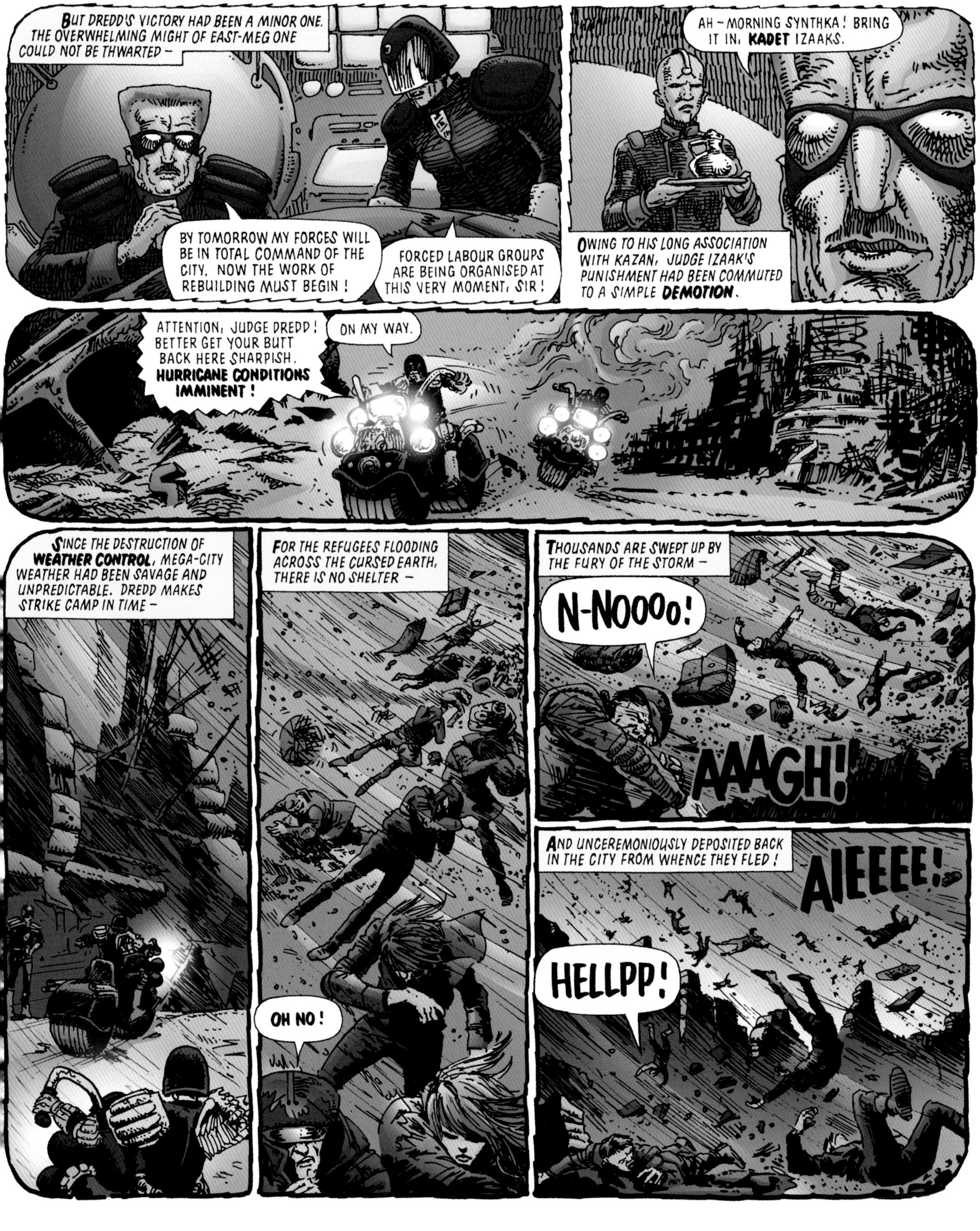
BUT DREDD'S VICTORY HAD BEEN A MINOR ONE. THE OVERWHELMING MIGHT OF EAST-MEG ONE COULD NOT BE THWARTED –
BY TOMORROW MY FORCES WILL BE IN TOTAL COMMAND OF THE CITY. NOW THE WORK OF REBUILDING MUST BEGIN!
FORCED LABOUR GROUPS ARE BEING ORGANISED AT THIS VERY MOMENT, SIR!
AH – MORNING SYNTHKA! BRING IT IN, KADET IZAAKS.
OWING TO HIS LONG ASSOCIATION WITH KAZAN, JUDGE IZAAK'S PUNISHMENT HAD BEEN COMMUTED TO A SIMPLE DEMOTION.
ATTENTION, JUDGE DREDD! BETTER GET YOUR BUTT BACK HERE SHARPISH. HURRICANE CONDITIONS IMMINENT!
ON MY WAY.
SINCE THE DESTRUCTION OF WEATHER CONTROL, MEGA-CITY WEATHER HAD BEEN SAVAGE AND UNPREDICTABLE. DREDD MAKES STRIKE CAMP IN TIME –
FOR THE REFUGEES FLOODING ACROSS THE CURSED EARTH, THERE IS NO SHELTER –
OH NO!
THOUSANDS ARE SWEPT UP BY THE FURY OF THE STORM –
N-NOOOo!
AAAGH!
AND UNCEREMONIOUSLY DEPOSITED BACK IN THE CITY FROM WHENCE THEY FLED!
AIEEEE!
HELLPP!

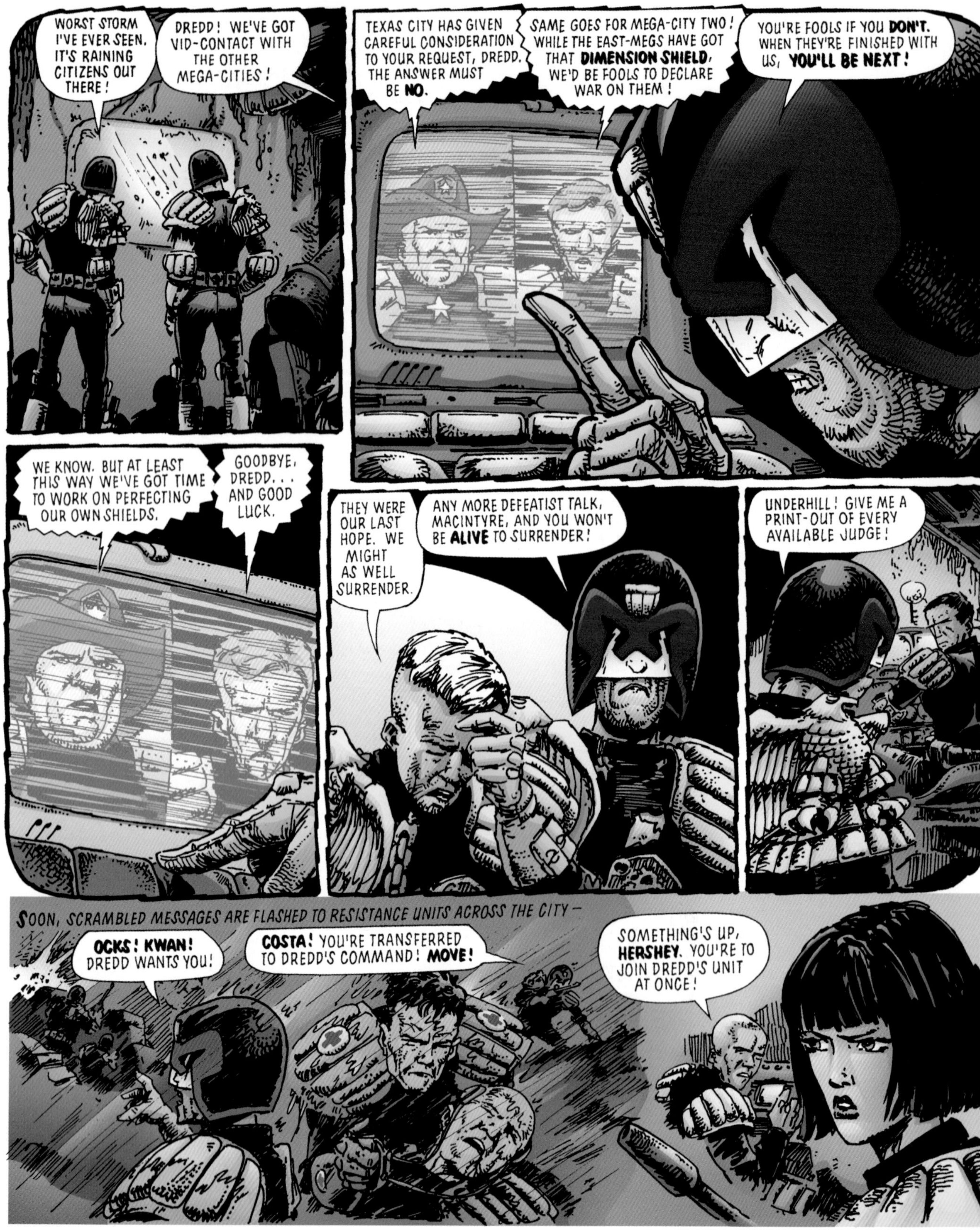
WORST STORM I'VE EVER SEEN. IT'S RAINING CITIZENS OUT THERE!
DREDD! WE'VE GOT VID-CONTACT WITH THE OTHER MEGA-CITIES!
TEXAS CITY HAS GIVEN CAREFUL CONSIDERATION TO YOUR REQUEST, DREDD. THE ANSWER MUST BE NO.
SAME GOES FOR MEGA-CITY TWO! WHILE THE EAST-MEGS HAVE GOT THAT DIMENSION SHIELD, WE'D BE FOOLS TO DECLARE WAR ON THEM!
YOU'RE FOOLS IF YOU DON'T. WHEN THEY'RE FINISHED WITH US, YOU'LL BE NEXT!
WE KNOW. BUT AT LEAST THIS WAY WE'VE GOT TIME TO WORK ON PERFECTING OUR OWN SHIELDS.
GOODBYE, DREDD. . . AND GOOD LUCK.
THEY WERE OUR LAST HOPE. WE MIGHT AS WELL SURRENDER.
ANY MORE DEFEATIST TALK, MACINTYRE, AND YOU WON'T BE ALIVE TO SURRENDER!
UNDERHILL! GIVE ME A PRINT-OUT OF EVERY AVAILABLE JUDGE!
SOON, SCRAMBLED MESSAGES ARE FLASHED TO RESISTANCE UNITS ACROSS THE CITY —
OCKS! KWAN! DREDD WANTS YOU!
COSTA! YOU'RE TRANSFERRED TO DREDD'S COMMAND! MOVE!
SOMETHING'S UP, HERSHEY. YOU'RE TO JOIN DREDD'S UNIT AT ONCE!

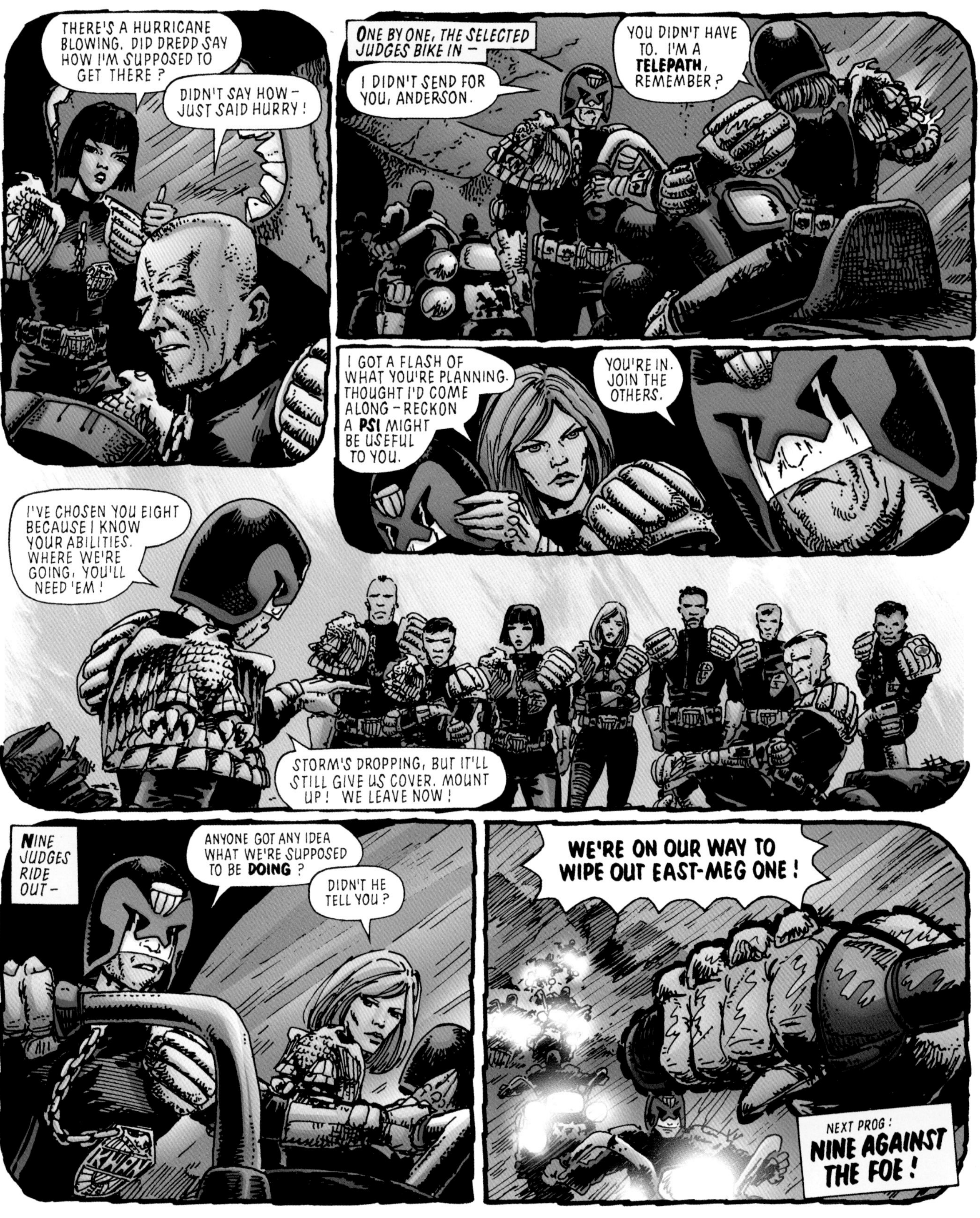
THERE'S A HURRICANE BLOWING. DID DREDD SAY HOW I'M SUPPOSED TO GET THERE ?
DIDN'T SAY HOW – JUST SAID HURRY !
ONE BY ONE, THE SELECTED JUDGES BIKE IN –
I DIDN'T SEND FOR YOU, ANDERSON.
YOU DIDN'T HAVE TO. I'M A TELEPATH, REMEMBER ?
I GOT A FLASH OF WHAT YOU'RE PLANNING. THOUGHT I'D COME ALONG – RECKON A PSI MIGHT BE USEFUL TO YOU.
YOU'RE IN. JOIN THE OTHERS.
I'VE CHOSEN YOU EIGHT BECAUSE I KNOW YOUR ABILITIES. WHERE WE'RE GOING, YOU'LL NEED 'EM !
STORM'S DROPPING, BUT IT'LL STILL GIVE US COVER. MOUNT UP ! WE LEAVE NOW !
NINE JUDGES RIDE OUT –
ANYONE GOT ANY IDEA WHAT WE'RE SUPPOSED TO BE DOING ?
DIDN'T HE TELL YOU ?
WE'RE ON OUR WAY TO WIPE OUT EAST-MEG ONE !
NEXT PROG : NINE AGAINST THE FOE !

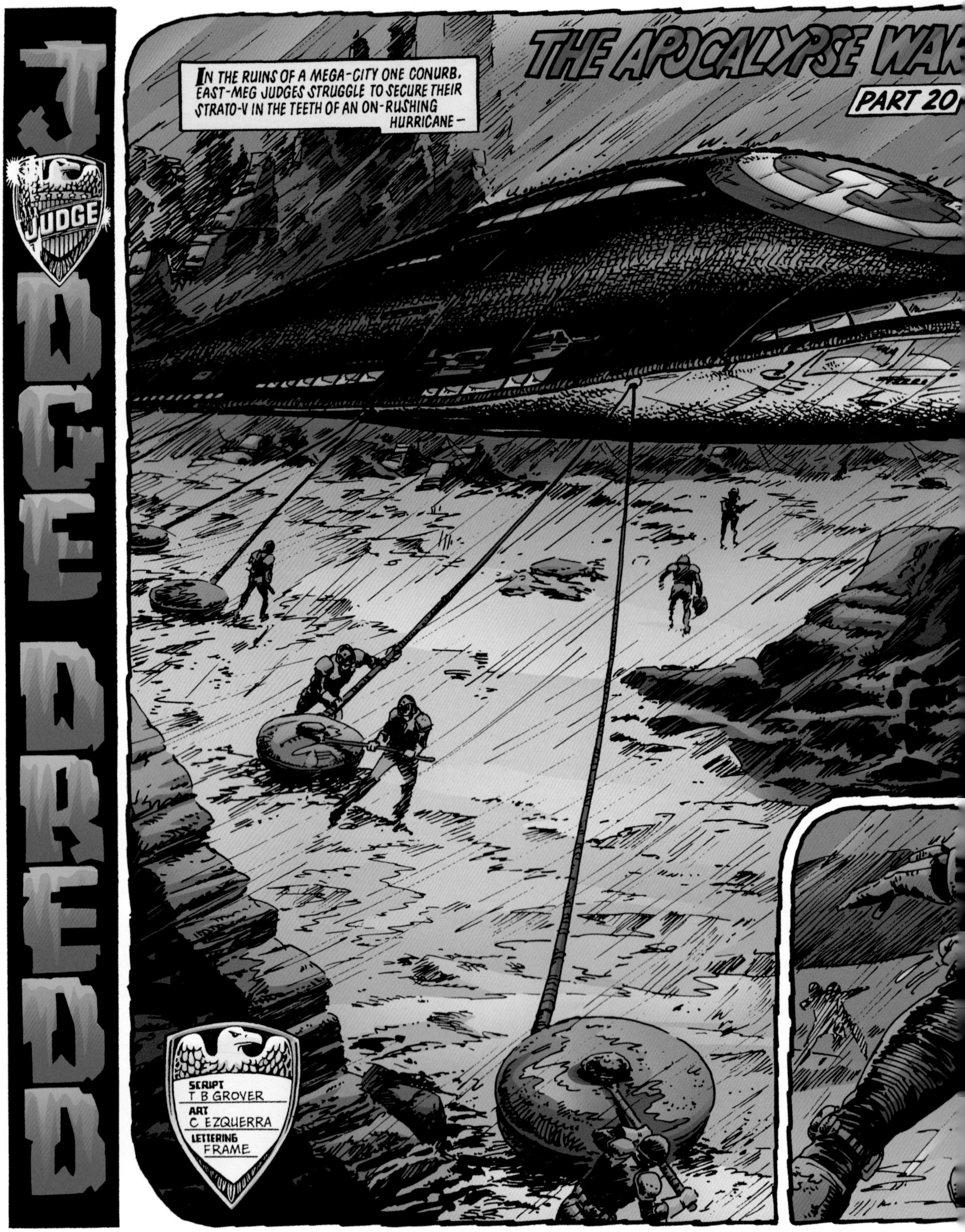
JUDGE DREDD
THE APOCALYPSE WAR
PART 20
IN THE RUINS OF A MEGA-CITY ONE CONURB, EAST-MEG JUDGES STRUGGLE TO SECURE THEIR STRATO-V IN THE TEETH OF AN ON-RUSHING HURRICANE –
SCRIPT
T B GROVER
ART
C EZQUERRA
LETTERING
FRAME

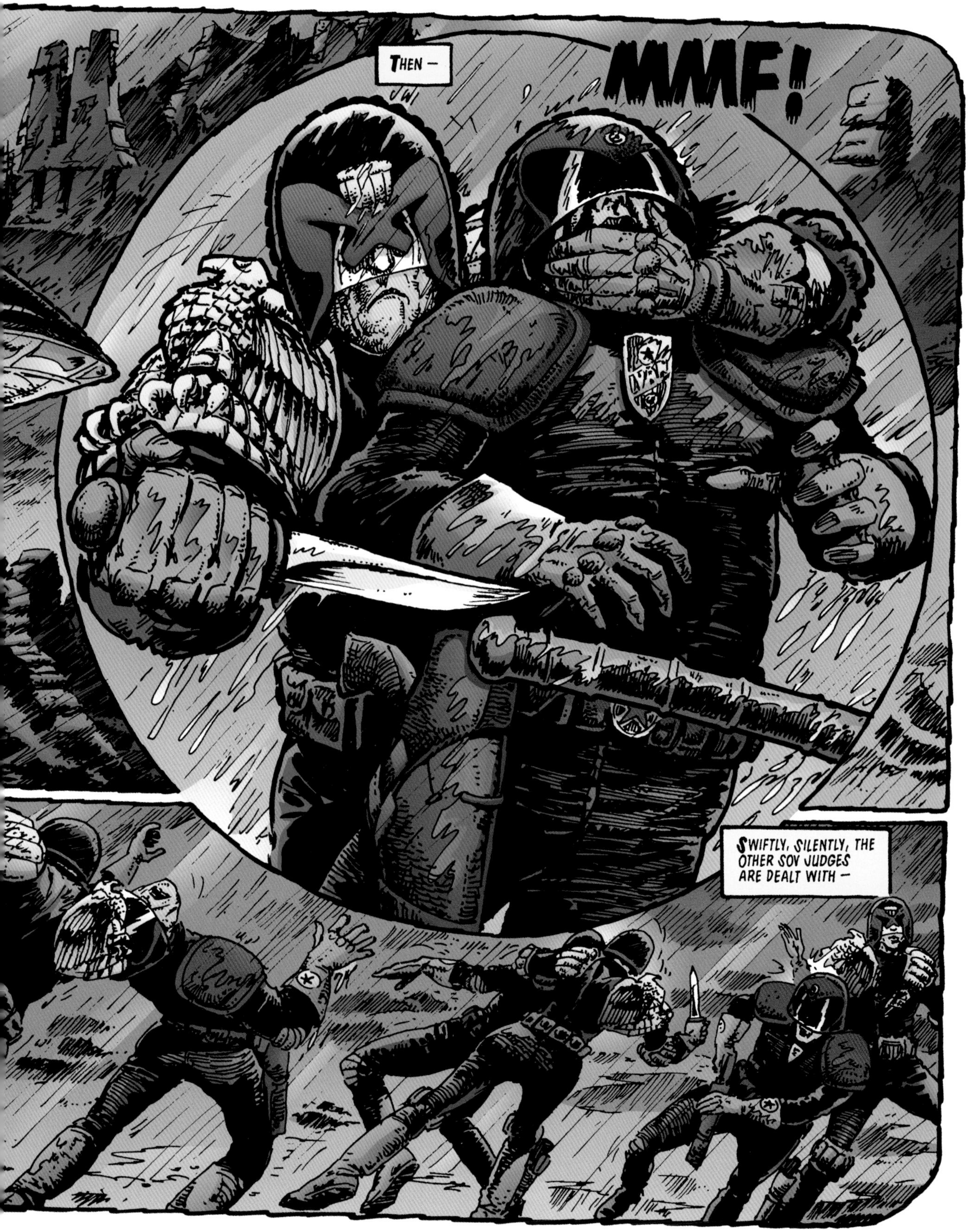
THEN –
MMF!
SWIFTLY, SILENTLY, THE OTHER SOV JUDGES ARE DEALT WITH –

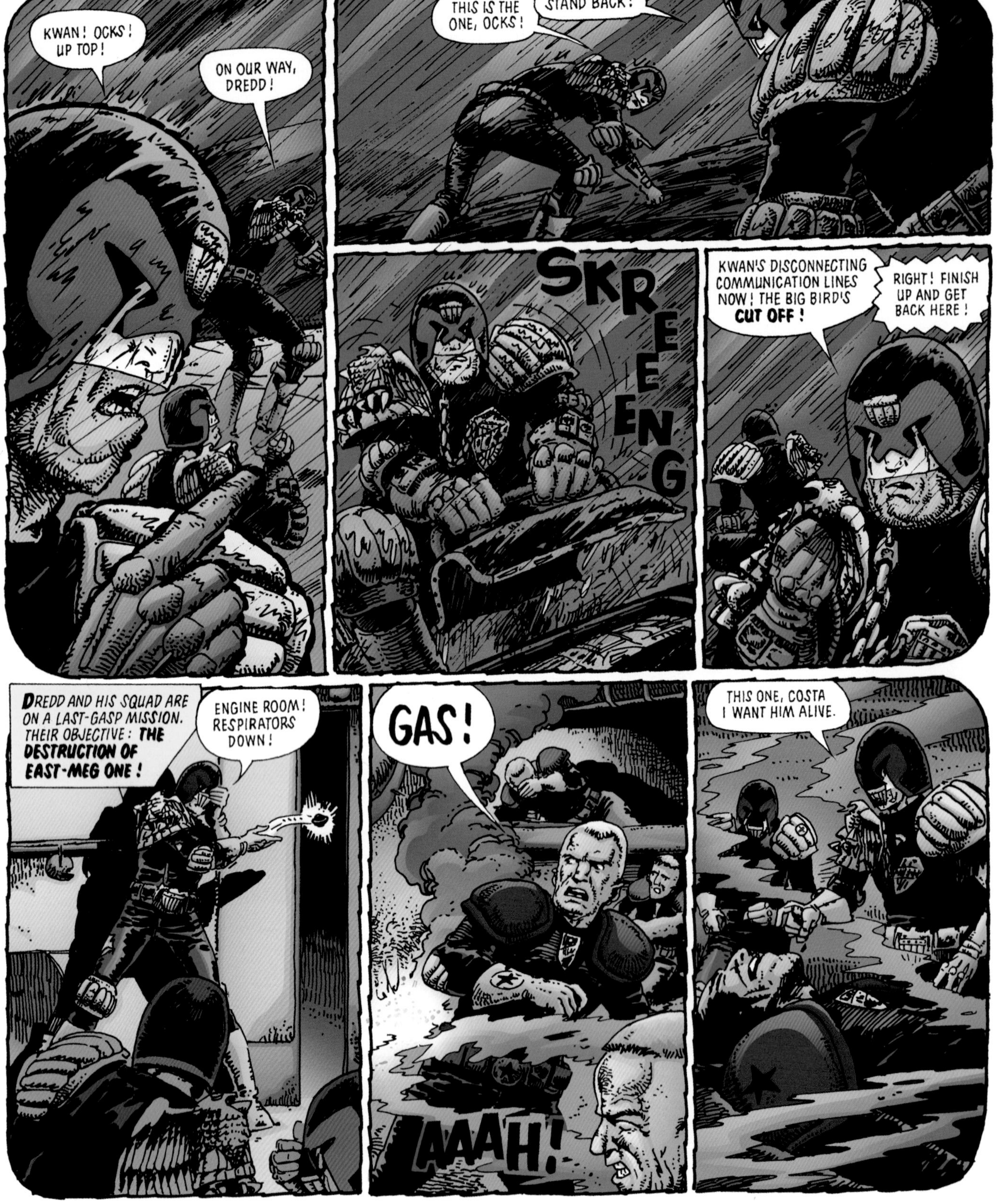
KWAN! OCKS! UP TOP!
ON OUR WAY, DREDD!
THIS IS THE ONE, OCKS!
STAND BACK!
SKREEENG
KWAN'S DISCONNECTING COMMUNICATION LINES NOW! THE BIG BIRD'S **CUT OFF**!
RIGHT! FINISH UP AND GET BACK HERE!
DREDD AND HIS SQUAD ARE ON A LAST-GASP MISSION. THEIR OBJECTIVE: **THE DESTRUCTION OF EAST-MEG ONE!**
ENGINE ROOM! RESPIRATORS DOWN!
GAS!
AAAH!
THIS ONE, COSTA I WANT HIM ALIVE.

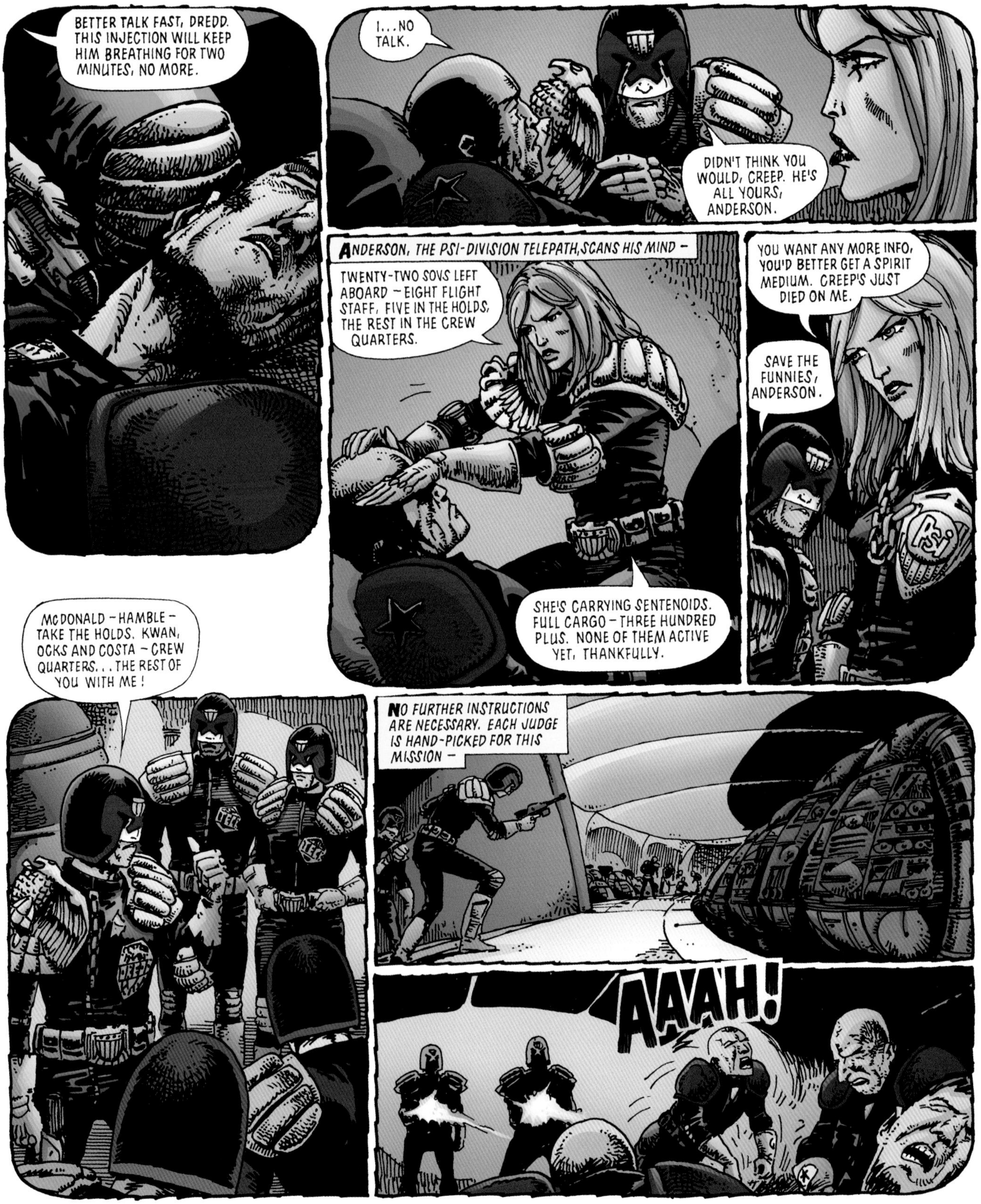

BETTER TALK FAST, DREDD. THIS INJECTION WILL KEEP HIM BREATHING FOR TWO MINUTES, NO MORE.
I...NO TALK.
DIDN'T THINK YOU WOULD, CREEP. HE'S ALL YOURS, ANDERSON.
ANDERSON, THE PSI-DIVISION TELEPATH, SCANS HIS MIND –
TWENTY-TWO SOVS LEFT ABOARD – EIGHT FLIGHT STAFF, FIVE IN THE HOLDS, THE REST IN THE CREW QUARTERS.
SHE'S CARRYING SENTENOIDS. FULL CARGO – THREE HUNDRED PLUS. NONE OF THEM ACTIVE YET, THANKFULLY.
YOU WANT ANY MORE INFO, YOU'D BETTER GET A SPIRIT MEDIUM. CREEP'S JUST DIED ON ME.
SAVE THE FUNNIES, ANDERSON.
McDONALD – HAMBLE – TAKE THE HOLDS. KWAN, OCKS AND COSTA – CREW QUARTERS... THE REST OF YOU WITH ME!
NO FURTHER INSTRUCTIONS ARE NECESSARY. EACH JUDGE IS HAND-PICKED FOR THIS MISSION –
AAAH!

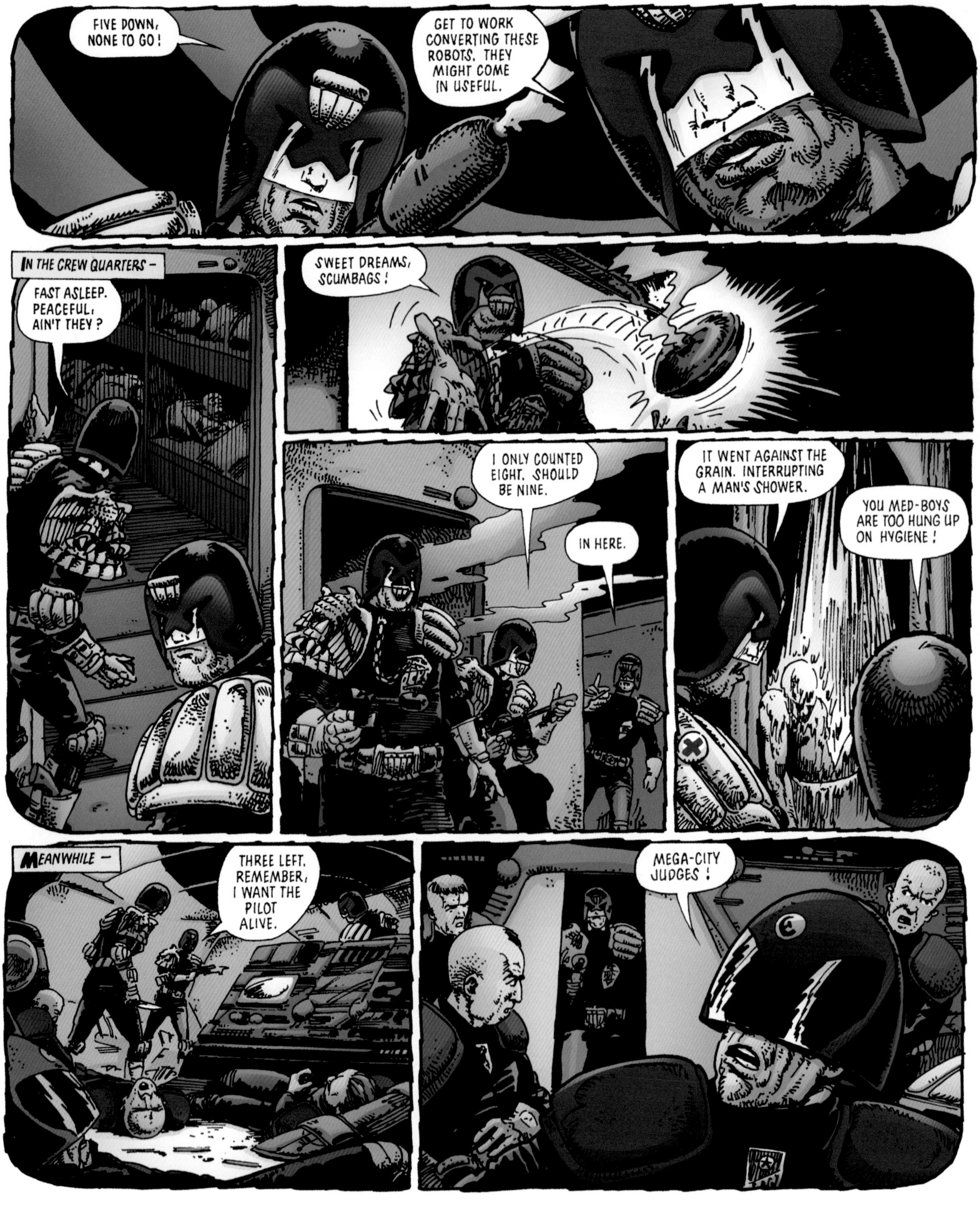
FIVE DOWN, NONE TO GO!
GET TO WORK CONVERTING THESE ROBOTS. THEY MIGHT COME IN USEFUL.
IN THE CREW QUARTERS –
FAST ASLEEP. PEACEFUL, AIN'T THEY?
SWEET DREAMS, SCUMBAGS!
I ONLY COUNTED EIGHT. SHOULD BE NINE.
IN HERE.
IT WENT AGAINST THE GRAIN. INTERRUPTING A MAN'S SHOWER.
YOU MED-BOYS ARE TOO HUNG UP ON HYGIENE!
MEANWHILE –
THREE LEFT. REMEMBER, I WANT THE PILOT ALIVE.
MEGA-CITY JUDGES!

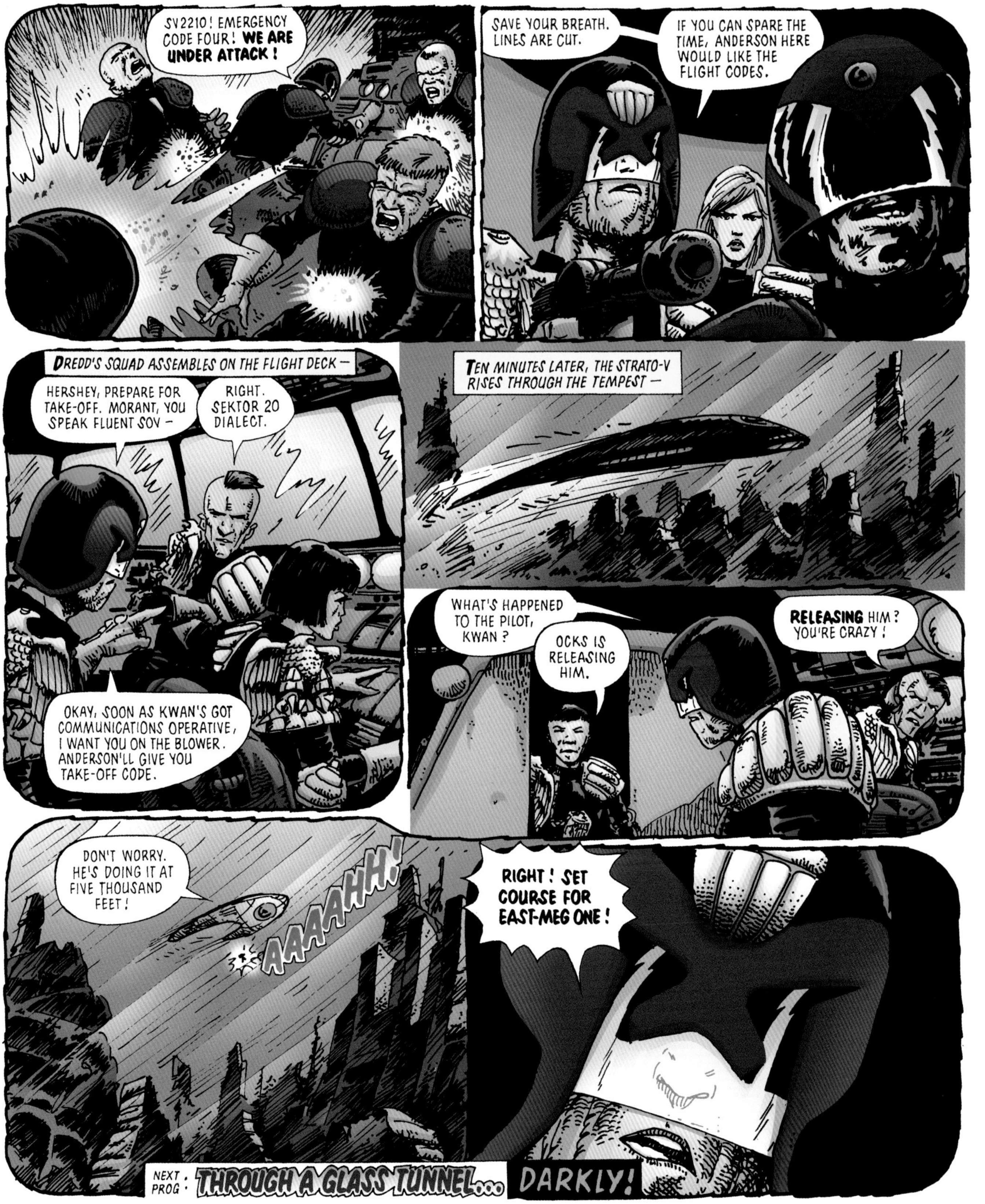

SV2210! EMERGENCY CODE FOUR! WE ARE UNDER ATTACK!
SAVE YOUR BREATH. LINES ARE CUT.
IF YOU CAN SPARE THE TIME, ANDERSON HERE WOULD LIKE THE FLIGHT CODES.
DREDD'S SQUAD ASSEMBLES ON THE FLIGHT DECK –
HERSHEY, PREPARE FOR TAKE-OFF. MORANT, YOU SPEAK FLUENT SOV –
RIGHT. SEKTOR 20 DIALECT.
OKAY, SOON AS KWAN'S GOT COMMUNICATIONS OPERATIVE, I WANT YOU ON THE BLOWER. ANDERSON'LL GIVE YOU TAKE-OFF CODE.
TEN MINUTES LATER, THE STRATO-V RISES THROUGH THE TEMPEST –
WHAT'S HAPPENED TO THE PILOT, KWAN?
OCKS IS RELEASING HIM.
RELEASING HIM? YOU'RE CRAZY!
DON'T WORRY. HE'S DOING IT AT FIVE THOUSAND FEET!
AAAAAHH!
RIGHT! SET COURSE FOR EAST-MEG ONE!
NEXT PROG: THROUGH A GLASS TUNNEL... DARKLY!

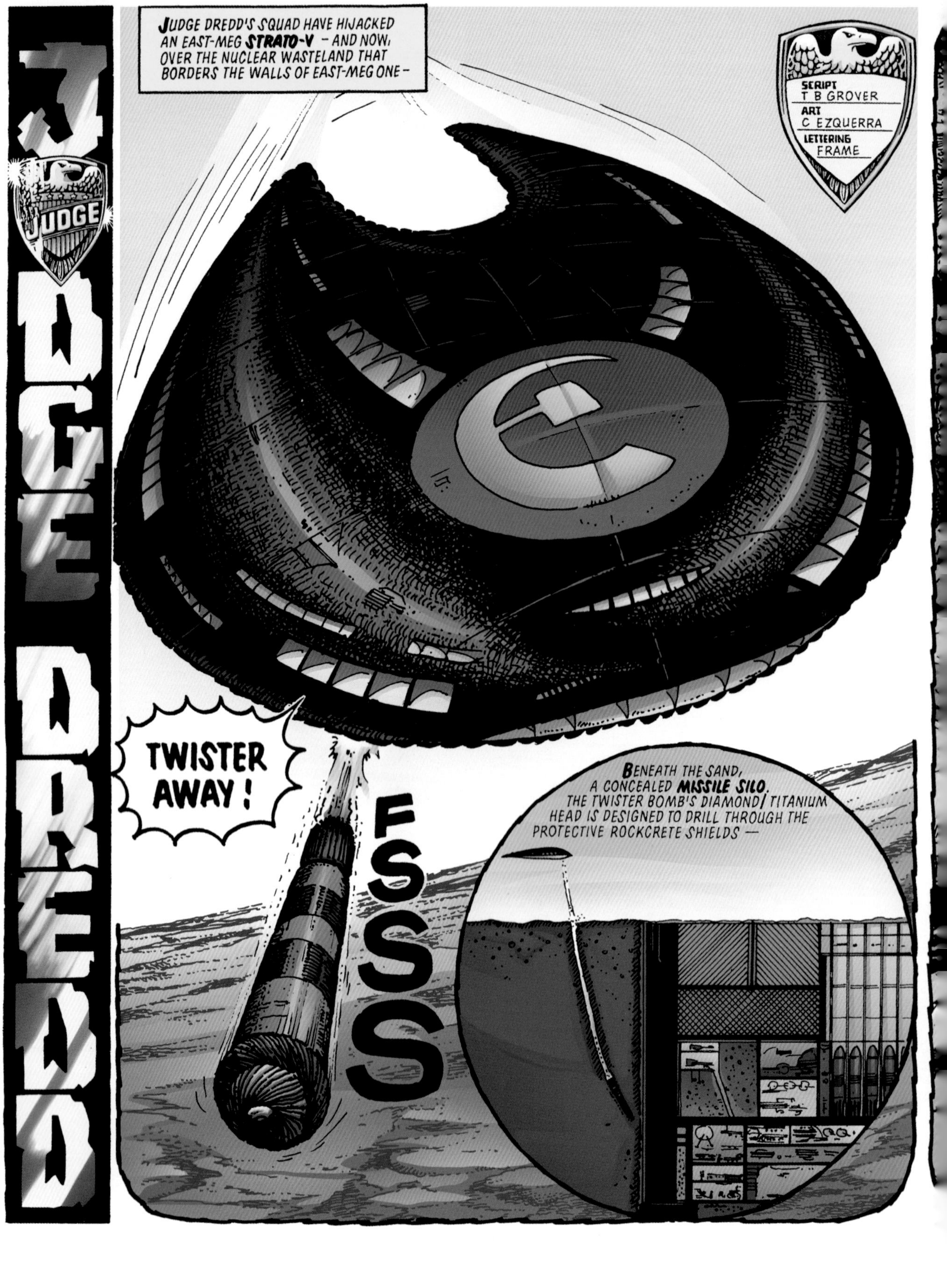
JUDGE DREDD
JUDGE DREDD'S SQUAD HAVE HIJACKED AN EAST-MEG STRATO-V - AND NOW, OVER THE NUCLEAR WASTELAND THAT BORDERS THE WALLS OF EAST-MEG ONE -
SCRIPT T B GROVER
ART C EZQUERRA
LETTERING FRAME
TWISTER AWAY!
FSSSS
BENEATH THE SAND, A CONCEALED MISSILE SILO. THE TWISTER BOMB'S DIAMOND/ TITANIUM HEAD IS DESIGNED TO DRILL THROUGH THE PROTECTIVE ROCKCRETE SHIELDS —

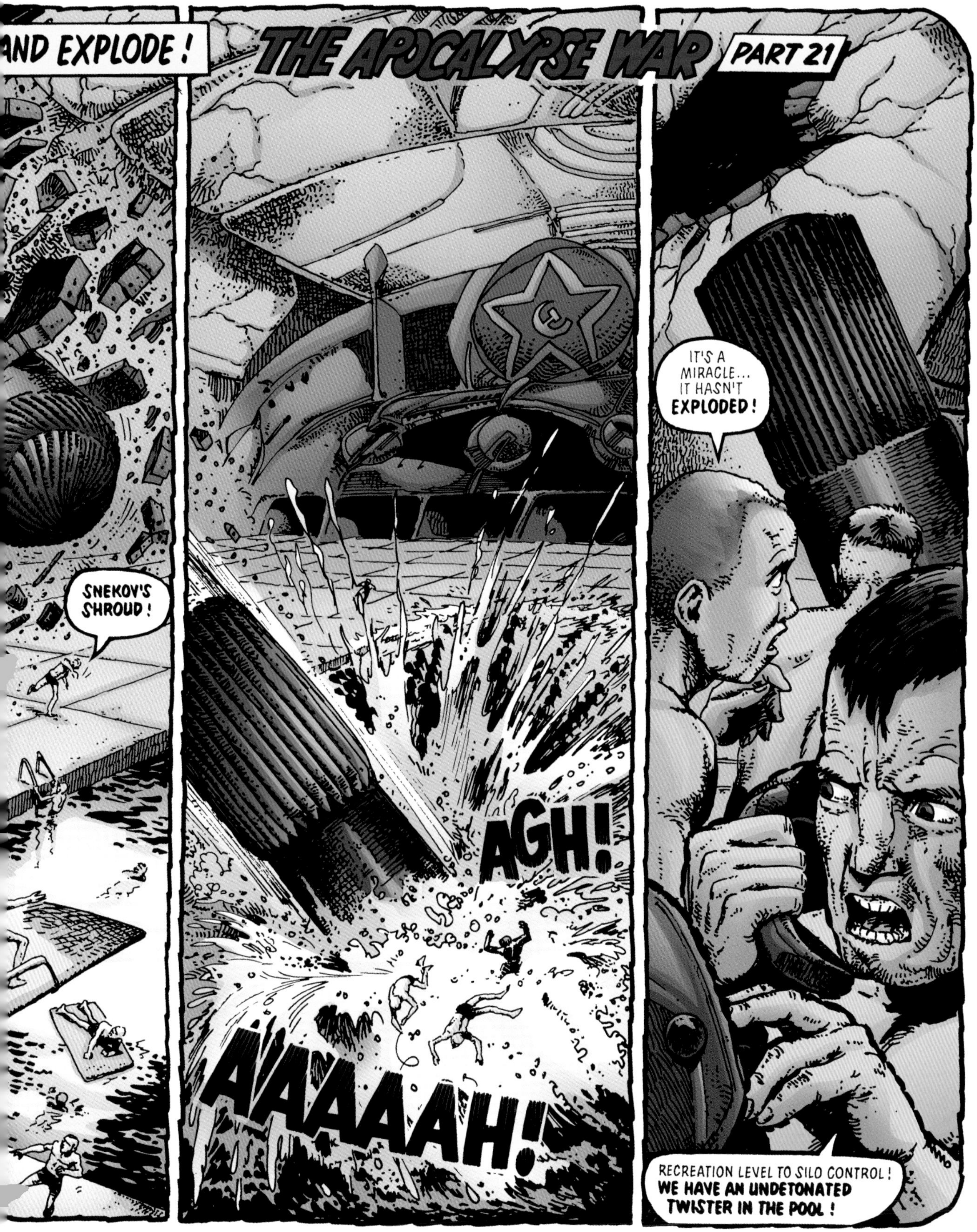
AND EXPLODE!
THE APOCALYPSE WAR
PART 21
SNEKOV'S SHROUD!
AGH!
AAAAAAH!
IT'S A MIRACLE... IT HASN'T EXPLODED!
RECREATION LEVEL TO SILO CONTROL! WE HAVE AN UNDETONATED TWISTER IN THE POOL!

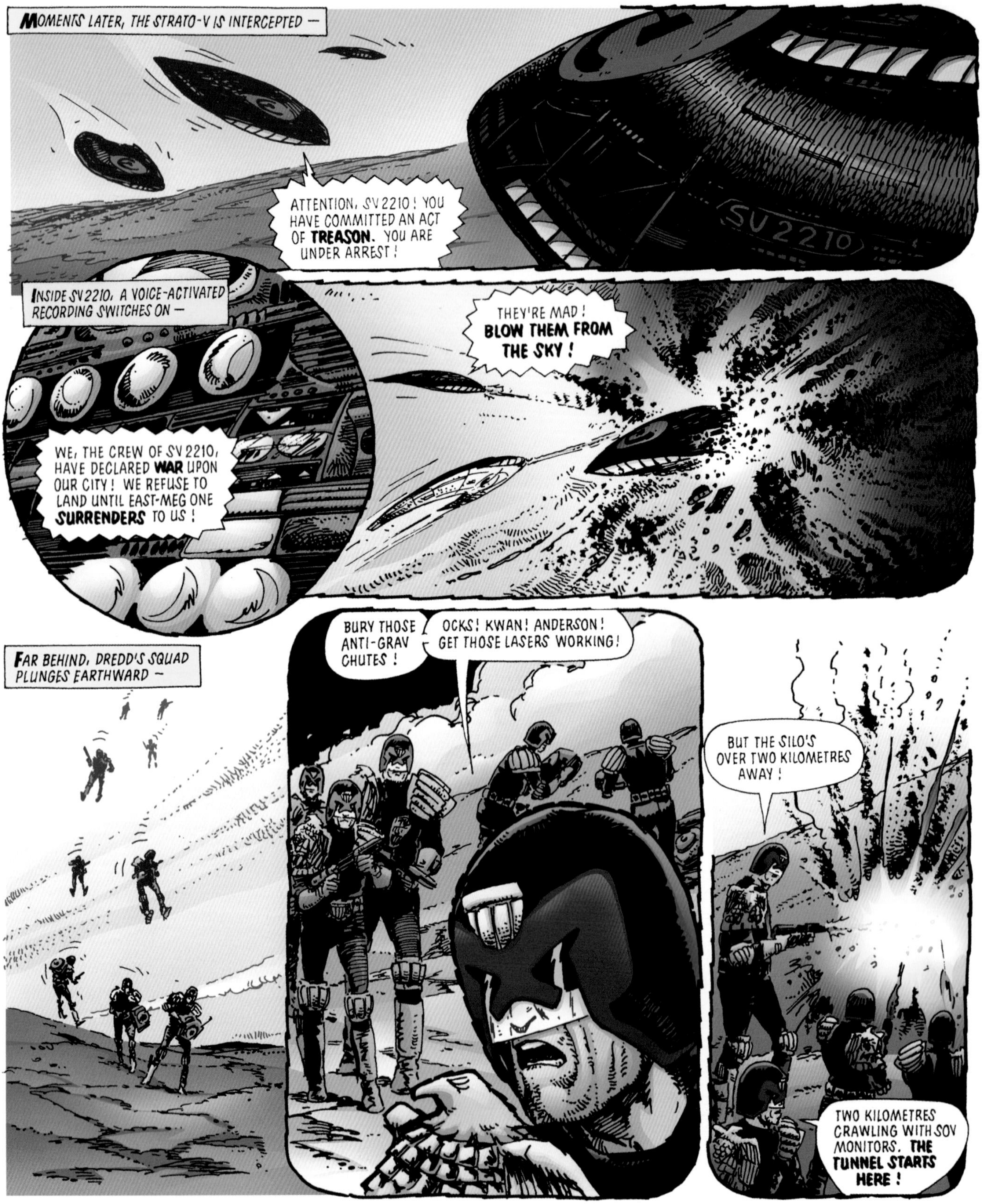
MOMENTS LATER, THE STRATO-V IS INTERCEPTED —
ATTENTION, SV 2210! YOU HAVE COMMITTED AN ACT OF TREASON. YOU ARE UNDER ARREST!
SV 2210
INSIDE SV 2210, A VOICE-ACTIVATED RECORDING SWITCHES ON —
WE, THE CREW OF SV 2210, HAVE DECLARED WAR UPON OUR CITY! WE REFUSE TO LAND UNTIL EAST-MEG ONE SURRENDERS TO US!
THEY'RE MAD! BLOW THEM FROM THE SKY!
FAR BEHIND, DREDD'S SQUAD PLUNGES EARTHWARD —
BURY THOSE ANTI-GRAV CHUTES!
OCKS! KWAN! ANDERSON! GET THOSE LASERS WORKING!
BUT THE SILO'S OVER TWO KILOMETRES AWAY!
TWO KILOMETRES CRAWLING WITH SOV MONITORS. THE TUNNEL STARTS HERE!

MEANWHILE, AN EMERGENCY TEAM FORGES THROUGH THE FLOODING SILO —

ALL UNAUTHORISED PERSONNEL CLEAR THIS LEVEL!

WATER'S JUST CLEARING THE WARHEAD ACCESS HATCH. I'LL KEEP YOU INFORMED.

THE PANEL'S BEEN FUSED SHUT! WE'LL NEED PRECISION LASERS!

BEYOND THE SILO, OTHER LASERS PIERCE THE DESERT SANDS —

IT'S WORKING, DREDD. THE INTENSE HEAT'S TURNING THE SAND INTO GLASS.

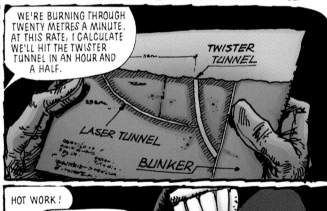

WE'RE BURNING THROUGH TWENTY METRES A MINUTE. AT THIS RATE, I CALCULATE WE'LL HIT THE TWISTER TUNNEL IN AN HOUR AND A HALF.

TWISTER TUNNEL

LASER TUNNEL

BUNKER

HOT WORK!

NOT HALF AS HOT AS IT'S GOING TO BE IN EAST-MEG ONE WHEN WE TAKE THAT SILO!

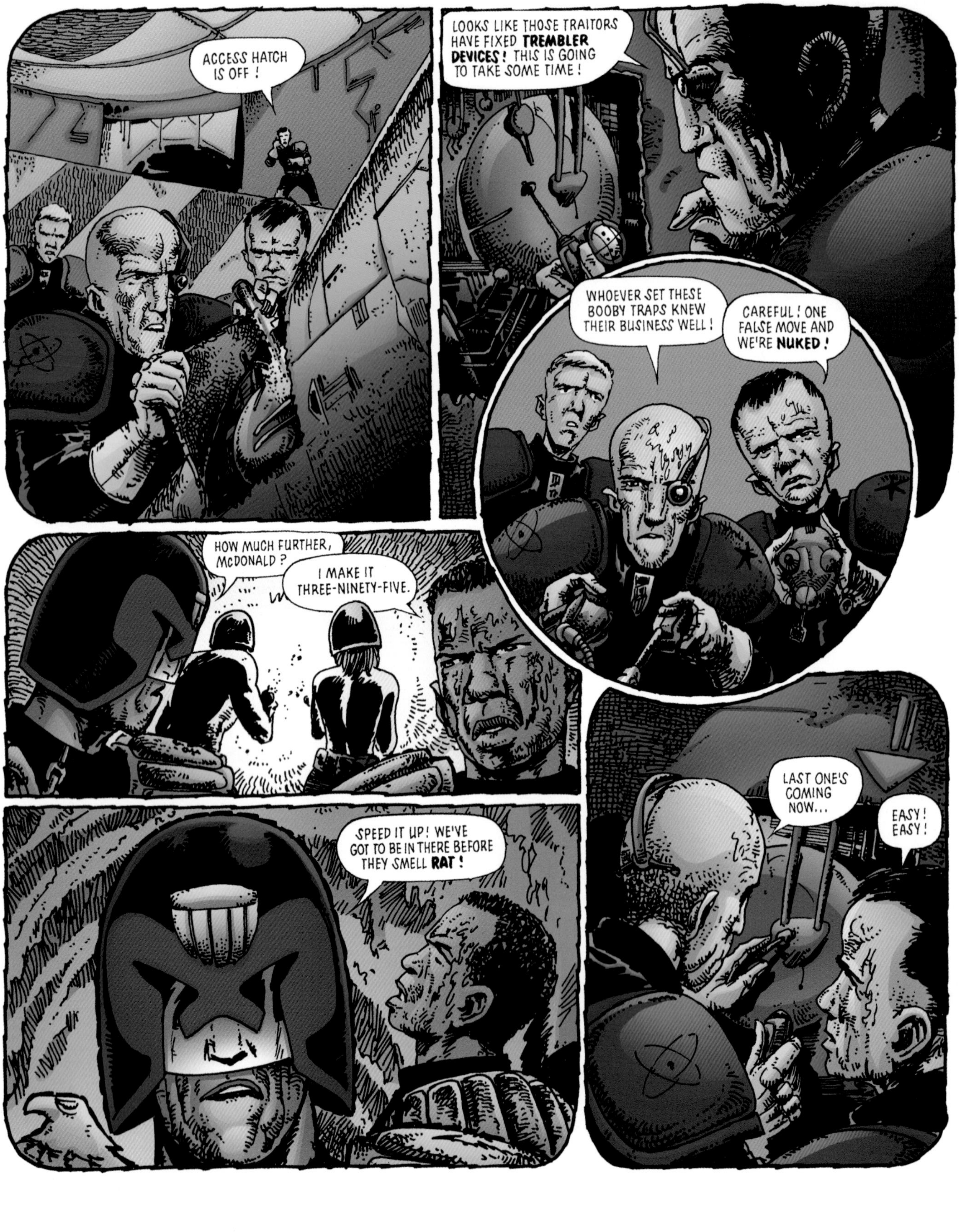
ACCESS HATCH IS OFF !
LOOKS LIKE THOSE TRAITORS HAVE FIXED TREMBLER DEVICES ! THIS IS GOING TO TAKE SOME TIME !
WHOEVER SET THESE BOOBY TRAPS KNEW THEIR BUSINESS WELL !
CAREFUL ! ONE FALSE MOVE AND WE'RE NUKED !
HOW MUCH FURTHER, McDONALD ?
I MAKE IT THREE-NINETY-FIVE.
SPEED IT UP ! WE'VE GOT TO BE IN THERE BEFORE THEY SMELL RAT !
LAST ONE'S COMING NOW...
EASY ! EASY !

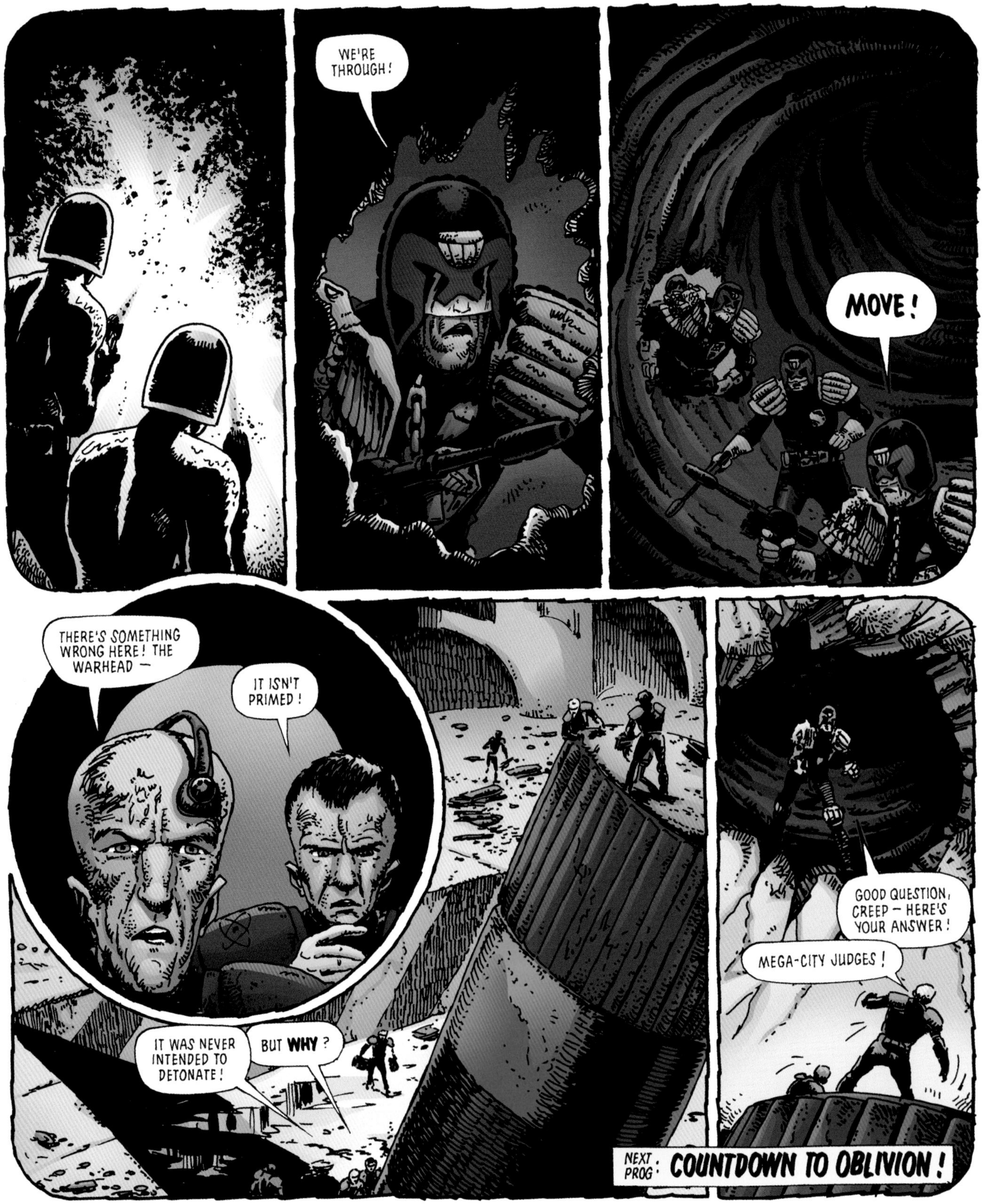
WE'RE THROUGH!
MOVE!
THERE'S SOMETHING WRONG HERE! THE WARHEAD —
IT ISN'T PRIMED!
IT WAS NEVER INTENDED TO DETONATE!
BUT WHY?
GOOD QUESTION, CREEP — HERE'S YOUR ANSWER!
MEGA-CITY JUDGES!
NEXT PROG: COUNTDOWN TO OBLIVION!

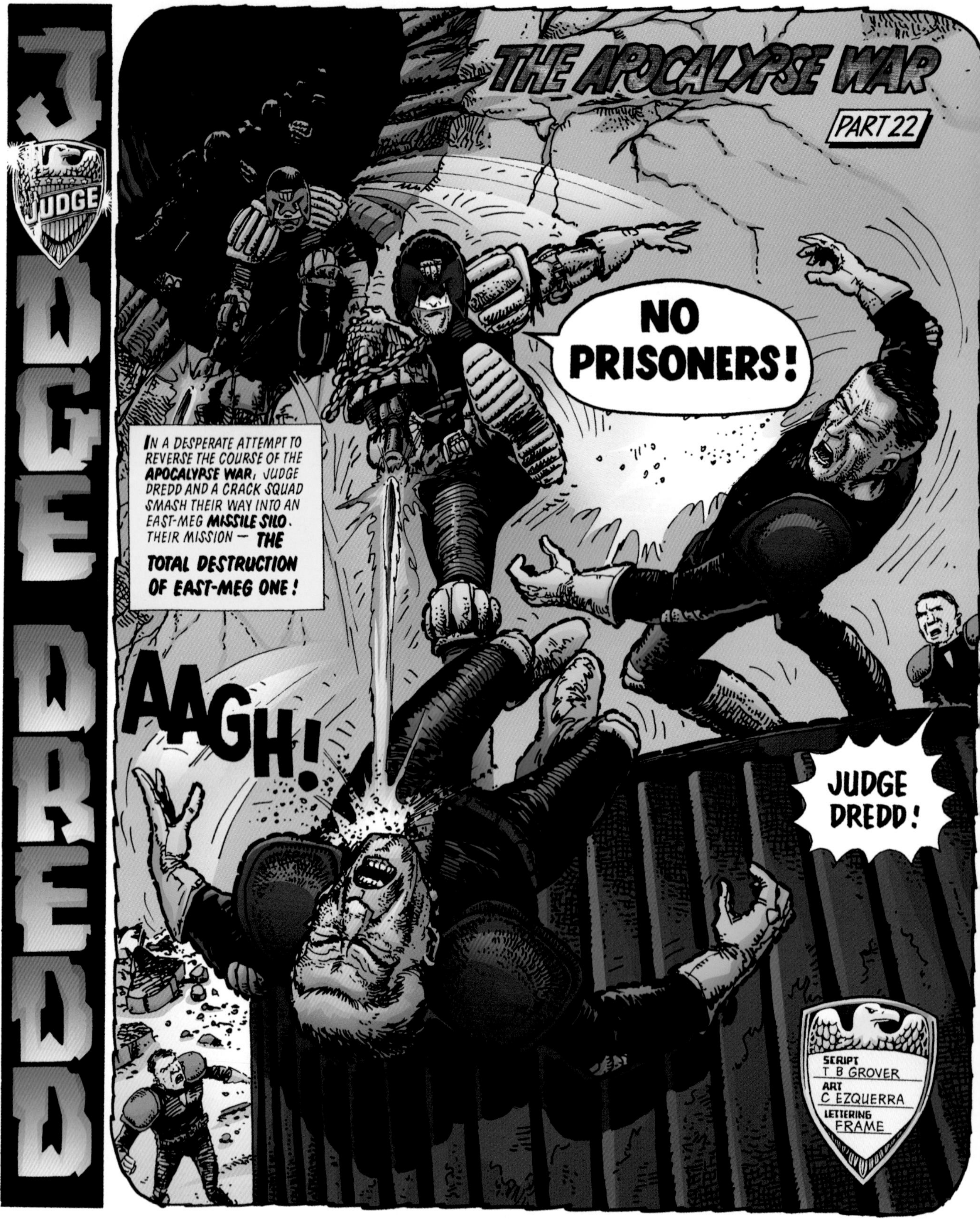
JUDGE DREDD
THE APOCALYPSE WAR
PART 22
IN A DESPERATE ATTEMPT TO REVERSE THE COURSE OF THE APOCALYPSE WAR, JUDGE DREDD AND A CRACK SQUAD SMASH THEIR WAY INTO AN EAST-MEG MISSILE SILO. THEIR MISSION — THE TOTAL DESTRUCTION OF EAST-MEG ONE!
NO PRISONERS!
AAGH!
JUDGE DREDD!
SCRIPT T B GROVER
ART C EZQUERRA
LETTERING FRAME

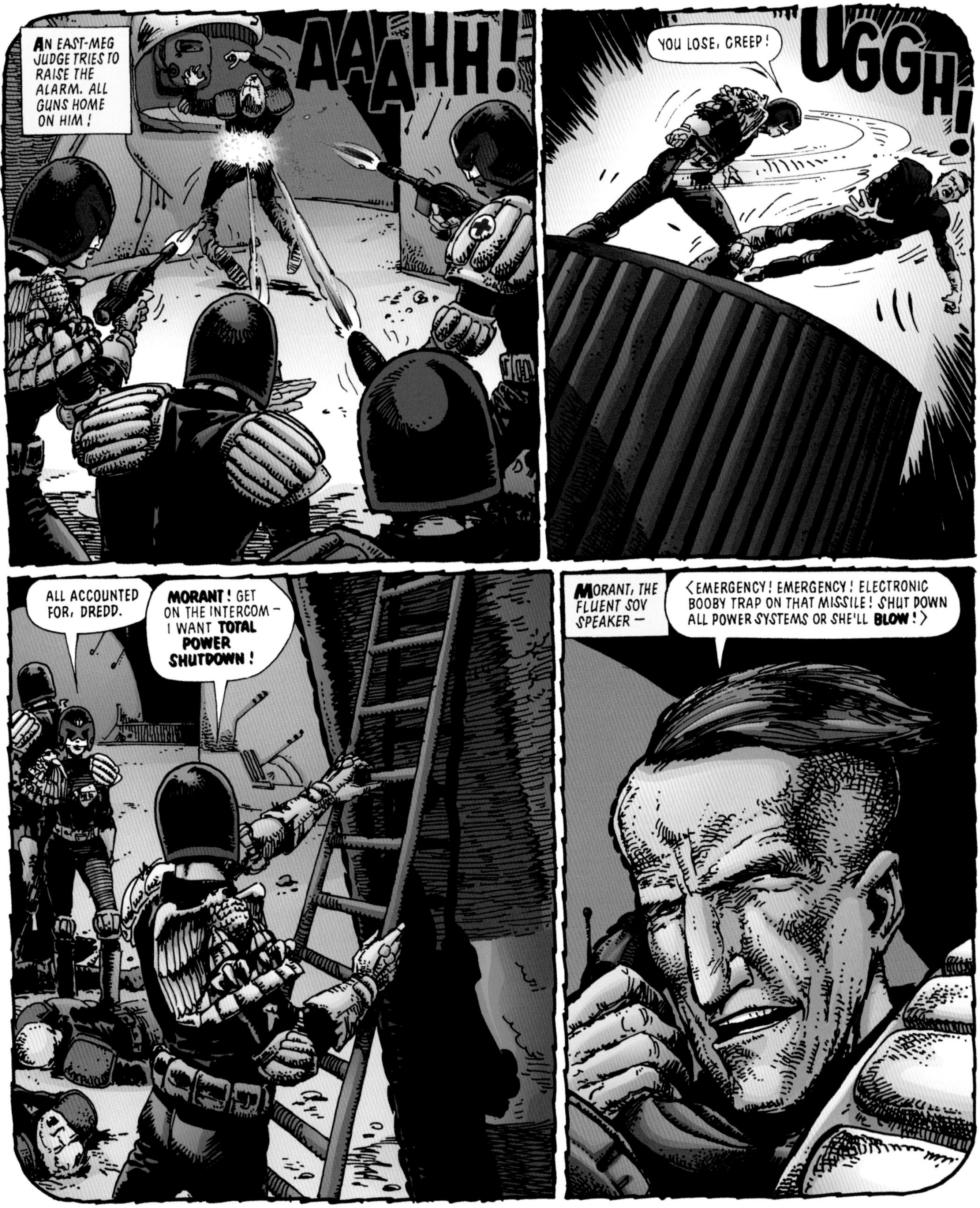
AN EAST-MEG JUDGE TRIES TO RAISE THE ALARM. ALL GUNS HOME ON HIM!
AAAAHH!
YOU LOSE, CREEP!
UGGH!
ALL ACCOUNTED FOR, DREDD.
MORANT! GET ON THE INTERCOM – I WANT TOTAL POWER SHUTDOWN!
MORANT, THE FLUENT SOV SPEAKER –
<EMERGENCY! EMERGENCY! ELECTRONIC BOOBY TRAP ON THAT MISSILE! SHUT DOWN ALL POWER SYSTEMS OR SHE'LL BLOW!>

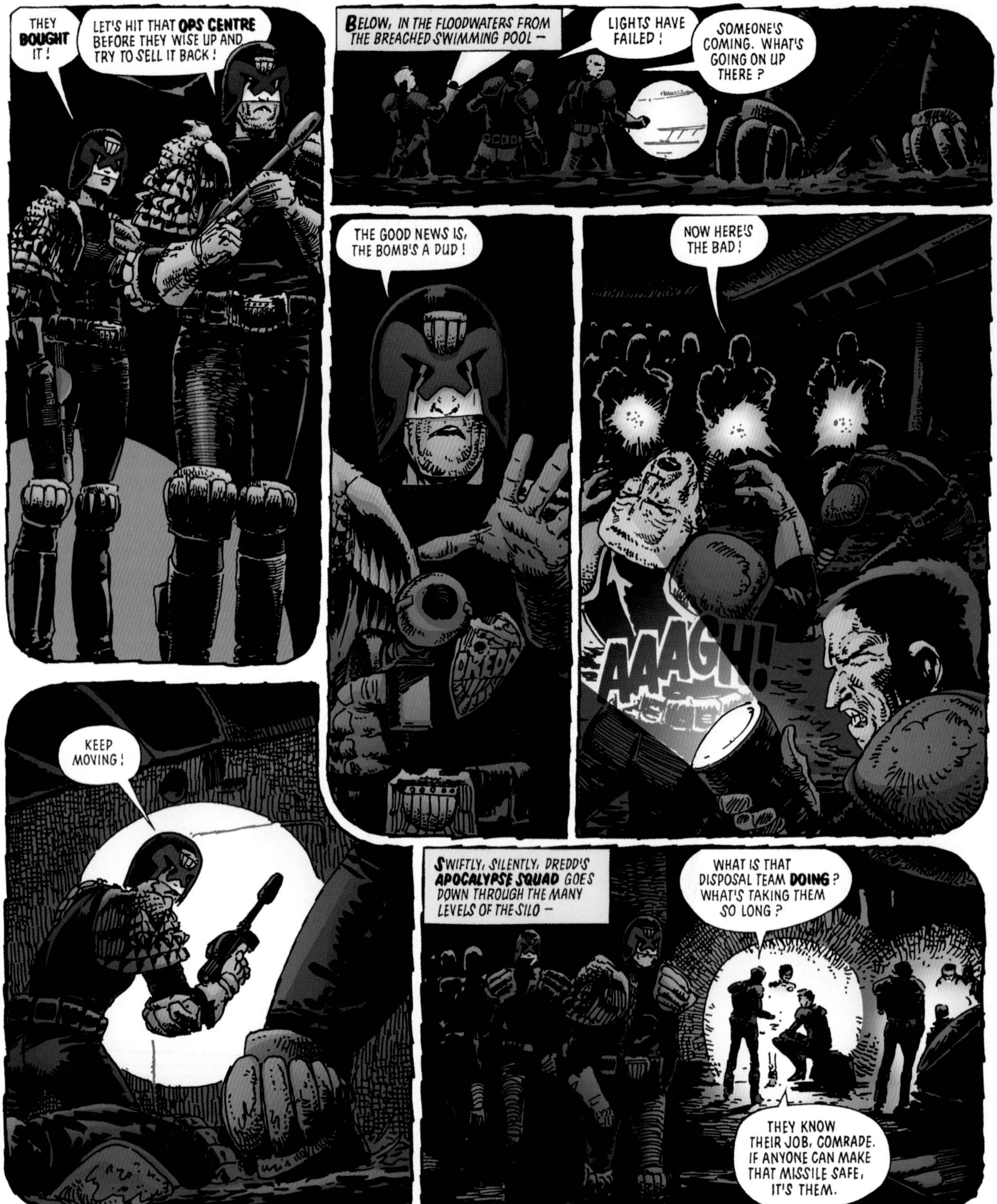

THEY BOUGHT IT!
LET'S HIT THAT OPS CENTRE BEFORE THEY WISE UP AND TRY TO SELL IT BACK!
BELOW, IN THE FLOODWATERS FROM THE BREACHED SWIMMING POOL —
LIGHTS HAVE FAILED!
SOMEONE'S COMING. WHAT'S GOING ON UP THERE?
THE GOOD NEWS IS, THE BOMB'S A DUD!
NOW HERE'S THE BAD!
AAAGH!
KEEP MOVING!
SWIFTLY, SILENTLY, DREDD'S APOCALYPSE SQUAD GOES DOWN THROUGH THE MANY LEVELS OF THE SILO —
WHAT IS THAT DISPOSAL TEAM DOING? WHAT'S TAKING THEM SO LONG?
THEY KNOW THEIR JOB, COMRADE. IF ANYONE CAN MAKE THAT MISSILE SAFE, IT'S THEM.

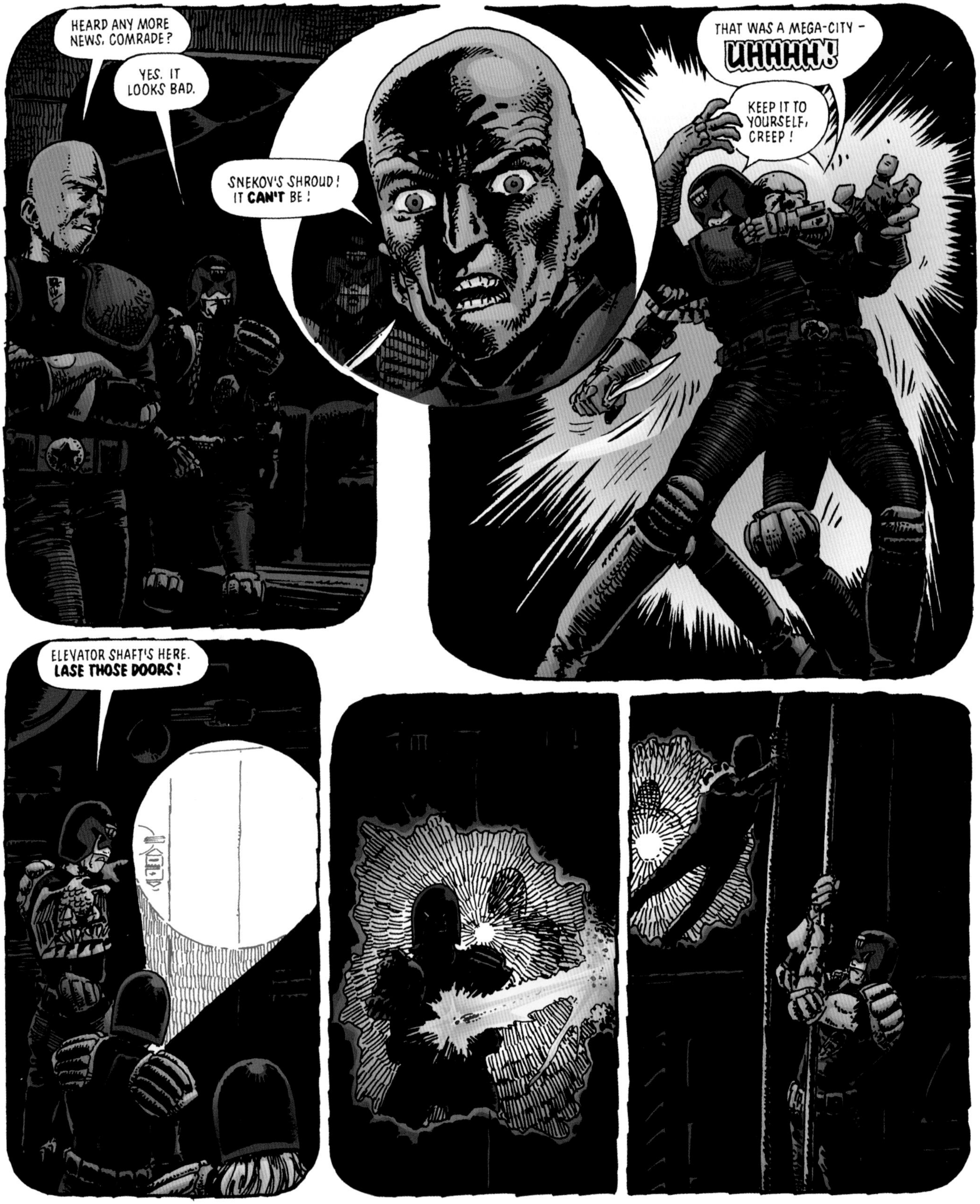
HEARD ANY MORE NEWS, COMRADE?
YES. IT LOOKS BAD.
SNEKOV'S SHROUD! IT CAN'T BE!
THAT WAS A MEGA-CITY - UHHHH!
KEEP IT TO YOURSELF, CREEP!
ELEVATOR SHAFT'S HERE. LASE THOSE DOORS!

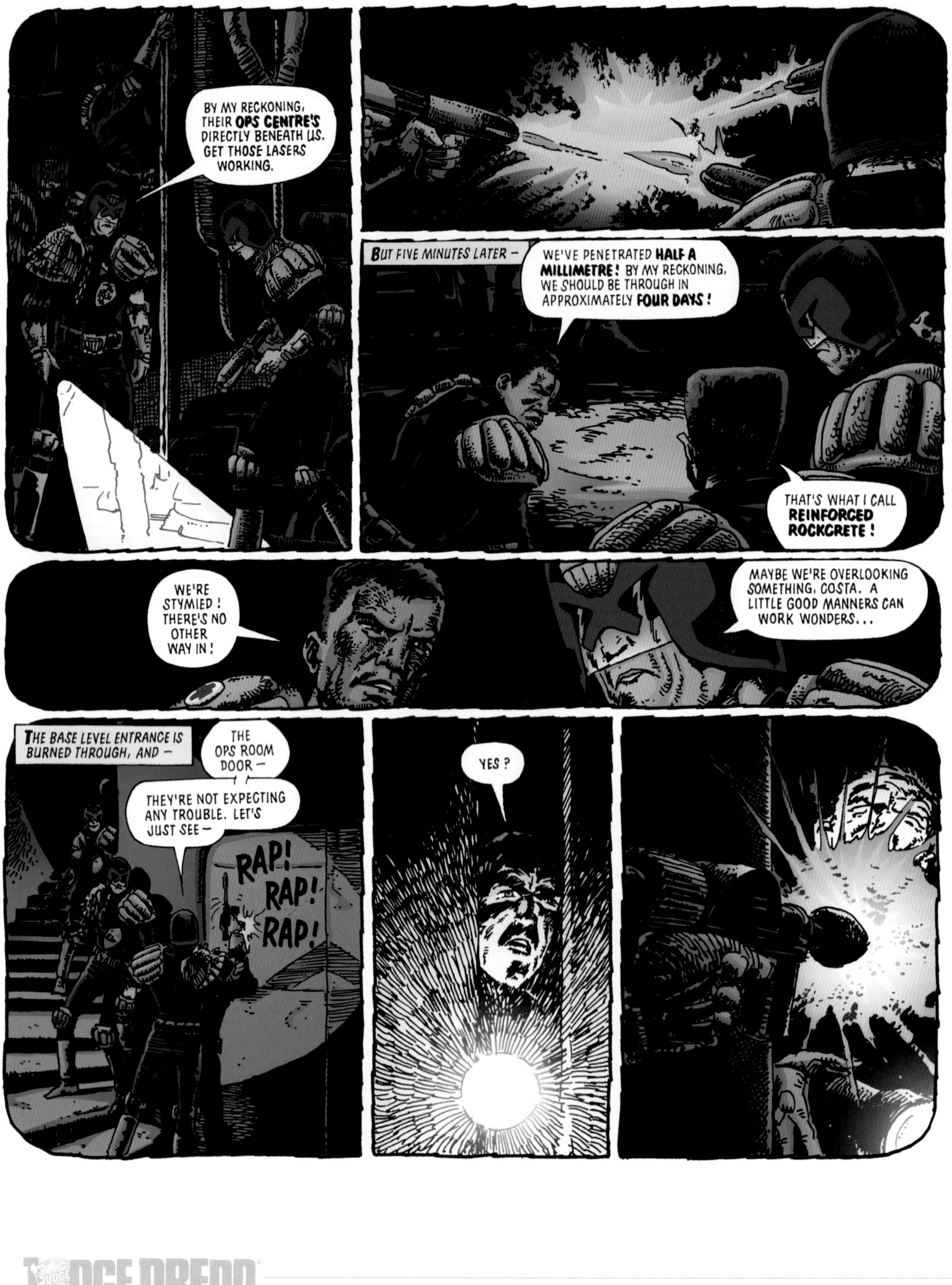

BY MY RECKONING, THEIR OPS CENTRE'S DIRECTLY BENEATH US. GET THOSE LASERS WORKING.
BUT FIVE MINUTES LATER —
WE'VE PENETRATED HALF A MILLIMETRE! BY MY RECKONING, WE SHOULD BE THROUGH IN APPROXIMATELY FOUR DAYS!
THAT'S WHAT I CALL REINFORCED ROCKCRETE!
WE'RE STYMIED! THERE'S NO OTHER WAY IN!
MAYBE WE'RE OVERLOOKING SOMETHING, COSTA. A LITTLE GOOD MANNERS CAN WORK WONDERS...
THE BASE LEVEL ENTRANCE IS BURNED THROUGH, AND —
THE OPS ROOM DOOR —
THEY'RE NOT EXPECTING ANY TROUBLE. LET'S JUST SEE —
RAP! RAP! RAP!
YES?

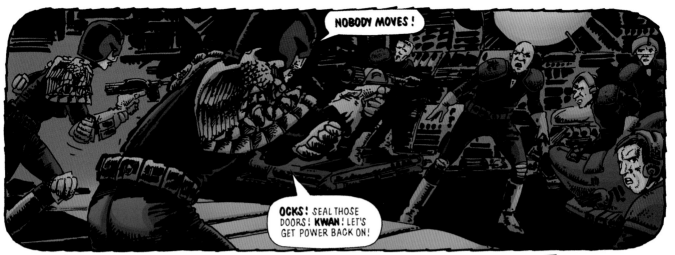

NOBODY MOVES!

OCKS! SEAL THOSE DOORS! KWAN! LET'S GET POWER BACK ON!

POWER FLOODS BACK —

I WANT TARGETING AND FIRING CODES FOR ALL MISSILES — NOW!

YOU'D TURN OUR OWN WEAPONS AGAINST US? NIET! NEVER!

I WOULD DIE A THOUSAND TIMES BEFORE I BETRAY MY CITY!

I'D SETTLE FOR JUST ONCE.

SORT HIM OUT, ANDERSON.

TARGETING CODE — PUNCH RED FOUR, TREBLE DOT DASH SEQUENCE.

FIRING CODE, GREEN ONE-SEVEN. WAIT FIVE, REPEAT.

SNEKOV'S SHROUD! THEY'VE GOT A TELEPATH!

HAMBLE AND McDONALD, THE TWO TEKS, OPERATE THE CODES —

TWENTY TADS IN SILO, DREDD.

TARGET ON EAST-MEG ONE.

READY TO FIRE!

THE RESPONSIBILITY IS MINE.

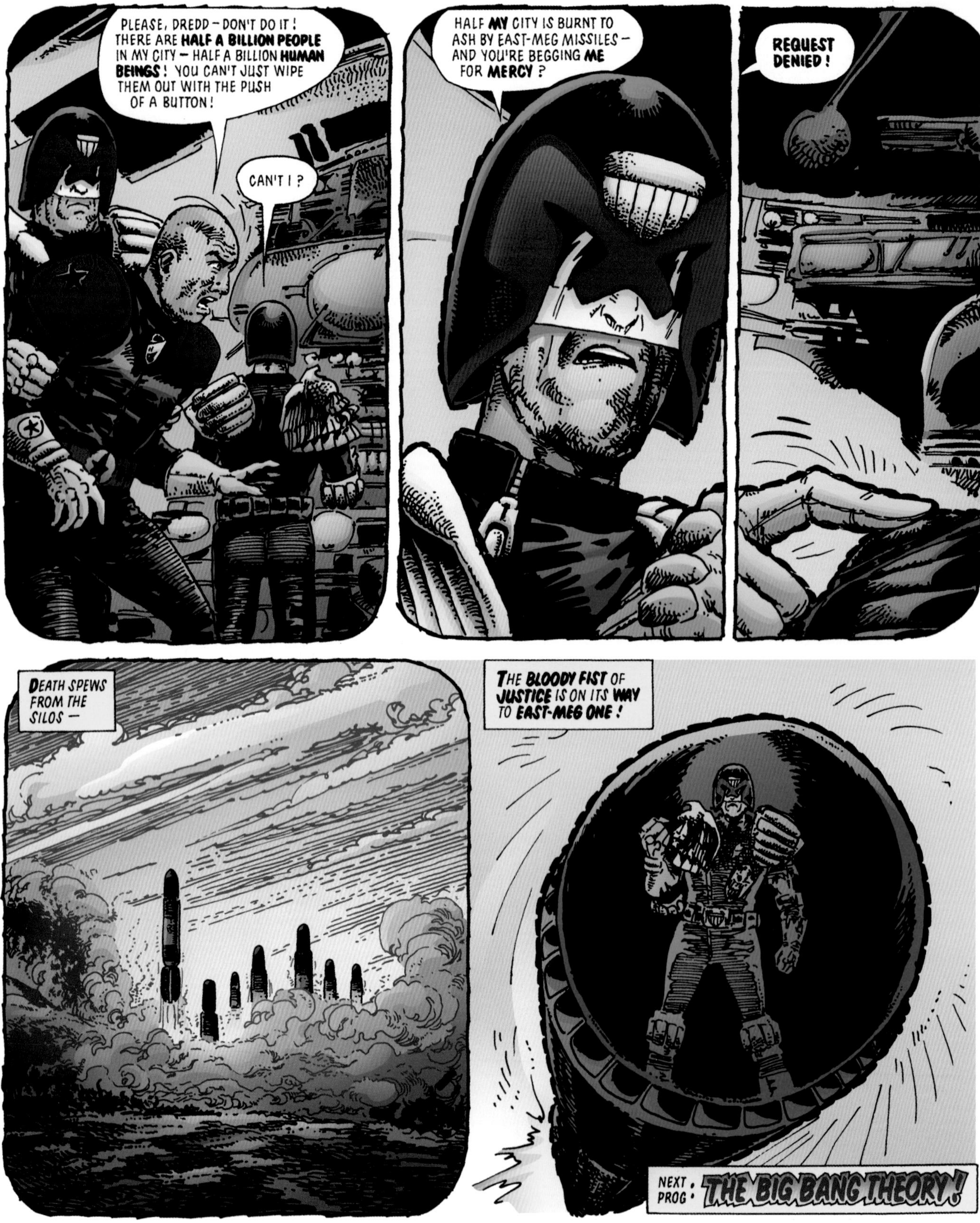
PLEASE, DREDD – DON'T DO IT! THERE ARE HALF A BILLION PEOPLE IN MY CITY – HALF A BILLION HUMAN BEINGS! YOU CAN'T JUST WIPE THEM OUT WITH THE PUSH OF A BUTTON!
CAN'T I?
HALF MY CITY IS BURNT TO ASH BY EAST-MEG MISSILES – AND YOU'RE BEGGING ME FOR MERCY?
REQUEST DENIED!
DEATH SPEWS FROM THE SILOS –
THE BLOODY FIST OF JUSTICE IS ON ITS WAY TO EAST-MEG ONE!
NEXT PROG: THE BIG BANG THEORY!

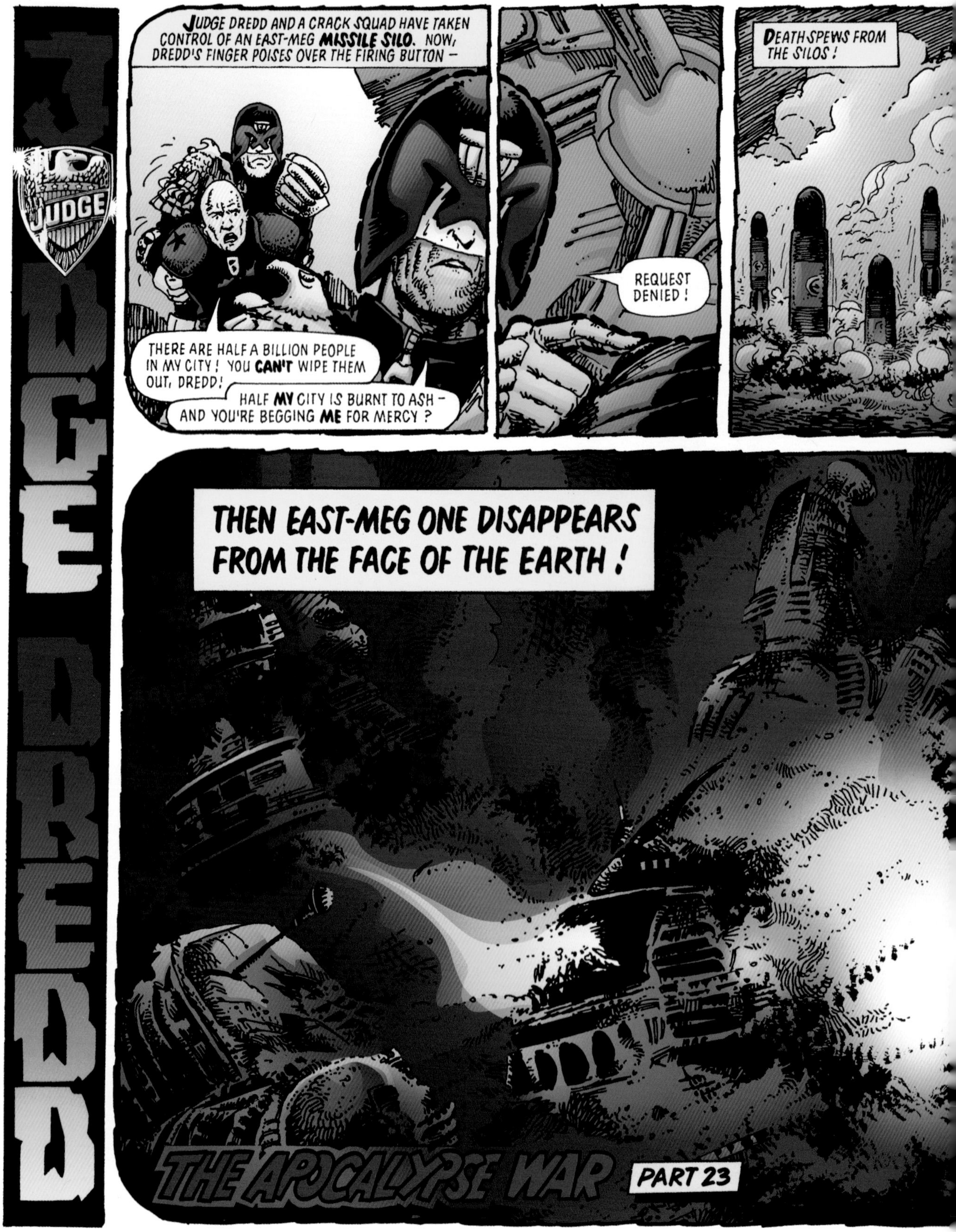
JUDGE DREDD
JUDGE
JUDGE DREDD AND A CRACK SQUAD HAVE TAKEN CONTROL OF AN EAST-MEG MISSILE SILO. NOW, DREDD'S FINGER POISES OVER THE FIRING BUTTON –
THERE ARE HALF A BILLION PEOPLE IN MY CITY! YOU CAN'T WIPE THEM OUT, DREDD!
HALF MY CITY IS BURNT TO ASH – AND YOU'RE BEGGING ME FOR MERCY?
REQUEST DENIED!
DEATH SPEWS FROM THE SILOS!
THEN EAST-MEG ONE DISAPPEARS FROM THE FACE OF THE EARTH!
THE APOCALYPSE WAR
PART 23

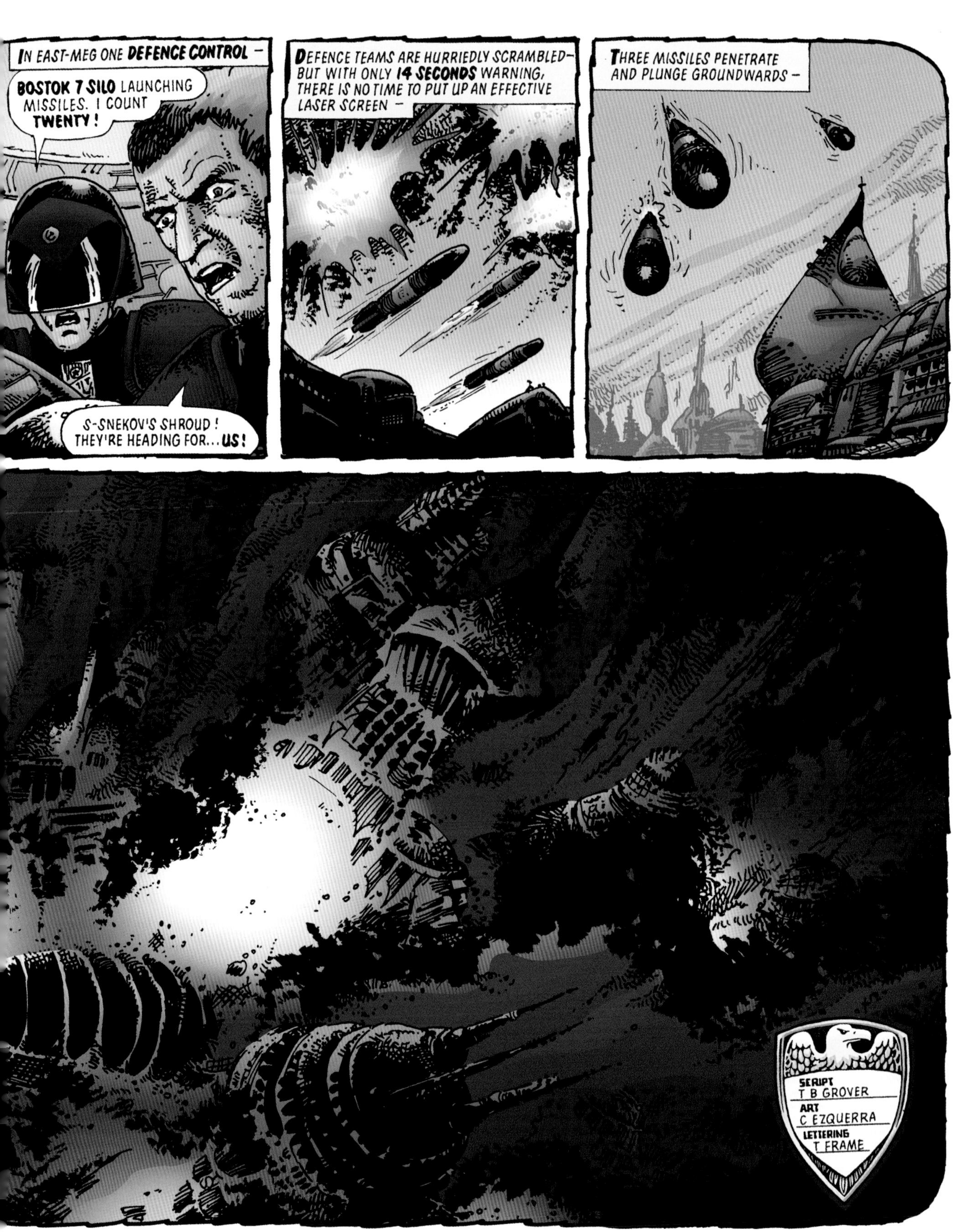

IN EAST-MEG ONE DEFENCE CONTROL –
BOSTOK 7 SILO LAUNCHING MISSILES. I COUNT TWENTY!
S-SNEKOV'S SHROUD! THEY'RE HEADING FOR... US!
DEFENCE TEAMS ARE HURRIEDLY SCRAMBLED– BUT WITH ONLY 14 SECONDS WARNING, THERE IS NO TIME TO PUT UP AN EFFECTIVE LASER SCREEN –
THREE MISSILES PENETRATE AND PLUNGE GROUNDWARDS –
SCRIPT T B GROVER
ART C EZQUERRA
LETTERING T FRAME

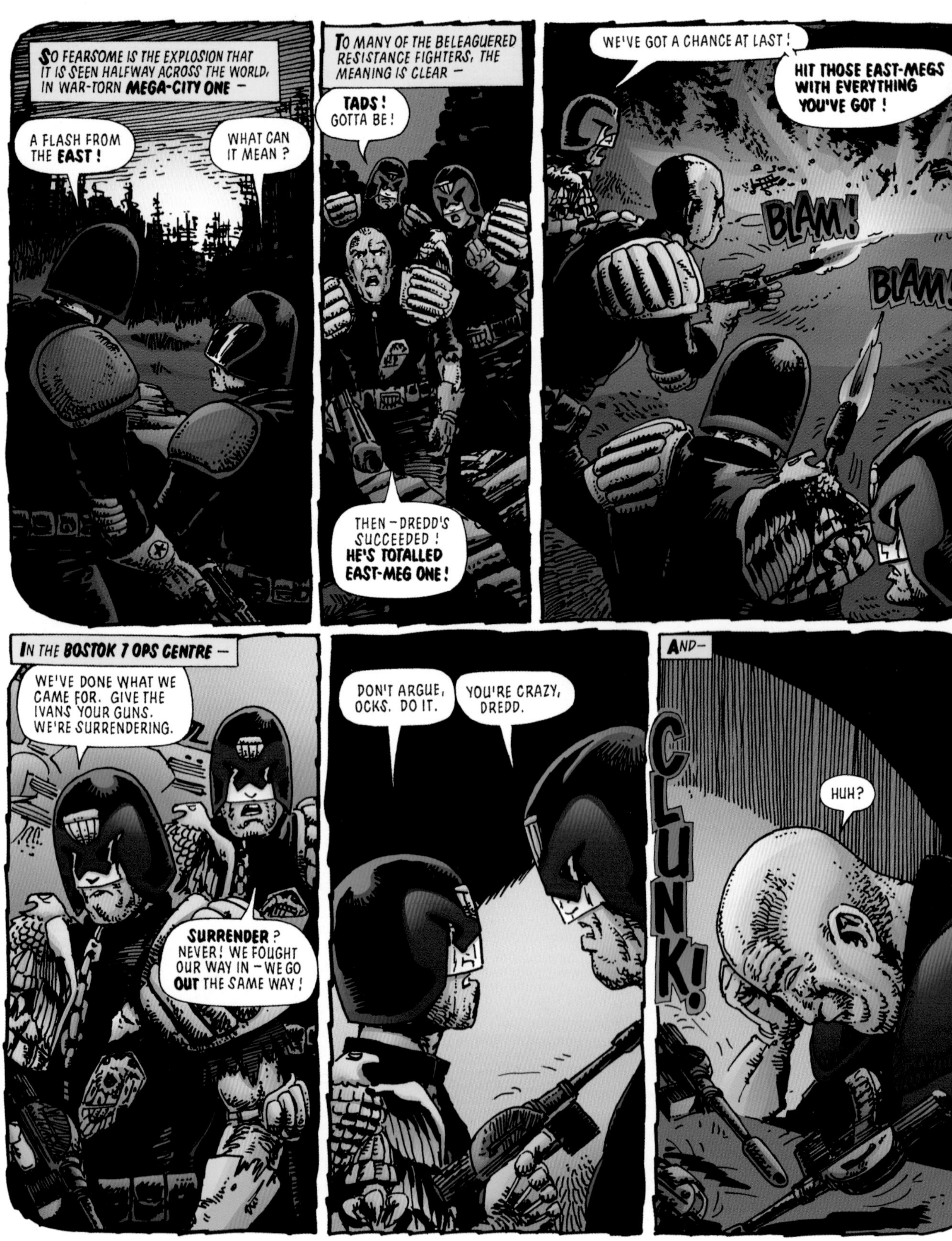

SO FEARSOME IS THE EXPLOSION THAT IT IS SEEN HALFWAY ACROSS THE WORLD, IN WAR-TORN MEGA-CITY ONE –
A FLASH FROM THE EAST!
WHAT CAN IT MEAN?
TO MANY OF THE BELEAGUERED RESISTANCE FIGHTERS, THE MEANING IS CLEAR –
TADS! GOTTA BE!
THEN – DREDD'S SUCCEEDED! HE'S TOTALLED EAST-MEG ONE!
WE'VE GOT A CHANCE AT LAST!
HIT THOSE EAST-MEGS WITH EVERYTHING YOU'VE GOT!
BLAM!
BLAM!
IN THE BOSTOK 7 OPS CENTRE –
WE'VE DONE WHAT WE CAME FOR. GIVE THE IVANS YOUR GUNS. WE'RE SURRENDERING.
SURRENDER? NEVER! WE FOUGHT OUR WAY IN – WE GO OUT THE SAME WAY!
DON'T ARGUE, OCKS. DO IT.
YOU'RE CRAZY, DREDD.
AND–
CLUNK!
HUH?

HALF A BILLION PEOPLE— **WIPED OUT!** YOU'LL PAY FOR THIS WITH YOUR LIVES!

I SUGGEST YOU CHECK THAT OUT WITH **WAR-MARSHAL KAZAN.** HE MAY JUST WANT TO SPEAK TO US.

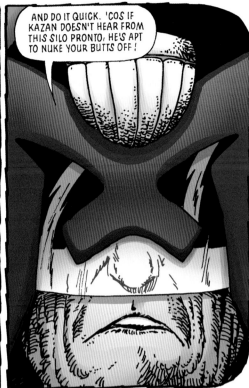

AND DO IT QUICK. 'COS IF KAZAN DOESN'T HEAR FROM THIS SILO PRONTO, HE'S APT TO NUKE YOUR BUTTS OFF!

HIGH ABOVE THE EARTH, EAST-MEG WAR-SATS REPORT—

TOTAL ANNIHILATION DEVICES, WAR MARSHAL— WITHOUT A DOUBT! THERE'S NOTHING LEFT— JUST A BIG, BLACK HOLE!

OUR CITY— GONE! IT— IT'S UNBELIEVABLE!

OUR WAR-SATS STAND READY TO DESTROY THE TRAITOR SILO, WAR MARSHAL!

WAR MARSHAL?

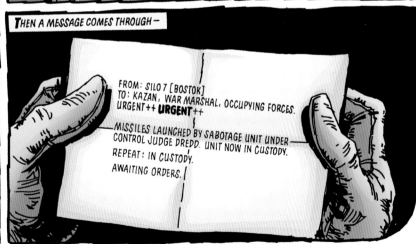

THEN A MESSAGE COMES THROUGH—

FROM: SILO 7 [BOSTOK]
TO: KAZAN, WAR MARSHAL, OCCUPYING FORCES.
URGENT++ **URGENT**++

MISSILES LAUNCHED BY SABOTAGE UNIT UNDER CONTROL JUDGE DREDD. UNIT NOW IN CUSTODY.
REPEAT: IN CUSTODY.

AWAITING ORDERS.

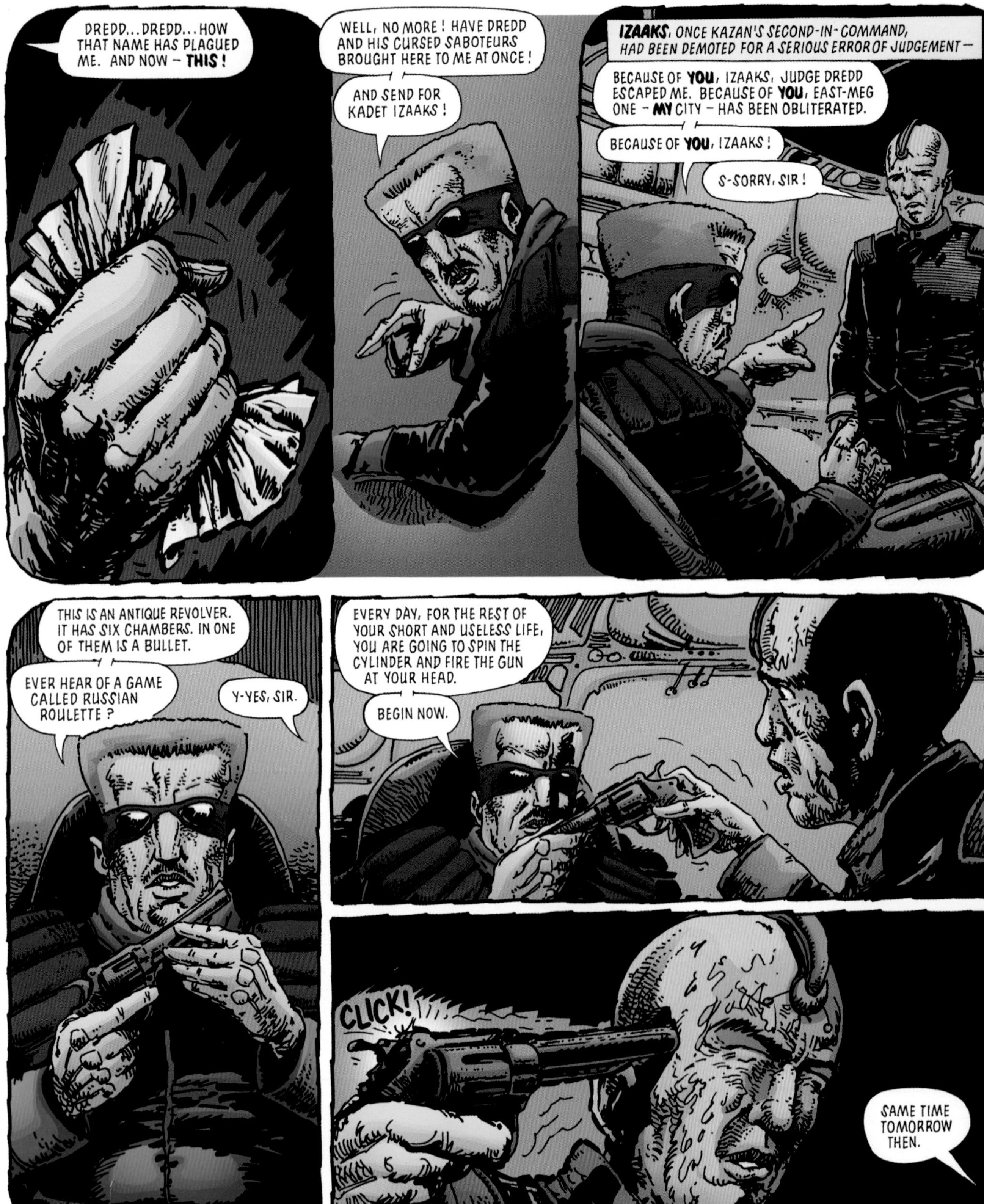
DREDD... DREDD... HOW THAT NAME HAS PLAGUED ME. AND NOW – THIS!
WELL, NO MORE! HAVE DREDD AND HIS CURSED SABOTEURS BROUGHT HERE TO ME AT ONCE!
AND SEND FOR KADET IZAAKS!
IZAAKS, ONCE KAZAN'S SECOND-IN-COMMAND, HAD BEEN DEMOTED FOR A SERIOUS ERROR OF JUDGEMENT –
BECAUSE OF YOU, IZAAKS, JUDGE DREDD ESCAPED ME. BECAUSE OF YOU, EAST-MEG ONE – MY CITY – HAS BEEN OBLITERATED.
BECAUSE OF YOU, IZAAKS!
S-SORRY, SIR!
THIS IS AN ANTIQUE REVOLVER. IT HAS SIX CHAMBERS. IN ONE OF THEM IS A BULLET.
EVER HEAR OF A GAME CALLED RUSSIAN ROULETTE?
Y-YES, SIR.
EVERY DAY, FOR THE REST OF YOUR SHORT AND USELESS LIFE, YOU ARE GOING TO SPIN THE CYLINDER AND FIRE THE GUN AT YOUR HEAD.
BEGIN NOW.
CLICK!
SAME TIME TOMORROW THEN.

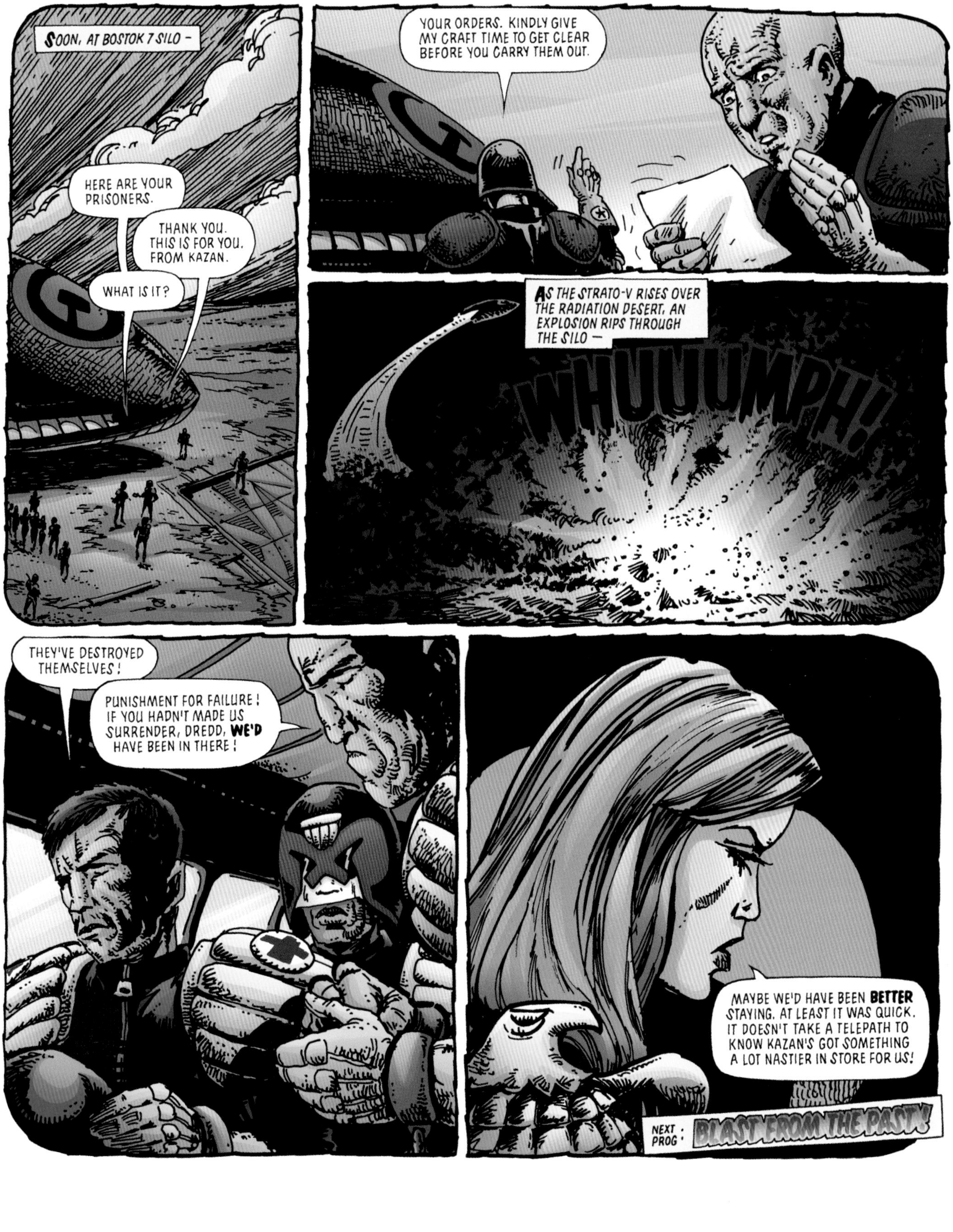

SOON, AT BOSTOK 7 SILO –
HERE ARE YOUR PRISONERS.
THANK YOU. THIS IS FOR YOU. FROM KAZAN.
WHAT IS IT?
YOUR ORDERS. KINDLY GIVE MY CRAFT TIME TO GET CLEAR BEFORE YOU CARRY THEM OUT.
AS THE STRATO-V RISES OVER THE RADIATION DESERT, AN EXPLOSION RIPS THROUGH THE SILO –
WHUUUMPH!!
THEY'VE DESTROYED THEMSELVES!
PUNISHMENT FOR FAILURE! IF YOU HADN'T MADE US SURRENDER, DREDD, WE'D HAVE BEEN IN THERE!
MAYBE WE'D HAVE BEEN BETTER STAYING. AT LEAST IT WAS QUICK. IT DOESN'T TAKE A TELEPATH TO KNOW KAZAN'S GOT SOMETHING A LOT NASTIER IN STORE FOR US!
NEXT PROG: BLAST FROM THE PAST!

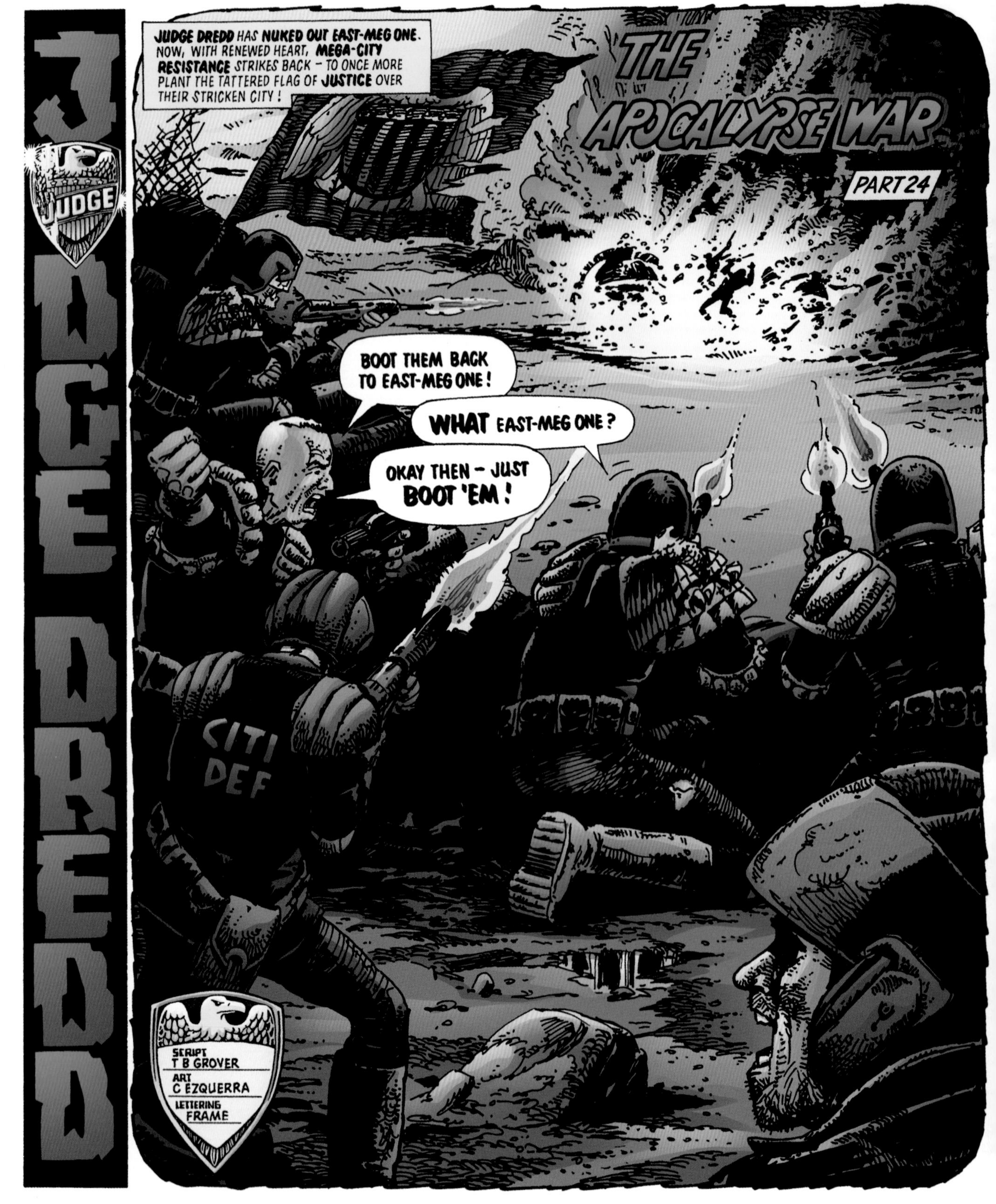
JUDGE DREDD
JUDGE DREDD HAS NUKED OUT EAST-MEG ONE. NOW, WITH RENEWED HEART, MEGA-CITY RESISTANCE STRIKES BACK – TO ONCE MORE PLANT THE TATTERED FLAG OF JUSTICE OVER THEIR STRICKEN CITY!
THE APOCALYPSE WAR
PART 24
BOOT THEM BACK TO EAST-MEG ONE!
WHAT EAST-MEG ONE?
OKAY THEN – JUST BOOT 'EM!
CITI DEF
SCRIPT T B GROVER
ART C EZQUERRA
LETTERING FRAME

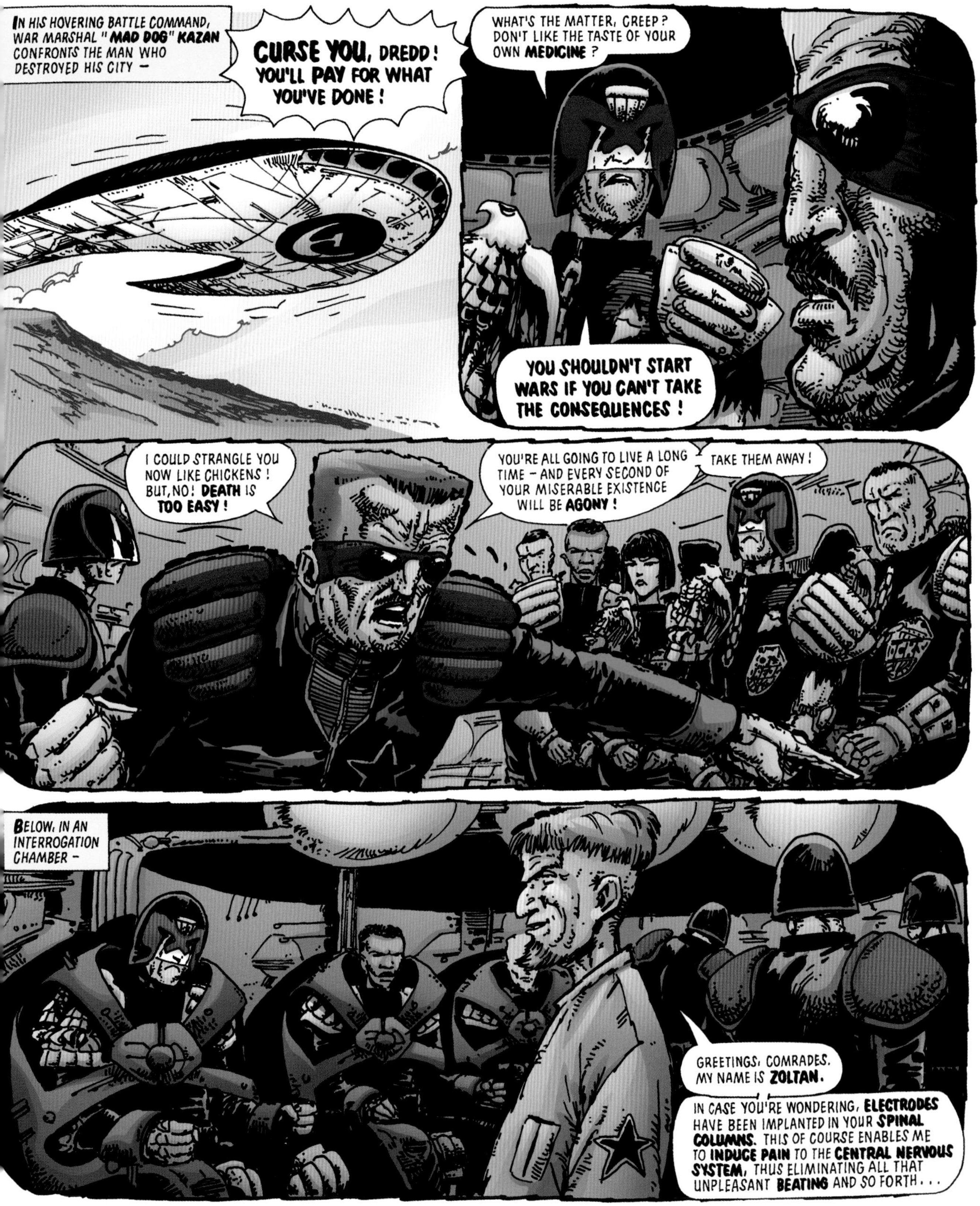
IN HIS HOVERING BATTLE COMMAND, WAR MARSHAL "MAD DOG" KAZAN CONFRONTS THE MAN WHO DESTROYED HIS CITY –
CURSE YOU, DREDD! YOU'LL PAY FOR WHAT YOU'VE DONE!
WHAT'S THE MATTER, CREEP? DON'T LIKE THE TASTE OF YOUR OWN MEDICINE?
YOU SHOULDN'T START WARS IF YOU CAN'T TAKE THE CONSEQUENCES!
I COULD STRANGLE YOU NOW LIKE CHICKENS! BUT, NO! DEATH IS TOO EASY!
YOU'RE ALL GOING TO LIVE A LONG TIME – AND EVERY SECOND OF YOUR MISERABLE EXISTENCE WILL BE AGONY!
TAKE THEM AWAY!
BELOW, IN AN INTERROGATION CHAMBER –
GREETINGS, COMRADES. MY NAME IS ZOLTAN.
IN CASE YOU'RE WONDERING, ELECTRODES HAVE BEEN IMPLANTED IN YOUR SPINAL COLUMNS. THIS OF COURSE ENABLES ME TO INDUCE PAIN TO THE CENTRAL NERVOUS SYSTEM, THUS ELIMINATING ALL THAT UNPLEASANT BEATING AND SO FORTH...

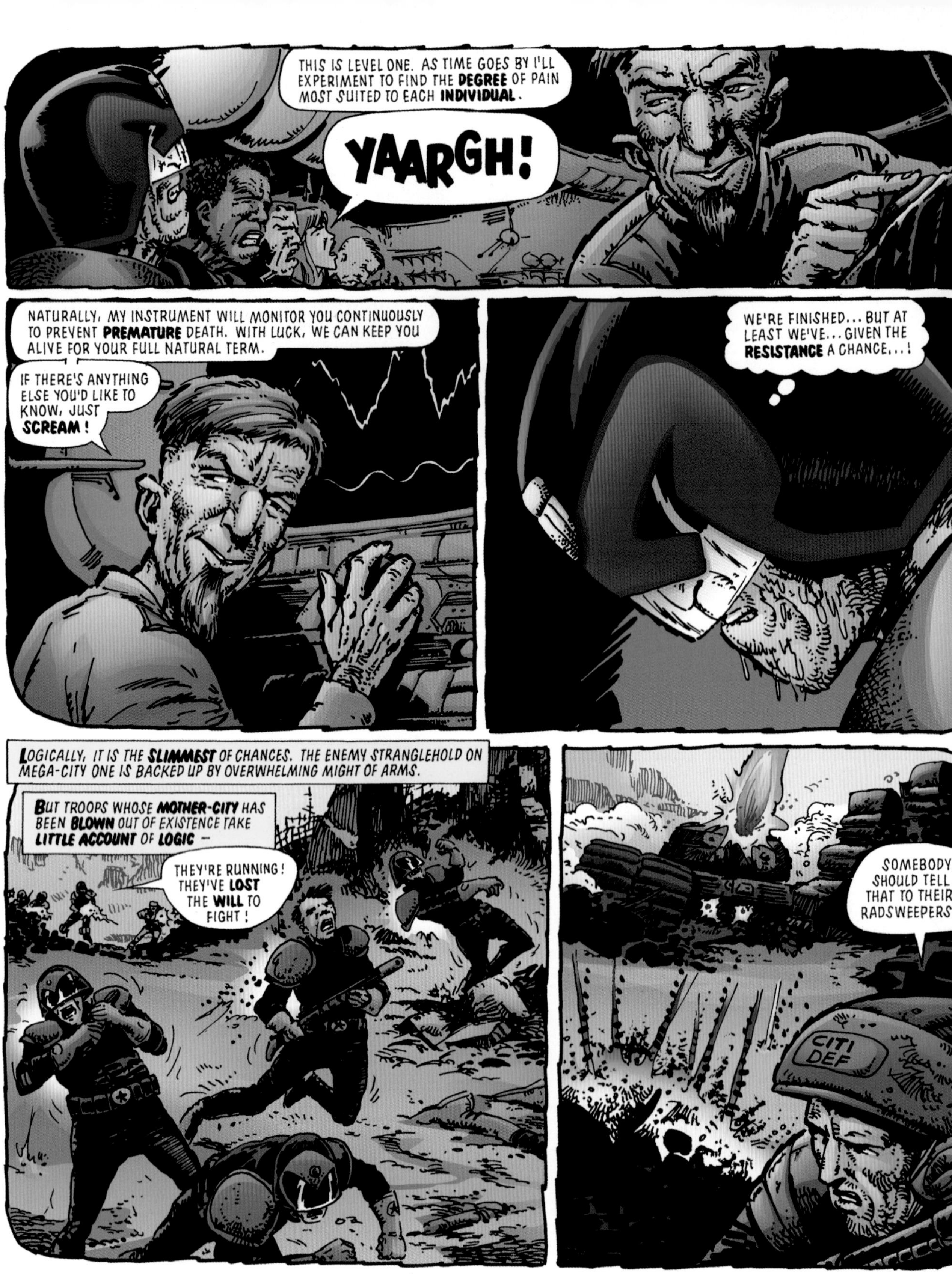
THIS IS LEVEL ONE. AS TIME GOES BY I'LL EXPERIMENT TO FIND THE DEGREE OF PAIN MOST SUITED TO EACH INDIVIDUAL.
YAARGH!
NATURALLY, MY INSTRUMENT WILL MONITOR YOU CONTINUOUSLY TO PREVENT PREMATURE DEATH. WITH LUCK, WE CAN KEEP YOU ALIVE FOR YOUR FULL NATURAL TERM.
IF THERE'S ANYTHING ELSE YOU'D LIKE TO KNOW, JUST SCREAM!
WE'RE FINISHED... BUT AT LEAST WE'VE... GIVEN THE RESISTANCE A CHANCE...!
LOGICALLY, IT IS THE SLIMMEST OF CHANCES. THE ENEMY STRANGLEHOLD ON MEGA-CITY ONE IS BACKED UP BY OVERWHELMING MIGHT OF ARMS.
BUT TROOPS WHOSE MOTHER-CITY HAS BEEN BLOWN OUT OF EXISTENCE TAKE LITTLE ACCOUNT OF LOGIC —
THEY'RE RUNNING! THEY'VE LOST THE WILL TO FIGHT!
SOMEBODY SHOULD TELL THAT TO THEIR RADSWEEPERS!
CITI DEF

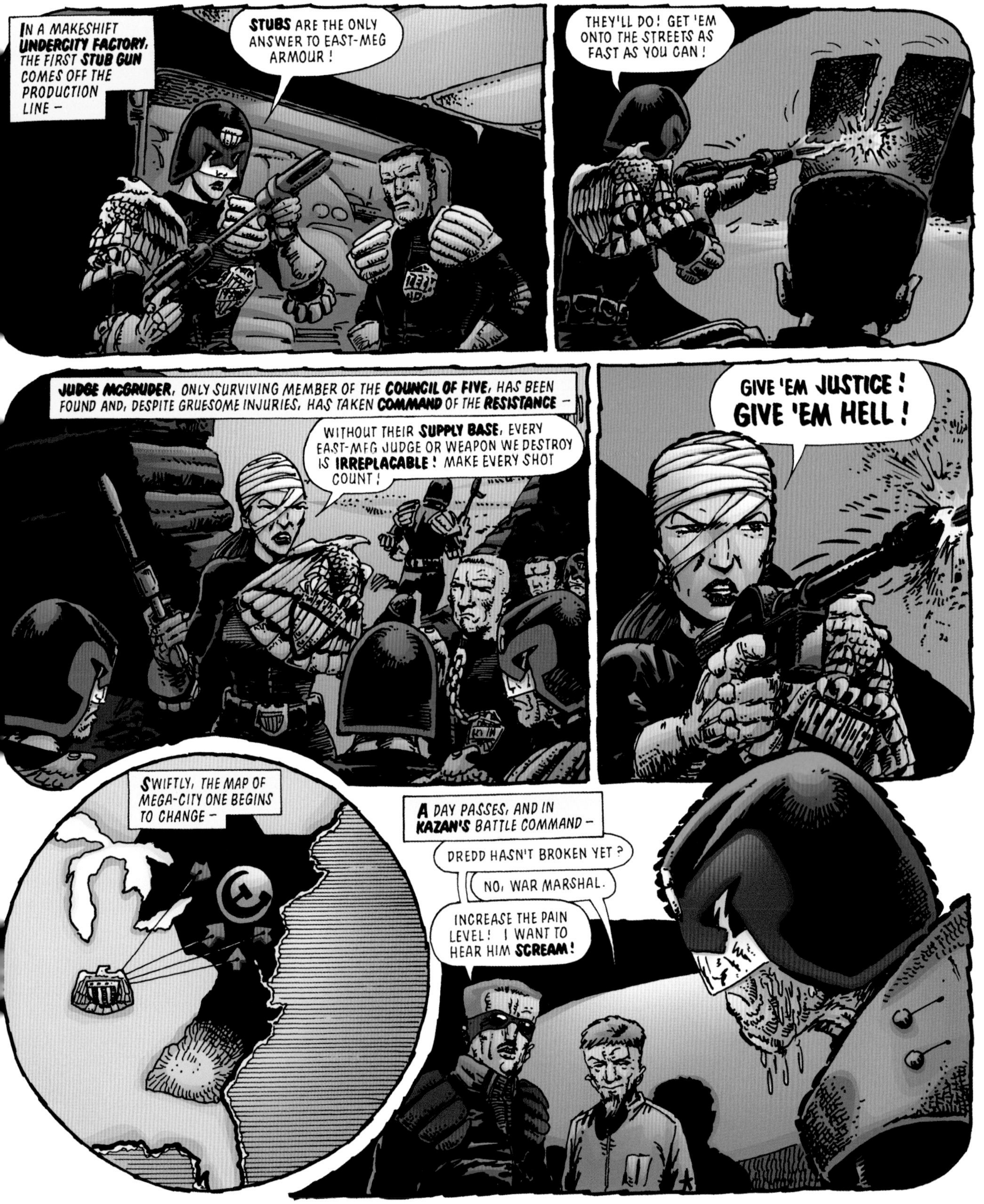
IN A MAKESHIFT UNDERCITY FACTORY, THE FIRST STUB GUN COMES OFF THE PRODUCTION LINE –
STUBS ARE THE ONLY ANSWER TO EAST-MEG ARMOUR!
THEY'LL DO! GET 'EM ONTO THE STREETS AS FAST AS YOU CAN!
JUDGE MCGRUDER, ONLY SURVIVING MEMBER OF THE COUNCIL OF FIVE, HAS BEEN FOUND AND, DESPITE GRUESOME INJURIES, HAS TAKEN COMMAND OF THE RESISTANCE –
WITHOUT THEIR SUPPLY BASE, EVERY EAST-MEG JUDGE OR WEAPON WE DESTROY IS IRREPLACABLE! MAKE EVERY SHOT COUNT!
GIVE 'EM JUSTICE! GIVE 'EM HELL!
SWIFTLY, THE MAP OF MEGA-CITY ONE BEGINS TO CHANGE –
A DAY PASSES, AND IN KAZAN'S BATTLE COMMAND –
DREDD HASN'T BROKEN YET?
NO, WAR MARSHAL.
INCREASE THE PAIN LEVEL! I WANT TO HEAR HIM SCREAM!

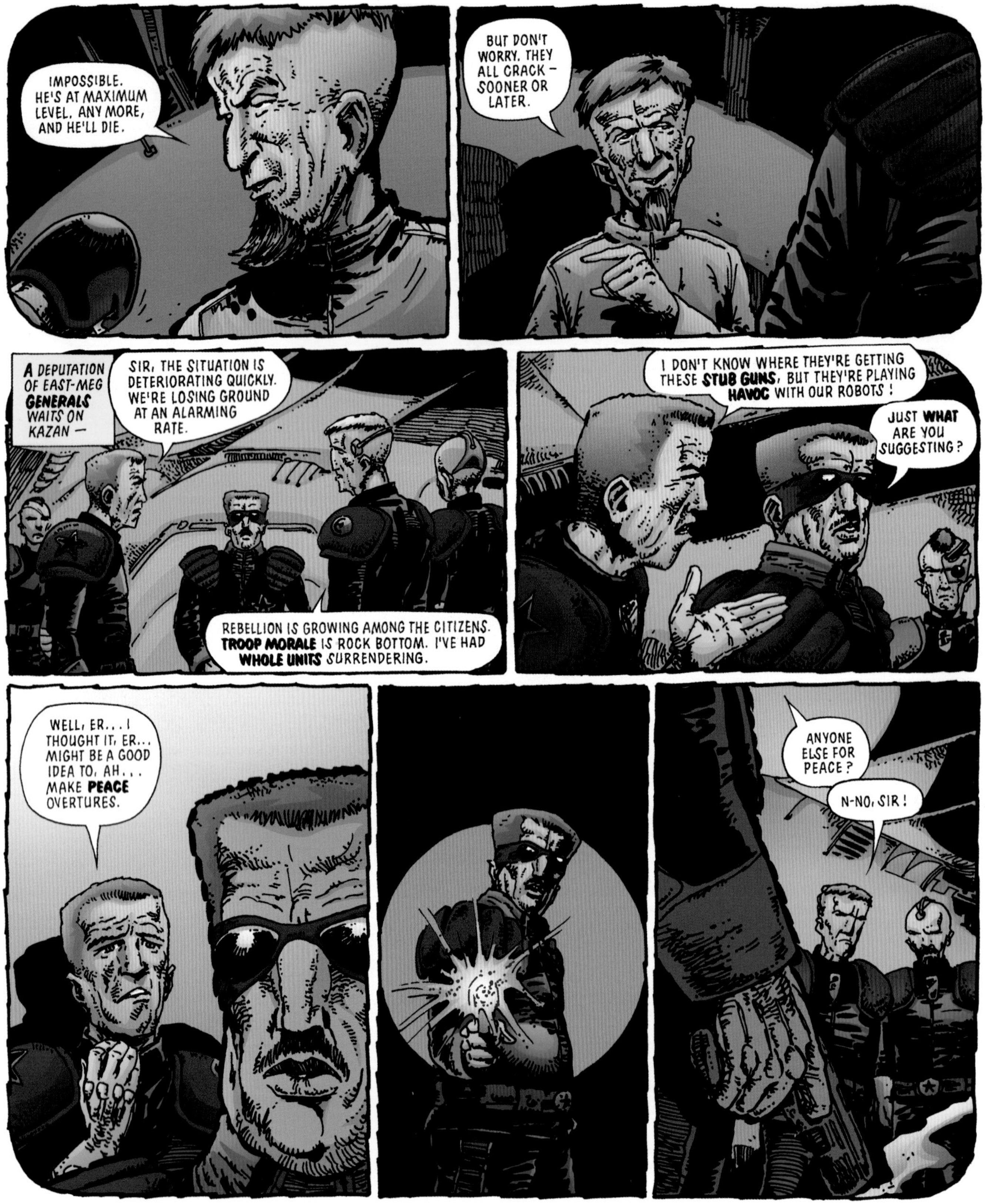

IMPOSSIBLE. HE'S AT MAXIMUM LEVEL. ANY MORE, AND HE'LL DIE.
BUT DON'T WORRY. THEY ALL CRACK - SOONER OR LATER.
A DEPUTATION OF EAST-MEG GENERALS WAITS ON KAZAN -
SIR, THE SITUATION IS DETERIORATING QUICKLY. WE'RE LOSING GROUND AT AN ALARMING RATE.
REBELLION IS GROWING AMONG THE CITIZENS. TROOP MORALE IS ROCK BOTTOM. I'VE HAD WHOLE UNITS SURRENDERING.
I DON'T KNOW WHERE THEY'RE GETTING THESE STUB GUNS, BUT THEY'RE PLAYING HAVOC WITH OUR ROBOTS!
JUST WHAT ARE YOU SUGGESTING?
WELL, ER... I THOUGHT IT, ER... MIGHT BE A GOOD IDEA TO, AH... MAKE PEACE OVERTURES.
ANYONE ELSE FOR PEACE?
N-NO, SIR!

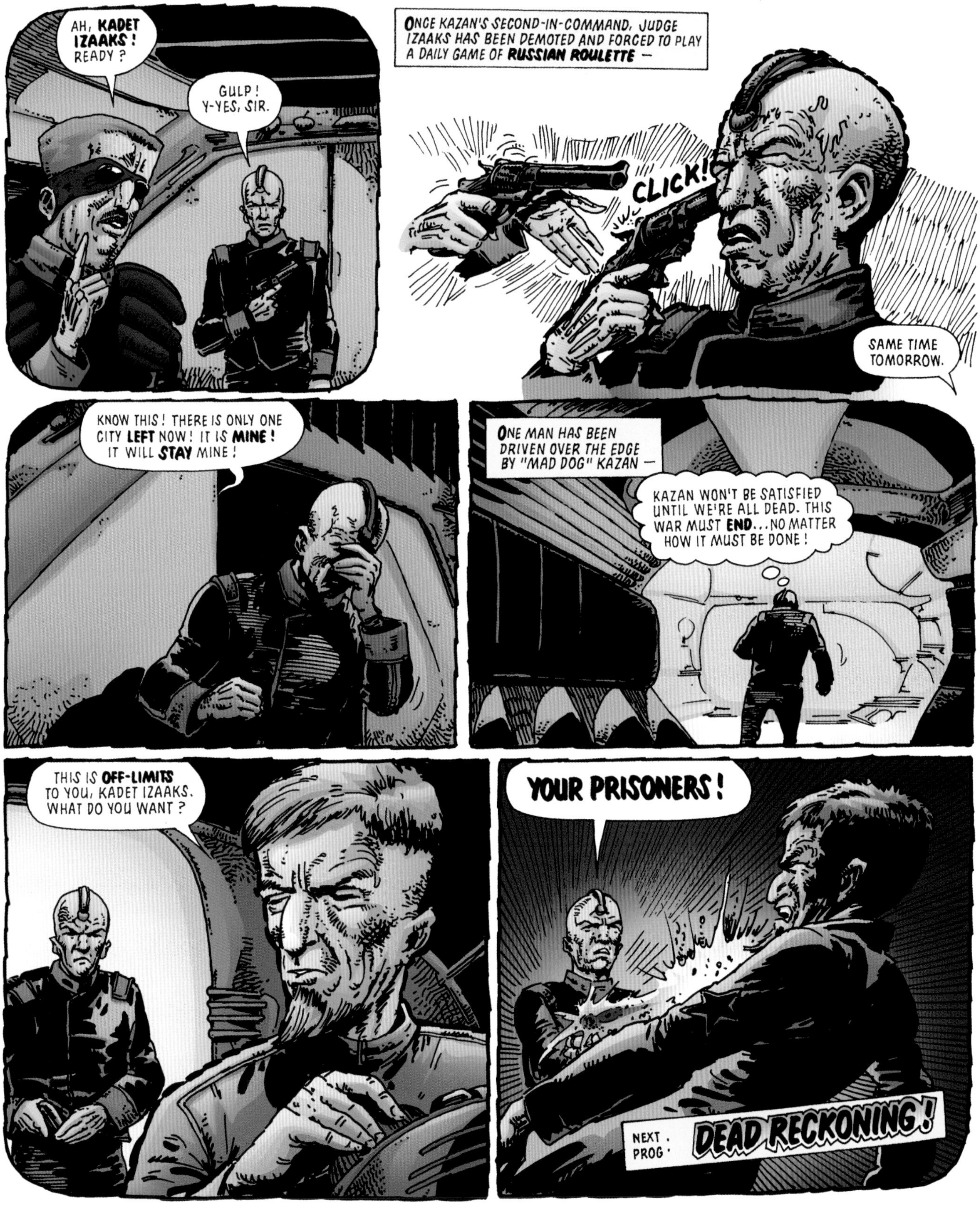
AH, KADET IZAAKS! READY?
GULP! Y-YES, SIR.
ONCE KAZAN'S SECOND-IN-COMMAND, JUDGE IZAAKS HAS BEEN DEMOTED AND FORCED TO PLAY A DAILY GAME OF RUSSIAN ROULETTE —
CLICK!
SAME TIME TOMORROW.
KNOW THIS! THERE IS ONLY ONE CITY LEFT NOW! IT IS MINE! IT WILL STAY MINE!
ONE MAN HAS BEEN DRIVEN OVER THE EDGE BY "MAD DOG" KAZAN —
KAZAN WON'T BE SATISFIED UNTIL WE'RE ALL DEAD. THIS WAR MUST END... NO MATTER HOW IT MUST BE DONE!
THIS IS OFF-LIMITS TO YOU, KADET IZAAKS. WHAT DO YOU WANT?
YOUR PRISONERS!
NEXT PROG: DEAD RECKONING!

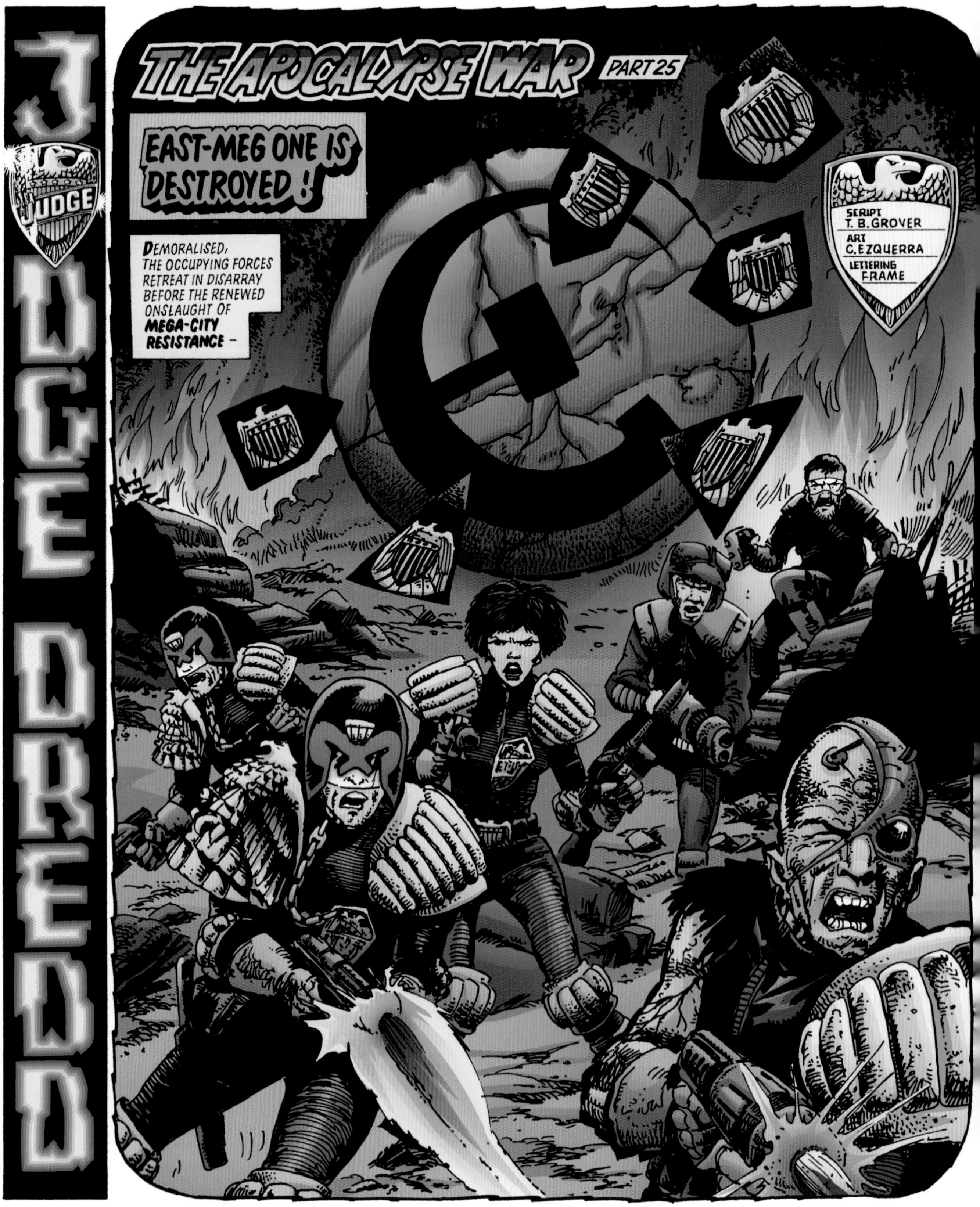
JUDGE DREDD
THE APOCALYPSE WAR
PART 25
EAST-MEG ONE IS DESTROYED!
DEMORALISED, THE OCCUPYING FORCES RETREAT IN DISARRAY BEFORE THE RENEWED ONSLAUGHT OF MEGA-CITY RESISTANCE –
SCRIPT T. B. GROVER
ART C. EZQUERRA
LETTERING FRAME

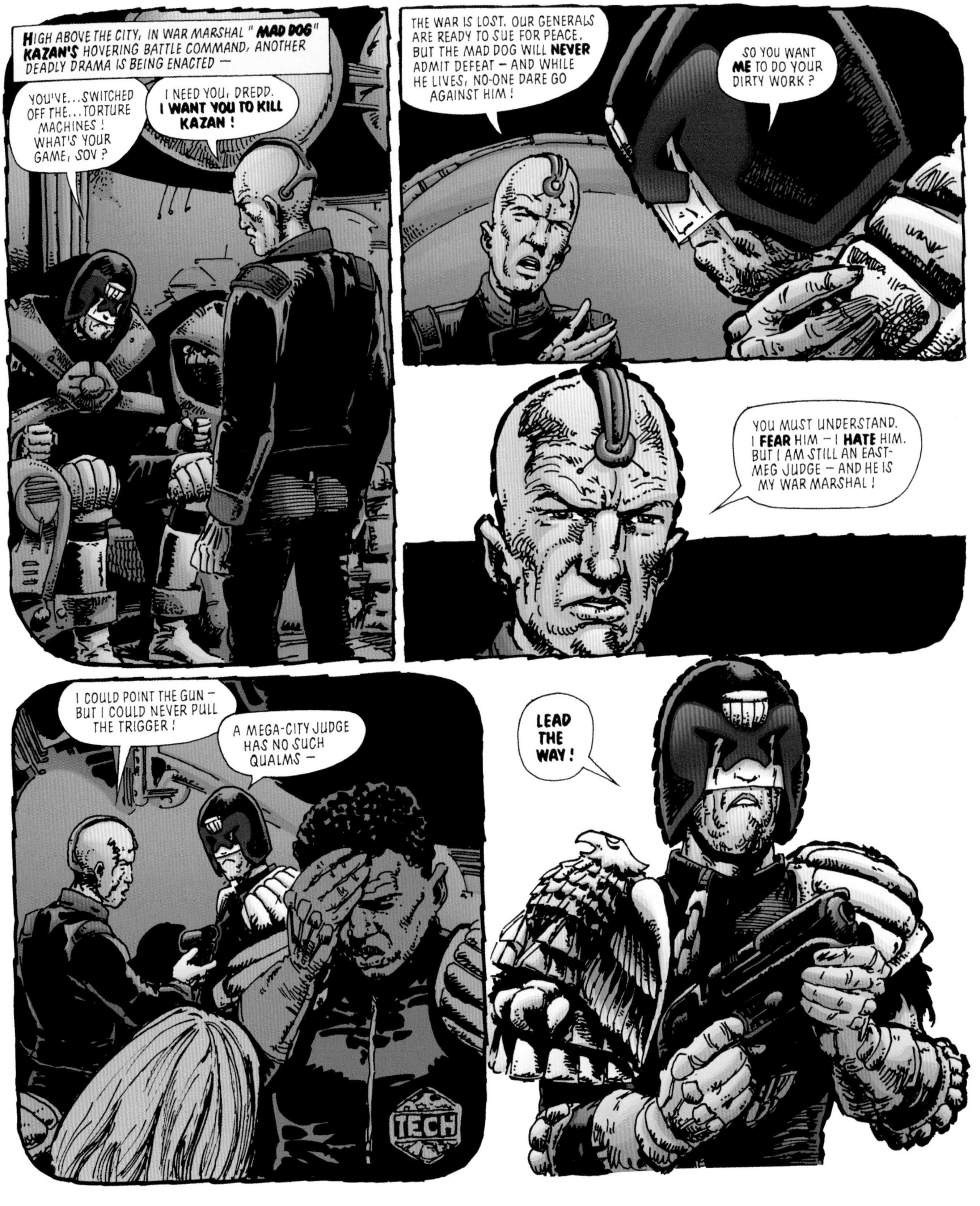
HIGH ABOVE THE CITY, IN WAR MARSHAL "MAD DOG" KAZAN'S HOVERING BATTLE COMMAND, ANOTHER DEADLY DRAMA IS BEING ENACTED —
YOU'VE...SWITCHED OFF THE...TORTURE MACHINES! WHAT'S YOUR GAME, SOV?
I NEED YOU, DREDD. I WANT YOU TO KILL KAZAN!
THE WAR IS LOST. OUR GENERALS ARE READY TO SUE FOR PEACE. BUT THE MAD DOG WILL NEVER ADMIT DEFEAT — AND WHILE HE LIVES, NO-ONE DARE GO AGAINST HIM!
SO YOU WANT ME TO DO YOUR DIRTY WORK?
YOU MUST UNDERSTAND. I FEAR HIM — I HATE HIM. BUT I AM STILL AN EAST-MEG JUDGE — AND HE IS MY WAR MARSHAL!
I COULD POINT THE GUN — BUT I COULD NEVER PULL THE TRIGGER!
A MEGA-CITY JUDGE HAS NO SUCH QUALMS —
TECH
LEAD THE WAY!

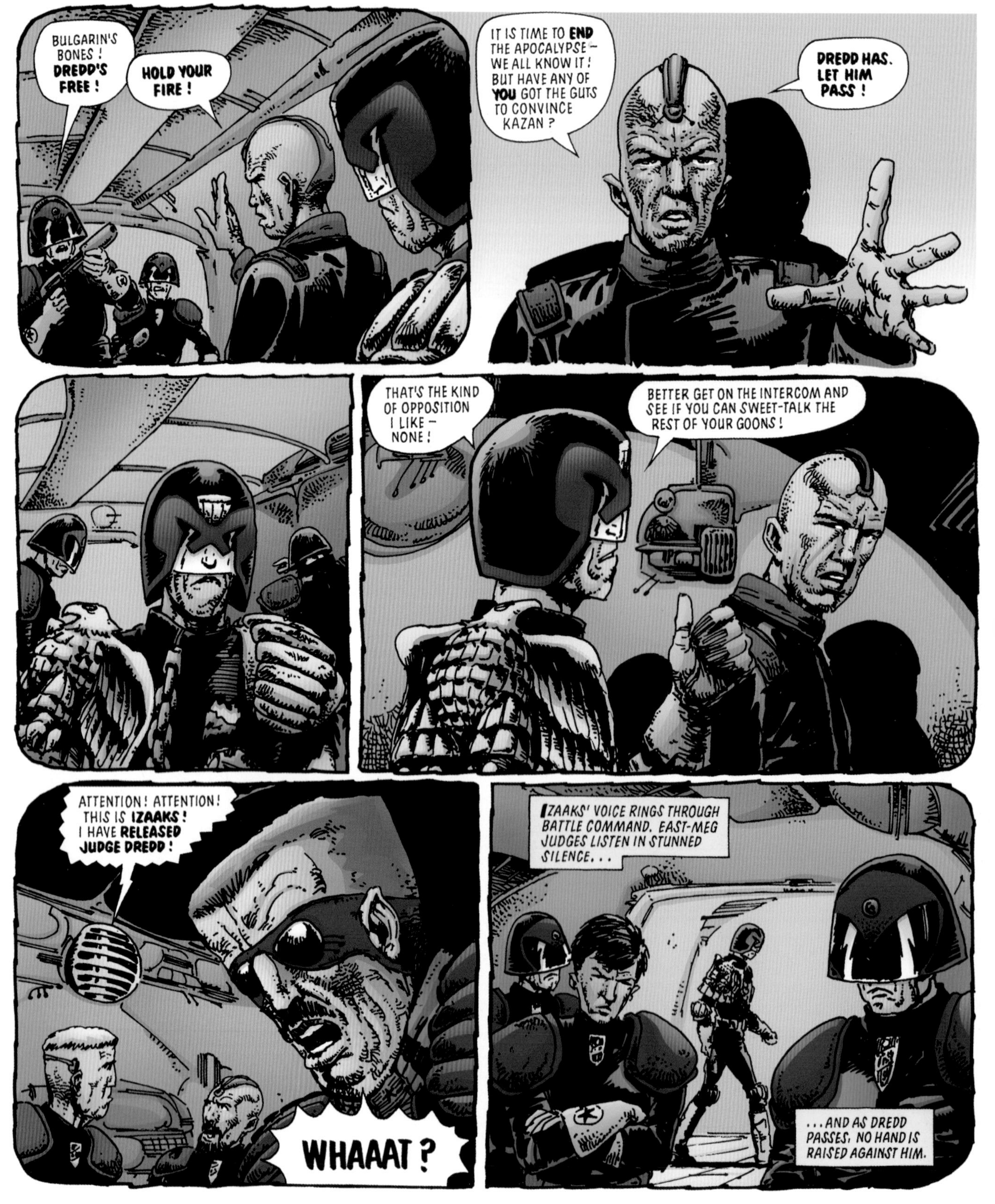
BULGARIN'S BONES! DREDD'S FREE!
HOLD YOUR FIRE!
IT IS TIME TO END THE APOCALYPSE — WE ALL KNOW IT! BUT HAVE ANY OF YOU GOT THE GUTS TO CONVINCE KAZAN?
DREDD HAS. LET HIM PASS!
THAT'S THE KIND OF OPPOSITION I LIKE — NONE!
BETTER GET ON THE INTERCOM AND SEE IF YOU CAN SWEET-TALK THE REST OF YOUR GOONS!
ATTENTION! ATTENTION! THIS IS IZAAKS! I HAVE RELEASED JUDGE DREDD!
WHAAAT?
IZAAKS' VOICE RINGS THROUGH BATTLE COMMAND. EAST-MEG JUDGES LISTEN IN STUNNED SILENCE...
...AND AS DREDD PASSES, NO HAND IS RAISED AGAINST HIM.

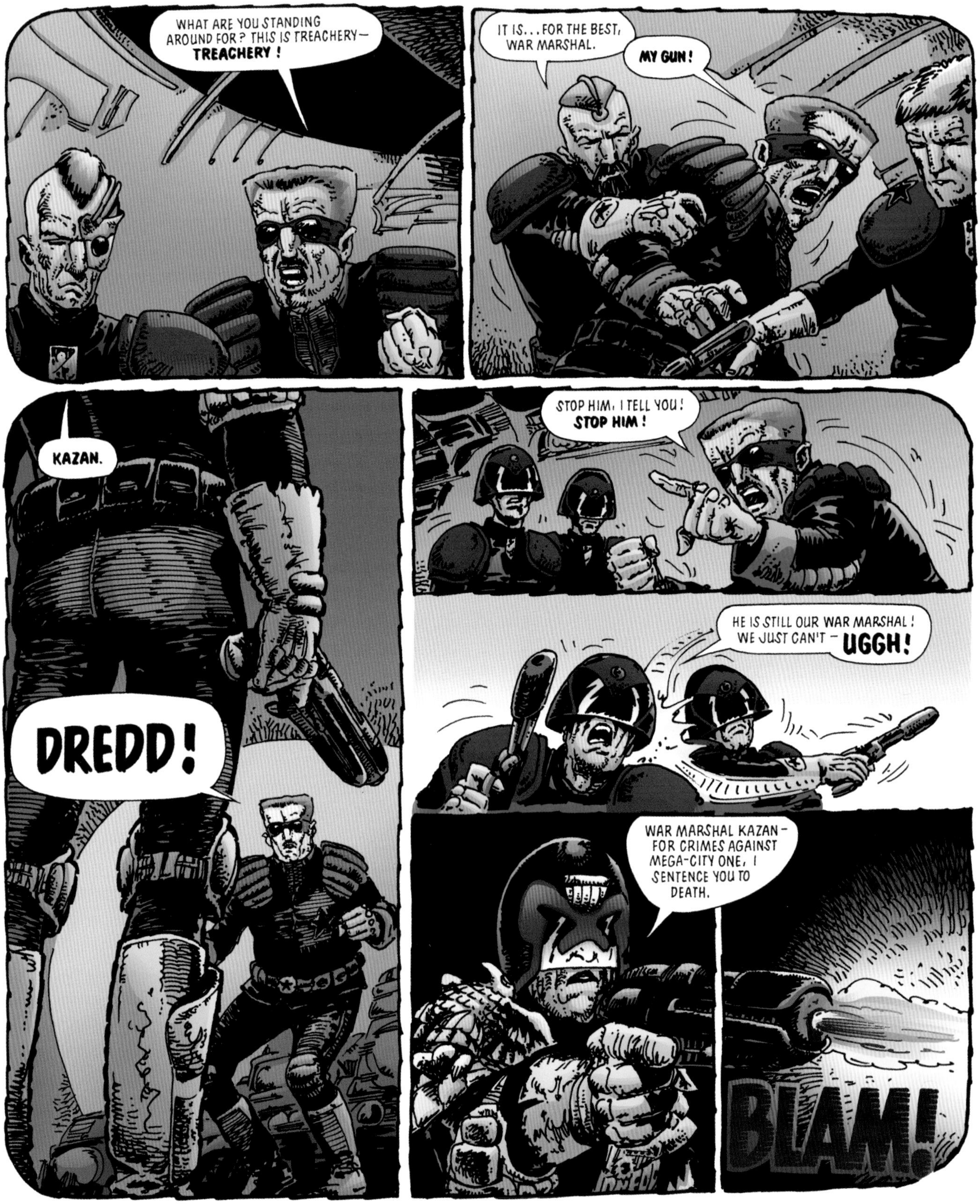

WHAT ARE YOU STANDING AROUND FOR? THIS IS TREACHERY— TREACHERY!
IT IS... FOR THE BEST, WAR MARSHAL.
MY GUN!
KAZAN.
DREDD!
STOP HIM, I TELL YOU! STOP HIM!
HE IS STILL OUR WAR MARSHAL! WE JUST CAN'T — UGGH!
WAR MARSHAL KAZAN— FOR CRIMES AGAINST MEGA-CITY ONE, I SENTENCE YOU TO DEATH.
BLAM!

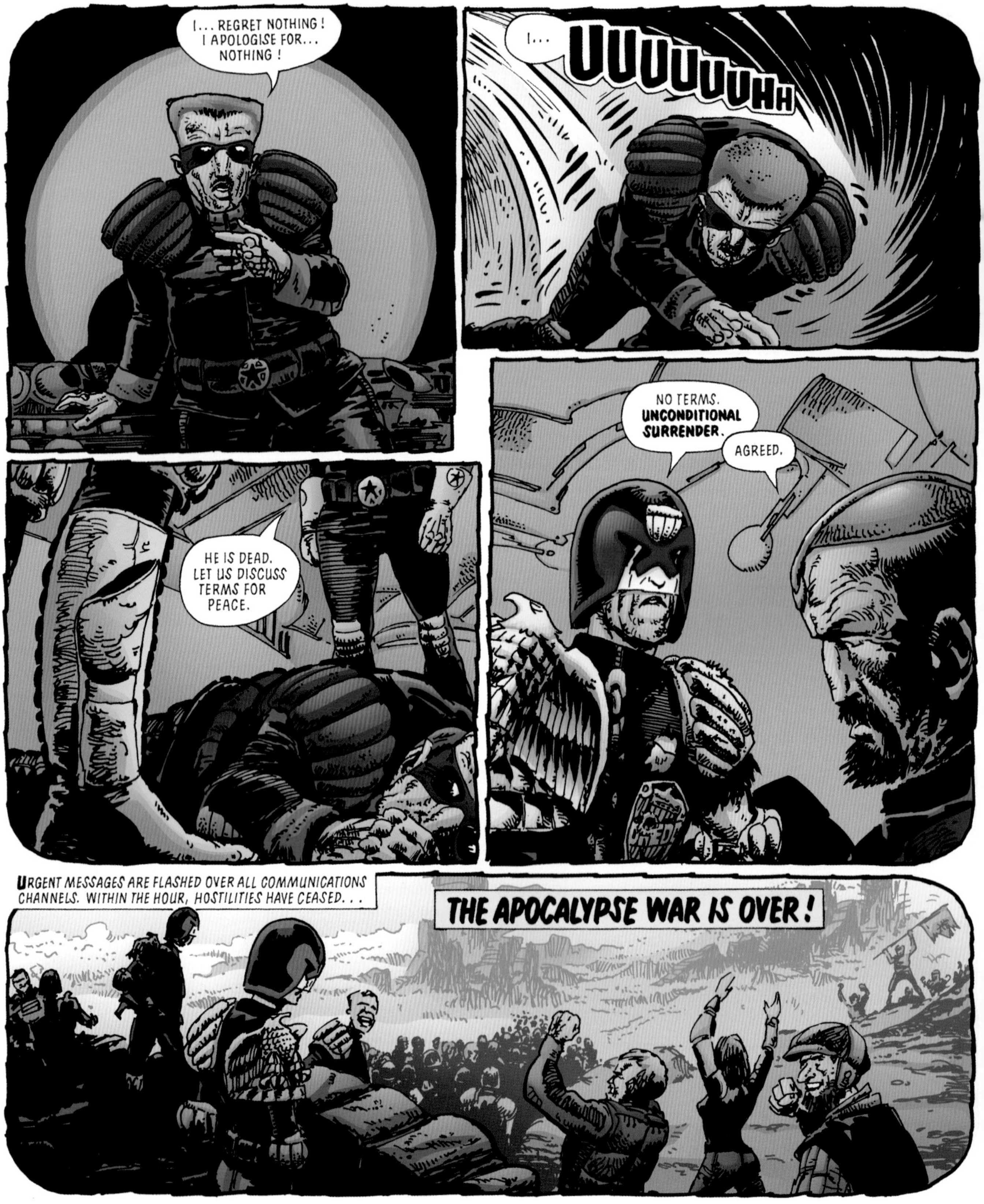
I... REGRET NOTHING! I APOLOGISE FOR... NOTHING!
I...
UUUUUUUHH
HE IS DEAD. LET US DISCUSS TERMS FOR PEACE.
NO TERMS. **UNCONDITIONAL SURRENDER.**
AGREED.
URGENT MESSAGES ARE FLASHED OVER ALL COMMUNICATIONS CHANNELS. WITHIN THE HOUR, HOSTILITIES HAVE CEASED...
THE APOCALYPSE WAR IS OVER!

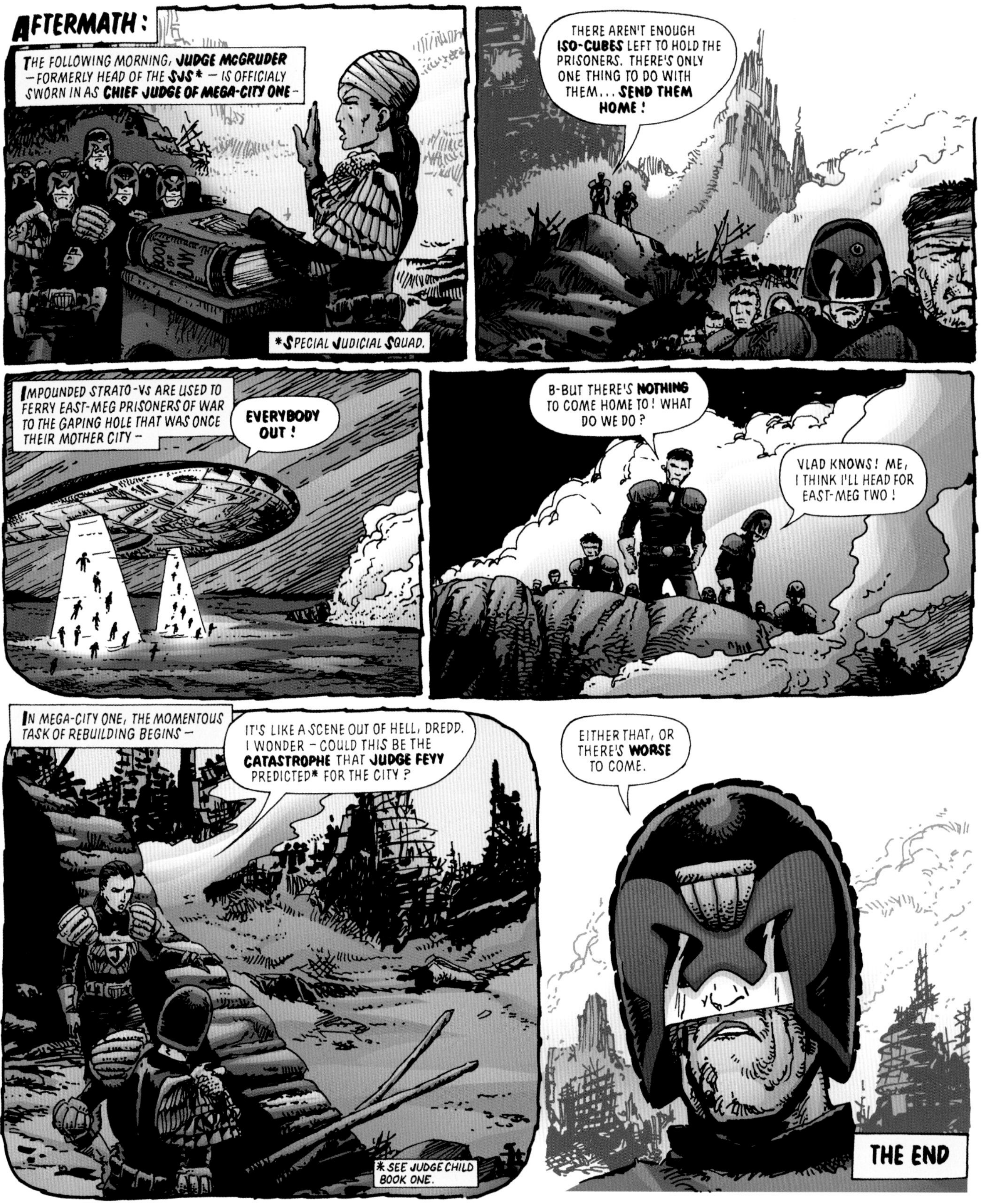

AFTERMATH:
THE FOLLOWING MORNING, JUDGE MCGRUDER — FORMERLY HEAD OF THE SJS* — IS OFFICIALY SWORN IN AS CHIEF JUDGE OF MEGA-CITY ONE —
*SPECIAL JUDICIAL SQUAD.
THERE AREN'T ENOUGH ISO-CUBES LEFT TO HOLD THE PRISONERS. THERE'S ONLY ONE THING TO DO WITH THEM... SEND THEM HOME!
IMPOUNDED STRATO-VS ARE USED TO FERRY EAST-MEG PRISONERS OF WAR TO THE GAPING HOLE THAT WAS ONCE THEIR MOTHER CITY —
EVERYBODY OUT!
B-BUT THERE'S NOTHING TO COME HOME TO! WHAT DO WE DO?
VLAD KNOWS! ME, I THINK I'LL HEAD FOR EAST-MEG TWO!
IN MEGA-CITY ONE, THE MOMENTOUS TASK OF REBUILDING BEGINS —
IT'S LIKE A SCENE OUT OF HELL, DREDD. I WONDER — COULD THIS BE THE CATASTROPHE THAT JUDGE FEYY PREDICTED* FOR THE CITY?
*SEE JUDGE CHILD BOOK ONE.
EITHER THAT, OR THERE'S WORSE TO COME.
THE END

COVER GALLERY

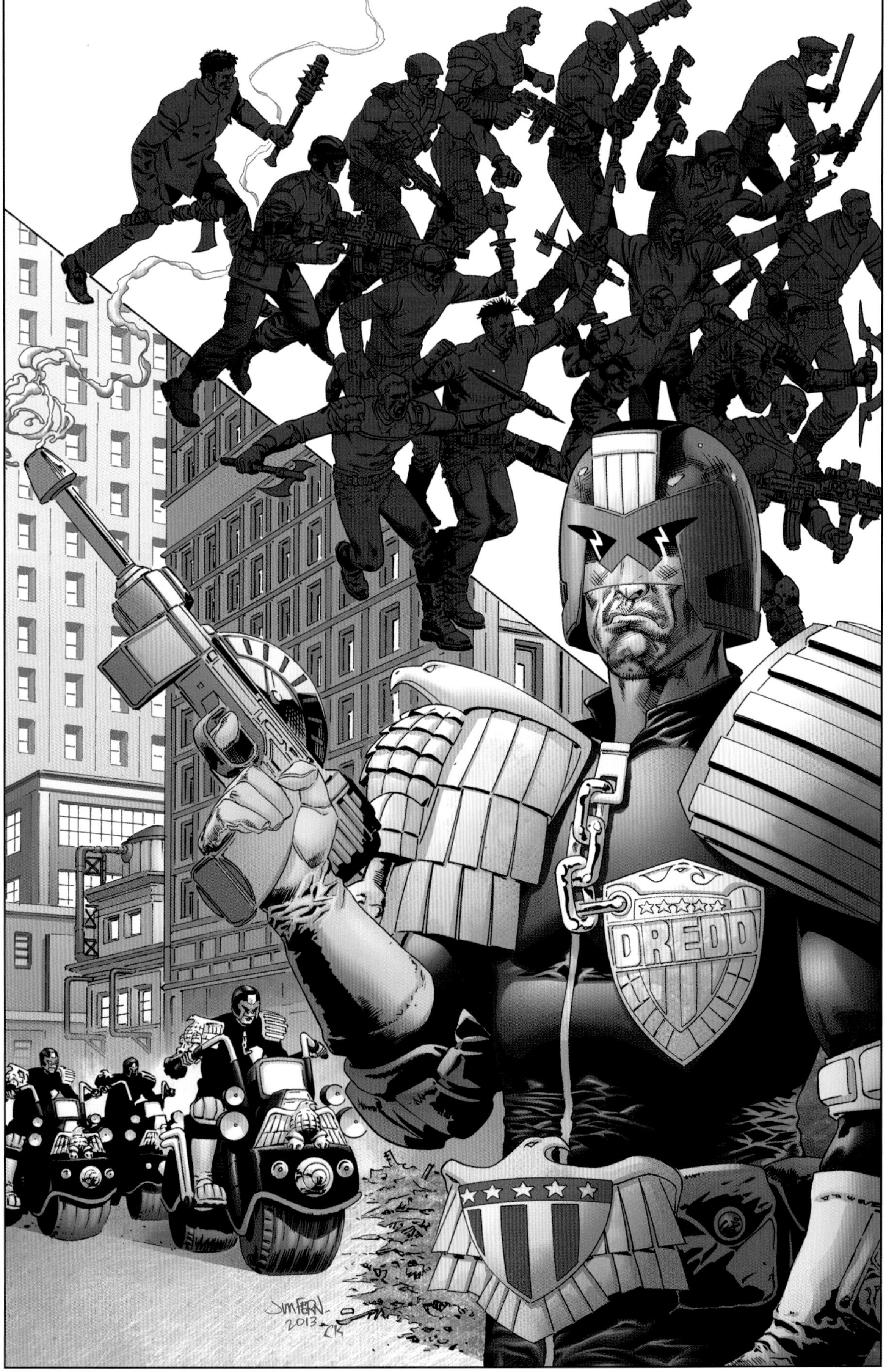
DREDD
JIM FERN 2013
CK

Art by JIM FERN
Color by CHARLIE KIRCHOFF

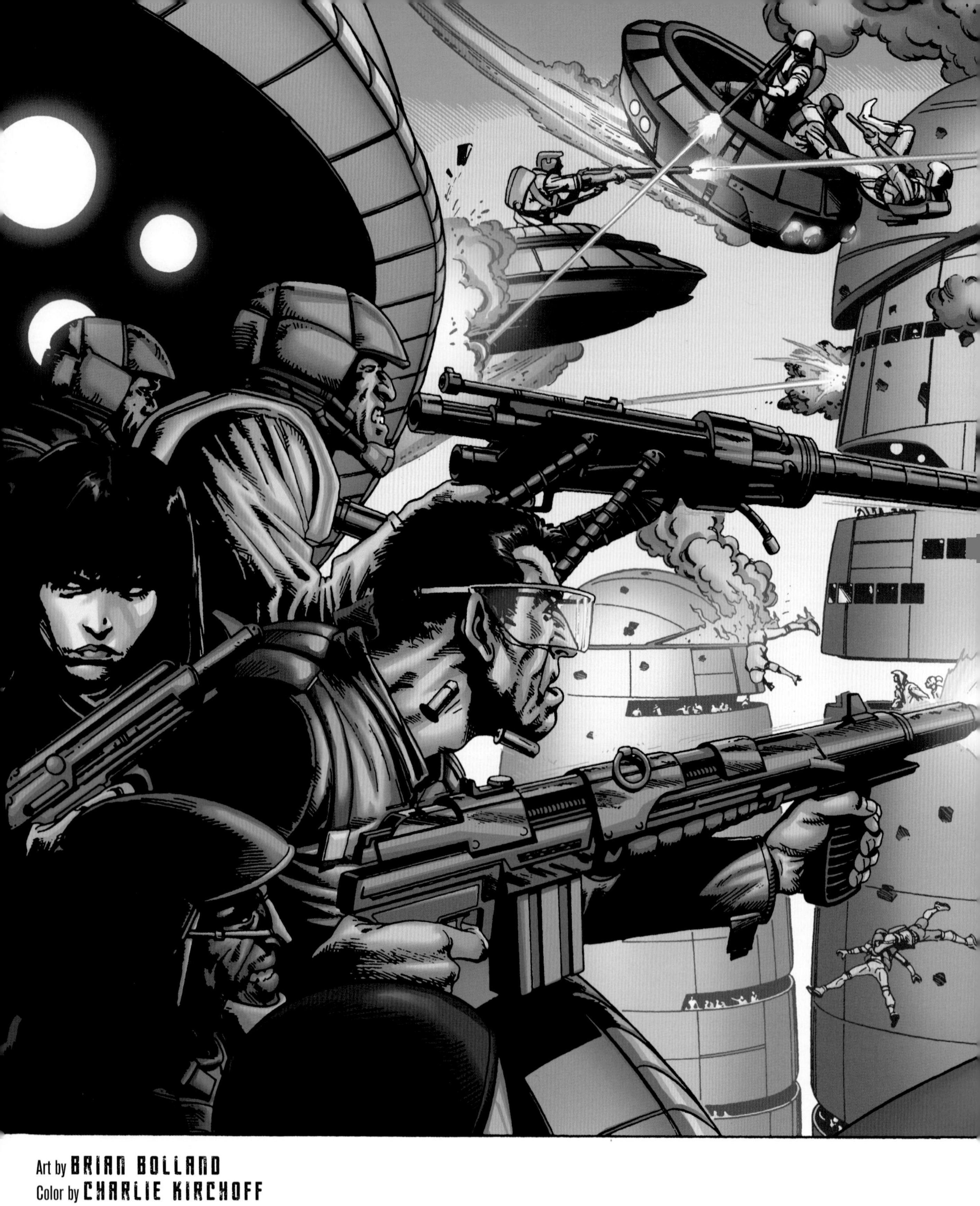

Art by BRIAN BOLLAND
Color by CHARLIE KIRCHOFF

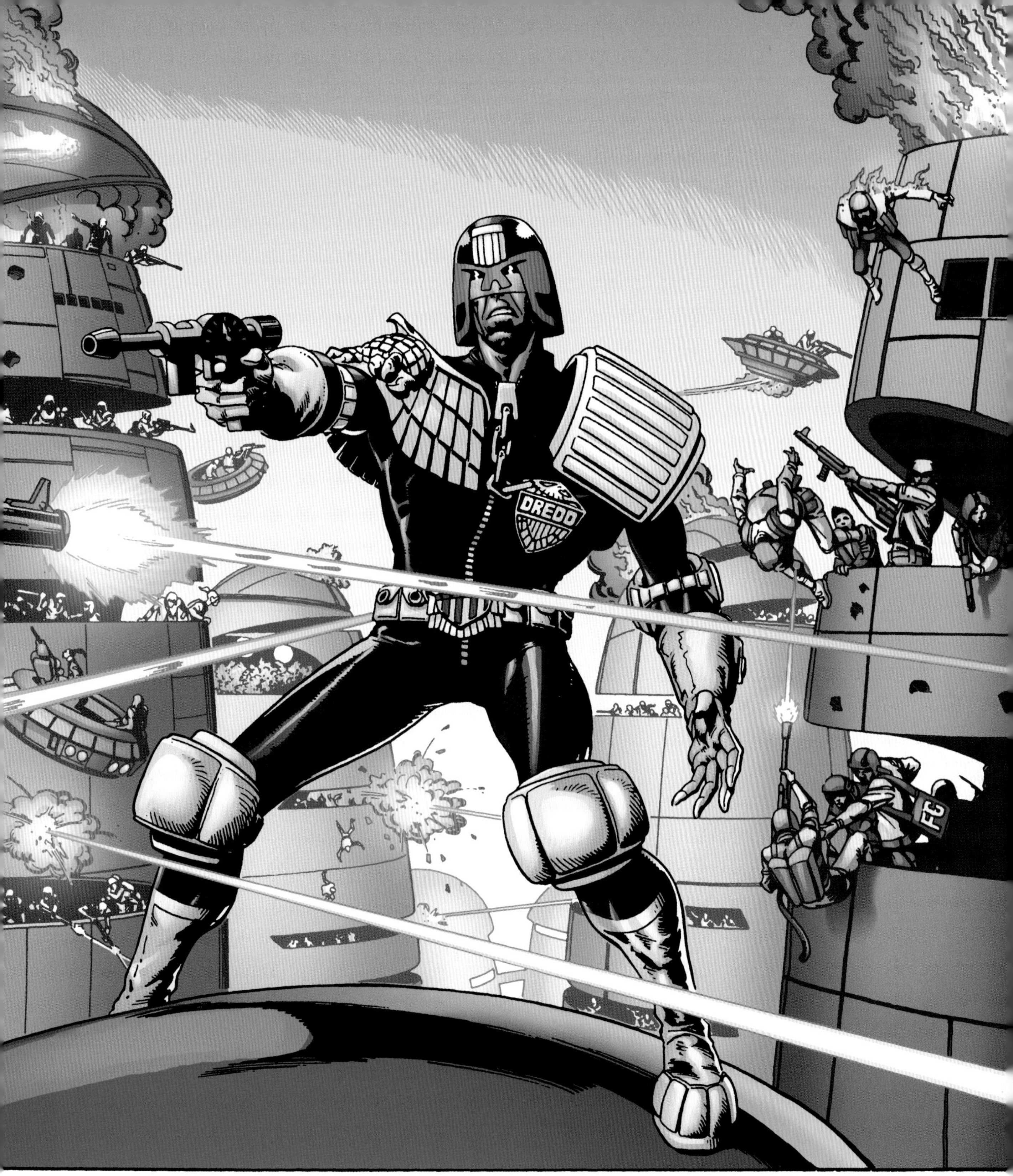
DREDD
FC

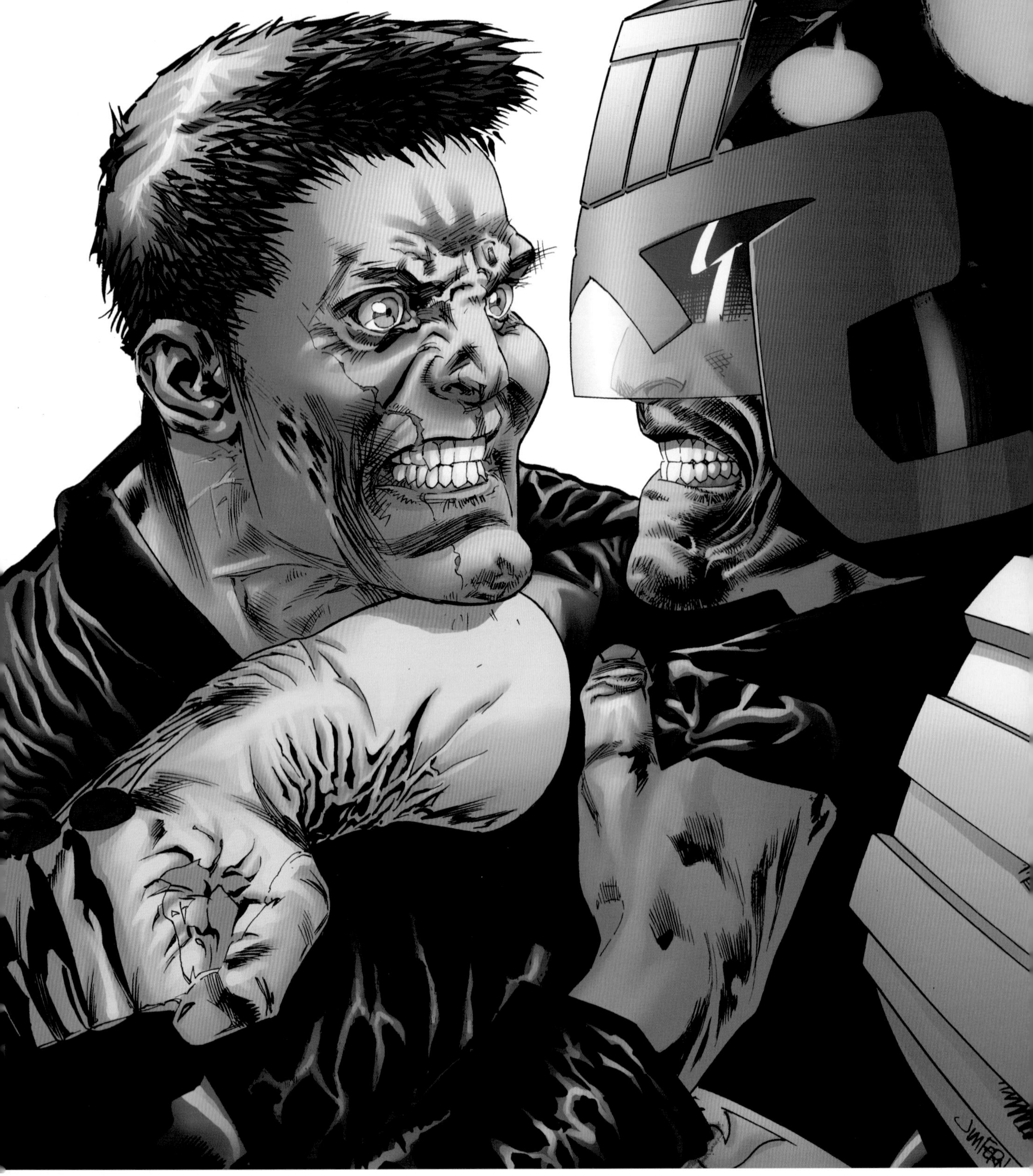

Art by **JIM FERN**
Color by **CHARLIE KIRCHOFF**

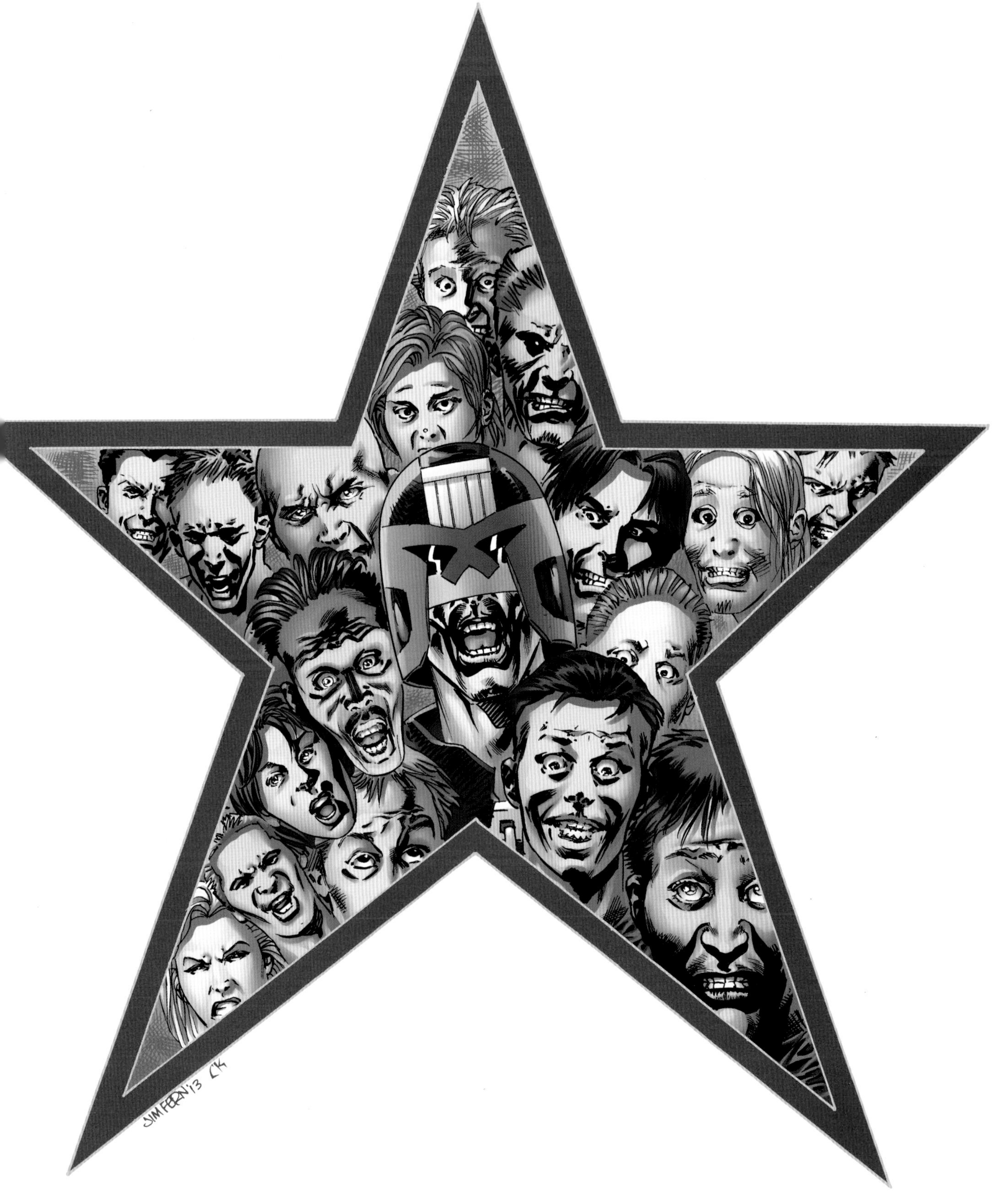
JIM FERN '13 CK

Art by **JIM FERN**
Color by **CHARLIE KIRCHOFF**

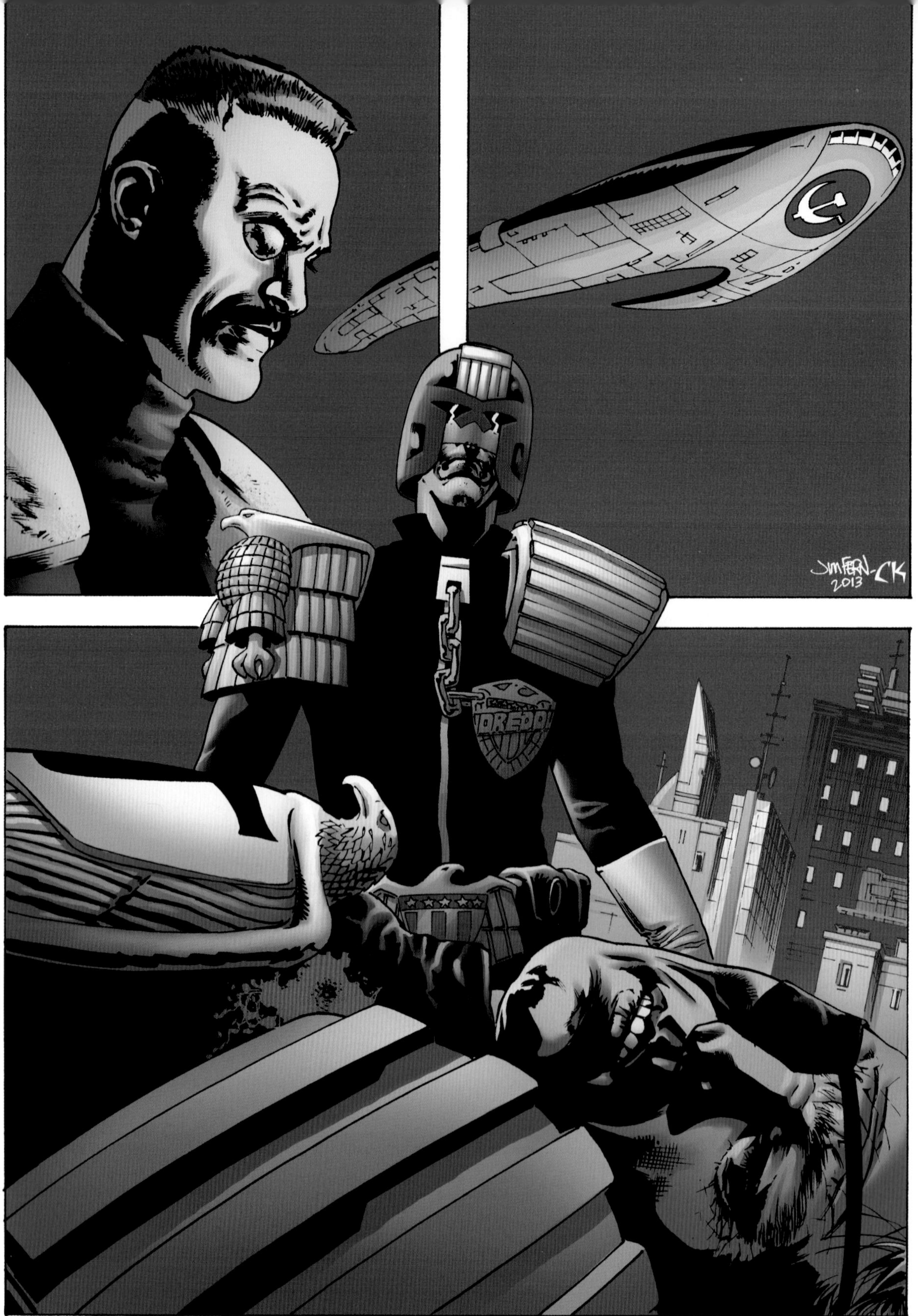
JIM FERN-CK
2013

Both pages:
Art by **JIM FERN**
Color by **CHARLIE KIRCHOFF**

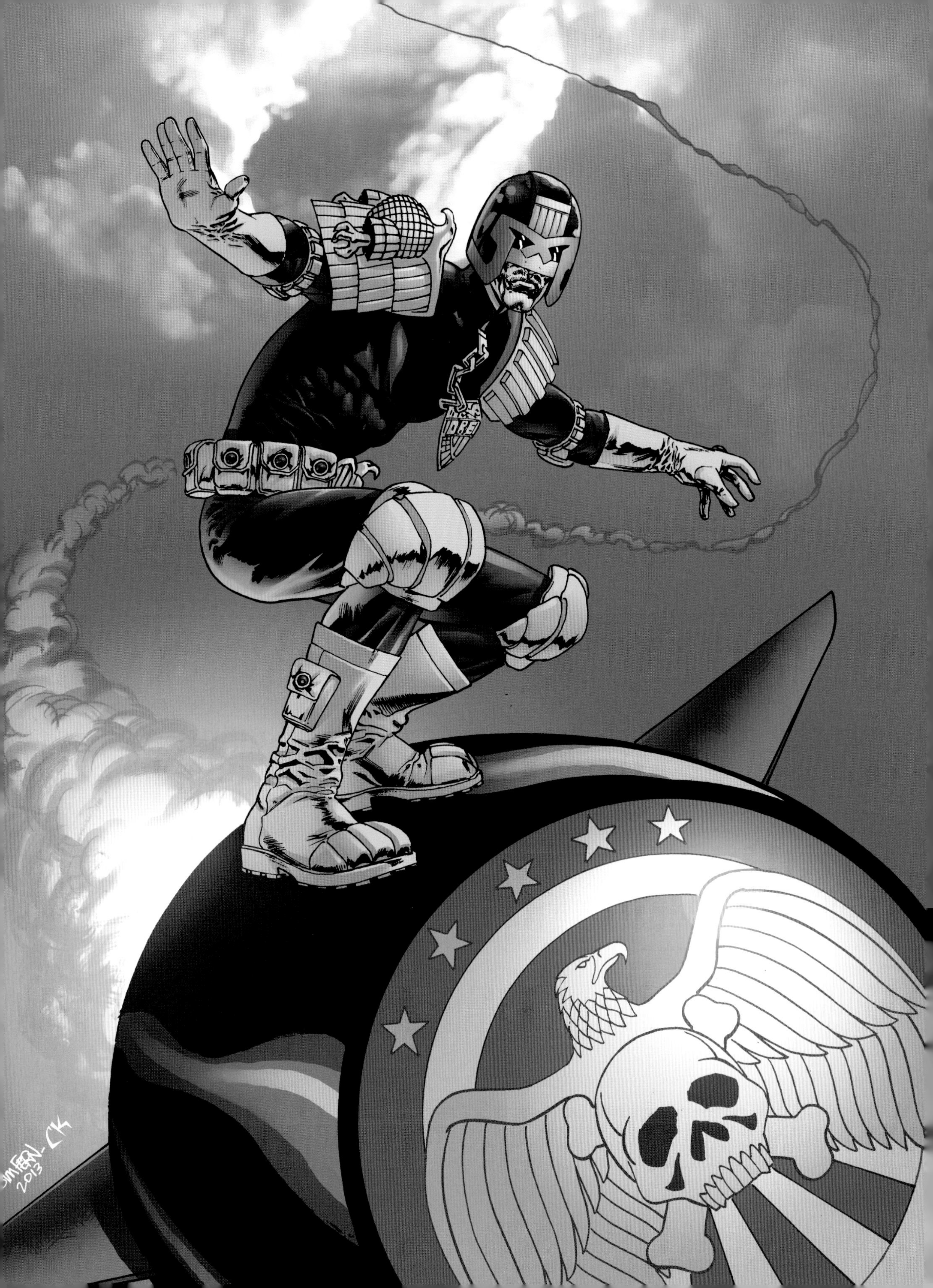

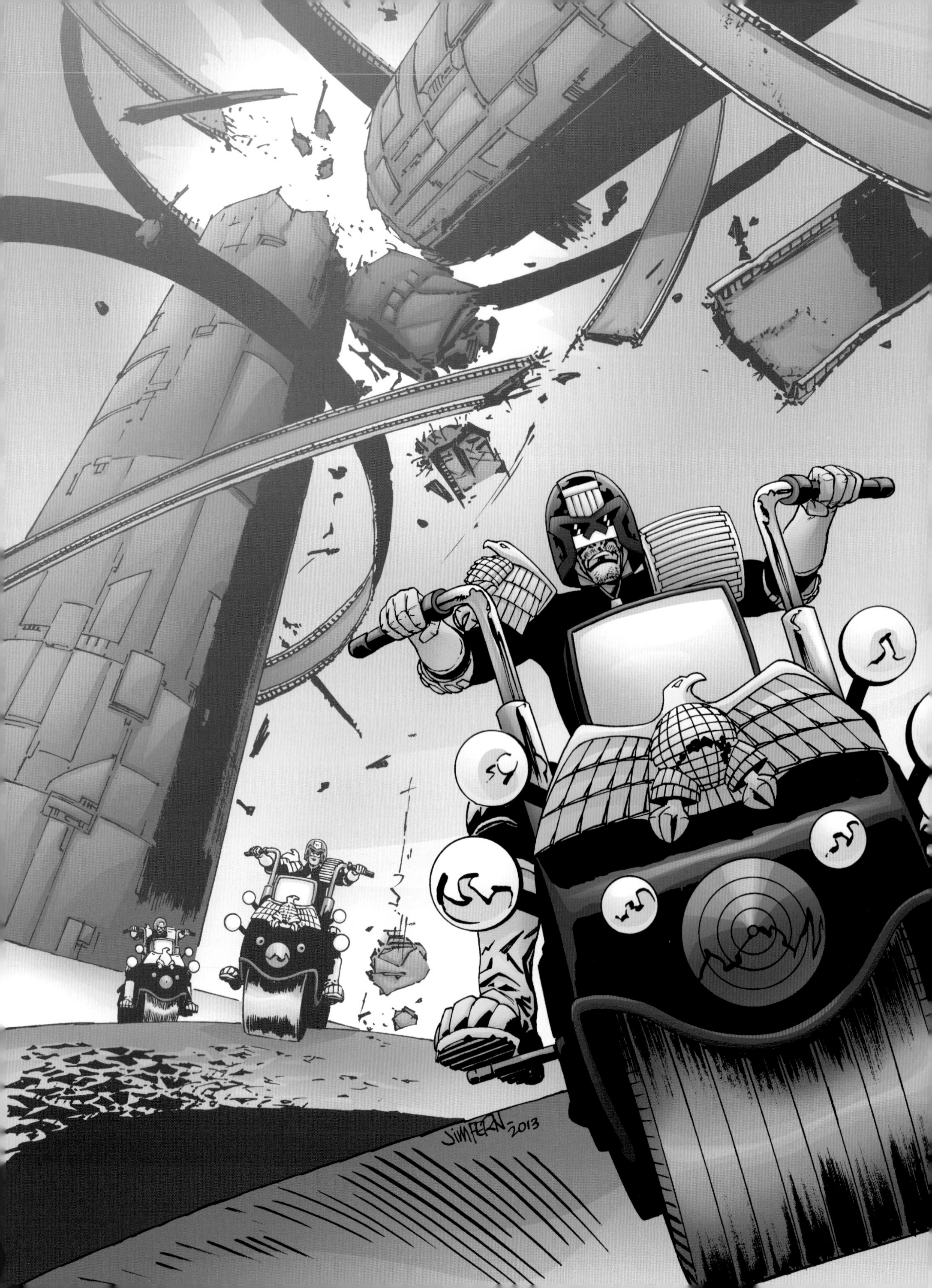
JIMFERN
2013

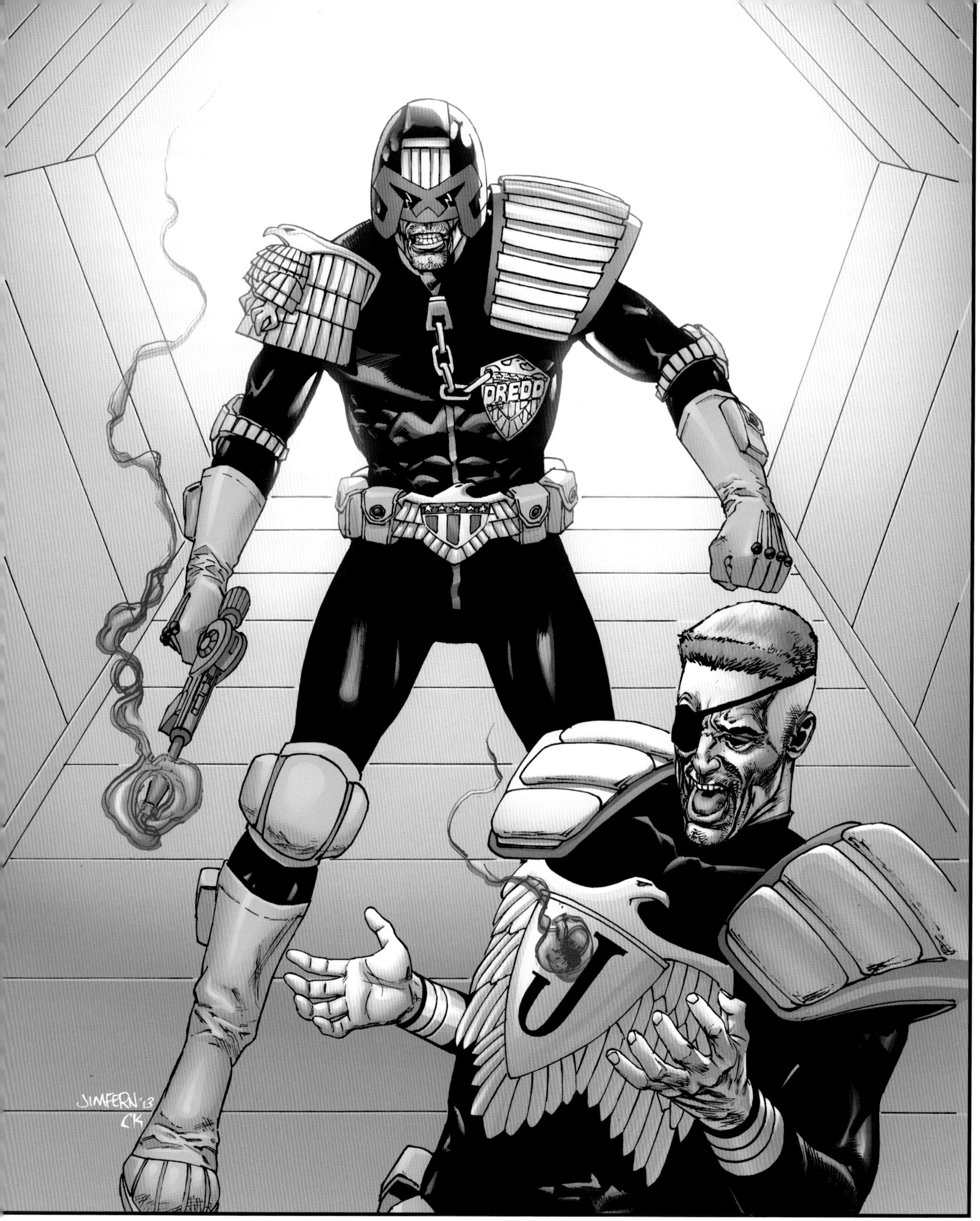
DREDD
J
JIMFERN '13
CK

vious page:
by JIM FERN
or by TOM MULLIN

Art by JIM FERN · Color by CHARLIE KIRCHOFF

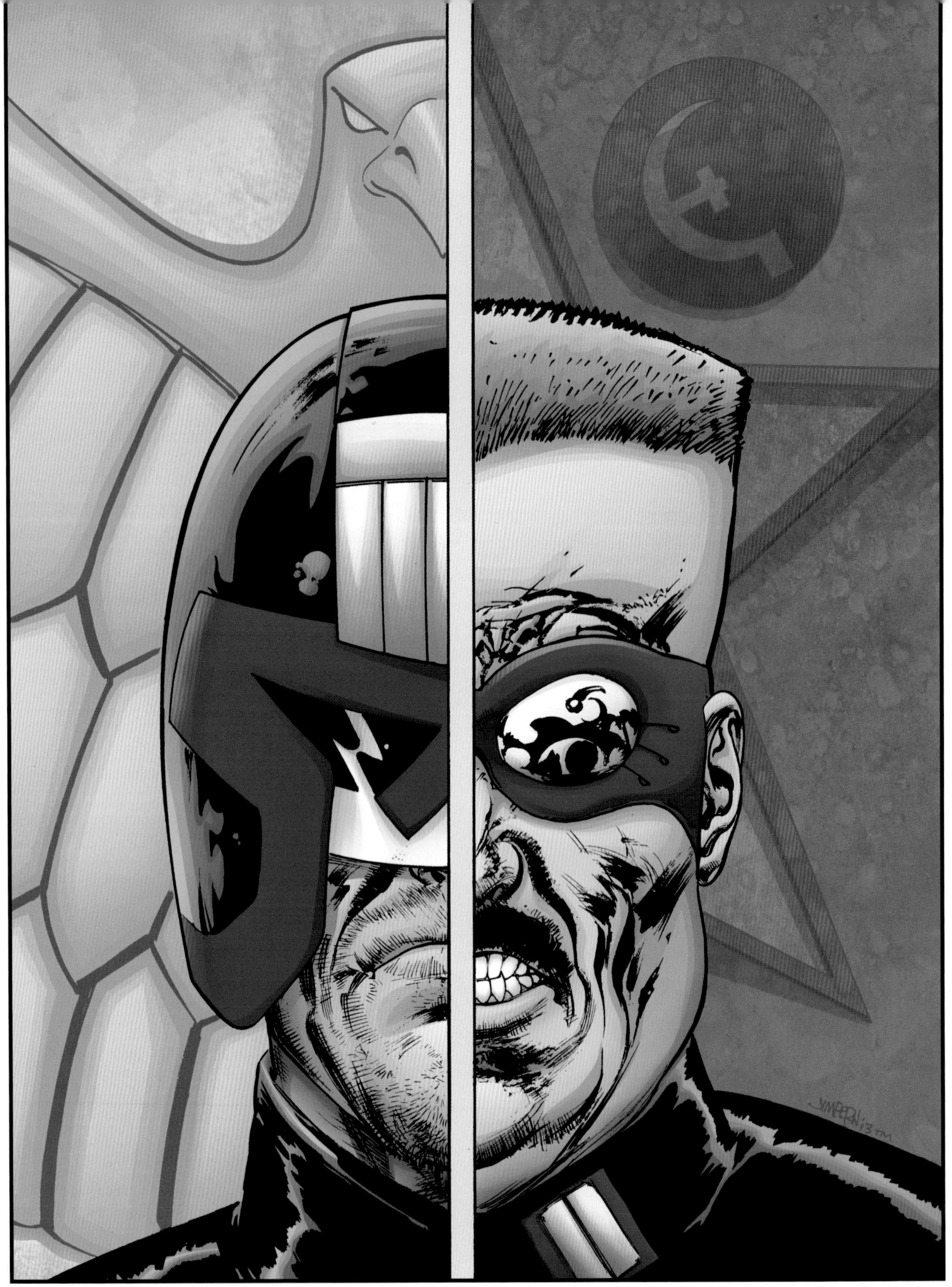

Art by JIM FERN
Color by CHARLIE KIRCHOFF

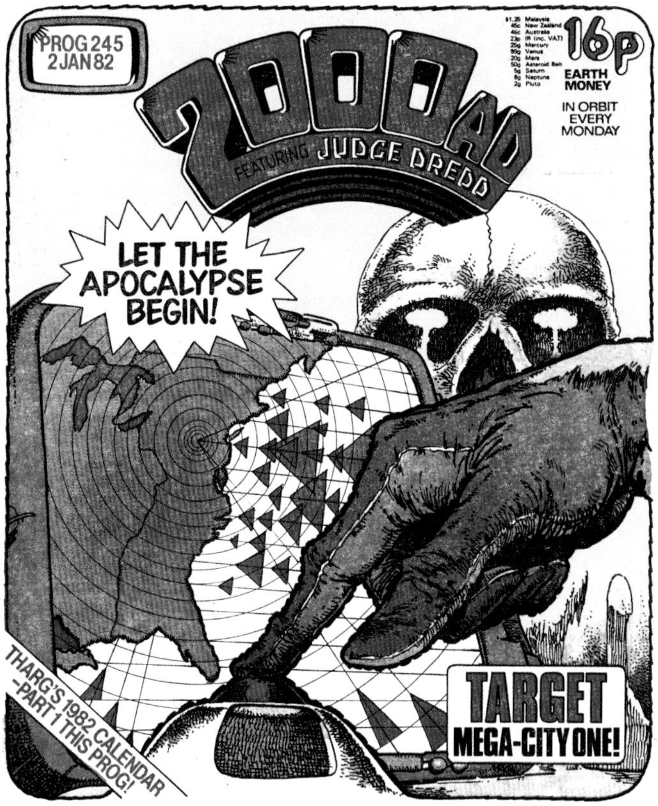
PROG 245
2 JAN 82
2000 AD
FEATURING JUDGE DREDD
16p
EARTH MONEY
IN ORBIT EVERY MONDAY
LET THE APOCALYPSE BEGIN!
THARG'S 1982 CALENDAR –PART 1 THIS PROG!
TARGET MEGA-CITY ONE!

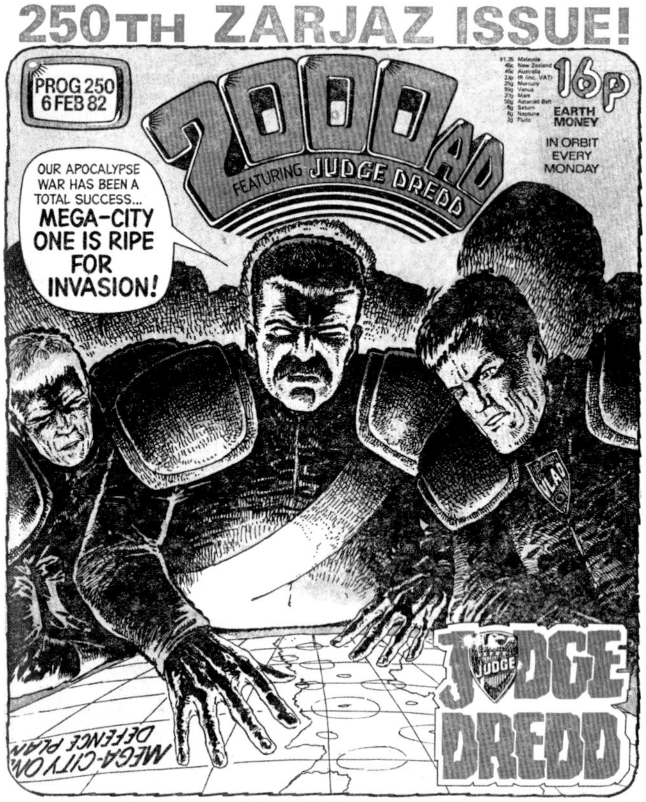
250TH ZARJAZ ISSUE!
PROG 250
6 FEB 82
2000 AD
FEATURING JUDGE DREDD
16p
EARTH MONEY
IN ORBIT EVERY MONDAY
OUR APOCALYPSE WAR HAS BEEN A TOTAL SUCCESS... MEGA-CITY ONE IS RIPE FOR INVASION!
MEGA-CITY ONE DEFENCE PLAN
JUDGE DREDD

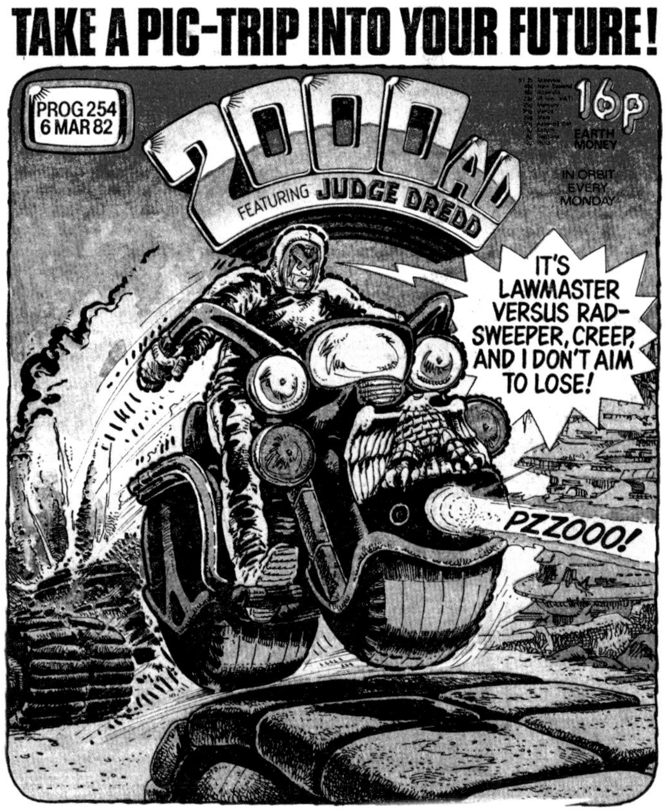
TAKE A PIC-TRIP INTO YOUR FUTURE!
PROG 254
6 MAR 82
2000 AD
FEATURING JUDGE DREDD
16p
EARTH MONEY
IN ORBIT EVERY MONDAY
IT'S LAWMASTER VERSUS RAD-SWEEPER, CREEP, AND I DON'T AIM TO LOSE!
PZZOOO!

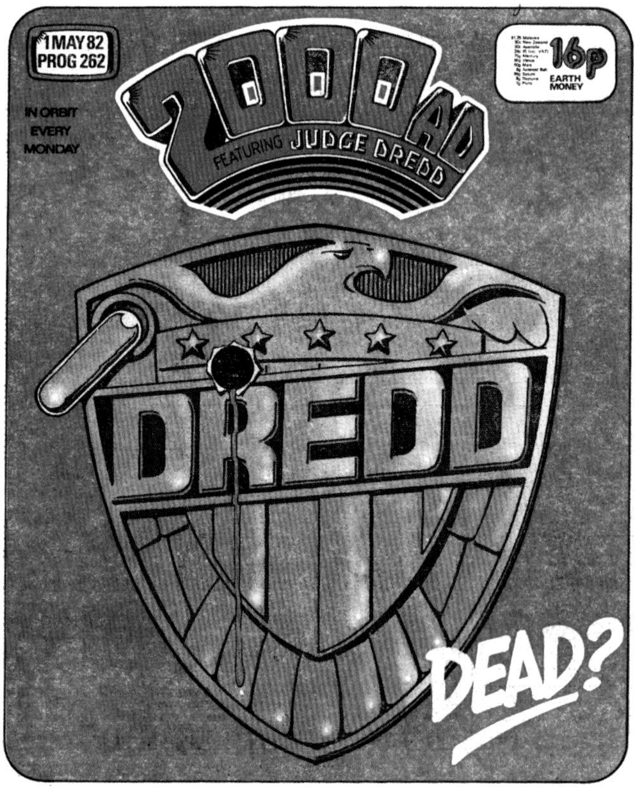
1 MAY 82
PROG 262
2000 AD
FEATURING JUDGE DREDD
16p
EARTH MONEY
IN ORBIT EVERY MONDAY
DREDD
DEAD?

TO ACTIVATE

Borag Thungg, Earthlets! Here is another zarjaz pull-out poster for you to display on your bedroom wall. To detach the poster open the staples in the middle of the comic. Then, using a pair of sharp scissors, neatly trim off the sides up to the black line. Lastly, paste the poster on to a piece of cardboard which has been cut to size. Look out for another amazing cover poster soon!

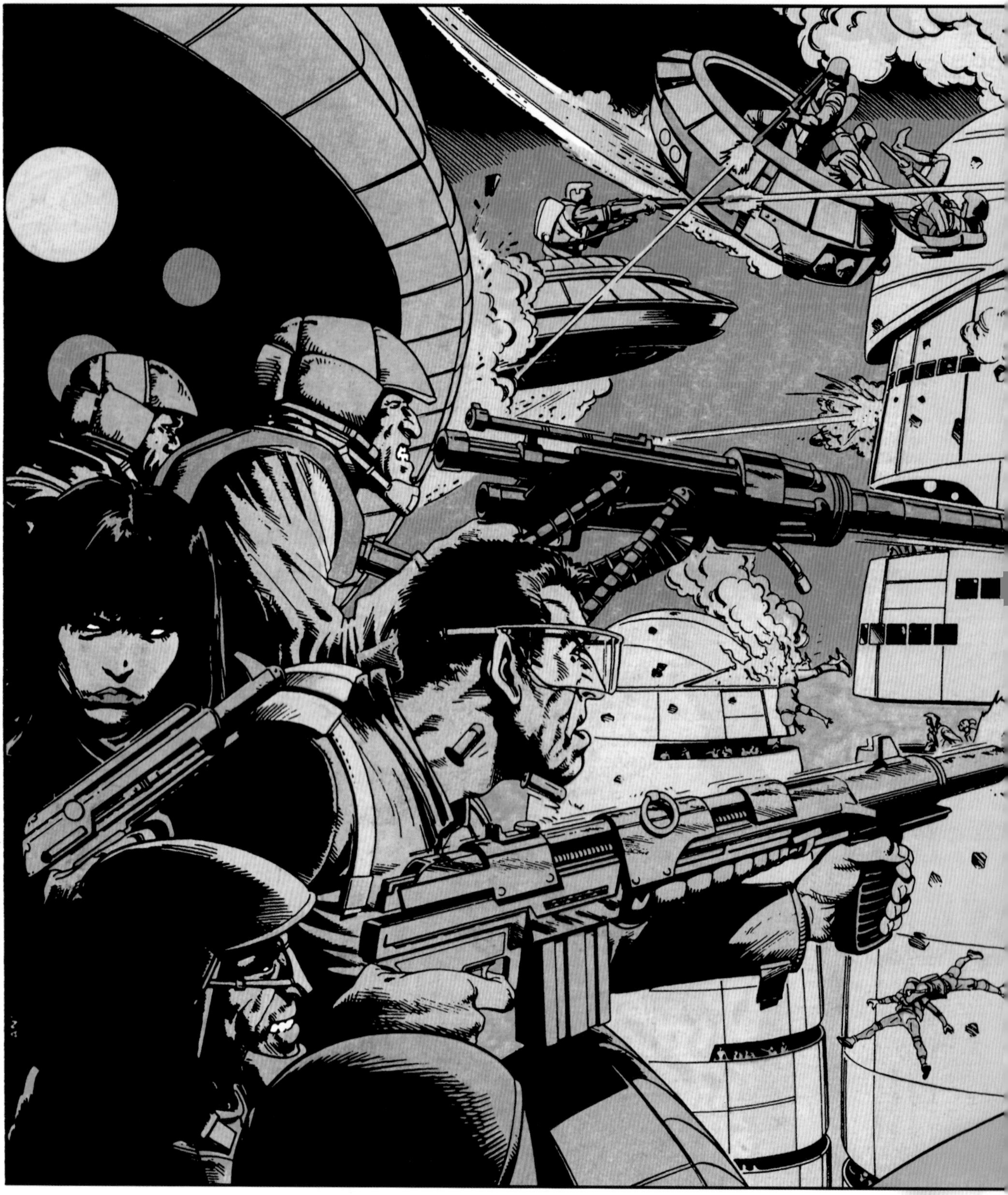

OG 236
OCT 81

ZARJAZ COVER POSTER THIS PROG

$1.25 Malaysia 45c New Zealand 45c Australia 23p IR (inc VAT)

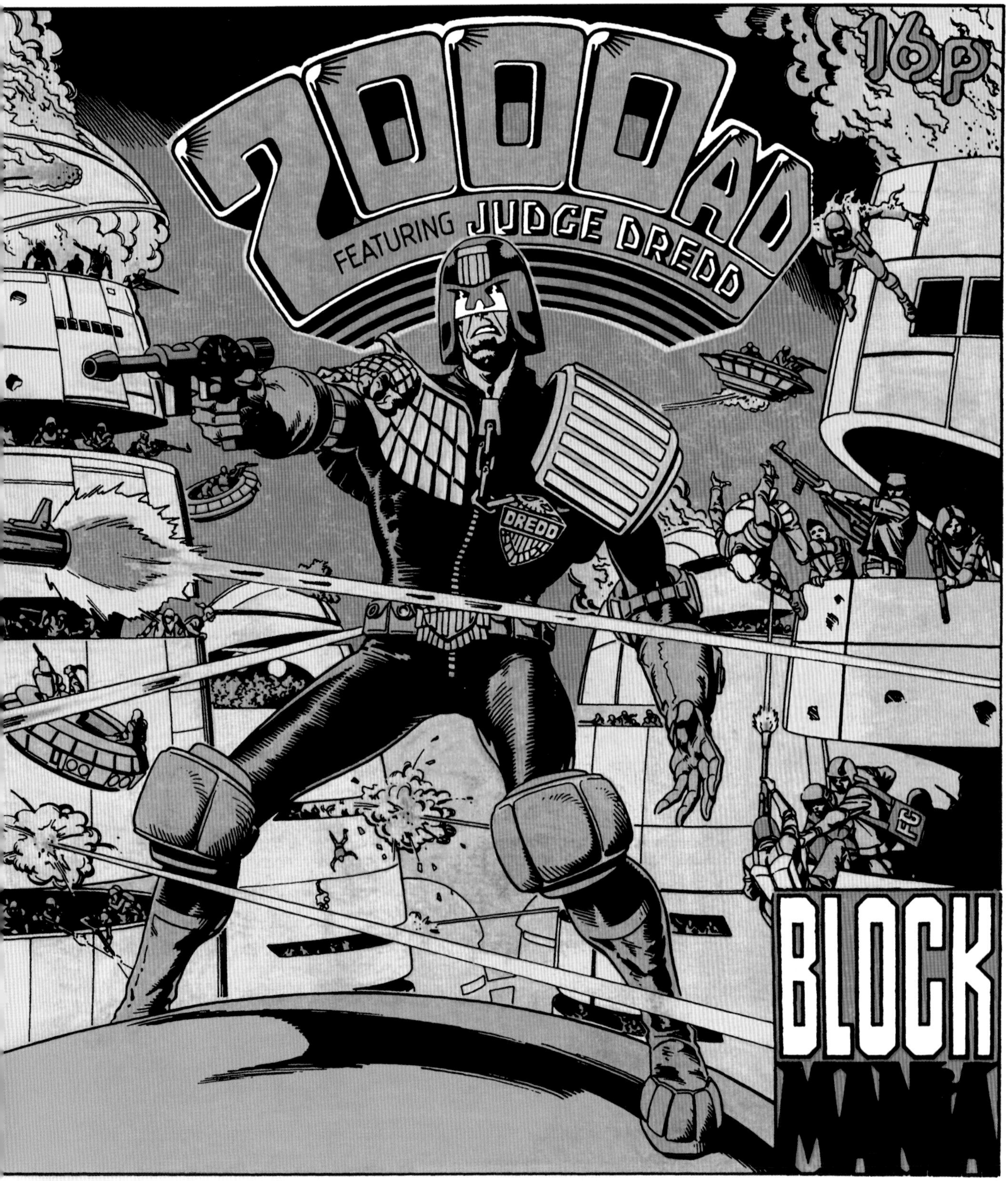

16p
2000 AD
FEATURING JUDGE DREDD
DREDD
BLOCK
MANIA

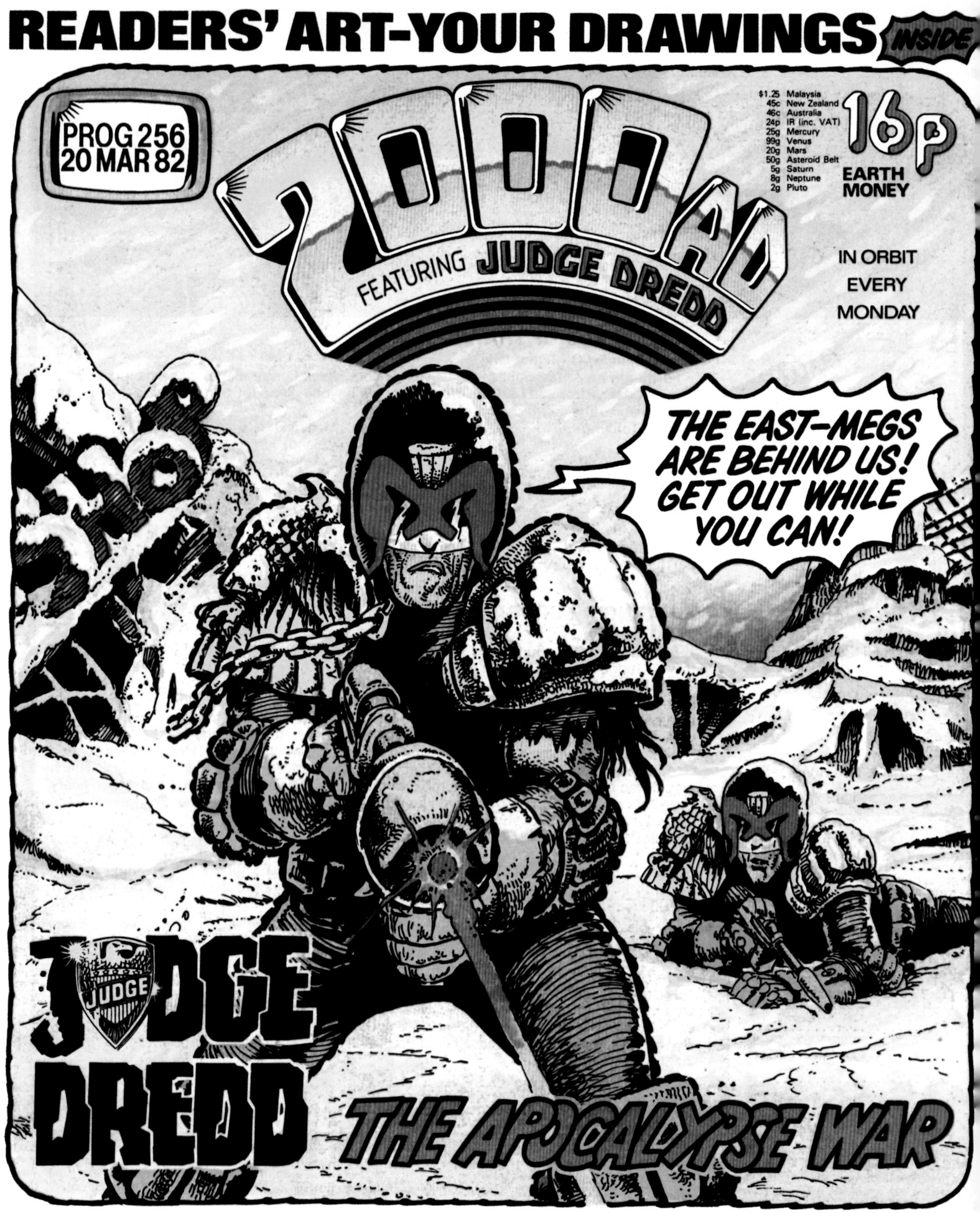
READERS' ART-YOUR DRAWINGS INSIDE
PROG 256
20 MAR 82
2000 AD
FEATURING JUDGE DREDD
$1.25 Malaysia
45c New Zealand
46c Australia
24p IR (inc. VAT)
25g Mercury
99g Venus
20g Mars
50g Asteroid Belt
5g Saturn
8g Neptune
2g Pluto
16p
EARTH MONEY
IN ORBIT EVERY MONDAY
THE EAST-MEGS ARE BEHIND US! GET OUT WHILE YOU CAN!
JUDGE
JUDGE DREDD
THE APOCALYPSE WAR

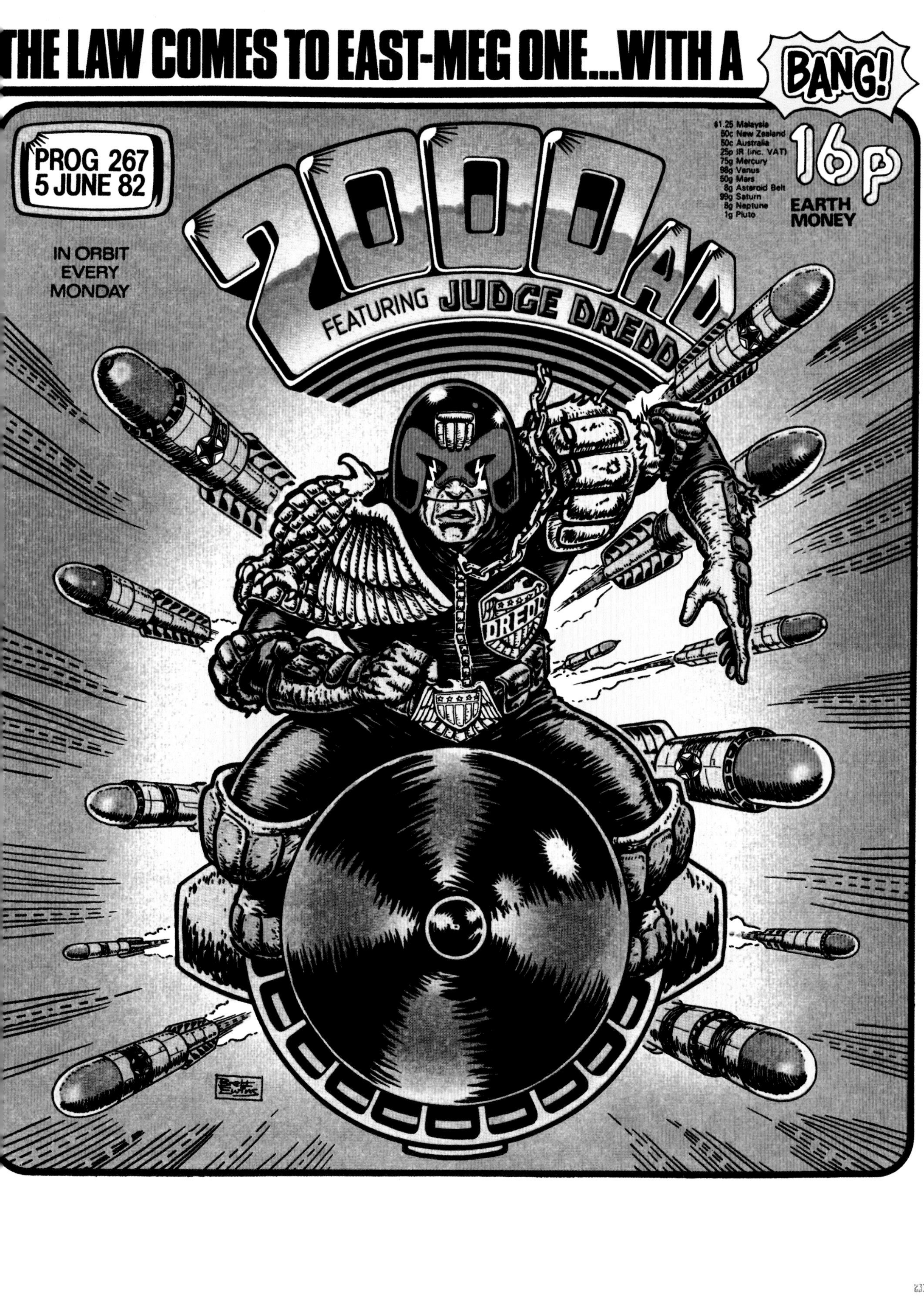
THE LAW COMES TO EAST-MEG ONE...WITH A BANG!
PROG 267
5 JUNE 82
IN ORBIT
EVERY
MONDAY
2000 AD
FEATURING JUDGE DREDD
$1.25 Malaysia
50c New Zealand
50c Australia
25p IR (inc. VAT)
75g Mercury
98g Venus
50g Mars
8g Asteroid Belt
99g Saturn
8g Neptune
1g Pluto
16p
EARTH
MONEY
DREDD
Brett Ewins

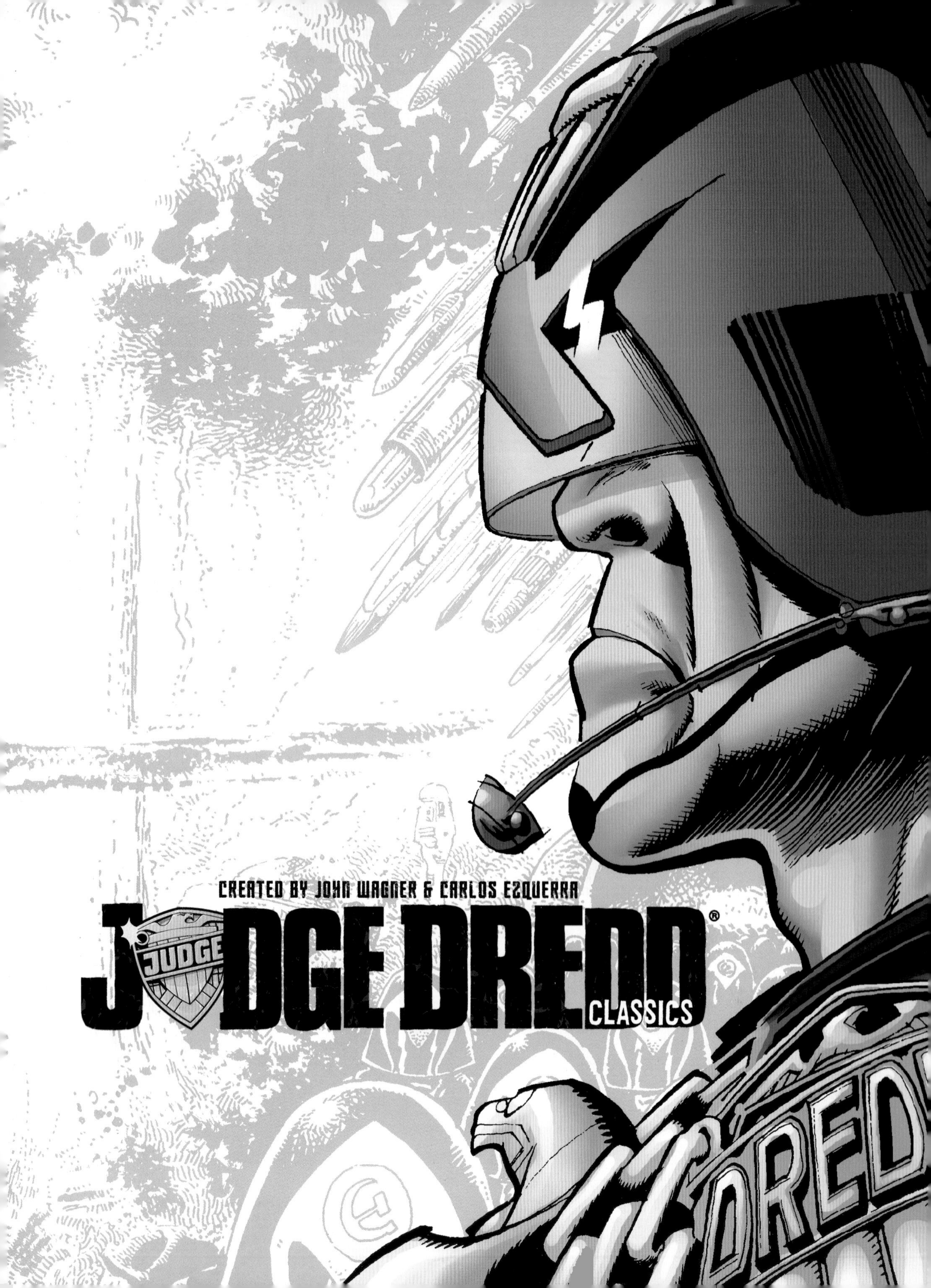
CREATED BY JOHN WAGNER & CARLOS EZQUERRA
JUDGE DREDD®
CLASSICS
DREDD